Property Development

THIRD EDITION

Other titles available from Law Society Publishing:

Client Care in Conveyancing (forthcoming, summer 2019)
Priscilla Sinder

Conveyancing Handbook (25th edn)
General Editor: Frances Silverman

Environmental Law for Conveyancing and Property Practitioners (forthcoming, summer 2019)
Andrew Wiseman

Risk and Negligence in Property Transactions
Editor: John de Waal QC

Titles from Law Society Publishing can be ordered from all good bookshops or direct (telephone 0370 850 1422 or visit our online shop at **www.lawsociety.org.uk/bookshop**).

PROPERTY DEVELOPMENT

THIRD EDITION

Gavin Le Chat

ISBN-13: 978-1-78446-087-7

First published in 2010
2nd edition 2014
This third edition published in 2019 by the Law Society
113 Chancery Lane, London WC2A 1PL

Typeset by Columns XML Design Ltd, Reading
Printed by TJ International Ltd, Padstow, Cornwall

The paper used for the text pages of this book is FSC® certified. FSC (the Forest Stewardship Council®) is an international network to promote responsible management of the world's forests.

Contents

APPENDICES

Contents of the CD-ROM

The CD-ROM accompanying *Property Development* contains the following documents.

About the author

Gavin Le Chat is a solicitor and, until his retirement in June 2018, he was a partner with Shoosmiths LLP. He grew up in South Africa where he graduated from Rhodes University and the University of Cape Town. Moving to England in 1978, Gavin attended the Cheshire College of Law and, upon being admitted in 1982, joined the commercial property team at the City firm Birkbeck Montague. After partnerships with Bayer-Rosin and Shoosmiths, he joined Howes Percival as a partner in 2010 and returned to Shoosmiths as a partner in 2011.

Gavin has over 35 years' experience and a detailed understanding of development work. During his career, he specialised in residential development and regularly advised developers, including national housebuilders, in connection with site acquisitions, contracts conditional on planning, options to purchase, planning promotion agreements, collaboration agreements and overage agreements.

Gavin particularly enjoyed strategic land work and acted for both developers and landowners in connection with option agreements and planning promotion agreements relating to substantial strategic land sites throughout the UK.

Preface

Since the publication of the second edition a new Electronic Communications Code has come into force and a revised National Planning Policy Framework (NPPF) has been published. The Digital Economy Act 2017 repealed the Electronic Communications Code contained in Schedule 2 to the Telecommunications Act 1984 and inserted a new Electronic Communications Code into the Communications Act 2003; in July 2018 the Ministry of Housing, Communities and Local Government published a new NPPF, which replaced the NPPF published in March 2012. A detailed summary of the 2017 Electronic Communications Code is contained in **Chapter 2** (see **2.14**) and **Chapter 5** has been updated to include references to the revised NPPF and a summary of the new (and much wider) categories of affordable housing set out therein.

This third edition contains a new chapter on collaboration agreements between landowners (**Chapter 15**) and discusses ways of achieving equalisation without incurring a double charge to capital gains tax (**15.3**). This is a complex subject, on which there is not much guidance available, and the chapter should be of interest and (hopefully) assistance to landowners (and their advisers) wishing to collaborate and to maximise the development potential of their land.

The chapters on investigating title, access, drainage, planning and contaminated land issues have been substantially revised and updated and include references to new cases and cases not previously mentioned. As stated in **Chapter 4** ('Drainage and other services'), Schedule 3 to the Flood and Water Management Act 2010 is still not in force and although s.42 of that Act has been implemented in Wales, it is not yet in force in England. The failure by the government to implement Schedule 3 and to fully implement s.42 has created uncertainty for developers and has led to the government being much criticised.

The chapters on conditional contracts, option agreements, promotion agreements and overage agreements have also been substantially revised and expanded. The author has attempted to adopt a balanced approach and to present the issues for both landowners and developers entering into these types of agreement. Promotion agreements continue to be popular with landowners (and their agents) as an alternative to entering into option agreements and **Chapter 13** includes a number of new paragraphs dealing with matters not previously discussed. Also, the precedents contained in the CD-ROM which accompanies the third edition now include, in addition to a 'pure' promotion agreement, a hybrid promotion/option agreement.

The law is as stated at January 2019.

Gavin Le Chat
January 2019

Acknowledgements

First, I would like to thank a number of my former colleagues at Shoosmiths for their help with this third edition. Tim Willis reviewed and suggested amendments to **Chapter 5** ('Planning') and Angus Evers reviewed and suggested amendments to **Chapter 6** ('Contaminated land issues'). Their respective suggested amendments have greatly improved these chapters. I also had many useful discussions with my former real estate partner, David Perry, which helped to clarify my thinking on a number of issues. The help that I received from Tim, Angus and David is much appreciated.

I would also to thank my wife, Sue, for her encouragement and patience and for giving up a considerable amount of her time to type up my revisions to the second edition from my handwritten notes. She deserves a medal.

Gavin Le Chat
January 2019

Table of cases

Table of statutes

Table of statutory instruments

Abbreviations

CA 2003	Communications Act 2003
CGT	capital gains tax
CIL	Community Infrastructure Levy
DEA 2017	Digital Economy Act 2017
EA 1989	Electricity Act 1989
EPA 1990	Environmental Protection Act 1990
FBT	farm business tenancy
FWMA 2010	Flood and Water Management Act 2010
HA 1980	Highways Act 1980
LA 2011	Localism Act 2011
LCA 1973	Land Compensation Act 1973
LPA 1922	Law of Property Act 1922
LPA 1925	Law of Property Act 1925
LRA 2002	Land Registration Act 2002
LTA 1954	Landlord and Tenant Act 1954
LTA 1987	Landlord and Tenant Act 1987
NPPF	National Planning Policy Framework
PA 2008	Planning Act 2008
PPG	Planning Practice Guidance
PWA 1996	Party Wall etc. Act 1996
RA 1977	Rentcharges Act 1977
SDLT	stamp duty land tax
SUD	sustainable drainage system
TCGA 1992	Taxation of Chargeable Gains Act 1992
TCPA 1990	Town and Country Planning Act 1990
TPO	tree preservation order
VAT	value added tax
WIA 1991	Water Industry Act 1991

PART I

Site acquisition

CHAPTER 1

Preliminary investigations

1.1 SITE INSPECTION

Whenever possible an early inspection of a potential development site should be carried out. It may sound trite, but there really is no substitute for carrying out a physical inspection of the land which is to be developed. The advantages to be gained from carrying out a site inspection will far outweigh any disadvantages, such as cost and the time spent travelling to the site. For example, a site inspection could reveal the existence of a ransom strip, the existence of a public right of way or the existence of informal or implied rights which would not be discoverable from an investigation of title, the existence of apparatus belonging to statutory undertakers or utility companies and potential boundary and right to light issues.

It would be sensible for the developer's lawyer to prepare a checklist of items to consider when visiting a site. This may include the following items:

- Are the boundaries of the site clearly defined?
- Is the site enclosed by fencing or walls along all boundaries?
- Do the on-site boundaries accord with the title plan? (This is very important – see **1.2**.)
- Are there any ditches and/or hedges running alongside any of the boundaries? (See **1.2**.)
- Is any apparatus belonging to a statutory undertaker or other service provider, such as an electricity substation, located on the site?
- Are there any overhead power lines crossing the site or electricity pylons or stays located on the site which may need diverting?
- Are there any buildings on adjoining land containing windows which overlook the site? (See **2.1**.)
- Are there any tracks or paths crossing the site? (See **2.3**.)
- Does the route of a public footpath shown on the definitive map follow the route of the footpath on the ground or has there been a diversion of the definitive route?
- Is there any evidence of an adjoining owner exercising rights over the site?
- Does the site directly abut the highway? (This is very important – see **3.1**.)
- Is there any evidence of an adjoining owner encroaching on to the site?

- Are there any trees on the site which may be protected? (See **2.6**.)
- Does the site have any unusual features, such as a watercourse which crosses the access to the site or which separates one part of the site from another part?
- Is there any evidence of flooding?
- Is there any Japanese knotweed or protected wildlife on the site?
- Is the frontage of the site wide enough to accommodate any visibility splays which may be required? (See **3.2**.)
- Is there any evidence of the site being used for recreational purposes (e.g. dog walking or bird watching) by members of the public? (See **2.17**.)
- Are there any buildings or other structures on adjoining land within 3 metres of the boundary of the site? (See **7.1.5**.)

1.2 BOUNDARIES AND PLANS

Along with carrying out a site inspection, one of the first things that a developer's lawyer should do is check that the title plan and any contract plan accurately identify the boundaries of the land being acquired. Disputes and mistakes in relation to boundaries and plans are all too common in the context of property development. It is probably not too much of an exaggeration to say that the majority of conveyancing errors involve plans. However, these mistakes can easily be avoided or reduced by taking some or all of the following steps:

- A site inspection of the development site should be carried out at an early stage with a view to checking that there is no discrepancy between the boundaries as indicated on the Land Registry filed plan or (if title to the site is unregistered) the title conveyance plan and the on-site boundaries.
- The developer should be made aware that the filed plan of a registered property is not definitive, that it is deemed to indicate only the general boundaries of the property, and that it is possible to apply to the Land Registry for a determination of the exact line of a boundary (see Land Registration Rules 2003 (SI 2003/1417), rules 118–120).
- Where a developer is purchasing only part of a seller's title, the contract plan and the transfer plan should be based on a coordinated boundary survey and, ideally, the boundaries of the land being purchased should be pegged out on site prior to exchange of contracts. In order to comply with the Land Registry's requirements[1] the transfer plan will need to:
  - be to a stated scale (the preferred scales are 1:1250–1:500 for urban properties and 1:2500 for rural properties);
  - show a north point;
  - show sufficient detail of surrounding roads and other features to enable the

[1] See Land Registry Practice Guide 40, *Land Registry plans*, Supplement 1 'The basis of Land Registry Plans' and Supplement 2 'Guidance for preparing plans for Land Registry applications'; and Land Registry Practice Guide 41, *Developing estates – registration services*.

land being purchased to be identified on the Ordnance Survey map or the vendor's title plan.

Ideally, the transfer plan should not be marked as 'for identification only' or with similar wording and it should not bear a statement of disclaimer.

- The developer should arrange for a topographical survey to be carried out (regardless of whether the developer is acquiring the whole or part of a vendor's site) at an early stage (and preferably prior to exchange of contracts) and the topographical or site survey plan should be compared with any title plan to ensure that there are no discrepancies. The topographical survey plan will show the physical features of the land in detail and the boundaries of the site as they are on the ground.
- Where a developer is selling part of a larger site to another developer, particularly where planning permission has not yet been granted or where outline planning permission has been granted but approval of reserved matters has not been obtained, it would be sensible to include a clause in the contract which allows for adjustments to be made to the boundaries of the land being sold (e.g. to reflect changes to the estate layout required by the planning authority) with the consent of both parties (acting reasonably and in good faith). The developer's lawyer should consider inserting a clause in the sale and purchase agreement similar to model clauses 1 or 2 in **Appendix D1**.
  - Model clause 1 (see **Appendix D1**) may be used where the land being sold has the benefit of an outline planning permission and the seller is retaining land which benefits from the same planning permission. If the planning authority requires changes to be made to the proposed estate layout before a full planning permission or reserved matters approval is granted then the seller will want to be able to make adjustments to the boundaries of the land being sold so that the transfer plan and the estate layout plan correspond.
  - Model clause 2 (see **Appendix D1**) may be used in a contract conditional on planning where the seller is selling part of his land.
- Where there is uncertainty about the ownership of boundary structures or there is a discrepancy between the on-site boundaries and the title plan, the developer should require the owner of the land to enter into a statutory declaration – in the case of a discrepancy this will assist the Land Registry in plotting the correct boundaries.
- The developer should ensure that its architects are aware of the legal boundaries of the site and that all planning and technical drawings, including the planning/estate layout drawing and the road and sewer layout drawings, are based on the title plan.

The developer's lawyer should check whether the title deeds contain any boundary declarations or impose any obligations in relation to the maintenance and repair of boundary structures. Enquiries regarding the location and ownership of boundary structures should also be made of the seller and if the title deeds are silent on the question of ownership of boundary structures then the developer should be made aware that there are a number of boundary presumptions (all of which can be rebutted by evidence) which may apply. These include the following:

1. Where two properties are separated by a hedge and a single ditch there is a presumption (in the absence of evidence to the contrary) that both the hedge and the ditch belong to the owner of the property on which the hedge is planted.[2] This rule (known as the hedge and ditch rule) does not apply if the position of the boundary can be ascertained from the title deeds or the ditch is not artificial (e.g. it is a natural watercourse) or the ditch was in existence before the boundary was drawn or the date on which the ditch was constructed is not known.
2. Where a property abuts a non-tidal river or stream it is presumed (in the absence of evidence to the contrary) that the boundary extends to the mid-point of the river bed or stream. This relates only to the soil itself and does not include ownership of the water.[3]
3. Where a property abuts a highway it is presumed (in the absence of evidence to the contrary) that the owner of the property owns the sub-soil up to the middle of the highway.[4] This presumption (known as the *ad medium filum* rule) can be rebutted by showing that it must be inferred from the surrounding circumstances that it was not intended to include the sub-soil of one half of the road in the conveyance/transfer of the property. For example, the presumption will not apply where the transferor is obliged to construct the road and to procure its adoption. The effect of vesting the road in the highway authority will be not to transfer the freehold title in the road to the authority but merely to vest in the authority the surface of the road and so much of the soil below the surface of the road as may be required for its protection, control and maintenance. In other words, the transferor will retain ownership of the soil beneath the road and the airspace above it.[5]
4. Where a ditch lies between a hedge or fence and the highway there is a presumption that the ditch does not form part of the highway and that it is owned by the owner of the adjoining land (see *Hanscombe* v. *Bedfordshire County Council* [1938] Ch 944 (Ch D)). However, there is no rule of law which prevents a ditch from being dedicated as part of a highway and this presumption may be rebutted (see *Chorley Corporation* v. *Nightingale* [1906] 2 KB 612 and *Halsbury's Laws of England* (5th edition, 2011), vol.4, para.322). For example, the ditch may have been constructed by the owners of

---

[2] See *Vowles* v. *Miller* (1810) 3 Taunt 137 (Court of Common Pleas); and *Emmet & Farrand on Title* (Sweet & Maxwell), para.17.034.
[3] See *Blount* v. *Layard* [1891] 2 Ch 681 (CA); and *Emmet & Farrand on Title* (Sweet & Maxwell), para.17.033.
[4] See *Emmet & Farrand on Title* (Sweet & Maxwell), para.17.036.
[5] See *Emmet & Farrand on Title* (Sweet & Maxwell), para.17.037.

the road as a drain for the purpose of taking surface water run off from the road. (A highway search may help in determining whether or not a ditch forms part of the adopted highway.)

It will also be necessary to establish whether any wall separating the site and an adjoining property is a party wall, since this may have implications for the developer. For example, the wall may be a party wall under the Party Wall etc. Act 1996 and it may be necessary for the developer to serve a notice on an adjoining owner before commencing development. A summary of the main provisions of the 1996 Act is contained in **7.1**. It is also possible that the wall may be a party wall governed by the provisions of the Law of Property Act (LPA) 1925, s.38. Under s.38 the owner of one half of a party wall is entitled to use the other half of the wall for support and protection.

1.3 GROUND INVESTIGATIONS AND SURVEYS

A developer should always satisfy itself that the ground conditions of a development site are satisfactory for development and that the land has not been contaminated (or contaminated to such an extent that the cost of carrying out the development will be substantially increased) by commissioning a ground investigation report before proceeding with the purchase of the site (unless there already exists a suitable ground investigation report upon which the developer will be able to rely). Where a developer is intending to rely on an existing report, the age of the report and the thoroughness of the report will need to be carefully checked and the developer's lawyer will want to ensure that the report is capable of being relied upon (see **6.3**). **Chapter 6**, which deals with contaminated land issues, explains how a developer may be liable for contamination even if the contamination was caused by another party.

A developer should also consider commissioning:

- a desktop archaeological survey. If there is any doubt as to the presence of archaeological remains then early consultation with the local planning authority's archaeological officer and Historic England is to be recommended;
- an asbestos survey. If the development will involve the demolition of an existing building then the developer's lawyer should raise enquiries regarding the existence and monitoring of asbestos within the building and the developer should consider commissioning an asbestos survey to determine whether any harmful asbestos is present in the building. Harmful asbestos may be removed only by specialist contractors.

1.4 SEARCHES

Various pre-contract searches should be carried out by the developer's lawyer, including the following:

- An index map search (using Land Registry form SIM) of the site development and adjoining land. An index map search should be carried out even if the title to the development site is registered – it may reveal a sub-surface mineral title (see **2.7.2** and **2.18.4**).
- A local search (using forms LLC1, CON29 and CON29O). It is recommended that most of the optional enquiries on form CON29O are raised, including those relating to public footpaths and common land and village greens.
- A chancel repair liability search.
- A CON29M Local mining and brine subsidence claim search (assuming that the site is located in an area affected by coal mining works or a Cheshire brine subsidence claim, see **2.7**).
- An environmental search. There are a number of companies which will provide environmental data on a site, although the search may be in the form of a letter addressed to the Environment Agency (see **Appendix B4**).
- A flood search. There are a number of companies that will provide a report which assesses the potential flood risk to a site, although information on flooding (such as whether the site is located within a flood plain) can be obtained from the Environment Agency.
- A highway search (in the form of a letter addressed to the highway authority – see **Appendix B2**). The search will usually reveal the extent of the public highways in the vicinity of the site and whether the site is affected by a public footpath or road improvements.
- Service enquiries of the various statutory undertakers and utility companies – see **Appendix B3**.
- A CON29DW Drainage and water search.
- A company search (if the title is unregistered and the seller is a company).
- Land charge searches against all the estate owners (if the title is unregistered) using form K15. The search will need to be sent to the Land Charges Department in Plymouth.[6]

Additional searches may be required if, for example, the development site is located in a tin mining area (e.g. Cornwall, Devon or Somerset) or a clay mining area (e.g. Cornwall, Devon or Dorset) or an area of archaeological interest or near a railway or canal. The results of all searches should be carefully checked and the developer promptly informed of any adverse entries. For example, if a coal mining search reveals the existence of mine shafts within the boundaries of a site then this should be drawn to the attention of the developer.

[6] Detailed information for the making of all kinds of applications to the Land Charges Department is contained in Land Registry Practice Guide 63, *Land charges – applications for registration, official search, office copy and cancellation.*

The developer should be made aware that:

1. The result of a highway search will not be definitive since it will be based on the council's records, which may not be accurate. Also, the highway authority will not usually confirm that a site abuts the public highway, but will provide a plan showing the extent (according to their records) of the public highways in the vicinity of the site.
2. A chancel repair search will not establish beyond all doubt that the land has no chancel repair liability. Again, the search will be based on certain records and will not be conclusive. Accordingly, if the land was formerly glebe land or the title indicates that there may be a potential chancel repair liability then, unless there has been a sale for value after 12 October 2013 without the chancel repair right having been noted on the title, it would be prudent to obtain a chancel repair indemnity policy (see **2.18.5**).
3. Where a local search reveals that a site is within a Mineral Consultation Area the planning authority has undertaken to consult with the local mineral extraction industries before granting planning permission to develop the site and planning permission may be refused if the proposed development would impede the extraction of the minerals.

1.5 DEVELOPMENT AND TITLE ENQUIRIES

The developer's lawyer should also raise general pre-contract development enquiries with the landowner (see **Appendix B1**). Commercial property standard enquiries (form CPSE 1 (version 3.7)) may be used, but they do not relate specifically to development land and, if they are used, the developer's lawyers may also wish to consider submitting a supplementary form of development enquiries. The developer's lawyer may also need to raise specific title enquiries after completing his investigation of title. The replies to these enquiries should be carefully checked and, if necessary, further enquiries should be raised.

CHAPTER 2

Investigating title: adverse matters

A potential development site may be affected by various adverse title matters which will need to be identified by the developer's lawyer and drawn to the attention of the developer as soon as they are discovered. The developer's lawyer should also prepare a legal report in which all adverse matters are highlighted (see **Appendix B5**) and send this to the developer prior to exchange of contracts.

2.1 RIGHTS TO LIGHT

The developer will need to consider whether its proposed development will breach or infringe any rights to light enjoyed by buildings on adjoining land. Rights to light may be expressly created by a deed, but in many cases they will arise as a result of the actual enjoyment of light from adjoining land for a period of 20 years or more. Under the Prescription Act 1832, s.3 enjoyment of light for 20 years raises an absolute presumption of a legal easement which may be rebutted only if the enjoyment of the easement is with the written agreement or written consent of the owner of the adjoining land. For this reason, rights to light can easily be overlooked and it would be prudent to inspect the development site in order to ascertain whether there are any buildings on adjoining land containing windows which overlook the site. The title to the site should also be checked for any right to light declarations.

Determining whether a right to light has been or may be breached is not always a straightforward matter. The basic rule established by *Colls* v. *Home and Colonial Stores Limited* [1904] AC 179 (HL) is that the quantity of light which an owner of a building has a right to expect is that 'which is required for the ordinary purposes of inhabitancy or business of the tenement according to the ordinary notions of mankind'. In other words, the measure of light should be sufficient for the use and enjoyment of a building for any ordinary purpose for which it is adapted. However, it is not easy to apply this rule in practice, as can be seen from the volume of case law on rights to light disputes.[1]

[1] See J Gaunt and P Morgan *Gale on the Law of Easements* (20th edition, Sweet & Maxwell, 2017).

If there is any uncertainty about whether a proposed development will infringe a right to light enjoyed by a building on adjoining land then the developer may wish to seek the advice of consultants who specialise in dealing with rights to light disputes, although, having regard to the complexities of rights to light disputes and the apparent inconsistencies between various decisions of the courts, it will be a brave developer who is prepared to proceed with a development in reliance on such advice. In such circumstances it is submitted that it would be more sensible for the developer to obtain a rights to light indemnity insurance policy or to enter into an agreement with the adjoining owner in which the adjoining owner either acknowledges that no right to light exists or agrees to release absolutely any right to light which may exist. However, where a developer enters into a right to light agreement with an adjoining landowner in which the adjoining owner agrees, for a consideration, to the site being developed in accordance with certain drawings, the developer will need to be aware that the agreement may not be effective if the developer makes changes to the drawings which result in a greater loss of light than would otherwise have been the case. Any right to light agreement should therefore be carefully checked in order to ascertain whether the landowner is totally abandoning any right to light claim or merely agreeing not to object to a specific development.[2]

Any developer which ignores rights to light does so at its peril. The cases of *Dennis Regan* v. *Paul Properties Limited* [2006] EWCA Civ 1391 and *HKRUK11 (CHC) Limited* v. *Heaney* [2010] EWHC 2245 (Ch) highlight some of the complexities of rights to light disputes and make it clear that in cases where a developer ignores complaints from those with rights to light, the courts are now more likely to consider granting an injunction against the development rather than awarding damages.

It is worth mentioning that, following consultation on rights to light, the Law Commission published its final report (*Rights to Light* (Law Com. No.356)) and draft bill on the subject on 4 December 2014. It is currently awaiting a response to its recommendations from the government. The most important recommendations are:

- a statutory notice procedure which would allow landowners to require neighbours to inform them within a specified period if they intend to seek an injunction or to lose the potential for that remedy to be granted;
- a statutory test (which takes account of the Supreme Court's decision in *Coventry* v. *Lawrence* [2015] UKSC 50) to clarify when courts may order damages to be paid rather than halting development or ordering demolition;
- an updated version of the procedure that allows landowners to prevent their neighbours from acquiring rights to light by prescription;
- amendment of the law governing where an unused right to light is treated as abandoned;
- a power for the Lands Chamber of the Upper Tribunal to discharge or modify obsolete or unused rights to light.

[2] *G&S Brough* v. *Salvage Wharf Limited and another* [2009] EWCA Civ 21.

The Law Commission is no longer recommending that prescription should be abolished as a means of acquiring rights to light. This represents a change to the recommendation published in its consultation paper in 2012.

2.2 SERVICE MEDIA AND WAYLEAVE AGREEMENTS

The development site may be affected by service media crossing the site and there may be agreements granting a statutory undertaker or utility company the right to lay its apparatus on, over or under the land.

The developer's lawyer should check whether any of the following cross the site:

- sewers;
- gas pipes;
- water pipes;
- electricity cables;
- telecommunications apparatus.

Appropriate enquiries should be made, not only of the landowner, but also of the various statutory undertakers and utility companies (see **Appendices B1** and **B3**). Failure to make such enquiries could be extremely costly for the developer and the developer's lawyer may be negligent if he fails to make such enquiries, unless it has been agreed that the developer is to be responsible for making all technical searches. For example, there may be a large foul sewer crossing the site which will need to be diverted in order to develop the site. Subject to compliance with the Building Regulations 2010, it may be possible to erect roads or buildings over public sewers, but this will require the consent of the local authority and the sewerage undertaker who will need to be satisfied that the proposed building works will not have an adverse effect upon the public sewer system and will inevitably cause delays. The Building Regulations 2010 (SI 2010/2214) prevent the building over, or within three metres of, any public sewer, without a full Building Regulations application and consent. (See Buildings Regulations, Approved Document H, 2002, s.H4 (incorporating the 2010 amendments) for guidance on when it may be permissible to build over, or within three metres of, public sewers.) Sewerage undertakers will not usually be willing to agree to sewers running through or under the back gardens of dwellings.

The results of all technical searches should be carefully checked and where a site is affected by sewers, electricity cables, gas pipes or other apparatus, the developer should enquire of the relevant statutory undertaker/utility company as to whether there is any agreement or wayleave consent relating to such service media. If the site is affected by such an agreement or consent, the developer should obtain a copy of the agreement and check whether the owner will have a right to determine the agreement or relocate the relevant apparatus. The developer should be also made aware of the statutory rights of the relevant statutory undertaker/utility company entitled to the wayleave. For example, under the Electricity Act 1989, a landowner requiring the removal of an existing electrical line from his land after the wayleave agreement has been terminated must serve a notice on the wayleave holder requiring it to remove its apparatus. A wayleave agreement will usually contain a provision allowing either party to terminate the agreement by giving the other party six- or 12-months' notice to terminate. In this case it will be necessary for the landowner to serve a notice to terminate and, once the agreement has been terminated, it will be necessary for the landowner to serve a further notice requiring the wayleave holder to remove its apparatus. It is important that the removal notice makes a clear reference to the removal of the apparatus from the landowner's land. The wayleave holder will be obliged to comply with the notice to remove unless, within three months of the date of the notice, an application is made to the Secretary of State for the grant of a new wayleave agreement or an order authorising the compulsory purchase of the land is made (see Electricity Act (EA) 1989, Sched.4, para.8(3)). The Secretary of State will not entertain an application for a wayleave where 'the land is covered by a dwelling or will be so covered on the assumption that any planning permission which is in force is acted on' (EA 1989, Sched.4, para.6(4)). The expression 'dwelling' includes any garden, yard, outhouses and appurtenances belonging to or usually enjoyed with that dwelling. However, the Secretary of State may entertain an application for a wayleave when it already exists, and the wayleave holder is applying to keep its apparatus on the land rather than to install new apparatus.[3]

Under the Water Industry Act (WIA) 1991, a landowner is entitled to serve a notice on the relevant statutory undertaker requiring a pipe or other apparatus belonging to the undertaker to be altered or removed on the ground that the alteration or removal is necessary to enable the landowner to develop his land, and the undertaker will be under a duty to comply with the requirement of the notice except to the extent that it is unreasonable (see WIA 1991, s.185). The undertaker will be entitled to recover from the landowner any expenses reasonably incurred in altering or removing its apparatus (WIA 1991, s.185(5)).

2.3 PUBLIC RIGHTS OF WAY

2.3.1 Discovering public rights of way

The developer should be advised that planning permission does not entitle it to obstruct or divert a public footpath or bridleway. If a developer erects a dwelling or builds a road across a public footpath without obtaining a stopping up or diversion order then this will amount to an obstruction and the highway authority has power to prosecute for and require the removal of obstructions. Accordingly, the developer's lawyer should ask the vendor and the highway authority to confirm whether or not the development site is affected by a public footpath or bridleway. The highway

[3] See *R. v. Secretary of State for Trade & Industry, ex p. Wolf* (2000) 79 P & CR 229 (QBD) and **4.7** of this book for discussion of the rights and duties of other service providers.

authority should also be asked to indicate on a plan the route of any public footpath or bridleway adjacent to, abutting or crossing the development site.

When carrying out a site inspection the developer's lawyer should check whether or not the route of a public footpath as shown on the definitive footpath map follows the same route as the route of the footpath on the ground. If there has been a diversion, the developer's lawyer should endeavour to ascertain for how long the diversion has existed and the landowner should be required to provide a statutory declaration confirming the position.

The developer's lawyer should also look for evidence of any other paths or tracks created by members of the public walking across the site, as these could pose an obstacle to development. Under the Highways Act (HA) 1980, s.31(1):

> Where a way over any land, other than a way of such character that use of it by the public could not give rise at common law to any presumption of dedication, has been actually enjoyed by the public as of right and without interruption for a full period of 20 years, the way is to be deemed to have been dedicated as a highway unless there is sufficient evidence that there was no intention during that period to dedicate it.

The use of the way by members of the public for a shorter period can also give rise to a presumption of dedication. Section 31(9) of HA 1980 states as follows:

> Nothing in this section operates to prevent the dedication of a way as a highway being presumed on proof of user for any less period than 20 years or being presumed or proved in any circumstances in which it might have been presumed or proved immediately before the commencement of this Act.

Any of the following, in the absence of proof of a contrary intention, will be sufficient evidence to show that there was no intention to dedicate the way as a highway:

- where the owner of the land expressly consented to the use of the way by members of the public. The use of a right of access that has been expressly granted or the use of a way with the written permission of the owner cannot be 'as of right'. User 'as of right' requires use without force, secrecy or permission;
- where the owner of the land has erected a notice inconsistent with the dedication of the way as a highway and has thereafter continued to maintain it (see HA 1980, s.31(3)). The notice must be visible to persons using the way and if it is subsequently torn down or defaced the owner may give the appropriate council notice that the way is not dedicated as a highway. In the absence of proof of a contrary intention, this will be sufficient evidence to negative the presumption of dedication;
- where the owner of the land has deposited with the appropriate authority a map and a statement in a valid form (i.e. in a prescribed form) indicating what ways (if any) have been dedicated as highways and where within 20 years from the date of the deposit the owner or his successor in title lodges a declaration in a valid form (i.e. in a prescribed form) to the effect that no additional way has

been dedicated as a highway since the date of the deposit or since the date of any previous declaration. In the absence of proof of a contrary intention, this will be sufficient evidence to negative the intention of the owner to dedicate any such additional way as a highway (HA 1980, s.31(6) (as amended by the Growth and Infrastructure Act 2013, s.13));
- where the owner periodically blocks the way. For dedication to be inferred, use must be 'without interruption'.

Under HA 1980, s.31A a council is obliged to keep a register containing details of maps, statements and declarations lodged with the council pursuant to s.31(6).

2.3.2 Procedures for stopping up and diverting public paths

If the site is affected by a public footpath or bridleway then it may be necessary for the developer to apply to the planning authority or the highway authority for a stopping up order or a diversion order. It would be prudent for the developer to discuss the matter with the planning authority before acquiring the site, in order to satisfy itself that the planning authority will not object to the making of a stopping up or diversion order.

There are two procedures that can be used to stop up or divert a public footpath or bridleway, namely, the procedure under HA 1980 or the procedure under the Town and Country Planning Act (TCPA) 1990.

Procedure under the Highways Act 1980

(A) PUBLIC PATH EXTINGUISHMENT ORDER

Where it appears to a council that it is expedient that a footpath or bridleway should be stopped up on the ground that it is not needed for public use, the council may, by order, extinguish the public right of way over the path or way (HA 1980, s.118). Such an order is referred to as a public path extinguishment order. If the order is unopposed then the council must confirm that it was unopposed, but if the order is opposed it will need to be confirmed by the Secretary of State.

To confirm the order the Secretary of State and the council must be satisfied that it is expedient so to do having regard to:

- the extent (if any) to which it appears that the path or way would be likely to be used by the public; and
- the effect which the extinguishment of the right of way would have as respects land served by the path or way (s.118(2)).

A public path extinguishment order must be in such form as may be prescribed by regulations made by the Secretary of State and must contain a map defining the land over which the public right of way is extinguished (s.118(3)).

A council which receives an application for a public path extinguishment order must determine the application as soon as reasonably practicable; and where an application has been made and the council has not determined the application within four months of receiving it, the Secretary of State may, at the request of the applicant and after consulting the council, by direction require the council to determine the application before the end of such period as may be specified in the direction (s.118ZA).

An application for a public path extinguishment order must be in such form as may be prescribed and accompanied by such information as may be prescribed, including a map showing the relevant land (s.118ZA).

(B) PUBLIC PATH DIVERSION ORDER

Where it appears to a council that, in the interests of the owner, lessee or occupier of land crossed by a footpath or bridleway, or in the interests of the public, it is expedient that the line of a footpath or bridleway should be diverted, the council may, by an order made by it create such new footpath or bridleway as appears to it requisite for effecting the diversion and extinguish the public right of way over so much of the path or way as appears necessary to it (s.119). This type of order is referred to as a public path diversion order. Again, the order must be confirmed by the council as unopposed or, if it is opposed, confirmed by the Secretary of State.

To confirm the order the Secretary of State and the council must be satisfied that:

- it is expedient to confirm the order; and
- the path or way will not be substantially less convenient to the public as a result of the diversion (s.119(6)).

An application for a public path diversion order must be made in such form as may be prescribed and accompanied by such information as may be prescribed, including a map which complies with s.119ZA(4).

If a person aggrieved by a public path extinguishment or diversion order wishes to question the validity of the order, on the ground that it is not within the powers of HA 1980 or on the ground that any requirement of the Act has not been complied with in relation to the order, he may apply to the High Court (Sched.2, para.2). The application must be made within six weeks from the date on which notice of the making or confirmation of the order was first published.

Procedure under TCPA 1990

A competent authority[4] may by order authorise the stopping up or diversion of any footpath or bridleway if it is satisfied that it is necessary to do so in order to enable

[4] TCPA 1990, s.257(4) defines a competent authority for the purposes of this section as: '(a) in the case of development authorised by a planning permission, the local planning authority who granted the permission or, in the case of a permission granted by the Secretary of State or by the Welsh Ministers, who would have had power to grant it; (b) in the case of development carried out by a government department, the local planning authority who would have had power to grant planning permission on an application in respect of the development in question if such an application had fallen to be made.'

development to be carried out in accordance with a planning permission granted under TCPA 1990, Part III or by a government department (TCPA 1990, s.257). The order must be necessary in the sense that without it, development could not be carried out. It is not sufficient that the making of the order would facilitate (i.e. make easier) the carrying out of the development.

Also, under a new subsection inserted into TCPA 1990 by the Growth and Infrastructure Act 2013, a competent authority may by order authorise the stopping up or diversion of any footpath or bridleway before a planning permission is granted. Section 257(1A) of TCPA 1990 states that a competent authority may by order authorise the stopping up or diversion of any footpath, bridleway or restricted byway if it is satisfied that an application for planning permission has been made under TCPA 1990, Part 3 and that if the application were granted it would be necessary to authorise the stopping up or diversion in order to enable the development to be carried out.

An order made under TCPA 1990, s.257 will not take effect unless confirmed by the Secretary of State or confirmed as an unopposed order by the authority who made it (s.259); and an order made under s.257(1A) may not be confirmed unless the Secretary of State or the authority who made it is satisfied that the planning permission in respect of the development has been granted and that it is necessary to authorise the stopping up or diversion to enable the development to be carried out in accordance with the permission.

Before an order under TCPA 1990, s.257 is submitted to the Secretary of State for confirmation or confirmed as an unopposed order, the authority by whom the order was made must:

- publish a notice in a prescribed form in at least one local newspaper;
- serve a similar notice on:
  - every owner occupier and lessee of the land which will be affected by the order;
  - every council, the council of every rural parish and the parish meeting of every rural parish not having a separate council; and
  - any statutory undertakers to whom there belongs or by whom there is used any apparatus under the relevant land;
- display the notice in a prominent position at the ends of so much of any footpath or bridleway as is to be stopped up diverted or extinguished by the order (Sched.14, Part II).

An order made under TCPA 1990, s.257 may provide for:

- the creation of an alternative highway for use as a replacement for the one authorised by the order to be stopped up or diverted;
- authorising or requiring works to be carried out in relation to any footpath or bridleway to be stopped up or diverted;

- the preservation of any rights of statutory undertakers in respect of any apparatus belonging to the statutory undertakers and located under, in, on, over or along the footpath or bridleway.

If no objections are made to the stopping up/diversion order, or if any objections made are withdrawn, the authority by whom the order was made may, instead of submitting the order to the Secretary of State, confirm the order.

If an objection is made by a local authority the Secretary of State must, before confirming the order, cause a local enquiry to be held.

If an objection is made by a person other than a local authority the Secretary of State must, before confirming the order, either:

- cause a local enquiry to be held; or
- give the person who made the objection an opportunity of being heard by a person appointed by the Secretary of State.

After considering the report of any person appointed to hold an enquiry or hear representations or objections, the Secretary of State may confirm the order, with or without modifications.

The Secretary of State may not confirm an order under TCPA 1990, s.257 which extinguishes a right of way over land in, on, along or across which there is apparatus belonging to or used by any statutory undertakers for the purposes of their undertaking, unless the undertakers have consented to the confirmation of the order (Sched.14, Part I, para.5(1)). Any such consent may be given subject to the condition that there are included in the order such provisions for the protection of the undertakers as they may reasonably require and such consent may not be unreasonably withheld.

If an objection is made by statutory undertakers on the ground that the order provides for the creation of a public right of way over land covered by works used for the purpose of their undertaking, or over the curtilage of such land, and the objection is not withdrawn, the order will be subject to special parliamentary procedure.

2.3.3 Differences between the two procedures

The differences between the two procedures may be summarised as follows.

The TCPA 1990 procedure can be used only if the stopping up or diversion is necessary in order to enable a development to be carried out in accordance with a planning permission, whereas the HA 1980 procedure can be used at any time.

It may be more difficult to obtain an order under HA 1980 than under TCPA 1990. Under HA 1980 the stopping up of a footpath or bridleway can only be authorised if the pathway is not needed for public use, and any diversion must not result in a substantially less convenient route or have an adverse effect on the public's enjoyment of the path or the land served by it.

Under the TCPA 1990 procedure an order can only be made once the planning permission has been granted or an application for the planning permission has been made. However, no order can be made if the development has already been carried out. If the development has been carried out then it will be too late to use the TCPA 1990 procedure and it will be necessary to use the HA 1980 procedure.

2.4 PRESCRIPTIVE RIGHTS AND IMPLIED EASEMENTS

As already mentioned, a good reason for carrying out a site inspection is that it may reveal rights over the site in favour of third parties which would not be revealed by an investigation of title. For example, the site may be subject to:

- a prescriptive right of way; or
- an implied easement.[5]

A prescriptive right may be acquired by long use (see **3.4**) and an easement may be implied when a landowner sells part of the land within his ownership.

Under the rule in *Wheeldon* v. *Burrows* (1879) 12 Ch D 31 (CA), if two plots of land are owned by the same person and one is sold, and if the plot which has been sold previously enjoyed a right over the retained plot which would have been an easement if the two plots had been in separate ownership, an implied easement will be created (subject to certain criteria being fulfilled). The criteria which need to be fulfilled are:

- the right enjoyed over the retained land must be continuous and apparent; and
- the right must be necessary to the reasonable enjoyment of the land sold.

For a detailed discussion of the meaning of 'continuous and apparent' see the judgment of Lewison J in *Wood and another* v. *Waddington* [2015] EWCA Civ 538.

Subject to certain exemptions, the rule in *Wheeldon* v. *Burrows* works only in favour of the party acquiring land. If the seller requires a right over the land being sold in favour of his retained land, he will need to reserve it expressly in the transfer to the purchaser, although in certain circumstances an easement of necessity may be implied in favour of the retained land. In his judgment in *Wheeldon* v. *Burrows* Thesiger LJ stated:

> on the grant by the owner of a tenement of part of that tenement as it is then used and enjoyed, there will pass to the grantee all those continuous and apparent easements (by which, of course, I mean quasi-easements), or, in other words, all those easements which are necessary to the reasonable enjoyment of the property granted, and which have been and are at the time of the grant used by the owners of the entirety for the benefit of the part granted . . . if the grantor intends to reserve any right over the tenement granted, it is his duty to reserve it expressly in the grant.

[5] Under the rule of *Wheeldon* v. *Burrows* (1879) 12 Ch D 31 (CA) or by Law of Property Act 1925, s.62.

The question of whether an implied right of way was necessary for the reasonable enjoyment of land was considered by the Court of Appeal in *Wheeler and another* v. *JJ Saunders Limited and others* [1995] 2 All ER 697 (CA). In this case the plaintiffs bought a farmhouse on land adjacent to a pig farm operated by two of the defendants. Both the plaintiffs' property and the farm had been in common ownership and there were two means of access to the plaintiffs' property at the time when it was conveyed to them, one of which crossed a part of the farm, but the conveyance did not include an express right of way over the farm. The Court of Appeal held that the access which crossed over the defendant's land was not necessary to the reasonable enjoyment of the plaintiffs' property since the other access would do just as well.[6]

The *Wheeldon* v. *Burrows* rule is extended by the Law of Property Act (LPA) 1925 which implies into transfers and leases all rights that the land enjoys at the time of the transfer/lease (s.62(1)):

> A conveyance of land shall be deemed to include and shall by virtue of this Act operate to convey, with the land, all buildings, erections, fixtures, commons, hedges, ditches, fences, ways, waters, watercourses, liberties, privileges, easements, rights, and advantages whatsoever, appertaining or reputed to appertain to the land, or any part thereof, or, at the time of conveyance, demised, occupied, or enjoyed with, or reputed or known as part or parcel of or appurtenant to the land or any part thereof.

It is common (and good) practice to exclude the rule in transfers of part by inserting a clause in the transfer in the form of model clause 3 in **Appendix D1**.

The difficulties which can arise if implied easements are overlooked are well illustrated by *P & S Platt Limited* v. *Crouch* [2002] EWHC 2195 (Ch). In this case the seller owned a hotel as well as adjoining land and an island with moorings. The seller agreed to sell the hotel and to grant the buyer an option to buy the adjoining land and island. The buyer bought the hotel but did not exercise the option. The seller then decided to remove advertising signs for the hotel on his adjoining land and refused the buyer access to the island and its moorings. The buyer argued that he had implied easements under s.62 in respect of both the advertising signs and the use of the island and its moorings. The court agreed.

2.5 EXPRESSLY GRANTED RIGHTS OF WAY AND OTHER EASEMENTS

2.5.1 The need for a deed of release or a statutory declaration or insurance?

If an investigation of title reveals that the development site is subject to certain rights (such as a right of way or a drainage easement) it will be necessary to ascertain:

---

[6] The Court of Appeal judgment referred to the dictum of Thesiger LJ in *Wheeldon* v. *Burrows* and the House of Lords decision in *Sovmots Investments Limited* v. *Secretary of State for the Environment and others* [1979] AC 144 (HL); *Brompton Securities Limited* v. *Secretary of State for the Environment* [1977] 2 All ER 385 (HL).

- whether the rights are ever exercised;
- whether the rights will affect the proposed development;
- whether the transfer or deed containing the rights contains any 'lift and shift' provisions;
- whether the rights can be accommodated within the site layout;
- whether a deed of release or an indemnity insurance policy will be required.

If the seller states that a right contained in a title document is no longer exercised then he should be required to provide a statutory declaration to this effect. The developer may also wish to consider obtaining a suitable title indemnity insurance policy, since the abandonment of an easement is extremely difficult to prove and the declaration alone may not satisfy a subsequent purchaser or his mortgagee.

2.5.2 Interference with easements and planning conditions

Acting in accordance with a planning condition is not a justification for interfering with an easement or preventing a person from exercising an easement. The authority for this is the Court of Appeal decision in *Wheeler and another* v. *JJ Saunders Limited and others* [1995] 2 All ER 697. In this case the court had to consider whether the grant of planning permission permitting the erection of two pig housing units constituted a defence to an action in nuisance (in the form of the smell from the pigs). The court held that, unlike Parliament, a planning authority has no jurisdiction to authorise a nuisance, save in so far as it has a statutory power to permit a change in the character of a neighbourhood.

It will be apparent from this case that where, in accordance with the requirement of a planning condition, a developer stops up a private road, it will not be a defence to an action in nuisance brought by the person having the benefit of a right of way over the road to claim that the stopping up of the road was authorised by planning permission.

The decision in *Wheeler* can be contrasted with the decision in *Allen* v. *Gulf Oil Refining Limited* [1980] UKHL 9. In the latter case, the House of Lords stated:

> where Parliament by express action or by necessary implication has authorised the construction and use of an undertaking or works, that carries with it an authority to do what is authorised with immunity from action based on nuisance.

The cases of *Hirose Electrical UK Limited* v. *Peak Ingredients Limited* [2011] EWCA Civ 987 and *Coventry and another* v. *Lawrence and others* [2012] EWCA Civ 26 illustrate that whether or not a nuisance authorised by a planning permission will be actionable will depend upon the character of the area in which the offending activity was carried out.

2.5.3 Varying the route of a right of way

A developer is not entitled to realign or alter the route of a right of way in the absence of agreement or a provision in the relevant deed of grant entitling the grantor to do so. The question of whether a servient owner is entitled to vary the route of an easement was considered by Lightman J in *Greenwich NHS Trust* v. *London and Quadrant Housing* [1998] 1 WLR 1749 (Ch D):

> In my view, a servient owner has no right to alter the route of an easement of way unless such a right is an express or implied term of the grant of the easement or is subsequently conferred on him. This view accords with the decision in *Deacon* v. *South Eastern RLY Co* [1889] 61 LT 337. In that case the question arose in respect of an easement of necessity and North J followed earlier authorities which were to this effect.

Notwithstanding that a servient owner has no right to alter the route of a right of way, the court may, in exceptional circumstances, be prepared to refuse to grant injunctive relief. For example, the court refused to grant injunctive relief in the *Greenwich NHS Trust* case, where the realignment of the right of way improved road safety. Also, the owners of the dominant land had failed to object to the realignment and the realignment was necessary to achieve an object of substantial public and local importance.

2.5.4 Interference with a right of way

A developer is not entitled to substantially interfere with the route of a right of way affecting a development site (e.g. by constructing a road over or laying a sewer under a section of the right of way and thereby temporarily preventing or restricting the exercise of the right of way by the dominant owner) in the absence of an express right to do so. It is established law that interference with an easement is actionable if the interference is substantial and even a temporary interference will be actionable if it is substantial. In *West* v. *Sharp* (2000) 79 P & CR 327 (CA) Mummery LJ described the test for an actionable interference in the following terms:

> Not every interference with an easement, such as a right of way, is actionable. There must be a substantial interference with the enjoyment of it. There is no actionable interference with a right of way if it can be substantially and practically exercised as conveniently after as before the occurrence of the alleged obstruction. Thus, the grant of a right of way in law in respect of every part of a defined area does not involve the proposition that the grantee can in fact object to anything done on any part of the area which would obstruct passage over that part. He can only object to such activities, including obstruction, as substantially interfere with the exercise of the defined right as for the time being is reasonably required by him.

In deciding whether a right of way can be substantially and practically exercised as conveniently after as before the occurrence of an obstruction, it is not open to the grantor/servient owner to dictate how the grantee/dominant owner exercises his right and the grantee/dominant owner will be entitled to enforce his right so as to follow his preferred modus operandi. In *B&Q plc* v. *Liverpool and Lancashire Properties Limited* [2001] 1 EGLR 92 (Ch D) Blackburn J stated as follows:

> The test of an actionable interference is not whether what the grantee is left with is reasonable, but whether his insistence upon being able to continue to use the whole of what he contracted for is reasonable. It is not open to the grantor to deprive the grantee of his preferred modus operandi and then argue that someone else would prefer to do things differently, unless the grantee's preference is unreasonable or perverse . . . If the grantee has contracted for the relative luxury of an ample right, he is not to be deprived of that right, in the absence of an explicit reservation of a right to build on it merely because it is a relative luxury, and the reduced, non-ample right would be all that was reasonably required.

Even if a developer, as the owner of the servient land, provides a dominant owner with an alternative access while temporarily blocking or obstructing the route of a right of way, there may be an actionable interference with the right, resulting in the grant of an injunction or damages (see *Lea* v. *Ward* [2017] EWHC 2231 (Ch)). An injunction is a discretionary remedy, but, in general, the courts do not treat those who deliberately interfere with an easement sympathetically. In *Lea* v. *Ward* the court held that there had been a substantial interference with a right of way enjoyed by Mr Lea's property over Mr Ward's neighbouring property even though Mr Ward had provided Mr Lea with an alternative access while completely blocking the route of his existing right of way for a period of five months. Mr Ward was fortunate that the court decided not to grant injunctive relief and only to award Mr Lea modest damages of £500. The court said that the provision of a new or alternative access was relevant to the consideration of what remedy should be granted and concluded that so long as Mr Ward agreed to remove part of the obstruction and to grant a new easement, it would not grant an injunction. The damages were modest because the interference with the easement was short-lived.

2.5.5 Summary

A developer will not be entitled to vary the route of a right of way granted by a deed of grant or a transfer, unless the document granting the easement contains suitable lift and shift provisions.

It will not be a good defence in an action brought by the dominant owner that the alternative route is no less convenient than the original route, although, in such circumstances, the courts may take the view that damages are an adequate remedy and refuse to grant injunctive relief.

A developer is not entitled to interfere, even temporarily, with a right of way, if the interference is substantial (see *West* v. *Sharp* (2000) 79 P & CR 327 (CA) and *Lea* v. *Ward* [2017] EWHC 2231 (Ch)).

2.6 TREE PRESERVATION ORDERS

If there are trees growing on a development site, the developer will need to ascertain whether or not they are protected. The local authority's replies to enquiries made using CON29[7] reveal whether there is an existing tree preservation order (TPO) and whether the local authority has decided to make a TPO in relation to the land. A TPO may prohibit the cutting down, topping, lopping, uprooting or wilful damage or destruction of trees without the consent of the local planning authority; and the developer should be made aware that it is a criminal offence to lop, top or fell a protected tree without such consent (TCPA 1990, s.198).

There are exceptions to the general prohibition. TPO offences do not apply to the cutting down, uprooting, topping or lopping of trees:

- which are dying or dead or have become dangerous; or
- in compliance with any obligations imposed by or under an Act of Parliament; or
- in so far as may be necessary for the prevention or abatement of a nuisance.

However, a developer would be well advised to exercise extreme caution when it is considering cutting down trees in reliance upon any of those exceptions. The developer should meticulously record its actions to allow it to defend any later action which may be brought by the local authority.

If the development site is affected by a TPO then the developer's lawyer should obtain a copy of the order from the local planning authority (including copies of all plans referred to in the order) and it will be necessary for the developer to consider whether the order will have any adverse effect on its development proposals. For example, the existence of a TPO could affect site design and prejudice viability if the locations of the protected trees limit the number of units or car parking permitted.

However, where a developer succeeds in its arguments with the local authority and full planning permission is granted for a development, which inevitably means that, in order to implement that permission, works will be necessary to TPO protected trees, the grant of that permission overrides the automatic prohibition in a TPO and separate TPO consent is not required.

Where a development site is located in a Conservation Area trees are protected but different and less formal rules apply (TCPA 1990, ss.211–212):

- A developer must give the local authority written notice of its intention to remove or undertake works to a tree.
- The local authority will have six weeks in which to consider the matters raised in the developer's notice and, if it believes that controls should be applied, it may make the tree subject to a TPO to give the local authority the desired level of control.

[7] Form CON29 Enquiries of the local authority (2016), enquiry 3.9.

- The local authority may confirm in writing that the developer may proceed with the works during the six-week period but the local authority is not obliged to respond.
- If the local authority fails to respond during the six-week period, the developer may, at the expiry of that period, undertake the notified works (but nothing more) within the period of two years from the expiry of the six-week period.

It will be important that the developer makes a full record of any application to the local authority to remove or undertake works to a tree in a Conservation Area and that it does not commence works to or remove a tree before the six-week period has expired.

2.7 MINES AND MINERALS

2.7.1 Mining searches

It is an accepted legal principle that ownership of land includes ownership of the airspace above the land and everything below the surface of the land. However, this principle is subject to certain exceptions. A party selling land may retain ownership of the minerals beneath the surface of the land by expressly excepting and reserving title to the mines and minerals; and no developer in England and Wales will ever acquire rights to work coal, gold or silver or to drill for oil. The Coal Authority, the Crown and oil companies all have rights to work these.

The developer's lawyer should check the gazetteer at **www.coal.gov.uk** to determine whether the land is situated in an area affected by previous, current or proposed working of coal or by brine subsidence. If the land is in an affected area, the developer's lawyer should carry out a CON29M search. The Coal Authority and the Law Society have published guidance for solicitors on the use and interpretation of CON29M searches.[8]

The developer's lawyer should also consider carrying out other mining searches, such as:

- a tin mining search for land in Cornwall, Devon and Somerset;[9]
- a clay mining search for land in Devon, Dorset and Cornwall;[10] and
- a limestone search for land in Dudley, Sandwell, Telford and Wrekin, Walsall and Wolverhampton.[11]

---

[8] The Coal Authority and the Law Society *Coal Mining and Brine Subsidence Claim Searches: Directory and Guidance* (6th edition, Law Society, 2006).

[9] Cornwall Consultants Limited provides a tin mining search. See **www.cornwallconsultants.co.uk**.

[10] A postcode search can be carried out online at **www.kabca.org** to determine whether the land is situated in an area affected by past mining of china clay or ball clay. If the land is in an affected area, solicitors should carry out a search with Imerys Minerals Limited or Sibelco UK Limited as appropriate (see **www.kabca.org** for contact details).

[11] A limestone mining search can be made of Dudley Metropolitan Borough Council, Sandwell Metropolitan Borough Council, Wolverhampton Borough Council, Walsall Metropolitan Borough Council and Telford and Wrekin Council.

2.7.2 Mineral exceptions and reservations and mining insurance

If a development site is affected by a mineral reservation, the wording and the extent of the reservation will need to be carefully checked. A mere reservation of ownership of mines and minerals to a third party should not of itself cause a developer any difficulty, unless there are minerals near the surface, in which case there would be a risk that the digging of foundations might give rise to a trespass. However, a right to win, work and carry away minerals is another matter, as is a right to 'let down the surface' of the land and a right to enter the surface of the land to extract minerals. Such rights could well present difficulties for potential purchasers and mortgagees (even if there is a provision for compensation to be paid in the event of damage being caused by such mining activities). Accordingly, if a development site is affected by mineral reservations then it would be prudent for the developer to obtain a mining rights indemnity policy. Although a developer may be prepared to take the commercial view that the planning authority would be unlikely to grant planning permission for the carrying out of mining activities beneath a residential estate, a mortgagee of the developer or a plot purchaser may not.

Usually, insurers will not be keen to issue a mining rights indemnity policy until planning permission for the proposed development has been granted, although some insurers may be prepared to issue a policy on a pre-planning basis for an additional premium. The insurers will normally require the following information in order to consider an insurance proposal:

- a copy of the actual planning permission authorising the development of the property;
- confirmation as to the market value of the property once fully developed;
- copies of any objection letters received by the local planning authority at the planning stage or, if no objection letters were received, written confirmation from the local planning authority to this effect;
- copies of all mining searches.

A developer's solicitor should be aware that it is possible for a mineral owner to apply to the Land Registry to be registered as the owner of the minerals under a separate sub-surface title (see **2.18.4**) and should always carry out a search of the Land Registry index map in respect of land being acquired (even if the title to the land is registered) in order to ascertain whether ownership of any mines and minerals beneath the land has been registered under a separate mineral title. If the search reveals the existence of a separate mineral title, the developer's solicitor should be aware that:

- there is a risk that the digging of foundations may give rise to a claim by the mineral owner for trespass. Clearly, the depth at which the minerals are located will be an important factor in determining whether the digging of foundations would be likely to give rise to a trespass and this may not be an issue if the mineral title states that the title includes only the mines and minerals lying at a specified depth below the surface of the land;
- potential plot purchasers may be concerned about the risk of minerals being worked in the future and possible subsidence, even if the reservation makes it clear that the mineral owner cannot enter the surface of the land to extract minerals and there is a requirement to make good any damage caused by subsidence.

Accordingly, where a separate sub-surface mineral title has been registered, the developer should consider:

- investigating the possibility of obtaining a mining rights indemnity policy; or
- requiring the purchase contract to be made conditional upon the seller acquiring the sub-surface mineral title or the grant of suitable sub-surface legal easements. However, the developer's solicitor should be aware that any approach to the mineral owner will make it impossible to obtain an indemnity policy.

The terms of any mining rights indemnity policy will need to be carefully considered in order to ensure that it provides the required cover. The policy should cover:

- claims for trespass;
- any reduction in the open market value arising from the exercise of the mineral rights;
- any sum payable to free the property from the rights;
- the cost of demolition of any dwellings to allow mineral extraction;
- subsidence caused by the enforcement of the mineral rights after the date of the policy.

2.8 RESTRICTIVE COVENANTS

Restrictive covenants are covenants which are negative in substance even though they may be expressed in positive terms. The test is whether the covenant restricts the use and enjoyment of the land affected. If it does, it is a restrictive covenant.

If the title to a development site is subject to a restrictive covenant, it will be necessary to consider whether the covenant will:

- prevent or restrict the proposed development; and
- be binding on or enforceable against the developer.

Determining whether a restrictive covenant will prevent or restrict the proposed development is not always a straightforward matter. For example, use of land for a purpose ancillary to the use prohibited by a restrictive covenant is not a breach of the covenant, unless the covenant also expressly prohibits ancillary uses. The Court of Appeal considered this in *Cooperative Retail Services Limited* v. *Tesco Stores Limited* (1998) 76 P & CR 328 (CA) and the High Court adopted the same approach in *Elliott* v. *Safeway Stores plc* [1995] 1 WLR 1396 (Ch D).

In the *Tesco Stores* case Tesco had constructed a new superstore on a site. Part of the site was subject to a restrictive covenant preventing use for food retailing, but the superstore was not erected on this part of the site, which was used exclusively as landscaping. The Co-op had the benefit of the covenant and sought to enforce it, arguing that the burdened land was an integral part of the whole site which was being used for food retailing. The High Court agreed. Tesco then appealed and the Court of Appeal overturned the earlier decision of the High Court. The Court of Appeal, while accepting that the act of making amenity land available for that purpose was ancillary or incidental to the carrying on of a food retailing business, held that the part of the site which was burdened by the covenant was not being used for food retailing.

In the *Safeway Stores* case land was subject to a restrictive covenant prohibiting the land from being used for the sale of fuel and lubricants. The party with the benefit of the covenant sought an injunction restraining Safeway from using part of the land which was burdened by the covenant as an access to a petrol filling station. However, the High Court ruled that Safeway was simply using the land as an accessway and that it was not in breach of the restrictive covenant prohibiting the land from being used for the sale of fuel.

The developer's lawyer, having discovered a restrictive covenant, should next consider whether the covenant is enforceable. A covenant may not be enforceable if, for example:

- there has been a change in the ownership of the land benefiting from the covenant; or
- there has been a change in the ownership of the land burdened by the covenant.

A person who is not the original covenantee will need to show that he is entitled to the benefit of the covenant and if a person seeks to enforce a covenant against a person who is not the original covenantor he will need to show that that person has become subject to the burden of the covenant (see **2.10**).

If the covenant is enforceable or may be enforceable then the developer's lawyer should consider taking one or more of the following courses of action:

- obtain a deed of release from the beneficiaries of the covenant;
- obtain a restrictive covenant indemnity insurance policy;
- apply to the Upper Tribunal under LPA 1925, s.84 for the restrictive covenant to be modified or discharged.

2.8.1 Deed of release of restrictive covenant

A deed of release may be obtained from the beneficiaries of the covenant (see **Appendix C11**). However, before approaching the beneficiaries for a deed of release, the developer's lawyer should first consider that if the beneficiaries decline, an insurer is unlikely to issue an indemnity insurance policy (see **2.8.2**).

Also, if the original beneficiary has disposed of part of the land which originally benefited from the restrictive covenant, the original beneficiary may not be able to release the covenant absolutely and it may be necessary to obtain additional deeds of release from the purchasers from the original beneficiary (or an indemnity insurance policy).

2.8.2 Restrictive covenant indemnity insurance policy

Before issuing such a policy the insurers will normally (but not always) require sight of the planning permission authorising the proposed development and confirmation that no objections have been raised on covenant grounds by any persons entitled to the benefit of the restrictive covenants. The developer may, therefore, need to make the contract for the purchase of the site conditional upon obtaining a restrictive covenant indemnity policy. Although some insurers will be prepared to issue a policy on a pre-planning basis, the additional risk to the insurer will be reflected in the premium payable. The developer should be aware that the insurers will be unlikely to issue an indemnity insurance policy in circumstances where the beneficiaries of the covenant have been approached and have refused to enter into a deed of release. A developer should, therefore, think twice before approaching the beneficiaries for a deed of release.

Although an indemnity policy can be useful in helping to overcome a title issue, it does have certain limitations, including the following:

- The policy will usually cover the insured against the costs of court action and any loss or damage that the insured may sustain by reason of any final judgment enforcing the restrictive covenants up to a pre-agreed aggregate limit. It will not cover loss of profit or consequential loss and no monies will be payable under the policy if the developer is unable to sell the site because of the defect. It should, however, cover any diminution in the value of the development site up to the amount of the sum insured.
- There will be exclusions under the policy and these will need to be carefully considered.
- Full disclosure of all material facts will need to have been made to the insurer, otherwise the insurer could elect to declare the insurance contract void.
- The policy may not be regarded as acceptable protection by a prospective purchaser from the developer. (Where a developer is purchasing a development site with the benefit of an existing restrictive covenant indemnity policy the developer's lawyer should always insist on seeing a copy of the original

insurance proposal and copies of all correspondence between the lawyer acting for the insured and the insurers.)
- The developer will need to ensure that the policy will exist for the benefit of the developer's successors in title and all mortgagees.

2.8.3 Application to modify or discharge a restrictive covenant

The Upper Tribunal (being the statutory successor to the Lands Tribunal) has powers (LPA 1925, s.84) to discharge or modify a restrictive covenant in certain circumstances, including where:

- by reason of changes in the character of the property or the neighbourhood the covenant ought to be regarded as obsolete;
- its discharge or modification would not injure the persons benefiting from it; or
- it prevents a reasonable use of the land for public or private purposes and either does not confer any practical benefit of substantial value or advantage on the persons benefiting from it or is contrary to the public interest and (in both cases) the payment of money will be an adequate compensation (LPA 1925, s.84(1)).

An application to the Upper Tribunal to discharge or modify a restrictive covenant can be made by 'any person interested in any freehold land affected by any restriction arising under covenant or otherwise as to the use thereof or the building thereon', thus including mortgagees and persons holding the benefit of an option to a purchase agreement or a conditional purchase contract. The Upper Tribunal is governed by the Tribunal Procedure (Upper Tribunal) (Land Chamber) Rules 2010 (SI 2010/2600) (the Rules) and an application to the Upper Tribunal will need to comply with rule 32 of the Rules and to include the address or description of the land affected by the covenant and the identity of any person whom the applicant believes may have the benefit of the covenant.

Developers can take comfort from a number of Lands Tribunal decisions in which s.84 was used to good effect, including the decisions in *Jilla's Application* [2000] 23 EG 147 and in *Davies Application* [2001] 03 EG 134. In both cases the Lands Tribunal held that the covenant was not obsolete and that discharging it would injure the beneficiaries of the covenant. Thus, the covenant could not be discharged on either of those grounds. However, the Tribunal was prepared to exercise its powers to modify the restrictive covenant to permit the development and ordered the developers to pay the beneficiaries modest compensation (£10,000 and £2,450) to reflect the reduction in value of the beneficiaries' land.

The Court of Appeal has provided guidance, in *Winter and another* v. *Traditional & Contemporary Contracts Limited* [2007] EWCA Civ 1088, as to how any compensation payable pursuant to a s.84 award should be calculated. The Court of Appeal held that awards should be based on the loss caused by the diminution in value of the land owned by the beneficiary of the covenant, not on the loss of opportunity to extract a share in the development value of the land which is subject to the covenant.

Notwithstanding the decisions in *Jilla's Application* and *Davies Application*, a developer should not submit an application to discharge or modify a restrictive covenant too hastily and not without careful consideration of the following:

- the chances of success – it is notoriously difficult to predict the outcome of an application to the Upper Tribunal under LPA 1925, s.84 and the developer should be aware that a large number of applications are unsuccessful and that the power of the Upper Tribunal to discharge or modify restrictive covenants is discretionary (see *George Wimpey Bristol Limited* v. *Gloucestershire Housing Association Limited* [2011] UKUT 91 (LC));
- the number of persons likely to oppose the application – usually the persons entitled to oppose an application will be those with the benefit of the restrictive covenant as original covenantee (or persons with the benefit by virtue of annexation, assignment or under a building scheme), persons claiming through them (such as tenants and mortgagees) and persons who remain entitled to grant or withhold consent under the provisions of the covenant;
- whether any compensation is likely to be payable to the beneficiary of the restrictive covenant, if so, and whether it is likely to be substantial;
- costs consequences – if the application is unsuccessful, the developer may be responsible for the objector's costs;
- whether anything can be done to improve the chances of an application being successful – for example, by delaying submitting the application until planning permission has been granted.

2.8.4 Land Registry entries: deeds of release and unknown covenants

If the Land Registry is not satisfied that a deed of release has brought about the full and unqualified release of certain covenants it will enter a note on the registered title stating that by a deed of release certain covenants 'were purported to be released'. In such circumstances, it would be prudent for the developer to require the vendor to obtain a restrictive covenant indemnity policy. It would also be prudent to obtain such a policy where the Land Registry has entered a note on a registered title stating that the land is subject to covenants contained in a conveyance, a copy of which was not produced to the Land Registry on first registration. The developer's lawyer may be negligent if he does not draw such entries to the attention of the developer.

2.9 POSITIVE COVENANTS

Positive covenants will not usually be a cause of concern for developers since, as a general rule, the burden of a positive covenant cannot be enforced against a successor in title of the original covenantor. However, this rule is subject to various exceptions, and it is possible to circumvent the rule by using certain devices. The following points should be noted:

- A covenant to make payments towards the upkeep of roads and sewers over which there are rights of way and drainage easements will be binding on a successor in title of the original covenantor, unless the successor in title declines to exercise the right. This is because of the rule in *Halsall* v. *Britzell* [1957] Ch 169 (Ch D) that a person cannot enjoy the benefit of a deed without complying with the obligations contained in the deed. The rule was applied in *Rhone* v. *Stephens* [1994] 2 AC 310 (HL) and more recently in *Wilkinson and others* v. *Kerdene Limited* [2013] EWCA Civ 44. However, in *Rhone*, the House of Lords refined the benefit and burden principle, stating that for the burden to be enforceable it must be relevant to the benefit and that for a successor in title to be bound by the burden he should, at least in theory, be able to choose between enjoying the right or renouncing it. The House of Lords held that an obligation to contribute towards the cost of maintaining a roof was not relevant to a right of support, that a person was not in a position to give up a right of support of a building and that the covenant to contribute towards the cost of maintaining the roof was therefore unenforceable against the successors in title of the original covenantor. By contrast, in *Halsall* the defendant could, at least in theory, choose between enjoying a right to use roads and sewers and paying his share of the cost or alternatively giving up the right and saving his money.
- On a sale of land, it is possible to make positive covenants binding on a successor in title of the purchaser by:
  - including a restrictive covenant in the transfer which prohibits the transferee from making a disposal without procuring that the disponee enters into a deed of covenant to perform the positive covenants in the transfer; and
  - requiring a restriction to be entered on the title to the burdened property prohibiting any disposition without a certificate signed by a conveyancer confirming that the requirement for a deed of covenant has been complied with.
- Positive covenants may be made binding on a successor in title of the original covenantor by creating an unbroken chain of indemnity covenants. If S sells land to B and the transfer of the land to B contains positive covenants by B, B will be liable for any breaches of the covenants even after B has parted with his interest in the land by virtue of privity of contract. If B subsequently sells the land to C and C fails to perform the positive covenants S will not be able to sue C for breach of covenant. However, S will be entitled to sue B and if B obtained a covenant of indemnity against future breaches of the positive covenants from C then B will be able to sue C in reliance on the covenant for indemnity.
- On a sale of land, it is possible to make positive covenants binding on a successor in title of the purchaser by creating a rentcharge and reserving a right of re-entry annexed to the rentcharge. A right of entry annexed 'for any purpose' to a legal rentcharge creates a legal interest in land (see LPA 1925, s.1(2)(e)) and will be binding on the successors in title of the purchaser. In the

words of the authors of *Megarry & Wade* 'a device commonly used in practice for securing the performance of covenants to build, repair, and so on, is to reserve a rentcharge, and to annex to it a right of entry allowing its proprietor to enter and make good any default in the observance of the covenants, charging the cost to the owner in possession. Such covenants will usually relate to the rentcharge since they will improve the security, but the words 'for any purpose' suggest that no particular connection is necessary; and in practice the rentcharge may be a nominal amount and may serve merely as a peg on which to hang enforcement of the covenants' (see *Megarry & Wade: The Law of Real Property* (8th edition, Sweet & Maxwell, 2012), p.1385). Rentcharges are sometimes used by developers as a device for ensuring the enforceability of positive service charge obligations contained in a freehold transfer of part of a residential estate (see **7.6.2**).

- It is also possible for a vendor of a freehold to reserve a right of re-entry as a means of enforcing positive covenants without creating a rentcharge (see *Megarry & Wade: The Law of Real Property* (8th edition, Sweet & Maxwell, 2012), p.1386).
- A local authority may enforce a covenant made pursuant to the Local Government (Miscellaneous Provisions) Act 1982, s.33 to carry out any works or do any other thing on or in relation to land.
- Planning obligations contained in a planning agreement made pursuant to TCPA 1990, s.106 will be binding on the successors in title of the party entering into such obligations (s.106(3)).
- An obligation to pay money after completion of the sale of land (such as an obligation to pay overage or an obligation to pay a deferred instalment of the purchase price) will not be binding on the purchaser's successors in title, but could give rise to an unpaid vendor's lien, which the vendor would be entitled to protect by registering a unilateral notice on the purchaser's title.

Deciding whether a covenant is positive or negative is not as straightforward as it might first appear. For example, a negative covenant may be expressed in positive terms, as illustrated in the following cases. In *Tulk* v. *Moxhay* (1848) 2 Ph 774 (Ch D) the court construed a covenant to keep and maintain a piece of land 'in an open state, uncovered with any buildings, in neat and ornamental order' as a negative obligation not to build on the land. In *Jarvis Homes* v. *Marshall* [2004] EWCA Civ 839 the court construed a covenant to use land 'as a private residence only' as a restrictive covenant not to use the land for any purpose other than as a private residence; and in *Powell* v. *Hemsley* (1909) 2 Ch 252 (CA) the court construed a covenant to submit plans for approval before carrying out any building work as a restrictive covenant not to build without first submitting plans.

2.10 ENFORCEMENT OF RESTRICTIVE COVENANTS

2.10.1 Original covenantee against original covenantor

As a general rule a covenant may be enforced by the original covenantee against the original covenantor without exception (by virtue of the privity of contract rule).

2.10.2 Original covenantee against successor of original covenantor

For the burden of a restrictive covenant to be enforceable by the original covenantee against successors in title of the original covenantor the following conditions must be satisfied:[12]

- The covenantee must have retained land at the date when the covenant was entered into and the retained land must be near the land burdened by the covenant.
- The covenantee's retained land must be sufficiently defined or identifiable.
- The covenantee's retained land must be adjacent to or near the burdened land.
- The covenant must 'touch and concern' the covenantee's retained land. In modern language, it must relate to the covenantee's retained land and it must be imposed for the benefit of or to enhance or preserve the value or to protect the amenity of the covenantee's retained land (see *P & A Swift Investments* v. *Combined English Stores Group plc* [1988] UKHL 3). A covenant designed to secure an overage payment may not be regarded as benefiting land and may not be enforceable as a restrictive covenant against a successor in title of the original covenantor (see *Cosmichome Limited* v. *Southampton City Council* [2013] EWHC 1378 (Ch) and *Bryant Homes Southern Limited* v. *Stein Management Limited* [2016] EWHC 2435 (Ch) (in which the court came to a different decision from the one reached in *Cosmichome Limited*)).
- The covenant must not be personal. Whether the burden of a covenant entered into before 1 January 1926 is personal to the original covenantor will depend on the wording of the covenant. Wording such as 'the covenantor for himself his heirs executors administrators and assigns' and 'the covenantor for himself and his successors in title' would suggest that the covenant is not intended to be personal and that it is intended to be binding on the covenantor's successors in title. Restrictive covenants entered into after 1 January 1926 will be treated as being given by the original covenantor and his successors in title, unless a contrary intention is expressed. The Law of Property Act 1925, s.79(1) states:

  > A covenant relating to any land of a covenantor or capable of being bound by him, shall, unless a contrary intention is expressed, be deemed to be made by the covenantor on behalf of himself his successors in title and the persons deriving title under him or them, and, subject as aforesaid, shall have effect as if such successors and other persons were expressed.

[12] These conditions were established by the decision in *Tulk* v. *Moxhay* (1848) 2 Ph 774.

- The covenant must have been protected by registration at the Land Registry or the Land Charges Department. In the case of unregistered land, a restrictive covenant entered into after 1 January 1926 must be registered as a Class D(ii) land charge to be enforceable against a purchaser for money or money's worth and, in the case of registered land, restrictive covenants must be noted in the charges register to be binding on the registered proprietor or the purchaser acquiring title under a registered disposition (by virtue of the Land Registration Act (LRA) 2002, ss.29, 30). A purchaser of registered land will not be concerned with any covenant not protected by notice on the registered title even if he has actual notice of the covenant.
- There must have been no common ownership of the land benefiting from the covenant and the burdened land since the covenant was imposed.

2.10.3 Successor of original covenantee against original covenantor

For the benefit of a restrictive covenant to be enforceable by a successor of the original covenantee, the following must apply:

- The covenant must not be personal to the original covenantee or limited. For example, a covenant 'for the benefit of the Transferor's adjoining land or any part thereof remaining unsold' will lapse if none of the adjoining land remains unsold. Also, where it is clear from the deed containing the covenant in favour of the transferor that, as a matter of construction, the expression 'the Transferor' does not include the successors in title of the transferor, the covenant will not be enforceable by the transferor's successors in title and will cease to be enforceable if the transferor dies or becomes insolvent or goes into liquidation (see **2.11.5**).
- The covenant must have been protected by registration.
- The covenant must 'touch and concern' the land in which the successor of the original covenantee has an interest (i.e. the covenant must affect the nature, quality, amenity or value of the covenantee's land and it must be imposed for the benefit of or to preserve or enhance the value of the covenantee's land or to protect the amenity of the covenantee's land).
- The benefit of the covenant must have passed to the successor of the original covenantee by annexation, express assignment or by virtue of the covenant being imposed as part of a building scheme.

In respect of pre-1925 covenants, it is not necessary to have express words of annexation. If, on the construction of the document containing the covenant, both the land which is intended to be benefited and an intention to benefit that land can clearly be established, the benefit will be annexed to the land.

In respect of post-1925 covenants, statutory annexation under LPA 1925, s.78 will apply provided that it is clear from the document containing the covenant that the covenantee has retained land which is capable of benefiting from the covenant and which can be readily identified (with the assistance of extrinsic evidence if necessary.)[13] The Law of Property Act 1925, s.78(1) states:

> A covenant relating to any land of the covenantee shall be deemed to be made with the covenantee and his successors in title and the persons deriving title under him or them and shall have effect as if such successors and other persons were expressed. For the purposes of this subsection in connexion with covenants restrictive of the user of land 'successors in title' shall be deemed to include the owners and occupiers for the time being of the land of the covenantee intended to be benefited.

It should be noted that s.78 is not mandatory and that it will not apply if it appears from the document containing the covenant that the parties intended the covenant to be personal to the covenantee and that the benefit should not run with the covenantee's land (see *Roake* v. *Chadha and another* [1983] 3 All ER 503 (Ch D)).

2.10.4 Successor of original covenantee against successor of original covenantor

For the enforcement of restrictive covenants by and against successors in title to the original parties, the rules set out above will have to be satisfied. For example, the benefit/burden of a covenant will not pass if it is personal to the original covenantee/original covenantor. The general rule is that the plaintiff will need to demonstrate that the benefit of the covenant has passed to him and that the burden of the covenant has passed to the defendant.

2.11 INTERPRETING RESTRICTIVE COVENANTS

2.11.1 Meaning of private residence

In *Jarvis Homes* v. *Marshall* [2004] EWCA Civ 839 the Court of Appeal held that:

- a covenant that the purchaser will not 'use or permit or suffer to be used the land hereby conveyed or any part thereof or any building or erection now or at any time hereafter erected thereon for any trade business or manufacture but will use the same as a private residence only' applied not only to the buildings but also to the garden; and
- the construction of a roadway over part of the garden leading to a proposed housing development on adjoining land would breach that covenant.

---

[13] See the decision in *Crest Nicholson Residential (South) Limited* v. *McAllister* [2004] EWCA Civ 410. Following the decision in *Federated Homes Limited* v. *Mill Lodge Properties Limited* [1980] 1 WLR 594 (CA) it was widely thought that LPA 1925, s.78 would result in an automatic statutory annexation. However, in the *Crest* case it was decided that for statutory annexation to apply, the identity of the land to be benefited must be ascertained from the document containing the covenant.

2.11.2 Meaning of a private dwellinghouse

In *Crest Nicholson Residential (South) Limited* v. *McAllister* [2004] EWCA Civ 410 Neuberger J held that the erection of more than one house on land subject to a covenant that 'the premises shall not be used for any purpose other than those of or in connection with a private dwellinghouse or for professional purposes' would give rise to a breach of covenant and that the expression 'a private dwellinghouse' in this covenant means 'a single dwellinghouse'.

This decision can be contrasted with the Court of Appeal decision in *Martin* v. *David Wilson Homes Limited* [2004] EWCA Civ 1027 in which the court had to consider the meaning of the expression 'a private dwellinghouse' in a covenant 'not to use or permit or suffer any buildings [erected on land] to be used for any other purpose than as a private dwellinghouse'. The court held that the expression 'a private dwellinghouse' in this covenant did not restrict the use/development of the land to a single dwellinghouse.

2.11.3 Covenants prohibiting access

As mentioned above, the court decided in *Jarvis Homes* that the construction of a roadway across land to provide access to a new housing development would constitute a breach of the covenant to use the land 'as a private residence only'. Neuberger LJ ruled that the owner of the burdened land was entitled to use it for all residential activities which might reasonably take place within the curtilage of a private dwellinghouse, but that using a substantial part of the burdened land as a roadway to provide access to an adjoining housing development fell outside the range of uses permitted by the covenant.

The decision in the *Jarvis Homes* case can be contrasted with the decision in *GLN (Copenhagen) Southern Limited* v. *ABC Cinemas Limited* [2004] EWCA Civ 1279. In the latter case the court held that using land to gain access to or to provide services to a cinema would not constitute a breach of the covenant not to use the land or any part of it as a cinema. As previously discussed, it would seem that if land burdened by a restrictive covenant is being used for a purpose which is ancillary to the prohibited use then this will not be a breach of covenant – the covenant will be breached only if the burdened land is used for the use which is specifically prohibited.

It will be apparent from the decisions in the *Jarvis Homes* and *GLN (Copenhagen) Southern Limited* cases that where access to a proposed development is across land affected by restrictive covenants, the wording of the covenants will need to be carefully analysed by the developer's lawyer.

2.11.4 Meaning of 'structure'

Would the existence of a covenant prohibiting the erection of a building or other structure on defined land prevent the construction of an access road across that land? It probably would not, so long as the road is not elevated. However, the erection of street lighting may be a breach of the covenant. Scammell states:

> Whilst making a road involves works of construction, prima-facie the construction of a road which was level with the surrounding land would not amount to the construction of a building or structure.[14]

2.11.5 Meaning of 'transferor's approval'

A restrictive covenant which prohibits the carrying out of any building works until plans have been approved by 'the Transferor' may be personal to the original transferor or may extend to and include the successors in title of the original transferor. It depends on the intention of the parties and the wording of the whole of the conveyance or transfer containing the covenant.

In the case of *Margerison* v. *Bates* [2008] EWHC 1211 (Ch), the High Court held that the expression 'the Vendor' referred only to the original vendor and that a restrictive covenant against alterations did not give the original vendor's successors in title the power to give or refuse consent to plans. The High Court reached the same conclusion in *City Inn (Jersey) Limited* v. *10 Trinity Square Limited* [2008] EWCA Civ 156 and *Churchill* v. *Temple and others* [2010] EWHC 3369 (Ch). In *City Inn (Jersey) Limited* a transfer contained a covenant not to make any external alterations or additions without the approval in writing of 'the Estate Officer for the time being of the Transferor' and the requirement to obtain the consent of 'the Estate Officer for the time being of the Transferor' was construed as referring solely to the original transferor even though it no longer owned any of the land which originally benefited from the covenant. The transfer defined the Port of London Authority as 'the Transferor' and Jacob LJ held that in circumstances in which the expression 'the Transferor' is a defined term, that term could only be given a different meaning if to give the term its defined meaning would lead to an absurdity. In *Churchill* the High Court held that the expression 'the Vendors' contained in a covenant 'not to make any structural alteration or addition to a permitted dwellinghouse without the written consent of the Vendors or their surveyor' referred only to the original vendors. The covenant clause did not contain any reference to the successors in title of the vendors and the expression 'the Vendors' had earlier been defined as the original vendors. These decisions can be contrasted with the decision in *Mahon* v. *Sims* [2005] 3 EGLR 67 (QBD) in which the High Court construed a requirement to obtain the consent of 'the Transferors' as including the successors in title of the original transferors even though there was no reference to successors in title in the transfer. In this case a covenant prohibited any building without obtaining the transferors' prior consent and the court held that, on the construction of the covenant, the words 'the Transferors' included the current owners. The expression 'the Transferors' was not a defined term and Hart J held that the covenant was apt to

---

[14] EH Scammell *Land Covenants* (Bloomsbury Professional, 1995), p.234.

include successors in title because that was the effect of LPA 1925, s.78 and because express words of annexation were used, making it clear that the benefit of the covenant was intended to run with the land.

The above cases illustrate the importance of:

- reading the wording of a restrictive covenant carefully and considering the terms of the whole of the document containing the covenant. If the covenant clause refers to 'the approval of the Transferor' and there are other clauses in the conveyance or transfer which refer to 'the Transferor and its successors in title' then this would suggest that it was intended that the covenant should be personal to the original transferor (unless the expression 'the Transferor' is a defined term and the definition includes successors in title); and
- drafting precision: the draftsman needs to consider, where a consent covenant is to be imposed, whether the covenant should benefit the transferor's successors in title and continue to apply after the transferor has sold the land benefiting from the covenant.

2.11.6 Will a covenant against 'annoyance or nuisance' prohibit development?

In the light of the decision in *Dennis and others* v. *Davies* [2008] EWHC 2961 (Ch) a lawyer acting for a developer should carefully consider any covenant prohibiting a nuisance or an annoyance. The High Court held in this case that the construction of an extension to a house which obscured the claimant's river views breached a restrictive covenant not to do or suffer to be done 'anything of whatsoever nature which may be or become a nuisance or annoyance to the owners or occupiers for the time being of the estate'. The test would appear to be: would reasonable people, having regard to the ordinary use of a house for pleasurable enjoyment, be annoyed and aggrieved by the works? According to the court this test is objective and the annoyance must be assessed objectively by robust and common-sense standards.

2.12 DAMAGES AND INJUNCTIONS FOR BREACH OF RESTRICTIVE COVENANT

A person with the benefit of a restrictive covenant is likely to want to have the breach stopped by an injunction. However, the breach must be capable of being remedied by an injunction and the court may refuse to grant an injunction where the party with the benefit of the covenant has delayed bringing enforcement proceedings. In *Gafford* v. *Graham* [1999] 41 EG 159 (CA) the defendant was in breach of a covenant that 'no building of any description shall be allowed on the land hereby conveyed or any part thereof until detailed plans thereof have been submitted to and approved in writing by the Vendors'. The plaintiff had acquiesced in the breach and the Court of Appeal refused to grant an injunction stating that a party who stands by while a permanent and substantial structure is unlawfully erected, ought not to be granted an injunction to have it pulled down. Such a party may, however, be entitled to damages, but only if his acquiescence was not such as to make it unconscionable for him to seek to pursue his right to claim damages. The damages will usually reflect the sum that the court considers would reasonably have been negotiated by the parties for the release of the covenant or, in the words of Nourse LJ, 'the sum which the plaintiff might reasonably have demanded as a quid pro quo for relaxing the restrictions in perpetuity'.

In the case of *Harris* v. *Williams-Wynne* [2005] EWHC 151 (Ch) the High Court considered whether a person who acquiesced in the breach of a covenant 'not to erect any buildings on the land' could still claim damages for the breach. The court distinguished *Gafford* and held that the defendant's inactivity was not fatal to the damages claim but the amount awarded was only a small proportion of the development value. The defendant, unhappy with the damages award, appealed, but the appeal was dismissed. In his judgment, Bernard Livesey QC, sitting as a deputy judge of the High Court, referred to the judgment of Nourse LJ in *Gafford* v. *Graham* and summarised the principles derived from the various cases referred to him as follows:

- First, damages for breach of contract at common law are likely to be only nominal where the breach is of a negative covenant, such as the present, having regard to the difficulty of establishing actual damage to the land for the benefit of which the covenant was provided: *Surrey County Council* v. *Bredero Homes Limited* [1993] 1 WLR 1361 (CA).
- Secondly, more substantial damages may be awarded for the same breach under the Chancery Amendment Act 1858 (Lord Cairns's Act), s.2, subject only to the proviso that the court 'has jurisdiction to entertain an application for an injunction against a breach of . . . covenant'.
- Thirdly, the court has such jurisdiction if at the date of the institution of proceedings it would then have had jurisdiction to grant an injunction, whether or not it would have been prepared to do so on the facts. Since the question is one of jurisdiction, it is not necessary for the claimant to include a claim for an injunction in order to found a claim for damages under the Act: see generally per Millett LJ in *Jaggard* v. *Sawyer* [1995] 1 WLR 269 (CA) at 284–5.
- Fourthly, the claimant may lose his entitlement to claim damages if he has been guilty of such acquiescence as to make it in all the circumstances unconscionable for him to rely upon his legal right: see e.g. *Gafford* v. *Graham* [1999] 41 EG 159 (CA).
- Fifthly, damages should be awarded in such a sum as the claimants might reasonably have demanded as a quid pro quo for relaxing the covenant had the defendants applied to them for relaxation: see *Wrotham Park* v. *Parkside Homes* [1974] 1 WLR 798 (Ch D). The assessment assumes a hypothetical negotiation on the basis that each party is willing to agree a proper and not a

ransom price. The proper price will have regard to the amount of profit which will predictably result to the person bound by the covenant as a consequence of its release.

- Sixthly, the correct date for assessing damages is normally the date before the building works in question are started: see *Amec Developments Limited* v. *Jury's Hotel Management (UK) Limited* (2001) 82 P & CR 22 (Ch D) per Anthony Mann QC; and *Lane* v. *O'Brien Homes* [2004] EWHC 303 (QB) per David Clarke J.
- Seventhly, in a suitable case damages may be measured by the benefit gained by the wrongdoer from breach, that is to say based on restitution rather than compensation: see especially *Attorney-General* v. *Blake* [2001] 1 AC 268 (HL). Awards of this kind will be made when they are 'the just response to a breach of contract': *Attorney-General* v. *Blake* at 284F.

None of the above principles were challenged at the appeal hearing.

In general, the courts do not look favourably on those who commit a wilful breach of a restrictive covenant (or who deliberately interfere with an easement). Although the grant of an injunction is always discretionary, there is a presumption that one will be granted if a restrictive covenant has been knowingly breached. This principle was expressed in *Araci* v. *Fallon* [2011] EWCA Civ 668 by Jackson LJ who said:

> Where the defendant is proposing to act in clear breach of a negative covenant, in other words to do something which he has promised not to do, there must be special circumstances (e.g. restraint of trade contrary to public policy) before the court will exercise its discretion to refuse an injunction.

In similar vein, the Tribunal judge in *George Wimpey Bristol Limited* v. *Gloucestershire Housing Association Limited* [2011] UKUT 91 (LC) (a case in which a housebuilder applied to the Upper Tribunal to modify covenants under LPA 1925, s.84(1) after having constructed houses in knowing breach of the covenants) said:

> if ground (a a) [no practical benefit] had been made out it is unlikely that I would have exercised my discretion that I have to modify the covenant. This is because I find on the evidence that the extensive works which Wimpey Homes have carried out on the application land were not an inadvertent action resulting from the discovery of the covenant at a late stage in the development programme. Rather they were the result of a deliberate strategy of forcing through the development on the restricted land in the face of many objections from those entitled to the benefit of the restriction, to the point where they had so changed the appearance and character of the application land that the Tribunal would be persuaded to allow them to continue with the development. It is appropriate for the Tribunal to make it clear that it is not inclined to reward parties who deliberately flout their legal obligations in this way.

2.13 INTERPRETING THE MEANING OF COVENANTS

As with all questions of construction it is always possible that the court may take a different view from that of the developer or its lawyers. For this reason, if there is any doubt about the meaning or effect of a covenant it would be sensible to investigate the possibility of obtaining a restrictive covenant indemnity insurance policy.

2.14 TELECOMMUNICATIONS APPARATUS

Enquiries should be made of the vendor to ascertain whether there are any mobile phone masts or other electronic communications apparatus on the proposed development site. If the site is affected by any such apparatus, the developer will need to consider the terms of any agreement or lease relating to the apparatus and whether the apparatus will have any adverse effect on its development proposals. The obligations on the part of the owner of the site and any early termination provisions should be carefully checked. It would not be unusual for the agreement to impose an obligation on the owner of the site not to interfere with the apparatus or obstruct the line of sight to the apparatus. If the proposed development is likely to breach this or any other obligation, the developer may need to enter into negotiations with the operator to remove or relocate the apparatus (which is likely to have cost implications for the developer).

The developer will need to be aware that if the rights conferred on the operator by the telecoms agreement/lease cease to be exercisable (or if the agreement/lease contains a break clause which allows the occupier of the land on which the electronic communications apparatus is located to terminate the agreement/lease early) and the agreement/lease is a code agreement under the 2017 Electronic Communications Code (the Code) then the agreement/lease will continue under para.30 of the Code (and the operator will be entitled to continue to exercise the rights) until it is determined in accordance with paras.31 and 32 of the Code. (The Code is set out in the Digital Economy Act (DEA) 2017, Sched.1 and came into force on 28 December 2017. DEA 2017 inserts the Code as Sched.3A into the Communications Act (CA) 2003 and repeals the Electronic Communications Code (the 1984 Code) contained in the Telecommunications Act 1984, Sched.2.) Also, subject to the provisions of para.40 of the Code, the operator will be entitled to keep its apparatus on the land after the right entitling it to do so comes to an end or ceases to bind the landowner (see below). Bringing a code agreement to an end and obtaining the removal of the electronic communications equipment will, therefore, be a two-stage process.

It should be noted that if a telecoms agreement is not a code agreement (because it is a lease to which Part 2 of the Landlord and Tenant Act (LTA) 1954 applies and its primary purpose is not to grant code rights – see para.29(2) of the Code) and it benefits from the security of tenure regime, or, if the telecoms agreement is a lease within LTA 1954, Part 2 and it benefits from security of tenure and was subsisting before the Code came into force, then, in order to regain possession of the land on which the electronic communications apparatus is located following the expiration or earlier determination of the lease, it will be necessary for the landlord:

- to serve a notice to quit pursuant to LTA 1954, s.25 on the operator; and
- to establish a ground for possession under LTA 1954, s.30(1).

Under para.20 of the Code, an operator can require a person (a relevant person) to confer a code right on it or to be bound by a code right which is exercisable by the operator. Code rights are set out in para.3 of the Code and include rights:

- to install electronic communications apparatus on, under or over land;
- to keep installed electronic communications apparatus which is on, under or over land;
- to inspect, maintain, adjust, alter, repair, upgrade or operate electronic communications apparatus;
- to carry out any works on land for or in connection with the maintenance, adjustment, alteration, repair, upgrading or operation of electronic communications equipment.

To acquire code rights an operator must give the relevant person (i.e. the occupier of the relevant land) a notice in writing setting out the required code right or rights and all the other terms of the agreement that the operator seeks, and stating that the operator seeks the person's agreement to those terms. If the relevant person does not agree to confer or otherwise be bound by the code right(s) within 28 days beginning with the day on which the notice is given, or if at any time after the notice is given, the relevant person notifies the operator in writing that the relevant person does not so agree, the operator will be entitled to apply to the court for an order imposing an agreement on the operator and the relevant person (CA 2003, Sched.3A, para.20). The court may make an order if (and only if) it thinks that both of the following conditions are met:

- the prejudice caused to the relevant person by the order is capable of being adequately compensated by money; and
- the public benefit likely to result from making the order will outweigh the prejudice to the relevant person. (In deciding whether this condition is met, the court must have regard to the public interest in access to a choice of high-quality electronic services.)

The court may not make an order if it thinks that the relevant person (i.e. the occupier of the relevant land) intends to redevelop all or part of the land to which the code right(s) would relate, or any neighbouring land, and could not reasonably do so if the order were made (CA 2003, Sched.3A, para.21). The relevant person would probably have to demonstrate that he has a firm and settled intention to redevelop, that all necessary consents and approvals have been obtained and that there is nothing to prevent development taking place.

As mentioned above, if a telecoms agreement/lease is a code agreement within the meaning given to that expression in para.29 of the Code, the operator will be entitled to exercise the rights contained in the agreement even after they cease to be exercisable under the agreement (CA 2003, Sched.3A, para.30). As also pointed out, a business lease that is governed by LTA 1954, Part 2 and whose primary purpose is not to grant code rights will not be a code agreement and will not enjoy protection under the Code. This will be the case whether or not the lease is contracted out of LTA 1954, Part 2 (see CA 2003, Sched.3A, para.29(3)). Nor will a telecoms agreement which was subsisting before the Code came into force benefit from the statutory continuation provisions contained in the Code if it is a lease within LTA1954, Part 2 that benefits from security of tenure or it is a lease whose primary purpose is not to grant code rights and that lease has been contracted out of LTA 1954, Part 2 (see below). However, a lease granted after the Code came into force whose primary purpose is to grant code rights will be a code agreement and LTA 1954, Part 2 will not apply to it. An operator cannot enjoy protection under both the LTA 1954 and the Code.

A site provider (i.e. a person who has conferred a code right on an operator or who is bound by a code right) is entitled to bring a code agreement to an end by giving the operator a notice which:

- specifies the date on which the site provider proposes the code agreement should end. This date must be a date falling after the end of the period of 18 months beginning with the date on which the notice is given and after the date that the code right(s) would have ceased to be exercisable or the code agreement would have come to an end if the exercise of the code rights had not been statutorily continued by para.30 of the Code;
- states the ground on which the site provider proposes to bring the code agreement to an end (CA 2003, Sched.3A, para.31(2) and (3)).

The ground stated in the notice must be one of the following:

- substantial breaches by the operator of its obligations under the agreement;
- persistent delays by the operator in making payments to the site provider;
- the site provider intends to redevelop all or part of the land to which the code agreement relates, or any neighbouring land, and could not reasonably do so unless the code agreement comes to an end;
- the operator is not entitled to the code agreement because the test under para.21 of the Code for the imposition of a code agreement on the site provider is not met (see above).

Where a site provider serves a notice on an operator pursuant to para.31 of the Code, the code agreement to which it relates will end, unless the operator and the site provider agree to the continuation of the code agreement or both of the following occur:

- Within the period of three months beginning with the day on which the notice is given, the operator gives the site provider a counter-notice in accordance with para.32(3) of the Code. (The counter-notice must state that the operator does not want the existing code agreement to come to an end, that the operator wants the site provider to agree to confer or otherwise be bound by the existing code right on new terms or that the operator wants the site provider to agree to confer or be otherwise bound by a new code right in place of the existing code right.)
- Within the period of three months beginning with the day on which the notice is given, the operator applies to the court for an order under para.34 of the Code (CA 2003, Sched.3A, para.32(1)).

If the court decides that the site provider has established any of the grounds stated in the site provider's notice it must order that the code agreement comes to an end.

A person with an interest in land (a landowner) has the right to require an operator to remove its electronic communications apparatus from the land if one or more of the following conditions (set out in para.37 of the Code) are met:

- Since the coming into force of the Code, the landowner has never been bound by a code right entitling the operator to keep the apparatus on, under or over the land. (This condition (and the following condition) will not be met if the land is occupied by a person who conferred a code right on an operator entitling the operator to keep its apparatus on, over or under the land and that right was not conferred in breach of a covenant enforceable by the landowner (CA 2003, Sched.3A, para.37(4)).)
- The apparatus is not, or is no longer, used for the purposes of the operator's network and there is no reasonable likelihood that it will be used for that purpose.
- The Code has ceased to apply to the operator, the retention of the apparatus is not authorised by a scheme contained in an order under CA 2003, s.117 and there is no other person with a right conferred by or under the Code to keep the apparatus on the land.
- The apparatus was kept on the land pursuant to a transport land right or a street work right, that right has ceased to be exercisable and there is no other person with a right to keep the apparatus on the land.

The right of a landowner or an occupier of land to require the removal of electronic communications apparatus under para.37 of the Code is enforceable only in accordance with para.40 of the Code. Under para.40, the landowner or occupier must give a notice to the operator requiring the operator to remove its apparatus and to restore the land to the condition it was in before the apparatus was installed. The notice must comply with para.89 (notices given by persons other than operators) and specify the period within which the operator must complete the works. The period must be a reasonable one. If, within the period of 28 days beginning with the day on which the notice was given, the landowner and the operator are unable to reach agreement regarding the removal of the apparatus, the landowner or occupier may make an application to the court for an order under para.44(1) (order requiring operator to remove apparatus) or an order under para.44(3) (order enabling landowner to sell apparatus).

Telecoms agreements that were in existence on the date that the Code came into existence will be subject to the Code, but with modifications (see DEA 2017, Sched.2, para.2). The modifications include:

- The expression 'Code rights' will be interpreted in the way set out in the 1984 Code (DEA 2017, Sched.2, para.3).
- Part 3 of the Code (which includes paras.16 and 17) (assignment of code rights and power for the operator to upgrade or share apparatus) will not apply in relation to an existing agreement, which will be enforceable in the terms in which it was drafted (DEA 2017, Sched.2, para.5(1)). (Under para.16 any code agreement will be void to the extent that it prevents or limits the assignment of the agreement to another operator or it makes the assignment subject to certain conditions, although a term that requires the assignor to enter into a guarantee agreement is permissible.)
- Part 5 of the Code (which includes paras.29–35) (termination and modification of agreements) will not apply to an existing agreement in respect of land if:

  (a) the existing agreement is a lease within LTA 1954, Part 2 and that lease benefits from security of tenure (i.e. security of tenure has not been excluded); or
  (b) the existing agreement is a lease of land whose primary purpose is not to grant code rights and that lease has been contracted out of LTA 1954, Part 2 (i.e. security of tenure has been excluded) (DEA 2017, Sched.2, para.6(2) and (3)).

  Otherwise paras.29–35 will apply to existing telecoms agreements with amendments (set out in DEA 2017, Sched.2, para.7). These include the ability to give shorter notice of termination. Under Sched.2, para.7(3), where the unexpired term of the existing agreement at the coming into force of the Code is less than 18 months, para.31 applies (with necessary modifications) as if for the period of 18 months referred to in para.31(3)(a) there was substituted a period equal to the unexpired term or three months, whichever is the greater.

It will be apparent from the above that, from a landowner's point of view, the provisions of the Code are fairly draconian and that a landowner should be very wary of entering into a telecommunications agreement and allowing a telecom operator to erect a mobile phone mast or other electronic communications apparatus on his land, although he may have no choice if the operator is successful in obtaining a court order.[15] However, where a landowner is prepared to enter into a telecommunications agreement/lease, the terms of the proposed agreement/lease should be carefully checked and negotiated by a specialist in this area.

---

[15] Pursuant to CA 2003, Sched.3A, para.20 (see also **4.7**).

2.15 POSSESSORY TITLE AND ENLARGEMENT

There are four main classes of registered title:[16]

- absolute freehold;
- absolute leasehold;
- good leasehold; and
- possessory.

The best type of title is absolute title, but

> [r]egistration with possessory title has the same effect as registration with absolute title, except that it does not affect the enforcement of any estate, right or interest adverse to, or in derogation of, the proprietor's title subsisting at the time of registration or then capable of arising.
>
> (LRA 2002, s.11(7))

If a development site includes land with possessory title it would be prudent not to erect any buildings or roads on the land with the possessory title, notwithstanding that the majority of lenders (but not all) will probably accept a property registered with possessory title as good security provided that the property has the benefit of a defective title indemnity insurance policy.

If land has been registered with freehold possessory title for 12 years or more then the developer may wish to require the vendor to apply to the Land Registry for the freehold possessory title to be upgraded to freehold absolute title. The registrar has the power to upgrade freehold possessory title to absolute title under LRA 2002, s.62, in the following circumstances:

- where he is satisfied as to the title to the estate;
- where the land has been registered with possessory title for at least 12 years and the registrar is satisfied that the registered proprietor is in possession.

It is also worth noting that it may be possible for a lease with 'a residue unexpired of not less than two hundred years of a term, which, as originally created, was for not less than three hundred years' to be enlarged into a fee simple (LPA 1925, s.153). This is only possible if no rent is payable or the rent payable is a peppercorn, or such other rent as shall have no monetary value.

2.16 ADVERSE POSSESSION

A development site will sometimes include a strip or strips of land to which there is no documentary title. It may be the case that the vendor has acquired title to the land by having been in adverse possession of the land for more than 12 years, or that the

[16] Land Registration Act 2002, s.10(1). Section 10(2)–(6) explains when each type of title will be available.

vendor is in the process of acquiring such title. This will need to be established and where the vendor has been in adverse possession of unregistered land for more than 12 years, he should be asked to provide a suitable statutory declaration and to submit an application to the Land Registry to be registered as proprietor of the land. The statutory declaration should be in the vendor's own words rather than using terminology borrowed from a precedent book, and should cover all matters of relevance, including the following:

- the circumstances under which adverse possession commenced, including the date on which the adverse possession started;
- the nature of the possession, specifying the purpose for which the land has been and is being used;
- details of all steps taken by the vendor (such as the erection and maintenance of fencing and the carrying out of works or other activities) to show that the vendor had an intention to possess the land;
- confirmation that the vendor's occupation has not been under a lease, tenancy or licence, or with the consent of any person;
- full particulars of any disputes concerning the vendor's possession.

In determining whether someone has acquired title to land by adverse possession different rules will apply, depending on whether the land is registered or unregistered. However, the meaning of 'adverse possession' will be the same under both the Limitation Act 1980 (which, by virtue of LRA 2002, s.96, now applies only to unregistered land) and LRA 2002.

2.16.1 Meaning of adverse possession

There is no statutory definition of 'adverse possession'. However, case law (see, e.g. the leading case of *JA Pye (Oxford) Limited* v. *Graham* [2001] EWCA Civ 117) has established that in order to obtain title to land by adverse possession a squatter must demonstrate that:

- he has factual possession of the land;
- he has the necessary intention to possess the land;
- his possession is without the owner's consent;
- he and any predecessors through whom he claims has/have been in factual possession of the land with the necessary intention to possess and without the owner's consent for at least 12 years (in the case of unregistered land) or 10 years (in the case of registered land) prior to the date of the application for registration.

2.16.2 Factual possession

It would seem that for possession to be factual:

- it must be single and exclusive;

- the squatter must exercise a degree of control over the land; and
- the squatter must deal with the land as an owner might.

Slade J in *Powell* v. *McFarlane* (1979) 38 P & CR 452 (Ch D) ruled that:

> Factual possession signifies an appropriate degree of physical control. It must be a single and [exclusive] possession, though there can be a single possession exercised by or on behalf of several persons jointly. Thus an owner of land and a person intruding on that land without his consent cannot both be in possession of the land at the same time. The question what acts constitute a sufficient degree of exclusive physical control must depend on the circumstances, in particular the nature of the land and the manner in which land of that nature is commonly used or enjoyed . . . Everything must depend on the particular circumstances, but broadly, I think what must be shown as constituting factual possession is that the alleged possessor has been dealing with the land in question as an occupying owner might have been expected to deal with it and that no-one else has done so.

If land was previously open ground, the erection of fencing would be strong (but not conclusive) evidence of factual possession.

2.16.3 Intention to possess

It was held in *Powell* v. *McFarlane* that an intention to possess means 'the intention, in one's own name and on one's own behalf, to exclude the world at large, including the owner with the paper title if he be not himself the possessor, so far as is reasonably practicable and so far as the processes of the law will allow'.

2.16.4 No owner's consent

Possession cannot be adverse if it is with the consent of the owner. As Slade LJ explained in *Buckinghamshire County Council* v. *Moran* [1989] 2 All ER 225 (CA):

> Possession is never adverse within the meaning of the 1980 Act if it is enjoyed under a lawful title. If, therefore, a person occupies or uses land by licence of the owner with the paper title and his licence has not been duly determined, he cannot be treated as having been in adverse possession as against the owner of the paper title.

2.16.5 The period of possession: unregistered land

The Limitation Act 1980, s.15(1) states:

> No action shall be brought by any person to recover any land after the expiration of twelve years from the date on which the right of action accrued to him or, if it first accrued to some person through whom he claims, to that person.

The time limit of 12 years will be extended in certain circumstances. For example, where the owner of the land is the Crown or the land is held by a charitable corporation sole the limitation period will be 30 years. Land owned by the Crown will include land held *bona vacantia* following the dissolution of a limited company. The time limit will also be extended where land is held on trust or by a person under a disability.

A squatter will be able to pass on his interest in the land on which he is squatting to a purchaser or under a will or an intestacy, but the party acquiring the squatter's interest must immediately follow the original squatter into possession and hold the land for the remainder of the 12 years.

2.16.6 Making an application for registration of title based on adverse possession of unregistered land

A person wishing to claim adverse possession of unregistered land may apply to the Land Registry to be registered as proprietor of the land using Land Registry form FR1. This form should be submitted together with:

- a plan showing the land in question;
- form DL in duplicate;
- evidence in support of the application;
- various searches, including:
  - an index map search;
  - land charge search certificates in respect of the squatter, the owner and any previous owners;
  - a company search (if the paper owner is a company); and
  - a commons registration search;
- the appropriate fee.

If the application is successful, the Land Registry will usually register the squatter with possessory title. The Land Registry will only register the squatter with absolute title or good leasehold title where it is satisfied beyond reasonable doubt that the squatter's adverse possession has barred the owner's title. Usually this will be the case only where the Land Registry is satisfied that the owner has consented to, or could have no valid grounds for objecting to, the squatter being registered as proprietor of the land. The squatter's title will not, as a rule, be subject to any charge created by the owner after the start of the adverse possession. However, if the charge was created before the commencement of the adverse possession time will start to run against the chargee if the mortgage repayments cease with the adverse possession.

2.16.7 The Land Registration Act 1925 regime

Where title to land is registered and a squatter is able to demonstrate that as at 13 October 2003[17] he has been in adverse possession for 12 years or more then he will

[17] The Land Registration Act 2002 came into force on 13 October 2003.

be entitled to be registered as the proprietor of the land by virtue of LRA 2002, Sched.12, para.18(1) which states:

> Where a registered estate in land is held in trust for a person by virtue of section 75(1) of the Land Registration Act 1925 immediately before the coming into force of section 97, he is entitled to be registered as the proprietor of the estate.

Under the Land Registration Act 1925, s.75 (which has now been repealed) the Limitation Act 1980 applied to registered land in the same way as it applied to unregistered land and once a squatter had been in adverse possession for 12 years the registered estate was held on trust for the squatter until the squatter applied for registration.

The right of a squatter to be registered as the proprietor of a registered estate under LRA 2002, Sched.12, para.18(1) will subsist indefinitely against a registered proprietor who is holding on trust. However, if the registered proprietor makes a disposition for value then the squatter's right to be registered may be lost. The right for the squatter to be registered will operate as an overriding interest and will bind the purchaser provided that the squatter is in actual occupation of the land, but not if the occupation 'would not have been obvious on a reasonably careful inspection of the land at the time of the disposition' and the purchaser 'does not have actual knowledge' of the squatter's interest (LRA 2002, Sched.3, para.2).

In the light of the decision in *Beaulane Properties Limited* v. *Palmer* [2005] EWHC 817 (Ch) a squatter whose adverse possession ended between 1 October 2000 and 13 October 2003 will need to show (in addition to satisfying the other requirements for adverse possession) that his use of the land was inconsistent with the owner's intended use in order to establish his claim to adverse possession.

2.16.8 The Land Registration Act 2002 regime

Where title to land is registered and 12 years' adverse possession has not been established by 13 October 2003, a squatter will find it considerably more difficult to become registered as the proprietor of a registered estate. Although a squatter of registered land will be able to apply to the Land Registry to be registered as the proprietor of the land (by complying with the provisions of LRA 2002, Sched.6), the scope for being registered as the proprietor of a registered estate is very limited.

The Land Registration Act 2002 provides that 'a person may apply to the registrar to be registered as the proprietor of a registered estate in land if he has been in adverse possession of the estate for the period of ten years ending on the date of the application' (LRA 2002, Sched.6, para.1(1)). The 10-year period is subject to certain exceptions; for example, if the land is Crown foreshore then the required period is 60 years.

Where an adverse possession claim is made under Sched.6, the application is made using form ADV1. On receipt of such an application the registrar must give notice of the application to:

- the proprietor of the estate to which the application relates;
- the proprietor of any registered charge on the estate;
- where the estate is leasehold, the proprietor of any superior registered estate;
- any person who is registered as a person to be notified under LRA 2002, Sched.6, para.2.

A person given such a notice may:

- do nothing (which would not be advisable as this will result in the applicant being registered as proprietor of the estate);
- consent to the application;
- object to the application;
- give a counter-notice to the registrar (using form NAP) within 65 business days requiring the registrar to deal with the application under LRA 2002, Sched.6, para.5.

If the registrar does not receive any objection to the application or any counter-notice from any of the persons given notice, the Land Registry will register the squatter as the new proprietor of the estate. It is important, therefore, that any person given the notice takes steps to oppose the application promptly and it would be prudent for the registered proprietor to serve a counter-notice on the registrar in accordance with the requirements of LRA 2002, Sched.6, para.5. The advantage of serving a counter-notice pursuant to para.5 is that the adverse possession claim will succeed only if one of three very limited conditions is satisfied (see below). However, it is crucial that the correct procedure is followed and that the counter-notice expressly requires the application to be dealt with under para.5. The importance of complying with the procedure set out in Sched.6 is illustrated by the decision in *King* v. *Suffolk County Council* [2016] 10 WLUK 277. In this case, King's adverse possession claim was notified to the county council and it was given a deadline for lodging a form NAP. The council failed to lodge a form NAP but did object to the application in an email prior to the expiration of the deadline. Following the commencement of proceedings, the council attempted to invoke para.5, but its attempts failed (because it had not served a counter-notice requiring the registrar to deal with the application under para.5) and the Tribunal dismissed the council's allegations that the claimant had not adversely possessed its land.

If the squatter's claim that he had been in adverse possession for 10 years was wrong then, notwithstanding the failure by the original proprietor to object to the squatter's application, the original proprietor would be entitled to apply to the Land Registry for rectification of the register of title and to have his name restored as the registered proprietor (see *Boxter* v. *Mannion* [2011] EWCA Civ 120).

If an application is required to be dealt with under LRA 2002, Sched.6, para.5 the applicant will be entitled to be registered as the new proprietor of the estate only if one of the following three conditions is met:

1. That it would be unconscionable because of an equity by estoppel for the registered proprietor to seek to dispossess the applicant and the circumstances

are such that the applicant ought to be registered as the proprietor. This condition is intended to embody the equitable principles of proprietary estoppel. According to the Land Registry an example of where this condition might apply is where the squatter has built on the registered proprietor's land in the mistaken belief that he was the owner of it and the proprietor has knowingly acquiesced in his mistake.

2. The applicant is for some other reason entitled to be registered as the proprietor of the estate. According to the Land Registry examples of where this condition might apply are where the applicant is entitled to the land under the will or intestacy of the deceased proprietor and where the applicant contracted to buy the land and paid the purchase price, but the legal estate was never transferred to him.
3. The land to which the application relates is adjacent to land belonging to the applicant and:
   (a) the exact line of the boundary between the two sites has not been determined under LRA 2002, s.60;
   (b) the applicant has been in adverse possession of the land to which the application relates for at least 10 years under the mistaken but reasonable belief that he is the owner of it; and
   (c) the estate to which the application relates was registered more than one year prior to the date of the application.

According to the Land Registry this condition may be useful in situations where the boundaries as they appear on the ground do not accord with the title plan.[18]

Where a squatter's application is rejected, he will be entitled to make a further application to be registered as the proprietor of the registered estate if he remains in adverse possession continuously for a further two years from the date of rejection of the previous application. However, the squatter will not be entitled to make such an application if:

- he is a defendant in proceedings for possession;
- he has had a judgment for possession given against him in the last two years;
- he has been evicted pursuant to a judgment for possession.

It will be apparent from the above that it is important that the registered proprietor does not sit back and do nothing after the squatter's application has been rejected. He should either immediately commence possession proceedings or grant the squatter a lease or licence.

[18] Land Registry Practice Guide 4 *Adverse possession of registered land* (see **gov.uk/government/organisations/land-registry**).

2.16.9 Adverse possession of highway land

It will never be possible for a squatter to obtain adverse possession of land dedicated as a public highway. The court held in *R. (on application of Smith)* v. *Land Registry* [2009] EWHC 328 (Admin) that the occupation of a highway verge amounted to an obstruction of the highway and was illegal under HA 1980.

2.17 TOWN AND VILLAGE GREENS

Applications to register land as a town or village green have increased over the past decade and have been used more and more as a means of delaying and preventing unwanted development (see e.g. *Oxfordshire County Council* v. *Oxford City Council* [2006] UKHL 25; *R. (Lewis)* v. *Redcar and Cleveland Borough Council and another* [2010] UKSC 11; *Newhaven Port and Properties Limited* v. *East Sussex County Council* [2012] EWHC 647 (Admin); *BDW Trading Limited (trading as Barratt Homes)* v. *Spooner and another* [2011] EWHC B7 (QB); and *Taylor* v. *Betterment Properties (Weymouth) Limited and another* [2012] EWCA Civ 250). Anyone can apply to register land as a town or village green if the local inhabitants have been using it 'as a right' (i.e. without permission or force) for sports or recreational purposes for 20 years or more and once the land has been registered as a town or village green it will be illegal to build on it.

To reduce the risk of acquiring land which has been or may be registered as a town or village green the following steps should be taken by the developer's lawyer:

1. The optional enquiry on form CON29O Enquiries of local authority (2016) relating to registered common land and town or village greens should be raised when the developer's lawyer submits his local search.
2. The following pre-contract enquiries of the vendor should be made:
   (a) Is the land being purchased enclosed by fencing or walls along all boundaries and when were the boundary structures erected?
   (b) Has any part of the land being purchased at any time been used for sporting or recreational purposes by any of the local inhabitants? If so, provide full details.
   (c) Is the vendor aware of any pending application or threat of an application to register the land or any part of it as a town or village green?
3. If the replies to these enquiries reveal that the land has been used in the past for recreational or sporting purposes by a significant number of local inhabitants then the vendor should be required to provide a statutory declaration setting out all the relevant facts, including the period during which the land was used for such purposes.
4. When carrying out a site inspection the developer's lawyer should look for any evidence of the land having been used for recreational purposes by members of the public, particularly where the site is open to the public.

Steps 2, 3 and 4 will not need to be taken where, prior to any person making an application to register land as a town or village green, an application for planning permission has been published or the land has been identified for development – see below.

The enquiries in form CON29O will not reveal the existence of any pending application to register land as a town or village green and, prior to the enactment of the Growth and Infrastructure Act 2013, there was the possibility that an application for registration may be submitted after the developer had acquired the land. This risk was substantially increased as a result of the Commons Act 2006, s.15 which came into force in April 2007; but it has effectively been removed by the Growth and Infrastructure Act 2013, s.16, which imposes restrictions on the right to register land as a town or village green under the Commons Act 2006, s.15(1) (see below).

Prior to the enactment of the Commons Act 2006 a landowner could protect his land against the threat of it being registered as a town or village green by putting up fencing or appropriate signage such as 'this is private land – keep out' or 'no public right of access permitted' or 'trespassers will be prosecuted' or 'the use of this land by members of the public is permitted with the landowner's consent which may be revoked at any time'. In the past taking these steps would have been sufficient to prevent the registration of the land as a town or village green (and this would have been the case even if the land had been used as a right by local inhabitants for sports or recreation for more than 20 years). However, under the Commons Act 2006, s.15(3) a landowner who takes steps to protect his land after 6 April 2007 (e.g. by erecting fencing or appropriate signs) will be deprived of the protection which was previously available to him (and an application to register land as a town or village green will succeed) where:

- a significant number of local inhabitants have before the date of the application indulged as of right in lawful sports and pastimes on the land for a period of at least 20 years; and
- the application to register the land as a village green is made within two years of the date of the protective steps taken by the landowner.

Under the Commons Act 2006, s.15(4) a landowner who took steps to protect his land before 6 April 2007 (e.g. by erecting fencing or appropriate signs) will also be deprived of the protection which was previously available to him (and an application to register land as a town or village green will succeed) where:

- a significant number of local inhabitants have indulged as of right in lawful sports and pastimes on the land for a period of at least 20 years; and
- the application to register the land as a village green is made within five years of the protective steps taken by the landowner.

Section 15(4) is subject to an exception and will not apply where planning permission was granted before 23 June 2006 and construction works, which have the effect of making the land permanently unusable by members of the public for recreational purposes, were commenced before that date.

The good news for developers is that the Growth and Infrastructure Act 2013, s.16 amends the Commons Act 2006, s.15(1) and removes the threat of development being delayed or frustrated by anyone making a village green application after an application for planning permission has been publicised or after land has been identified for development in a development plan document or a neighbourhood development plan. Under the Commons Act 2006, s.15C the right to apply to register land as a town or village green will no longer be available if one of the following trigger events has occurred:

- an application for planning permission in relation to the land under TCPA 1990, s.70 or s.293A has been publicised;
- a draft of a development plan document or a proposal for a neighbourhood development plan which identifies the land for potential development has been published for consultation;
- a development plan document which identifies the land for potential development has been adopted;
- a neighbourhood development plan which identifies the land for potential development exists (see Growth and Infrastructure Act 2013, Sched.4).

The right to apply for registration will become exercisable again if any publicised planning application is withdrawn or if planning permission is refused and all means of challenging the refusal have been exhausted or if any planning permission which has been granted expires before the commencement of development or if any of the other terminating events referred to in the Commons Act 2006, Sched.1A occur.

In July 2013, the government consulted on proposals to amend the trigger and terminating events and decided to extend the trigger and terminating events to include land which is:

- affected by a local development order permitting operational development;
- affected by a neighbourhood development order permitting development; or
- subject to an application for an order under the Transport and Works Act 1992.

The Growth and Infrastructure Act 2013 came into force on 1 October 2013 and also gives landowners a new way to protect against town and village green registrations. The Act allows a landowner to deposit a statement in a prescribed form with the commons registration authority for the purpose of bringing to an end any period during which persons have indulged as of right in lawful sports and pastimes on the land to which the statement relates (see Growth and Infrastructure Act 2013, s.15(1)). The statement must be accompanied by a map identifying the land to which the statement relates. The depositing of such a statement does not prevent a new period commencing.

2.18 OVERRIDING INTERESTS, LEGAL EASEMENTS, EQUITABLE EASEMENTS, MANORIAL RIGHTS AND CHANCEL REPAIR LIABILITY

2.18.1 Overriding interests

The developer's solicitor will need to consider whether the development site is subject to any overriding interests. Overriding interests are interests which will be binding on a purchaser of registered land even though they do not appear on the seller's title. They include interests which override first registration and interests which override registered dispositions. Unregistered interests which override first registration are listed in LRA 2002, Sched.1 and include:

- a leasehold estate in land granted for a term not exceeding seven years from the date of the grant, except for a lease the grant of which falls within LRA 2002, s.4(1)(d), (e) or (f);
- an interest belonging to a person in actual occupation, so far as relating to land of which he is in actual occupation, except for an interest under a settlement under the Settled Land Act 1925;
- a legal easement or profit a prendre;
- a customary right;
- a public right;
- a local land charge;
- an interest in any coal or coal mine, the rights attached to any such interest and the rights of any person under the Coal Industry Act 1994, ss.38, 49 or 51;
- in the case of land to which title was registered before 1898, rights to mines and minerals (and incidental rights) created before 1898; and
- in the case of land to which title was registered between 1898 and 1925 inclusive, rights to mines and minerals (and incidental rights) created before the date of registration of the title.

Unregistered interests which override registered dispositions are listed in LRA 2002, Sched.3 and include:

- a leasehold estate in land granted for a term not exceeding seven years from the date of the grant, except for:

  (a) a lease the grant of which falls within LRA 2002, s.4(1)(d), (e) or (f); and
  (b) a lease the grant of which constitutes a registrable disposition (registrable dispositions are listed in LRA 2002, s.27(2))

  (Sched.3, para.1);
- a leasehold estate in land under a relevant social housing tenancy (Sched.3, para.1A);
- an interest belonging at the time of the disposition to a person in actual occupation, so far as relating to the land of which he is in actual occupation, except for:

(a) an interest under a settlement under the Settled Land Act 1925;
(b) an interest of a person of whom enquiry was made before the disposition and who failed to disclose the right when he could reasonably have been expected to do so;
(c) an interest:

    (i) which belongs to a person whose occupation would not have been obvious on a reasonably careful inspection of the land at the time of the disposition; and
    (ii) of which the person to whom the disposition is made does not have actual knowledge at that time;

(d) a leasehold estate in land granted to take effect in possession after the end of the period of three months beginning with the date of the grant and which has not taken effect in possession at the time of the disposition

(Sched.3, para.2);

- an interest which, immediately before the coming into force of Sched.3, was an overriding interest under Land Registration Act 1925, s.70(1)(g) by virtue of a person's receipt of rents and profits, except for an interest of a person of whom enquiry was made before the disposition and who failed to disclose the right when he could reasonably have been expected to do so (Sched.3, para.2A (as inserted by LRA 2002, Sched.12, para.8));
- a legal easement or profit a prendre, except for an easement, or a profit a prendre which is not registered under the Commons Act 2006, Part I, which at the time of the disposition:

    (a) is not within the actual knowledge of the person to whom the disposition is made; and
    (b) would not have been obvious on a reasonably careful inspection of the land over which the easement or profit is exercisable.

    (The exception does not apply if the person entitled to the easement or profit proves that it has been exercised in the period of one year ending with the day of the disposition.)

    (Sched.3, para.3);

- a customary right (Sched.3, para.4);
- a public right (Sched.3, para.5);
- a local land charge (Sched.3, para.6);
- an interest in any coal or coal mine, the rights attached to any such interest and the rights of any person under the Coal Industry Act 1994, ss.38, 49 or 51 (Sched.3, para.7);
- in the case of land to which title was registered before 1898, rights to mines and minerals (and incidental rights) created before 1898 (Sched.3, para.8); and

- in the case of land to which title was registered between 1898 and 1925 inclusive, rights to mines and minerals (and incidental rights) created before the date of registration of the title (Sched.3, para.9).

Under LRA 2002, s.117 and Land Registration Act 2002 (Transitional Provisions) (No.2) Order 2003 (SI 2003/2431), rule 2 the following overriding interests lost their overriding status at midnight on 12 October 2013:

- a franchise;
- a manorial right;
- a right to rent that was reserved to the Crown on the granting of any freehold estate;
- a non-statutory right in respect of an embankment or sea or river wall;
- a right to payment in lieu of tithe;
- a right in respect of the repair of a church chancel.

As explained below, the loss of overriding status does not mean that manorial rights and chancel repair liability are no longer relevant. Manorial rights and chancel repair liability did not cease to exist after 12 October 2013 and are still of significance.

2.18.2 Legal easements

For an easement to be a legal easement, it must be granted by a transfer or a deed in fee simple or for a term of years absolute.

A legal easement granted after 12 October 2003 cannot be an overriding interest. Under LRA 2002, s.27 the express grant of a legal easement out of registered land is a registrable disposition and will not operate at law until the relevant registration requirements are met (i.e. it will not be enforceable against a purchaser unless it has been registered on the grantor's title and (if registered) the grantee's title). Form AP1 must be used to meet the registration requirements.

However, an easement that was an overriding interest before the coming into force of LRA 2002, Sched.3 (such as an unregistered expressly granted legal easement), but which would not be an overriding interest under Sched.3, para.3 if created after the coming into force of LRA 2002 (because it is a legal easement which is not within the knowledge of a purchaser or not obvious from a careful inspection), will be binding on a purchaser of registered land (see LRA 2002, Sched.12, para.9). Schedule 12, para.9(2) states that 'in relation to an interest to which this paragraph applies, Schedule 3 has effect as if the interest were not excluded from paragraph 3'. Paragraph 9 applies to

> an easement or profit a prendre which was an overriding interest in relation to a registered estate immediately before the coming into force of Schedule 3 but which would not fall within paragraph 3 of that Schedule if created after the coming into force of that Schedule.

A legal easement that has not been expressly granted, such as a prescriptive right or an implied easement, will be an overriding interest under LRA 2002, Sched.3, para.3 and binding on a purchaser if:

- it is within the knowledge of the purchaser;
- it is obvious from a reasonably careful inspection of the land;
- it has been exercised in the period of one year ending with the date of the transfer to the purchaser; or
- it is registered under the Commons Act 2006, Part I.

2.18.3 Equitable easements

All easements that are not legal easements will be equitable easements. They include:

- an easement granted for life;
- an easement arising under a contract that was not completed;
- an easement arising by proprietary estoppel (e.g. where the owner of the dominant land has exercised a right in the mistaken belief that he is entitled to do so and the owner of the servient land has acquiesced in his mistake). A good example of an easement arising by proprietary estoppel is the case of *Chaudhary* v. *Yavuz* [2011] EWCA Civ 1314. This case also highlights the need to protect an equitable easement by the registration of a unilateral or agreed notice or (in the case of unregistered land) a D(iii) land charge at the Land Charges Department. The facts of the case are as follows.

  C constructed a metal staircase on land owned by V with the consent of V. The staircase provided access to a first floor flat owned by C and access to an adjoining first floor flat owned by V. V sold his property to Y without any formal right of way over the staircase having been granted to C. Following the sale Y removed the connection between the staircase and the flat owned by C. C then sought a declaration that he was entitled to a right of way over the staircase. It was accepted between the parties that C had become entitled to an equitable easement as a result of a proprietary estoppel, but Y maintained that, in the absence of registration, it was not binding on him. The county court judge agreed but held that as C had been in actual occupation of the staircase, he had an overriding interest under LRA 2002, Sched.3, para.2. He also held that, even if this was incorrect, C was entitled to an easement by estoppel as the right was binding by way of a constructive trust. The Court of Appeal disagreed and held that:

  (a) there had been no occupation by C of any part of the staircase such as to constitute an overriding interest under LRA 2002, Sched.3, para.2; and
  (b) no constructive trust had been created;

- an easement that is of uncertain duration or that is terminable (in the case of an easement granted in fee simple). For example, a right to use a road until such time as it is adopted as a public highway is an equitable easement.

Equitable easements created before the coming into force of LRA 2002 could be overriding interests. However, an equitable easement created after 12 October 2003 cannot be an overriding interest under LRA 2002, Sched.3, para.2 and will not be binding on a purchaser of registered land, unless it has been protected by the registration of an agreed or unilateral notice on the grantor's title. In the case of unregistered land, an equitable easement will need to be protected by the registration of a D(iii) land charge at the Land Charges Department against the name of the grantor. Also, it is good practice to register a caution against first registration in respect of the grantor's land, so that the Land Registry notes the easement on the title to the grantor's land when it is first registered.

2.18.4 Manorial rights

Manorial rights are rights that were originally retained by the lord of the manor over land known as copyhold land. The tenure of copyhold allowed a tenant to have possession of land belonging to the lord of the manor subject to certain rights being reserved in favour of the lord of the manor, including sporting rights, rights to mines and minerals and rights to hold fairs and markets on the land. Copyhold was abolished as a form of tenure on 1 January 1926 by the Law of Property Act (LPA) 1922 when all copyhold land was enfranchised. On enfranchisement all copyhold tenure was converted into freehold tenure, but, under LPA 1922, Sched.12 certain rights were preserved, including rights of the lord of the manor to mines and minerals and rights in respect of fairs, markets and sporting rights. However, these rights could be extinguished by written agreement between the lord of the manor and the tenant. (LPA 1922, s.138(12) allowed the lord and the tenant to agree in writing that any of the rights could be treated as a manorial incident and be extinguished as if they were a manorial incident.)

One of the problems with manorial rights is that it can be difficult to ascertain whether or not land is subject to such rights – there is no register of manorial rights which can be inspected and an investigation of title will be insufficient to establish whether any such rights exist.

The good news for developers is that as from 13 October 2013 manorial rights lost their overriding status (see LRA 2002, s.117). However, it does not follow from this that they are no longer relevant, that they can be ignored. Manorial rights continue to be enforceable against a landowner and are capable of being protected by the registration of a unilateral notice or an agreed notice of the rights on the register of title to the land affected or (in the case of unregistered land) a caution against first registration before the owner of the land makes a disposal for value of the land. Once there has been a disposal for value without the manorial rights having been protected by registration the rights will be lost (see LRA 2002, s.29).

There are different procedures for entering unilateral notices and agreed notices on a landowner's title. An application for an agreed notice will not be approved by the Land Registry unless it is made with the consent of the registered proprietor or the Land Registry is satisfied as to the validity of the applicant's claim. However, in the case of an application for a unilateral notice, the consent of the registered proprietor is not required and the Land Registry does not have to be satisfied as to the validity of the applicant's claim. The Land Registry must notify the registered proprietor of the entry of the unilateral notice on his title and the registered proprietor may apply to have the entry cancelled by lodging a form UN4. If a form UN4 is lodged the Land Registry must notify the beneficiary of the unilateral notice and if the beneficiary exercises his right to object to the cancellation of the unilateral notice the objection will be dealt with in the procedure for disputed applications (see LRA 2002, s.73(5)–(8)). In practice most applications for an agreed notice will be made without the consent of the registered proprietor and the application will need to be accompanied by sufficient evidence to satisfy the registrar of the validity of the applicant's claim.

The Land Registry Practice Guide 66, *Overriding interests that lost automatic protection in 2013* contains guidance as to the type of evidence that will be required to establish the validity of a claim for the purposes of an agreed notice relating to manorial rights and states that the applicant will normally need to produce:

- evidence that the land in question was previously copyhold of the manor in question (this will usually be provided by producing a copy of the deed of enfranchisement or compensation agreement);
- evidence that it was the custom of the manor in question that the lord had the rights claimed, for example by evidence from the court rolls;
- evidence that the rights in question survived enfranchisement (this will usually be provided by producing a copy of the deed of enfranchisement or compensation agreement);
- evidence of the applicant's title to the particular manorial rights claimed (this will usually consist of an abstract or epitome of title showing the applicant's title to the lordship of the manor and that the rights have not been severed from the lordship).

If manorial rights have not been protected in the way described above then a purchaser for value after 12 October 2013 will take free of such rights.

Rights to mines and minerals often derive from manorial rights and, as mentioned above, can be protected by registering a notice on the title to the land affected or a caution against first registration before the land is sold to a purchaser for value. It is also possible for a mineral owner to make a voluntary application to the Land Registry to be registered as the owner of the minerals under a separate sub-surface title. This can be done at any time – it did not have to be done before 13 October 2013. There is a rebuttable presumption that land includes mines and minerals, so an absolute title to a property does not prevent an application by a mineral owner. Also, if the application is successful, no indemnity is payable unless it is noted on the surface title that mines and minerals are included. The applicant will need to prove to the Land Registry that he owns the minerals, but, if ownership can be established, he will be registered as the owner of the minerals under a separate title. The Land Registry Practice Guide 65, *Registration of mines and minerals* contains guidance on dealing with the registration of mines and minerals under LRA 2002 and states that the conventional 15-year root of title will rarely be sufficient to allow the grant of an absolute title to mines and minerals.

2.18.5 Chancel repair liability

Chancel repair liability is a liability which originated in medieval times. It derives from ancient rules which allow the Church of England or Church of Wales to claim the cost of carrying out repairs to the church chancel dating from the medieval period or earlier from the owners of land previously owned by the church.

Chancel repair liability is archaic and unpopular and one of the problems with the liability is that, as with manorial rights, it is not easy to ascertain whether a property is subject to the liability. Another problem with the liability is that it is a joint and several liability and, although the liability will usually be apportioned between various landowners, the church is able to pursue an individual landowner for the full amount.

The case of *Aston Cantlow with Billesley Parochial Church Council* v. *Wallbank* [2003] UKHL 37 highlighted the issue of chancel repair liability. Until recently most practitioners acting for a purchaser of land would have carried out a chancel repair search as a matter of course and, if the search revealed that there was a potential chancel repair liability, they would have advised their client to take out a chancel repair indemnity policy. (As discussed below, in future this practice is likely to change – it will no longer be necessary to obtain an indemnity policy where there has been a previous sale for value of the land since 13 October 2013 without the chancel repair right having been protected by registration.) Before the *Wallbank* case most practitioners would not have been concerned about chancel repair liability, unless the property in question was located near a medieval church or on land known to have been former ‘glebe land’ or monastery land.

The cost of obtaining a chancel repair indemnity policy is relatively low and, in the case of a development site, there is no need for the sum insured to be for the gross development value of the site. The sum insured should cover the likely cost of carrying out repairs to the chancel in the future and the policy should cover the insured and his successors in title and all mortgagees and provide in perpetuity cover. The policy should be obtained prior to exchange of contracts or completion should be made conditional upon the policy being obtained, and solicitors acting for the developer/buyer should require that the seller is obliged to pay the premium.

Chancel repair liability, like manorial rights, ceased to be an overriding interest on 13 October 2013 (see Land Registration Act 2002 (Transitional Provisions) (No.2) Order 2003, SI 2003/2431) but, as with manorial rights, may be protected by the registration of a unilateral or an agreed notice on the title affected or (in the case of unregistered land) the registration of a caution against first registration before the land is sold to a purchaser for value. As from 12 October 2013, a purchaser paying valuable consideration for registered land will acquire the land free from any chancel repair liability if the liability has not been protected by the registration of a notice; and a purchaser paying valuable consideration for unregistered land will acquire the land free from any chancel repair liability if no caution against first registration has been registered.

It should be noted that owners of land will continue to be bound by any existing chancel repair liability (whether or not a notice has been registered on the owner's title) until the land is sold for valuable consideration (provided that no prior protection has been obtained).

Notwithstanding that manorial rights ceased to be overriding interests on 13 October 2013, the purchaser's solicitor will need to consider whether or not to carry out a chancel repair search. If there has been no disposal of the vendor's land for valuable consideration since 13 October 2013 it is still possible that a notice of a manorial right or a right to chancel repair may be entered on the title to the vendor's land prior to completion and a chancel repair search should be carried out and, if a potential liability exists, an indemnity policy should be obtained.

2.18.6 Summary

To sum up:

- A legal easement created by express grant out of registered land after 12 October 2003 cannot be an overriding interest. It will be a registerable disposition and will not be binding on a purchaser unless it has been registered on the grantor's and the grantee's titles (see LRA 2002, s.27).
- A legal easement that has not been expressly granted, such as a prescriptive right, will be an overriding interest and binding on a purchaser of registered land if it is known to the purchaser or obvious from an inspection or it has been exercised during the previous year (see LRA 2002, Sched.3, para.3).
- An easement that was an overriding interest before the coming into force of LRA 2002, Sched.3, but which would not be an overriding interest under Sched.3, para.3 if created after the coming into force of LRA 2002, will be binding on a purchaser of registered land (see LRA 2002, Sched.12, para.9).
- An equitable easement, such as an easement arising by proprietary estoppel, created after 12 October 2003, cannot be an overriding interest under LRA 2002 and will not be binding on a purchaser, unless it has been protected by the registration of the appropriate notice.
- The grant of an equitable easement out of registered land is not a registerable disposition but it needs to be protected by the registration of an agreed or unilateral notice and the grant of an equitable easement out of unregistered land needs to be protected by the registration of a D(iii) land charge at the Land Charges Department against the name of the grantor.

- Manorial rights and rights in respect of chancel repair lost their overriding status at midnight on 12 October 2013, but landowners will continue to be bound by any existing liability and the rights are still capable of being protected by registration – the registration did not have to take place before 12 October 2013 for the protection to apply.
- As from 12 October 2013, a purchaser paying valuable consideration for land after 12 October 2013 will acquire the land free from any manorial rights and rights in respect of chancel repair only if (in the case of registered land) the rights have not been noted on the owner's title or (in the case of unregistered land) no caution against first registration has been registered (see LRA 2002, s.29).
- Once there has been a disposition for value without a protective notice having been registered on the owner's title prior to the disposition, any manorial rights or rights in respect of chancel repair liability will be lost.
- Rights in respect of mines and minerals can be protected by registration of a unilateral notice or an agreed notice as well as by the mineral owner applying to the Land Registry to be registered as the owner of the minerals under a separate sub-surface title. This can be done at any time and the mineral owner did not have to apply to be registered as the owner of the minerals before 13 October 2013.

2.19 DISPOSALS OF ASSETS OF COMMUNITY VALUE

A developer proposing to acquire a pub, a village shop, a village hall, a community centre, a sports field or any other building or land which furthers the social wellbeing or social interests of the local community, will need to check whether or not it has been listed as an asset of community value. If it has been so listed, no disposal of the property may take place until certain conditions have been satisfied. Under the Localism Act (LA) 2011, s.95 a person who is an owner of land included in the local authority's list of assets of community value must not enter into a relevant disposal of the land unless each of the following conditions is met:

- the owner has notified the local authority in writing of his wish to enter into a relevant disposal of the land;
- either:

  (a) an interim moratorium period of six weeks beginning with the date on which the local authority received notification of the intended disposal has ended without the local authority having received a potential bid to purchase the land from any community interest group, or

  (b) a full moratorium period of six months beginning with the date on which the local authority received notification of the intended disposal has ended;

- the relevant disposal takes place within the period of 18 months beginning with the date on which the local authority received notification of the intended disposal.

For the purposes of s.95 a relevant disposal is a disposal of the freehold estate in land with vacant possession or the grant or assignment of a 'qualifying lease' (i.e. a lease which has a term of at least 25 years from the date of its grant) with vacant possession; and the disposal is made when it takes place or, if it is made pursuant to a binding agreement, when the agreement is entered into.

Section 95 does not apply to:

- residences and land connected to a residence (as defined in the Assets of Community Value (England) Regulations 2012 (SI 2012/2421), Sched.1, para.2), although a residence may be listed as an asset of community value if it is a building that is only partly used as a residence and, but for residential use, the land would be eligible for listing;
- the disposals listed in the 2012 Regulations, Sched.3, which include (inter alia) disposals made pursuant to a s.106 agreement or a legally enforceable option to buy or right of pre-emption (unless the relevant land was listed before the option or right was granted);
- the various disposals listed in LA 2011, s.95(5), which include (inter alia) a disposal by way of gift, a disposal by personal representatives of a deceased person in satisfaction of an entitlement under the will, or on the intestacy, of the deceased person, and the disposal of land on which a business is carried on as a going concern.

The provisions of LA 2011 relating to assets of community value came into force on 21 September 2012. They do not restrict in any way who the owner of a listed asset can sell his property to, or at what price. Nor do they confer a right of first refusal on community interest groups or place any restriction on what an owner can do with his property after it has been listed. However, unless an exemption applies, the owner of a listed asset will not be able to dispose of the asset unless he has complied with the moratorium requirements of LA 2011, s.95. If an owner of a listed asset makes a disposal and fails to comply with these requirements the disposal will be ineffective.

CHAPTER 3

Access

The developer will need to ensure that there is adequate access to the development site, which sounds simple enough, but there are a number of potential pitfalls to avoid. The pitfalls are not always easy to spot and particular care needs to be taken when considering the access position. Access issues can be both difficult and costly to resolve.

3.1 RANSOM STRIPS

Even where a development site would appear to directly abut a public highway there may be a ransom strip between the development site and the public highway. For example, there may be a grass verge between the development site and the highway which does not form part of the highway and which is owned by a third party. To avoid the problem of ransom strips, a developer's lawyer should always carry out:

- a site inspection;
- an index map search of the land adjoining the development site and obtain official copy register entries of title relating to any titles revealed by the search;
- a highway search. The highway authority should be asked to indicate on a plan the extent of the public highway abutting the development site and to confirm that the site directly abuts the public highway and that there are no public footpaths or bridleways crossing the development site. However, the results of highway searches should not be regarded as definitive and should be treated with caution (see **1.4**). The developer and/or its highway consultants should always overlay the title plan and the highway search plan to check that there is no intervening strip of land between the highway and the site boundary across which access to the site is to be gained.

The title plan should also be carefully inspected as it may reveal a possible gap between the property and the highway.

If the site inspection reveals the existence of a ditch between the highway and a hedge or fence running along the frontage of the site it will need to be established whether the ditch is part of the site or part of the highway (see **1.2**). As stated in **1.2**, there will be a rebuttable presumption that the ditch is owned by the owner of the site and the owner should be required to provide a statutory declaration which supports this presumption.

3.2 VISIBILITY SPLAYS

Visibility splays are long narrow triangular pieces of land which are located on either side of a road where it joins a main road junction. They allow the driver of a motor vehicle approaching the junction to have a clear and uninterrupted view of any on-coming traffic.

Where a development site directly abuts a public highway and a new access is to be created the developer will need to ensure that the frontage of the site is of sufficient length to accommodate any visibility splay or sight line requirements of the planning or highway authority. It may be a condition of the planning permission that visibility splays must be created and, if this is the case, the developer will need to satisfy itself that the visibility splay requirements do not involve third party land over which it has no control.

3.3 APPARATUS CROSSING THE ACCESS

The developer will need to check whether there are any sewers, pipes or cables running along the front of the development site and appropriate enquiries should be made (see **2.2**). If there are, the developer will need to obtain the consent of the relevant statutory undertaker or utility company to build over or divert such service media. In the case of a small development, the additional cost involved in building over or diverting such service media may mean that it is not worth proceeding with the proposed development.

3.4 PRESCRIPTIVE RIGHTS OF WAY

If the development site does not directly abut a public highway then the developer will need to ensure that there are adequate rights of way benefiting the site. Such rights may be acquired, for example, by express grant or by prescription following long use.

If an investigation of title reveals that there is no formal right of way to a site (i.e. there is no transfer or other deed containing an express right of way in favour of the site) the developer will need to ascertain whether a prescriptive right of way exists and whether it is sufficient for the developer's purposes. The extent of the right of way will need to be carefully considered and it will also be necessary to consider whether the right will be affected by any change in the character or use of the site and/or any intensification in the use of the right of way.

The developer's lawyer should be aware that a prescriptive right of way to a potential development site will not be adequate where there is a requirement for the estate roads to be adopted (see **3.7**). He should also bear in mind that a prescriptive right of way does not include a right to lay service media.

3.4.1 Acquisition

In order to acquire a right of way by prescription under the Prescription Act 1832 certain qualifying conditions must be satisfied:

- The user must be 'as of right' (i.e. *nec vi, nec clam, nec precario*, meaning without force, secrecy, or permission). A right of way cannot be acquired by prescription if the use is with force or the permission/licence of the owner of the servient land or if the right is exercised secretly. It should be noted that mere acquiescence or toleration by the owner of the servient land will not be sufficient to demonstrate that the use of the way was with the permission of the owner. For permission to be implied there must be some positive, overt act by the servient owner. (The case of *London Tara Hotel* v. *Kensington Close Hotel Limited* [2011] EWCA Civ 1356 is a good illustration of this.)
- There must have been at least 20 years' continuous use of the right. Use for 20 years raises the presumption of a prescriptive right of way but can be defeated by a failure to meet the 'as of right' condition. Use for 40 years is stronger and will give rise to an absolute and indefeasible right which can only be defeated if it can be demonstrated that the right was enjoyed pursuant to a written consent or agreement.[1]

Where there is no formal/documentary right of way, the developer's lawyer should ensure that a statutory declaration is obtained from the vendor and, where appropriate, previous owners of the site, which clearly demonstrate(s) that the site benefits from a prescriptive right of way. In addition, it would be prudent for the developer to obtain a defective title indemnity insurance policy since a statutory declaration will rarely be conclusive. However, indemnity insurance policies do have certain limitations and the developer should be made aware of these limitations (see **2.8.2**). The safest course of action would be for the developer to require the vendor to obtain a deed of easement from the owner of the right of way. Indeed, if mortgagees are involved, the mortgagees may insist on a deed of easement. The problem with this approach, however, is that if the owner of the right of way refuses to enter into a deed of easement then it is unlikely that any insurer would be prepared to provide indemnity insurance cover.

[1] See Prescription Act 1832, s.2 and J Gaunt and P Morgan *Gale on the Law of Easements* (20th edition, Sweet & Maxwell, 2017), paras.4.107–4.136.

3.4.2 Change of use

A developer should be aware that changing the use of land benefiting from a prescriptive right of way (such land is known as the dominant land or dominant tenement) may be an abuse of the right and result in the right of way being lost or suspended. The cases of *Attwood and others* v. *Bovis Homes Limited* [2001] Ch 379 (Ch D) and *McAdams Homes Limited* v. *Robinson and another* [2004] EWCA Civ 214 demonstrate that an easement acquired by prescription cannot continue to be used if there is a radical change in the use or character of the dominant land and this results in a substantial increase in the burden on the servient land (see **4.1** for the facts of these cases). Both cases involved drainage easements. But will there be an abuse of a prescriptive right of way if there is a substantial change in the use or character of the dominant land without there being any increase in the burden on the servient land? The answer to this question would appear to be in the affirmative,[2] although the position is complex and not entirely clear. In *Attwood and others* v. *Bovis Homes Limited* Neuberger LJ expressed the view that the authorities on prescriptive rights of way are open to different interpretations and tentatively suggested as follows:

> I would tentatively suggest that the rule may be that, if there is a subsequent radical change in the use of the dominant tenement, a right of way acquired by prescription can only continue to be used in connection with the dominant tenement if the court can be satisfied that the change cannot result in the use of the way being greater in quantum or different in character from that which it was for any continuous period of 20 or 40 years during the period of use of the way in connection with the original use of the dominant tenement . . . The onus would be on the owner of the dominant tenement and would, I suspect, normally be difficult to satisfy in relation to a right of way.

In *McAdams Homes Limited* he said:

> Where there is a change in the use of or the erection of new buildings on land without having any effect on the nature or extent of the use of the easement, the change, however radical, will not affect the right of the dominant owner to use the easement.

However, from the cases referred to in *Gale on the Law of Easements* (20th edition, Sweet & Maxwell) at paras.9.05–9.17, it would appear that a right of way acquired by prescription cannot be used for all purposes and that the right will be limited to the ordinary and reasonable user for which the way might be used at the time when the right was acquired. In *RPC Holdings Limited* v. *Rogers* [1953] 1 All ER 1029 (Ch D), a case involving a right of way acquired by prescription and a change in the use of the dominant land from a field to a camping site for caravans, the court decided that the track leading to the dominant land could only be used for agricultural purposes. Harman J said:

---

[2] See J Gaunt and P Morgan *Gale on the Law of Easements* (20th edition, Sweet & Maxwell, 2017), para.9.05.

> It seems to me ... that I am not to conclude from the mere fact that while the property was in one state the way was for all purposes for which it was wanted, therefore, that is a general right exercisable for totally different purposes which only came into existence at a later date. Sitting as a juryman I can feel no doubt that the way here was a way limited to agricultural purposes, and that to extend it to the use proposed would be an unjustifiable increase in the burden of the easement.

The authors of *Gale on the Law of Easements*, as well as referring to the above statement, also refer to the following statement by Bovill CJ in *Williams* v. *James* (1866–67) LR 2 CP 577:

> In all cases of this kind which depend upon user the right acquired must be measured by the extent of the enjoyment which is proved. When a right of way to a piece of land is proved, then that is, unless something appears to the contrary, a right of way for all purposes according to the ordinary and reasonable user to which that land might be applied at the time of the supposed grant. Such a right cannot be increased so as to affect the servient tenement by imposing upon it any additional burden.

They also refer to the case of *Wimbledon and Putney Commons Conservators* v. *Dixon* (1875) 1 Ch D 362 in which James LJ said:

> I am satisfied that the true principle is . . . that you cannot from evidence of user of a privilege connected with the enjoyment of property in its original state, infer a right to use it, into whatsoever form or for whatever purpose that property may be changed, that is to say, if a right of way to a field be proved by evidence of user, however general, for whatever purpose, qua field, the person who is the owner of that field cannot from that say, I have a right to turn that field into a manufactory, or into a town, and then use the way for the purposes of the manufactory or town so built.

According to the authors of *Gale on the Law of Easements*, the purpose to be served by a prescriptive right is determined by the purpose for which the way was used during the whole period relied on to establish it (para.9.13).

3.4.3 Intensification of user

A mere intensification in the use of a right of way acquired by prescription without a change in the use of the dominant land will not be an abuse of the right of way. In *British Railways Board* v. *Glass* [1965] Ch 538 (CA) the Court of Appeal held that the defendant had acquired a prescriptive right of way over a level crossing in favour of a field which was used as a caravan park and that a mere increase in the number of caravans using the site did not amount to an excessive user. Also, in *Giles* v. *County Building Construction (Hertford) Limited* (1971) 22 P & CR 978 (Ch D) the court held that demolishing two houses and erecting six flats, a bungalow and seven garages did not involve a radical change in the character or use of the dominant land and so did not involve excessive user.

In the *British Railways Board* case Harman LJ stated:

> it is clear that a mere increase in the numbers of the caravans using the site is not an excessive user of the right. A right to use a way for this purpose or that has never been to my knowledge limited to a right to use the way so many times a day or for such and such a number of vehicles so long as the dominant tenement does not change its identity. If there be a radical change in the character of the dominant tenement, then the prescriptive right will not extend to it in that condition. The obvious example is a change of a small dwelling-house to a large hotel, but there has been no change of that character according to the facts found in this case.

In *Wood* v. *Waddington* [2015] EWCA Civ 538, a case involving a right of way dispute and the application of the Law of Property Act (LPA) 1925, s.62, the law on intensification of user was summarised by a unanimous Court of Appeal, where Lewison J said at paras.79 and 80:

> Even where a right is acquired by prescription or implication the right is 'a right for all purposes according to the ordinary and reasonable use to which the dominant tenement might be applied at the time of the implied or supposed grant' *McAdams Homes Ltd v Robinson* [2004] EWCA Civ 214, [2005] 1 P&CR at [79 (iii)]. It is also clear on the authorities that a mere intensification of use is not something to which the servient owner is entitled to object. In *McAdams Homes* Neuberger LJ said at [50] that the servient owner's entitlement to object depended on the answers to two questions:
>
> (i) Whether the dominant land had undergone a radical change in the character or a change in the identity of the site as opposed to a mere change or identification of the use of the site;
> (ii) Whether the use of the dominant land as changed would result in a substantial increase or alteration in the burden on the servient land.
>
> It is clear from Neuberger LJ's judgment at [51] that the servient owner is only entitled to object if both questions are answered affirmatively.

3.4.4 Prescriptive rights of way over common land and village greens

In two cases heard in the Court of Appeal it was decided that it was not possible to acquire a vehicular right of way by prescription:

- over common land[3] (since vehicular access over common land is a criminal offence (LPA 1925, s.193(4)) unless authorised by the owner); or
- over a private track[4] (since it is an offence (Road Traffic Act 1988, s.34(1)(a)) to drive a motor vehicle without lawful authority over any land which is not a road).[5]

Fortunately, for property developers (and other landowners) the House of Lords in *Bakewell Management Limited* v. *Brandwood and others* [2004] UKHL 14 overruled these decisions. According to the House of Lords, a prescriptive right of way over a track could be obtained by long use even if that use had been illegal. The

---

3 *Hanning* v. *Top Deck Travel Group Limited* (1994) 68 P & CR 14 (CA).
4 *Massey* v. *Boulden* [2002] EWCA Civ 1634.
5 A 'road' being a public highway or a road to which the public has access.

House of Lords held that if an easement over land could be lawfully granted by the landowner, an easement could be acquired by prescription, whether the use relied on was illegal in the criminal sense or merely in the tortious sense, and there was no valid reason of public policy to bar that acquisition.

It is important to appreciate, however, that while the decision in the *Bakewell* case establishes that it is possible to acquire a prescriptive right of way over a track or common land, it does not establish that a prescriptive right of way can be acquired over a town or village green. The disturbance or interference of the soil of a town or village green will be deemed to be a public nuisance (under Commons Act 1876, s.29) and it is not possible for an owner of land to authorise its illegal use. Accordingly, whereas the owner of common land is able to authorise a vehicular right of way over it, the owner of a town or village green cannot, in view of the illegality principle, authorise the creation of a track over a town or village green.

Under the Countryside and Rights of Way Act 2000, s.68 it was possible for the owner or occupier of a property served by a track over common land or a town or village green to buy a legal right of way over the track from its owner but, unfortunately, this possibility no longer exists.[6]

3.4.5 Prescriptive right of way over a public footpath

The case of *Sheringham Urban District Council* v. *Holsey* (1904) 91 LT 225 suggests that it is not possible to acquire a prescriptive right of way over a public footpath. The case concerned a lane which in 1811 had been set out as a public footpath under an award made by Inclosure Commissioners under the Sheringham Inclosure Act 1809. For over 40 years, carts had been continuously used in the lane. Because of the narrow width of the lane, foot passengers were necessarily obstructed and had to wait until carts had completed their passage to use the lane. Joyce J held that the use of the carts was a public nuisance and no length of time could legalise the use of the passage by the carts.

3.4.6 Summary

- A right of way acquired by prescription cannot be used for all purposes and will be limited to the ordinary and reasonable purposes for which the way might be used at the time when the right of way was acquired.
- A right of way acquired by prescription cannot continue to be used if there is a radical change in the use of the dominant land and this results in a substantial increase in the burden on the servient land.
- It would appear that a right of way acquired by prescription cannot continue to be used if there is a radical change in the use of the dominant land even if the change does not increase the burden on the servient land, although the position is not entirely clear.

[6] Section 68 was repealed by the Commons Act 2006, s.51.

- A mere intensification in the use of a right of way acquired by prescription will not amount to excessive user and will not be an abuse of the right.
- It is possible to acquire a prescriptive right of way over a private track or common land.
- It is not possible to acquire a prescriptive right of way over a public footpath or a town or village green.
- Interference with a public footpath or the soil of a town or village green is a public nuisance and a right to commit a public nuisance cannot be acquired by prescription.

3.5 EXPRESSLY GRANTED RIGHTS OF WAY

If a right of way has been granted by deed it will be necessary to consider whether the right is adequate, for instance:

- Is the physical extent of the right of way clear?
- Does the right permit a full, free and unrestricted right of way over a roadway which connects to an adopted highway?
- Does the right include pedestrian and vehicular use?
- Is the right for all purposes?
- Who is to be responsible for repairing and maintaining the road over which the right has been granted?
- Does the right permit the owner of the dominant land to enter the servient land for the purpose of repairing, maintaining, renewing and improving the road over which the right has been granted?
- Will the right cease to be exercisable if there is a change in the use of the dominant land? The developer will need to consider whether the proposed development will result in a change in the nature or use of the dominant land or in an intensification of the use of the right of way or both and, if so, whether the right will be lost or suspended.
- Does the grantor own the right of way land? The developer's solicitor will need to ensure that the grantor has title to the right of way land and is able to grant the right.

3.5.1 Extent of right

It will be necessary to carefully consider the physical extent of the right of way and to ensure that it connects with the boundary of the property and that there is no gap between the end of the right of way and the property. The developer's lawyer should pay special attention to the wording of the document containing the right and any plan referred to. If the right of way is over a road which has been adopted or which is the subject of a road adoption agreement, the developer's lawyer should obtain a copy of that agreement and check both the wording of the agreement and all plans attached to it in order to ascertain the extent of the area which has been or will be adopted.

3.5.2 Change of use and excessive user

It would appear that changing the use of land benefiting from a right of way granted by deed will not be an abuse of the right (and will not result in the right being suspended or lost) so long as:

- the change in the use of the dominant land does not result in an increase in the use of the right of way which is excessive, or which interferes with other users;
- the deed does not restrict the use of the right to a particular purpose;
- the surrounding circumstances do not dictate that the right was intended to be restricted.

A right of way granted by deed may be used for all purposes, irrespective of the purpose for which the dominant land was used at the date of the grant, unless something in the deed or surrounding circumstances dictates a more restrictive interpretation.[7] For example, the deed may expressly limit the use of the right of way to a particular purpose or purposes, such as 'for purposes in connection with the use and enjoyment of the property as agricultural land', in which case a change in the use of the dominant land to industrial or commercial use would result in the servient land being used for a purpose which goes beyond the scope of the easement.

The grant of a right of way in general terms will authorise user with vehicles and pedestrian user provided that the way to which the grant refers is suitable at the date of grant for use by vehicles.[8] Notwithstanding that the right of way is for all purposes it will be limited by the physical characteristics of the way at the date of its grant. In *Todrick* v. *Western National Omnibus Co. Limited* [1934] Ch 190 (Ch D) it was held that the grant of a right of way, with or without vehicles, over a road 7 feet 9 inches wide did not authorise user by heavy vehicles.

In light of the judgment of Neuberger LJ in the *Attwood and others* v. *Bovis Homes Limited* [2001] Ch 379 (Ch D) and *McAdams Homes Limited* v. *Robinson and another* [2004] EWCA Civ 214, the developer's lawyer should be aware that it may be the case that a right of way granted by deed cannot continue to be used if there is a radical change in the use of the land benefiting from the right and this results in a substantial increase in the burden on the servient land. As mentioned in **4.1**, these cases concerned prescriptive and implied drainage easements, but the courts are likely to adopt the approach of Neuberger LJ in relation to the excessive

[7] See J Gaunt and P Morgan *Gale on the Law of Easements* (20th edition, Sweet & Maxwell, 2017), paras.9.61–9.81.

[8] See J Gaunt and P Morgan *Gale on the Law of Easements* (20th edition, Sweet & Maxwell, 2017), paras.9.35–9.37.

user of prescriptive/implied drainage easements when considering whether there has been an excessive use of an expressly granted right of way.

The question of excessive use of an expressly granted right of way was considered in *Jelbert* v. *Davis* [1968] 1 WLR 589 (CA) and *Rosling* v. *Pinnegar* (1987) 54 P & CR 124 (CA). In *Jelbert* agricultural land had been conveyed together with 'the right of way at all times and for all purposes over the driveway . . . leading to the main road in common with all other persons having the like right'. The use of the dominant land was changed to a caravan site and the Court of Appeal held that although the use of the right of way by caravans was not outside the wording of the grant, it was excessive and would interfere with the use of the way by 'other persons having the like right'. The Court of Appeal reached the same conclusion in *Rosling* where a Georgian mansion had been conveyed with a right of way over a lane at all times and for all purposes with or without vehicles. The mansion was opened to the public and the local residents sought an injunction preventing the owner of the mansion from causing persons to use the right of way as a result of public or general invitation. The Court of Appeal held that the mere fact that there had been a change in the use of the mansion was not itself a breach of the terms of the grant, but the increased use of the lane was excessive in that it interfered unreasonably with the use of the lane by other persons entitled to use it.

The decisions in *Jelbert* and *Rosling* clearly establish that a right of way granted by deed will be lost or suspended if there is a change in the use of the land benefiting from the right and this interferes unreasonably with the use of the way by others.

3.5.3 New right of way to be granted

If a new right of way is to be granted over a newly constructed access road (or over an access road which is to be constructed by the vendor pursuant to its contractual obligations) the developer will need to ensure that:

- the right of way leads from the development site up to and directly connects with an adopted highway (see **7.4.1**);
- the right granted provides for full free and unrestricted access at all times and for all purposes and covers both pedestrian and vehicular access;
- the right granted includes a right to connect to the access road and all necessary ancillary rights, such as a right to carry out repairs to the access road;
- the right granted includes (if the access road has not yet been constructed) appropriate 'step in' rights which allow the developer to complete the construction of the access road in the event of the vendor failing to comply with its contractual obligations;
- the scope of the easement is not open to doubt. For example, the developer will want to ensure that the exercise of the right is not subject to any preconditions and that it will not be capable of being terminated prematurely (e.g. before it is adopted). Clearly, a right of way which will terminate in the event of it

becoming the subject of a road adoption agreement will not be adequate. Even a right of way which will terminate in the event of the road being adopted is not ideal (see **7.4.1**);

- the exercise of the right of way should not be conditional upon the payment of a maintenance contribution (see **7.4.1**) and (unless the right of way is temporary) the use of the way should not be terminable.

The developer's lawyer will also need to ensure that obligations are imposed on the vendor as the owner of the access road, including:

- to repair and maintain the access road until it is adopted;
- (if the access road has not yet been constructed) to construct the access road in a good and workmanlike manner using good quality materials and in accordance with the requirements of the highway authority and to adoptable standards;
- (if the access road has not yet been constructed) to complete the construction of the road to base course level within a specified period;
- (if the access road has not yet been constructed) to apply the wearing course within a specified period;
- to enter (or use reasonable endeavours to enter) into an adoption agreement with the highway authority as soon as reasonably possible and by a specified date – it will not be possible to have adopted any roads constructed on the developer's land in the future unless the access road is adopted (see **7.4.1**);
- to provide such bond or other security as the highway authority shall require.

The obligations above are all positive obligations and, as such, will not be binding on the vendor's successors in title. However, as already mentioned, there are ways of making the obligations enforceable against successors in title (see **2.9** and **12.10.2**) and the appropriate steps should be taken to achieve this.

3.5.4 Implied ancillary rights

The grant of an easement by deed will include the grant of such ancillary rights as are reasonably necessary to its exercise or enjoyment.[9] The grant of a right of way will, therefore, include an ancillary right to enter the land over which the right of way exists and to alter the surface of the servient land to accommodate the right and to carry out repairs to it. Repairs can include making alterations to and improving the subject of the easement.[10] The grant may, depending on the circumstances at the time when the right was granted, also include ancillary visibility splay rights (see *Carter* v. *Cole* [2009] EWCA Civ 410).

---

[9] See e.g., *Bulstrode* v. *Lambert* [1953] 1 WLR 1064 and *Pwllbach Colliery* v. *Woodman* [1915] AC 634.

[10] See J Gaunt and P Morgan *Gale on the Law of Easements* (20th edition, Sweet & Maxwell, 2017), para.1.92.

Rather than having to rely on implied rights, the developer's lawyer should always ensure that the transfer to the developer includes all necessary ancillary rights.

3.5.5 Summary

- A right of way granted by deed may be used for all purposes unless the deed restricts the use of the right to a particular purpose or the surrounding circumstances dictate that the right was intended to be restricted.
- A right of way granted by deed cannot continue to be used if there is a change in the use of the dominant land and this results in an excessive use of the way or an unreasonable interference with the use of the way by others.
- A right of way granted by deed may also be lost or suspended if there is both a radical change in the use of the dominant land and a substantial increase in the burden on the servient land.
- A mere increase in the use of a right of way without any change in the character or use of the dominant land cannot be objected to.

3.6 RIGHT OF WAY BENEFITING PART OF A SITE

A developer should be aware that a right of way benefiting part of a site cannot be used to gain access to other parts of the site. Suppose that a development site consists of several separate titles and that the land comprised in one of those titles has the benefit of a right of way. The right of way attaches only to the individual title and cannot be extended to the site as a whole.

The question of whether a right of way benefiting one piece of land can be used to gain access to an adjoining piece of land was considered in *Peacock* v. *Custins* [2001] 2 All ER 827 (CA). In this case, the claimants owned a 15-acre parcel of land ('the first parcel') which enjoyed the benefit of a right of way over a strip of land owned by the defendants. The claimants also owned a 10-acre parcel of land ('the second parcel') which was adjacent to the first parcel. The first parcel and the second parcel were farmed as one unit and the right of way used for the purpose of gaining access to both the first parcel and the second parcel. The Court of Appeal held that the right of way was granted for the sole purpose of benefiting the first parcel and that the use of the way for the purpose of gaining access to the second parcel went beyond the scope of the easement. This decision follows the decision in *Harris* v. *Flower & Sons* (1905) 74 LJ Ch 127. In the words of Romer LJ:

> If a right of way be granted for the enjoyment of close A, the grantee, because he owns or acquires close B, cannot use the way in substance for passing over close A to close B.

The decisions in *Peacock* and *Harris* can be distinguished from the decision in *National Trust for Places of Historic Interest or Natural Beauty and another* v. *White and another* [1987] 1 WLR 907 (Ch D). In the latter case the National Trust had the benefit of a right of way to an historic site and it was held that they and their visitors were entitled to use the way as a means of gaining access to a car park on nearby land for the purpose of visiting the historic site. According to the authors of *Gale on the Law of Easements* (20th edition):

> The principle seems to be that access to land which is ancillary to the use of the way for the purpose of the grant is permissible but access to land which is ancillary to the enjoyment of the dominant tenement is not.
>
> (para.9.50)

3.7 ROAD AGREEMENTS AND ROAD ADOPTION

A local highway authority may agree to adopt roads constructed on private land and to enter into a road adoption agreement with a developer pursuant to the Highways Act (HA) 1980, s.38. Under a s.38 agreement the developer's estate roads will be vested in the highway authority, subject to the roads having been constructed in accordance with the provisions of the agreement, following a 12-month maintenance period, during which the developer will be obliged to make good any defects in the road.

A person wishing to enter into a s.38 agreement with a local highway authority will need to have the necessary power to dedicate the relevant roads as a highway and prior to entering into a s.38 agreement it will be necessary for the developer's lawyer to deduce title to the development site to the highway authority. This could be problematic if any section of the estate roads will pass over land registered with possessory title or over land to which there is no documentary title, although some highway authorities may be prepared to adopt a practical approach and may be satisfied if a defective title indemnity insurance policy is obtained.

Where the owner of land on which it is proposed to build a road or part of a road is unknown and the highway authority is not prepared to enter into a s.38 agreement, the following options for adoption may be available:

- Under HA 1980, s.228 when any street works have been executed in a private street, the highway authority may, by notice displayed in a prominent position in the street, declare the street to be a highway maintainable at the public expense, unless within one month of the date of the notice the owner or the majority of the owners of the street object and the magistrates' court does not overrule the objection. A 'private street' is any street not maintainable at public expense (HA 1980, s.203) and a 'street' is any road, lane, footway, alley or passage (HA 1980, s.329(1)). Whether this option for adoption is available or not will clearly depend upon the highway authority.
- Under HA 1980, s.228(7) if all street works have been executed in a private street to the satisfaction of the highway authority, then, on the application of the majority in rateable value of the owners of properties in the street, the highway

authority shall, within the period of three months from the date of the application, by notice displayed in a prominent position in the street, declare the street to be a highway maintainable at the public expense. Section 228(7) does not apply to part of a street.

- Under HA 1980, s.229(1) the majority in number of the owners of land having a frontage on a built-up private street may by notice require the highway authority to declare the street to be a highway maintainable at the public expense. Section 229(1) will not apply:
  - unless a payment has been made or security has been given under s.219 by the owner of land having a frontage on the street and the payment has not been refunded or the security released or realised (s.229(2));
  - where the street is part of a street, unless it is a part not less than 100 yards in length (s.229(4)).

A developer should be aware that where a development site is accessed via a private road it will not be possible to have the estate roads adopted. For estate roads to be adopted they must connect to an existing adopted highway.

3.8 LAND COMPENSATION ACT CLAIMS

When acquiring a development site, the development of which will involve the construction of major road works, a developer will need to be aware of a potential liability under the Land Compensation Act (LCA) 1973, Part 1. Under LCA 1973, Part 1, s.1 a person may make a claim for compensation against the highway authority where the value of his land is depreciated by physical factors, such as noise, fumes and lighting, caused by the new roads or their use. The compensation will be payable by the highway authority. However, the developer will invariably end up paying the compensation as agreements entered into pursuant to HA 1980, ss.38 and 278 usually contain a covenant by the developer to indemnify the highway authority in respect of any claims made against the highway authority under LCA 1973, Part 1, s.1.

3.9 REGISTRATION OF RIGHT OF WAY

All new legal easements expressly granted or reserved out of a registered title after 13 October 2003 are registerable dispositions and will need to be registered using form API (Land Registration Act (LRA) 2002, s.27(2)(d)), otherwise they will have no effect at law. Accordingly, the creation of a legal right of way (whether by a transfer or a separate deed of grant) out of a registered title will give rise to a registerable disposition which will not be binding on the successors in title of the grantor until the transfer/deed has been registered. An application should be made for a note of the right of way to be entered on both the grantor's and the grantee's titles, but even if the grantee's land is not registered, an application should still be made for a note of the right to be made on the grantor's registered title.

It is worth noting that all easements created before 13 October 2003 that were overriding interests (such as an unregistered expressly granted legal easement) will continue to bind a purchaser (LRA 2002, Sched.12, para.9). Therefore, a pre-13 October 2003 expressly granted legal easement will be binding on a purchaser even if it is not noted on the title to the land being acquired.

In the case of unregistered land, the grant of a right of way that is a legal easement is not a registerable transaction, but it is good practice to register a caution against first registration in respect of the grantor's land. This will ensure that the Land Registry registers the easement when the grantor's land is first registered. The grant of a right of way that is an equitable easement (such as a right of way that will terminate upon the way becoming adopted) out of unregistered land will need to be protected by the registration of a D(iii) land charge against the name of the grantor. Again, it is good practice to also register a caution against first registration in respect of the grantor's land.

CHAPTER 4

Drainage and other services

Having satisfied itself about the access to the site, the developer will need to think about drainage issues and the supply of services (such as electricity, water, gas and telecommunications). There are a number of key issues to be considered, including the following:

- Are any existing drainage and other service media rights adequate?
- Are any new drainage and other service media rights required?
- How easy will it be to connect to the existing mains drainage system and the existing mains water, gas and electricity network systems? If the site does not already benefit from drainage and other services then the developer will need to make enquiries of the various statutory undertakers and utility companies in order to identify the proximity of services into which the new development can link, and, if the site is not in close proximity to a public sewer or other mains services, it may be necessary for the developer to acquire easements over third party land or to requisition the supply of services.
- Are the existing adopted sewers to which it is proposed to make a connection of sufficient capacity? Even if the site is in close proximity to adopted foul sewers it would be prudent for the developer to check with the sewerage undertaker that the sewers are of sufficient capacity to allow the developer to make a connection to the adopted sewerage system at the point required by the developer.
- Where will the surface water go? It may be that there are no storm water sewers under the highway adjoining the site or that the drainage authorities will not allow the discharge of surface water into the sewers adjoining the site, in which case the developer will have to consider an alternative drainage solution, such as discharging the surface water into a ditch or watercourse or an attenuation or balancing pond.
- Dealing with surface water has been made more difficult by the Flood and Water Management Act (FWMA) 2010 and planning guidance. Under FWMA 2010, Sched.3 the run off of surface water into a foul sewer will no longer be permitted and no development may be commenced until a sustainable drainage system (SUD) for the proposed development has been approved by an approving body (defined in Sched.3, para.6) (see **4.5**). The implementation of Sched.3

has been subject to continuous delays and it is not yet in force. However, under the revised National Planning Policy Framework, any major development should incorporate sustainable drainage systems and planning authorities are currently using a combination of planning conditions and s.106 agreements to deliver SUDS.

4.1 PRESCRIPTIVE DRAINAGE RIGHTS

Drainage rights, like rights of way, may be expressly granted or acquired by prescription. Again, the developer will need to consider whether any existing rights are adequate and whether the proposed development will result in any existing drainage easement being lost or suspended.

A developer's lawyer should be aware that a drainage easement acquired by prescription will not be adequate where there is a requirement for the estate sewers to be adopted (see **4.6**).

4.1.1 Change of use

The question of whether a drainage easement acquired by prescription will be lost if there is a change in the use of the dominant land was considered in *Attwood and others* v. *Bovis Homes Limited* [2001] Ch 379 (Ch D) and in *McAdams Homes Limited* v. *Robinson and another* [2004] EWCA Civ 214.

In the *Attwood* case Bovis had bought some agricultural land intending to develop it as a large housing estate. The land drained through another nearby farm, and the farmer argued that the right of drainage was for agricultural purposes only (and thus could not be extended to residential purposes). Fortunately for Bovis, the court disagreed and held that a drainage easement acquired by prescription would not be defeated by a substantial change in the nature of the dominant land, unless the owner of the servient land could prove that the change had substantially increased the burden on his land.

The *McAdams Homes* case concerned an implied drainage easement. A site which was formerly used as a bakery was sold in 1982 with the benefit of implied drainage rights over the vendor's retained land. In 2001 the bakery was demolished and two houses were built on the site. The owners of the retained land blocked the drains serving the site and the developers were forced to construct an alternative drainage system. The developers commenced proceedings to recover the cost of the new system and the court held that the rights of drainage enjoyed by the former bakery were not available to the new houses since the change in the use of the site had been radical and this change had resulted in an increased flow of water through the drain and represented a substantial increase in the burden on the servient land.

In his judgment in the *McAdams Homes* case Neuberger LJ helpfully stated that the following principles can be derived from various cases concerning prescriptive and implied easements:

- Where the dominant land is used for a particular purpose at the time an easement is created, an increase in the intensity of that use cannot of itself be objected to by the owner of the servient land.
- Excessive use of an easement by the dominant land will render the owner of the dominant land liable in nuisance.
- A change in the use of the dominant land, without having any effect on the nature or extent of the use of the easement, will not affect the right of the dominant owner to use the easement.
- A radical change in the use of the dominant land (as opposed to mere change or intensification in the use of the site) which results in a substantial increase in the burden of the servient land does affect the right of the dominant owner to use the easement.

4.1.2 Intensification of use

As we have already seen, a right of way acquired by prescription will not be defeated by a mere intensification of use of the right of way. Having regard to the judgment of Neuberger LJ in *McAdams Homes Limited* it is also likely that a drainage easement acquired by prescription will not be lost or suspended if there is an intensification of the use of the drainage easement without any change in the use of the dominant land.

4.2 EXPRESSLY GRANTED RIGHTS OF DRAINAGE

As with expressly granted rights of way, it would appear that the benefit of a drainage right expressly granted or reserved for the benefit of defined land will not be defeated by a change in the use of that land unless:

- the right has been expressly limited in some way in the relevant deed; or
- the surrounding circumstances (e.g. the capacity of the sewer) indicate a restrictive use of the right; or
- there has been an excessive use of the right which has caused a nuisance to others.

As mentioned above, the question of excessive use of an implied drainage easement was considered in the *McAdams Homes Limited* case by Neuberger LJ, who stated:

> If the owner of a drain expressly or impliedly grants an easement to another party to use the drain for certain purposes, the easement cannot be determined, nor the purposes cut down or modified, merely because of some subsequent defect in the public sewerage system into which the drain discharges. The position, would, of course, be very different if, in a case where the issue was whether the other party was making excessive use of the easement, it was established that his alleged excessive use of the drain was causing, or even substantially contributing to, the backing up.

As we have already seen, according to Neuberger LJ there will be an excessive use of an implied drainage easement if there is both a radical change in the use of the dominant land and a substantial increase in the burden on the servient land, and it is likely that this principle will be applied in the case of expressly granted drainage easements.

4.2.1 New drainage rights to be granted

If new drainage easements are to be granted to the developer, similar considerations to those already mentioned in relation to new rights of way will apply. The developer will need to ensure that:

- the drainage easements are adequate for the proposed development;
- the sewers are of sufficient capacity and connect to existing adopted sewers;
- the drainage easements include both foul and surface water sewers;
- there is a right to connect to and use the sewers, a right to lay a new sewer within the vendor's retained land for the purpose of making such a connection and a right to enter the vendor's retained land for the purpose of connecting to, repairing, renewing and inspecting the sewers;
- the drainage easements include appropriate step in rights which allow the developer to remedy any breach of the vendor's obligations referred to below;
- various obligations are imposed on the vendor as the owner of the land through which the sewer will pass, including:
  - an obligation to repair and maintain the sewer until it is adopted;
  - (if the sewer has not yet been constructed) an obligation to construct the sewer in accordance with the requirements of the relevant statutory undertaker and planning conditions and to complete such construction before a specified date;
  - (if the sewer has not yet been constructed) an obligation to construct the sewer in a good and workmanlike manner and to adoption standard;
  - an obligation to enter (or use reasonable endeavours to enter) into an appropriate adoption agreement as soon as reasonably possible;
  - an obligation to provide such bond or other security as the relevant statutory undertaker shall require.

The developer will also need to consider whether the sewers located on the adjoining land will be of sufficient capacity to serve both the adjoining land and the development site once the development site has been fully developed, and whether there will be a need for attenuation/pumping or the raising of site levels. Suitable additional obligations may need to be imposed on the vendor.

As already mentioned in relation to rights of way, the creation of a new drainage easement (whether by a transfer or a separate deed of grant) out of a registered title will need to be registered against the grantor's title using form AP1 (see **3.9**). In the case of unregistered land, the grant of a drainage easement is not a registrable disposition, but it is good practice to register a caution against first registration in respect of the grantor's title.

4.2.2 Perpetuity period

Prior to the Perpetuities and Accumulations Act 2009 coming into force, where a transfer granted to a purchaser the right to connect to and use any sewers which might be laid under the vendor's retained land in the future, or a right to lay new sewers under the vendor's retained land, it was necessary, in order to comply with the rule against perpetuities, for the wording of the right granted to include the words 'during the Perpetuity Period' (which would usually be defined as 'the period of 80 years commencing with the date of this Transfer', which is the maximum perpetuity period permitted under the Perpetuities and Accumulations Act 1964). Without these words the 'wait and see' rule would have applied, and the grant of the right would have been void, unless the right was exercised within the perpetuity period of 21 years. However, as from 6 April 2010 easements are no longer subject to the rule against perpetuities. The rule applies only to the interests set out in the Perpetuities and Accumulations Act 2009, s.1. These are generally trust interests and do not include other types of interests such as easements, options and rights of pre-emption. Accordingly, it is no longer necessary to refer to any perpetuity period in a transfer or deed granting rights.

4.2.3 Implied ancillary drainage rights

A drainage easement will include a right to enter the land over which the drainage easement exists for the purpose of repairing and maintaining the relevant pipe, drain or sewer. However, the implied right to repair and maintain will not extend to relaying or improving or enlarging the relevant pipe, drain or sewer – this is not reasonably necessary to the exercise or enjoyment of the drainage easement. Accordingly, where a developer is to be granted a new right to use an existing foul sewer located on adjoining land, it should always require an express additional right to enter the adjoining land for the purpose of connecting to and thereafter repairing, maintaining and renewing and, if necessary, upgrading or enlarging the foul sewer. While a right to use the foul sewer on the adjoining land may imply ancillary rights of entry and connection, it is clearly better practice to include in the transfer all necessary ancillary rights.

4.3 FOUL SEWERS: CONNECTION TO PUBLIC SEWER SYSTEM

A developer will have a right under the Water Industry Act (WIA) 1991, s.106 to connect a development to the public sewer system. Under s.106(1) of that Act the owner or occupier of any premises is entitled to have his drains or sewers communicate with the public sewer of any sewerage undertaker and to discharge foul and surface water from those premises into the public sewer. A sewerage undertaker is entitled to refuse permission for a connection to be made to the public sewer system only if it appears to the undertaker that the mode of construction or the condition of the sewer does not satisfy standards reasonably required by the undertaker or if the proposed connection would be prejudicial to the sewerage system (s.106(4)). The undertaker will not be able to refuse permission for a connection to be made at the point of connection required by the developer on the ground that the sewer system lacks capacity or that the proposed connection will overload the system (see *Barratt Homes* v. *Welsh Water* [2008] EWCA Civ 1552); and once a planning permission authorising development has been granted there will be limited scope for the sewerage undertaker to refuse permission for the developer to connect to the public sewer system.

The automatic right to communicate with public sewers under WIA 1991, s.106(1) has been qualified by FWMA 2010, s.42(1), which inserts a new section (s.106B) into WIA 1991. However, although s.42 is in force in Wales, it is not yet in force in England and there is uncertainty as to when the provisions of s.42(1) will be implemented in England. (Section 42 was brought into force in Wales by the Flood and Water Management Act 2010 (Commencement No.8 and Transitional Provisions) Order 2012 (SI 2012/2048), art.2(1), which states that 'Section 42 of the Flood and Water Management Act 2010, to the extent not already commenced, comes into force on 1 October 2012 in relation to sewerage undertakers whose areas are wholly or mainly in Wales'. Article 2(1) is subject to the transitional provisions set out in art.3.) Under s.106B, a person may exercise the right to connect a newly built lateral drain or sewer (see **4.6** for definitions of 'lateral drain' and 'sewer') to the public sewer network only if two conditions are satisfied. The first condition is that an agreement was entered into under WIA 1991, s.104. The second condition is that the agreement included a provision about the standards (being standards published by the Secretary of State or, where the sewer or drain is located wholly or mainly in Wales, the Welsh Ministers) according to which the drain or sewer was to be constructed and a provision made for the automatic adoption of the sewer or drain by the sewerage undertaker upon the occurrence of specified events. (It will be possible to depart from these standards by express consent of the parties to the s.104 agreement.) Where the two conditions are met the sewerage undertaker may not refuse to allow a connection to be made to the public sewer network.

It will be important, therefore, once s.42(1) becomes effective, that the developer enters into the s.104 agreement as soon as possible and it would be sensible for the developer to approach the sewerage undertaker at an early stage to negotiate the s.104 agreement and to secure agreement on the technical details for making the proposed connection to the public sewer system. Any delay may have an adverse effect on the developer's development programme and the sale of dwellings.

Section 42 does not apply to drainage systems required to be approved in accordance with FWMA 2010, Sched.3 or in other circumstances specified by the Secretary of State or the Welsh Ministers in regulations (i.e. surface water drainage systems) (see WIA 1991, s.106B(6)). Subsections 42(2) and 42(3) of FWMA 2010 have been repealed by the Water Act 2014.

If the route of the foul sewers for a proposed development will need to pass over land owned by third parties then the developer will need to approach those parties to see whether they would be willing to enter into a suitable deed of easement. The deed of easement should be in a form which will be acceptable to the sewerage undertaker and should include various covenants on the part of the grantor, including a restrictive covenant not to erect any building or other structure or plant any tree over the sewer or within a certain distance on either side of the sewer and, most importantly, a positive covenant to enter into a sewer adoption agreement with the relevant drainage authority upon request by the developer (see **Appendix C14**). The deed should also contain a covenant by the grantor not to make any disposal without procuring that the disponee enters into a deed of covenant with the developer in which the disponee covenants to perform the obligations contained in the deed of easement, and there should be a requirement (where the grantor's title is registered) for a restriction against dealing to be entered on the title to the grantor's land. The deed, being a registerable disposition under the Land Registration Act 2002, will need to be registered on the grantor's registered title using form AP1 to be binding on the grantor's successors in title, and the registration should be dealt with promptly (in case the grantor decides to sell his land shortly after the deed of easement has been completed); a note of the deed will also need to be registered on the developer's title using form AP1. If the grantor's title is unregistered then the easement created by the deed, being a legal easement, will be binding on the grantor's successor's in title, but the restrictive covenants contained in the deed will need to be registered as a land charge within class D(ii). The grantee's lawyer should also ensure that a note of the deed is endorsed on the conveyance which is the root of title to the grantor's land.

4.4 REQUISITIONING SEWERS

If the third parties are not prepared to co-operate with the developer, the developer will have no alternative other than to requisition the relevant sewerage undertaker to provide the necessary sewers. The Water Industry Act 1991 imposes a duty on a sewerage undertaker to provide a public sewer to be used for the drainage for domestic purposes of premises in a particular locality in its area if so required by, amongst others, the owner or occupier of any premises in that locality (s.98), subject to certain conditions being satisfied (s.99). The duty is not restricted to residential dwellings and extends to commercial and industrial premises (see **4.7.3**). A landowner will not be entitled to refuse a water or sewerage undertaker permission to lay a sewer or water pipe across his land, since under WIA 1991 a water or sewerage undertaker has an express right to lay pipes under any land which is not in, under or over a street (s.159). This right is subject to the relevant undertaker giving reasonable notice to the landowner and payment of compensation. Under WIA 1991,

Sched.12 compensation is payable for any depreciation in the value of the land caused by the presence of the pipe together with an allowance for disturbance and actual losses. A water/sewerage undertaker also has powers to purchase compulsorily any land which it requires for the purposes of, or in connection with, the carrying out of its functions (s.155).

It should be noted that, although a water undertaker has an express power to discharge water into a watercourse (s.165), a sewerage undertaker has no power to discharge water on to another person's land or watercourse without the landowner's consent (see *British Waterways Board* v. *Severn Trent Water Limited* [2001] EWCA Civ 276). If, therefore, a sewerage undertaker wishes to discharge water from a development site via a sewer into a watercourse on another person's land, it will be necessary to obtain the consent of the owner of the watercourse. The sewerage undertaker could utilise its compulsory purchase powers to purchase the watercourse, but this would require the payment of compensation by the developer to the owner.

4.5 DEALING WITH SURFACE WATER

As well as thinking about foul sewers, the developer will need to consider where the surface water is to go and the following questions should be asked:

- Are there storm water sewers within the highway or surface water sewers within the vicinity of the development site into which surface water will be able to flow?
- Will balancing ponds within the development site be required?
- Is it possible to discharge surface water into an adjoining ditch or watercourse?
- Will soakaways or a balancing pond provide a satisfactory drainage solution?

If it is intended that the surface water should be discharged into a ditch or watercourse adjoining the proposed development site then the developer will need to check that this arrangement will be acceptable to the relevant drainage authority and the Environment Agency. It will also be necessary to ascertain who owns the ditch or watercourse and it may be necessary for the developer to enter into a suitable deed of easement with the owner. Although a landowner cannot object to the natural run off of surface water from his neighbour's land, a landowner is not entitled to discharge surface water from his land on to his neighbour's land if that water has been artificially accumulated there or artificial erection on his land has caused the surface water to flow on to his neighbour's land in a manner in which it would not have done, but for such erection.[1]

If there are no public storm water sewers or surface water sewers within the vicinity of the development (which would have been revealed by the developer's

[1] See J Gaunt and P Morgan *Gale on the Law of Easements* (20th edition, Sweet & Maxwell, 2017), para.6.24.

technical/service enquiries) then it may be necessary to construct a storm water soakaway system or balancing pond in order to satisfy the requirements of the drainage and planning authorities. Whether this will be possible will depend on ground conditions.

Developers will need to be aware of the requirement under FWMA 2010 to include sustainable surface water drainage as part of any development. Surface water run off has caused serious flooding over recent years when conventional drainage systems have become overloaded and unable to cope with the increased volume of surface water. To help tackle this problem the government included provisions for sustainable drainage in FWMA 2010, Sched.3. As mentioned above, Sched.3 is not yet in force. However, local planning authorities are required by planning guidance to ensure that SUDS are in place when considering planning applications for 10 or more dwellings, unless it is demonstrated that they are clearly inappropriate. They are currently using a combination of planning conditions and planning obligations to deliver SUDS. The latest version of the National Planning Policy Framework (revised in July 2018) states as follows:

> Major developments should incorporate sustainable drainage systems unless there is clear evidence that this would be inappropriate. The systems used should:
>
> (a) take account of advice from the lead local flood authority;
> (b) have appropriate proposed minimum operational standards;
> (c) have maintenance arrangements in place to ensure an acceptable standard of operation for the lifetime of the development; and
> (d) where possible, provide multifunctional benefits.
>
> (para.165)

Schedule 3 deals only with the drainage of surface water and para.16 of the schedule amends WIA 1991, s.106(1) by removing the automatic right for a landowner to make a connection for the discharge of surface water to the public sewer system. The right under s.106(1) will in future be subject to WIA 1991, s.106A(2) which states that:

> A person may exercise the right under section 106(1) in respect of surface water only if
>
> (a) the construction of the drainage system was approved under [FWMA 2010, Sched.3] and
> (b) the proposals for approval included a proposal for the communication with the public sewer.

Under FWMA 2010 surface water may not be discharged into a foul sewer and no construction work which has drainage implications may be commenced unless a drainage system for the work has been approved by the approving body (Sched.3, para.7(1)). A drainage system is a structure designed to receive rainwater, excluding a public sewer under WIA 1991, s.219(1) (i.e. a sewer vested in a sewerage undertaker in its capacity as such) and a natural watercourse (i.e. a river or stream). An application for approval of a drainage system under Sched.3, para.7 must be made to an approving body (as defined in para.6). If the construction work requires planning permission, the application for approval may be a free-standing application or a combination of an application for approval under para.7 with an application for planning permission. If the application is a combined application the planning authority must:

- consult the approving body (if different) in determining the application for planning permission; and
- inform the approving body (if different) of its determination of the application for planning permission.

An approving body must grant approval if it is satisfied that the drainage system (if constructed as proposed) will comply with national standards for sustainable drainage (Sched.3, para.11(1)). However, before determining an application the approving body must consult:

- any sewerage undertaker with whose public sewer the drainage system is proposed to communicate;
- the Environment Agency, if the drainage system involves the discharge of water into a watercourse in England;
- the Natural Resources Body for Wales, if the drainage system directly or indirectly involves the discharge of water into a watercourse in Wales;
- the relevant highway authority for a road which the approving body thinks may be affected;
- the Canal and River Trust, if the approving body thinks that the drainage system may directly or indirectly involve the discharge of water into or under a waterway managed by the Trust;
- an internal drainage board, if the approving body thinks that the drainage system may directly or indirectly involve the discharge of water into an ordinary watercourse (within the meaning of the Land Drainage Act 1991, s.72).

An approving body must adopt a drainage system if it satisfies the following conditions:

- that the drainage system was constructed in pursuance of proposals approved under para.7;
- that the approving body is satisfied that the drainage system was constructed, and functions, in accordance with the approved proposals or that the approving body can issue or has issued a certificate under para.12(2);
- that the drainage system is a sustainable drainage system, as defined by regulations made by the minister (Sched.3, para.17).

The adoption duty does not apply to the following drainage systems:

- a drainage system or any part of a drainage system designed only to provide drainage for a single property;
- any part of a drainage system which is a publicly maintained road.

The delay by the government in implementing Sched.3 has been much criticised and created ongoing uncertainty, but, whether it is implemented in its current form or in an amended form, developers will need to consider SUDS at the land acquisition stage.

4.6 DRAINAGE ADOPTION

A sewerage undertaker may agree to adopt sewers constructed on private land and to enter into a sewer adoption agreement with a developer pursuant to WIA 1991, s.104. Under a s.104 agreement the developer's estate sewers will be vested in the undertaker, subject to the sewers having been constructed in accordance with the provisions of the agreement, following a 12-month maintenance period, during which the developer will be obliged to make good any defects in the sewers.

Prior to entering into a s.104 agreement the drainage authority will want to be satisfied that the developer owns the development site and it will be necessary for the developer's lawyer to deduce title to the development site to the drainage authority. This could be problematic if any section of the estate sewers will pass over land registered with possessory title or over land to which there is no documentary title, although some drainage authorities may be prepared to adopt a practical approach and may be satisfied if a defective title indemnity insurance policy has been obtained.

A developer should be aware that where a development site is served by private sewers it will not be possible to have the developer's estate sewers adopted. For estate sewers to be adopted they must connect to existing adopted sewers.

Under the Water Industry (Schemes for Adoption of Private Sewers) Regulations 2011 (SI 2011/1566) all private gravity sewers and lateral drains that were connected to a public sewer before 1 July 2011 were automatically adopted on 1 October 2011. If any such sewer or lateral drain had been the subject of a s.104 adoption agreement the agreement was treated as terminating immediately before the vesting of the sewer or drain in the water company. (The terms 'sewer' and 'lateral drain' are defined in WIA 1991, s.219. Essentially, to be classified as a sewer, a drainage pipe must serve more than one property. A drain serves only one property and a lateral drain is that part that extends beyond the property boundary to the point where it meets the sewer.) If any sewer or lateral drain connected to the public sewer network between 1 July 2011 and the date that FWMA 2010, s.42 becomes operative is the subject of a s.104 adoption agreement then, again, the adoption agreement will be treated as terminating on the vesting date (i.e. the earlier of the date specified in the adoption agreement and the date six months after s.42(1) comes into force) and ownership of the sewer or lateral drain will pass to the water and drainage companies.

For the future, assuming that FWMA 2010, s.42 is eventually implemented, it will not be possible for a private foul sewer or lateral drain to connect to a public sewer unless the developer has entered into a s.104 adoption agreement with the water company and the agreement imposes a mandatory build standard (see **4.3**); and, assuming that FWMA 2010, Sched.3 comes into force, it will not be possible for a surface water sewer to connect to a public sewer unless the requirements of FWMA 2010, Sched.3 have been complied with (see **4.5**). The drainage authority will be obliged to adopt a surface water drainage system which satisfies the conditions set out in FWMA 2010, Sched.3, para.17.

For the present, the situation remains that the drainage authority is not obliged to adopt a private sewer connected to the public sewer network after 1 July 2011. Nor is it obliged to adopt any newly constructed sustainable surface water drainage system.

4.7 RIGHTS IN RESPECT OF SERVICES

As well as ensuring that there are adequate drainage arrangements, the developer will need to arrange for the supply of electricity, water, gas, telecommunications and other services to the development site. The developer will need to identify the proximity of mains services in the vicinity of the site and, again, it may be necessary for service easements to be acquired over adjoining land. If the developer is to be granted service easements, similar considerations to those mentioned in relation to rights of way and drainage will apply.

4.7.1 Requisitioning services

The developer should be aware that, as well as being able to requisition sewers, it is also possible to requisition the supply of electricity and water (but not gas or telecommunications).

4.7.2 Electricity

The Electricity Act (EA) 1989 (as amended by the Utilities Act 2000) imposes a duty on an electricity distributor to make a connection between its distribution system and any premises when requested to do so by the owner or occupier of the premises (s.16(1)(a)). However, an electricity distributor will be exempted from making a connection if:

- the electricity distributor is prevented from doing so by circumstances not within its control;
- making the connection would or might involve a breach of safety regulations;
- it is not reasonable in all the circumstances for the distributor to be required to do so (s.17).

Where any electric line or electric plant is provided by an electricity distributor pursuant to EA 1989 the distributor may require any expenses reasonably incurred in providing the relevant apparatus to be defrayed by the person requiring the connection to such extent as is reasonable in all the circumstances (s.19).

A landowner will not be entitled to refuse an electricity distributor permission to lay an electric line across his land unless there is a dwelling on the land or he can persuade the Secretary of State that a wayleave should not be granted. Under EA 1989 an electricity distributor may serve a notice on the owner or occupier of land requiring him to give 'the necessary wayleave' (Sched.4, para.6). If the owner or occupier fails to give the wayleave within the period (being not less than 21 days) specified in the notice then the Secretary of State may, on the application of the electricity distributor, grant the necessary wayleave subject to such terms and conditions as he thinks fit. Before granting the necessary wayleave, the Secretary of State must afford the owner or occupier of the land an opportunity of being heard by a person appointed by the Secretary of State. The purpose of the hearing will be to consider why it is necessary for the electric line to cross the land in question and the effects of the line on the use and enjoyment of the land. The Secretary of State will not grant a wayleave if the land is covered by a dwelling or it has the benefit of a planning permission permitting residential development, although the Secretary of State will entertain an application to retain existing apparatus (as opposed to installing new apparatus) (see **2.2**). The Secretary of State can only grant or refuse 'the necessary wayleave'. He has no power to vary the application. In most cases it is usual for the electricity distributor to negotiate with the landowner in order to try to reach an amicable settlement without the need for a hearing.

4.7.3 Water

The Water Industry Act 1991 imposes a duty on a water undertaker 'to provide a water main to be used for providing such supplies of water to premises in a particular locality in its area as (so far as those premises are concerned) are sufficient for domestic purposes' (s.41(1)). This duty is subject to:

- the undertaker being required to provide the main by a notice served on it by the owner or occupier of premises within any locality within the water undertaker's area;
- the premises consisting of buildings or part of buildings or that they will so consist when proposals for the erection of buildings are completed; and
- certain financial conditions being satisfied (s.42).

'Domestic purposes' means drinking, washing, cooking, central heating and sanitary purposes (s.218(1)). The premises do not have to be used for domestic purposes and may be used for commercial purposes, but not for the purpose of the business of a laundry or for any purpose of a business of preparing food or drink for consumption off the premises (s.218(3)).

As indicated above, it will not be possible for a landowner to object to a water undertaker laying a water pipe under his land since a water undertaker has an express statutory power to lay a water pipe under private land (s.159). The power is exercisable after giving reasonable notice to the owner and the occupier of the land and the owner has no right to object.

4.7.4 Gas

The Gas Act 1986 (as amended by the Gas Act 1995 and the Utilities Act 2000) imposes a duty on a gas transporter to develop and maintain an efficient and economical pipeline system for the conveyance of gas and to comply, so far as it is economical to do so, with any reasonable request to connect to that system and convey gas by means of that system to any premises or to connect to that system a pipeline system operated by an authorised transporter (s.9). The Gas Act 1986 also imposes a duty on a gas transporter to connect premises to a gas main upon request by the owner or occupier where the premises are within 23 metres of the main or where the owner or occupier has laid a properly specified gas supply pipe (s.10). Unlike an electricity distributor or a sewerage or water undertaker, a gas transporter has no statutory right to acquire a wayleave over private land, although it does have compulsory purchase powers (s.9(3) and Sched.3).

4.7.5 Telecom services

There is no express statutory duty on a telecommunications operator to provide telecommunications services. However, the Electronic Communications Code set out in the Digital Economy Act 2017 refers to the interest of the public having access to a choice of high-quality electronic communications services and establishes a procedure which enables an operator to install telecommunications apparatus on private land. Under the Code the consent of the occupier of the land must be obtained before any rights can be conferred on the operator. However, if no such consent is forthcoming, the operator may apply to the county court for an order conferring the required rights. The court will make the order only if it is satisfied that any prejudice caused by the order is capable of being adequately compensated for by money and the public benefit likely to result from the making of the order outweighs the prejudice to the relevant person. In determining the extent of the prejudice and the weight of the benefit, the court will have regard to the public interest in access to a choice of high-quality electronic communications services (see Communications Act 2003, Sched.3A, para.21).

CHAPTER 5

Planning

Having investigated the title to the development site and considered access and drainage issues, the developer's lawyer will need to consider the planning situation, which should include a review of all relevant planning documentation. Where a developer is proposing to acquire a site with the benefit of an existing planning permission the developer should request copies of all relevant planning documents from the vendor, including the planning decision notice, the planning agreement, the planning application together with all plans and drawings which accompanied the planning application and all relevant correspondence (including copies of all letters and email exchanges and telephone and meeting notes) where discussions, consultations, understandings or agreements may have taken place or been reached between the applicant and the local authority.

The plans and drawings (together with any site plan attached to a planning agreement) should be carefully checked and compared with the title plan to ensure that there are no discrepancies and that the development will fit within the boundaries of the development site as shown on the title plan.

The developer will also want to be clear as to the extent of any actual or potential liability for payment of the Community Infrastructure Levy (CIL) imposed pursuant to the Community Infrastructure Levy Regulations 2010 (SI 2010/948). If the development site is in London, any CIL liability could also include additional Mayoral CIL.

The amount of CIL payable can be significant dependent upon the nature and size of any new or proposed development (see **5.4**).

5.1 PLANNING CONDITIONS

Where a site benefits from an existing planning permission which the developer intends to implement, the conditions attaching to the relevant planning permission should be carefully checked.

Under the Town and Country Planning Act (TCPA) 1990 (as amended), a local authority has power to grant planning permission unconditionally or subject to such conditions as it thinks fit (s.70(1)). However, this power is not unfettered and a local planning authority will be bound by a number of decisions of the courts and planning policies, including the policy guidance contained in the revised National Planning Policy Framework dated July 2018 published by the Ministry of Housing, Communities and Local Government and the Planning Practice Guidance (PPG) first published online by the government on 6 March 2014 (see **www.gov.uk/government/collections/planning-practice-guidance**), and updated electronically from time to time so as to ensure that the guidance reflects changes in planning policy or case law.

Footnote 1 of the July 2018 version of the National Planning Policy Framework makes it clear that 'this document replaces the first National Planning Policy Framework published in March 2012'. The July 2018 version is already colloquially known by practitioners as 'NPPF2' and that is the reference that will be adopted in this chapter to distinguish it from the March 2012 version (which will be referred to as 'NPPF1').

When first published in March 2012, NPPF1 replaced a number of planning policy statements and planning guidelines, which had been referred to and used by practitioners for many years, including Circular 05/2005: Planning Obligations. (A full list of the documents replaced by NPPF1 is set out in Annex 3 of NPPF1.)

NPPF2 stipulates in para.55 that a planning condition must be:

- necessary (i.e. there must be a definite planning reason for the condition such that permission would have been refused without it);
- relevant to planning (i.e. a condition must relate to planning objectives and must not be used to control matters that are subject to specific control elsewhere in planning legislation);
- relevant to the development to be permitted (i.e. the condition must be justified by the nature or impact of the development permitted);
- enforceable (in both policy and practical terms);
- precise (i.e. the condition must make clear to the applicant what needs to be done to comply with it); and
- reasonable in all other respects (e.g. it would be unreasonable to impose a condition which placed an unjustifiable and disproportionate burden on the applicant).

The above requirements are separately referred to in the PPG as the six tests.

Paragraph 55 of NPPF2 is similar to para.206 of NPPF1. Paragraph 55 also states that 'Conditions that are required to be discharged before development commences should be avoided, unless there is a clear justification' and footnote 23 of NPPF2 states that, when in force, TCPA 1990, s.100ZA(4)–(6) will require the applicant's written agreement to the terms of a pre-commencement condition, unless prescribed circumstances apply.

5.1.1 Conditions limiting the progress of development

A planning permission will often contain conditions known as pre-commencement or Grampian conditions.

These are conditions which prohibit commencement of development or restrict the use or occupation of a development until certain actions have been taken or requirements have been satisfied. They may be drafted as positive obligations requiring the developer to undertake various matters within his control (e.g. submit various documents for local authority approval) before commencing development or as negative obligations (e.g. no development to commence until ...) or a combination of the two.

It has long been accepted that a planning condition requiring a developer to do something beyond its control, such as the carrying out of works on land outside the application site, will not be valid. However, in *Grampian Regional Council* v. *City of Aberdeen District Council* [1984] JPL 590 (HL) the House of Lords drew a distinction between positive and negative planning conditions and held that a negative condition prohibiting development without the co-operation of a third party may be validly imposed.

Paragraphs 005 and 010 of the section in the PPG entitled 'Use of Planning Conditions' reinforce the decision of the court in *Grampian Region Council* and make it clear that it is unreasonable to impose a positive condition which the applicant would be unable to comply with without the consent or authorisation of a third party, whereas a negatively worded condition which achieves the same end would be permissible. Paragraph 005 provides that:

> No payment of money or other consideration can be positively required when granting planning permission. However, where the 6 tests will be met, it may be possible use a negatively worded condition to prohibit development authorised by the planning permission until a specified action has been taken ...

Paragraph 010 explains that it may be possible, in exceptional circumstances, to impose a planning condition prohibiting development until the applicant has entered into a planning obligation under TCPA 1990, s.106 and provides that:

> A negatively worded condition limiting the development that can take place until a planning obligation or other agreement has been entered into is unlikely to be appropriate in the majority of cases ...
>
> However, in exceptional circumstances a negatively worded condition requiring a planning obligation or other agreement to be entered into before certain development can commence may be appropriate in the case of more complex and strategically important development where there is clear evidence that the delivery of the development would otherwise be at serious risk. In such cases the 6 tests must also be met.

If a planning permission contains pre-commencement or Grampian conditions then the developer will need to satisfy itself that it will be able to comply with the relevant requirements and that it will not be prevented from commencing development or selling dwellings. If a Grampian condition requires the co-operation of a third party or an action to be taken on land outside the control of the developer then the developer could be prevented from carrying out development or held to ransom.

The updated PPG makes it clear that care should be taken when considering using conditions that prevent any development authorised by the planning permission from beginning until the condition has been complied with. This includes conditions stating that 'no development shall take place until …' or 'prior to any works starting on site …'.

The PPG states that such conditions should only be used where the local planning authority is satisfied that the requirements of the condition (including the timing of compliance) are so fundamental to the development permitted that it would have been otherwise necessary to refuse the whole permission (and from 1 October 2018 the applicant has given written consent to such a condition – see below).

From 1 October 2018, s.100ZA(5) provides that planning permission for the development of land may not be granted subject to a pre-commencement condition without the written agreement of the applicant to the terms of the condition (except in the circumstances set out in the Town and Country Planning (Pre-commencement Conditions) Regulations 2018 (SI 2018/566)).

5.1.2 Highway works

Planning permissions sometimes contain a negative condition which prohibits the commencement of development of a site until certain off-site highway works have been completed. If a planning permission contains such a condition then the implementation of the planning permission will effectively be dependent upon the highway authority entering into an agreement with the developer pursuant to the Highways Act 1980, s.278. What will be the position if the highway authority refuses to enter into a s.278 agreement? Will the highway authority be able to hold the developer to ransom? This question was raised in *R.* v. *Warwickshire County Council, ex p. Powergen plc* [1997] 3 PLR 62 (CA). The court held that although a highway authority is entitled to refuse to enter into a s.278 agreement, its discretion to do so will be very limited if it was consulted about the works prior to the planning consent being granted. Forbes J in the first instance decision stated as follows:

> In my opinion, where the benefit to the public of the proposed highway works, in respect of which an agreement with the highway authority is sought under section 278 of the 1980 Act, has been fully considered and determined in the planning process, because the highway works in question form a detailed and related aspect of the application for development of land in respect of which planning consent has been properly obtained through the planning process, then the highway authority's discretion whether to enter into the section 278 agreement will necessarily be somewhat limited.
>
> [1997] 2 PLR 60

It is important to note that the court's decision may have been different if the highway authority had not been consulted as part of the planning process.

Clearly, where a planning permission requires off-site highway works to be carried out, it would be prudent for the developer to check that the highway authority is prepared to enter into a s.278 agreement or (at the very least) that the highway authority was fully appraised of, and consulted about, the works, before proceeding to purchase the development site.

On a practical level, it is imperative that the programme of development includes sufficient time for the detailed highway specification of works to be worked up and agreed with the highway authority as that will be a critical element of any subsequent highways agreement with it.

The developer will also need to satisfy itself that the off-site highway works can be carried out entirely within the confines of the highway and that the works will not involve land not forming part of the highway (e.g. land owned by a third party). This is very important and can easily be overlooked, with disastrous consequences.

5.1.3 Approval of third party

If the planning permission contains appropriately drafted negative conditions which ultimately require the approval or co-operation of a third party (such as a condition imposing visibility splay requirements involving land owned by a third party or a condition requiring the construction of an access over third party land or other off-site works) then the developer will want to ensure that such approval or co-operation can be obtained on reasonable terms and that it will not be ransomed. Ideally, such approval should be obtained before exchange of contracts or the contract should be made conditional upon such approval or co-operation being obtained (see **9.1**).

As from 1 October 2018, the Town and Country Planning (Pre-commencement Conditions) Regulations 2018 will provide an opportunity for a developer to invoke a statutory route of objection to the imposition of pre-commencement conditions without its express written agreement. That may prevent a ransom situation arising, although ultimately it is far better for the proposed developer to have legal control of all land required for its development in any event.

5.1.4 Purchase of part of larger site with conditions prohibiting development or restricting occupation

If a developer is acquiring part of a larger site with the benefit of an existing planning permission which relates to the whole site, there is a potential trap. The developer will need to be aware that a breach of a planning condition or failure to comply with a planning condition by the owner of the remainder of the site may prevent the commencement of development or the sale of dwellings on its own site. As already mentioned, it is often a condition of a planning permission that no development shall be commenced or dwellings occupied until certain matters have been approved by the council (such as the approval of a drainage strategy) or until certain works or other actions have been undertaken by the developer. For example, it may be a condition of a planning permission that no open market dwellings are to be occupied until affordable housing units have been constructed and/or transferred to a registered social landlord. If the vendor has agreed to construct the affordable housing units on its retained land and it fails to comply with this obligation then the developer will not be able to sell the open market dwellings which it has built on its site, which would be fairly disastrous! Another example of such a condition is one which states that no development is to be commenced until ground investigations have been carried out and the whole of the site has been remediated in accordance with a scheme of remediation approved by the council. The effect of such a condition is that a developer purchasing part of a larger development site would not be able to commence the development of its part of the site until the whole of the site had been remediated (unless the planning permission contained phasing provisions which specifically allowed for the site to be developed and remediated in phases). In the above-mentioned circumstances the developer should impose an obligation on the vendor, as the owner of the remainder of the site, to comply with the planning conditions contained in the planning permission in so far as they relate to the remainder of the site (and within timescales which will enable the developer to commence the development of its site immediately following completion and to sell dwellings as soon as they have been constructed). In addition, the developer should obtain a suitable indemnity from the vendor and consider imposing a requirement for:

- the transfer to the developer to include step in rights which allow the developer to comply with the relevant planning conditions in the event of the vendor's default and to carry out all necessary works at the cost of the vendor; and/or
- a retention to be made out of the purchase price and held by the developer's solicitors until the relevant planning conditions have been discharged; and/or
- a bank guarantee, performance bond, parent company guarantee, or some other form of security.

5.1.5 Reserved matters approval: timing issues

Two of the most standard conditions in an outline planning permission are the conditions which require that the application for reserved matters be made within three years of the date of the permission and that the development be commenced within three years or (if later) two years from final approval of reserved matters. These conditions can give rise to difficulties (as illustrated in the case of *R.* v. *Leicester City and another, ex p. Powergen UK plc* [2000] EG 64 (CS)), particularly where the development site is substantial and it is intended to be developed in phases. A developer purchasing part of a development site which has the benefit of an outline planning permission will need to ensure that there is sufficient time left for it to apply for reserved matters approval.

5.1.6 Phasing

Where there is a large development site which it is intended should be developed in phases, the developer will need to consider whether the planning conditions allow for this. As indicated in **5.1.4**, if a planning condition prohibits the development of a site until that site has been remediated in accordance with a remediation strategy which has been approved by the local planning authority, it would not be possible to develop part of the site until the whole of the site has been remediated. Ideally, where a planning permission permits a site to be developed in phases, all pre-commencement conditions should apply to each phase separately. Also, the s.106 agreement pursuant to which the planning permission was granted should treat each phase of development as a separate chargeable development for the purposes of CIL and all planning obligations should be apportioned between the various phases and expressed to bind separate phases of development (see **5.2.9**).

In this respect, it is always helpful to discuss potential draft conditions with the planning case officer of the local planning authority dealing with the planning application. In that way it will be possible to phrase conditions which are phase specific and which do not restrict or impede development progressing as a result of a need to comply with site-wide planning conditions.

A similar discussion will also need to be had in relation to s.106 agreement planning obligations (see **5.2** below), which again will need to be drafted so that obligations are made specific to an individual phase of the development wherever possible. Failure to get this drafting in place could mean that the developer of a phase could be caught by site-wide obligations which could stop or delay development of that phase.

5.2 PLANNING AGREEMENTS

A planning authority will often require a landowner to enter into a planning obligation pursuant to TCPA 1990, s.106 (commonly known as a s.106 agreement) as a prerequisite to the grant of a planning permission. A s.106 agreement must be in the form of a deed and it will need to comply with the formal requirements set out in s.106.

5.2.1 Parties

Under TCPA 1990 'any person interested in land' may enter into a s.106 agreement (s.106(1)). Accordingly, a developer with the benefit of either a contract to purchase conditional on planning or an option to purchase agreement will not be precluded from entering into a s.106 agreement. However, the local planning authority will usually also require the owner of the development site and all other parties with a legal interest in the site, such as a mortgagee and a tenant with a long leasehold interest which cannot be terminated prematurely to enable development to commence, to be made a party to the s.106 agreement. If a mortgagee is not made a party to a s.106 agreement then the planning obligations will not be binding on a purchaser of the site from the mortgagee, which is why the local planning authority should ensure that the s.106 agreement contains a clause which states that the mortgagee will be bound by the planning obligations if it enters into possession of the site, or has appointed a receiver, or has exercised its powers of sale. From the local planning authority's point of view, the s.106 agreement should contain an appropriate clause in the form of model clause 4 in **Appendix D1**.

A common misconception with regard to s.106 agreements is that all parties with a legal interest in the site affected must be a party to the agreement. That will usually be the case but, under TCPA 1990, only those whose agreement is essential to give effect to the obligations in the agreement must be a party. The distinction can be vital because it is perfectly valid to omit those parties with a current legal interest whose minor interest can be extinguished before the obligations bite, e.g. a tenant (who may well object) whose interest can be extinguished under the terms of a lease need not become a party to the agreement. Most local authorities will require proof that there is no need for a tenant or a licensee to be made a party to the s.106 agreement, but they should ultimately accept the position.

A similar situation can arise where the obligations under an existing s.106 agreement need to be varied but some individual plots have been sold. To require every party with a current legal interest in the land within the scope of the original agreement to enter into a new agreement would be a logistical impossibility, particularly on a large site. Clearly it is also otiose where the obligations will fall to be carried out by the developer and the various new plot owners have neither the financial resources nor the ability to carry out works on land outside their own plots.

Where a developer has the benefit of a contract or an option to purchase land which is conditional upon the grant of planning permission, the local planning authority will usually require the developer, as a party with an interest in the land, to be made a party to any s.106 agreement required as a prerequisite to the grant of the planning permission. However, the developer will not want to be bound by the obligations contained in the s.106 agreement until it has purchased the site and an appropriate clause should be inserted in the s.106 agreement (in the form of model clause 5 in **Appendix D1**).

Where a local planning authority is selling land as the freeholder to a developer and the sale is conditional upon the grant of planning permission, the local planning authority will not be able to enter into any required s.106 agreement in its capacity as both landowner and planning authority. This is because , in law, a person cannot contract with himself. In addition, the council cannot be in a position whereby it is effectively wearing 'two hats' and it is both landowner and enforcing authority.

One way of overcoming this difficulty is for the developer and the local planning authority to enter into an agreement pursuant to the Local Government Act 1972, s.111 in which the developer covenants with the local planning authority that it will enter into a s.106 agreement (in the form of the draft s.106 agreement to be attached to the s.111 agreement) on acquiring the application site from the local planning authority and that the planning permission will not be implemented until the site has been acquired by the developer. The Local Government Act 1972, s.111 states that a local authority has:

> power to do any thing (whether or not involving the expenditure, borrowing or lending of money or the acquisition or disposal of any property or rights) which is calculated to facilitate, or is conducive or incidental to, the discharge of any of their functions.

Section 111 powers are ancillary to the use of other statutory powers and are not unlimited (see *McCarthy & Stone (Developments) Limited* v. *Richmond upon Thames London Borough Council* [1992] 2 AC 48, in which the court held that charging for pre-planning application advice to a developer was 'at best, incidental to the incidental and not incidental to the discharge of the functions' – and therefore unlawful).

Some local planning authorities include reference to the Localism Act 2011, s.1 as well as s.111 powers. Section 1 is a general power of competence for local authorities in England. The explanatory notes to the Localism Act 2011 described the s.1 power as:

> a general power of competence for local authorities in England. It gives these authorities the same power to act that an individual generally has and provides that the power may be used in innovative ways, that is, in doing things that are unlike anything that a local authority – or any other public body – has done before, or may currently do

There are still limits on the use of this power, however, and the 2011 Act, s.2 sets out the boundaries of the general power, requiring local authorities to act in accordance with statutory limitations or restrictions.

5.2.2 Enforceability of planning obligations and release from liability

Notwithstanding that the planning obligations contained in a s.106 agreement may be positive obligations, they will be enforceable against the person entering into the obligations and against any person deriving title from that person (TCPA 1990, s.106(3)). However, the s.106 agreement 'may provide that a person shall not be bound by the obligation in respect of any period during which he no longer has an interest in the land' (s.106(4)). The owner of a site and the developer will both usually want to ensure that they will not be liable for any breaches of covenant occurring after they have parted with their interests in the development site and an appropriate clause to this effect should be inserted in the s.106 agreement (see model clause 6 in **Appendix D1**).

5.2.3 Conditionality

The obligations contained in a s.106 agreement should not be enforceable until all possibility of a statutory planning challenge/judicial review has passed and the planning permission has been implemented. Ideally, a s.106 agreement should be conditional and should only have effect upon the later of:

- the date of commencement of development; and
- the date which is six weeks (or preferably more if you are a purchaser) after the planning permission has been issued in circumstances in which no legal proceedings have been commenced by any person to challenge the validity of the permission.

It should be noted here that there are two possible routes to legal challenge dependent on whether the decision to grant planning permission has been made by a local planning authority or by the Secretary of State for Housing, Communities and Local Government.

In cases where a local planning authority makes the decision to grant, the correct route is a judicial review of that decision, whereas if the Secretary of State (or one of his appointed planning inspectors) makes the decision, this gives rise to a statutory right of appeal under TCPA 1990, s.288 (as amended).

The court process is not the same in both cases and so legal advice should be sought if you are faced with this situation. In both cases, however, the claim is required to be lodged with the Planning Court six weeks after the date of the decision notice or decision letter. That time commences from the date of the decision notice/letter itself.

In some cases, claims will be lodged with a court on the very last day of the six-week period, but notification of that claim may not actually filter through to a purchaser's solicitor until after that six-week period has expired. It is essential that some time is added to the six-week period, therefore, to allow for service of court documents. That will avoid a scenario whereby a purchaser may elect to proceed with a contract on an unconditional basis (because they believe that no legal challenge has been made), only to be subsequently advised that the claim was made in time.

To allow for this, the drafting of the contractual provisions should allow not only for the six-week legal challenge period, but also some additional time for notification of claims/service of documents. Generally, eight weeks in total is an acceptable compromise.

5.2.4 Definition of 'commencement of development'

Most s.106 agreements will contain a definition of 'commencement of development'. Commencement of development is not a term that is defined in TCPA 1990, but it is most commonly defined by reference to TCPA 1990, s.56, which defines the time when development is begun by reference to the carrying out of a 'material operation' on the application site.

The definition is wide, for sound planning reasons, but does not take any account of commercial reality. The definition is important since the obligations contained in the s.106 agreement will normally become binding on the commencement of development and some payments may be triggered by the commencement of development.

The practitioner's role is therefore to consider the practical requirements of a site and define commencement of development to exclude, where practicable, those matters which will be required to be done at a very early stage. In many cases this will be site clearance and preparation works which need to be carried out pursuant to the planning permission. These can be costly and the developer will want to minimise its exposure to any additional s.106 agreement obligations at that stage.

Therefore, while these works will effectively 'implement' the planning permission, the developer will be keen to exclude certain categories of 'material operations' which would otherwise trigger potential financial and other obligations under the s.106 agreement.

The list of exclusions will not be identical in every case but will frequently include the following:

- site investigations or surveys;
- the demolition of existing buildings;
- the clearance of the development site;
- the remediation of the development site (including the removal of contamination);
- ground modelling works;
- the construction of off-site highway works;
- alteration and/or provision of access to the site;
- provision of utility services to the site;
- erection of fencing or hoarding;
- erection of boards advertising the development;
- the construction of a site compound or marketing suite; and
- any ecological or nature conservation works associated with the development.

Critically, in phased developments it is important that this list of exclusions is phase specific (as discussed at **5.1.6**), to ensure that each phase benefits from the exclusions.

5.2.5 Financial contributions: content and timing

An s.106 agreement will often require the landowner to make various financial contributions to the local council, the county council (in its role as highway, education and waste authority), the parish council, and/or other organisations such as primary care trusts. To avoid creating an agreement with an unwieldy number of parties, and all the disagreement and potential delays an increased number of parties generally brings, it is advisable wherever practicable to try to persuade the local authority and the county council that payments should be made initially to those two bodies and for them to distribute the sums as required. Much will depend on the circumstances of each case but where the obligations also involve actions or works to be undertaken by the developer, with reciprocal obligations placed on the recipient of any monies, the inclusion of all recipients as parties to the agreement is likely to be more practical.

Typical contribution heads are:

- education;
- highways;
- travel;
- libraries;
- amenity waste facilities;
- health care provision;
- provision of open space;
- improvement of existing open space;
- maintenance of open space;
- provision of sports facilities for various age groups;
- provision of play equipment;
- public art;
- provision or upgrading of street furniture; and
- improvements to parking facilities.

Contributions may also be sought for more questionable uses such as policing, CCTV cameras and monitoring facilities and the upgrading of water supply or sewerage facilities where other sources of funding are available or there is an existing responsibility on others, e.g. water or sewerage operators.

The list of potential heads of contribution has consistently grown over recent years but it should still be remembered that contributions should only be sought where the development of the site gives rise to such a requirement – the local authority or county council may well have a policy stating in general terms that contributions for a particular reason should be sought, but that does not absolve them of the responsibility of showing a nexus between the policy and the proposed development, e.g. education contributions should not be sought merely on a policy basis where there is an excess of school places in the vicinity of the development site; similarly, payments towards water services or sewerage improvements should be fully investigated to ensure that they are required because of the development and resisted where monies are sought for improvements to facilities which should have been adequate but for persistent lack of proper maintenance by the operators charged with that duty.

The local authority or county council will often want the financial contributions to be made on or before development is commenced. The developer, on the other hand, will want to delay the timing for the making of the payments.

Any demand for monies (other than to cover a party's reasonable legal fees) to be made before commencement of development should be resisted. The essence of a s.106 agreement is that its obligations arise because of the detrimental effects of the proposed development; it follows therefore that until such time as the development commences there is no legitimate justification why those monies should be paid.

Notwithstanding the above the usual position is that some monies will be paid (in whole or in part) upon commencement of development (i.e. on the day of or within a defined period after commencement of development), with payment of other monies being made at agreed trigger points throughout the development (e.g. on the occupation of the 50th dwelling).

Where an obligation is imposed on a developer in a s.106 agreement to lay out a play area or an open space area and to transfer such areas to the council upon request following a maintenance period, there will usually also be an obligation to pay commuted sums to the council for the future maintenance of the play area/open space area. The obligation to pay commuted sums should not arise until the play area/open space area has been transferred to the council (since the council will not be responsible for the maintenance of such areas until they have been transferred to it and cannot have any legitimate reason to require the monies to be paid in advance). Having agreed to transfer such land to the council the developer will be keen to ensure that a timely transfer takes place to avoid being responsible for maintaining the land indefinitely. To ensure that the council does take a transfer of the land involved it is advisable to include a clause in the s.106 agreement placing an obligation upon the council to accept the transfer (on terms which can also be set out in a schedule) either within a defined period of time following completion of the laying out of the play area or open space to an agreed scheme (and standard) of work or upon expiry of a maintenance period.

5.2.6 Termination

The developer should seek to include a clause in the s.106 agreement to the effect that it will terminate in the following circumstances:

- if the planning permission expires before the development is begun;
- if the planning permission is revoked or quashed in any legal proceedings; or
- if the permission is altered or varied save with the consent of the developer.

5.2.7 Approvals

Where the consent or approval of the council to a particular matter is required under a s.106 agreement the council should not be able to unreasonably withhold or delay the giving of such consent or approval, and a clause to this effect should be inserted in the s.106 agreement.

5.2.8 Residential units: liability of individual owners and occupiers and their mortgagees

The developer of a residential site should also seek to include a clause in the s.106 agreement to the effect that all individuals owning or occupying single plots on the site and any mortgagee will be excluded from liability under the agreement. Statutory undertakers should be excluded from liability as well.

Many planning authorities will try to resist exclusions, citing a need to be able to force the issue if the developer defaults and pointing out that indemnities can be offered by the developer to plot purchasers in respect of financial contributions. Those arguments should be resisted. The simple facts are that for indemnities to have any meaning there needs to be confidence that the developer is good for the money and in tough economic times there is no such certainty, even with large developers. In a worst-case scenario, individuals are highly unlikely to be able to meet the financial contributions required and any potential liability is highly likely to depress sales or the rate of take up of tenancies. Theoretically mortgagees will be able to meet those financial contributions but will be understandably reluctant to lend on such properties and mortgage lending is likely to be prejudiced. In respect of works to be carried out on a site, neither the various occupiers nor their mortgagees will have the necessary rights over land to carry out works on a part of the site outside their ownership. Notwithstanding the above, most councils are sensitive to publicity – consider what press reaction there would be to a council trying to enforce financial contributions from individuals where a developer defaults – and should agree to a clause being inserted in the s.106 agreement in the form of model clause 7 in **Appendix D1**.

5.2.9 Purchase of part of larger site

Where a developer is acquiring part of a larger site which is subject to a s.106 agreement, it may be possible to expressly limit a developer's liability to such part of the development site as it has a legal interest in. Where such limitation is not acceptable to the council the developer will be bound to comply fully with all of the obligations contained in the s.106 agreement (notwithstanding that it is purchasing only part of the site) and will need to think about ways of mitigating its liability. Some obligations will be easier to enforce than others and some, though theoretically possible, will effectively be impossible for the council to achieve under the s.106 mechanism. For example, payment of monies relating to a defaulting developer's area of the site can be made by any other developer with sufficient funds, whereas, no matter how much a council may press an issue, works required to be undertaken on land in the ownership and control of the defaulting developer cannot be undertaken by any other developer, unless they have step in rights to complete those works. In those circumstances the whole development could be halted until such time as the required works are undertaken but that, of itself, does not ensure that those works will be undertaken or guarantee the timeframe in which they will occur.

Ideally, where a planning permission permits phased development, all financial contributions payable under the associated s.106 agreement should be apportioned and expressed to bind separate phases of development (i.e. the contributions should be phase specific) and any obligation relating to the delivery of works or placing restrictions on the occupation of dwellings should be ring fenced and only bind the owner of the land within the specific phase of the development to which the works or restrictions relate. This should be discussed with the planning authority at an early stage.

In the purchase of part of a development site the following points should be considered:

- Is it necessary to impose an obligation on the vendor (as the owner of the remainder of the site) to comply with the obligations contained in the s.106 agreement and to discharge the planning conditions contained in the planning permission authorising the development of the whole of the development site, so as not to prevent or delay the commencement of development of the land being sold and the sale of dwellings erected thereon and to indemnify the purchaser/developer against any losses, claims and liabilities arising as a result of any breach of the obligations contained in the s.106 agreement?
- Is any security (such as a guarantee, performance bond or legal charge) required in order to ensure that the vendor (as the owner of the remainder of the site) complies with the covenants and obligations contained in the s.106 agreement?
- Are step in rights needed? Such rights may benefit the planning authority in that they ensure that works will be completed by one of the developers on site, but, equally, they can be beneficial to the developers in that they allow others to step in to undertake or complete works anywhere on the site. Where such works are triggers in a s.106 agreement, and thereby capable of jeopardising or delaying work on the wider site, it is clearly in the developer's own interest to ensure that its site cannot be prejudiced by defaults elsewhere.
- Is it necessary for a retention to be made? Ideally, the retention should cover the cost of complying with the s.106 obligations, but this may not be practical. Nevertheless, the retention should be substantial.
- If the vendor is to be required to enter into a positive covenant with the developer to comply with the obligations contained in the s.106 agreement then the vendor should also be required:
    - to covenant not to transfer, sell, lease or otherwise deal with the remainder of the site without procuring that any transferee, purchaser, lessee or other relevant party enters into a deed of covenant with the developer containing a covenant to observe and perform the obligations contained in the s.106 agreement – as previously indicated, this will be needed because the covenant by the vendor is positive and therefore not binding on its successors in title; and
    - to agree to a restriction being entered on the vendor's title prohibiting any transfer or other disposition of the land, unless a certificate signed by a solicitor is produced confirming that the necessary deed of covenant has been entered into.

It is likely that the vendor will want any requirement for a deed of covenant not to apply in the case of certain 'excluded disposals' or 'permitted disposals' (see **12.10.2**).

5.2.10 Affordable housing

There are only certain types of housing which may be considered as affordable housing for planning purposes. These were defined in Annex 2 of NPPF1 and included social rented housing, affordable rented housing and intermediate housing. Social rented housing is defined in NPPF1 as housing for which target rents are determined through the national regime; affordable rented housing is defined in NPPF1 as housing subject to rent controls that require a rent of no more than 80 per cent of the local market rent (including any service charges); and intermediate housing is defined in NPPF1 as housing for sale and rent at a cost above social rent but below market levels to eligible households whose needs are not met by the market. Low cost market housing was not considered to be affordable housing in NPPF1.

The categories of affordable housing are now considerably wider in NPPF2, which defines it as:

> **Affordable housing:** housing for sale or rent, for those whose needs are not met by the market (including housing that provides a subsidised route to home ownership and/or is for essential local workers); and which complies with one or more of the following definitions:
>
> a) **Affordable housing for rent:** meets all of the following conditions: (a) the rent is set in accordance with the Government's rent policy for Social Rent or Affordable Rent, or is at least 20% below local market rents (including service charges where applicable); (b) the landlord is a registered provider, except where it is included as part of a Build to Rent scheme (in which case the landlord need not be a registered provider); and (c) it includes provisions to remain at an affordable price for future eligible households, or for the subsidy to be recycled for alternative affordable housing provision. For Build to Rent schemes affordable housing for rent is expected to be the normal form of affordable housing provision (and, in this context, is known as Affordable Private Rent).
>
> b) **Starter homes:** is as specified in Sections 2 and 3 of the Housing and Planning Act 2016 and any secondary legislation made under these sections. The definition of a starter home should reflect the meaning set out in statute and any such secondary legislation at the time of plan-preparation or decision-making. Where secondary legislation has the effect of limiting a household's eligibility to purchase a starter home to those with a particular maximum level of household income, those restrictions should be used.
>
> c) **Discounted market sales housing:** is that sold at a discount of at least 20% below local market value. Eligibility is determined with regard to local incomes and local house prices. Provisions should be in place to ensure housing remains at a discount for future eligible households.
>
> d) **Other affordable routes to home ownership:** is housing provided for sale that provides a route to ownership for those who could not achieve home ownership through the market. It includes shared ownership, relevant equity loans, other low

> cost homes for sale (at a price equivalent to at least 20% below local market value) and rent to buy (which includes a period of intermediate rent). Where public grant funding is provided, there should be provisions for the homes to remain at an affordable price for future eligible households, or for any receipts to be recycled for alternative affordable housing provision, or refunded to Government or the relevant authority specified in the funding agreement.

It will be noted that both starter homes and discounted market sales housing have been introduced into this list, a clear indication that low cost market housing is back in favour, albeit with strings attached. In addition, NPPF2 acknowledges the rise in affordable private rented housing and includes provision for this in the affordable housing definition.

Where there is a requirement for a developer to provide affordable housing the affordable housing provisions contained in the s.106 agreement will need to be carefully considered. There is likely to be a requirement that the developer must offer to transfer the affordable housing dwellings to a private registered provider (as defined in the Housing and Regeneration Act 2008, s.80) or other social housing provider and/or a requirement that the affordable housing dwellings must be transferred to a private registered provider or other social housing provider before any private dwellings (or a specified number of private dwellings) are occupied; and the developer will need to consider various matters, including the following:

- Does the s.106 agreement specify where the units are to be located? Does the location of the affordable housing need to be approved by the council? The most usual requirement will be that the type of housing, the proportion to be rented and the overall location of the units must be approved by the council.
- Most commonly a s.106 agreement will impose a requirement that affordable housing land and/or affordable housing units must be transferred to a private registered provider or other social housing provider, but some go further and require that the private registered provider or other social housing provider must be one which is nominated or approved by the council. The developer may wish to resist any attempt by the council to impose such a requirement because it is likely to affect the price that the developer ultimately receives. However, where the council's list of approved providers is extensive and includes on it registered providers frequently used by the developer the developer will need to consider whether there is any commercial advantage to be gained by arguing the point with the council.
- Developers should note the decision in *Jelson Limited* v. *Derby City Council* [1999] 4 PLR 11 (Ch D) in which the court held that a provision in a s.106 agreement requiring a developer to transfer affordable housing land (at a price and on terms determined in the s.106 agreement) to a housing association to be nominated by the planning authority was void because it did not comply with the Law of Property (Miscellaneous Provisions) Act 1989, s.2. Under s.2 a contract for the sale or other disposition of an interest in land must be in writing, incorporate all agreed terms and be signed by all the parties to the contract (although terms may be incorporated by reference) and, in this instance, the

housing association was not a party to the agreement. In *RG Kensington Management Co. Limited* v. *Hutchinson IDH Limited* [2002] EWHC 1180 (Ch) Neuberger J (as he then was) declined to follow *Jelson* stating at para.57 of the judgment that:

> the purpose and effect of section 2 is to be assessed by reference to the words used by the legislature ... Those words are to be given their natural meaning unless there is some very good reason to the contrary. The closing words of section 2(3) require the contract, or the parts of the contract to be signed by 'each party to the contract', not by 'each party to the prospective conveyance or transfer'.

- The decision in *Jelson* did not represent a complete bar on the transfer of affordable housing land to a housing association nominated by the council unless that housing association was a party to the s.106 agreement. A negatively worded clause can ultimately achieve that objective and be inserted in the body of the s.106 agreement under which the developer covenants not to sell the affordable housing land other than to [an approved] private registered provider/social landlord on the terms (or similar) set out in the schedule dealing with affordable housing.
- Does there need to be a mechanism for selling the affordable housing units on the open market or for changing the tenure of the units if there is no social landlord willing to purchase the affordable housing units or to purchase the units on the terms required by the planning authority? Developers often have concerns that they will be unable to find a registered provider to take the affordable housing units. One way of dealing with this concern would be to include a clause such as model clause 8 in **Appendix D1** in the s.106 agreement.
- The price payable by the registered provider for the affordable housing units – does the agreement require the affordable housing land to be transferred for a nominal sum and/or the completed units to be sold for a sum to be approved by the council, or will the developer be entitled to a commercial price to be agreed with the social landlord? Developers should strenuously resist any attempt by the council to limit or approve the price payable for affordable housing land or dwellings – councils have a legitimate interest in ensuring that the units will be affordable but councils do not have any authority to dictate details of what is essentially a private agreement between the parties.
- Does the s.106 agreement require the developer to transfer the land on which the affordable housing units are to be constructed to a private registered provider/social landlord before any development is commenced? If so, the developer will need to be aware of a possible value added tax (VAT) trap and take appropriate steps to avoid it (see **7.2**).
- The timing of the transfer of the affordable housing units to the registered provider – the developer should resist any clause which prohibits private/open market dwellings from being occupied until the affordable housing dwellings have been transferred to the private registered provider/social landlord,

although the developer may have to reach a compromise with the council over this. The potential for delay is clear: there may be no registered provider willing to take the units or the contract with the registered provider/social landlord may fail to be completed for any number of reasons and it is therefore essential that those circumstances are taken into account and a fall-back position agreed at the outset to allow the release of the open market units. The terms of the fall-back position will be site and circumstance specific but could include offering the units/land to a wider list of housing providers and/or to the council for a specific period. (Another reason for resisting any restriction on the sale or occupation of private/open market dwellings is that it may not be practical (because of the layout of the development site) or make economic sense (for cash flow reasons) to construct the affordable units before commencing the construction of the private units.)

- Nomination rights of the council – are these likely to be acceptable to the private registered provider/social landlord?
- Registered providers are likely to require exclusion for themselves and their mortgagees from both financial obligations and also those obligations which require works to be carried out on a site where the land involved is not in the ownership of the registered provider. Nevertheless, they should still be willing to accept a covenant to retain and utilise the affordable housing units as social housing until such time as the occupiers of those units acquire them, by staircasing to 100 per cent of the equity or exercising a statutory right to buy.
- The affordable housing provisions will need to be acceptable to a private registered provider/social landlord and the lawyers acting for a private registered provider/social landlord will usually want to see mortgagee protection provisions incorporated into the s.106 agreement whereby the covenants and restrictions contained in the s.106 agreement will not be binding on any mortgagee or chargee or any party acquiring affordable housing units from them (see model clause 9 in **Appendix D1**).

This last point is important to a registered provider as many will seek to raise funds to build or fund new affordable home development by 'charging' existing housing stock. A badly worded 'mortgagee in possession' clause in the s.106 agreement which imposes onerous obligations on a mortgagee/funder prior to a potential sale of the affordable houses can badly impact on the valuation of existing stock for charging purposes.

The more impediments that are put in the way of a funder being able to secure possession of the relevant affordable housing stock, the more likely the funder's valuation will be at an 'existing use value' which can be 30–50 per cent below market value. By contrast, a better worded and less onerous clause could result in a valuation which is nearer a market valuation subject to the tenancy.

Some local authorities will accept provisions of the type in model clause 9 without the wording in the second square brackets, but most will require a mortgagee of a registered provider to use reasonable endeavours to sell the affordable housing dwellings to another registered provider or to offer to sell the affordable dwellings to the council before being permitted to sell them on the open market free from the affordable housing provisions. Such a requirement will generally be acceptable to a registered provider (and critically its funders) subject to the following:

- the mortgagee cannot be expected to delay selling the dwellings on the open market for more than three months;
- the mortgagee must be free to sell the dwellings on the open market at a price which disregards the affordable housing restrictions. This requirement is unlikely to be acceptable to most local planning authorities, particularly where it is to have a right to buy the affordable dwellings. From the registered provider's point of view if the affordable housing restriction is ignored the value of the affordable units will not be restricted to their existing use value and, as mentioned above, this will assist the registered social landlord in maximising its funding; and
- the price to be paid for the affordable dwellings by another private registered provider or the council should be a sum equal to the open market value of the dwellings (and not a nominal consideration), although the registered provider and the council will sometimes compromise and agree that the mortgagee of the registered provider will not be required to dispose of the affordable dwellings for a price lower than that required to recover all monies due under the mortgage or charge.

5.2.11 Bonds

On larger sites there may be a requirement for a bondsman or surety to enter into the s.106 agreement to guarantee the performance by the landowner and/or developer of certain obligations. The developer's lawyer will need to ensure that the bond provisions will be acceptable to the bondsman and it would be sensible to send a copy of the draft s.106 agreement to the bondsman for approval at an early stage. It will be important to the bondsman that its liability is quantifiable and limited to a specified maximum aggregate amount. A bondsman will not usually be prepared to guarantee sums which are not fixed or which may vary. A bondsman will also want to know that it will be released from all liability by a specified date or (if earlier) once all of the sums which are being guaranteed by the bondsman have been paid.

Clearly, a bonding requirement will have cost implications for the developer and, for this reason, should be resisted. Also, there seems no justification for a bond in the case of financial contributions which must be paid before the commencement of development or before a specified number of dwellings have been occupied.

5.2.12 Site plan

The site plan attached or to be attached to the s.106 agreement will need to be carefully checked. The developer will want to ensure that it accords with the title plan and the plans which accompanied the planning application. The usual situation is for the site location plan approved as part of the planning application to be used to denote the red line area which will be bound by the obligations in the s.106 agreement with a separate site layout plan or plans on which more detail can be shown to identify areas for affordable housing, public open space, etc.

5.2.13 Draft planning permission

The developer will want to ensure that the terms of the proposed planning permission are acceptable to it before entering into the s.106 agreement and, ideally, a draft planning permission should be attached to the agreement.

5.2.14 Council's obligations

The developer's lawyer should ensure that the s.106 agreement imposes an obligation on the council to utilise all financial contributions for the purposes for which they were provided and to repay to the developer the whole or any unexpended part of the contributions if the contributions have not been spent in full within a specified period.

5.3 PLANNING GAIN

Often a developer will be willing to agree to the planning obligations which a planning authority wishes to include in a s.106 agreement without too much argument, since it will be keen to obtain a planning permission and to commence development; and local planning authorities will sometimes take advantage of their ability to impose planning obligations on a developer by trying to impose planning obligations which are unreasonable. However, NPPF2 (which follows para.204 of NPPF1) states that planning obligations should only be sought where they are:

- necessary to make the development acceptable in planning terms;
- directly related to the development; and
- fairly and reasonably related in scale and kind to the development (para.56).

These are the same legal tests as set out in the Community Infrastructure Levy Regulations 2010, reg.122(2).

NPPF2 also states (at para.54) that planning obligations should only be used where it is not possible to address unacceptable impacts through a planning condition.

5.4 COMMUNITY INFRASTRUCTURE LEVY

5.4.1 What is Community Infrastructure Levy?

It is tempting to describe CIL as a property tax, but strictly speaking it is not a tax – it is a charge on development that will be payable on most forms of development in local planning authority areas where a document setting out rates for charging CIL (known as a charging schedule) is in force. CIL was introduced by the Planning Act (PA) 2008 and came into force on 6 April 2010. Part II (ss.205–225) of PA 2008 (as amended by the Localism Act 2011) provides the basic framework for CIL and gives a charging authority a discretion to charge CIL in respect of the development of land in its area. The Community Infrastructure Levy Regulations 2010 (SI 2010/948) (as amended by the Community Infrastructure Levy (Amendment) Regulations 2011 (SI 2011/987), 2012 (SI 2012/2975), 2013 (SI 2013/982), 2014 (SI 2014/385), 2015 (SI 2015/836) and 2018 (SI 2018/172)) (the Regulations) contain detailed regulations relating to the application of CIL. They deal with matters such as ascertaining who is liable to pay CIL, when does the liability arise and how is the amount payable in respect of any CIL liability to be calculated.

The Community Infrastructure Levy (Amendment) Regulations 2015 (SI 2015/836), which came into force on 20 March 2015, extended the categories of development that are capable of exemption from CIL by introducing mandatory social housing relief to persons who are not local housing authorities, private registered providers of social housing in England or registered social landlords in Wales, who let dwellings at no more than 80 per cent of market rent to households whose needs are not adequately met by the commercial housing market.

Concerns over the extent to which CIL provides an effective mechanism for funding infrastructure, resulted in the government setting up the Community Infrastructure Levy review group. This recommended changes that 'would improve its operation in support of the Government's wider housing and growth objectives'.

The government's Housing White Paper (*Fixing Our Broken Housing Market*, Ministry of Housing, Communities and Local Government, 7 February 2017) reported that:

> The independent review of CIL and its relationship with Section 106 planning obligations, published alongside this White Paper, found that the current system is not as fast, simple, certain or transparent as originally intended. **The Government will examine the options for reforming the system of developer contributions including ensuring direct benefit for communities, and will respond to the independent review and make an announcement at Autumn Budget 2017**.

The government's subsequent response to the Housing White Paper was published in March 2018 and in announcing a period of consultation (which closed on 10 May 2018) stated:

> In the 2017 Autumn Budget, the Chancellor announced a package of reforms, aimed at complementing proposed changes to the NPPF and making the system of developer contributions more transparent and accountable by:
>
> - Reducing complexity and increasing certainty for local authorities, developers and communities
> - Supporting swifter development
> - Improving market responsiveness of CIL
> - Increasing transparency over where developer contributions are spent, and
> - Introducing a new tariff to support the development of strategic infrastructure
>
> Rather than replacing the CIL regime wholesale – as was suggested by the independent Review – the consultation aims instead to give Local Planning Authorities (LPAs) more flexibility in their approach to CIL, as well as considering limiting the use of s106 agreements to an extent. This should mean that organisations already benefiting from the charity exemption from CIL will continue to do so.

The government's message is therefore very much one of 'mend not end' CIL. December 2018 saw the release of the consultation document 'Reforming developer contributions: technical consultation on draft regulations', which is seeking views on further changes to the Regulations; it is anticipated that further amendments to the Regulations will be issued in spring 2019.

Despite the unintended consequences of some aspects of CIL which the amendments to the Regulations and (hopefully) the further reforms to CIL will bring, the purpose of CIL remains one which seeks to ensure that the costs of providing infrastructure to support the development of an area can be funded, wholly or partly, by owners or developers of land. CIL must be used to fund new infrastructure or to improve, replace, maintain and operate existing infrastructure and cannot be used by a charging authority for any other purpose (reg.59). (A charging authority will be the local planning authority unless the Regulations provide otherwise.) The expression 'infrastructure' is defined in PA 2008 and includes:

- roads and other transport facilities;
- flood defences;
- schools and other educational facilities;
- medical facilities;
- sporting and recreational facilities;
- open spaces (PA 2008, s.216(2)).

The above list may be amended or varied (with existing items being excluded or new items being added) by the Regulations (PA 2008, s.216(3)) and since the enactment of PA 2008 affordable housing has been excluded from the list. At present, therefore, CIL cannot be used to fund the provision of affordable housing and any requirement for affordable housing will need to be covered in a s.106 planning agreement.

5.4.2 The charging schedule and setting the rate of CIL

A charging authority which proposes to charge CIL must issue a document setting rates or other criteria by reference to which the amount of CIL chargeable is to be determined, and, in setting such rates or other criteria, it must have regard to the matters referred to in PA 2008, s.211.

A charging authority may set differential rates for different zones or different intended uses of development (reg.13).

In setting rates in a charging schedule, a charging authority must aim to strike a balance between the desire to fund the cost of providing infrastructure from CIL and the potential effects of the imposition of CIL on the economic viability of development across its area (reg.14).

A charging authority which proposes to issue or revise a charging schedule must first prepare a preliminary draft charging schedule for consultation (reg.15) and before submitting a draft charging schedule for examination in accordance with PA 2008, s.212 it must publish on its website the draft charging schedule and the other information referred to in reg.16 of the Regulations. Any person may make representations about a draft charging schedule to an examiner (reg.17).

A draft charging schedule must contain the rates (set at pounds per square metre) and the other information referred to in reg.12(2) of the Regulations.

5.4.3 CIL liability

The liability to pay CIL arises when chargeable development (as defined in reg.9 of the Regulations) occurs. Chargeable development is any 'development for which planning permission is granted' and 'planning permission' includes planning permission granted by a local planning authority under TCPA 1990, ss.70, 73 and 73A and various other kinds of planning permission (reg.5). It does not include planning permission granted for a limited period.

There will be no CIL liability if no charging schedule is in force when planning permission is granted. Also, the following works are not to be treated as development and will not give rise to any CIL liability:

- the creation of a building into which people do not normally go;
- the creation of a building into which people go intermittently for the purpose of inspecting or maintaining fixed plant or machinery;
- work to an existing building of the above kind (so long as the building remains a building of the above kind);
- the change of use of any building previously used as a single dwellinghouse to use as two or more separate dwellinghouses;
- minor development where on completion of the development the gross internal area of the new building will be less than 100 square metres (regs.6 and 42).

A collecting authority (as defined in reg.10) must issue a liability notice as soon as practicable after the day on which a planning permission first permits development (reg.65). (Subject to the provisions of reg.10 the charging authority will be the collecting authority.) For an outline planning permission which permits phased development, the day on which the planning permission first permits a phase of the development is the day of final approval of the last reserved matter associated with the phase or, if earlier, and it is agreed in writing by the collecting authority before commencement of any development, the day on which final approval is given under any pre-commencement condition associated with that phase (reg.8(3A)). For a full planning permission which permits phased development, the day on which the planning permission first permits a phase of the development is the day on which final approval is given under any pre-commencement condition associated with the phase or, where there are no pre-commencement conditions, the day on which planning permission is granted. (A pre-commencement condition is defined in reg.8(3B) as a condition imposed on a phased planning permission which requires further approval to be obtained before a phase can commence.) For an outline planning permission which is not a phased planning permission, the day on which the planning permission first permits development is the day of the final approval of the last reserved matter associated with the permission (reg.8(4)).

It would appear that there will be no liability to pay CIL if a charging schedule is not in force on the date of grant of a planning permission even if a charging schedule is in place on the date that the planning permission 'first permits development' (reg.128(1)). However, the position will be different if after the grant of an outline planning permission a charging schedule is adopted and a s.73 planning permission is subsequently granted to vary the outline permission (see below).

A liability notice must comply with the requirements of reg.65(2) of the Regulations and:

- be issued on a form published by the Secretary of State (or a form to substantially the same effect);
- include a description of the chargeable development;
- state the date on which it was issued;
- state the chargeable amount;
- where the chargeable amount may be paid in instalments, include a copy of the charging authority's current instalment policy;
- state the amount of any charitable relief or relief for exceptional circumstances;
- where social housing relief has been granted, state the particulars of each person benefiting from the relief and the amount of relief from which each person benefits.

The collecting authority must serve the liability notice on:

- the relevant person (as defined in reg.65(12)) – this will usually be the person who applied for planning permission;
- if a person has assumed liability to pay CIL, that person; and
- each person known to the authority as an owner of the relevant land (i.e. any freeholder and any leaseholder with over seven years of lease term remaining at

the time the development is first permitted – see reg.4 for definition of 'owner' and 'material interest') (reg.65(3)).

Where a planning permission exists permitting phased development and containing conditions allowing separate reserved matter applications to be made in respect of each phase, each phase will be treated as a separate chargeable development and give rise to a separate CIL liability (reg.9(4)). (There are proposals by the government to extend this to both outline and full permissions permitting phased development.)

Where the grant of planning permission made pursuant to an application to vary or remove a condition of a planning permission under TCPA 1990, s.73 does not affect the amount of CIL payable (because there is no increase in the floor area of the chargeable development), the chargeable development will be the chargeable development permitted by the original planning permission.

Where the grant of planning permission made pursuant to an application to vary or remove a condition of a planning permission under TCPA 1990, s.73 would have an effect on the amount of CIL payable, the chargeable development will be the most recently commenced development (i.e. the later development permitted by the s.73 permission) (reg.9(7)), unless at the time when the original planning permission was granted there was no CIL liability (because no charging schedule was in force), in which case CIL will be payable only on the uplift and the amount of CIL payable (the chargeable amount) will be the chargeable amount for the development under the s.73 permission less the amount that would have been the chargeable amount for the development permitted by the original planning permission (reg.128A).

Where CIL has been paid in respect of a chargeable development and a new s.73 permission is later granted in relation to that chargeable development, the person liable to pay CIL for that chargeable development will be entitled to request the charging authority to credit the CIL already paid against the amount due under the s.73 permission (reg.74A). The charging authority will be obliged to comply with such a request, subject to the request being accompanied by proof of the amount of CIL that has already been paid.

Where CIL is paid in relation to a building that is not completed, the CIL paid can be credited against the CIL due in relation to a revised scheme on the same site (see reg.74B).

5.4.4 When does CIL become payable?

Where a liability to pay CIL exists the chargeable amount will become payable on the commencement of development. Development will be treated as commencing 'on the earliest date on which any material operation begins to be carried out on the relevant land' (reg.7(2)) and, except where planning permission is granted by way of general consent or where planning permission is granted which permits phased development, the relevant land will be 'the land to which the planning permission relates' (reg.2(1)). Where planning permission is granted which permits the development to be implemented in phases, the relevant land will be the land to which the phase relates.

The expression 'material operation' in reg.7(2) has the same meaning as in TCPA 1990, s.56(4) and includes:

- any work of construction in the course of the erection of a building;
- demolition works;
- the digging of a trench which is to contain the foundations, or part of the foundations, of a building;
- any operation in the course of laying out or constructing a road or part of a road;
- any change in the use of any land which constitutes material development.

A person intending to commence chargeable development must submit a commencement notice to the collecting authority no later than the day before the day on which the chargeable development is to be commenced (reg.67). A commencement notice must comply with the requirements of reg.67(2) and on receiving a valid commencement notice the collecting authority must send an acknowledgement of the notice to the person who submitted it. The notice may be withdrawn at any time before the commencement of the chargeable development.

CIL must be paid within 60 days of the commencement of a chargeable development, unless the charging authority has published an instalment policy.

Any interested person (as defined in reg.112(2)) may request a review of the calculation of a chargeable amount (reg.113) and, if aggrieved at the decision on the review, may appeal on the ground that the chargeable amount has been calculated incorrectly (reg.114).

5.4.5 Calculation of the chargeable amount

CIL will be charged on the gross internal floor area of a chargeable development and, as mentioned above, a charging authority must express CIL rates in pounds per square metre.

The amount of CIL payable in respect of a chargeable development (referred to in the Regulations as 'the chargeable amount') must be calculated by the charging authority in accordance with reg.40 of the Regulations. This will involve applying the formula contained in reg.40(5) and (7). Put simply, the chargeable amount will be the relevant rate at which CIL is chargeable multiplied by the net gross internal area of the chargeable development. The net gross internal area will be the gross internal area of the whole chargeable development less the aggregate of the gross internal areas of the following:

- the retained parts of an existing building(s) that will form part of the chargeable development and that have been in lawful use for a continuous period of at least six months within the period of three years ending on the day on which the relevant planning permission first permits the chargeable development (such a building is referred to in reg.40 as an 'in-use building');

- the other retained parts of an existing building(s) that will form part of the chargeable development (i.e. those parts which are not 'in-use') and that may be lawfully and permanently used without the need for further planning permission in the same way as the completed development will be used; and
- the parts of an existing building(s) that are to be demolished and that have been in lawful use for a continuous period of at least six months within the period of three years ending on the day on which the relevant planning permission first permits the chargeable development (see reg.40(7)).

For a mixed use scheme, where different rates of CIL apply to different uses comprised in the scheme, the chargeable amount will be calculated separately in relation to each of the proposed uses and then aggregated to derive an overall CIL liability. Where the scheme involves demolition of existing buildings, which meet the vacancy test, the formula for calculating the chargeable amount provides for the gross internal area of those buildings to be apportioned pro rata between the various uses of the scheme.

The formula also provides for the chargeable amount to be increased in line with increases in the All-in Tender Price Index from the year in which the charging schedule was adopted until the year in which the planning permission was granted.

5.4.6 Payment in kind

A charging authority is entitled to accept a conveyance or transfer of land (referred to in the Regulations as 'a land payment') or an infrastructure payment from a person who would be liable to pay CIL in satisfaction of the whole or part of the CIL liability (regs.73 and 73A).

Where CIL is paid by way of a land payment the value of the land acquired by the charging authority will be the amount of CIL paid.

The charging authority may not accept a land payment as a payment in kind unless an agreement to convey or transfer the land to the charging authority has been entered into before the chargeable development is commenced. The agreement must be in writing and state the value of the land to be acquired and may not form part of a planning obligation entered into under TCPA 1990, s.106.

Where CIL is paid by way of an infrastructure payment, the value of the infrastructure provided will be the amount of CIL paid. An infrastructure payment is defined in reg.73A(2) as the provision of one or more items of infrastructure by a person who would be liable to pay CIL in respect of a chargeable development on the commencement of that development.

5.4.7 Who is liable to pay CIL?

A person with a material interest in a chargeable development will be liable to pay the amount of CIL chargeable in respect of that development, unless another person has assumed (and not withdrawn) the liability. A material interest includes a freehold interest or a leasehold interest the term of which will expire more than seven years after the date on which the planning permission first permits development (reg.4 and see reg.8). As mentioned above; 'first permits development' is defined in reg.8.

The liability to pay CIL is joint and several and where two or more persons own land jointly they will be jointly and severally liable for any CIL liability attaching to their land (reg.37). Also, where two or more persons have assumed liability to pay CIL in respect of a chargeable development they will be jointly and severally liable for the CIL payable in respect of that chargeable development (reg.37(2)).

Any person may assume liability to pay CIL in respect of a chargeable development by submitting an assumption of liability notice to the collecting authority (reg.31). An assumption of liability notice must be in a form published by the Secretary of State and served before development is commenced. A person who has assumed liability for CIL may transfer the assumption of liability to another person by submitting a liability transfer notice to the collecting authority (reg.32). He may also withdraw an assumption of liability at any time before commencement of the chargeable development (reg.31(6)). To be valid a transfer of liability notice must comply with requirements of reg.32(2) and (3). While a collecting authority must acknowledge receipt of an assumption of liability notice and a transfer of liability notice, there is no requirement for a collecting authority to acknowledge receipt of a notice of withdrawal of liability, which is surprising.

Where a person who has assumed liability to pay CIL dies before the chargeable development is commenced, the assumption of liability will cease to have effect (reg.39).

Where a chargeable development is commenced and nobody has assumed liability to pay CIL in respect of that development, the liability will be apportioned between each person who has a material interest in the relevant land (reg.33(2)). Accordingly, where there is a large development site which benefits from a single planning permission relating to the entire site and the site is in a number of different ownerships and nobody has assumed liability for CIL, each owner will be liable for a proportion of the amount payable in respect of CIL, unless the planning permission is a phased planning permission, in which case each phase of the development will be treated as a separate chargeable development (see reg.9(4)) and each owner of a phase will only be liable for the CIL payable in respect of the development of their phase.

The amount of CIL payable by each owner of a material interest in a chargeable development must be calculated by applying the formula contained in reg.34(2). This will involve ascertaining the open market value of the material interest belonging to an owner and the aggregate of the open market values of each material interest in the relevant land. It is worth noting that the amount of CIL payable by an owner will be a proportion of the market value of the chargeable development and will not depend upon the size or floor space of the buildings to be erected on the land of each owner.

Where a person has assumed liability to pay CIL in respect of a chargeable development and the collecting authority has been unable to recover the amount of CIL payable by that person the collecting authority may determine that the liability be transferred to the owners of the relevant land (reg.36). The collecting authority may not make such a determination before it has made all reasonable efforts to recover CIL from the person who assumed the liability.

It would appear that where nobody has assumed liability to pay CIL in respect of a chargeable development and one of three owners of a material interest in that chargeable development becomes insolvent (and the collecting authority is unable to recover the amount of CIL payable by that owner), the other two owners will not be liable for the whole amount of the CIL liability. The formula for apportioning liability contained in reg.34 suggests that, if one owner of a material interest in the relevant land becomes insolvent, the other owners will only be liable to pay an amount which is proportionate to the value of their interest in the relevant land. In such circumstances the collecting authority would have to pursue the insolvent owner for its portion of CIL and they would have the full range of enforcement powers in the Regulations available to them, including enforcing the local land charge imposed under reg.66, with the effect that, if the collecting authority was unable to recover the portion of CIL due from the insolvent owner as a creditor, they would be able to recover it from the successors in title to that owner's material interest in the relevant land.

5.4.8 Recovery of CIL

The Regulations provide a collecting authority with considerable powers to recover CIL, including:

- applying to a magistrates' court for a liability order (reg.97) and, following the making of the order, levying the outstanding amount of CIL by distress and sale of goods of the debtor (reg.98);
- applying to a magistrates' court for the issue of a warrant committing a debtor to prison (reg.100);
- applying to an appropriate court for a charging order (i.e. an order imposing a charge on any asset of the debtor of a kind mentioned in s.2(2) of the Charging Orders Act 1979) (reg.103); and
- applying to the county court for consent to enforce the local land charge imposed under reg.66 (reg.107). For the purpose of enforcing the local land charge the collecting authority will have the same powers and remedies under the Law of Property Act 1925 and otherwise as if it were a mortgagee by deed having powers of sale and lease and of appointing a receiver (reg.107(7)).

5.4.9 Payment in instalments and phased payments

A charging authority may allow CIL to be paid in instalments (reg.69). If a charging authority wishes to allow persons to pay CIL in instalments it must publish on its website an instalment policy containing the information set out in reg.69B(2) of the Regulations.

As already mentioned, if there is no instalment policy any CIL liability must be discharged within 60 days of starting development.

Assuming that a charging schedule is in place, it will be important, in the case of a large development site, that a planning permission is granted which permits the development to be implemented in phases for the following reasons:

- if the planning permission does not allow the site to be developed in phases this will have cash flow implications for the person developing the site, since the whole amount of the CIL payable will need to be paid on the commencement of development; and
- if the owner of the site intends to develop part of the site and to sell the remainder of the site to another person he will not want to have any CIL liability in respect of the part of the site being sold. (As mentioned above, each phase will be treated as a separate chargeable development.)

5.4.10 Relationship between CIL and s.106 agreements

Regulation 122 of the Regulations states that a planning obligation (i.e. an obligation under TCPA 1990, s.106) may only constitute a reason for granting planning permission for development if the obligation is:

- necessary to make the development acceptable in planning terms;
- directly related to the development;
- fairly and reasonably related in scale and kind to the development.

Under reg.59 of the Regulations CIL may only be used to fund the provision, improvement, replacement, operation or maintenance of infrastructure to support the development of the area of a charging authority, although a charging authority may apply CIL to fund infrastructure outside its area where to do so would support the development of its area.

A developer should not have to pay for the same infrastructure twice and reg.123 of the Regulations appears to deal with this. Under reg.123(2), after the date on which a charging authority first adopts a charging schedule, an obligation in a s.106 agreement 'may not constitute a reason for granting planning permission' to the extent that the obligation provides for the funding or provision of:

- infrastructure projects or types of infrastructure that it intends will be or may be funded by CIL and which are contained in a list published on its website; or
- where no such list exists, any infrastructure.

Since April 2015, therefore, when determining planning applications, local planning authorities (or inspectors on appeal) have not been entitled to take into account a financial contribution 'for the funding or provision of an infrastructure project' where five or more separate planning obligations have already been sought for the funding or provision of that project from other sources (i.e. financial contributions secured in other s.106 agreements). All payments, counting back to 6 April 2010, are taken into account. Such payments are commonly referred to as 'pooled contributions'.

However, the interaction of CIL and the s.106 agreement regime does cause problems in certain instances, particularly where contributions need to be made to ensure the impact caused by the development proposal is adequately mitigated.

In March 2018 the Ministry of Housing, Communities and Local Government issued its consultation paper 'Supporting housing delivery through developer contributions: Reforming developer contributions to affordable housing and infrastructure'. This stated:

> The CIL Review Team's 'A new approach to developer contributions, 2017' identified that the pooling restriction could have distortionary effects, and lead to otherwise acceptable sites being rejected for planning permission. The research report highlighted that the restriction was a key concern for both local authorities and developers, and that it was seen as making the process longer, slower and more difficult than before.

5.4.11 Relationship between CIL and s.73 planning applications

As mentioned above, where the effect of a planning permission granted under TCPA 1990, s.73 is to vary or remove a condition subject to which a planning permission was granted:

- if this does not result in any change to the amount of CIL payable under reg.40 of the Regulations, the chargeable development will be the development for which planning permission was granted by the previous permission;
- if this results in a change in the amount of CIL payable under reg.40, the chargeable development will be the most recently commenced or re-commenced chargeable development (reg.9(7)) (but note the provisions of reg.128A).

5.4.12 Exemptions and relief

A charitable institution will be exempt from any liability to pay CIL if the chargeable development will be used wholly or mainly for charitable purposes, unless any of the qualifications referred to in reg.43(2) of the Regulations apply. Also, a charitable institution may be eligible for relief from liability to pay CIL if the provisions of regs.44 and 45 apply.

A chargeable development which comprises or is to comprise (in whole or in part) social housing dwellings will be eligible for relief from liability to CIL under reg.49 if the dwellings are 'qualifying dwellings'. To be a qualifying dwelling at least one of the following conditions must be satisfied:

- the dwelling must be let by a local housing authority on a demoted tenancy or an introductory tenancy or a secure tenancy or an arrangement that would be a secure tenancy but for the Housing Act 1985, Sched.1, para.42A or 12 (reg.49(3));
- the dwelling must be occupied in accordance with shared ownership arrangements within the meaning of s.70(4) of the Housing and Regeneration Act 2008 and on the day on which a lease is granted the percentage of the value of a qualifying dwelling paid as a premium must not exceed 75 per cent of the market value and the annual rent payable must not be more than 3 per cent of the value of the unsold interest and in any given year the annual rent payable must not increase by more than the percentage increase in the retail price index for the year to September immediately preceding the anniversary of the day on which the lease was granted plus 0.5 per cent.(reg.49(4));
- in England the dwelling must be let by a private registered provider of social housing on an assured tenancy (including an assured shorthold tenancy) or one of the other types of tenancy referred to in reg.49(5) and one of the criteria described in reg.49(6) must be met;
- in Wales the dwelling must be let by a registered social landlord on an assured tenancy (including an assured shorthold tenancy) or one of the other types of tenancy referred to in reg.49(7)(a) and the rent must be no more than 80 per cent of market rent.

A person wishing to claim social housing relief must:

- assume liability to pay CIL in respect of the chargeable development for which relief is claimed;
- be an owner of the relevant land;
- submit the claim to the collecting authority in writing on a form published by the Secretary of State;
- submit the claim before commencement of the chargeable development; and
- not commence development before the collecting authority has notified the claimant of its decision (reg.51).

The amount of the social housing relief must be calculated in accordance with reg.50. The formula for calculating social housing relief is complicated but essentially no CIL will be payable on the net additional floorspace which is affordable housing.

Social housing relief will be subject to clawback if the social housing dwellings cease to be 'qualifying dwellings' (as defined in reg.49 – see above).

Under reg.49A of the Regulations discretionary social housing relief may be available for certain discount market sale housing.

Under reg.57 of the Regulations a person may claim relief from liability to pay CIL if there are exceptional circumstances. For the relief to be available:

- the relevant charging authority must have elected to make the relief available in its area;
- the claimant must have entered into a s.106 agreement; and
- the charging authority will need to be satisfied that the cost of complying with the s.106 agreement exceeds the amount of the CIL liability and that to require CIL would have an unacceptable impact on the economic viability of the development (reg.55).

5.4.13 Mayoral CIL

Mayoral CIL will be payable in Greater London, in addition to any CIL payable to a local authority under an adopted charging schedule. Mayoral CIL applies to all development in Greater London, other than development to be used wholly or mainly for the provision of medical or health services or for the provision of education, at specified rates for specified zones.

5.4.14 Transaction implications

Land acquisitions and sales

Where land is being sold with the benefit of a planning permission which relates to a wider area, the buyer could be liable as an owner of a 'material interest' in the chargeable development for a proportion of the CIL liability relating to the whole of the chargeable development (i.e. the land being sold and the land being retained by the seller) if the seller does not assume liability or, having assumed liability, defaults on payment. (On the question of how the CIL liability is to be apportioned see **5.4.7**.) Similarly, the seller could be liable as an owner of a 'material interest' for a proportion of the CIL liability relating to the whole of the chargeable development if the buyer does not assume liability or, having assumed liability, defaults on payment. The buyer and the seller will need to decide how any CIL liability should be apportioned between them and the sale and purchase agreement should contain appropriate clauses (including, if one of the parties has agreed to assume liability for the chargeable development, an obligation to submit and not withdraw an assumption of liability notice) to protect the position of both the buyer and the seller. The transfer should also contain an appropriate indemnity by the party assuming liability or (where liability is to be apportioned) appropriate cross-indemnities. (It would appear that any assumption of liability notice must relate to the whole of a chargeable development and that it is not possible for a buyer and a seller to agree that the buyer will serve an assumption of liability notice in respect of the part of the chargeable development which is to be sold and that the seller will serve an assumption of liability notice in respect of the part of the chargeable development being retained by the seller.)

Where land is being sold with the benefit of a planning permission which permits development in phases and the buyer is acquiring a phase the buyer will only be liable for the land to be developed by him (because each phase is treated as a separate chargeable development), so there is no need for any CIL liability to be apportioned or for the sale contract to contain any CIL liability provisions (unless the seller has agreed to assume liability for any CIL payable in respect of the phase).

Where land is being sold with the benefit of a planning permission which relates to a wider area and the seller has agreed to be responsible for compliance with all the obligations contained in a s.106 agreement and the payment of the whole amount of CIL payable in respect of the chargeable development, the buyer will need to be aware that he could be liable for a proportion of the CIL as the owner of a material interest if the seller fails to pay the CIL and the question of security for performance of the seller's obligation to pay CIL should be considered. For example, the buyer could require that the seller retain a sum from the sale proceeds and that the retention monies be placed into an escrow account.

Contracts conditional on planning

Where a contract for the sale of land is conditional upon the grant of a planning permission that does not contain any onerous conditions the buyer's solicitor will want to ensure that the list of onerous conditions includes a condition which has a detrimental effect on the financial viability of the proposed development when taken together with any requirement to pay CIL and all other conditions attaching to the planning permission and the obligations contained in any associated s.106 agreement. The buyer's solicitor may also want to make the contract conditional upon any requirement to pay CIL not having a detrimental effect on the financial viability of the proposed development.

Option agreements

The developer's solicitor should ensure that any liability to pay CIL in respect of the option land will be treated as a development cost and taken into account in calculating the market value of the option land or deducted from the sum payable in respect of the purchase price.

The landowner's solicitor should ensure that the option agreement imposes an obligation on the developer to provide the landowner with an indemnity against all CIL liability (see **10.11**). The landowner may also wish to impose an obligation on the developer to submit an assumption of liability notice on the collecting authority (see **5.4.7**).

Overage agreements

Where planning overage is to be paid by a developer following the grant or implementation of a new planning permission which enhances the value of the land acquired by the developer, the developer may wish to include a clause in the overage agreement stating that the cost of obtaining the new planning permission and the cost of complying with the obligations contained in any associated planning agreement and any CIL liability should be deducted from the overage payment.

Promotion agreements

The landowner and the promoter should be made aware that the carrying out of infrastructure works in accordance with a planning permission authorising the development of the promotion land will trigger any liability to pay CIL. The promoter will not want to be responsible for the CIL liability (even if he will be reimbursed the cost of paying the CIL) because usually he will not be reimbursed any deductible expenditure unless (and until) the promotion land is sold. However, where there is a possibility that the promotion land may be sold in tranches, the landowner should insist on the promoter providing him with an indemnity (see **13.4**).

Collaboration agreements

Where land is owned or will be owned by two or more developers who have agreed to enter into a collaboration agreement with a view to jointly applying for planning permission to develop the whole site (i.e. all of the land which is or will be in their separate ownerships) and constructing common infrastructure, they will need to decide how any CIL liability is to be apportioned between them. They will need to be aware that they will all be liable for CIL as the owner of a 'material interest' in a chargeable development. As mentioned above, it will not be possible for each developer to serve an assumption of liability notice in respect of the land in its ownership (since only one assumption of liability notice may be served in respect of a chargeable development) and where nobody has served an assumption of liability notice each developer, as the owner of a material interest in the chargeable development, will be liable under reg.34 to pay a proportion of the CIL payable in respect of the chargeable development. (Under reg.34 the amount of CIL payable by each developer will depend upon the open market value of that developer's material interest in the chargeable development.) Accordingly, it would be sensible for the developers to agree in the collaboration agreement how any CIL liability should be apportioned between them. For example, they could agree that any CIL liability will be apportioned between them in agreed proportions with each developer liable to pay a fixed percentage of the total CIL liability or they could agree that the CIL payable on the chargeable development will be apportioned between them on a gross internal floor area basis. It would also be sensible for each developer to provide the other developers with an appropriate indemnity and/or suitable security (such as a bank bond or parent company guarantee).

Affordable housing

Where land is being sold with the benefit of a planning permission which includes social housing the buyer will need to be aware that social housing relief from liability to pay CIL does not apply to all types of affordable housing (see **5.4.12**). It only applies to social rented, affordable rented and shared ownership housing. The buyer will also need to remember to submit the claim for relief before commencing development and not to commence development until after the collecting authority has notified the buyer of its decision.

5.5 JUDICIAL REVIEW INSURANCE

If a developer is proposing to purchase a site which has the benefit of a newly granted planning permission (i.e. one which is less than six weeks old) then it will need to be aware that the planning permission may be challenged by a third party and, in such circumstances, it would be prudent for the developer to obtain a judicial review insurance policy. However, as discussed at **2.8.2**, insurance policies do have limitations and, ideally, the purchase should be made conditional upon there being no planning challenge within the period expiring two weeks after the planning challenge period expires.

The insurers are likely to require the following information to enable them to consider an application for a judicial review insurance policy:

- confirmation as to the amount of cover required. It should not be necessary to insure the site for its gross development value – a sum insured/limit of indemnity which equals the purchase price for the site plus legal and other costs and the cost of any works which may be carried out during the judicial review period should be sufficient;
- a copy of the proposed site layout plan;
- a copy of the relevant planning permission;
- copies of all letters of objection in respect of the planning permission;
- copies of any planning agreements or other relevant agreements between the local authority and the developer;
- a copy of the planning officer's report;
- confirmation from the local planning authority and the owner of the site that they have not received notice of any planning challenge;
- confirmation that the site is not in a Conservation Area and that it has no particular historic interest;
- copies of all local newspaper reports or publicity concerning the development;
- a letter from the local planning authority confirming that it has posted all relevant statutory notices and complied with all relevant statutory requirements relating to the planning permission;
- details of the age of the property and the nature of the previous, current and proposed uses of the property.

The policy should indemnify the owner for the time being of the development site and its mortgagee against:

- all sums which the owner shall become legally liable to pay as damages or compensation;
- the difference between the market value of the development site on the date of any court order determining the judicial review application and ordering the cancellation of the planning permission and the market value of the development site before the date of the judicial review application;
- the cost of any works carried out by the owner before the date of the court order;
- all sums paid with the written consent of the insurer to free the development site from the judicial review application; and
- interest payable on capital monies borrowed by the owner to purchase the site and carry out works.

CHAPTER 6

Contaminated land issues

A developer should be aware that liability for contaminated land may arise under the common law tort of nuisance and also under statute and that it would be unwise to purchase a development site without first having thoroughly investigated the ground conditions. The fact that a site consists of bare land or a green field does not mean that there is nothing to worry about – what is currently a greenfield site may have previously been used for landfill purposes.

6.1 COMMON LAW LIABILITY

The case of *Blue Circle Industries* v. *Ministry of Defence* [1999] Ch 289 (CA) is a good illustration of the way in which common law liability may arise. In this case Blue Circle Industries plc (BCI) owned an estate consisting of a large Victorian house surrounded by landscaped gardens and marshland, which adjoined land at Aldermaston owned by the Atomic Weapons Establishment (AWE). In July 1989, following a storm which caused the ponds situated on AWE's land to overflow, the marshland owned by BCI became contaminated with radioactive material. The contamination was discovered 14 days later, but its extent and importance were not disclosed to BCI at that time. In the meantime, BCI had put the estate up for sale. In May 1992 Sun Microsystems Limited (Sun) became interested in purchasing the estate and on 23 September 1992 made an offer to purchase the estate for £10 million. The offer was rejected by BCI but Sun increased the offer to £10.1 million on 27 December 1992. However, in January 1993 the Ministry of Defence (MOD) disclosed the contamination and Sun broke off further negotiations. BCI then issued proceedings for damages against the MOD. The judge awarded BCI damages in the sum of £6,045,617.65, which comprised mainly the loss of a 75 per cent chance of selling the estate and clean-up costs. The MOD appealed contending that the loss should be limited to the cost of reinstatement of the marshland or the diminution in its value as at the date of damage, and not the loss of the sale to Sun. The Court of Appeal disagreed and held that BCI was entitled to compensation for damage to the land and all resulting losses, including diminution in the value and saleability of the land.

6.2 STATUTORY LIABILITY

6.2.1 The contaminated land regime

The statutory contaminated land regime is set out in the Environmental Protection Act (EPA) 1990, Part 2A. It was brought into being by the Environment Act 1995, s.57 and came into force on 1 April 2000 in England and on 15 September 2001 in Wales. The provisions of Part 2A need to be read in conjunction with a number of regulations, including the Contaminated Land (England) Regulations 2006 (SI 2006/1380) (as amended), the Contaminated Land (Wales) Regulations 2006 (SI 2006/2989) (as amended), the statutory guidance for England set out in the Defra *Environmental Protection Act 1990: Part 2A: Contaminated Land Statutory Guidance*, dated April 2012 (which replaced Defra Circular 01/2006) and the statutory guidance for Wales set out in the Welsh Government Guidance Document No.WG19243, *Contaminated Land Statutory Guidance 2012* (which replaced the National Assembly for Wales guidance to enforcing authorities under EPA 1990, Part 2A) (Statutory Guidance). There are related regulations and statutory guidance for radioactive contaminated land.

6.2.2 Meaning of 'contaminated land'

Contaminated land is defined in EPA 1990, s.78A(2) (as amended by the Water Act 2003, s.86) as:

> any land which appears to the local authority in whose area it is situated to be in such a condition, by reason of substances in, on or under the land, that:
>
> (a) significant harm is being caused or there is a significant possibility of such harm being caused; or
>
> (b) significant pollution of controlled waters is being caused or there is a significant possibility of such pollution being caused.

Harm is defined in EPA 1990, s.78A(4) as 'harm to the health of living organisms ... and, in the case of man, includes harm to his property'.

6.2.3 Duty on local authority to identify contaminated land

Under EPA 1990 every local authority is obliged to inspect land in its area from time to time for the purpose of identifying contaminated land (s.78B). In the case of a site which may be particularly hazardous the local authority must refer the site to the Environment Agency (or to Natural Resources Wales if the site is in Wales), although the final decision to determine a site as contaminated land rests with the local authority. If the site is then designated as a 'special site' by the Environment Agency/Natural Resources Wales, responsibility for the site as the enforcing authority transfers to the Environment Agency/Natural Resources Wales and only they will have the power to determine when and how the site should be remediated.

According to the Statutory Guidance, local authorities should adopt a strategic approach to the identification of contaminated land.

This approach should:

- be rational, ordered and efficient, and reflect local circumstances;
- be set out in a written strategy, which should be finally adopted and periodically reviewed;
- ensure that priority is given to investigating areas that the authority considers most likely to pose a risk to human health or the environment.[1]

6.2.4 Remediation notices

Once a site has been identified as contaminated land or a special site, the enforcing authority (i.e. the local authority or the Environment Agency/Natural Resources Wales) will be under a duty to notify the owner and any occupier of the site and to prepare a remediation notice specifying what must be done by way of remediation (EPA 1990, s.78E). The remediation notice will need to be served on the 'appropriate person' of which there may be more than one (see **6.2.8**). The remediation notice may require the appropriate person(s) to carry out further investigations; it may require certain works to be carried out or it may require the site to be monitored. However, in specifying things to be done under a remediation notice the enforcing authority can only require reasonable steps to be taken and it must have regard to the cost which is likely to be involved and the seriousness of the harm. A remediation notice must not be served where the enforcing authority is satisfied that appropriate things are being, or will be, done by way of remediation.

6.2.5 Consultation

Before serving any remediation notice the enforcing authority must carry out a formal consultation exercise with the owner and any occupier of the contaminated land and there is a moratorium on serving a remediation notice on any such person within three months of them being notified of the determination of the land as contaminated land (EPA 1990, s.78H). However, this duty to consult does not apply where it appears to the enforcing authority that there is an imminent danger of serious harm or serious pollution of controlled waters being caused. In these circumstances the enforcing authority has the power to remediate the site and to recover the cost from the appropriate person. In deciding whether to recover the costs of remediation from the appropriate person the enforcing authority must have regard to any hardship which this may cause and to any guidance issued by the Secretary of State.

---

[1] See paras.2.3–2.8 of the Defra *Environmental Protection Act 1990: Part 2A: Contaminated Land Statutory Guidance*, dated April 2012 and paras.2.3–2.8 of the Welsh Government Guidance, Document No.WG19243, *Contaminated Land Statutory Guidance 2012*.

Where remediation is carried out voluntarily to avoid a remediation notice being served, or if the enforcing authority carries out remediation itself to avoid an imminent danger of serious harm or serious pollution of controlled waters being caused, the person who carries out the remediation (the 'responsible person') must prepare a 'remediation statement' setting out what has been done by way of remediation (EPA 1990, s.78H(7) and (8)).

If the enforcing authority is of the view that there is nothing by way of remediation that could be specified in a remediation notice, it must publish a 'remediation declaration', which will record why the authority considers that no remediation is required even though the land has been formally identified as contaminated land (EPA 1990, s.78H(6)). This situation will arise if remediation has not been carried out because it would be unreasonable.

6.2.6 Failure to comply with a remediation notice

If a person on whom an enforcing authority serves a remediation notice fails to comply with any of the requirements of the notice, he will be guilty of an offence and liable, on conviction, to a fine. He will also be liable to reimburse the enforcing authority any costs incurred by it in remediating the site.

6.2.7 Appeals

There is a right of appeal against a remediation notice. The appeal will be heard by the Secretary of State for sites in England and by the National Assembly for sites in Wales, and must be made within 21 days of the date of service of the remediation notice (EPA 1990, s.78L (as revised by the Contaminated Land (England) Regulations 2006 (SI 2006/1380), reg.8)). Any appeal must be on one or more of the grounds set out in the regulations (Contaminated Land (England) Regulations 2006 (SI 2006/1380), reg.7(1) and Contaminated Land (Wales) Regulations 2006 (SI 2006/2989), reg.7(1)).

6.2.8 Persons responsible for remediation

The 'appropriate person' responsible for complying with the remediation notice will be the person(s) who caused or knowingly permitted the contaminated substances to be present in the land (such a person is referred to in the Statutory Guidance as a Class A person) (EPA 1990, s.78F(2)). However, if no such person is to be found after reasonable inquiry then the appropriate person will be the owner or occupier for the time being of the contaminated land (such a person is referred to in the Statutory Guidance as a Class B person) (EPA 1990, s.78F(4)). The expression 'owner' does not include a mortgagee not in possession. However, it will include a tenant if he is a person receiving the rack rent of the land.

What does the expression 'knowingly permitted' mean? It would appear that:

- Notification by the local authority to an owner or occupier of contaminated land that his land is contaminated will not make him a knowing permitter of contamination that he is not already aware of.
- The legislation clearly distinguishes between those who cause or knowingly permit the presence of pollutants and those who are simply owners or occupiers of land.
- The test of knowingly permitting requires four elements – knowledge of a substance, the power to remove that substance (for example, owning the land), the opportunity to exercise that power (for example, having planning permission to develop the land), and a failure to do so.[2]
- A mortgagee cannot be a knowing permitter prior to the exercise of its security.

It will be apparent that the Part 2A regime follows the principle that, where feasible, the polluter pays. In the first instance, any person who caused or knowingly permitted the contaminating substances to be present in the land will be responsible to undertake the remediation and to meet its cost; and only if it is not possible to find any such person will responsibility pass to the current owner or occupier of the land.

There are, however, exceptions to the principle that the polluter pays. For example, a Class A person selling a contaminated site may avoid liability for the cost of remediation by providing the buyer with sufficient information about the contamination (see **6.2.9**).

In addition, responsibility for the cost of remediation will be subject to certain limitations. These will apply where hardship might be caused and in other circumstances mentioned in the Statutory Guidance. In these circumstances the responsibility for paying for the cost of remediation may be waived or reduced.

6.2.9 Exclusion from liability for remediation

Under the Part 2A regime, a Class A person (i.e. the original polluter or 'a knowing permitter') may be excluded from liability if he satisfies one of a number of exclusion tests. However, there are certain difficulties with these tests:

- The tests must be applied in the order set out.
- The tests must not be applied if there is not at least one person left who will bear responsibility for remediation. In other words, someone must be left to face the music.

The exclusion tests are as follows:

1. Excluded activities. This test will exclude those involved in activities such as lending, insuring and advising.
2. Payment for remediation. This test will exclude a seller who has made a

[2] See para.8.4.5.1 of the Inspector's report in the appeal by Jim 2 Limited against the contaminated land remediation notice in respect of land at Stonegate Housing Estate, Willenhall, Walsall (Planning Inspectorate appeal reference APP/CL/15/3).

sufficient payment to a buyer for particular remediation, which the buyer then fails to carry out (or fails to carry out properly).

3. Sold with information. This test will exclude those who sold the land, or let it on a long lease, and provided the buyer or lessee with sufficient information about the contamination.
4. Changes to substances. This test will exclude those who would otherwise be liable where another party introduces a substance or takes action which has the result of causing the original substance to cause harm.
5. Escaped substances. This test will exclude those who would otherwise be liable where the contamination has resulted from the escape of substances from other land, where it can be shown that another Class A person was actually responsible for that escape.
6. Introduction of pathways or receptors. This test will exclude those who are liable solely because of the subsequent introduction by another party of relevant pathways or receptors.

Developers will need to be aware that under tests 4 and 6 they will be ostensibly liable (under the strict statutory position) if their development activities result in the contamination present in their site causing harm or escaping or if they create a pathway or receptor. A good illustration of the application of test 6 in practice is the appeal by Jim 2 Limited against the contaminated land remediation notice in respect of land at Stonegate Housing Estate, Willenhall, Walsall (Planning Inspectorate appeal reference APP/CL/15/3). The Secretary of State determined that a number of previous owners of the land, including the original polluters, would have been excluded from liability under test 6 because the land (a former gasworks) had been redeveloped for housing by the appellant and another developer.

6.2.10 Apportionment of liability for remediation

Under EPA 1990, s.78F(6) where there are two or more persons responsible for the remediation of land it will be down to the enforcing authority to decide, in accordance with guidance issued by the Secretary of State, which of them is to be treated as an appropriate person responsible for the remediation.

In determining liability between members of a Class A liability group (as it is termed in the Statutory Guidance) the enforcing authority is likely to follow the general principle that liability should be apportioned to reflect the relative responsibility of each of the members for creating the contamination or allowing it to continue.[3]

The Statutory Guidance (para.7.73) also states:

> Where the enforcing authority is determining the relative responsibilities of members of the liability group who have knowingly permitted the continued presence, over a period of

[3] See para.7.64 of the Statutory Guidance.

time, of a significant contaminant in, on or under land, it should apportion that responsibility in proportion to: (a) the length of time during which each person controlled the land; (b) the area of land which each person controlled; (c) the extent to which each person had the means and a reasonable opportunity to deal with the presence of the contaminant in question or to reduce the seriousness of the implications of that presence; or (d) a combination of the foregoing factors.

6.2.11 Recovery of cost of remediation

An enforcing authority has power to remediate contaminated land itself if it considers it necessary for the purpose of preventing the occurrence of any serious harm or if a person on whom the enforcing authority has served a remediation notice fails to comply with any of the requirements of such notice (EPA 1990, s.78N).

The enforcing authority will be entitled to recover the reasonable cost of the remediation from the appropriate person (s.78P(1)) and in deciding whether to recover such cost it must have regard to:

- any hardship which the recovery may cause; and
- any guidance issued by the Secretary of State (s.78P(2)).[4]

6.2.12 Apportionment of cost of remediation

Where there are two or more appropriate persons responsible for remediation the cost of remediation is to be apportioned between them 'in proportions determined by the enforcing authority in accordance with guidance issued for the purpose by the Secretary of State' (EPA 1990, s.78F(7)).

According to the Statutory Guidance:

> 8.5 In making any cost recovery decision, the enforcing authority should have regard to the following general principles:
>
> (a) The authority should aim for an overall result which is as fair and equitable as possible to all who may have to meet the costs of remediation, including national and local taxpayers.
>
> (b) The 'polluter pays' principle should be applied with a view that where possible the costs of remediating pollution should be borne by the polluter. The authority should therefore consider the degree and nature of responsibility of the relevant appropriate person(s) for the creation, or continued existence, of the circumstances which lead to the land in question being identified as contaminated land.
>
> 8.6 In general, the enforcing authority should seek to recover all of its reasonable costs. However, the authority should waive or reduce the recovery of costs to the extent that it considers this appropriate and reasonable, either: (i) to avoid any undue hardship which the recovery may cause to the appropriate person; or (ii) to reflect one or more of the specific considerations set out in the statutory guidance …

[4] See section 8 of the Statutory Guidance.

6.3 AVOIDING LIABILITY

It will be apparent from the above that under the Part 2A regime a buyer of a contaminated site may be liable for the remediation of the site even if the contamination was caused by the seller or a previous owner. Although the Part 2A regime follows the principle that, where feasible, the polluter pays, there are exceptions to this principle, and it is also possible for liability for contamination to be transferred from a seller to a buyer. A developer should be aware that it may be liable for the remediation of a contaminated site in any of the following ways:

- As the owner of the site. If the original polluter or any other person who knowingly permitted the contamination to remain in the land cannot be traced then the developer will be liable (even if he had no knowledge of the contamination) by virtue of the fact that he is the owner of the land.
- As a knowing permitter. If the developer knows about the contamination and does nothing to stop the problem then he may be liable.
- If the seller has provided the developer with sufficient information to make the developer aware of the contamination. The Statutory Guidance states that in transactions where the buyer is a 'large commercial organisation' permission from the seller for the buyer to carry out his own survey will normally be taken as sufficient indication that the buyer had the necessary information. However, there is no definition of 'large commercial organisation' or 'permission' and it is not immediately clear what these expressions mean. For example, would permission from the seller's agent suffice?
- If the seller has permitted the developer to carry out his own environmental survey.
- If the development works cause the original contamination to migrate to another party's land.
- If the purchase contract contains environmental provisions which state that the purchaser shall be responsible for all environmental liabilities arising as a result of any existing contamination present in the land being sold (including the remediation of the land) – contracts for the sale and purchase of land often contain environmental provisions which make the purchaser liable for dealing with any historic contamination which may be present in the land being sold or which migrates to an adjoining property. Such provisions are referred to in the Statutory Guidance as 'agreements on liabilities' (see paras.7.29 and 7.30).
- As a condition of a planning permission for the redevelopment of the site. In practice, the vast majority of contaminated sites are remediated through the planning system rather than through the Part 2A regime. A contaminated site does not need to have been determined to be contaminated land under the Part 2A regime for the local planning authority to impose a remediation condition on any planning permission for its redevelopment.

In view of the potential liabilities facing a developer, it should protect its position by thoroughly investigating the environmental condition of the development site which it is proposing to acquire before entering into the purchase contract. Solicitors acting for developers should also be aware of their professional duties under the Law Society's Practice Note on contaminated land in relation to due diligence.[5] As part of the process of checking the environmental condition of the land, the developer should take some or all of the following steps:

- Raise pre-contract environmental enquiries with the seller.
- Commission an environmental search and/or raise environmental enquiries with the Environment Agency/Natural Resources Wales. There are a number of companies which will provide a report containing environmental data on a property. Also, the Environment Agency/Natural Resources Wales will, for a fee, provide information on the contamination of a property, the existence of former landfills on or in the vicinity of a property and water pollution problems associated with a site (see **Appendix B4**). Information about flood risk is also available from the Environment Agency's and Natural Resources Wales's websites.
- Commission a ground investigation report. This will typically be a Phase 2 environmental survey, which will involve taking samples of soil and groundwater for analysis. (The most basic type of environmental survey is a desktop survey. It does not involve any testing of ground conditions. Another type of environmental survey is a Phase 1 environmental survey. This is a desktop survey and a non-intrusive site inspection. A Phase 2 environmental survey is the most comprehensive type of environmental survey. It will give a more detailed picture of the contamination in the ground than a desktop survey or a Phase 1 survey. However, it cannot guarantee that the site is free from contamination – the survey will be based on samples taken from a specific location and other hotspots of contamination may have been missed. A Phase 2 environmental survey should always be carried out if the transaction is a substantial commercial property transaction or if land is being developed.)
- Consider making the contract conditional on the receipt of a satisfactory ground investigation report.
- Include a clause in the sale and purchase contract stating that the seller shall retain liability in respect of the presence in the seller's land of: contamination caused by the seller; the escape, migration, emission or discharge of dangerous substances from the seller's land prior to the date of completion of the sale; or any personal injury caused by exposure to dangerous substances in the seller's land prior to the date of completion of the sale (see clause 18 of **Appendix E1** on the CD-ROM). However, while reasonable sellers will usually accept retaining liability for the escape, migration, emission or discharge of dangerous substances from the seller's land prior to the date of completion of the sale, or any personal injury caused by exposure to dangerous substances in the seller's land prior to the date of completion of the sale, most will not accept

[5] Available to those with a My Law Society login at **www.lawsociety.org.uk/support-services/advice/practice-notes/contaminated-land/**.

retaining liability for contamination they have caused themselves (on the basis that the developer will be required to remediate the site as a condition of any planning permission he obtains and the seller will not underwrite the developer's remediation costs).

- Obtain an indemnity from the seller. A seller will not usually be willing to provide an indemnity, except perhaps if it is limited to cover contamination caused by the seller and will usually expect the developer to provide an indemnity to the seller instead. However, any indemnity is likely to be worthless unless the seller is a seller of substance or the indemnity is backed up by some suitable form of security (such as insurance).
- Obtain environmental insurance cover. Several companies offer insurance products which provide cover in relation to all or a selection of potential environmental liabilities, but the cost of the policy can be high and there will be the inevitable exclusion clauses. Such exclusions usually include an exclusion for the redevelopment or change of use of land, so unless such an exclusion can be removed, an environmental insurance policy for a development site is of little use.
- Impose a contractual obligation on the seller to procure a fresh report addressed to the developer from the author of any environmental reports (such as ground investigation reports) prepared for the seller, or a letter of reliance acknowledging that the developer is relying on the report and that the author of the report owes the developer a duty of care. (The developer's lawyer should request a copy of any letter of engagement or deed of appointment signed by the environmental consultant and evidence of his professional indemnity insurance.)
- Impose a contractual obligation on the seller to assign the benefit of any environmental report prepared for the seller to the developer. (The developer's lawyer will need to check that the reports are capable of being assigned. He should also obtain and consider the terms of any letter of engagement or deed of appointment, which should set out the scope of the environmental consultant's duties, and request evidence of the environmental consultant's professional indemnity insurance.) However, most sellers will prefer to procure a letter of reliance from the environmental consultant to the buyer, so that they will continue to have the benefit of the reports after completion of the transaction.

When appointing an environmental consultant to carry out an environmental survey or remediation works at a contaminated site, there are a number of important things which a developer should do, including the following:

- Ensure that the correct type of consultant for the investigation is engaged and/or any reports which were commissioned by the seller and on which the developer is relying are appropriate. There are important differences between a geo-technical investigation and a geo-environmental investigation:
  - a geo-technical investigation will look at drainage characteristics, frost

resistance of the soils, long-term stability of the site (including potential for subsidence and heave) and specific potential problems associated with the chemical content of the soil, e.g. sulphate, which will determine the type of buried concrete to be used in foundations;
- a geo-environmental investigation will investigate chemical content of soil and water, identify potential pathways and receptors and whether remediation will be required.

Clearly the two types of investigation are not the same and it can be an expensive mistake where the limited chemical analysis from a geo-technical report is mistakenly accepted as a full chemical analysis that would have been obtained from a geo-environmental report.

- Select a reputable firm with a proven track record.
- Ensure that the consultant has the necessary experience.
- Ensure that the consultant is properly briefed.
- Ensure that there is a deed of appointment which clearly sets out the scope of the consultant's services and which obliges the consultant to provide a warranty or letter of reliance in favour of a purchaser, tenants and any purchaser's mortgagee. Ideally, consultants should not be appointed on their standard terms of business, which often contain unacceptably low liability caps.
- Ensure that the consultant has adequate professional indemnity insurance cover.
- Ensure that any letter of reliance or deed of warranty to be entered into by the consultant is freely assignable.

6.4 REMEDIATION TAX RELIEF

A developer should be aware that tax relief is available for companies spending money on the remediation of contaminated land, although a number of conditions will need to be satisfied by a company for it to qualify for remediation tax relief.[6] These conditions are:

- the land must be in the UK and it must be, or have been, acquired by a company for the purposes of a trade carried on by the company;
- at the time of the acquisition, all or part of the land must be in a contaminated or derelict state;
- the company must incur capital expenditure which is 'qualifying land remediation expenditure' (Corporation Tax Act 2009, s.1144).

In order for expenditure to be qualifying land remediation expenditure it must meet the following conditions:

[6] Remediation tax relief was introduced by the Finance Act 2001, Sched.22.

- the expenditure must be on land, all or part of which is in a contaminated or derelict state;
- the expenditure must be on relevant land where remediation is directly undertaken by the company or on the company's behalf;
- the expenditure must be incurred on employee costs, on materials, or on subcontractors' costs;
- it must be the case that the expenditure would not have been incurred had the land not been in a contaminated or derelict state;
- the expenditure must not be subsidised; and
- the expenditure must not be incurred on landfill tax.

A company entitled to claim remediation tax relief will be entitled to a deduction of an amount equal to 150 per cent of the qualifying land remediation expenditure when calculating taxable profit for corporation tax purposes.

The tax relief is claimed by way of an election in writing to HM Revenue & Customs specifying the accounting period to which it relates, and must be claimed within two years of the end of the relevant accounting period in which the costs were occurred.

In order to avoid disputes with HM Revenue & Customs as to whether the contamination existed at the time the land was acquired, a developer acquiring land with a view to obtaining remediation tax relief should obtain environmental reports that detail the exact extent of any contamination that exists at the time of acquisition.

CHAPTER 7

Miscellaneous issues

As well as matters such as access, drainage, title, planning and environmental issues, there are a host of other matters which will need to be considered by a developer. This chapter deals with some of these matters.

7.1 PARTY WALL ETC. ACT 1996

Where a developer is proposing to carry out works to an existing party wall or to carry out excavation works within 3 or 6 metres of a building or structure on an adjoining property then it may need to comply with the provisions of the Party Wall etc. Act (PWA) 1996. The general principle of PWA 1996 is that all work (including certain excavations) which might have an effect upon the structural strength or support function of a party wall or might cause damage to the neighbouring side of the wall must be notified to the adjoining owner.

The developer's lawyer should be aware that under PWA 1996 a wall may be a party wall even if it is not a party wall under the general law. 'Party wall' is defined in PWA 1996, s.20 as follows:

(a) a wall which forms part of a building and stands on lands of different owners to a greater extent than the projection of any artificially formed support on which the wall rests; and
(b) so much of a wall not being a wall referred to in paragraph (a) above as separates buildings belonging to different owners.

Accordingly, a wall may be a party wall under PWA 1996 even if it stands on land belonging to one owner. As Gaunt and Morgan explain:

> a wall may be a party-wall for the purposes of the 1996 Act even though it stands entirely on one person's land, provided that it separates buildings belonging to different owners. Whereas at common law the question whether a wall is a party-wall is to be determined by

> reference to the interests in it of adjoining owners, the determining factor for the 1996 Act is not title but the position and use of the wall . . . party-wall is essentially a wall forming part of a building.[1]

To summarise, a wall will be a party wall under PWA 1996 if:

- it straddles the boundary line between two properties in different ownerships (and is part of one building or separates two buildings or consists of a 'party fence wall'); or
- it stands wholly on land belonging to one owner and separates buildings in different ownerships.

7.1.1 What does PWA 1996 cover?

PWA 1996 covers the following works:

- the construction of a new building at or on the line of junction between two properties (s.1);
- the carrying out of repairs and other works to an existing party wall (ss.2–5);
- the carrying out of excavation works within 3 to 6 metres of a building or structure on an adjoining property (depending upon the depth of the works) (s.6).

7.1.2 Erection of new building on line of junction

If a building owner wishes to erect a party wall or a party fence wall[2] on the line of junction between his property and an adjoining owner's property then he must serve a notice on the adjoining owner, which indicates his desire to build and describes the intended wall (s.1(2)). The adjoining owner may either consent or refuse consent to the building of the wall. If the adjoining owner consents to the building of the wall then the wall must be built on half of the land of each owner or in such other position as may be agreed between the two owners. But if the adjoining owner refuses to give his consent to the building of the wall then the building owner may only build the wall as an external wall of a building or a party fence wall on his own land.

If a building owner wishes to build on the line of junction between his property and an adjoining owner's property a wall placed wholly on his land then he must serve a notice on the adjoining owner at least one month before he intends to start building works, which indicates his desire to build and describes the intended wall (s.1(5)). The adjoining owner will not be entitled to object to the notice but may be entitled to compensation if any damage is caused to his property.

---

[1] See J Gaunt and P Morgan *Gale on the Law of Easements* (20th edition, Sweet & Maxwell, 2017), para.11.08.

[2] A party fence wall is defined as a wall which is not part of a building and which stands on lands of different owners and is used or constructed to be used for separating such adjoining lands.

7.1.3 Meaning of 'owner'

For the purposes of PWA 1996 the expression 'owner' includes:

- a party in receipt of rents;
- a party in possession (but not a mortgagee or a tenant where the term of the lease is 12 months or less);
- a party with the benefit of an agreement for lease or a contract to purchase an interest in land.

Accordingly, where it is necessary to serve a notice under PWA 1996 on an adjoining owner it may be necessary to serve a notice on more than one party.

7.1.4 Works to an existing party wall

Under PWA 1996, s.2 a building owner has various rights, including:

- a right to demolish and/or rebuild a party wall;
- a right to increase the height or thickness of a party wall;
- a right to insert a damp proof course;
- a right to cut into a party structure for any purpose;
- a right to cut away from a party wall, external wall or boundary wall any footing or any projecting chimney breast or other projection on or over land of the building owner in order to erect, raise or underpin any such wall or for any other purpose; and
- a right to execute any other necessary works incidental to the connection of a party structure with premises adjoining it.

Before exercising any right conferred on him by s.2 a building owner must first serve a notice on any adjoining owner (referred to in PWA 1996 as a party structure notice) stating:

- the name and address of the building owner;
- the nature and particulars of the proposed work including, in cases where the building owner proposes to construct special foundations, plans, sections and details of construction of the special foundations together with reasonable particulars of the loads to be carried thereby; and
- the date on which the proposed work will begin (s.3).

A party structure notice must be served at least two months before the date on which the proposed work will begin and, having been served with a party structure notice, an adjoining owner will be entitled to serve a counter-notice on the building owner setting out:

- in respect of a party fence wall or party structure, a requirement that the building owner build in or on the wall or structure to which the notice relates

such chimney copings, breasts, jambs or flues, or such piers or recesses or other like works, as may reasonably be required for the convenience of the adjoining owner; and
- in respect of special foundations to which the adjoining owner consents under s.7(4), a requirement that the special foundations be placed at a specified greater depth than that proposed by the building owner or that they be constructed of sufficient strength to bear the load to be carried by columns of any intended building of the adjoining owner (s.4).

A counter-notice must specify the works required to be executed by the adjoining owner and be accompanied by plans, sections and particulars of such works and it must be served within the period of one month beginning with the date on which the party structure notice is served.

A building owner on whom a counter-notice has been served must comply with the requirements of the counter-notice unless the execution of the works required by the counter-notice would be injurious to him or cause unnecessary inconvenience or unnecessary delay in the execution of the works pursuant to the party structure notice.

If an owner on whom a party structure notice or a counter-notice has been served does not serve a notice indicating his consent to it within a period of 14 days beginning with the date on which the party structure notice or counter-notice was served, he shall be deemed to have dissented from the notice and a dispute shall be deemed to have arisen between the parties.

7.1.5 Excavation works near adjoining building

Under PWA 1996, s.6 a building owner must serve a notice where he intends either to:

(a) excavate within 3 metres of an adjoining owner's building or structure where the excavation will go to a depth below the bottom of the foundations of the neighbouring building, or
(b) excavate within 6 metres of an adjoining owner's building or structure where the excavations will go below a line drawn 45 degrees downwards from the bottom of the foundations of the neighbouring building.

The notice must be served at least one month before the excavation works begin and must indicate whether the building owner intends to underpin or otherwise strengthen or safeguard the foundations of the adjoining owner's building. The notice must be accompanied by plans and sections showing the site and depth of any excavation and the site of any new building. The building owner may, and if required by the adjoining owner, must at his own expense, underpin or otherwise strengthen or safeguard the foundations of the adjoining owner's building. If the adjoining owner does not serve a notice indicating his consent to the proposed work within 14 days of the date of the notice served by the building owner, the adjoining owner is deemed to have dissented from the notice and a dispute shall be deemed to have arisen between the parties.

7.1.6 Resolution of disputes

If a dispute arises between a building owner and an adjoining owner in respect of any matter connected with any work to which PWA 1996 relates then the dispute must be determined by a surveyor appointed in accordance with the provisions of PWA 1996, s.10. Unless the parties agree to the appointment of a single surveyor, each party must appoint a surveyor and the two surveyors must then appoint a third surveyor. The agreed surveyor, or the three surveyors, or any two of them, must settle by award any matter in dispute. If no two surveyors can agree, the selected third surveyor must make an award forthwith. The award must deal with the work required, the manner of executing it, costs and supervision of the work. The award will be conclusive subject to appeal to the county court within 14 days of delivery of the award (s.10(17)). The court may rescind the award or modify it in such manner as the court thinks fit.

7.2 VALUE ADDED TAX

It is beyond the scope of this book to discuss tax issues in any detail. However, a brief word about value added tax (VAT) and stamp duty land tax (SDLT) is necessary.

7.2.1 Is VAT payable?

As a general rule, the majority of property transactions will be exempt for VAT purposes. There are, however, a number of exceptions to this rule, including (but not limited to) the following:

- Disposals or grants of interests in 'new' buildings will be standard rated if the buildings are not to be used for residential or charitable purposes. A new building is one completed three years before the grant of the relevant interest.
- Disposals of dwellings and buildings used for residential/charitable purposes will generally be zero rated.
- The disposal of a property where the seller has elected to waive exemption from VAT. The effect of waiving exemption or opting to tax (as the process is also known) is that VAT will be chargeable at standard rate, unless the transaction can be regarded as a transfer of a business as a going concern.

The sale of a freehold or leasehold investment property will be regarded as a transfer of a business as a going concern if all of the conditions specified in HM Revenue & Customs Notice 700/9 are met. The main conditions are:

- the property or part of the property must be let;
- the property will be used by the buyer in carrying on the same kind of business as that carried on by the seller (e.g. the letting of the property);
- where the seller is a taxable person, the buyer must be a taxable person already or become one as the result of the transfer;
- in respect of property which would be standard rated if it were supplied, the buyer must notify HM Revenue & Customs that he has opted to tax the property by the relevant date, and must notify the seller that the option has not been disapplied by the same date;
- where only part of the 'business' is sold it must be capable of operating separately; and
- there must not be a series of immediately consecutive transfers of 'business'.

The developer's lawyer will need to check whether VAT will be payable on the purchase price for the development site and appropriate enquiries should be made of the vendor's solicitors. If VAT is payable (e.g. because the vendor has elected to waive exemption from VAT) then the following information should be requested from the vendor:

- evidence that the vendor is registered for VAT;
- a copy of the vendor's election to waive exemption from VAT in respect of the property;
- a copy of the vendor's letter notifying HM Revenue & Customs of the election;
- a copy of the letter of acknowledgement of the election received by the vendor from HM Revenue & Customs.

The developer should not exchange contracts until this information has been provided.

In addition, it should be a term of the purchase contract that the vendor will provide the developer with a valid VAT invoice addressed to the developer on completion.

Where there is any doubt about the VAT treatment of a transaction, it would be prudent to include suitable clauses in the contract to enable the VAT treatment actually adopted to be reversed or corrected if necessary.

7.2.2 Sales to housing associations

A developer selling land to a housing association will need to beware of a possible VAT trap. A developer who has purchased land and been charged VAT may have elected to waive exemption from VAT and reclaim the VAT. If subsequently it sells the land to a housing association, the supply may be exempt and the developer will be required to repay to HM Revenue & Customs the VAT it reclaimed. One way of avoiding this problem is for the developer to make a zero-rated supply by constructing the affordable housing units for the housing association. The sale and construction documentation will need to be carefully drafted and the land should not be transferred to the housing association until after all the affordable housing units have been built (or at least partially built to 'golden brick' level, i.e. to a level of at least one brick above the damp proof course). A common structure in transactions with housing associations is for there to be a land agreement which provides for the affordable housing land to be transferred to the housing association when the affordable housing dwellings reach golden brick level and a separate development agreement containing building obligations and stage payment provisions (see **Appendix E12** and **E13** on the CD-ROM).

Often a developer, having acquired a large development site and entered into a contract with an affordable housing provider for the construction and sale of the affordable housing units, will agree to sell part of the development site to another developer and to assign the benefit of part of the affordable housing contract or contracts (which may include a land contract and a separate development agreement) to that developer. As it is not possible to assign the burden of a contract it will be necessary for the original developer, the affordable housing provider and the assignee/new developer to enter into a deed of novation and assignment of part of the affordable housing contract(s). However, this will be possible only if the affordable housing contract(s) permit the developer to assign part of its interest in the contract(s) and an obligation has been imposed on the affordable housing provider to enter into a deed of novation with an assignee upon request by the developer. Under such a deed the assignee/new developer will step into the shoes of the original developer and take on the obligations of the original developer in so far as they relate to the land being sold. The deed of novation should contain:

- a covenant by the assignee directly with the affordable housing provider to perform and be bound by the obligations of the original developer under the affordable housing contract(s) as if the assignee had been named as an original party to the affordable housing contract(s) but only in so far as the obligations relate to the affordable housing units which are to be constructed on the part of the development site being sold to the assignee;
- a covenant by the affordable housing provider with the assignee to observe and perform the obligations on the part of the provider contained in the affordable housing contract(s);
- a declaration by the affordable housing provider that it releases and discharges the original developer from the obligations on the part of the original developer contained in the affordable housing contract(s) in so far as they relate to the land being sold to the assignee;
- a covenant by the original developer with the assignee to observe and perform the obligations on the part of the original developer contained in the affordable housing contract(s) in so far as they relate to the part of the development site being retained by the original developer (see **Appendix E12** on the CD-ROM).

7.3 STAMP DUTY LAND TAX

SDLT is a self-assessed tax which is charged on 'land transactions'. A land transaction is defined in the Finance Act 2003 as 'any acquisition of a chargeable interest' (s.43) and a chargeable interest is defined as (s.48(1)):

(a) an estate, interest, right or power in or over land in the UK; or
(b) the benefit of an obligation, restriction or condition affecting the value of any such estate, interest, right or power,

other than an exempt interest.

Exempt interests include:

(a) an interest or right (other than a rentcharge) held for the purpose of securing the payment of money or the performance of any other obligation;
(b) a licence to use or occupy land; and
(c) a tenancy at will.

Certain land transactions may be relieved from SDLT (Finance Act 2003, s.58A and Sched.6A). In addition, a land transaction may be exempt from a charge to SDLT if there is no 'chargeable consideration' for the transaction or if the transaction is one of the other exempt transactions listed in the Finance Act 2003, Sched.3. Chargeable consideration is defined in Sched.4, para.1:

> The chargeable consideration for the transaction is, except as otherwise expressly provided, any consideration in money or money's worth given for the subject-matter of the transaction, directly or indirectly, by the purchaser or a person connected with him.

It is important to remember that SDLT is payable on a transaction and not on a document. Accordingly, SDLT will be payable on the acquisition of a chargeable interest in land whether or not there is an instrument or a document recording or implementing the transaction. For example, suppose that A and B enter into a building licence under which A agrees to build dwellings on the land owned by B and to pay B a licence fee of £3 million and B agrees to transfer the completed dwellings to A or such parties as A shall direct and that A shall be entitled to all the proceeds of sale. Even if A never takes a transfer of a completed unit it will be liable to pay SDLT on the licence fee. Although a licence to use or occupy land is an exempt interest, where a house builder is granted a licence to enter and remain upon land for the purpose of carrying out building works and obligations are imposed on the owner of the land to transfer completed dwellings to such parties as the house builder shall direct then the interest granted is not an exempt interest, since the house builder will have the benefit of a right or power over the land and the benefit of an obligation, restriction or condition.

The difference between major and other interests is important in relation to the computation of the tax and the reporting obligations. A major interest (Finance Act

2003, s.117) (i.e. a freehold or leasehold interest) is notifiable, unless it is exempt. A non-major interest is also notifiable if SDLT is payable or would be payable but for a relief.

It is worth remembering that SDLT was introduced to counter the avoidance of stamp duty on land transactions, typically by 'resting on contract'. SDLT is still relatively new, having come into force as from 1 December 2003, and the guidelines of HM Revenue & Customs on the tax do not clearly cover a number of practical situations. Additionally, the Finance Act 2003, s.75A sought to reduce the effectiveness of SDLT avoidance schemes by imposing a notional land transaction in place of scheme transactions. The use of any SDLT saving scheme should therefore be approached with great caution.

7.3.1 Part exchanges

There is a useful relief from SDLT for a house builder who sells a new house in exchange for the plot purchaser's existing house (Finance Act 2003, s.58A). The builder will not be liable to pay any SDLT on the acquisition of the existing house if certain conditions are met, but the plot purchaser will be liable to pay SDLT on the new house. The conditions which need to be satisfied in order for the relief to apply include the following:

- The plot purchaser must be an individual.
- The plot purchaser must have occupied the existing house as his only or main residence at some time during the period of two years immediately before the acquisition of the new house.
- The plot purchaser must intend to occupy the new house as his only or main residence.
- The acquisition of the new house by the plot purchaser must be in consideration of the acquisition of the existing house by the builder.
- The area of land acquired by the builder or any connected company together with the existing house must not exceed an area inclusive of the site of the dwelling of 0.5 hectare (a larger area is permitted where this is regarded as required for the reasonable enjoyment of the existing dwelling as a dwelling having regard to its size and character).

When acting for a developer in connection with a part exchange transaction, the developer's lawyer may wish to include a clause in the part exchange contract in the form of model clause 10 in **Appendix D1**.

7.3.2 Obligation to carry out works

The developer should be aware that if the whole or part of the consideration for a land transaction consists of the carrying out of construction works or other works which enhance the value of land then the value of the works will be taken into account as chargeable consideration for SDLT purposes, unless certain conditions are satisfied (Finance Act 2003, Sched.4, para.10).

The conditions, all of which will have to be satisfied in order to avoid the cost of the works being treated as chargeable consideration, are the following:

- The works must be carried out after the 'effective date' of the transaction (typically the effective date will be when the lease or transfer is completed and the balance of the purchase price is paid).
- The works must be carried out on land acquired or to be acquired under the transaction or on other land held by the purchaser or a person connected with the purchaser.
- It must not be a condition of the transaction that the works are carried out by the vendor or a person connected with the vendor.

An example of a land transaction involving construction works where the value of such works will be treated as chargeable consideration is one where, as part of the consideration, a developer agrees to construct a house on land which is being retained by the vendor. The open market cost of building the house will be added to and will form part of the chargeable consideration.

7.3.3 Linked transactions

The question of whether transactions are linked is important and will need to be carefully considered. If two or more transactions are linked then this may mean that SDLT at the higher rates is payable on both or all the transactions (see the Finance Act 2003, s.108).

Transactions are linked if they form part of a single scheme arrangement or series of transactions between the same vendor and purchaser or persons connected with either of them.

Special rules apply in relation to options. The grant of an option and the exercise of the option are separate chargeable transactions. However, the grant and the exercise of the option may be linked transactions. The consideration for the option should be added to the consideration payable upon the exercise of the option so that, if appropriate, the higher rates of SDLT will be applicable to both the option fee and the purchase price payable in the event of the option being exercised.

7.3.4 Overage payments

Special rules also apply in relation to overage payments. SDLT is chargeable on overage payments and the liability to pay SDLT will arise on the signing of the overage agreement. This will be the case even if the amount of the overage payment is contingent, uncertain or unascertained at the time when the overage agreement is signed.

It will be possible for a developer to apply to HM Revenue & Customs to defer the payment of SDLT if the overage payment is uncertain or contingent and all or part of the overage payment is payable more than six months after the effective date of the transaction. However, there can be no guarantee that HM Revenue & Customs will agree to a deferment.

The application must be made within 30 days of the date of the overage agreement and it will be necessary for the developer to estimate the amount of the overage which is likely to be payable. The estimate will need to be reasonable and supported by appropriate reports and projections.

Developers will need to remember to file amended SDLT returns in the following circumstances:

- When a contingency is satisfied – for example, the grant of planning permission. If this results in an overage payment greater than the reasonable estimate at the time of the sale of the land, a further payment of SDLT will need to be made on the recalculated amount.
- When a contingency ceases to be capable of being satisfied – for example, planning permission is not granted within a specified period. In such circumstances, a repayment may be due.
- When the amount of the overage payment becomes ascertained. Every time that there is a payment of overage which before had not been ascertained, it will be necessary for the developer to file an amended SDLT return. Depending upon the SDLT previously paid, there may also be a need for a further payment of SDLT.

7.3.5 Sub-sales

A typical sub-sale occurs where A contracts to sell land to B (the original contract), B contracts to sell the same land to C (usually at a higher price) and there is a direct transfer of the land by A to C. The transfer will state that A has received from C at B's direction the purchase price payable under the original contract between A and B and that B has received from C any excess consideration. Sub-sale relief will be available on such a transaction (such that SDLT will be payable only on the purchase price payable under the contract between B and C (the secondary contract)) so long as:

- the original contract between A and B had not been 'substantially performed' when the secondary contract was entered into. Substantial performance will occur if the original purchaser takes possession of the whole or a substantial part of the property or if the original purchaser pays a substantial amount of the consideration;
- the original contract is completed or substantially performed at the same time as the secondary contract; and
- the relief is claimed by A in a land transaction return (see Finance Act 2013, Sched.39, para.16).

7.4 SALES OF PART

7.4.1 Reserving rights for benefit of retained land

Where a landowner is selling part of his land to a developer he will need to consider whether he requires any rights to be reserved over the land being sold in favour of his retained land. For example, if the only access to the retained land is across the land being sold then, in order to avoid becoming landlocked and a ransom situation arising, the landowner will need to reserve a right of way over the land being sold. In addition, he may need rights in respect of drainage and services. This will require careful drafting of the transfer and the developer's lawyer should not agree to a covenant being imposed on the developer to construct an access road and sewers to the boundary with the retained land, since this may not be acceptable to the local planning authority and/or the highway/drainage authority. Instead, the developer should be required to construct the estate roads as close to the boundary with the retained land as the local planning authority and the highway authority shall permit and to grant the landowner the following rights (see **Appendix C2**):

- a right of way at all times and for all purposes over all the estate roads;
- a right to make connections to the estate roads;
- a right of way over a specified area or areas ('the road corridor') linking the estate roads and the retained land;
- a right to construct a link road within the road corridor and to lay sewers and other service media within the road corridor (subject to obtaining all necessary consents and approvals) with visibility splays (if necessary);
- a right of way over the road corridor and any link road constructed in the future within the road corridor;
- a right to connect to and use any existing service media and the estate sewers and other service media installed by the developer after the date of the transfer;
- a right to lay new service media within the land being sold in order to connect to the estate sewers and other service media installed by the developer after the date of the transfer;
- a right to use any sewers and/or other service media laid in the future within the road corridor;
- a right to enter and remain upon such parts of the land being sold as shall not be built upon to:
  - connect to any existing service media;
  - connect to the estate roads and estate sewers and any other service media installed by the developer after the date of the transfer;
  - lay new service media in order to connect to the estate sewers and any other service media installed by the developer after the date of the transfer;
  - construct a road within the road corridor and thereafter connect to, repair, re-lay, alter, clean, maintain, replace, enlarge and renew any road constructed within the road corridor;

  - install service media within the road corridor and thereafter connect to, repair, re-lay, alter, clean, maintain, replace, enlarge and renew any service media installed within the road corridor;
  - repair, clean, maintain, replace and renew (where necessary) the estate roads and the estate sewers and any other service media installed by the developer;
  - repair, re-lay, alter, clean, maintain, replace, enlarge and renew any service media installed by the landowner;
  - repair, maintain, decorate, replace, renew and clean any buildings or fences on the retained land or any boundary fences or party walls between the land being sold and the retained land;

- step in rights entitling the landowner to enter the land being sold to construct the estate roads (including visibility splays) the estate sewers and other service installations in the event of the developer failing to do so within a specified period.

The definitions of 'estate roads,' 'estate sewers' and 'road corridor' in the transfer reserving the above-mentioned rights will need to be carefully worded. For example, it would be prudent, from the landowner's point of view, to specify that the carriageway and the footpaths of the estate roads are to have a minimum width (which should be determined by a highway consultant acting for the landowner) and that they are intended to serve both the property and the retained land and all buildings from time to time erected on the retained land and to lead from the adopted highway up to and directly connect with and fully abut the boundary of the retained land between specified points (or as close thereto as the highway authority and the local planning authority shall permit). (The landowner will need to ensure that the carriageway of the estate roads and its footpaths are of sufficient width and capacity to serve the retained land if and when the retained land is developed in the future and the landowner should seek advice from a highway consultant as to what the widths of the carriageway and the footpaths should be in order to comply with the highway authority's requirements.) Also the definition of 'road corridor' should make it clear that it is the corridor of land lying between the boundary of the retained land shown marked on the transfer plan between specified points and the section of the estate roads lying closest to that boundary and that it is intended that the corridor of land should connect with and fully abut at ground level both that section of the estate roads and the boundary of the retained land between points marked on the transfer plan.

The developer may wish to qualify the reserved rights and to include a clause in the transfer stating that:

- the reserved rights shall not be exercised over land which has been or is intended to be developed by the construction of buildings or their curtilages;
- any rights of entry shall be exercised only upon reasonable notice;

- all requisite consents from the relevant authorities for making connections to and constructing roads, sewers and other service media must be obtained before the construction rights are exercised;
- the person exercising the rights shall cause as little disturbance as reasonably possible and shall make good any damage caused to the reasonable satisfaction of the developer/transferee as soon as reasonably possible;
- connections to estate sewers and other service media shall only be made to the extent that there is sufficient capacity and the developer/transferee shall not be obliged to upsize or oversize the estate sewers and other service media – the developer will not want to be obliged to incur any additional cost of upsizing or oversizing the estate sewers such that they are of sufficient capacity to serve both the land transferred to it and the retained land once fully developed, except perhaps if the transferor is prepared to bear the additional cost;
- the person exercising the rights shall (if so requested) consent to the estate roads and the estate sewers becoming adopted and pending adoption shall contribute a fair and reasonable proportion (according to user) of the costs of repairing and maintaining the estate roads and the estate sewers – the transferor's solicitor should not agree to the exercise of the right of way being made conditional upon the payment of maintenance costs because if the transferor fails to pay the maintenance costs the transferor will not be entitled to exercise the right of way and there is a danger that the easement could be lost (see *Carter* v. *Cole* [2006] EWCA Civ 398 and *Gale on the Law of Easements* (20th edition, Sweet & Maxwell), para.1.100);
- the right of way over the estate roads shall not be exercised until the estate roads have been constructed to base course level – this should not be an issue for the transferor so long as the developer/transferee is obligated to complete the construction of the estate roads to base course level within a specified period and the transferor is granted appropriate step in rights which are enforceable against successors in title of the developer;
- the right of way over the estate roads shall cease upon the estate roads becoming adopted – this qualification seems unnecessary and should be resisted by the transferor's solicitor because an easement that is terminable cannot be a legal easement and will take effect as an equitable interest (and need to be protected by the registration of an agreed or unilateral notice);
- the developer/transferee shall be entitled to alter the position of the estate roads and/or the estate sewers and/or other service media provided that the exercise of the reserved rights shall not be materially or unreasonably prejudiced and any alteration of the position of the estate roads shall not make the exercise of the right of way any less convenient or commodious. From a developer's point of view, lift and shift provisions are important and, properly drafted, they should not be an issue for the transferor. The transfer should grant the developer an express right to alter the route of the estate roads and the estate sewers, subject to obtaining the approval of the transferor to the alteration (such approval not to be unreasonably withheld or delayed) and all other necessary

consents and approvals, and subject to the parties entering into a deed of easement which reflects the new arrangement and which is in a form to be approved by both parties (acting reasonably) or which is in the form of a draft deed of easement to be attached to the transfer.

The transfer should also impose various infrastructure and planning obligations on the developer, including:

- not to commence any development of the property without obtaining the approval of the transferor (such approval not to be unreasonably withheld or delayed) to the position of the estate roads and the road corridor and having obtained such approval not to construct the estate roads other than in the position approved by the transferor;
- not to make any disposition of the road corridor other than to the transferor;
- not to make any other disposition of the property or any part of it (other than an excluded/permitted disposal) without procuring that the disponee enters into a deed of covenant with the transferor containing a covenant to perform the positive obligations on the part of the transferee contained in the transfer;
- not to erect or place or permit to be erected or placed any building, tree, shrub or other structure on the road corridor;
- not to create any rights or incumbrances over the road corridor;
- to commence the construction of the estate roads and the estate sewers within a specified period (e.g. within 12 months of obtaining the relevant technical approvals);
- to use reasonable endeavours to obtain all relevant technical approvals as soon as reasonably practicable;
- to complete the construction of the estate roads and the estate sewers within a specified period;
- to secure the installation of gas, water, electricity and telecommunications with connection points to or close to the boundary of the retained land within a specified period;
- to construct the estate roads and the estate sewers in a good and workmanlike manner and to the standard required for adoption;
- to keep the estate roads and the estate sewers in good and substantial repair until such time as they are adopted;
- (assuming that it is intended that the estate roads and sewers should be adopted) to enter into or use reasonable endeavours to enter into an agreement for the making up and adoption of the estate roads and/or an agreement for the adoption of the estate sewers as soon as reasonably practicable – this is an important obligation for the transferor because it will not be possible to have adopted any roads constructed on the retained land in the future, unless they connect to an adopted road;
- upon receipt of written notice from the transferor to enter into an agreement (in its capacity as landowner) for the adoption of any road constructed by the

transferor within the road corridor and/or an agreement for the adoption of any sewers laid by the transferor within the road corridor;

- within 10 days of a request in writing from the transferor to transfer the road corridor to the transferor for nil consideration and with full title guarantee and the benefit of vacant possession and free from all incumbrances (the transfer to be in a form to be approved by the transferor (such approval not to be unreasonably withheld) and to contain all necessary rights, including (but not limited to) rights to use the estate roads ,the estate sewers and the service media within the land transferred to the developer, and such covenants as shall be reasonably required). It is important to remember that the rights granted for the benefit of the retained land will not benefit the road corridor land (see **3.6**) (see **Appendix C2**). (Full title guarantee implies that the disposing party has the right to dispose of the land and that the disposal is free from all charges, encumbrances and adverse rights, except any charges, encumbrances or adverse rights about which the seller does not know and could not reasonably be expected to know (Law of Property (Miscellaneous Provisions) Act 1994, s.2).);
- to enter into any wayleave agreement, deed of easement, adoption agreement or other document at the request of the transferor or if required by the provider of services as a condition of installing service media or allowing connections to be made to existing service media for the benefit of the retained land – this is an important obligation for the transferor because it ensures that the transferor can require the transferee/developer to enter into any wayleave or other agreement required by service providers before they will install services within the land transferred for the benefit of the retained land;
- to act in good faith towards the transferor and not to do or omit to do anything that would ransom the transferor or prevent the transferor from gaining access to and from the retained land or developing the retained land (it being acknowledged that the transferor intends to develop the retained land in the future).

In addition to the above obligations, the landowner may wish to consider imposing an obligation on the developer:

- not to carry out any development on the land being sold other than the development permitted by an existing planning permission;
- not to vary an existing planning permission or any planning agreement or submit a new or revised planning application without the approval of the transferor;
- not to make any disposition other than a permitted disposal (e.g. a transfer to a plot purchaser).

The above obligations are likely to be resisted by a developer but may be required where control over the type of development carried out on the land being sold is particularly important to the landowner or the landowner wants to ensure that the development is carried out by the developer with whom he has agreed to contract.

The landowner will also need to think about implied easements over his retained land (see **2.4**).

7.4.2 Granting rights over retained land

Where a landowner is selling part of his land to a developer the developer may wish to be granted rights over the retained land in the transfer to it. For example, the developer may want to be granted a right to lay a sewer and/or other service media within the retained land. The reason for the developer wanting to lay service media within the retained land rather than an alternative route may be that it is less costly. However, the landowner should think carefully before agreeing to this and should consider the possible impact that such a right may have on the future development of his retained land. For example, laying a sewer through the middle of the retained land may prevent or substantially hinder the future development of the retained land, whereas laying service media along or close to the boundaries of the retained land may be less objectionable and something that the landowner could accept. If the landowner is prepared to grant the developer a right to lay sewers and other service media across his retained land, this should be subject to:

- the landowner having the right to approve the proposed route of the sewer or other service media (such approval not to be unreasonably withheld, but with the landowner to be entitled to withhold his approval if the route of the sewer or other service media would be likely to have a materially adverse effect on the development of the retained land); and
- the developer and the landowner entering into a deed of easement to be approved by both parties (acting reasonably) and containing (but not limited to) lift and shift provisions.

The landowner should be aware that, although lift and shift provisions are desirable, once a sewer is adopted the right to lift and shift will be lost.

7.4.3 Sales of serviced parcels

Where a developer is proposing to sell part of a development site on the basis that it will provide all necessary infrastructure to the boundaries of the land being sold and that it will comply with all the planning obligations affecting the site, there are a number of obligations (including infrastructure and planning compliance obligations) which should be imposed on the developer in the sale and purchase contract (see clause 11 of **Appendix E2** on the CD-ROM). Also, if completion will take place before the necessary infrastructure has been provided, it would be prudent for a retention to be made from the purchase price and for the contract to contain a default/step in rights clause (see model clause 11 in **Appendix D1**).

7.5 RELIANCE AGREEMENTS AND COPYRIGHT

Where a vendor has commissioned specialist reports in respect of a property (such as reports from planning consultants, highway consultants, environmental consultants, etc.) the developer's lawyer should ensure that the vendor is obliged to:

- assign the benefit of the reports to the developer (assuming that the reports are capable of being assigned);
- procure that the consultants enter into a duty of care deed/letter or reliance agreement/letter in favour of the developer; or
- procure that the reports are re-addressed to the developer (see **Appendix C16** for an example of a letter of reliance).

Where a report is to be assigned or a letter of reliance provided the developer's lawyer should request evidence of the consultants' professional indemnity insurance policy and a copy of the letter of engagement or deed of appointment (in order to check the scope of the consultants' duties and, in the case of an assignment, ensure that the report is assignable).

Where a developer is proposing to construct buildings in accordance with plans/drawings prepared for the vendor the developer will also want to ensure that it obtains the approval of the vendor's architect to use the plans/drawings and that such use will not be a breach of copyright. The developer should require a clause in the same or similar form as model clause 12 to be inserted in the sale and purchase contract (see **Appendix D1**).

7.6 PLOT SALES

7.6.1 General points

There are a number of things which a developer and its lawyer can do in order to ensure that plot sales proceed smoothly, including the following:

1. Prepare a full set of documents for sending to the buyer's solicitor, including copies of all relevant title documents, planning documents, road and sewer adoption agreements, all relevant ground investigation reports (or an executive summary thereof), the approved estate layout plan, etc.
2. Obtain a letter from the local planning authority confirming that all relevant planning conditions have been discharged – this information is likely to be required by the solicitor acting for the plot purchaser.
3. Submit two copies of a site survey plan to the Land Registry for approval. Ideally, the site survey plan should be based on the latest ordnance survey map. The Land Registry will compare the external boundaries shown on the site survey plan with the boundaries of the registered title and the latest

ordnance survey map and, providing that there are no discrepancies, it will approve the site survey plan.[3]

4. Submit two copies of the estate layout plan to the Land Registry for approval. Plans marked 'for identification only' or 'not to scale' will not be acceptable. Ideally, the plans should be based on the latest ordnance survey map and contain sufficient details of the surrounding areas to enable the site to be clearly identified. The plans should be to a stated scale (the preferred scales are 1:1250–1:500 for urban properties and 1:2500 for rural properties) and they should clearly define and number the precise extent of each plot.[4]
5. Submit two copies of the developer's standard form of draft transfer/draft lease to the Land Registry for approval.[5] The developer's lawyer will need to ensure that the standard form of lease contains the prescribed clauses set out in the Land Registration Rules 2003 (SI 2003/1417), Sched.1A: all leases granted out of a registered title on or after 19 June 2006 must (with certain exceptions) contain a set of prescribed clauses, which must appear at the beginning of the lease. The developer's lawyer will also need to remember that if a transfer grants rights over land which is not registered then it will be necessary to deduce the developer's title to that land in order to establish that the developer has the necessary authority to grant the rights.

7.6.2 Plot sale documentation and management of common parts

Freehold plots

Where a development comprises freehold dwellings with common parts or communal areas the developer will need to think about the following:

- How are common parts, such as shared private access drives, to be maintained?
- How will public open space areas and other communal areas (such as landscaped areas, visitors' car parking spaces, balancing ponds/lagoons and attenuation tanks) be maintained?
- Does any s.106 agreement require any of the above areas to be transferred or offered for adoption to the local authority? (If there is such a requirement the developer will need to consider how such areas should be maintained if the local authority decides not to take a transfer of or adopt such areas; and the form of the plot transfer will need to provide for such areas to be treated as common parts to be maintained by the developer or a management company until such time as they may be adopted or transferred to the local planning authority.)

---

[3] See Land Registry Practice Guide 41, *Developing estates – registration services.*

[4] See Land Registry Practice Guide 41, *Developing estates – registration services*, Supplement 2 'Estate plan approval'.

[5] See Land Registry Practice Guide 41, *Developing estates – registration services*, Supplement 4 'Plot sales – transfers and leases'.

- If there is a need for the plot transfer to contain service charge provisions, should a management company be formed for the purpose of providing specified services?
- Should the management company be a professional management company or a residents' management company (i.e. a management company owned by the residents)?
- If the management company is to be a residents' management company, should the company be limited by guarantee with the residents becoming members of the company or should each resident be allocated shares in the company and issued with a share certificate? One of the advantages of a company limited by guarantee is that the owners of dwellings can become members of the company without the need to issue share certificates which invariably get lost.
- Should the freehold interest in the common parts be transferred to the management company and, if so, when? It is common to transfer the freehold interest in the common parts of a residential estate to a management company once the last dwelling has been sold. The problem with this is that it may take several years to dispose of all the dwellings and control of any residents' management company will not pass to the residents until the last dwelling has been sold; and the developer will be responsible for providing the services specified in the plot transfer and filing company accounts until the sale of the last dwelling on the estate.
- How should the positive service charge obligations be enforced against successors in title of the first plot purchaser? For example, should the obligations be enforced by way of a deed of covenant scheme or a rentcharge scheme?

DEED OF COVENANT SCHEME

Under the deed of covenant scheme the plot transfer should contain:

- a covenant by the management company to provide specified services and a covenant by the transferee to pay a service charge;
- a covenant by the transferee not to transfer the property without procuring that the party taking a transfer from the transferee enters into a deed of covenant with the management company;
- (where the residents are to be allotted shares in the management company) a covenant by the transferee not to transfer the property without also transferring his shares in the management company;
- a requirement for a restriction to be entered on the title to the property prohibiting future transfers without a certificate from the management company confirming that the requirement for the new transferee to enter into a deed of covenant has been complied with.

An issue for the plot purchaser to consider is the possibility of the management company going into liquidation or failing to provide the services. From the plot purchaser's perspective, the transfer should contain:

- a covenant by the transferor that if the management company shall go into liquidation or cease to exist or if the management company shall at any time default in the performance of any of the covenants on its part contained in the transfer then the transferor shall perform such covenants until the appointment of a new management company. (If the management company is a residents' management company then this covenant should cease to apply once the common parts have been transferred to the management company);
- a provision stating that if the management company goes into liquidation for any reason (whether compulsory or voluntary) or fails in a material way to observe and perform the covenants on its part contained in the transfer then the transferor shall be entitled to appoint a new management company and following the appointment of a new management company the transferee will enter into an appropriate deed with the transferor to vary the provisions of the transfer by substituting the new management company for the management company in liquidation/default;
- a covenant by the transferor to pay the service charge relating to unsold dwellings.

RENTCHARGE SCHEME

A rentcharge is defined in the Rentcharges Act (RA) 1977, s.1 as an annual or periodic sum charged on or issuing out of land, except rent reserved by a lease or tenancy or any sum payable by way of interest.

RA 1977 prohibits the creation of any rentcharges other than those referred to in s.2(3) of the Act. The permitted rentcharges include an estate rentcharge which is defined as a rentcharge created for the purpose:

(a) of making covenants to be performed by the owner of the land affected by the rentcharge enforceable by the rent owner against the owner for the time being of the land; or
(b) of meeting, or contributing towards, the cost of the performance by the rent owner of covenants for the provision of services, the carrying out of maintenance or repairs, the effecting of insurance or the making of any payment by him for the benefit of the land affected by the rentcharge or for the benefit of that and other land.

A rentcharge created for the purpose mentioned in (a) above (i.e. a covenant supporting rentcharge) must be for a nominal amount and a rentcharge created for the purpose mentioned in (b) above (i.e. a rentcharge created for the purpose of recovering service charge costs) must be an amount which is reasonable in relation to the services provided by the rent owner (RA 1977, s.2(5)).

The deed or transfer creating the rentcharge may include an express right of entry which is exercisable on a breach of any of the covenants contained in the deed/transfer (and not just on a breach of the covenant to pay the rentcharge); and if a right of entry is annexed to a legal rentcharge it will create a legal interest in land under the Law of Property Act (LPA) 1925, s.1(2)(e) and be enforceable against the successors in title of the land burdened by the rentcharge. (A rentcharge will be a legal rentcharge if it is created by deed and it is in possession (i.e. the rent owner is entitled to immediately receive the rent) and it is either perpetual or for a term of years absolute.)

If the owner of the land affected by the rentcharge fails to pay the annual or periodic sum due under the rentcharge the rent owner will have available to him the statutory remedies described in LPA 1925, s.121. The remedies are implied into every rentcharge by statute, subject to any expression of a contrary intention in the instrument creating the rentcharge (LPA 1925, s.121(5) and (7)). They include:

- (if the annual sum or any part of it is unpaid for 40 days after the due date for payment) a right to enter into possession of and hold the land charged and take the income from the land until the annual sum and all arrears are fully paid; and
- a right by deed to demise the land charged to a trustee for a term of years on trust and by any reasonable means to raise and pay the annual sum and all arrears.

It will be apparent that the statutory right of re-entry under LPA 1925, s.121 does not provide the rent owner with an absolute right of re-entry and forfeiture. Also, it does not allow the rent owner to re-enter the land charged if there has been a breach of any of the positive covenants imposed on the first transferee when the land was transferred to him. For these reasons, it is important, where positive covenants are to be enforced by a rentcharge scheme, that the transfers reserving the rentcharge contain an express declaration that if the rentcharge or any part of it is at any time in arrears and unpaid for more than 21 days after it has become due or there is at any time a breach of any of the positive transferee obligations then the management company may re-enter the property and repossess and enjoy the property as if the transfer had never been made (or re-enter the property and distrain or take possession of the property and the income from the property until the arrears have been paid).

The plot transfer for a rentcharge scheme should:

- reserve to the management company a yearly rentcharge to be charged for ever upon and issuing out of the property. (It is common for an estate rentcharge transfer to reserve a fixed rentcharge of £1.00 and a variable rentcharge which represents a proportion of the costs incurred by the management company in providing the services specified in the transfer);
- contain a covenant by the management company to provide specified services and a covenant by the transferee with the management company (and a separate covenant with the transferor) to pay the rentcharge;
- contain a right for the management company to re-enter and repossess the property if the rentcharge or any part of it is at any time in arrears and unpaid for more than 21 days after it has become due and lawfully demanded or if there is at any time a breach of any of the other positive transferee obligations.

The right of re-entry may be a cause of concern for a plot purchaser and/or his mortgagee. To help overcome this concern the right of re-entry should not include a right for the transferor to repossess the property in perpetuity. Such a right would appear to be draconian and disproportionate to any breach of the obligation to pay the rentcharge. The plot transfer should also contain a provision stating that the management company shall not be entitled to exercise any rights of re-entry pursuant to the rentcharge unless the management company has served notice of any breach of the transferee covenants on the owner of the property and his mortgagee, and the breach shall not have been remedied within a reasonable period or two months of the date of notice.

Another cause for concern is the statutory right for the rent owner to grant a lease to a trustee (under LPA 1925, s.121(4)). Little consideration has previously been given to this remedy but the case of *Roberts and others* v. *Lawton and others* [2016] UKUT 395 (TCC) highlights the issue for a property owner where a rentcharge owner employs the remedy. In this case, several residential owners were in arrears with their rentcharges and the rent owner granted leases to two of its directors for terms of 99 years. The property owners objected but the court held that the rent owner was entitled to grant the leases under the terms of s.121(4). The problem for a property owner is that under s.121(4) there is no requirement for any lease granted pursuant to this section to be surrendered if the arrears due to the rent owner are subsequently paid and the presence of the lease is likely to make the freehold unsaleable.

If the rentcharge is a legal rentcharge created over registered land the following registration requirements will need to be complied with:

- The grant or reservation of a legal rentcharge or a right of entry annexed to a legal rentcharge must be registered under Land Registration Act (LRA) 2002, s.27(2)(e). Until the registration is completed the rentcharge/right of entry does not operate at law and will only be equitable (LRA 2002, s.27(1)). The rentcharge should be registered with its own title (Land Registration Rules 2003 (SI 2003/1417), rule 2(2)).
- Notice of the rentcharge must be entered on the title of the burdened land (LRA 2002, Sched.2, Part 1, para.6). This will ensure that the rentcharge is enforceable against subsequent transferees of the burdened land.
- Notice of any right of entry must be entered on the title of the burdened land (LRA 2002, Sched.2, Part 1, para.7(2)(a)).

The requirements for registration of a legal rentcharge over registered land are explained by the authors of the *Encyclopaedia of Forms and Precedents* (5th edition), LexisNexis (vol.33) as follows:

> Although not compulsory, if the person having the benefit of a newly created estate rentcharge wishes to obtain substantive registration of the rentcharge, this may be achieved by that person applying on Land Registry Form FR1 at the same time as application is made for registration of the land transferred. If no such separate application is made then the rentcharge will be noted as an incumbrance against the transferee's title,

> but the rentcharge will not be substantively registered and will take effect in equity only and not in law: see the Land Registration Act 2002 s27(2)(e). A rentcharge granted out of a registered estate has a dual character as regards registration. It constitutes a disposition which is required to be completed by registration, and an interest capable of substantive registration if it is a legal rentcharge within the Law of Property Act 1925 s1(2)(b): see the Land Registration Act 2002 s27(2)(e).

The main drawbacks of the rentcharge scheme are the right of re-entry, the statutory right for the rent owner to grant a lease to a trustee and the registration requirements. The right of re-entry (if it involves a right to repossess the land charged) and the statutory right to grant a lease of the land charged will be of particular concern to a mortgagee of the plot purchaser. A plot purchaser should think twice before entering into a rentcharge arrangement.

Flat leases

Where the development includes a block or blocks of flats and there is a requirement for a management company, the developer will need to think about the following:

- The developer will need to be aware that if it transfers the freehold interest in the block to the management company, it will lose the ability to sell the ground rents to a ground rent investor. If the developer's objective is to maximise the value of its investment, alternatives to transferring the freehold interest in the block to the management company will need to be considered. One option would be for the developer to interpose a reversionary lease between the freehold and the flat leases by granting the management company a long headlease of the block subject to and with the benefit of the occupational flat leases and requiring the management company, by way of a covenant in its headlease, to collect the ground rent and insurance rents and to pass them up to the freeholder. This effectively allows the developer to retain the benefit of ground rents. Where the block containing the flats includes commercial rack rent space the demise to the management company will need to exclude such space.
- The developer will also need to consider the rights of first refusal afforded to 'qualifying tenants' under the Landlord and Tenant Act (LTA) 1987, Part 1 and to think about ways of disposing of the freehold interest in the block without falling foul of the pre-emption rights contained in LTA 1987. One way of achieving this would be for the developer to enter into a forward sale agreement with a ground rent investor before 50 per cent of the flats in the block have been sold on long leases. (As discussed in **Chapter 16**, a disposal pursuant to a contract entered into before 50 per cent of the flats in a block have been sold is not a 'relevant disposal' under LTA 1987.) Completion of the sale of the freehold interest in the block would need to be made conditional upon all the flats having been sold on long leases by a longstop date. Other options open to the developer would be for the developer to transfer the freehold to an associated company which has been an associated company of the developer

for at least two years and to sell the shares in the associated company or to delay selling the freehold until all the flats have been sold and a headlease of the block granted to the management company. The grant of the headlease to the management company would be a 'relevant disposal', but following the grant of the headlease, the developer would be free to sell its freehold interest in the block without having to first offer to sell the freehold to the 'qualifying tenants' because the disposal would not be a disposal made by the immediate landlord of the 'qualifying tenants'.

- In addition to the above-mentioned considerations, the developer will need to ensure that any structure set up by the developer complies with the UK Finance Mortgage Lenders' Handbook (see **Chapter 16**).

CHAPTER 8

Obtaining vacant possession

A developer purchasing a property subject to existing leases or tenancies will want to ensure that it is able to obtain vacant possession of the property when it is ready to commence development.

Where a property is subject to a business lease, an agricultural tenancy or an assured shorthold tenancy, it will be necessary to serve a statutory notice on the tenant in order to bring the lease/tenancy to an end and it will be crucial that the notice is served strictly in accordance with the requirements of the relevant statutory provision.

8.1 EXCLUDED BUSINESS LEASES

If the property is subject to a business lease which was granted before 1 June 2004 and which excludes the security of tenure provisions of the Landlord and Tenant Act (LTA) 1954 then the developer's lawyer will need to check that the court order authorising the exclusion of security of tenure was properly obtained and is valid. The developer's lawyer should check and/or ask the vendor's solicitors to confirm that the lease granted is not materially different from the lease which was submitted to the court prior to the making of the exclusion order. He should also request a copy of the order, and check that it pre-dates the grant of the lease. In the case of *Metropolitan Police District Receiver* v. *Palacegate Properties Limited* [2000] 3 All ER 663 (CA) the court was asked to consider whether an agreement between a landlord and tenant to exclude security of tenure would be invalid if the terms of the lease granted differed from the draft lease placed before the court. The court held that the terms of the lease should bear a substantial similarity to those placed before the court. However, minor changes, which have no bearing upon the court's function in determining whether the tenant has understood that he was giving up protection, will not affect the validity of any agreement to exclude security of tenure.

If the property is subject to a business lease which excludes security of tenure and which was granted after 1 June 2004 then the developer's lawyer will need to check that:

- the landlord served a notice containing a 'health warning' in prescribed form on the tenant and any guarantor of the tenant before entering into the agreement for lease or (if there was no agreement for lease) the lease (the contracting out process must be completed before the landlord and the tenant commit themselves to entering into the lease);
- the tenant signed a declaration in prescribed form acknowledging receipt of the warning notice or a statutory declaration if the notice was served less than 14 days before the agreement for lease was exchanged or the lease granted;
- the lease contains a reference to the warning notice served by the landlord, a reference to the declaration/statutory declaration by the tenant and an agreement to exclude security of tenure;
- there was no change in the identity of the landlord or the tenant after the agreement for lease was exchanged and the contracting out process completed.

It is perhaps worth noting that for security of tenure to be excluded the tenancy granted must be for a fixed term and that a tenancy will be a fixed-term tenancy even if it contains a break clause.[1] Periodic tenancies cannot be excluded from LTA 1954.

8.2 SHORT LEASES

A lease granted for a fixed term not exceeding six months and not containing an option to renew will be excluded from the security of tenure provisions of LTA 1954 (even without a court order) provided that the tenant (or the predecessor of his business) has not been occupying the premises for more than a year. There is therefore a limit on the number of successive six-month tenancies that can be granted.

8.3 BREAK CLAUSES (BUSINESS LEASES)

If the property is subject to a business lease which contains an option to determine (also known as a break clause) allowing the landlord to terminate the lease by serving notice in writing on the tenant then the developer will need to check the wording of the break clause carefully. The following points should be noted:

- The time limits laid down by the lease for the exercise of the break clause will need to be strictly observed.[2]
- If a break clause is ambiguous the courts will construe it against the landlord.
- A slight variation in the order of the words of a break clause can change its meaning and produce a different (and unintended) result.[3]

1 See *Scholl Manufacturing Co. Limited* v. *Clifton (Slim Line) Limited* [1967] Ch 41 (CA) at 51.
2 See *United Scientific Holdings Limited* v. *Burnley Borough Council* [1978] AC 904 (HL).
3 See *Associated London Properties Limited* v. *Sheridan* [1946] 1 All ER 20 (KBD).

- Any preconditions to the exercise of the break clause will need to be strictly complied with (usually only a break clause in favour of a tenant will be subject to preconditions).
- The break notice will need to be served in accordance with the notice provisions contained in the lease (which should be carefully checked).
- The break notice must be served on the current tenant.

The developer should be aware that (unless the lease is outside the provisions of LTA 1954) in the event of the developer serving a break notice on the tenant, the tenancy will continue until it is terminated as prescribed by statute and that it will be necessary for the developer to serve (in addition to the notice served in accordance with the break clause) a notice to quit pursuant to LTA 1954, s.25 (and to establish a ground for possession under LTA 1954) in order to bring the tenancy to an end. For example, suppose that the break clause entitles the landlord to determine the lease on 25 December 2010 by giving to the tenant not less than three months' notice in writing. In order to comply with LTA 1954, s.25(2) a statutory notice to quit should be served not less than six months and not more than 12 months before 25 December 2010. But suppose the landlord fails to serve the statutory notice and that he serves only a notice to determine in accordance with the break clause four months before 25 December 2010. Will the landlord have lost his right to determine the lease? The short answer to this question is: no. However, in order to bring the tenancy to an end the landlord will also have to serve the tenant with a s.25 notice to quit specifying as the date of termination of the tenancy a date not earlier than six months and not later than 12 months from the date of service of the notice. In the words of Lord Diplock in *Scholl Manufacturing Company Limited* v. *Clifton (Slim Line) Limited* [1967] Ch 41 (CA):

> A tenancy with a break clause is a tenancy for a term of years certain within the meaning of the Act; but until the latest date at which notice may be given subject to the break clause it is also one which, apart from the Act, could be brought to an end by notice to quit given by the landlords. By serving notice in accordance with the provisions of the break clause, but not in the prescribed form, the landlords converted it into a tenancy for a term of years certain expiring on the earlier date specified in the break clause, but the Act itself prevents such a notice from bringing the tenancy to an end. It will continue thereafter by virtue of the Act until brought to an end by notice in the prescribed form appropriate to a tenancy for a term of years certain expiring at that earlier date.

The tenant may be able to extend his lease and possibly delay the commencement of the proposed development by applying to the court for a new tenancy, making the developer prove his intention to carry out the redevelopment work. If a tenant is minded to put the landlord to proof of its intention to redevelop, and is prepared to take the adverse litigation costs of doing so, it can take at least 15 months, from service of a s.25 notice, to force a protected tenant to leave. The developer should therefore consider serving the s.25 notice at the earliest possible opportunity – as already mentioned, a s.25 notice may be served up to 12 months, but not less than six months, before the lease term will expire.

In order to successfully oppose the grant of a new lease under LTA 1954 and for the exercise of the break clause to be valid, it will be necessary for the developer to establish a ground for possession under LTA 1954, s.30. The most common grounds for obtaining possession are that the landlord:

- has offered to provide the tenant with suitable alternative accommodation (LTA 1954, s.30(1)(d)); and
- intends to demolish or reconstruct the demised premises or a substantial part of the demised premises or to carry out substantial works of construction on the demised premises and could not do so without obtaining possession (LTA 1954, s.30(1)(f)).

It will be apparent that there are a number of strands to s.30(1) and the developer will be able to rely on any one of those strands.

In order to successfully oppose the grant of a new lease on redevelopment grounds (LTA 1954, s.30(1)(f)) the developer will need to demonstrate by the time the case comes to trial that it has a firm and settled intention to redevelop. A developer who is seeking to oppose the grant of a new lease on redevelopment grounds should ensure that all necessary consents and approvals have been obtained, that the necessary finance for the project is or can be available, and that the project will not be held up by some impediment, such as a tenant of another part of the site who cannot be removed. Intention means more than mere thought or desire. In the words of Lord Evershed MR in *Fleet Electrics* v. *Jacey Investments Limited* [1956] 3 All ER 99 (CA):

> there must be a firm and settled intention not likely to be changed, or in other words that the proposal for doing the work has moved 'out of the zone of contemplation into the valley of decision'.

Any tenant whose statutory right of renewal is successfully opposed on redevelopment grounds or on the ground that the landlord can provide suitable alternative accommodation (alone) will be entitled to compensation for disturbance (LTA 1954, s.37(1), Part II). The amount of compensation will be the rateable value of the demised premises, unless the tenant has occupied the demised premises for more than 14 years, in which case it will be twice the rateable value of the demised premises. The relevant date for the purposes of ascertaining the rateable value will be the date of service of the landlord's s.25 notice to quit or the landlord's notice of opposition to a s.26 request by the tenant for a new tenancy.

Under the Landlord and Tenant Act 1927 a tenant of business premises whose lease renewal is successfully opposed may also be entitled to compensation for authorised alterations which benefit the landlord by adding to the letting value of the premises. The tenant will be entitled to compensation only if:

- he served a notice on the landlord of his intention to make the improvement together with a specification and plan showing the proposed improvement; and

- the landlord did not serve a notice of objection on the tenant within three months of the date of service of the tenant's notice offering to carry out the improvement himself in consideration of a reasonable increase in rent (s.3(1)).

8.3.1 Effect of exercise of break clause on underlessees

What effect will the exercise by a landlord of an option to determine contained in a head lease of business premises have on an underlessee? In the event of a head lease being forfeited an underlessee will be entitled to apply to the court for relief (see Law of Property Act 1925, s.146(4)). However, where a head lease is terminated by a superior landlord exercising an option to determine the position is different and the exercise of the option will bring to an end any underlease granted out of the head lease.[4] But the underlessee, rather than the lessee, being a tenant in occupation of business premises, will have a statutory right to remain in possession of the demised premises and (subject to the superior landlord establishing a ground for possession under LTA 1954) he will be entitled to a new tenancy.

8.4 AGRICULTURAL TENANCIES

8.4.1 Farm business tenancies

The date when an agricultural tenancy or lease begins is critical. The date when a tenancy begins for this purpose is defined in the Agricultural Tenancies Act 1995, which covers all tenancies beginning on or after 1 September 1995.

A tenancy which begins on or after 1 September 1995 is referred to as a farm business tenancy (FBT) even though it may be a long lease. A fixed-term FBT for two years or less will expire without notice. A periodic FBT or an FBT for longer than two years can only be terminated on at least 12 months' notice to expire on the term date of the tenancy. Until such notice is given the tenancy continues as a tenancy from year to year (Agricultural Tenancies Act 1995, s.5(1)).

8.4.2 Agricultural Holdings Act tenancies

Tenancies beginning before 1 September 1995 are protected under the Agricultural Holdings Act 1986. These tenancies have considerable protection, and specialist agricultural advice on any possible termination is always required.

Generally speaking the tenant will have security of tenure for his lifetime and subject to certain requirements there may be rights for up to two successions to the tenancy on the tenant's death.

---

[4] See *Weller* v. *Spiers* (1872) 26 LT 866 and *Keith Bayley Rogers & Co.* v. *Cubes Limited* (1976) 31 P & CR 412 (Ch D).

There are very limited grounds for gaining possession,[5] one of which is that a notice to quit can be served once there has been a grant of planning permission over the land for a non-agricultural use. This will only allow possession of the area covered by the planning permission, and even if the notice is uncontested, it may still take up to two years after planning permission is actually granted before possession can be obtained. Compensation may be payable to the tenant.

8.5 RESIDENTIAL TENANCIES

Security of tenure in relation to residential tenancies is too complex to deal with comprehensively in a book of this nature, but the following points should be noted:

1. A residential tenant may never be evicted from his home without a court order.
2. Most residential tenancies will be assured shorthold tenancies. These enable the landlord to recover possession through the courts usually as a matter of formality, after the tenancy has lasted for six months or, if longer, at the end of the contractual term.
3. A minority of residential tenancies will be assured tenancies. These give the tenant security of tenure and the landlord will only be allowed to evict the tenant by establishing to the court's satisfaction one of a limited number of grounds. One of those grounds is, however, the provision by the landlord of suitable alternative accommodation. Unless the tenant is working, that accommodation does not even have to be in the locality.
4. In order to recover possession of a dwelling let on an assured shorthold tenancy for a fixed term the landlord must serve not less than two months' notice in writing on the tenant stating that he requires possession of the dwellinghouse. The notice must be given on or before the day on which the tenancy comes to an end (Housing Act 1988, s.21(1)(b) and (c)).
5. To recover possession of a dwelling let on an assured shorthold tenancy which is a periodic tenancy the landlord must give a notice in writing to the tenant stating that, after a date specified in the notice, being the last day of a period of the tenancy and not earlier than two months after the date the notice was given, possession of the dwellinghouse is required (Housing Act 1988, s.21(4)).
6. The service of notices under Housing Act 1988, s.21(1)(b) and (4) requires special care and attention – it is all too easy to get them wrong!
7. Tenancies granted before 15 January 1989 (or replacing tenancies that were so granted) will generally still benefit from the Rent Act 1977, but usually even these tenants can be moved if the landlord secures for them suitable alternative accommodation.

[5] See cases A to G in the Agricultural Holdings Act 1986, Sched.3.

PART II

Transaction structures

CHAPTER 9

Conditional contracts

Developers often enter into contracts conditional on planning as a means of securing an interest in land which has development potential but without being under an obligation to buy the land unless the planning condition is satisfied (see **Appendix E1** on the CD-ROM). Drafting a sale and purchase contract which is to be conditional upon the grant of planning permission requires care and attention: the contract will need to contain a number of important provisions and both the developer's lawyer and the landowner's lawyer will need to obtain detailed instructions from their respective clients in order to ensure that the contract complies with the developer's and landowner's requirements.

The case of *Jolley* v. *Carmel Limited* [2000] 3 EGLR 68 (CA) illustrates some of the difficulties associated with conditional contracts and how the courts are likely to interpret contracts which fall short of drafting precision. In this case the contract was deficient in a number of respects and the High Court held that in order to give business efficacy to the transaction certain terms should be implied into the contract (see **9.8**).

9.1 SATISFACTORY PLANNING PERMISSION

A sale and purchase contract conditional on planning should contain a definition of 'satisfactory planning permission' which, once granted, triggers completion. The difficulty is finding a definition which is acceptable to both the developer and the landowner. This will invariably involve striking a balance between the developer's desire not to buy if any of the planning conditions are unworkable and the landowner's need to know that the sale will go through and that the developer will not be able to wriggle out of the contract on a technicality.

The developer may initially suggest that satisfactory planning permission should be defined as 'planning permission together with any required planning agreement which is in a form and containing conditions acceptable to the developer in its absolute discretion'. It is unlikely that such a definition will be acceptable to a well-advised landowner since this will make the contract more like an option to purchase (but it may be worth a try!). However, it may be acceptable if the developer offers to pay the landowner a substantial non-refundable deposit on exchange of contracts or if the planning/conditional period is very short.

A well-advised landowner will usually require the contract to be made conditional upon the grant of a planning permission for defined works or a specified use, with a right for the developer to reject a permission only if it is granted subject to a finite list of conditions defined in the contract as onerous conditions (see **9.4** for examples of onerous conditions). If this is acceptable to the developer, the developer's lawyer will need to ensure that there are provisions in the contract which make it clear that a planning permission should not be regarded as satisfactory unless both the planning permission is free from any onerous conditions and any planning agreement required as a prerequisite to the grant of the planning permission does not contain any onerous obligations.

If the developer is paying a fixed price for a residential development site, it may want the definition of 'satisfactory planning permission' or the definition of 'development' to refer to a minimum number of dwellings or to dwellings having a minimum gross internal floor area. For example, suppose that a developer is prepared to pay £5 million for a site on the basis that it will be able to construct 60 residential dwellings on it. If the planners are willing to grant a planning permission for only 10 dwellings, this will have a detrimental effect on the financial viability of the project and the developer will not want to be obliged to proceed with the purchase.

The parties to the contract will need to decide whether the contract is to be conditional upon the grant of outline or full/detailed planning permission or outline planning permission followed by reserved matters approvals. If the contract is to be conditional upon full/detailed planning permission then the parties may wish to define what is meant by 'full/detailed planning permission' since there is no statutory definition of 'full/detailed planning permission' (see **10.6** for a possible definition of 'planning permission'). From a developer's point of view, it would probably be preferable for the contract to be made conditional upon the grant of a full/detailed planning permission, since this will remove the uncertainties associated with outline consents.

The developer will need to consider whether the contract should be made conditional upon the grant of a planning permission which is capable of implementation. For example, the contract could state that the planning condition is not to be treated as satisfied until all reserved matters approvals associated with the planning permission have been obtained and all pre-commencement conditions (i.e. conditions in the form 'no development may be commenced until …') have been discharged so as to enable the lawful commencement of building works to start. Both parties would probably want the definition of 'pre-commencement conditions' to exclude certain pre-commencement conditions, such as a condition prohibiting the commencement of development until the site has been remediated or a condition prohibiting the commencement of development until existing buildings have been demolished or certain other works (whether on site or off site) have been carried out (see **Appendix E1** on the CD-ROM for a suggested definition of 'capable of implementation' and a suggested definition of 'pre-commencement condition').

If the contract is to be conditional upon the grant of a planning permission which is capable of implementation, the developer will need to ensure that the condition is capable of being waived (see **9.15**) so that it is not at risk of being timed-out and it can waive the planning condition if there is insufficient time to obtain reserved matters approvals and/or discharge pre-commencement planning conditions before the planning period expires. Usually, there will be a requirement for each party to notify the other party within a short, specified period after the grant of a planning permission as to whether or not they regard the planning permission as satisfactory. If the parties agree that the planning permission must be one which is capable of implementation, the contract will need to make it clear that, notwithstanding the grant of the planning permission, the planning permission is not to be treated as granted unless it is both capable of implementation and immune from challenge (unless the developer has elected to waive these requirements).

From a developer's point of view, a planning permission should not be regarded as satisfactory unless and until it is immune from challenge (see **9.14**) and the contract should contain a definition of 'planning condition' in the following or similar terms:

> the grant of a Satisfactory Planning Permission which (unless the Buyer elects in writing to waive this requirement) is Immune from Challenge [and which (unless the Buyer elects in writing to waive this requirement) is Capable of Implementation].

It should be noted that where a satisfactory planning permission is an outline planning permission it will not be capable of implementation until all necessary reserved matters approvals have been obtained and all pre-commencement conditions have been discharged.

9.2 CONDITIONS PRECEDENT AND CONDITIONS SUBSEQUENT

The distinction between conditions precedent and conditions subsequent is complicated and not entirely clear and there appear to be different views between some of the commentators as to whether a contract that is conditional upon the grant of planning permission is a condition precedent type of contract or a condition subsequent type of contract. Conditions precedent are sometimes called contingent conditions precedent.

The authors of *Chitty on Contracts* (33rd edition, Sweet & Maxwell, 2018) explain the difference at para.2.159 as follows:

> A condition is precedent if it provides that the contract is not to be binding until the specified event occurs. It is subsequent if it provides that a previously binding contract is to determine on the occurrence of the specified event: e.g. where A contracts to pay an

> allowance to B until B marries. A provision entitling a party to terminate a contract on the occurrence or non-occurrence of a specified event would likewise amount to, or give rise, to a condition subsequent.

They go on to discuss the effects of agreements subject to contingent conditions precedent and say:

> Where an agreement is subject to a contingent condition precedent, there is, before the occurrence of the condition, no duty on either party to render the principal performance promised by him: for example, a seller is not bound to deliver, and a buyer is not bound to pay. Nor in such a case, does either party undertake that the condition will occur. But an agreement subject to such a condition may impose some degree of obligation on the parties or on one of them.
>
> (para.2.160)

It would seem therefore that one of the fundamental characteristics of a condition precedent type of contract (i.e. a contract containing a condition precedent) is that it cannot be binding until the condition has been satisfied. As the authors of *Megarry & Wade: The Law of Real Property* (8th edition, Sweet & Maxwell, 2012) explain (at para.15.006), although a contract to sell land subject to a condition precedent creates 'a binding contract between the parties it is not a contract for the sale of land until the condition precedent is fulfilled'. However, they also go on to say 'neither party can waive the condition precedent because the existence of the contract depends on it' and they describe a condition subsequent type of contract as one 'where there is an immediate, binding contract for the sale of land which may be terminated by one or (sometimes) both parties if a condition to which it is subject is not performed' (para.15.008).

The views expressed by the authors of *Megarry & Wade* that a condition precedent cannot be waived and that a condition in a contract making the sale of land conditional on the grant of planning permission is a condition subsequent would appear to be questionable and at odds with the views of Kim Lewison and other commentators. In his book *The Interpretation of Contracts* (Sweet & Maxwell, 2017) Kim Lewison says (at section 9 of Chapter 16):

> Conditions precedent are normally contingent conditions. In other words, unless and until the condition is satisfied, no contract comes into existence, or liability under a contract is suspended. There may be obligations imposed in relation to the fulfilment of the condition, but such obligations are collateral to the substance of the agreement which is to come into operation once the condition has been fulfilled. For example, a sale of land may be conditional on planning permission being obtained. The purchaser may be under an obligation to use his best endeavours to obtain such permission, but that is collateral to the main substance of the agreement.

He goes on to add:

> One important difference between the types of condition is whether fulfilment of the condition is within the power of one of the contracting parties. If it is, the condition is more likely to be promissory rather than contingent. In *Michaels v Harley House*

> *(Marylebone) Ltd*, Robert Walker L.J. said: 'He recognised the important difference (mentioned by Goff J. in *Eastham v Leigh London and Provincial Properties Ltd*) between a true condition precedent which is not within a contracting party's power to bring about, even though he may undertake to use his best endeavours to bring it about, and a promissory condition which the party does have the power to fulfil or to cause to be fulfilled'.

Kim Lewison is clearly of the view that a condition in a contract making the contract conditional on planning permission is a condition precedent. If, as would seem to be the case, a key characteristic of a condition precedent is that it is not within a contracting party's power to fulfil, then, as obtaining planning permission is outside the control of the contracting parties, it follows that a contract conditional on planning permission must be a condition precedent type of contact. In a contract conditional on a buyer obtaining planning permission there is often a clause allowing the buyer to waive the condition before it is satisfied and a clause stating that the contract will terminate (or may be terminated) if the condition has not been satisfied by a specified date. The comment in *Megarry & Wade* that 'only a condition subsequent is capable of waiver' is difficult to understand.

9.3 MEANING OF 'ABSOLUTE DISCRETION'

A person who has absolute discretion to decide whether or not a planning permission is satisfactory will not have a completely unfettered discretion. He cannot act arbitrarily, capriciously or in bad faith. However, he is entitled to take into account his own interests and to act in his best commercial interests (see the cases of *Abu Dhabi National Tanker Co.* v. *Product Star Shipping Limited (The Product Star) (No.2)* [1993] 1 Lloyd's Rep 397 (CA), *Socimer International Bank Limited (in liquidation)* v. *Standard Bank London Limited* [2008] EWCA Civ 116 and *Ludgate Insurance Co. Limited* v. *Citibank NA* [1998] Lloyd's Rep IR 221 (CA)). Also, there is no requirement for a person with an absolute discretion to act in an objectively reasonable way and it is unlikely that the courts would intervene unless the exercise of the discretion was perverse (see *Chitty on Contracts* (33rd edition, Sweet & Maxwell, 2018), para.1.059). The court held in *Socimer* that

> a decision maker's discretion will be limited, as a matter of necessary implication, by concepts of honesty, good faith and genuineness, and the need for the absence of arbitrariness, capriciousness, perversity and irrationality.

However, the court did not agree that a further term should be implied that the decision maker had to act in a reasonably objective way and in *Ludgate* the court held as follows:

> It is very well established that the circumstances in which a court will interfere with the exercise by a party to a contract of a contractual discretion given to it by another party are extremely limited.

It will be apparent from the above that any attempt by a landowner to challenge the decision of a developer exercising an absolute discretion will be unlikely to succeed, unless the landowner is able to prove that the developer acted in bad faith or dishonestly and there is clear evidence that the developer's decision was perverse. The developer is entitled to act in his own best interests and does not have to act reasonably (in an objective sense).

9.4 ONEROUS CONDITIONS

Assuming that the landowner and the developer have accepted the principle of the contract containing a list of onerous planning conditions, they will need to consider which type of planning conditions are to be construed as onerous (i.e. which type of conditions will result in a planning permission not being 'satisfactory').

From a developer's point of view, a planning condition should be regarded as onerous if it would have the effect of making the development economically unviable – the developer will be expecting a certain return on capital and if, because of the planning gain requirements of the planning authority, the developer's expectations cannot be met then it will not want to be bound to proceed with the project. For this reason it would be prudent to stipulate in general terms that any planning condition is to be construed as onerous if it would have the effect of preventing or delaying the proposed development or if it would have a detrimental effect on the financial viability of the proposed development in the opinion of the developer (acting reasonably). However, this may be regarded as too general/wide by certain vendors and the developer may need to be more specific.

Usually a vendor and a developer will have little difficulty in agreeing that the following conditions should be regarded as onerous:

- a condition which makes the planning permission personal to the purchaser or to any specific person or class of persons;
- a condition which makes the planning permission limited in time (i.e. temporary) (excluding any requirement to commence development by a certain date);
- a condition which limits the occupation and/or use of the whole or any material part of the property (other than any part of the property on which affordable housing dwellings are to be located) to any designated occupier or class of occupier (by imposing a geographical qualification on proposed occupiers or otherwise).

Where the vendor is not prepared to agree to general wording along the lines mentioned above, the developer should try to ensure that any planning gain condition (i.e. a condition requiring financial contributions to be made towards things such as highway improvements, recreational facilities, education, health, travel and so on and conditions requiring works to be carried out) and any other planning obligation will be construed as onerous if the cost of complying with the condition/planning obligation and all the other planning gain conditions and planning obligations would substantially increase the cost of carrying out the proposed development or would exceed a certain aggregate amount or would have the effect of increasing, by more than a specified percentage or amount, the cost of carrying out the proposed development.

The impact of Community Infrastructure Levy (CIL) on the proposed development will also need to be considered by the developer and, from the developer's point of view, it would be prudent to include as an onerous condition a condition which, when taken together with any requirement to pay CIL and all other conditions attaching to the relevant planning permission and obligations contained in any associated planning agreement, has a detrimental effect on the financial viability of the proposed development.

A well-advised developer will also want to ensure that conditions which require the approval or co-operation of a third party (such as a condition imposing visibility splay requirements involving land owned by a third party or a condition requiring road improvements on land owned by the highway authority or some other third party) are to be construed as onerous if such approval or co-operation cannot be obtained or obtained on terms or at a cost (subject to a maximum amount) or within a period that is reasonable and proper.

The developer will need to consider whether affordable housing provisions are likely to be a factor and will probably want to insert a provision in the contract to the effect that a planning condition (whether in a planning permission or planning agreement) is to be regarded as onerous if:

- it requires more than a certain number or percentage of dwellings erected pursuant to the planning permission to be affordable housing dwellings; or
- it would be unacceptable to a prudent affordable housing provider or its mortgagee acting reasonably.

From the developer's point of view, it would be prudent to insert a sweeper clause in the contract to the effect that a planning condition is to be construed as onerous if it is by an objective standard unreasonable or unduly restrictive or if it would be unacceptable to a prudent property developer acting reasonably.

In the case of a mixed use development, the buyer/developer will need to consider including additional conditions in the list of onerous conditions, such as a condition which restricts or limits trading hours, ceiling heights, parking, the delivery of goods, or the operation or use of the buildings which are to be erected.

For a detailed list of onerous conditions refer to the definition of 'onerous condition' in **Appendix E1** on the CD-ROM.

9.5 PLANNING APPLICATIONS

The sale contract should contain a definition of 'planning application' and a definition of 'development'. These definitions will need to be carefully drafted and there are a number of points which will need to be considered by both parties to the contract:

- Should there be a reference to a full/detailed planning permission, an outline planning permission or an outline planning permission followed by the approval of such reserved matters as shall be identified by the developer buyer? (Remember that there is no statutory definition of full/detailed planning permission and it may be preferable to define 'planning permission' as suggested at **10.6**.)
- Should the planning permission be capable of implementation?
- Should the vendor/landowner be entitled to approve the developer's planning application before it is submitted to the local planning authority?
- Should there be a reference to a minimum number of dwellings or to a minimum floor area?
- Should the application be in joint names?
- Should the developer be allowed to vary or withdraw a planning application and/or submit a new application?
- Should there be a reference to a layout drawing which has been approved by the vendor/landowner?

If the vendor/landowner is to have a right to approve the developer's planning application then this should only be on the basis that such approval will not be unreasonably withheld or delayed, that the vendor/landowner shall be entitled to refuse approval only if the developer has failed to comply with certain planning obligations (e.g. to maximise the market value of the property and the extent of the net developable land within the application) or if the planning application is not in accordance with local or national planning policies, that such approval shall be deemed to be given if no objection to the application is raised (with reasons being given) within 10 working days of the vendor receiving a copy of the application and that in the event of a dispute the matter is to be referred to and settled by an independent expert.

From the developer's point of view, it is important that the developer should be entitled to vary a planning application and/or to withdraw a planning application and/or submit a new planning application at any time. The landowner may wish to resist this, and it may be necessary for the developer to compromise and to agree that it will only be entitled to vary a planning application/submit a new planning application:

- in circumstances where it is reasonable to do so (e.g. where the local planning authority has indicated that it would be minded to grant planning permission but only if variations were made to the application); and/or

- with the prior written consent of the landowner (not to be unreasonably withheld or delayed); or
- if leading planning counsel advises in writing that there is little prospect of the existing planning application succeeding and/or that it would be sensible to vary the application and/or lodge a fresh planning application.

9.6 PLANNING PERIOD AND TERMINATION

The sale contract will need to provide that if a satisfactory planning permission has not been granted (or any other condition has not been satisfied) by a certain date then the contract may be terminated. From a developer's point of view, the contract should not terminate automatically if a satisfactory planning permission has not been granted (or any other condition has not been satisfied) by a specified date. Ideally, the contract should stipulate that if a satisfactory planning permission has not been granted (or any other condition has not been satisfied) by a specified date then either party shall be entitled to terminate the contract by serving, say, not less than five days' notice in writing on the other party and if at the expiry of such notice the planning condition (or any other condition) shall remain unsatisfied then (unless the developer shall have elected to waive the planning condition or any other outstanding condition) the contract shall immediately terminate and the deposit paid by the developer shall be returned to it.

From a developer's point of view, it may be desirable to insert a clause in the contract which allows the developer to terminate the contract at any time.

9.7 EXTENSION OF PLANNING PERIOD

From the developer's point of view, the contract should provide for the initial planning period or the conditional period (as it is sometimes also called) to be automatically extended if on the expiry of the initial planning period:

- a planning decision is awaited;
- the outcome of an appeal is awaited;
- the outcome of a planning challenge/judicial review is awaited;
- a resolution to grant planning permission subject to a planning agreement being entered into has been passed;
- an independent expert's determination on a particular matter is awaited or an opinion from counsel on whether a planning permission is a satisfactory planning permission is awaited;
- a planning permission has been granted but the planning condition has not been satisfied owing to the fact that the planning challenge period has not expired (see **9.14**);

- the developer has lodged a reserved matters application and a planning decision is awaited;
- a planning permission has been granted but one or more pre-commencement conditions remains to be satisfied;
- a planning permission has been granted but completion of an infrastructure agreement (such as a s.38 road adoption agreement or a s.104 sewer adoption agreement) required in connection with the proposed development is awaited.

Where a planning decision or the outcome of an appeal or expert's determination is awaited, the planning period should be extended to expire by a period of more than two months after the date of the relevant decision (to allow for a planning challenge/judicial review to pass).

The extension provisions will need to be carefully drafted so as to ensure that the initial planning period can be extended more than once and also that it can be extended (and more than once) after the expiry of the initial planning period if there has already been an extension on the expiry of the initial planning period (see clause 6 of **Appendix E1** on the CD-ROM).

As discussed in the chapters on option agreements and promotion agreements, the landowner is likely to want the extension provisions to be subject to a longstop date (see **10.3** and **13.3.1**).

9.8 DEVELOPER'S OBLIGATIONS AND MEANING OF BEST AND REASONABLE ENDEAVOURS

From the landowner's point of view, the contract should impose various planning obligations on the developer, including:

- to submit (or to use reasonable endeavours to submit) the planning application to the local planning authority within a specified period and thereafter pursue the application with all due diligence;
- to use reasonable endeavours or 'all reasonable endeavours' to obtain a satisfactory planning permission and as soon as reasonably possible;
- to appeal against a planning refusal or the imposition of an onerous condition;
- to keep the landowner fully informed of the progress of the planning application and to promptly notify the landowner of any planning decision;
- to provide the landowner with a copy of the planning application and all other relevant documents and drawings and such other information as the landowner may from time to time reasonably request in writing; and
- not to implement any planning permission granted until after completion of the sale to the developer.

Entering into such obligations, apart from the obligation to submit a planning application by a specified date and the obligation to appeal, should not pose too much of a problem for the developer, although the developer will probably also want to resist entering into an all reasonable endeavours obligation. What is the difference between a reasonable endeavours obligation, a best endeavours obligation and an all reasonable endeavours obligation? An obligation to use reasonable endeavours does not require a party to act in a way which is prejudicial to its commercial interests and probably only requires a party to take one reasonable course of action (see *Yewbelle Limited* v. *London Green Developments Limited* [2006] EWHC 3166 (Ch)), whereas an obligation to use best endeavours requires a party to pursue all options available to it and even if they are detrimental to its commercial interests (see *Rhodia International Holdings Limited and another* v. *Huntsman International LLC* [2007] EWHC 292 (Comm)). However, even an obligation to use best endeavours only requires a party to take all those steps which a prudent, determined and reasonable person, acting in his own interests, would take (see *IBM United Kingdom Limited* v. *Rockware Glass Limited* [1980] FSR 335 (CA)). It does not require a party to take any action which would result in his own certain ruin or show utter disregard for his own interests (see *Terrell* v. *Mabie Todd and Co. Limited* [1952] 69 RPC 234 (QBD)) or impose an obligation to litigate or appeal against a decision that was doomed to failure or would be unreasonable in all the circumstances (*Malik Co.* v. *Central European Trading Agency Limited* [1974] 2 Lloyd's Rep 279 (QBD)). An obligation to use all reasonable endeavours is probably less onerous than a best endeavours obligation and closer to a reasonable endeavours obligation, but, from a developer's point of view, should still be resisted, as there can be no certainty as to how the courts will interpret such an obligation.

In *UBH (Mechanical Services) Limited* v. *Standard Life Assurance Company*, *The Times*, 13 November 1986 it was stated, obiter, that all reasonable endeavours is probably a middle position somewhere between best endeavours and reasonable endeavours 'implying something more than reasonable endeavours but less than best endeavours'. This would seem logical and to reflect the natural and ordinary meaning of the expressions. However, in *Rhodia* the judge stated, obiter, that:

> [an] obligation to use reasonable endeavours to achieve the aim probably only requires a party to take one reasonable course, not all of them, whereas an obligation to use best endeavours probably requires a party to take all the reasonable courses he can. In that context, it may well be that an obligation to use all reasonable endeavours equates with using best endeavours.

This passage is sometimes used as support for the view that all reasonable endeavours is synonymous with best endeavours, but this is far from clear. Perhaps all that the judge in *Rhodia* is saying is that all reasonable endeavours is like best endeavours in the sense that they both require a party to take more than one course of action.

The landowner may seek to place the developer under an obligation to allow the landowner to attend and/or make representations at planning meetings. The developer will normally wish to resist this but may agree if the landowner agrees to attend planning meetings as an observer and not to speak!

In *Jolley* v. *Carmel Limited* [2000] 3 EGLR 68 (CA) the contract did not impose an express obligation on the buyer to pursue the planning application and it did not specify a date by which planning permission must be granted, but the court held that the buyer was under an implied obligation to use reasonable endeavours to obtain a planning permission within a reasonable time.

9.9 APPEALS

Most developers will not want to be under an obligation to appeal against a planning refusal or the imposition of onerous conditions and will prefer to have the ability to submit a revised or new planning application or to appeal at their sole discretion (together with an ability to discontinue an appeal at their sole discretion at any time).

From the developer's point of view, any obligation to appeal (or to submit a revised or new planning application) should be qualified, so that the developer does not have to appeal (or submit a revised or new application) if it obtains a written opinion from leading counsel experienced in planning matters to the effect that an appeal (or a revised or new planning application) does not have a reasonable prospect of success. There will often be a difference of opinion between a developer and a landowner as to what constitutes a reasonable prospect of success. The landowner may want the contract to refer to 'a better than 50 per cent chance of success' whereas the developer will prefer, and with some justification, that the contract refers to 'a better than 60 per cent chance of success'. The prospect of the appeal succeeding should be reasonable and a better than 50 per cent chance of success is not good odds! The problem, however, is that counsel is unlikely to advise that an appeal stands a better than 60 per cent chance of success, so if the landowner agrees that the developer will not be obliged to appeal unless counsel advises that there is a better than 60 per cent chance of the appeal succeeding, the landowner may effectively be removing the obligation to appeal.

The parties to the contract will also need to consider whether the developer should be obliged to appeal against a deemed refusal to grant a planning permission. Again, most developers will want to have the ability to appeal against the non-determination of a planning application (i.e. if the local planning authority fails to determine the planning application within the relevant statutory period) but will not wish to be obliged to do so (because it is preferable not to appeal until the planning authority's reasons for refusing to grant planning permission are known).

If the contract is silent about appeals then an obligation on the part of the developer to use reasonable endeavours to obtain planning permission will not involve pursuing an appeal (see *Hargreaves Transport Limited* v. *Lynch* [1969] 1 All ER 455 (CA)), whereas an obligation to use best endeavours to obtain planning permission will include pursuing an appeal where the appeal stands a reasonable chance of success (see *Obagi* v. *Stanborough (Developments) Limited* (1995) 69 P & CR 573 (Ch D)).

9.10 LANDOWNER'S OBLIGATIONS

The developer will want to ensure that the contract imposes various obligations on the landowner, including:

- an obligation to assist the developer (at the cost of the developer) in obtaining a satisfactory planning permission;
- an obligation to enter into any planning agreement required as a precondition of a satisfactory planning permission being granted (see **9.11**);
- an obligation to procure that any mortgagee and tenant of the landowner also enters into any required planning agreement;
- an obligation not to apply for planning permission or to take any other action which would prejudice the grant of a satisfactory planning permission or adversely affect the proposed development;
- an obligation to oppose any application to register the property or any part of it as a town or village green and to commence proceedings to challenge the validity of any registration of the property as a town or village green;
- an obligation not to do or permit anything to be done on the property which shall or may result in a material change in the state or character or condition of the property or which shall or may make more difficult the development of the property;
- an obligation not to transfer, convey, agree to transfer, lease or agree to lease, charge, mortgage or grant any easement or otherwise deal with or dispose of the property or any part of it (see below and **9.21**).

The above obligations are very important and should not be overlooked.

The landowner should not have any difficulty entering into a planning agreement as long as:

- the planning agreement is in a form and contains obligations approved by the landowner (such approval not to be unreasonably withheld or delayed) (see **9.11** and **13.4**);
- it is a term of the planning agreement that the obligations contained in the agreement will not become binding until the planning permission has been implemented;
- the developer agrees to use reasonable endeavours to procure that the landowner will be released from all liabilities under the planning agreement after parting with his interest in the site; and
- the developer agrees that in the transfer of the site to the developer it will provide the landowner with an appropriate indemnity in respect of all the liabilities in the planning agreement (and any CIL liability).

The landowner may not be prepared to agree to an absolute prohibition against dealing and is likely to want some flexibility in this regard (see **13.5**). However, it is of fundamental importance to the developer that the landowner should not be permitted to make a disposal unless the disponee enters into a deed of covenant with the developer containing a covenant to observe and perform all of the obligations on the part of the landowner contained in the contract. The reason for this is that, although the contract will be binding on the landowner's successor in title (assuming that it has been protected by registration – see **9.21**) and the successor will be obliged to sell the property to the developer, the positive obligations contained in the contract (such as the obligation to enter into a planning agreement) will not be binding on the successor, unless the successor has entered into a deed of covenant with the developer. (The positive obligations will not be binding on the landowner's successor in title because the burden of a positive covenant cannot be enforced against a successor in title of the original covenantor – see **2.9**.) In addition to the requirement for a disponee to enter into a deed of covenant, the developer should require a restriction to be registered on the landowner's title to the property prohibiting any dealing unless the developer's solicitor has certified that the requirement for a deed of covenant has been complied with.

9.11 PLANNING AGREEMENT CONDITION

The contract should be made conditional, not only upon the grant of a satisfactory planning permission, but also upon the vendor/landowner entering into any planning agreement required as a prerequisite to the grant of a satisfactory planning permission. From the developer's point of view, the planning agreement should be in a form and contain obligations acceptable to the developer in its absolute discretion, but, from the landowner's perspective, the planning agreement should be in a form and contain obligations acceptable to the developer and the landowner (both acting reasonably) or in a form which does not contain any onerous conditions and which contains various stipulations, such as a release from liability clause (see **9.10** and **13.4**).

Where the developer will not have an absolute discretion to decide if a planning agreement is in an acceptable form, the developer's lawyer should ensure that the contract contains a provision stating that the planning agreement must:

- not contain any onerous conditions;
- be in a form and contain affordable housing provisions (including mortgagee protection provisions) which would be acceptable to a prudent affordable housing provider (acting reasonably) and its mortgagee (unless the developer elects to waive this requirement);
- not impose obligations on buyers of any dwellings or on their mortgagees (unless the developer elects to waive this requirement).

The developer will usually want to resist any attempt by the landowner to have the ability to approve the form of any required planning agreement, but, if forced to concede on this point, any right of approval should be qualified by adding the words 'such approval not to be unreasonably withheld or delayed'. Also, the developer may wish to include a clause in the contract stating that the landowner shall be deemed to be acting unreasonably in refusing to provide approval where the obligations:

- on the part of landowner contained in the planning agreement comply with the tests referred to in para.56 of the National Planning Policy Framework dated July 2018;
- are in accordance with local or national planning policies at the time the planning agreement is to be entered into;
- are reasonable having regard to the size of the application site and the extent of the proposed development on it; or
- are obligations which a prudent landowner acting reasonably would agree to in order to obtain a planning permission.

From the landowner's perspective, the above clause is too wide and should only be accepted if it is watered down. For example, whenever the word 'or' occurs it should be amended to read 'and', so that all of the strands of the clause need to apply before the landowner is deemed to be acting unreasonably.

The developer should not be made a party to the planning agreement, except for the purpose of consenting to its terms. However, if the local planning authority insists on the developer being made a party, the developer should agree to this only if the agreement contains a clause stating that the developer shall have no liability under the agreement unless it takes ownership of the site.

9.12 CIL CONDITION

The developer may also wish to make the contract conditional upon any requirement to pay CIL not having, in the opinion (or reasonable opinion) of the developer, a detrimental effect (or a materially adverse effect) on the financial viability of the proposed development (CIL Condition). A CIL Condition may not be necessary where a charging schedule is in force at the time when the conditional contract is entered into and the developer is able to calculate the amount of CIL payable, unless there is a prospect that the charging schedule may be revised by the charging authority during the existence of the contract.

Even if the contract contains a CIL Condition the developer's solicitor should still ensure that any list of onerous conditions includes a condition which (when taken together with any requirement to pay CIL and all the other conditions attaching to the relevant planning permission and the obligations contained in any associated planning agreement) has a detrimental effect on the financial viability of the proposed development in the opinion (or reasonable opinion) of the developer.

9.13 PLANNING LONGSTOP DATE

As already mentioned, the contract should provide for the planning period to be extended in certain circumstances (see **9.7**). However, a vendor may be prepared to agree to this only if the extension provisions are subject to a longstop date. Is this reasonable? Possibly not, particularly if the developer is obliged to appeal against a planning refusal, but a compromise may need to be reached between the parties.

9.14 THIRD PARTY CHALLENGES/JUDICIAL REVIEW

Notwithstanding that a satisfactory planning permission has been granted, a developer will not wish to be under an obligation to complete the purchase of a site until the possibility of a planning challenge/judicial review has passed. This can be achieved by defining 'planning condition' as 'the grant of an acceptable planning permission which is immune from challenge' (see **9.1**) or by inserting a clause in the contract in the same or similar form to model clause 13 or 14 in **Appendix D1**.

Another way of dealing with the issue of planning challenges is to define 'planning condition' as in model clause 15 in **Appendix D1**.

If the vendor will not agree to the inclusion of any of the above clauses in the contract, the developer may wish to explore the possibility of taking out a judicial review insurance policy (see **5.5**). The developer's lawyer should be aware that if the contract does not contain a judicial review protection clause and the developer has not been advised of this then he will be negligent.[1]

Currently, a planning challenge must be made within six weeks of the date of the decision notice (see **5.2.3**), but this period could be changed by statute or the Civil Procedure Rules for complying with planning challenges.

9.15 WAIVER OF CONDITIONS

The developer's lawyer should ensure that the contract gives the developer the ability to waive the planning condition (and any other condition) so that it can elect to complete the purchase of the property notwithstanding that a satisfactory planning permission may not have been granted or that some other condition remains to be satisfied. There may be good commercial reasons why a developer would wish to elect to complete without a satisfactory planning permission.

Any requirement that a satisfactory planning permission must be immune from challenge and capable of implementation should also be capable of waiver by the developer.

---

[1] See *Stoll* v. *Wacks Caller* [2009] EWHC 2299 (Ch). This case illustrates the danger where a lawyer, acting for a developer in the acquisition of land conditional upon the grant of planning permission, fails to include a judicial review protection clause in the contract or agrees to complete the purchase before the judicial review period has expired.

9.16 DISPUTES

The sale contract may need to contain a dispute resolution clause which provides for any planning dispute between the parties (e.g. regarding a planning application or a planning permission or a planning agreement) to be determined by a planning consultant or planning counsel or an independent surveyor experienced in planning matters. Such a clause will not be necessary where there is no right for the landowner to approve a planning application or a planning agreement and the developer is to have an absolute discretion to decide whether a planning permission is satisfactory, but otherwise the contract should contain a dispute resolution clause.

9.17 SECTION 106 COSTS AND ABNORMAL COSTS – PRICE ADJUSTMENT?

The developer will need to consider whether the cost of obtaining a satisfactory planning permission (including any planning gain costs payable under a planning agreement) and any other abnormal costs (such as the cost of dealing with contamination or digging deeper foundations as a result of abnormal ground conditions) should be deducted from the purchase price payable to the landowner. From a developer's point of view, this would seem both reasonable and desirable, particularly where the purchase price is fixed and does not take account of any abnormal costs. The landowner, however, will probably wish to resist any attempt by the developer to deduct such costs from the purchase price because there would then be uncertainty for the landowner.

One of the main difficulties for a developer wishing to enter into a contract conditional on planning is having to agree a fixed purchase price when there are a number of unknown factors that could adversely affect the economic viability of the transaction. In calculating the purchase price which he is prepared to pay, the developer will usually make various assumptions in relation to some or all of the following:

- the s.106 costs payable pursuant to any planning obligations associated with the planning permission (i.e. planning gain costs);
- abnormal costs (such as the cost of carrying out ground treatment works (including site remediation works), the cost of diverting existing services within the property, and the cost of bringing services to the boundary of the property and making connections to the public sewer and water mains networks);
- the number of dwellings which the planning permission will permit to be constructed and the floor area of such dwellings;
- the number of affordable housing dwellings which the planning permission or planning agreement will require to be constructed and the tenure mix and the size of such dwellings.

If the developer's assumptions in relation to any of the above matters should turn out to be incorrect, the economic viability of the project could be seriously prejudiced, with disastrous consequences for the developer, unless the contract gives the developer an absolute discretion to decide whether or not a planning permission is satisfactory and the ability to terminate the contract if it considers any planning permission granted to be unsatisfactory.

Whilst having an ability to terminate the contract is clearly desirable, it is not entirely satisfactory, since the developer is likely to have spent considerable time applying for and obtaining a planning permission. It would be far better, from the developer's point of view, for the contract to provide for:

- the purchase price to be reduced by the amount by which any assumed s.106 costs and any assumed abnormal costs exceed the actual s.106 costs and the actual abnormal costs;
- the purchase price to be adjusted where any assumptions made in relation to floor area and/or affordable housing prove to be incorrect.

Having agreed a fixed price, a seller may have difficulty in accepting a price reduction, unless the deductible costs are subject to a cap. However, this may leave the developer feeling exposed, and the parties may need to compromise and agree that if the deductible costs exceed the cap then, unless the developer or the seller is prepared to meet the excess, either party will be entitled to terminate the contract by giving notice in writing to the other. (For examples of price adjustment clauses and a definition of 'abnormal costs', see **Appendix E1** on the CD-ROM.)

9.18 RANSOM STRIPS

If a development site adjoins other land which has the potential for development in the future, the landowner may wish to retain a strip or strips of land along some of the boundaries of the development site. Most developers will want to resist the creation of ransom strips. However, they may have no alternative other than to agree to this, in which case they may wish to suggest that the ransom strips should be transferred into the joint names of the landowner and the developer, so that they retain a degree of control over the ransom strips.

9.19 INFRASTRUCTURE AGREEMENT CONDITION

The developer may wish to consider making the sale contract conditional not only upon the grant of a satisfactory planning permission and the vendor entering into any required s.106 agreement, but also upon the vendor entering into any infrastructure agreement required to be entered into by the developer in connection with the proposed development. As discussed in **Chapter 4**, once the Flood and Water Management Act (FWMA) 2010, s.42 has been implemented, a developer will not be permitted to make a connection to the public sewer network until it has entered into a s.104 agreement and, by making the contract conditional upon the vendor entering into any required infrastructure agreement, the developer will be able to ensure that completion of the development and the sale of dwellings are not delayed because, for example, there is no signed sewer adoption agreement in place.

In addition to an infrastructure agreement condition, the developer may wish to make the sale conditional upon its sustainable surface water drainage strategy being approved by the local planning authority. As discussed in **Chapter 4**, once FWMA 2010, Sched.3 is in force, a developer will not be permitted to commence any development until its sustainable drainage strategy has been approved by the local planning authority or an approving body.

9.20 OVERAGE

A landowner entering into a contract conditional on planning with a developer may require the developer to enter into an overage agreement on completion of the sale. Again, the developer will probably wish to resist this. However, in order to secure the purchase of the site it may have no alternative other than to agree to pay overage, in which case the landowner's overage proposals and the various issues discussed in **Chapter 12** will need to be carefully considered.

9.21 PROTECTION OF CONTRACT

A contract for the sale of land that is conditional upon the grant of a satisfactory planning permission creates an equitable interest in the land and, notwithstanding that the planning condition remains to be satisfied, it will create a binding contract between the contracting parties (but not a contract for the sale of the land until the satisfactory planning permission is granted) (see *Megarry & Wade: The Law of Real Property* (8th edition, Sweet & Maxwell, 2012), para.15.007).

The developer's solicitor will need to protect the contract by registering a unilateral or an agreed notice of the contract on the landowner's title or (in the case of unregistered land) by registering the contract as a land charge within Class C(iv), since another purchaser for value without notice of the contract would take the land free of it. This should be done immediately after contracts have been exchanged.

As already mentioned, in addition to protecting the contract by registration of an agreed or unilateral notice, the developer's solicitor should ensure that the landowner is prohibited from selling or making any other disposal of the land to another party without procuring that the disponee enters into a deed of covenant to observe and perform all of the obligations on the part of the landowner contained in the contract – without such a deed the positive obligations of the landowner will not be enforceable against the disponee.

As well as the requirement for a deed of covenant, there should be a requirement for a restriction against dealing to be entered on the landowner's title prohibiting any dealing without a certificate from a conveyancer confirming that the requirement for a deed of covenant has been complied with or does not apply.

9.22 CAPITAL GAINS TAX: THE DISPOSAL DATE

Where a sale of land is conditional on the grant of planning permission, the date of the disposal for capital gains tax purposes will be the date when the condition is satisfied. The authors of *Barnsley's Land Options* (6th edition, Sweet & Maxwell, 2016) state that 'Where a conditional contract is made for the sale of land the date of disposal is the date when the contract becomes unconditional' (see para.12.026). They refer to the Taxation of Chargeable Gains Act 1992, s.28(2), which states that

> if the contract is conditional (and in particular if it is conditional on the exercise of an option) the time at which the disposal and acquisition is made is the time when the condition is satisfied.

9.23 ADVANTAGES

From the developer's point of view, the main advantage of entering into a contract conditional on planning is that the developer is not obliged to purchase the land if it is unsuccessful in obtaining a satisfactory planning permission. If planning permission is refused or granted subject to onerous conditions which make the development unworkable then (under a well-drawn contract) the developer will be entitled to rescind the contract and to recover its deposit.

9.24 DISADVANTAGES

One of the disadvantages for a developer entering into a contract conditional on planning is that it cannot be certain of the amount of the planning gain costs which will be payable under a planning agreement. These costs may substantially increase the overall cost of acquiring the land and if the contract provides for a fixed purchase price and does not allow the developer to deduct planning gain costs from the purchase price or to terminate the contract if the planning gain costs are unacceptable to the developer, the developer will need to be satisfied that the purchase price which it has agreed to pay for the land reflects the likely planning gain costs. (The developer would be well advised to speak to the planners and to carefully consider the provisions of any planning brief relating to the development site before agreeing the purchase price with the landowner.)

Another disadvantage for a residential developer entering into a contract conditional on the grant of an outline planning permission is that until full/detailed permission is granted, or reserved matters approvals are obtained, it cannot be certain about the number of dwellings which the local planning authority will permit to be constructed on the development site.

CHAPTER 10

Option agreements

10.1 WHAT IS AN OPTION?

An option to purchase land is like a conditional contract except that the developer is not usually obliged to purchase the land in the event of a satisfactory planning permission being granted. This is the main difference between an option and a conditional contract.

A typical example of a 'call option' is where a landowner grants to a developer the right, during a specified period of time, to call for a sale and purchase of the land following the grant of a planning permission which is in a form acceptable to the developer. The developer is not obliged to exercise the right to buy in the event of a satisfactory planning permission being granted. However, if the developer does decide (in its absolute discretion) to exercise its right to buy, a binding contract for the sale and purchase of the land will come into existence.

In a typical strategic land call option agreement where the option land has not yet been allocated for development the developer will usually be required to promote the land for development before lodging a planning application and to use reasonable endeavours to obtain a satisfactory planning permission (see **Appendices E3** and **E4** on the CD-ROM for examples of strategic land call option agreements).

There are a number of key issues which a developer and a landowner will need to think about before entering into an option agreement of the kind described above, including the following.

10.2 FORMALITIES

In order to create a valid option, certain formalities must be observed:

- the option agreement must be in writing and signed by all the parties to the agreement; and
- the option must be granted by a deed or supported by consideration.

10.3 OPTION PERIOD

The option agreement should refer to an option period at the end of which the option agreement will terminate. Commercially it is important to specify an option period and to avoid contractual uncertainty.

Prior to the Perpetuities and Accumulations Act 2009 coming into force it was crucial that the option period did not exceed 21 years – an option granted for a period of more than 21 years would have breached the rule against perpetuities, unless it was exercised within 21 years of its grant; and although an option with no time limit would not have been void *ab initio*, it would have needed to have been exercised within 21 years of its grant (Perpetuities and Accumulations Act 1964, s.9(2)). However, as mentioned previously (see **4.2.2**), the rule against perpetuities no longer applies to options, so the option period may be whatever length the parties to the option agreement decide.

The option period should be realistic: the developer will want to ensure that it has sufficient time to make planning representations and to promote the option land for development. But, whatever the length of the option period, the option agreement should, from the developer's point of view, contain a clause which automatically extends the initial option period if at the expiration of that period:

- the developer is awaiting the result of a planning application or an appeal;
- there has been a planning challenge in respect of the satisfactory planning permission and proceedings are pending;
- the local planning authority has resolved to grant a satisfactory planning permission subject to the creation of a planning agreement;
- an expert's determination or counsel's opinion is awaited on a particular matter;
- a satisfactory planning permission has been granted but the judicial review period has not passed;
- the provisions of any tax freezer clause (see **10.19**) have been invoked;
- the developer has submitted a reserved matters application and a planning decision is awaited;
- any pre-commencement conditions remain to be satisfied;
- a third party has lodged an application to register the option land or any part of it as a town or village green.

The extension provisions will need to be very carefully drafted and the developer's lawyer should ensure that the option agreement contains wording which makes it clear that the option period may be extended on more than one occasion and to the latest of the various extension dates (see clause 4 of **Appendix E3** on the CD-ROM).

A landowner's solicitor will sometimes want to insert a provision in the option agreement stating that notwithstanding the planning extension provisions the option period shall not extend beyond a certain specified date. The difficulty with this, from the developer's point of view, is that if, say, an appeal against a planning refusal has been lodged, it would not make sense for the option agreement to come to an end until the appeal proceedings have been exhausted. Certainly, if the developer is under an obligation to appeal against a planning refusal then the developer should not agree to the planning extension provisions being subject to an artificial longstop date.

In addition to planning extension provisions, the option agreement should (from the developer's point of view) include a provision stating that if, on or before the expiry of the option period (including any period of extension thereof), the developer has served a price notice but the price has not been agreed or determined, the option period shall be extended and shall expire on the date three months from the date on which the price is agreed or determined.

If the option agreement contains tranching provisions (see **10.13**) then the developer should consider inserting a provision stating that the option agreement will not lapse when the original option period expires if, prior to the expiration of the original option period, the developer has served an exercise notice on the landowner to purchase part of the land benefiting from satisfactory planning permission and that the option shall continue until the developer has completed the purchase of the final tranche or until the date occurring three years after the date of the actual completion of the first tranche (whichever is the earlier) (subject to complying with all the timescales contained in the price notice and exercise notice provisions).

Also, if the proposed development area includes the landowner's property and adjoining or neighbouring land belonging to other landowners, the developer may wish to consider inserting a clause in the option agreement stating that the option period shall be extended if, at the expiration of the option period (including any period of extension thereof), the developer has served a price notice in respect of the adjoining or neighbouring land on the other landowners and the purchase price has not been agreed or determined (see **10.15**).

Finally, it would be sensible for the developer to include a clause in the option agreement stating that if the developer obtains a satisfactory planning permission that relates to only part of the landowner's property, the provisions of the option agreement shall continue to apply in respect of the balance of the landowner's property and the developer shall be entitled to exercise the option separately in relation to the balance of the landowner's property once it benefits from a satisfactory planning permission.

10.4 OPTION FEE

An option fee will usually be payable to the landowner and if the option fee will form part of the purchase price then this should be clearly stated in the option agreement. (If no option fee is payable, the option must be granted by deed, otherwise it will be invalid.)

Where an option agreement allows a developer to extend the original option period by paying a further option fee on or before a specified date, it would be sensible (from the landowner's point of view) to make time of the essence in relation to the payment (see *Rennie* v. *Westbury Homes (Holdings) Limited* [2007] EWCA Civ 1401).

10.5 CAPACITY

The developer's solicitor will need to be satisfied that the party granting the option has the power to do so. It is probably not prudent for executors/personal representatives to enter into option agreements.

10.6 SATISFACTORY PLANNING PERMISSION AND OPTION OBJECTIVES

Usually the exercise of the option will be dependent upon the grant of a satisfactory planning permission and, as discussed in relation to conditional contracts, it will be necessary to define the terms 'planning permission' and 'satisfactory planning permission'.

As discussed at **9.1**, there is no statutory definition of full or detailed planning permission and it will be important to make clear what is meant by 'planning permission'. One option would be to define 'planning permission' as:

> planning permission for the Development granted pursuant to a Planning Application or any subsequent Appeal followed by the obtaining of [such of those matters as shall be reserved for approval in such planning permission as the Developer shall identify] [all matters reserved for approval in such planning permission] and the discharge of [such Pre-Commencement Conditions as the Developer shall require to be discharged] [all Pre-Commencement Conditions].

If it is not intended that reserved matters approvals will need to be obtained or pre-commencement conditions discharged, this should be made clear, although the developer is likely to want to keep its options open. Where reserved matters approvals are to be obtained and/or pre-commencement conditions discharged, the option agreement should contain a clause which entitles the developer (in its absolute discretion) to elect in writing to waive either one or both of these requirements at any time. Such a right of waiver will be very important to the developer.

A developer is likely to want a planning permission in relation to an option to be regarded as satisfactory only if it is in the form which (together with any associated planning agreement) is acceptable to the developer in the developer's absolute discretion. This, the developer may claim, is consistent with the fact that, under an option, the developer is not usually obliged to proceed to purchase in any event.

The developer may also claim that making the definition of 'satisfactory planning permission' objective will result in the option being more like a conditional contract and that it is not usual to pay a landowner an upfront non-refundable payment on entering into a conditional contract. However, this would not be correct as under an option agreement the developer will not be obliged to buy the landowner's property if a satisfactory planning permission is granted. If the developer doesn't like the planning permission that has been granted, it will not be obliged to exercise the option. But in any event the bottom line for the landowner is that the landowner will not want the developer to be able to exercise the option if the planning permission contains adverse conditions or it is inconsistent with option agreement objectives.

From a landowner's point of view, the option agreement should contain a definition of 'adverse conditions' or 'onerous conditions' and a list of option objectives which the developer must endeavour to achieve (such as to maximise the value of the option land) and 'satisfactory planning permission' should be defined in the following (or similar) terms:

> a Planning Permission authorising the Development which together with any associated Planning Agreement is consistent with the Option Objectives and does not contain any Adverse Conditions.

If this is acceptable to the developer, the option agreement will need to contain a carefully considered definition of 'adverse conditions' (see **9.4**). Also, the developer should insist that a planning permission should not be regarded as satisfactory unless it is free from all planning challenges and (unless the developer elects to waive this requirement) capable of lawful implementation. This would mean that all pre-commencement planning conditions would need to be discharged and all necessary reserved matters approvals obtained before a planning permission could be regarded as satisfactory (unless this requirement was waived by the developer). The developer may also wish to suggest that a planning permission should not be regarded as satisfactory unless the option land benefits from all easements required to facilitate access and services to the land.

Sometimes a landowner will want to ensure that the definition of 'satisfactory planning permission' is not too general and that it refers to a specific type of development (e.g. residential or primarily residential). This should not cause a developer too much difficulty, although it may still wish to retain a certain degree of flexibility (e.g. by referring to 'primarily residential development or mixed use development comprising residential and retail and/or commercial and/or industrial'), particularly if there is a possibility the planners may require a mixed use development.

Sometimes, in addition to imposing an obligation on the developer to use reasonable endeavours to maximise the extent of the landowner's land within a planning permission, a landowner will want to ensure that there is a minimum land take requirement and to include a provision in the option agreement stating that a planning permission shall not be regarded as satisfactory unless it permits at least 50 per cent of the landowner's land to be developed for beneficial purposes. In other words, at least 50 per cent of the land comprised within the planning permission must be net developable land for the planning permission to be regarded as satisfactory. This will give the landowner the certainty of knowing, where there is also a minimum price requirement, that he is guaranteed to receive a minimum ascertainable sum in the event of the option being exercised. For example, if there is a minimum price requirement of £300,000 per net developable acre and the landowner owns 20 acres of land, he will know that he cannot receive a purchase price of less than £3,000,000 (i.e. £300,000 × 10 acres), assuming that the developer is obliged to buy the option land as a whole (and there are no tranching provisions). If the option agreement is to contain tranching provisions, the landowner may want the agreement to specify that each tranche must be of a minimum size (e.g. 10 acres) and to include a minimum price linked to gross acreage (e.g. £300,000 per gross acre).

It is not all that common for an option agreement to contain a list of option objectives (and for the developer to be obligated to use reasonable endeavours to achieve those objectives), although option agreements do often impose planning obligations on a developer, such as to maximise the value of the option land and the extent of the net developable land within a planning permission and to minimise the requirements of the planning authority in a planning agreement (see **10.12**). From the landowner's point of view, it would be prudent to:

- include, in addition to imposing an obligation on the developer to use reasonable endeavours to maximise the extent of the landowner's land within a planning permission, a list of option objectives similar to the objectives often found in promotion agreements (see **13.2**);
- impose an obligation on the developer to use reasonable endeavours to achieve the option objectives; and
- insert a clause in the option agreement stating that a planning permission and any associated planning agreement are not to be regarded as satisfactory unless they are consistent with the option objectives and planning policy guidance and do not contain any adverse/onerous conditions.

10.7 PURCHASE PRICE

The purchase price for the option land may be a fixed sum but, more often than not, it will be based on the open market value of the land and there will be a definition of 'market value'.

In a typical developer's call option agreement, market value will be defined as the price at which the option land might reasonably be expected to be sold on the open market as at a specified date (e.g. the date of the price notice) having regard to all relevant factors, including the existence of all rights and covenants affecting the option land and the terms of the satisfactory planning permission and any relevant planning agreement. It is important to specify the date on which the option land is to be valued (see *Redlawn Land Limited* v. *Cowley* [2010] EWHC 766 (Ch)). There will usually be a list of assumptions, including some or all of the following:

- a willing seller and a willing buyer;
- a reasonable period in which to negotiate the sale taking into account the nature of the option land and the state of the market;
- that values will remain static during that period;
- that the option land will be freely exposed to the open market;
- that no account will be taken of the bid by a purchaser with a special interest;
- that the option land has no special value attributable to the fact that any other land might be dependent upon it for access or services;
- that the option land has no ransom value;
- that the option land is vacant; and
- that the option land is not subject to the option agreement.

Market value is sometimes defined by reference to the RICS *Appraisal and Valuation Manual* (commonly known as the Red Book) or the RICS *Valuation – Professional Standards UK January 2014*. Lawyers and agents advising landowners tend to favour the Red Book definition and method of calculating market value. The latest edition of the Red Book is the RICS *Valuation – Global Standards 2017*, which followed the RICS *Valuation – Professional Standards UK January 2014* (revised April 2015). It took effect on 1 July 2017, the same date that the RICS *International Valuation Standards 2017* was published, and incorporates these standards.

'Market Value' is defined in Valuation Standard 3.2 of the RICS *Appraisal and Valuation Manual* (9th edition) as follows:

> the estimated amount for which an asset or liability should exchange on the valuation date between a willing buyer and a willing seller in an arm's length transaction after proper marketing and where the parties had acted knowledgeably, prudently and without compulsion.

Valuation Standard 3.2 states that:

- valuations based on market value shall adopt the definition and the conceptual framework settled by the International Valuation Standards Council;
- in applying market value, regard must also be had to the conceptual framework set out in paras.31–35 of the International Valuation Standards Framework, including the requirement that the valuation amount reflects the actual market state and circumstances as of the effective valuation date;
- market value ignores any existing mortgage, debenture or other charge over the property; and
- where the price offered by prospective buyers generally in the market would reflect an expectation of a change in the circumstances of the property in the future, this element of 'hope value' is reflected in market value.

Many developers prefer not to refer to the Red Book and to require the option agreement to contain a detailed list of development costs which are to be deducted from the purchase price or taken into account in calculating market value. The reason for this is certainty. There can be no doubt about whether a particular development cost should be deducted from the purchase price if it is included in a list of development costs. Also, in calculating market value in accordance with the Red Book, pre-planning costs will not be deductible. For example, the cost of promoting the option land for development and obtaining a satisfactory planning permission will not be a deductible development cost. The option land will be valued with the benefit of the satisfactory planning permission, but the cost of promoting the land for development and the costs incurred by the developer in securing the satisfactory planning permission (including planning application fees, the fees of highway consultants and other consultants and the cost of pursuing an appeal) will not be reflected in the calculation of the market value of the option land and will not be deductible from the purchase price, unless the option agreement expressly provides for this.

Where development costs are to be deducted from the purchase price, the landowner will want to ensure that there can be no double deduction of such costs. This may happen if there is a formula for calculating the purchase price which requires development costs to be deducted, and the calculation of the market value of the option land also involves the deduction of development costs. The problem of double deduction can easily be avoided by inserting a clause in the agreement such as model clause 16 in **Appendix D1**.

If a potential development site is owned by a number of different landowners, it may be appropriate or desirable for the purchase price which is to be paid to each individual landowner to be based on the equalised value of their combined land holdings (see **Appendix E4** on the CD-ROM). The equalised value is calculated by multiplying the open market value of the whole of the development site by the number of acres comprised within an individual landowner's ownership and dividing the resulting figure by the total number of acres within the whole of the development site. From an individual landowner's point of view, the advantage of calculating the purchase price by reference to equalised value is that he will not be prejudiced if his land consists mainly of infrastructure land and/or public open space and/or affordable housing. An example of an equalisation purchase price formula is contained in Example 5 of **10.8**. Although the principle of equalisation would seem to be fair, there will always be some landowners who believe that their land is more valuable (e.g. because it will provide the access to the site or it has some other ransom value), which can cause difficulties. For this reason, a developer may not be willing to agree to an equalisation purchase price formula with an individual landowner unless and until all of the relevant landowners accept the principle of equalisation.

From the landowner's point of view, it would be prudent to specify a minimum purchase price in order to ensure that the developer is incentivised not to be too generous in agreeing planning gain or other development costs. However, most developers will be reluctant (at least initially) to agree to this, unless the minimum price is at a level which is sufficiently low so as not to be a cause for concern. Often the minimum purchase price will be arrived at by multiplying a specified sum by the number of gross acres or net developable acres comprised within the option land. If a developer is prepared to agree to a minimum purchase price provision then it will probably want the minimum price to relate to net developable land and to exclude land required for infrastructure, public open space, affordable housing and any other non-beneficial use. The landowner may object to the exclusion of affordable housing and it may be necessary for the parties to agree a different minimum price for the affordable housing land. However, a well-advised landowner will not agree to the exclusion of affordable housing from the definition of net developable land.

From the landowner's point of view, it would seem sensible for the minimum purchase price to be index linked to guard against the effects of inflation and the retail price index would appear to be a suitable index for this purpose, although the developer may prefer to refer to a land-based index. However, developers generally are not keen on the idea of indexation because of the uncertainty to which this gives rise. A compromise may be to agree that there will be no indexation for the first few years of the option or to agree that the sum per acre payable will be increased annually by a fixed percentage.

Where the developer is willing to agree to a minimum purchase price and equalisation is to apply, the purchase price should be calculated in accordance with the formula set out in Example 6 of **10.8** and the parties will need to consider what should happen if the purchase price as agreed between the parties or determined by an independent valuer is lower than the minimum price. For example, should the option lapse if the developer fails to serve an exercise notice within a specified period of the purchase price being agreed or determined or should the option continue until the purchase price equals or exceeds the minimum purchase price (see **10.16**)?

Where a developer is to have the ability to draw down the option land in tranches, only a fair and reasonable proportion of any development costs that are to be deducted from the purchase price should be deducted (see **10.9**).

Where the option land is large and likely to have a substantial value once planning permission has been granted, the developer may seek to include deferred payment provisions and/or tranching provisions (see **10.13**) in the option agreement. However, the landowner should be aware that the inclusion of deferred payment provisions could give him a tax problem, since the exercise of the option will trigger an immediate liability to pay capital gains tax: a liability to pay capital gains tax arises on the 'disposal of assets' which will be the date of the exercise of the option and not the date when the option land is conveyed/transferred to the developer or the date when the purchase price is paid.

Where the option agreement is to contain tranching provisions, the landowner may wish to insert a clause in the agreement stating that the developer shall not be entitled to acquire more than one tranche in any tax year if acquiring two or more tranches in the same tax year would have adverse tax consequences for the landowner.

10.8 EXAMPLES OF PURCHASE PRICE FORMULAE

The following are examples of purchase price formulae which may be used in calculating the purchase price for option land:

Example 1: purchase price formula (based on market value of option land)

$[(A - (B + C)) \times [\ ]\%] - D$

Where:

A = Market Value of the Option Land (i.e. all of the land within the Property that is the subject of the Satisfactory Planning Permission or a Tranche (as the case may be))

B = Development Costs [less any sum previously deducted in respect of Development Costs on the purchase of a previous Tranche]

C = Planning Promotion Costs

D = Option Fee plus (if appropriate) the Further Option Fee

Provided that:

(a) there shall be no double deduction of any costs or expenditure incurred by the Developer so that the Developer shall not be entitled to deduct a Development Cost and/or a Planning Promotion Cost if it has already been deducted in calculating the Market Value or if it was deducted on the purchase of a previous Tranche;
(b) where any Development Costs and/or Planning Promotion Costs relate to land other than the Property, only a fair and reasonable proportion of them shall form part of the Development Costs and/or Planning Promotion Costs;
(c) the Option Fee shall be deducted only once; and
(d) where the Option Land comprises a Tranche, only a fair and reasonable proportion of the Development Costs and Planning Promotion Costs shall be deducted.

Note: The formula in Example 1 is appropriate/suitable where the proposed development area comprises only land belonging to the landowner and does not include any adjoining or neighbouring land.

Example 2: purchase price formula (based on market value of option land)

$(A \times [\ ]\%) - (B + C + D)$

Where:

A = Market Value of the Option Land (i.e. all of the land within the Property that is the subject of the Satisfactory Planning Permission or a Tranche (as the case may be))

B = Development Costs [less any sum previously deducted in respect of Development Costs on the purchase of a previous Tranche]

C = Planning Promotion Costs

D = Option Fee

Provided that:

(a) there shall be no double deduction of any costs or expenditure incurred by the Developer so that the Developer shall not be entitled to deduct a Development Cost and/or a Planning Promotion Cost if it has already been deducted in calculating the Market Value or if it was deducted on the purchase of a previous Tranche;
(b) where any Development Costs and/or Planning Promotion Costs relate to land other than the Property, only a fair and reasonable proportion of them shall form part of the Development Costs and/or Planning Promotion Costs;
(c) the Option Fee shall be deducted only once; and
(d) where the Option Land comprises a Tranche, only a fair and reasonable proportion of the Development Costs and Planning Promotion Costs shall be deducted.

The formula in Example 2 is similar to the formula in Example 1 but it will produce a different result. The formula in Example 2 will produce a lower figure and therefore a better result from a developer's point of view. The developer will argue that the formula in Example 2 is correct since the developer's discount should apply only to the market value and not the development costs. This would probably be true if market value meant gross market value, but usually it will mean net market value (because development costs will be taken into account in calculating open market value).

Example 3: purchase price formula

(A × [ ]%) – OF

Where:

A = Market Value

OF = Option Fee plus (if appropriate) the Further Option Fee

The formula in Example 3 above does not require any deduction to be made in respect of development costs and is generally preferred by landowners. If this formula is used then, from the developer's point of view, it needs to be made clear in the definition of 'market value' that the development costs will be taken into account in calculating market value.

Example 4: purchase price formula (based on price per net developable acre)

((£ × (A/B)) × C) – (D + OF)

Where:

£ = [ ] (insert price to be paid for each acre within the Net Developable Area)

A = the figure of the Index last published for the month immediately preceding the Price Notice

B = the Base Figure (i.e. the figure of the Index last published for the month preceding the date of the option agreement)

C = the Net Developable Area (i.e. the part of the Option Land which is capable of beneficial development and which excludes land required for infrastructure or affordable housing [with no value]) measured in acres (calculated to two decimal places)

D = the Development Costs plus Planning Promotion Costs

OF = Option Fee

The formula in Example 4 is relevant where the price is to be based on the net developable area of the land benefiting from a satisfactory planning permission and indexation is required. It will be necessary to consider whether development costs should be deducted: they should not be deducted if they are reflected in the price payable per net developable acre.

Example 5: equalisation formula

$(A \times (B/C)) - OF$

Where:

A = (the Market Value of the Development Site (i.e. all the land within the Satisfactory Planning Permission owned or controlled by the developer by virtue of an option agreement in favour of the developer) less all Development Costs and Planning Promotion Costs) multiplied by [ ]%

B = the total area of the Option Land (i.e. the whole of such part of the Property as shall be comprised within the Satisfactory Planning Permission or a Tranche (as the case may be)) measured in acres (calculated to two decimal places)

C = the total area of the Development Site (i.e. the land within the Satisfactory Planning Permission at the time when the Price Notice is served that is owned by or controlled by the developer by virtue of an option agreement) measured in acres (calculated to two decimal places)

OF = Option Fee

[Provided that (a) the Developer shall not be entitled to double count any expenditure in assessing the Market Value so that any item which has been reflected in the calculation of Market Value cannot also be deducted as a Development Cost; (b) any Development Cost cannot be deducted more than once so that if a Development Cost was deducted on the purchase of a previous Tranche it will not be deducted again; and (c) the Option Fee can only be deducted once.]

The equalisation formula in Example 5 is appropriate where the landowner's land forms or may form part of a larger development site. Under this formula the landowner will receive a proportion of the market value of the whole of the development site (based on the size of his land holding or, if the option is exercised in tranches, part of it). Note that A in the above formula could be defined as: (Market Value × [ ]%) – (Development Costs + Planning Promotion Costs). This definition is better for the developer. It would mean that the multiplier would only apply to the Market Value and that the developer would be reimbursed in full for all the Development Costs and Planning Promotion Costs.

Example 6: equalisation formula with minimum purchase price

'Price' means the price payable for the Option Land which shall be the greater of:

(a) the sum calculated in accordance with the following formula:

(A × (B/C)) – D

Where:

A = (the Market Value of the Development Site (i.e. the land within the Satisfactory Planning Permission at the time when the Price Notice is served that is owned or controlled by the developer by virtue of an option agreement) less all Development Costs and Planning Promotion Costs) multiplied by [ ]%

B = the total area of the Option Land (i.e. the whole of such part of the Property as shall be comprised within the Satisfactory Planning Permission or a Tranche (as the case may be)) measured in acres (calculated to two decimal places)

C = the total area of the Development Site measured in acres (calculated to two decimal places)

D = the Option Fee plus (if paid) the Further Option Fee [and the legal and surveyors costs referred to in clause [ ]]

and

(b) the sum calculated in accordance with the following formula:

£ × (A/B)

Where:

£ = [ ] (insert minimum purchase price to be paid for each acre of Net Developable Area) multiplied by the total Net Developable Area of the Development Site measured in acres (and a proportionate amount for any part of a net acre)

A = the total Net Developable Area (i.e. land which is capable of beneficial development and which excludes land required for infrastructure or affordable housing [with no value]) of the Option Land measured in acres (including any part of an acre)

B = the total Net Developable Area (i.e. land which is capable of beneficial development and which excludes land required for infrastructure or affordable housing [with no value]) of the Development Site measured in acres (including any part of an acre)

The formula in Example 6 is appropriate where equalisation is required and there is to be a minimum purchase price. The formula does not provide for indexation, but this may be required by the landowner. Instead of using a formula to calculate the minimum price, it could be defined simply as: 'the sum calculated by multiplying the number of gross acres of land (calculated to two decimal places) comprised within the Option Land by the sum of £[ ]'.

10.9 DEVELOPMENT COSTS

The developer should ensure that any list of development costs includes (in addition to all the usual development costs, such as the cost of acquiring land or easements required to facilitate access or the provision of services to the development area, ground treatment/remediation costs and infrastructure and planning gain/s.106 costs) any Community Infrastructure Levy (see **5.4**) which may be payable as well as any other tax or levy which may be payable upon the grant or implementation of any planning permission.

From the landowner's point of view, the developer should be obliged to maintain an open book policy in relation to development costs and to provide the landowner with such evidence of all costs incurred or likely to be incurred in connection with the development of the option land as the landowner shall require in order to verify the amount of the development costs. There should also be a provision stating that where any of the development costs relate to the development of land other than the option land (i.e. the land belonging to the landowner that benefits from the satisfactory planning permission) or, where equalisation applies, the development area (i.e. the land, including the landowner's property, owned or controlled by the developer) then only a fair and reasonable proportion of them shall form part of the development costs to be deducted from the purchase price or taken into account in calculating the market value of the option land. This will allay the possible concern of the landowner that all of the development costs may be deducted from the purchase price payable to him. Also, where the option agreement contains tranching provisions (see **10.13**) there should be a provision stating that only a fair and reasonable proportion of the development costs shall be deducted from the purchase price payable for the tranche.

10.10 EQUALISATION

If there is a possibility that the option land may be developed, or is likely to be developed, in conjunction with adjoining or neighbouring land as part of a comprehensive scheme, or that the infrastructure works to be carried out by the developer will benefit the option land and adjoining land then, unless the equalisation purchase price formula applies, the landowner may wish to impose an obligation on the developer to use reasonable endeavours to enter into option agreements or collaboration agreements with the adjoining landowners which require all the development costs (including planning and infrastructure costs) to be apportioned fairly between the various landowners and/or the purchase price payable to each landowner to be calculated on an equalised basis. In such circumstances the parties may wish to consider inserting a provision similar to model clauses 17 and 18 in **Appendix D1**.

An alternative to the above clauses would be to include an additional assumption in the definition of 'market value', stating that it is to be assumed that the proportion of the net developable land within the option land equals the proportion that the gross acreage of the option land bears to the gross acreage of the whole of the development area (see the definition of 'market value' in **Appendix E3** on the CD-ROM). From a landowner's point of view, this may be preferable, since it does not involve a reasonable endeavours obligation on the part of the developer and gives the landowner the certainty that equalisation will apply.

10.11 LANDOWNER'S OBLIGATIONS

The developer will want to ensure that various obligations are imposed on the landowner, including:

- to enter into such planning agreements as the developer requires. This should not be a problem for the landowner so long as: the landowner has the right to approve the planning agreement; the planning agreement is consistent with the option objectives and planning policy guidance and does not contain any onerous/adverse conditions; it is a term of the planning agreement that the obligations contained therein will not be binding until the relevant planning permission has been implemented; the developer agrees to use reasonable endeavours to ensure that the planning agreement contains a clause whereby the landowner will be released from all liability under the agreement upon parting with his interest in the land; and the developer agrees to provide the landowner with an appropriate indemnity. Usually, a developer will be prepared to provide a landowner with an indemnity in respect of planning obligations and any CIL liability when, following the exercise of the option, the option land is transferred to it. This is acceptable if the planning agreement contains a release from liability clause and the developer is acquiring the whole

of the option land, but, for the reasons mentioned at **13.4**, it is unacceptable where the developer has the ability to acquire the option land in tranches;
- to procure that the landowner's mortgagee and any other person with an interest in the option land will enter into any planning agreement to which the landowner is a party upon request;
- to support the developer's planning application;
- not to make any application for planning permission without the approval of the developer;
- not to do anything that damages or changes the character of the option land;
- not to do anything which might adversely affect the development of the option land or reduce its value or which might prejudice the prospects of obtaining a satisfactory planning permission;
- not to sell or otherwise deal with the option land (but see **10.18**);
- to permit the developer access to the option land for the purpose of carrying out ground investigations;
- not to do or permit anything to be done whereby the development of the option land is made more difficult or more costly;
- not to enter into any telecommunications agreements or agreements with statutory undertakers without the approval of the developer (but note that, as discussed at **2.14**, a landowner can be compelled to enter into a telecoms agreement);
- to oppose any application to register the option land or any part of it as a town or village green and to challenge the validity of any registration of the option land or any part of it as a town or village green.

The developer may also wish to include a clause in the option agreement whereby the landowner irrevocably appoints the developer his attorney for the purpose of executing any planning agreement which the landowner fails to execute within 10 working days of receipt. Most well-advised landowners will be reluctant to agree to this, except perhaps where the landowner has the ability to approve both the planning agreement and the planning permission that is to be granted pursuant to it and, having approved the draft planning permission and the draft planning agreement (whether by express or deemed approval), he fails to execute the agreement within a reasonable period.

The landowner is likely to want to have the right to approve the form of any planning agreement and all planning gain costs in order to ensure that the planning obligations are fair and reasonable and that they reflect the option objectives and the obligations imposed on the developer in the option agreement (see **10.12**). If the landowner is to receive a minimum purchase price, he may be less concerned about the prospect of planning gain and other development costs substantially reducing the purchase price, although for most landowners this will be a major concern. Many developers will be reluctant to agree to the landowner having the ability to approve a planning agreement. However, if the landowner is adamant that he must have such a right (and he should be) then this should only be on the basis that such approval will not be unreasonably withheld, that it will be deemed to have been given if no objection (with reasons being given) is made within a specified period, that the landowner will be entitled to withhold his approval only on specified grounds and that in the event of a dispute the matter is to be referred to an independent expert for determination. From the developer's point of view, the landowner should be entitled to withhold his approval to a planning agreement only if the agreement contains provisions which directly and materially adversely affect the landowner's retained land and/or if the agreement imposes obligations which are not in accordance with local or national planning policies at the time the agreement is to be entered into or which infringe the tests referred to in para.56 of the National Planning Policy Framework dated July 2018. However, in addition to these grounds for refusing approval, the landowner will want to be entitled to refuse his approval to a planning agreement if it contains adverse/onerous obligations and obligations which are not consistent with the option objectives.

Ideally, the option agreement should set out criteria for determining whether the landowner is acting reasonably in refusing to approve a draft planning agreement. The developer's lawyer may wish to include a clause in the option agreement in the form of model clause 19 in **Appendix D1**, although, as discussed above, without any amendment the clause is unlikely to be acceptable to a well-advised landowner.

10.12 DEVELOPER'S PLANNING OBLIGATIONS

The option agreement will usually oblige the developer to promote the option land for development (assuming that the option land has not already been allocated for development) and to lodge a planning application and use reasonable endeavours to obtain a satisfactory planning permission. The landowner may want the developer to be obliged to lodge a planning application 'at the earliest possible opportunity'. However, the developer will not wish to be under an obligation to lodge a planning application by a specified date and will usually want to have an absolute discretion in this regard. The developer will argue, with some justification, that it is not in either party's best interests for a planning application to be lodged prematurely; but the developer may have to compromise and agree to lodge a planning application when it is reasonable or commercially sensible to do so, having regard to the prospect of obtaining a satisfactory planning permission and what is commercially achievable and/or the advice of its planning consultants. Another possibility would be for the parties to agree that the developer will lodge a planning application in accordance with an agreed timescale contained in a planning strategy that has been approved by the landowner and the developer (such approval not to be unreasonably withheld or delayed).

Nor will the developer wish to be under an obligation to appeal against a planning refusal or the grant of a planning permission that is not a satisfactory planning permission (e.g. because it contains onerous planning conditions). As a compromise, the developer could agree to the landowner having a right to terminate the option agreement if, following a planning refusal or the grant of a planning permission containing an onerous condition, the developer does not submit a revised or new planning application or lodge an appeal or lodge an application under the Town and Country Planning Act 1990, s.73 to vary or discharge the onerous condition within a specified period. Another option would be for the developer to be under an obligation to appeal or lodge a new or revised planning application if counsel experienced in planning matters advises that there is a reasonable prospect (or better than 50 per cent chance) of an appeal or new planning application succeeding.

The landowner's lawyer may wish to impose various other obligations on the developer, such as an obligation to use reasonable endeavours:

- to maximise the development value of the option land and the area of the option land to be included within a planning permission;
- to maximise the extent of the net developable land in a planning permission;
- to minimise the requirements of the local planning authority in respect of any planning agreement (e.g. planning gain requirements) and the requirement for affordable housing and infrastructure;
- to maximise the area of the development site to be included within a satisfactory planning permission (this will be relevant where the purchase price is based on an equalisation formula and the land to be developed will include the land of more than one landowner).

Such obligations should not cause the developer too much difficulty so long as they are qualified by words such as:

> so far as reasonably practicable and commercially achievable and having due regard to local and national planning policies current at the relevant time and the terms of the National Policy Framework dated July 2018 or similar document issued by any government department and the prospect of obtaining a Satisfactory Planning Permission.

As discussed at **10.6**, it would be sensible, from the landowner's perspective, for the above obligations to be included, along with others, in a list of option objectives which the developer must use reasonable endeavours to achieve, and for a planning permission not to be regarded as satisfactory unless it is consistent with the objectives (and planning policy guidance).

10.13 TRANCHING PROVISIONS

Where the option land is large, the developer may wish to have the ability to draw down the land in tranches or phases. This will assist the developer with its cashflow but can give rise to certain difficulties. For example, the commencement of development of a tranche may trigger planning obligations and the payment of CIL across the whole of the development area. In addition, the developer and the landowner will need to think about the following:

- Should the developer be permitted to purchase more than one tranche in a single tax year? The landowner needs to be aware that if the developer has the right to purchase two or more tranches in the same tax year this may have adverse tax consequences for him.
- Is it desirable to specify a minimum and/or a maximum size for each tranche?
- If a minimum size is to be specified, should this relate only to land which is developable? In other words, should land required for infrastructure, social housing and other non-profitable uses be excluded?
- Is it desirable to specify a maximum number of tranches?
- How should each tranche be valued? For example, should each tranche be valued separately, or should the valuer should be required to value the development site as a whole and then apportion its value to a particular tranche by comparing the area of the tranche and the area of the development site as a whole? Under the first method the open market value of the tranche is calculated and a proportion of the development costs for the development site as a whole is deducted from that value to the extent that they have not previously been taken into account. Under the second method the open market value of the whole of the development site is ascertained, all of the development costs are deducted from that value and the price for the tranche will be a proportion of the balance. Most developers would probably prefer to value the option land as a whole, to exercise their option in respect of the whole of the option land, and to pay the purchase price for the land in instalments. However, this would need to be provided for in the option agreement. In other words, any deferred payment terms would need to be agreed and set out in the option agreement. A well-advised landowner would not agree to deferred payment terms without obtaining tax advice from a tax specialist (see **10.7**.and **13.11**).
- The shape of a tranche: from the landowner's point of view, a tranche should be regular in shape and the land remaining after the sale of a tranche should be capable of being used for its existing use and capable of being developed.

10.14 THE FORM OF TRANSFER: EASEMENTS AND COVENANTS

The parties to the option agreement will need to agree the form of the transfer of the option land or any tranche to the developer and to attach a draft form of transfer to the agreement or to include in a schedule the provisions that must be included in the transfer.

If the option agreement is to contain tranching provisions, the tranche transfer will need to reserve easements (such as rights of way, drainage rights and rights to connect to and use services) over the tranche being sold for the benefit of the remainder of the option land. Also, if the landowner owns land adjoining the option land then easements may need to be granted over the option land in favour of the landowner's retained/adjoining land. Sometimes the landowner will require the developer to be under an obligation to bring roads and services to the boundary of the landowner's adjoining/retained land. The developer will not be able to do this without obtaining all necessary technical approvals and planning permission, and, as mentioned at **7.4**, the developer should not agree to be bound by a covenant which requires it to construct an access road to the boundary with the landowner's retained land. Instead, the developer should grant the landowner a right to use the estate roads constructed by the developer and a right of way over a specified area linking the estate roads and the retained land (see **7.4.1** and **Appendix C1**; also see **Appendix E3** on the CD-ROM).

In addition to reserving rights for the benefit of unsold tranches and any other retained land, the tranche transfer will need to impose various infrastructure and planning obligations on the developer (see **7.4.1** and **13.10**) and the developer may require rights to be granted over the retained land (but note **7.4.2**).

10.15 PRICE NOTICES

It will usually be a term of a developer's call option agreement that following receipt of a satisfactory planning permission the developer may serve on the landowner a notice at any time during the option period (and on as many occasions as the developer may wish) requiring the purchase price for the option land to be agreed or determined. (From the developer's point of view, it is obviously preferable to know the purchase price before exercising the option.) However, the landowner may want the agreement to stipulate that the price notice must be served within a specified period after the grant of a satisfactory planning permission (e.g. at any time within six months after the grant of satisfactory planning permission) for it to be valid; and, if the option is to be capable of being exercised in phases/tranches, the landowner may also want the agreement to stipulate that a second price notice must be served within a specified period after the service of the first price notice (e.g. within 24 months of the date of the first price notice) and that each subsequent price notice must be served within a specified period after the service of the previous price notice. The majority of developers will probably not find any reason to object to these time constraints, although they may wish to consider inserting an additional clause in the agreement to the effect that the time periods will not apply unless and until the satisfactory planning permission becomes immune from all planning challenges and capable of immediate and lawful implementation. If this is acceptable to the landowner then, as previously mentioned in relation to contracts conditional on planning, the expression 'capable of immediate and lawful implementation' will need to be clearly defined. Also, a developer may not wish to agree to any time constraints on serving price notices where there is to be a minimum purchase price or where the proposed development area includes adjoining land belonging to other landowners with whom the developer will need to agree a purchase price (see **10.16**).

From the landowner's point of view, the developer should not be permitted to serve a price notice until after a satisfactory planning permission has been granted.

Also, the landowner's lawyer may wish to try to include a clause in the option agreement stating that the price notice must include the developer's opinion of the price and appropriate evidence as to how that figure has been calculated.

10.16 EXERCISE NOTICES

Where the developer will require the ability to exercise the option in tranches the option agreement should allow the developer to serve any number of price and exercise notices.

From the landowner's point of view, the developer should not be entitled to serve an exercise notice before a satisfactory planning permission has been granted and, following the service of a price notice, a purchase price has been agreed for the land referred to in the price notice.

There are a number of additional points which a landowner will need to consider in relation to exercise notices:

- Should the developer be obliged to serve an exercise notice within a specified period following agreement or determination of the purchase price of the option land? This would make sense from the landowner's point of view and the landowner may wish to consider including a clause in the option agreement stating that to be valid not only must an exercise notice relate to the same part of the option land as is comprised in the associated price notice, but it must also be served within two months of the purchase price being agreed or determined. However, the developer may not be willing to agree to this if the proposed development area includes the land belonging to the landowner and adjoining or neighbouring land belonging to other landowners and the purchase price for the option land is to be calculated using an equalisation formula (see **10.8**). In such circumstances, the developer may not be prepared to serve an exercise notice on the landowner until after it has served a price notice on the other landowners and agreed a purchase price with them.
- Should the option lapse if the developer fails to comply with this requirement?
- Should the developer be precluded from serving an exercise notice if less than, say, 50 per cent of the land belonging to the landowner benefits from the satisfactory planning permission?
- Should the developer be precluded from serving a price notice and an exercise notice if less than, say, 50 per cent of the land belonging to the landowner that is comprised within the satisfactory planning permission is net developable land?
- Should the developer be required to pay a deposit on exercising the option? If a deposit is to be paid, the developer will want to ensure that time is not of the essence in relation to the making of such payment. The developer will often refuse to pay a deposit, particularly if it has paid a substantial option fee. Sometimes the parties will compromise and agree a 'reduced' deposit of 5 per cent of the purchase price. The deposit will usually be paid to the landowner's solicitor as stakeholder. However, if the deposit is paid to the landowner's

solicitor as agent for the landowner and the transaction is standard-rated (e.g. because the landowner has opted to tax), value added tax (VAT) will be payable on the deposit. If the landowner has not opted to tax but intends to do so before completion of any sale of the option land, he should not require the deposit to be paid to his solicitor as agent. The reason for this is that if the deposit is paid to the landowner's solicitor as agent and the landowner has not yet opted to tax, he will have made an exempt supply on receipt on the deposit and consent may then be required from HM Revenue & Customs if he wants to opt to tax before completion.

- If the option agreement contains tranching provisions and the developer exercises its option in respect of part of the option land, should the developer be forced to buy the remainder of the option land (by means of a put-option in favour of the landowner)? This would ensure that all liability under a planning agreement and all liability for CIL passes to the developer.

Where the option agreement specifies a minimum purchase price and there is a requirement for an exercise notice to be served within a specified period of the purchase price being agreed or determined, it should be made clear that the option agreement will not come to an end if the developer fails to serve an exercise notice where the agreed or determined purchase price is below the minimum purchase price. In other words, the requirement to serve an exercise notice within a specified period of the purchase price being agreed or determined should not apply unless the purchase price equals or exceeds the minimum purchase price or the parties agree otherwise. The parties could agree that if the purchase price, as agreed between the parties or determined by an independent valuer, is less than the minimum purchase price then the developer will be entitled to elect to serve an exercise notice if either:

- the landowner serves a notice on the developer stating that he is willing to accept the lower price; or
- the developer serves a notice on the landowner stating that it is willing to pay the minimum purchase price on the basis that the overpayment may be deducted from the purchase price payable on the sale of the next tranche or a subsequent tranche.

The parties could also agree to extend the option agreement for a specified period or for a period commencing on the date on which the purchase price was agreed or determined following the service of the price notice and expiring three months after the date on which it is agreed or determined that the purchase price equals or exceeds the minimum price (whichever is the earlier) and that if during the extension period it is agreed or determined that the purchase price equals or exceeds the minimum price then the developer will be entitled to exercise the option and if it fails to do so the option will lapse.

When exercising the option, the developer will need to take care to comply with the requirements of the option agreement and its notice provisions and, if there is more than one landowner, it will be necessary to serve an exercise notice on each individual landowner.[1]

10.17 TERMINATION

From the landowner's point of view, the option agreement should contain a clause which allows the landowner to terminate the agreement in the event of the developer becoming insolvent or in the event of the developer committing a fundamental breach of a material obligation and that breach not being remedied within a specified period. Most developers, having paid an option fee and incurred substantial planning costs, will be reluctant to agree to the landowner having a right to terminate the agreement, except perhaps in the case of the developer's insolvency.

10.18 DEALING

From the developer's point of view, there should be an absolute prohibition against dealing, but, if this cannot be agreed, the landowner should not be permitted to transfer or charge the whole or any part of the option land, unless the transferee/chargee covenants with the developer that the transferee/chargee will observe and perform all of the obligations on the part of the landowner contained in the option agreement.

The landowner should also be prohibited from creating any tenancy which cannot be brought to an end by the landowner prior to completion of the sale and purchase of the option land and from granting any easements or entering into any statutory agreements or telecommunications agreements without the approval of the developer.

The developer should also consider whether there should be an absolute prohibition against any sale or disposal of the option land by the landowner to another property developer or strategic land promoter and whether the developer should have a right of pre-emption or first refusal to buy in the event of the landowner wishing to dispose of the option land or any part of it. For the reasons mentioned in **11.13**, most landowners will probably want to resist granting the developer a right of pre-emption.

Where the option land is subject to an existing agricultural tenancy the developer will need to consider whether it is a farm business tenancy or an Agricultural Holdings Act tenancy (see **8.4**) and the parties will need to consider the effect of the tenancy on the requirement for vacant possession to be given on completion.

Where the option land is subject to an existing charge or mortgage it will be necessary for the landowner to obtain the consent of the existing chargee/mortgagee to the option agreement (see **10.23**). Ideally, the existing chargee/mortgagee should

---

1 See Law of Property Act 1925, s.61(c) and *Hollies Stores Limited* v. *Timms* [1921] 2 Ch 202 (Ch D).

be required to enter into a deed of adherence with the developer (see **Appendix C10** for an example of a deed of adherence).

Any restrictions on dealing imposed on the landowner should be protected by the registration of a restriction on the landowner's title and the option agreement should include a requirement for a restriction against dealing to be entered on the landowner's title.

10.19 TAX FREEZER

A landowner will sometimes require a tax freezer clause to be inserted in the option agreement. Under a standard tax freezer clause, a landowner is entitled to delay/suspend a sale of the option land for a specified period if at the time of the disposal the capital gains tax rate exceeds a certain fixed percentage (usually 59 per cent or 60 per cent). From the developer's point of view, a tax freezer clause should be strongly resisted and, if the developer has no alternative other than to agree to such a clause, any period of suspension should not exceed 18–24 months (in order to ensure that it is possible to implement the satisfactory planning permission before it lapses).

10.20 MORE THAN ONE OWNER

Where a development site is owned by a number of different landowners the developer will need to consider whether there should be a single option agreement to which each landowner is a party or whether it would be better to have a separate agreement with each landowner. It will also be necessary to consider how the purchase price is to be calculated. For example, should each individual landowner receive a sum based on the open market value of his land or should the equalisation principles discussed in **10.10** apply, with the development site being valued as a whole and each individual landowner receiving a proportion of the open market value of the whole of the development site? Should a landowner be entitled to receive a proportion of any payment due under the option agreement if his land is not included within a satisfactory planning permission or if his land is not included within the land which is the subject of an exercise notice? These are some of the questions which will need to be considered and it may be necessary or desirable for the various landowners to enter into a separate landowner's collaboration agreement which deals, among other things, with how the option fee and the purchase price should be apportioned between them and how any disputes should be resolved. However, before entering into any collaboration agreement, the landowners should seek tax advice and be made aware of the potential tax issues for landowners who wish to share sale proceeds (see **Chapter 16**).

10.21 PLANNING CHALLENGES

As already mentioned, a planning permission may be challenged after it has been granted. The developer will, therefore, need to ensure that, following the grant of planning permission and the exercise of the option, it will not be obliged to complete the purchase of the option land if there is a planning challenge, unless and until planning permission is subsequently quashed, modified or invalidated. One way of achieving this is to ensure that there is no requirement for the developer to exercise the option within the period of two months following the grant of a satisfactory planning permission. Another way is to provide for completion to take place two months and 10 working days following the service of an exercise notice and to include a clause in the option agreement stating that the period of two months and 10 working days is to be suspended if there is a legal challenge and proceedings are commenced prior to completion, and that this time period will only continue running once the proceedings have been finally determined and the satisfactory planning permission upheld. A third way of avoiding the planning challenge issue is to define satisfactory planning permission as a planning permission which is immune from planning challenges (see **10.6**).

10.22 PROTECTION OF OPTION

It is essential that, having secured the option, the developer protects the option by registration. An option creates an equitable interest in land and to ensure its enforceability against subsequent owners it must be registered (in the case of unregistered land) as a C(iv) land charge against the name of the landowner using Land Registry form K1 or (in the case of registered land) protected by entry on the landowner's title of a notice and/or a restriction. The notice may be an agreed notice or a unilateral notice. (See Land Registry Practice Guidance 19 for further information about registering an agreed or unilateral notice and Land Registry Practice Guide 63 for further information about registering land charges.)

In the case of registered land, the best way of protecting the option is to register an agreed or unilateral notice of the agreement on the landowner's title using form AN1 together with a restriction against dealing. An agreed notice will require the applicant to be the registered proprietor or the registered proprietor to consent to the entry of the notice. It is worth noting, however, that if a note of the option agreement is entered on the landowner's title by agreement then a copy of the option agreement will need to be lodged at the Land Registry. This will mean that the option agreement will be available for public inspection (which, for reasons of confidentiality, may not be desirable), although it may be possible to apply to the Land Registry using forms EX1 and EX1A to have the option agreement designated as an 'exempt information document' and to delete commercially sensitive information from the agreement (i.e. lodge an edited version of the option agreement) (see Land Registration Rules 2003 (SI 2003/1417), rule 136).

The developer's lawyer should ensure that the option agreement contains a clause stating that the landowner consents to the registration of a notice of the agreement in the charges register of the title to the option land. The landowner's lawyer, on the other hand, should ensure that the option agreement imposes an obligation on the developer to cancel any such notice and any restriction against dealing entered on the landowner's title within a specified period of the option agreement coming to an end. In addition, the landowner should be entitled to apply to the Land Registry as the agent of the developer to cancel any notice or restriction entered on his title if the developer is in default of its obligation to remove the restriction when the option expires.

10.23 MORTGAGEE'S CONSENT

It is also essential that the developer remembers to obtain an existing mortgagee's consent to the grant of the option. An option granted prior to a mortgage will be binding on a mortgagee and any purchaser from him provided that the option has been protected by registration (Law of Property Act (LPA) 1925, s.104(1)). However, where the option is granted after the creation of the mortgage, the option will not be binding on the mortgagee. In these circumstances, a transfer or conveyance by the mortgagee in exercise of its statutory power of sale will override the option (and this will be the case even if the option has been protected by registration). For this reason, the developer should require all existing mortgagees to enter into a separate deed of adherence with the developer containing the following covenants:

- that if the mortgagee shall take possession of the option land or exercise its power of sale or any other remedies available to it, it will comply with all the obligations on the part of the landowner contained in the option agreement;
- that if the mortgagee shall sell the option land, it will procure that the buyer enters into a suitable deed of covenant with the developer;
- that the mortgagee will not exercise its statutory or any other powers or remedies in a manner which is inconsistent with the terms of the option agreement; and
- that the mortgagee will enter into a planning agreement or infrastructure agreement upon request by the developer.

At the very least an existing mortgagee should be required to provide its consent to the landowner entering into the option agreement. However, the developer should be made aware that an existing mortgagee who has not entered into a deed of adherence will not be obliged to enter into any planning agreement required as a prerequisite to the grant of a planning application.

10.24 ASSIGNMENT

The parties to the option agreement will need to consider whether the developer should be allowed to assign the benefit of the agreement to another developer or whether it should be personal to the developer.

As a general rule, in the absence of a contra indication, the benefit of an option to buy land is freely assignable. However, to vest the benefit of an option in an assignee at law, notice of assignment must be given to the grantor (LPA 1925, s.136(1)).

10.25 OVERAGE

Having purchased the option land the developer may decide to apply for planning permission to build dwellings on open space land or on other land not authorised to be built on by the satisfactory planning permission or to submit a new or revised planning permission which enhances the value of the option land. From the landowner's point of view, it would seem sensible, therefore, to include overage provisions in the option agreement requiring the developer to pay overage if it obtains a new or revised or further planning permission which enhances the value of the option land (even if the developer is under an obligation to maximise the value of the option land). In addition to planning overage, the landowner may wish to consider including sales overage provisions in the option agreement (see **Chapter 12**).

10.26 GUARANTOR

Where the developer is a newly formed company or a company with very few assets the landowner should consider requiring a parent company or another company in the same group as the developer to guarantee the obligations of the developer under the option agreement and also to guarantee the performance and observance of the obligations on the part of the developer contained in the transfer of the option land to it.

10.27 PUT OPTIONS

A put option is a right for a landowner to require another party to purchase his land. A developer will not usually wish to be placed in a position where it is forced to buy land if the landowner so decides. However, a developer may be prepared to enter into a put option as part of some larger scheme. For example, in order to minimise his capital gains tax liability, a landowner may prefer to enter into a series of put and call options with a developer (rather than selling the whole of the site in one go).

10.28 AN OPTION FOR AN EASEMENT

It is not possible for anyone to acquire an easement benefiting land which he does not own. However, if a party wishes to acquire an easement benefiting land which he thinks he may own in the future then this can be achieved by the owner of the servient land granting that party an option to call for an easement in the future (see **Appendix E5** on the CD-ROM).

The following points should be noted in relation to an option to call for an easement:

- An option to call for an easement qualifies as an interest in land.
- An option to call for an easement for the benefit of land which is to be identified in the future will not create a proprietary interest and will not be binding on the successor in title of the grantor if the successor acquires the servient land before the dominant land is identified.
- An option to call for an easement for the benefit of an area of land within an identified larger area will create an equitable interest binding the whole of the larger area until the smaller area is identified.[2]

10.29 STAMP DUTY LAND TAX

Stamp duty land tax (SDLT) is charged on land transactions at *ad valorem* rates, and, depending on the amount of the option fee, the grant of an option may attract a charge to SDLT. As already mentioned, the exercise of the option will give rise to a separate charge to SDLT and the grant and the exercise of an option may be treated as linked transactions (see **7.3.3**).

The grant of an option for consideration is a notifiable land transaction and must be reported to HM Revenue & Customs within 30 days. However, if no consideration is given for the option then there will be no need to notify HM Revenue & Customs.

Where the developer is to have the right to extend the option period by paying the landowner a further option fee, the further option fee may be regarded as contingent consideration and result in SDLT being chargeable on the grant of the option on both the option fee and the further option fee, unless the developer successfully applies to HM Revenue & Customs to defer the payment of SDLT on the further option fee.

10.30 VALUE ADDED TAX

The grant of an option for consideration may also attract VAT. For example, if the landowner has elected to waive exemption from VAT (also known as opting to tax)

[2] See J Gaunt and P Morgan *Gale on the Law of Easements* (20th edition, Sweet & Maxwell, 2017), para.2.35.

in respect of the option land then VAT will be payable on any option fee and, following the exercise of the option, on the purchase price. If the landowner has not 'opted to tax' then the developer's lawyer may wish to include a clause in the option agreement stating that the landowner undertakes not to exercise the right to waive exemption from VAT and (save where VAT must be charged under statute) the purchase price shall be free from VAT. (The advantages to the developer of the landowner not opting to tax are that not only will VAT not be payable on the purchase price, but the liability to pay SDLT will be reduced.) However, the landowner should not agree to such a clause without obtaining tax advice. There may be good tax reasons as to why the landowner needs to opt to tax before completion of the sale of the option land to the developer.

10.31 CAPITAL GAINS TAX

For capital gains tax purposes, the date of the disposal will be the date on which the option is exercised (Taxation of Chargeable Gains Act 1992, s.28(2)) (see **9.22**).

10.32 ADVANTAGES

Options have the following advantages:

- They secure for the developer the right to purchase land without any obligation to buy the land: usually the developer will not be obliged to purchase the option land even if a satisfactory planning permission is granted (this is the main difference between options and conditional contracts).
- They are particularly useful in the context of strategic land buying where land has not been identified for development in a development plan document or a neighbourhood development plan but the developer considers that the land has a reasonable prospect of being allocated or released for development in the future.
- They are useful in the context of site assembly where a proposed development involves piecing together various parcels of land in different ownerships.
- They usually entitle the developer to buy land at a discounted price where the value of the land has not been market tested.

10.33 DISADVANTAGES

Options have the following disadvantages:

- They often involve much negotiation and can take considerable time and effort to complete.

- They are speculative and often involve the developer in paying a substantial non-refundable option fee (which will be lost if the option is not exercised) and incurring substantial planning and other costs, including legal fees and agent's fees.
- In the event of the developer obtaining planning permission and serving a price notice on the landowner, it will be necessary for the developer and the landowner to agree a purchase price for the option land. The landowner will be at a serious disadvantage at this point in that the developer will have considerably more experience and expertise than the landowner in purchase price negotiations. This is one of the reasons why minimum purchase price provisions and the other protective provisions mentioned above are so important for the landowner. It also explains why landowners and their agents tend to prefer promotion agreements to option agreements. If, instead of entering into an option agreement, the developer and the landowner were to enter into a promotion agreement, their interests would probably be more aligned.

CHAPTER 11

Pre-emption agreements

11.1 WHAT IS A PRE-EMPTION AGREEMENT?

A right of pre-emption is sometimes referred to as a right of first refusal to buy. In a pre-emption agreement the landowner agrees not to dispose of his land within a certain period without giving the grantee the opportunity to buy in preference to anybody else. Unlike an option, a right of pre-emption imposes no duty on the landowner to sell his land; he may sell or not as he pleases and, if he decides to sell, the grantee will be in the position of a preferred purchaser.

11.2 LEGAL STATUS

The legal status of a pre-emption agreement is not entirely clear. Does it give rise to a personal obligation/a personal contract which will be binding only on the grantor or does it create an interest in land which will be binding on the grantor's successors in title? The answer to this question has implications for issues such as the protection of the right of pre-emption and whether the Law of Property (Miscellaneous Provisions) Act 1989, s.2 applies to the right. The Court of Appeal held in *Pritchard* v. *Briggs* [1980] Ch 338 (CA) that a right of pre-emption did not create an interest in land. This decision has been much criticised and generated considerable uncertainty about the status of rights of pre-emption, but it has not yet been overruled by the Supreme Court. The Land Registration Act 2002 has helped to remove some of the uncertainty but it is relevant only in relation to rights of pre-emption created over registered land. Under the Land Registration Act 2002 a right of pre-emption created over registered land on or after 13 October 2003 will, like an option, give rise to an interest in land which will be capable of binding successors in title of the grantor (s.115). Accordingly, whether a right of pre-emption will create a personal obligation or an interest in land will depend upon the date of its creation and whether or not it relates to registered or unregistered land: if the right of pre-emption relates to unregistered land then, in the light of the decision in *Pritchard* v. *Briggs*, it will give rise to a personal contract; but if it relates to registered land and was created on or after 13 October 2003 then it will give rise to an interest in land.

11.3 KEY ISSUES

Before entering into a pre-emption agreement the parties should consider a number of key issues, including:

- the price to be paid for the land;
- the formalities which will need to be complied with in order to create a valid right of pre-emption;
- the triggering of the right of pre-emption;
- the exercise of the right;
- the consequences of not exercising the right;
- the duration of the right;
- whether the burden of the right is to be binding on the grantor's estate;
- whether the benefit of the right is to be assignable;
- protecting the right.

11.4 PRICE

The price for the pre-emption property will need to be specified. It may be a fixed sum or the open market value of the property or the price at which the landowner is prepared to sell or a sum equal to the price offered by a third party on a bona fide arm's length basis. Whatever purchase price is specified the agreement should contain a dispute resolution clause. If the purchase price is the open market value of the property then in default of agreement between the parties it will need to be determined by an independent valuer; or it may be necessary for an arbitrator to determine whether an offer made by a third party is genuine (and not a device set up by the landowner to frustrate the right of pre-emption).

11.5 FORMALITIES

Under the Law of Property (Miscellaneous Provisions) Act 1989, s.2 a contract for the sale or other disposition of an interest in land must be in writing, contain all the terms agreed between the parties and be signed by or on behalf of the parties. Accordingly, if the right of pre-emption was created on or after 13 October 2003 and it relates to registered land then, as an interest in land, it will need to comply with s.2. However, if the decision in *Pritchard* v. *Briggs* is correct, a right of pre-emption over unregistered land or a right of pre-emption over registered land created before 13 October 2003 will not need to comply with s.2. Nevertheless, it would still be prudent to ensure that such a right is contained in a contract which incorporates all agreed terms and which is signed by all relevant parties.

11.6 TRIGGER EVENTS

The pre-emption agreement should specify what will trigger the grantee's entitlement to buy the grantor's property. The parties will need to consider whether the right of pre-emption should be triggered by any disposition which the grantor is proposing to make or only certain dispositions, such as a proposed sale. From the developer's point of view, the right of pre-emption should be in the widest possible terms, i.e. it should be triggered, not only in the case of the landowner wishing to sell his property, but also in the case of the landowner wishing to create a mortgage or charge or grant a lease or option or transfer his land or any part of it and 'whether or not for valuable consideration'. This may be unacceptable to the landowner, but whatever the parties decide the agreement should contain a definition of 'disposition' or 'disposal' which lists the various types of disposals which will trigger the right of pre-emption. The landowner should be aware that if he agrees to the right of pre-emption being triggered by 'a sale or any other disposition' then this may catch a proposed assent by his personal representatives to a beneficiary under his will.

11.7 EXERCISING THE RIGHT

The parties will need to decide upon a mechanism for exercising the right. For example, following the occurrence of a trigger event the grantor could be required to:

- offer to sell his property to the grantee on certain agreed terms which have been specified in the pre-emption agreement (which offer the grantee can either accept or reject); or
- invite the grantee to make an offer to purchase the property on whatever terms the grantee thinks appropriate (which offer the grantor can either accept or reject).

Whatever procedure is agreed the agreement should stipulate that if the grantee wishes to accept an offer made by the grantor or vice versa then notice of acceptance must be served within a specified period.

The parties will also need to think about what should happen if an offer is rejected. For example, if the grantee rejects an offer to sell made by the grantor:

- Should the grantor be free to sell the property to whomsoever he pleases and on any terms?
- Should the grantee be entitled to a second bite of the cherry if the grantor fails to sell to a third party within a specified period of the date on which the grantee rejected the grantor's initial offer?

11.8 THE PRE-EMPTION PERIOD

The pre-emption agreement should refer to a pre-emption period at the end of which the agreement will terminate, and this will be a matter for negotiation between the grantor and the grantee. As mentioned previously (see **4.2.2**), the rule against perpetuities no longer applies to rights of pre-emption, so there is no statutory restriction on the length of the pre-emption period.

11.9 TRANSFER OF BURDEN OF RIGHT ON DEATH

As a matter of contract, the grantor's personal representatives will be bound by the obligations contained in the pre-emption agreement, unless there is an express clause stating that the obligations are personal to the grantor or this can be inferred from the wording of the agreement. The landowner may, therefore, wish to make the obligation to sell his land personal to him and to include a provision to the effect that the right of pre-emption will not be binding on the grantor's personal representatives or successors in title.

11.10 ASSIGNMENT OF BENEFIT OF RIGHT

As a general rule, a right of pre-emption will be assignable, unless there is a clause in the agreement making the right personal to the grantee or the wording of the agreement indicates a contrary intention. Again, the landowner may wish to insert a clause in the agreement to the effect that the grantee will not be entitled to assign the benefit of the agreement to a third party.

As previously mentioned in relation to options, if the right of pre-emption is assignable and the grantee assigns the right to a third party then notice of the assignment will need to be given to the grantor to enable the assignee to enforce the right in his own name (Law of Property Act 1925, s.136).

11.11 PROTECTING THE RIGHT

A right of pre-emption governed by the Land Registration Act 2002 should always be protected by the registration of a notice and/or a restriction on the grantor's title. It should be a term of the pre-emption agreement that the grantor consents to the entry of an agreed notice on his title. Although a unilateral notice may be registered, it is vulnerable to cancellation in certain circumstances.

Protecting a right of pre-emption created over unregistered land is more difficult. A right of pre-emption relating to unregistered land should be registered under the Land Charges Act 1972 as a C(iv) land charge. However, as the authors of *Barnsley's Land Options* point out, this will only provide the grantee with limited protection.[1] For example, it will not be possible to protect the right of pre-emption against a third party who, between the date of creation of the right and the trigger event, acquires rights over the land. If the grant of an option or the creation of a charge will not trigger the right of pre-emption then the option holder or the mortgagee will take free of the right of pre-emption.

In view of the limited protection afforded by a C(iv) land charge, the grantor should be persuaded to make an application for voluntary first registration of his title at the Land Registry and the pre-emption agreement should impose an obligation on the grantor to lodge such an application within a specified period, and to agree to a notice of the right of pre-emption and a restriction against dealing being entered on the registered title.

11.12 ADVANTAGES

A developer who is acquiring land for development may find it useful to enter into a pre-emption agreement with the landowner if the landowner owns adjoining or neighbouring land which he does not want to sell at the present time, particularly if the developer is concerned that the adjoining land might be acquired by another developer in the future. In other words, a pre-emption agreement could be used as a bolt on to another deal.

11.13 DISADVANTAGES

From the landowner's point of view, the creation of a right of pre-emption will have the following disadvantages:

- It must be doubtful whether any third party will seriously consider purchasing land which he knows is subject to a right of pre-emption in favour of another party. In other words, there must be a probability that the landowner is sterilising his land during the pre-emption period.
- Even if a third party does make an offer to purchase the land that transaction must be put on hold whilst the pre-emption mechanism is activated. The landowner therefore runs the risk that the developer with the right of pre-emption decides not to proceed and the third party loses interest in the meantime and withdraws.

[1] M Dray, A Rosenthal and C Groves *Barnsley's Land Options* (4th edition, Sweet & Maxwell, 2004), pp.223–5.

CHAPTER 12

Overage agreements

Overage agreements are becoming more and more common in the context of development work. They can be complex and there are a number of key issues which will need to be considered if mistakes and negligence actions are to be avoided.

12.1 WHAT IS OVERAGE?

In short, overage refers to the right for a landowner to receive further payments if, and when, certain events occur, such as the grant of planning permission.

A typical example of overage (or clawback or uplift as it is also sometimes called) is where a farmer agrees to sell land to a developer for its agricultural value with the right reserved for the farmer to receive an additional sum or top-up payment in the event of the developer subsequently obtaining planning permission which enhances the value of the land. This is called planning overage (see **Appendix E6** on the CD-ROM). Another example of planning overage is where a developer buys land that benefits from an existing planning permission for a fixed sum and agrees to pay the seller an additional sum if, following completion of the sale, the developer obtains a new or revised planning permission which has the effect of increasing the gross internal floor area of the dwellings permitted to be constructed under the original planning permission or the developer obtains a further planning permission which permits the construction of dwellings or other buildings on any part of the land sold on which such construction was not permitted by the original planning permission.

An example of a different kind of overage is where a developer buys land for a fixed sum and agrees to pay the landowner an additional sum if, following the grant of planning permission for residential development, the sales revenue generated by the sales of completed dwellings or completed open market dwellings exceeds a certain threshold sum. This type of overage is called sales overage (see **Appendices E7** and **E8** on the CD-ROM). Where sales overage is to be paid, the developer will usually want to exclude all revenue generated by the sales of affordable housing dwellings when calculating the sales revenue and to deduct the cost of incentives paid to buyers from the overage payment.

Other examples of overage include profit overage and development overage. Profit overage is relevant where a purchaser sells on a property for a quick profit within a short period after acquiring the property. It is a mechanism for avoiding a potential embarrassment where a vendor sells his property for below its best price. Development overage is similar to planning overage except that it is triggered, not by the enhanced value created by the grant of planning permission, but by the enhanced value of a site following practical completion of a development on it.

12.2 WHY ENTER INTO AN OVERAGE AGREEMENT?

From a developer's point of view, one advantage of entering into a planning overage agreement is that it enables the developer to purchase land which has the potential for development without any real risk. There is no risk in the sense that the developer will pay a price for the land based on its current use value. In difficult market conditions, this may be particularly attractive for a developer. For the landowner, the advantage of entering into a planning overage agreement is that he is able to sell his land for a fixed sum based on its current use value and at the same time retain a proportion of its 'hope' value.

Sometimes a landowner may be reluctant to sell his land for its current use value if he believes that planning permission may be granted in the foreseeable future which will enhance its value. If the developer offers to pay the landowner overage then this may be the incentive which the landowner needs to sell the land, but the overage payment will need to be properly protected (see **12.10**).

12.3 OVERAGE PAYMENTS

The overage payment may be:

- a fixed sum;
- a percentage of the enhanced value of the land following the grant of planning permission;
- a percentage of the amount by which the total net sales revenue exceeds the anticipated sales revenue (which may, for example, be a fixed amount or an amount calculated by multiplying the total net area (in square feet) of all open market dwellings by a specified price per square foot or an amount to be calculated by reference to the number of dwellings permitted to be erected by a planning permission and the values of different house types);
- a percentage of the amount by which the sale price of a completed unit exceeds a specified price per square foot/metre;
- a sum equal to the difference between the gross internal floor area in square feet of the dwellings permitted to be constructed on the land under an existing planning permission and the gross internal floor area in square feet of the

dwellings permitted to be constructed on the land following the grant of a new or amended planning permission multiplied by a specified price per square foot.

For example, the overage payment may be a percentage of the difference between the agricultural value of the land (which might have been the original purchase price) and its value with the benefit of planning permission for residential and/or industrial development.

A developer will sometimes require inflation to be factored into the overage calculation. (For example, if the overage is a percentage of the difference between the original purchase price and the value of the land with the benefit of planning permission or if profit overage is payable, the developer may want the original purchase price to be index linked.) The developer may also require certain costs to be deducted from the overage payment (or to be taken into account when calculating the market value of the overage land), such as:

- planning costs (i.e. costs incurred by the developer in obtaining planning permission including the cost of consultants and planning application and other statutory fees);
- planning gain costs payable under a planning agreement;
- the Community Infrastructure Levy or any other tax or levy which is required to be paid by statute on the grant of planning permission or the commencement of development or any tax or levy payable to a local planning authority under a planning agreement, such as a supplementary planning gain tax, or a roof tax;
- incentives paid to buyers of completed dwellings. This will apply only if the overage payment is to be based on the sales revenue received by the developer (the landowner will often require the cost of incentives to be capped);
- the cost of any extras ordered by the buyer. The landowner should not agree to the cost of extras being deducted when the overage payment is calculated. The cost of extras is not a cost that is incurred by the developer. It represents the amount paid by a plot purchaser for items not included in the standard specification of the house builder and should be ignored for the purposes of calculating overage;
- the cost to the developer of acquiring and selling a part exchange property and any losses suffered by the developer in respect of part exchange properties (e.g. where the developer sells a part exchange property for less than the price which the developer paid for it);
- development costs (if the overage payment is to be calculated by reference to a formula which requires the deduction of development costs then development costs should not be deducted or taken into account in calculating the market value of the overage land, since this could result in a double deduction of the development costs);
- the cost of acquiring additional land or easements to facilitate access to the site and/or the provision of services;

- build cost inflation (i.e. any increase in building costs between the date of the overage agreement and the date of the grant or implementation of the relevant planning permission). An index often used to measure build cost inflation is the Building Cost Information Service (BCIS) General Building Cost Index published by the Royal Institution of Chartered Surveyors; and
- stamp duty land tax payable on the overage sum.

If the overage is to be calculated by reference to a formula, the formula will need to be checked very carefully to ensure that it produces the result intended. Two formulae which appear similar can produce very different results! It may therefore be sensible to include a preamble or statement of intent and/or a working example to illustrate how the overage should be calculated. The case of *George Wimpey UK Limited* v. *VI Construction Limited* [2005] EWCA Civ 77 highlights the need to check an overage formula very carefully and to have a clear understanding of how the formula will work. In this case, the formula was so complex that no one noticed that part of the formula had been missed out of the final agreement.

Where there is a possibility that the overage land may be the subject of a number of planning permissions (because, for example, the development is to be carried out in phases) giving rise to a number of separate overage payments, the landowner will want to ensure that any sums which are to be deducted in calculating the overage (such as the original purchase price for the overage land and development costs) are not deducted more than once (i.e. that there is no double deduction of costs) and the developer will want to ensure that it receives credit for any sums previously paid towards overage.

Where the overage land forms part of a larger development site and overage will become payable following the grant of planning permission relating to the entire site, it will be necessary to consider how the enhanced value should be apportioned between the two sites. For example, should it be apportioned on a pro rata acreage basis and should any deductions (such as the cost of acquiring additional land or any land required as an access) be made?

12.4 EXAMPLES OF OVERAGE FORMULAE

The following are some examples of overage formulae:

Example 1: planning overage

[(A – B) – C] × [ ]%

Where:

A = the Market Value of the Planning Land

B = the Base Value

C = Planning Costs

(See **Appendix E6** on the CD-ROM for definitions of 'market value', 'planning land', 'base value' and 'planning costs'.)

The formula in Example 1 is suitable where it is intended that overage should be paid on the grant of each and every planning permission during the overage period. The overage payment will be a proportion of the difference between the value of the overage land benefiting from a planning permission and the value of that land immediately before the grant of the relevant planning permission (i.e. the base value). The base value on the first payment of overage following the first grant of planning permission which enhances the value of the overage land will be the original purchase price for the overage land or (if the planning permission relates only to part of the overage land) a pro rata proportion thereof. On each occasion that a planning permission is granted the base value will need to be adjusted. If a subsequent planning permission relates to the same land as a previous planning permission then the base value will be the open market value of that land with the benefit of the immediately preceding planning permission; and if the subsequent planning permission relates to part of the land which has been the subject of a previous planning permission and land in respect of which no planning permission has been granted then the base value of the relevant land will be a pro rata proportion of the open market value of the land with the benefit of the previous planning permission plus a pro rata proportion of the original base value.

Example 2: planning overage

[(A – B) – C] × [ ]%

Where:

A = Enhanced Value (i.e. the Market Value of the Development Land as at the date of, and with the benefit of, the relevant Planning Permission, assuming that the Development Land has the benefit of any easements, wayleaves, sight-line covenants and other agreements necessary to provide access, visibility splays or services to or from the Development Land)

B = Base Value (i.e. the Market Value of the Development Land immediately prior to the grant of the relevant Planning Permission with no expectation of the grant of the relevant Planning Permission)

C = Planning Costs (i.e. the costs incurred by the Buyer in obtaining a Planning Permission including (but not limited to) the cost of external advisers and consultants and planning application and other statutory fees)

Development Land means such part or parts of the Property in respect of which Planning Permission is granted during the Overage Period.

Planning Permission means outline or detailed planning permission for Development.

Development means development of the whole or any part or parts of the Property, with or without other land that increases the area of Development Land within the Property or which by material change of use increases the value of the Property.

The formula in Example 2 may also be used where it is intended that overage should be paid on the grant of each and every planning permission during the overage period.

Example 3: sales overage (unit by unit basis)

[ ]% × (A – (B × C))

Where:

A = the Net Sale Proceeds for a relevant Market Unit

B = [insert the base price figure per square feet]

C = the Gross Internal Area in square feet of the relevant Completed Market Unit

Net Sale Proceeds means the Sale Proceeds for a Disposal less Incentives.

Sale Proceeds means the gross consideration passing from a purchaser to the Developer for a Completed Market Unit on each Disposal including the value of any non-monetary consideration and aggregating sums payable under separate contracts for land and buildings and including a premium paid on the grant of a lease.

Incentives means (a) the cost to the Developer of any carpets, curtains, soft furnishings or white goods or any other incentives that it provides to a purchaser on a Disposal of a Market Unit including (but not by way of limitation) the payment of a purchaser's legal fees, survey fee, stamp duty land tax (SDLT) and estate agent's commission on the sale of a purchaser's property and (b) the price received by the Developer for the supply of customer extras to a purchaser of a Market Unit.

(See **Appendix E7** on the CD-ROM for definitions of 'market unit', 'completed market unit', 'disposal' and 'gross internal area'.)

Example 4: sales overage

[ ]% × (A – B)

Where:

A = the Total Sales Proceeds (i.e. the total of the Sales Proceeds for all Dwellings less all Sales Incentives and the cost of any Extras ordered by a buyer)

B = the Anticipated Sale Proceeds (i.e. the Net Sales Area expressed in square feet multiplied by £[ ])

Sale Proceeds means the aggregate sale price for all of the Dwellings as paid by the first buyers (including the value attributed to any PX Property less PX Costs) together with the Deemed Disposal Value of any Dwelling in respect of which a sale has not yet been completed by the Longstop Date (if applicable).

Net Sales Area means the total amount (in square feet) of net sales area (as defined by the then current RICS Code of Measuring Practice) of all the Open Market Dwellings (but, for the avoidance of doubt, this shall be calculated on the area of the main building at a Dwelling which shall include the area of a conservatory [and a garage] but not the area of a store room, outhouse, [garage] or other ancillary building or area).

Sales Incentives means any proper and normal payment, incentive, contribution or consideration whatsoever made to the purchaser of a Dwelling including (but not by way of limitation) the cost to the Developer of any carpets, curtains, soft furnishings or white goods and the payment of a purchaser's deposit, legal fees, survey fee, stamp duty land tax and estate agent's commission on the sale of a purchaser's property.

Where the overage formula contains a reference to the gross internal floor areas of a dwelling or dwellings, the overage agreement will need to contain a suitable definition of 'gross internal area'. The expression 'gross internal area' is often defined by reference to the Code of Measuring Practice (6th edition) published by the Royal Institution of Chartered Surveyors. Under the 6th edition of the Code of Measuring Practice, the gross floor area of a building includes a garage and a conservatory (but not open vehicle parking areas and greenhouses). The parties to the overage agreement should consider whether areas such as garages and/or conservatories are to be included or excluded in any calculation of the gross internal floor area of a dwelling and the definition of 'gross internal area' should be drafted to reflect the agreement reached between the parties.

12.5 SALES OVERAGE AND AFFORDABLE HOUSING

Where sales overage is to be paid, there are a number of matters that the landowner and the buyer/developer will need to consider, including:

- The timing of the sales overage payment. Should the overage be paid after the sale of the last of the dwellings permitted to be constructed under the relevant planning permission or should the overage be paid every six months or after the sale of each dwelling (i.e. on a plot-by-plot basis)? If the overage is to be paid following the sale of the last of the dwellings to be constructed, which is the mechanism often favoured by developers, there will need to be a longstop date on which any unsold dwellings will be deemed to have been sold for their market value. This will necessitate a valuation of the unsold dwellings as at the longstop date (see **12.6**).
- Whether the revenue generated by the sale of affordable housing dwellings should be included within the sales overage calculation. If it is intended that

only revenue from the sale of open market dwellings should be included in the sales overage calculation, the expression 'market units' will need to be carefully defined and it should expressly exclude affordable housing dwellings.

- Whether, on a sale of part of the land affected by the sales overage obligations, the buyer/developer should be released from those obligations to the extent that they relate to the land being sold. Clearly, there should not be any release unless and until the party buying the land enters into a deed of covenant with the landowner, as the party entitled to the overage (see **12.10.2**). However, the landowner may take the view that, notwithstanding a sale, the original buyer/developer should remain liable for the payment of all overage. Also, covenant strength may be an issue where the party buying the land from the developer is of lesser covenant strength. From the landowner's point of view, the landowner should have the right to approve the covenant strength of the party proposing to buy part of the land affected by the overage obligations from the developer and be entitled to refuse to release the developer from those obligations (to the extent that they relate to the land being sold) unless the covenant strength of the proposed buyer is at least equal to the covenant strength of the developer.
- How on a sale of part should the liability to pay overage be dealt with? Should the developer and the buyer of part from the developer each be responsible for a pro rata proportion (based on gross internal floor areas) of the total sales overage payable (to be calculated once all the dwellings that are to be constructed on both the area of land being sold and the area being retained by the developer have been built)? Alternatively, should the sales revenue threshold sum (i.e. the anticipated sales revenue figure above which overage becomes payable) be apportioned between the two areas of land with each party to pay overage only if the revenue generated by the sale of the dwellings on their land exceeds the apportioned threshold sum? The latter alternative is likely to be favoured by the developer.

12.6 TRIGGER FOR PAYMENT

The trigger for the payment of overage may be any of the following:

- the grant of a planning permission;
- the implementation of a planning permission;
- a disposal with the benefit of a new planning permission;
- the earlier of the implementation of a planning permission and a disposal (other than a specified permitted disposal) with the benefit of a new planning permission;
- (in the case of sales overage) the sale of the last of the dwellings to be constructed pursuant to an existing planning permission or any new or revised planning permission.

If the overage payment is linked to a new planning permission then the landowner will probably want the payment to be triggered as soon as possible, which would be on the grant of the planning permission. From the developer's point of view no overage should be payable until the planning permission is implemented (as opposed to granted) and the planning permission should relate only to an application made by or on behalf of the developer (and not the landowner or any other party). The planning permission may contain conditions which are unacceptable to the developer and it may decide that it does not actually wish to implement the permission, or it may be an outline permission requiring a reserved matters approval to be obtained before development can be commenced.

If the landowner is adamant that the overage payment is to be triggered by the grant of a planning permission (as opposed to its implementation) then the developer could, as a compromise, suggest that the overage should be payable only upon the grant of a planning permission containing no onerous conditions and which is capable of implementation. However, the expression 'capable of implementation' will need to be carefully defined. From a developer's point of view, a planning permission should not be regarded as implementable until all the pre-commencement conditions have been discharged and all necessary third party approvals and reserved matters approvals, easements and infrastructure agreements have been obtained to enable a lawful start on building works on the site. From the landowner's point of view, the developer should be obliged to use reasonable endeavours to discharge all pre-commencement conditions and to obtain all necessary reserved matters approvals as soon as reasonably possible after the grant of the planning permission.

Under no circumstances should overage be payable until all possibility of a planning challenge has passed. The developer should insist that the overage provisions contain a statement to the effect that a planning permission shall not be deemed to have been granted until all possibility of a planning challenge (including a judicial review) has passed, leaving in place a valid planning permission.

Where overage is payable on sales revenues, the landowner should insist on the overage agreement containing deemed disposal provisions stating that if on a specified date there are any unsold dwellings, they shall be deemed to have been sold on that date for their market value. This will prevent the developer from retaining unsold units in order to delay or avoid the payment of overage, but the specified period should be reasonable to allow the developer sufficient time to sell all of the units in the open market. The risk for the developer is that there may be a downturn in market conditions after the overage payment in respect of the unsold units has been paid and it will not be possible to realise the same value for those units as the value used to calculate the overage payment.

It is worth noting that where sales overage is payable on the sale of the last dwelling constructed, a developer will not be able to avoid paying sales overage by not building out all of the dwellings. In *Renewal Leeds Limited* v. *Lowry Properties Limited* [2010] EWHC 2902 (Ch) the buyer/developer was obliged to pay the seller sales overage 20 working days after completion of the final sale of a completed residential unit. The buyer/developer completed a substantial part of the development but left four houses incomplete and unsold. The court, rather surprisingly, held that it was an implied term of the contract that the developer would complete, market and sell the houses as soon as reasonably practicable and that the seller was entitled to specific performance of these implied obligations.

The landowner may also require the overage agreement to contain deemed disposal provisions which would apply in the case of a sale of a unit to a connected party or if the consideration for the disposal is other than cash. In the case of a deemed disposal the unit will be deemed to have been sold for its market value.

Where the trigger for the payment of overage is a disposal of the land or part of the land benefiting from a new planning permission or there is a requirement for a disponee to enter into a deed of covenant with the overage beneficiary (see **12.10.2**), careful consideration will need to be given as to how the expression 'disposal' should be defined. The landowner's lawyer will need to ensure that it is not so narrowly defined that the developer is able to avoid paying overage and it would probably be better for the trigger for the payment of overage to be the earlier of a disposal with the benefit of planning permission or the implementation of a planning permission. The landowner's lawyer should consider expanding the definition of 'disposal' so that it includes not only a freehold transfer (whether or not for valuable consideration), the grant of a lease (whether or not for valuable consideration) and an assent, but also a share sale, a change in the ownership or control of the developer, a building licence, the grant of an option to purchase and a transfer made after the overage period expires where the transfer was made pursuant to a conditional contract or an option agreement entered into during the overage period. The landowner's lawyer may wish to include an additional clause in the overage agreement stating that, notwithstanding the expiration of the overage period, the obligations contained in the overage agreement shall continue to apply in the event of the buyer making a disposal pursuant to a contract of option agreement entered into during the overage period.

Where the trigger for the payment of overage is the implementation of a planning permission, overage should be payable regardless of who implements the planning permission. The trigger should not be limited to implementation 'by the Buyer'.

12.7 FURTHER PLANNING PERMISSIONS

The landowner and the developer will need to consider whether the provisions of the overage agreement should continue to apply after the first grant of planning permission and the payment of overage to the landowner.

The landowner should be aware that the developer could obtain a low value permission, pay overage on it, and then reapply for a more valuable permission. However, the developer will probably not want the landowner to be allowed a second bite at the cherry since this could cause problems on a sale of the development site. A possible compromise might be to provide for the obligation to pay overage to come to an end after a planning permission has been fully implemented and all the overage monies paid to the landowner. Once a planning permission has been fully implemented there is not likely to be much incentive for a developer to apply for a higher value planning permission. But the meaning of 'fully implemented' will need to be carefully defined.

The landowner should also be aware that the developer could initially apply for planning permission to develop part of the site and then at a later date or dates apply for planning permission(s) to develop the rest of the site. From the landowner's point of view, it would seem both reasonable and sensible for the obligation to pay overage to continue until the whole or a substantial part of the site has been developed.

If it is intended that overage should be payable following the grant or implementation of each and every planning permission granted during the overage period then the overage agreement should contain a clause to this effect. The parties should not be left in any doubt about this.

One of the problems with continuing overage obligations (i.e. overage obligations which continue to apply throughout the overage period and even after overage has been paid) is that, in order to protect the overage payment, there is usually a requirement that on a sale (or other disposition) of the land affected by the overage obligations, the seller must procure that the buyer enters into a deed of covenant containing a covenant with the beneficiary of the overage to comply with the overage obligations. This can be a major issue for a developer, unless the requirement for a deed of covenant is dispensed with and does not apply in the case of certain disposals, such as a sale to a plot purchaser (see **12.10.2**). Clearly, a plot purchaser will not want to have to enter into a deed of covenant containing a covenant to pay overage.

12.8 OVERAGE PERIOD

The overage agreement should, except where it relates to sales overage, contain a clause stating that the agreement will terminate after a specified period. The overage period should be long enough to give the landowner a reasonable time to realise the 'hope' value in his land.

The overage period does not have to be a fixed period: for example, the parties to the overage agreement could agree that the overage period will be the period commencing on the date of the agreement and expiring on the earlier of a fixed period (e.g. 30 years after the date of the agreement) and the happening of some event, such as the payment of overage following the first grant of planning permission or the practical completion of a development on a substantial part of the overage land.

In the case of sales overage, the overage agreement should continue until the last of the dwellings permitted to be constructed under the relevant planning permission has been sold and any overage that is due or outstanding has been paid to the overage beneficiary. Accordingly, it is inappropriate to include an overage period in an overage agreement that relates to sales overage. However, as discussed above, there will need to be a longstop date on which there shall be a deemed disposal of any unsold dwellings (see **12.5** and **12.6**).

12.9 RELEASE

The overage agreement should contain a mechanism for releasing the developer from all liability upon the agreement terminating. Ideally, from the developer's point of view, the release should be automatic and should not be dependent upon the landowner signing a deed of release. However, for this mechanism to operate successfully, it will be necessary for the overage agreement to contain a provision whereby the developer's solicitor is authorised by the landowner to instruct the Land Registry to remove any protective entries on the developer's title upon the agreement terminating. If the landowner will not agree to an automatic release then he should be obliged to enter into a deed of release within a specified period (e.g. immediately upon receipt of the overage monies) and if he fails to comply with this obligation then the developer should be entitled to execute the deed of release and to sign a form to cancel any restriction on the title to the overage land as the attorney of the landowner.

On a sale by the developer of part of the land affected by the overage obligations the developer may wish to be released from those obligations to the extent that they related to the part being sold. As discussed above in relation to sales overage, there should be no release until the party buying the land enters into an appropriate deed of covenant with the landowner and, in addition, the landowner may wish to be satisfied as to the covenant strength of the buyer before agreeing to any release (see **12.5**).

Where the payment of overage is to be protected by a deed of covenant and a restriction, the developer is likely to require (unless self-certification applies) that the overage agreement contains a clause stating that in the event of the developer making a permitted disposal the landowner shall hand over a certificate addressed to the Land Registry confirming that the restriction does not apply to the disposal.

12.10 PROTECTING THE OVERAGE PAYMENT

The landowner will need to take steps to ensure that the overage payment is adequately protected since the obligation to pay overage is a positive obligation and will not be binding on future owners of the overage land. By virtue of the privity of contract rule, the obligation to pay overage will continue to be binding on the party who originally covenanted to pay the overage even after that party has parted with his interest in the land affected by the overage obligations, unless that party has been expressly released from the obligations.

The landowner's lawyer should be aware that if he fails to advise the landowner to take steps to protect the landowner's entitlement to overage then he will be negligent (see *Akasuc Enterprise Limited* v. *Farmar and Shirreff* [2003] EWHC 1275 (Ch)).

12.10.1 Legal charge

The landowner may wish to secure the overage payment by taking a first legal charge over the overage land. The difficulty with this is that it may prevent the developer from using the overage land as security, unless the landowner concedes priority to the developer's lender. In addition, a legal charge may not provide the protection required by the landowner. It will be protecting future unknown/ unascertained payments and it would appear that the legal charge could be defeated by a liquidator if the developer became insolvent before the payments were due, i.e. before the occurrence of the trigger date (see *Groveholt Limited* v. *Hughes* [2005] EWCA Civ 897). Also, where sales overage is to be paid on the sale of the last dwelling on a development site, a legal charge will not be appropriate.

If the developer is prepared to enter into a legal charge in favour of the landowner, an obligation should be imposed on the landowner in the legal charge to hand over a deed of release/discharge upon the termination of the overage agreement, subject to all outstanding overage having been paid. The landowner will not want to be obliged to hand over a deed of release/discharge where the obligation to pay overage will continue after the first grant of a planning permission and the payment of overage, although he may be prepared to provide the developer with a deed of release/discharge of part following the grant or implementation of a planning permission to develop part of the overage land (see **12.9**).

Where an overage payment does not become payable until after the sale of the last completed dwelling (as in the case of sales overage) or where the obligation to pay overage will continue after the first grant of planning permission and the payment of overage, an obligation should be imposed on the landowner to hand over a deed of release of part or (in the case of registered land) a deed of discharge of part (form DS3) or consent to dealing on the sale of a completed dwelling and on completion of certain other dealings, such as the sale of affordable housing land or affordable housing dwellings or partially completed affordable housing dwellings to a registered social landlord, the transfer of an electricity substation and the transfer of land to a local authority for roads, open space, etc.

In addition, an obligation should be imposed on the landowner to enter into any infrastructure agreement (such as a road or sewer adoption agreement) or planning agreement upon reasonable request in writing from the developer. This should not be an issue for the landowner, so long as it is made clear that the landowner will only enter into such an agreement in his capacity as mortgagee and without incurring any personal liability and the agreement is to be in a form to be approved by the landowner at the cost of the developer.

12.10.2 Deed of covenant and restriction on title

In order to ensure that the obligation to pay overage will be binding on the developer's successors in title the landowner should:

- impose an obligation on the developer to procure on any transfer or other disposal (including the grant of a lease for a premium and the creation of a charge) that the disponee enters into a deed of covenant containing a direct covenant with the landowner to observe and perform all the obligations contained in the overage agreement;
- require the developer to consent to the registration of a restriction or to apply to the Land Registry for the registration of a restriction on the title to the overage land prohibiting any dealing with the land unless the landowner's solicitor certifies that the requirement for the disponee to enter into a deed of covenant has been complied with; and
- require the developer to provide the landowner with details of the developer's title once it has been registered to enable the landowner to check whether the necessary restriction has been entered on the developer's title.

In addition, the overage agreement should contain a covenant by the developer not to make any disposition unless the requirement for a deed of covenant has been complied with. There will need to be a definition of 'disposition'. Usually, it will include a transfer of the whole or any part of the overage property (whether or not for valuable consideration) by the registered proprietor or by the registered proprietor of any charge and the grant of a lease of the whole or any part of the overage property by the registered proprietor or by the registered proprietor of any charge and an assent. However, the landowner should consider expanding this definition in order to ensure that the terms 'disposition' or 'disposal' are not so narrowly defined that the developer is able to avoid the payment of overage (see **12.6**).

From the developer's point of view, none of the above should be a problem so long as: the restriction against dealing does not apply to the creation of a legal charge; the developer's lawyer (as opposed to the landowner or his lawyer) is able to provide the required certificate; and (where overage will not become payable until after the development has been completed and all the units have been sold or the obligation to pay overage is a continuing obligation (see **12.7**)) the requirement for a deed of covenant does not apply in the case of certain 'excluded disposals' or 'permitted disposals', such as the sale of a completed dwelling to a bona fide purchaser, the transfer of public open space or other land which is to be adopted to a local authority, the sale of affordable housing land or affordable housing dwellings to a private registered provider or other social housing provider, disposals made pursuant to a planning agreement, the creation of a legal charge, a transfer of any land or the grant of a lease required for an electricity sub-station, the grant of a wayleave agreement or a deed of easement to a service supply company or statutory body, etc.

Where the overage agreement contains a definition of 'excluded disposals' or 'permitted disposals' (and the requirement for a disponee to enter into a deed of covenant with the landowner is not to apply in the case of such a disposal) the landowner's lawyer should ensure that:

- the definition of 'excluded disposals' or 'permitted disposals' expressly excludes a disposal to a connected person (as defined in the Income and Corporation Taxes Act 1988, s.839);
- (where the creation of a legal charge or other security is a permitted disposal) the creation of the legal charge or other security will be a permitted disposal only if it is created at arm's length in favour of a genuine financial institution making a loan to the developer and the financial institution enters into a deed of covenant with the original landowner containing, amongst other covenants, a covenant that if it enters into possession or exercises its power of sale or any other remedies available to it, it will be bound by the overage obligations and liable to ensure that on a sale the buyer enters into a deed of covenant with the original landowner;
- where it is intended that permitted disposals should include the transfer of affordable housing, there is no doubt about this – the definition of 'permitted disposals' or 'excluded disposals' should expressly refer to affordable housing. (In *Burrows Investments Limited* v. *Ward Homes Limited* [2017] EWCA Civ 1577 the Court of Appeal had to decide whether a transfer of affordable housing units to a social housing provider was a permitted disposal. The definition of 'permitted disposals' in the overage agreement did not expressly refer to affordable housing units, but the court held that 'a residential disposal' included a disposal of affordable housing units.)

The following points should be noted in relation to restrictions.

The implementation of the Land Registration Act 2002 on 13 October 2003 introduced new requirements for the registration of restrictions.

Schedule 4 to the Land Registration Rules 2003 (SI 2003/1417) provides numerous 'standard form' restrictions that can be applied for, without further fee, in the 'additional provisions' panel in transfer forms TP1/TR1. Any other form of wording applied for after 13 October 2003 will be deemed a non-standard restriction and will attract a fee.

An application for the registration of a non-standard restriction cannot be made in the body of a transfer and must be made in a separate form RX1. In addition, an application for a non-standard restriction must be accompanied by an additional fee for each application.

The Land Registry will ignore any restriction that is applied for within the body of a transfer that is not in the form of a standard restriction, unless a completed form RX1 and fee accompany the application.

Where the registration of a restriction is required on the registration of a lease the application for the restriction must be made in form RX1 and cannot be made in the body of the lease.

No fee will be payable for an application in form RX1 for a standard restriction lodged at the same time as the application to register the lease, but where a later application is made a fee will be payable.

An application in form RX1 for a non-standard restriction will require a fee for each application, whether made at the same time as the registration of the lease or not.

A restriction in the following form (form L) will meet the requirements of the Land Registry:

> No [disposition or specify type of disposition] of the registered estate [(other than a charge)] by the proprietor of the registered estate [or by the proprietor of any registered charge, not being a charge registered before the entry of this restriction] is to be registered without a certificate signed by [a conveyancer] [the applicant for registration [or their conveyancer]] [ ] [or their personal representatives] [or their conveyancer] that the provisions of [specify clause paragraph or other particulars] of [specify details] have been complied with [or that they do not apply to the disposition].

The wording of the restriction will need to be carefully considered by both the developer and the landowner. From the developer's point of view, the restriction against dealing should be limited to transfers and should not apply to the creation of a legal charge (and possibly other types of disposals, such as the sale of a completed dwelling).

Consideration will need to be given to the question of who is to provide the certificate required under the restriction. One of the problems with the landowner giving the certificate is that the landowner may die or become bankrupt/insolvent or difficult to find. The developer will usually want its solicitor to provide the certificate, particularly in circumstances where delays in providing the certificate could prejudice plot sales. The landowner may be prepared to agree to this if it is a requirement under the restriction that the developer's solicitor must acknowledge that he owes a duty of care to the landowner when he provides the certificate, although this will give rise to a non-standard restriction.

A restriction which requires a certificate that the overage monies have been paid will not work where the overage monies do not become payable until after the development has been completed and all of the units have been sold.

If it is agreed that the restriction against dealing should not apply in the case of certain disposals (such as the sale of a completed dwelling or the creation of a legal charge) and that certain disponees should not be required to enter into a deed of covenant with the landowner then the restriction should state that there is to be no disposition by the proprietor of the registered estate without a certificate that the provisions of the clause requiring disponees to enter into a deed of covenant 'have been complied with or do not apply'.

Where the restriction requires the certificate to be provided by the landowner or the landowner's conveyancer, the overage agreement should impose an obligation on the landowner to provide the certificate within a specified period (e.g. within five days of receipt of the duly executed deed of covenant). Ideally (from the developer's point of view at any rate) the overage agreement should contain a clause stating that the developer is entitled to sign the certificate as agent of the landowner if the landowner fails or refuses to provide the certificate within the stipulated time. Also, the landowner should be obliged to cancel the restriction when the overage agreement comes to an end.

The Land Registry will usually enter the restriction which has been placed on the developer's title on the title of a purchaser acquiring part of the site (e.g. a completed dwelling) from the developer (which can cause considerable problems for the purchaser). These problems can be avoided by:

(a) imposing an obligation on the landowner in the overage agreement to provide a form RX3 or a form RX4 on any disposal to a plot purchaser to enable the plot purchaser to cancel/withdraw any restriction entered on the plot purchaser's title; and
(b) including a provision in the overage agreement to the effect that if the landowner fails to provide the required form within a specified period then the developer will be entitled to do so as the attorney of the landowner.

Where the overage provisions are contained in a transfer to the developer it would also be sensible to include model clause 20 in **Appendix D1** in the transfer to the developer.

12.10.3 Restrictive covenants

Another way of protecting the overage payment is for the landowner to require the developer to enter into a restrictive covenant not to use the overage land for any purpose other than the existing use, with the landowner agreeing to enter into a deed of release or modification of the restrictive covenant upon receipt of the overage payment from the developer. However, it would not be prudent for a landowner to rely on a covenant prohibiting development as the sole mechanism for protecting the overage. Subject to the covenant not being a device designed solely to protect the overage payment (see below), it would be binding on the developer's successors in title (since it is restrictive), but for the covenant to be enforceable the landowner will need to retain land which is capable of benefiting from the covenant. The landowner will also need to ensure that if he sells the retained land or any part of it, he retains the benefit of the restrictive covenant and it does not pass to his successors in title. Any transfer of part of the retained land should contain a declaration that the benefit of the restrictive covenant is not intended to pass to the transferee and that it is to remain with and be enforceable only by the transferor. Without such a declaration the landowner would be unable to provide an absolute release of the restrictive covenant upon payment of the overage.

A fundamental issue with using restrictive covenants to protect overage payments is that the mechanism will not be effective if the purpose of the covenant is only to secure the overage payment and the covenant does not confer any other benefit on the retained land. As previously mentioned (see **2.10.2**), a restrictive covenant must 'touch and concern' the covenantee's land (i.e. it must be imposed for the benefit of or to preserve or enhance the value of the covenantee's land). If the sole purpose of the restrictive covenant is to secure an overage payment, the covenant will not be regarded as touching and concerning the covenantee's land and it will not be binding on the successors in title of the original covenantor. This principle was established in *Cosmichome Limited* v. *Southampton City Council* [2013] EWHC 1378 (Ch). In *Bryant Homes Southern Limited* v. *Stein Management Limited* [2016] EWHC 2435 (Ch), another case involving restrictive covenants and overage, the court found that a covenant restricting use genuinely benefited the retained land even though it did also secure an overage payment. The mechanism used to impose the covenant assisted the court with this interpretation and the facts of the case will be important in determining whether the restrictive covenant is a device designed solely for the purpose of protecting an overage payment or not.

Another drawback to relying on restrictive covenants to protect overage payments is that the developer will have the right to apply to the Upper Tribunal for the restrictive covenant to be modified or released under the Law of Property Act 1925, s.84. If the application was to be successful then the Upper Tribunal may award compensation to the landowner, but this would be based on the reduction in value of the landowner's retained land and not the enhanced value of the overage land without the restriction. As mentioned in **2.8.3**, the Court of Appeal in *Winter and another* v. *Traditional & Contemporary Contracts Limited* [2007] EWCA Civ 1088 held that s.84 awards must be based on the effect of the development on the land owned by the beneficiary of the covenant, not on the loss of the opportunity to extract a share of the development value.

12.10.4 Bank bond/security deposit/parent company guarantee

The difficulty with protecting overage which does not become payable until the development has been completed (and all the newly constructed units sold) is that a legal charge over the overage land or a restriction on the title to the overage land will not provide adequate or complete protection (since deeds of release of part and/or consents to dealing will need to be provided as plots are sold off). Another option may be for the developer to offer to provide the landowner with a bank bond, a security deposit or a parent company guarantee. The difficulty with a bank bond is that the liability of the bank under the bond will need to be limited to a specified amount; and the bond will also need to be limited in time. The cost of providing the bond is also likely to be high. Perhaps the best and safest option for the landowner, therefore, is to require the overage to be paid on a plot-by-plot basis.

12.11 PLANNING OBLIGATIONS

The landowner will often require the developer to enter into various planning obligations, such as an obligation to provide the landowner with copies of all planning applications lodged and copies of all planning decisions received by the developer. This should not cause the developer any difficulty. However, the landowner may wish to impose further obligations on the developer, including an obligation to apply for planning permission, an obligation to maximise the development value of the site, an obligation to appeal against a planning refusal and an obligation to implement any planning permission granted within a reasonable timescale. The developer will need to think carefully before agreeing to take on these obligations, and may wish to resist or, at least, qualify the obligations in some way. The developer should be aware that it may want or need to sell the land in the future and that such obligations may be unacceptable to the purchaser and/or the purchaser's mortgagee: the purchaser may wish to use the land for a purpose which would not maximise its value and will probably not want to be obliged to pursue a planning application.

12.12 SUCCESSORS IN TITLE

The landowner and the developer will need to consider whether the provisions of the overage agreement are to be binding on the developer's successors in title. If it is intended that the overage obligations should be binding on the developer's successors in title then this should be made clear in the overage agreement.

The developer will not want the overage agreement to be binding on the purchasers of individual dwellings or their mortgagees and a clause to this effect should be inserted in the agreement.

12.13 VENDOR'S LIEN

A vendor will have an equitable lien over land which he has sold until the whole of the purchase price has been paid and an obligation to pay overage could give rise to an equitable lien. The developer's lawyer should therefore ensure that the overage agreement contains a clause such as model clause 21 in **Appendix D1**.

12.14 DISPUTES

The overage agreement should contain a dispute resolution clause to allow for any dispute between the parties regarding the calculation of the overage payment or the performance of obligations or the construction or interpretation of the agreement to be referred to and determined by an independent third party; and the parties will need to decide whether the independent third party should act as an expert or an arbitrator.

12.15 GOOD FAITH AND IMPLIED TERMS

The case of *Renewal Leeds Limited* v. *Lowry Properties Limited* [2010] EWHC 2902 (Ch) demonstrates that it is not unknown for developers to attempt to avoid paying overage, and the landowner's lawyer will need to think about ways in which the developer may attempt to wriggle out of paying overage. It would be sensible for the overage agreement to contain a good faith clause in terms such as the following:

> In all things relating to the Overage Payment the Buyer and the Seller shall act with good faith towards each other and (without prejudice to the generality thereof) the Buyer shall not do or permit any act, matter or thing the effect of which is to reduce or adversely affect the amount or prospects of payment of the Overage Payment.

Case law shows that courts will uphold good faith provisions. However, they are likely to be interpreted narrowly and not so as to prevent a person acting in his own best interests. (For examples of cases involving good faith provisions see *Chitty on Contracts* (33rd edition, Sweet & Maxwell, 2018), paras.1.051–1.056.)

It is also clear from case law that the courts are prepared to imply a term into an overage agreement, but only in order to give business efficacy to that agreement (*Sparks* v. *Biden* [2017] EWHC 1994 (Ch) and *Renewal Leeds Limited* v. *Lowry Properties Limited* [2010] EWHC 2902 (Ch)). In *Sparks* v. *Biden* the document containing the overage obligations imposed an obligation on Mr Biden to pay Mr Sparks the overage payment on the sale of the last newly constructed dwelling. However, the agreement did not impose an obligation on Mr Biden to sell any of the houses, and, after obtaining planning permission and constructing the houses authorised to be built, Mr Biden decided to let all but one and to occupy the other himself. Mr Sparks argued that a term should be implied into the agreement obliging Mr Biden to market and sell each newly constructed house within a reasonable timeframe. The court agreed with him.

12.16 STAMP DUTY LAND TAX

A developer will need to be aware that the signing of an overage agreement will give rise to an immediate liability to pay stamp duty land tax, although it may be possible to have this liability deferred (see **7.3.4**).

CHAPTER 13

Land promotion agreements

As an alternative to entering into an option agreement, a developer will sometimes enter into a promotion agreement with a landowner (see **Appendix E10** for a hybrid promotion/option agreement and **Appendix E11** for a 'pure' promotion agreement on the CD-ROM).

13.1 WHAT IS A LAND PROMOTION AGREEMENT?

A land promotion agreement is really a type of joint venture agreement. Typically, a land promotion agreement will be between a landowner and a developer or between a landowner and a planning promoter. The developer or planning promoter will agree to promote the landowner's property for development, to apply for and use reasonable endeavours to obtain planning permission and, having secured planning permission, to market the property for sale in the open market. In return for providing these services, the developer or planning promoter will receive a fee. The fee will usually be a sum equal to a proportion of the net sale proceeds (i.e. a proportion of the gross sale proceeds generated by a sale of the promotion land after various costs, such as planning costs, have been deducted and reimbursed or paid to the promoter/developer and the landowner).

Promotion agreements are similar to option agreements in many ways. Many of the key issues which need to be considered in relation to promotion agreements are the same as those which need to be considered when dealing with option agreements, although there are fundamental differences between the two types of agreement. For example, a promoter does not usually have an option to purchase the whole of the landowner's property after planning permission has been granted (although, if the property is large, the landowner may be prepared to grant the promoter an option to purchase part of the property after selling part of it on the open market) and sometimes, following a sale of part of the landowner's property on the open market, a promoter will be obliged to buy another part of the landowner's property.

As mentioned above, a landowner will sometimes agree to enter into a hybrid promotion and option agreement with a developer. Under this type of agreement, the developer will have an option to purchase part of the development site following the grant of planning permission and the sale of the first tranche on the open market. Hybrid agreements are preferred by developers whose priority is to build houses and not to obtain planning permission for landowners.

The key points which the parties to a promotion agreement will need to think about include the following.

13.2 OBJECTIVES

The promotion agreement should contain a list of objectives, which may include all or some of the following:

- to use reasonable endeavours to obtain a planning permission which maximises the open market value of the property in the shortest time reasonably practicable;
- (if necessary to achieve the above objective) to use reasonable endeavours to procure that the property (or as much of it as shall be recommended by the promoter's planning consultants for inclusion in a development plan document (such as an adopted Local Plan or neighbourhood plan)) is allocated as a site suitable for development in a development plan document;
- to maximise as far as reasonably practicable the area of the property and the extent of the net developable land in a planning permission;
- to submit a planning application as soon as it is commercially sensible to do so and to use reasonable endeavours to secure a satisfactory planning permission;
- to pursue a planning application with all due diligence and to appeal against a planning refusal or the grant of a planning permission that contains an onerous condition;
- to minimise so far as reasonably practicable and having regard to local and national planning policies the requirement for affordable housing;
- to minimise so far as reasonably practicable the cost of infrastructure;
- to minimise so far as reasonably practicable and having regard to local and national planning policies the requirements of the local planning authority in respect of any planning agreement;
- following the grant of a satisfactory planning permission, to carry out the agreed infrastructure works required in order to sell the property as fully serviced development land; and
- following the grant of a satisfactory planning permission, to market the property for sale and to effect sales with a view to maximising the sale proceeds so far as reasonably practicable.

Most of the above objectives should not pose a problem for the promoter/developer, although it will need to consider whether it is willing to be under an obligation to appeal (see **13.3**) or to carry out infrastructure works (see **13.8**). The landowner will also need to consider very carefully whether the developer should be required or permitted to install infrastructure (see **13.8**).

The promotion agreement should impose an obligation on the promoter to use reasonable endeavours to achieve the promotion objectives. In principle, this should not be a problem for the promoter. However, the promoter may wish to qualify the obligation, so that is does not have to comply with an objective if it would compromise the likely success of a planning application or if the objective does not accord with or is inconsistent with planning policy guidance or it is not reasonably achievable. The landowner, on the other hand, may wish to make the requirement for the promoter to maximise the extent of the net developable land more meaningful by imposing a further requirement that for a planning permission to be regarded as satisfactory at least 50 per cent of the land comprised within the planning permission must be net developable land.

13.3 PROMOTION PERIOD AND SALES PERIOD

The promoter will usually have a fixed period (often known as the initial promotion period) to obtain a satisfactory planning permission, which may be extended in certain circumstances (see **13.3.1**). If upon the expiration of the initial promotion period (or any extension thereof) the promoter has not secured a satisfactory planning permission, the promotion agreement will terminate. However, if a satisfactory planning permission is granted before the initial promotion period expires, the promotion agreement will usually continue and the promoter will have a fixed period (often known as the sales period) to market and sell the land comprised within the satisfactory planning permission.

13.3.1 Extensions to the promotion period

From the promoter's point of view, the promotion agreement should contain provisions, similar to those often found in option agreements, which automatically extend the initial promotion period in the following circumstances:

- if at the expiration of the initial promotion period the result of a planning application or an appeal is awaited;
- if at the expiration of the initial promotion period the local authority has resolved to grant a planning permission;
- if at the expiration of the initial promotion period challenge proceedings in respect of a planning permission have been instituted (e.g. by way of a judicial review) and the result is awaited;
- if at the expiration of the initial promotion period planning permission has been granted but it is not immune from challenge (because the judicial review period has not expired);
- if at the expiration of the initial promotion period an independent expert has been asked to make a determination or counsel has been asked to provide advice and the determination has not been published or the advice has not been provided.

Most landowners will not have any objection to the initial promotion period being extended in any of the above circumstances, although they may require the extension provisions to be subject to a planning longstop date and insist on a clause being inserted in the promotion agreement stating that if any extension of the initial promotion period would extend the promotion period beyond the planning longstop date, the promotion period will be taken to end on the planning longstop date.

Where the proposed development is large and likely to be developed in phases, the promoter will want to ensure that the promotion period is long enough to give it sufficient time to obtain an outline planning permission to develop the whole of the development area and also to obtain reserved matters approvals in respect of each phase.

13.3.2 Sales period and extensions to sales period

The promoter will not want the promotion agreement to terminate if at the expiration of the promotion period a satisfactory planning permission which is immune from challenge has been granted and the landowner's property or part of it remains to be sold. This is very important and the agreement should contain a clause stating that if the property or any part of it is at any time during the promotion period the subject of a satisfactory planning permission which is immune from challenge, the agreement shall continue until all of the land comprised within the satisfactory planning permission has been sold and the sale proceeds distributed in accordance with the provisions of the agreement.

Such a clause should be acceptable in principle to the landowner, although the promotion agreement cannot be allowed to continue indefinitely, and its continuation should be subject to a sales longstop date. In other words, the promotion agreement should continue until all the consented land (i.e. the land benefiting from the satisfactory planning permission) has been sold or until the sales longstop date occurs (whichever is the earlier). A sales longstop date may be resisted by a promoter, but if the satisfactory planning permission lapses before the property is sold, the landowner will not want the agreement to continue.

From the promoter's point of view, a sales longstop date should be extended in the following circumstances:

- if after an initial marketing period no acceptable offer to purchase the consented land or any part of it has been received and any further marketing of the land is to be suspended for a fixed period – in such circumstances the sales longstop date should be extended by the length of the sales suspension period;
- if an acceptable offer to purchase the consented land or any part of it has been agreed and contracts exchanged prior to the sales longstop date but at the sales longstop date the sale has not been completed – in such circumstances the promotion agreement should continue until the sale has been completed and the sale proceeds distributed in accordance with the provisions of the promotion agreement.

Sometimes a promoter may try to persuade a landowner to grant it an option to purchase the consented land or part of it for a minimum price if the consented land has not been sold by the longstop date. This will be a matter for negotiation.

Where the proposed development area is large and there is a possibility that it may be developed in phases, it may be necessary to have more than one sales longstop date and to include a clause in the promotion agreement stating that:

- if satisfactory planning permission shall permit the development of the landowner's property or part of it in phases or if any phasing strategy agreed as part of the marketing strategy shall require the consented land to be sold in tranches then, in respect of the first phase/tranche, the sales longstop shall be the date occurring, say, 36 months after the date on which the satisfactory planning permission becomes immune from challenge and, in respect of each subsequent phase/tranche, the sales longstop date shall be the date occurring, say, 24 months after the date of the sale of the previous phase/tranche; and
- if a satisfactory planning permission does not include the whole of the landowner's property then on every subsequent grant of a satisfactory planning permission during the promotion period a further sales longstop date shall occur and shall be the date occurring, say, 36 months after the date that the relevant satisfactory planning permission becomes immune from challenge.

13.4 THE PROMOTER'S PLANNING OBLIGATIONS

The promotion agreement should impose various planning obligations on the promoter and the parties will need to think about matters such as the following:

- Should the promoter be obliged to appoint planning and other consultants to assist it in meeting the promotion objectives? (Neither the promoter nor the landowner should have any reason to object to this.)
- Should the appointment of each member of the professional team be subject to the approval of the landowner? (The developer is likely to want to resist having to obtain such approval on the ground that it has more expertise than the landowner in appointing consultants.)
- Should the landowner have the right to approve the planning application? Without such a right the landowner would be unable to ensure that the application is consistent with the promotion objectives, although the promoter is likely to want the right to be qualified (see **9.5**).
- Should the promoter be required to prepare a draft master plan and design statement for approval by the landowner?
- Should the promoter be obliged to maximise the open market value of the site?
- Should the planning application be for an outline or a detailed/full planning permission or an outline planning permission followed by the approval of such

reserved matters as shall be identified by the promoter? The promoter will usually wish to have flexibility in deciding which type of planning application to lodge.

- Should the promoter be obliged to use reasonable endeavours to ensure that any obligations imposed under any planning agreement are fair and reasonable and consistent with planning policy guidance and the promotion objectives?
- Should the landowner have the right to approve all planning agreements? From the landowner's point of view, having the right to approve a planning agreement will be essential, although the promoter is likely to want any such ability to be qualified. The landowner will not want to be obligated to enter into a planning agreement unless it is consistent with the promotion objectives and contains obligations which are in accordance with or consistent with planning policy guidance and stipulations such as:

  - the planning agreement will not come into effect until the relevant planning permission is granted;
  - any obligation imposed by the agreement will be conditional upon the commencement of development;
  - the landowner will be released from all liability under the planning agreement if the landowner disposes of his interest in the whole of the development site; and
  - the landowner will not be liable for any breach of the planning agreement unless at the date of the breach he holds an interest in the part of the development site in respect of which the breach occurs.

  As mentioned above, the promoter is likely to require any right of approval given to the landowner to be qualified, such that the landowner's approval of the planning agreement cannot be unreasonably withheld or delayed and the landowner will be deemed to have approved the draft planning agreement if he gives no reasons in writing for withholding approval within a specified period of receiving the draft planning agreement. Also, the promoter may only be prepared to be obligated to use reasonable endeavours (as opposed to being under an absolute obligation) to ensure that the planning agreement contains a release from liability provision (because this is not something in its control).

- Should the promoter be obliged to indemnify the landowner in respect of all liability under a planning agreement? From the promoter's point of view, this requirement may seem unreasonable, since usually there will be no liability under the planning agreement unless the associated planning permission has been implemented and, furthermore, any purchaser of the promotion land will be required to indemnify the landowner in the transfer to the purchaser. Also, the promoter may argue, if the planning agreement contains a release from liability clause (whereby the landowner will be released from all liability under the planning agreement upon sale of the whole of the consented land and the landowner will not be liable for any breach of the agreement unless he has an interest in the land in respect of which the breach occurs), why should the landowner be concerned about liability under the planning agreement and require an indemnity from the promoter? The answer to this question is because, even where the planning agreement contains a release from liability clause, the consented land may be sold and developed in phases and the commencement of development of part of the development area may trigger planning obligations and the payment of the Community Infrastructure Levy (CIL) across the whole of the development area. From the landowner's point of view, the promoter should always be required to indemnify the landowner in respect of the obligations contained in any required planning agreement where the agreement does not contain a release from liability clause. However, even where the agreement contains such a clause, the landowner should still insist on the promoter providing an indemnity if there is a possibility that the development area may be developed in phases. The promoter is likely to resist providing an indemnity on the ground that it has no interest in the development site, but where the promoter agrees to provide an indemnity this should only be on the basis that:

- the promoter will be reimbursed all costs incurred by it in complying with planning obligations and/or the payment of CIL out of the sale proceeds;
- the buyer will be required to provide the landowner and the promoter with an appropriate indemnity; and
- upon the buyer providing such an indemnity, the indemnity given by the promoter shall cease to apply in so far as it relates to the land being sold.

- Should the promoter be obliged to prepare and follow a planning strategy and master plan for approval by the landowner? This should not be an issue for the promoter, subject to the right of approval being qualified.
- Should the promoter be obliged to prepare and follow a phasing strategy which has been approved by the landowner? (A phasing strategy will be required in the case of a large development site that is likely to be developed in phases.)
- Should the promoter be obliged to submit the planning application at the earliest opportunity or should the promoter be entitled to submit the planning application when it deems it commercially sensible to do so (and not before the property has been allocated for development) or when its planning consultants advise that there is a good or reasonable prospect of success? As discussed in relation to options, the promoter will usually want to have some flexibility in this regard and it will not be in either party's best interests for the application to be lodged prematurely (see **10.12**). If the landowner is adamant that the planning application must be submitted by no later than a specified date, the promoter may be prepared to agree to this if the landowner accepts that the submission of the application may be delayed if the planning consultants appointed by the promoter recommend that it would be sensible for good planning reasons to delay submitting the application.

- Should the promoter be obliged to appeal against a planning refusal or the grant of a planning permission that contains an onerous condition? As discussed in relation to conditional contracts and options, most developers will not wish to be under an obligation to appeal. They will usually want to have the flexibility to lodge a fresh planning application or to make an application to the local planning authority for an onerous condition to be discharged or to appeal if counsel experienced in planning matters advises that there is a reasonable prospect of success or to terminate the agreement (see **9.9** and **10.12**). From the landowner's point of view, the promoter should be obliged to appeal against a planning refusal or to lodge a new or revised planning application (including an application for an onerous condition to be discharged) if there is a reasonable prospect (i.e. better than 50 per cent chance) of the appeal or the new/revised application being successful before the promotion period expires.
- Should the promoter be obliged to pursue planning challenge proceedings in relation to a competing site or to defend planning challenge proceedings commenced by others?
- Should the landowner have the right to approve the form of any planning permission granted or should the promoter have an absolute discretion to determine whether a planning permission is acceptable? Without such a right the landowner will be unable to ensure that the planning permission is consistent with the promotion objectives, the agreed planning strategy and planning policy guidance, and that it does not contain any onerous conditions.
- Should a planning permission be regarded as satisfactory only if (together with any associated planning agreement) it satisfies an objective test, such as that it must be consistent with the promotion objectives and in line with any agreed planning strategy and not contain any onerous conditions? As already discussed in relation to conditional contracts and options, there will need to be a definition of 'planning permission' and 'satisfactory planning permission' which are acceptable to both parties (see **9.1** and **10.6**). As mentioned above, the landowner may wish to impose a requirement that for a planning permission to be regarded as satisfactory, not only must it be consistent with the promotion objectives and not contain any adverse conditions, but, in addition, at least 50 per cent of the land comprised within the planning permission must be net developable land (see **14.3.4** for definition of net developable land).
- Should the promoter be entitled to amend a planning application or to withdraw and submit a new application or to submit multiple planning applications? From the promoter's point of view, it is important that it should be free to vary or amend a planning application or to withdraw and submit a new planning application and to submit more than one planning application at any time during the promotion period. (However, a well-advised landowner will want to have the ability to approve any new or revised application.) Also, if any planning permission granted is an outline planning permission, the promoter should be entitled to submit a reserved matters application at any time during the subsistence of the promotion agreement (whether before or after the

expiration of the promotion period). This may need to be done in order to prevent the outline planning permission from lapsing or in order to achieve a sale to a prospective buyer who requires the sale to be made conditional upon the grant of a satisfactory reserved matters approval.

The landowner's responses to some of the above questions are likely to be very different from those of the promoter. It is inevitable that a well-advised landowner will require a degree of control in relation to planning matters and the right balance will need to be struck in order to ensure that both parties' interests are safeguarded and neither party feels exposed. The landowner will usually be concerned about maximising the development value of his land and ensuring that planning gain obligations are fair and reasonable, that any planning permission granted and any associated planning agreement are consistent with the promotion objectives, that he will be protected against any liability under a planning agreement to pay CIL, and that the promoter actively and diligently promotes his land for development. The promoter/developer, on the other hand, will not want to be forced to lodge a planning application prematurely or to proceed with a development unless it is economically viable and, where the landowner's consent or approval is required, it will want to ensure that the landowner is not able to act unreasonably or to delay matters and that, in the event of a dispute, there is a mechanism for settling the dispute. The promoter will want to try to ensure that the landowner is entitled to withhold his approval to a planning application, a planning permission and a planning agreement only on specified grounds (see **9.5** and **9.11**).

13.5 OBLIGATIONS OF LANDOWNER

The promoter will want to ensure that various obligations are imposed on the landowner, including:

- not to object to any planning application submitted by the promoter or otherwise to do anything which is or may be prejudicial to the proposed development and/or the grant of planning permission;
- not to apply for any planning permission without the approval of the promoter;
- to take all reasonable steps to assist the promoter in obtaining planning permission, including entering into a planning agreement and any other necessary infrastructure agreements (e.g. relating to the adoption of roads and/or sewers) upon request in writing from the promoter (see **10.11**);
- to procure that any tenant of the promotion land and any mortgagee enter into any planning agreement to which the landowner is a party for the purpose of consenting to its terms;
- to promptly sign any contract and execute any transfer in order to achieve a sale of the promotion land or (if it is to be sold as fully serviced parcels) a tranche;
- not to do or omit to do anything which would be prejudicial to or delay a sale;

- not to permit any trespass or encroachment to be made or any easement or other right to be acquired over the promotion land;
- to oppose any application to register the promotion land or any part of it as a town or village green and to challenge the validity of any registration of the promotion land or any part of it as a town or village green;
- to provide vacant possession of the promotion land or a tranche (as appropriate) on completion of a sale;
- not to transfer, convey, lease, charge or deal with the property in any way (see **10.18**);
- to be wholly responsible for discharging all mortgages, financial charges and financial encumbrances (including any overage payment due to a third party) upon completion of the sale;
- to sell the property or a tranche (as appropriate) following the grant of planning permission to the buyer offering the best or highest price in the open market – this obligation will be especially relevant if the promoter is to receive a fee which equates to a proportion of the sale proceeds realised on the sale of the property.

Depending on the obligations contained in a promotion agreement, the courts may take the view that it is an implied term of the promotion agreement that the landowner is obliged not to sell or transfer the promotion land. In *Berkeley Community Villages Limited and another* v. *Pullen and others* [2007] EWHC 1330 (Ch) the court held that the proposed sale of land that was the subject of a promotion agreement would be a breach of the obligations on the part of the landowners to co-operate and use reasonable endeavours to promote the land so as to achieve the grant of planning permission and not to do anything that could prejudice the obtaining of planning permission. The sale of the land would have given rise to a breach of the landowner's obligations because it would have prevented the promoter from obtaining planning permission, since the new landowner would not have been bound by the obligation to enter into a s.106 planning agreement.

Most of the above obligations should not trouble a landowner, although the obligation to enter into a planning agreement should be qualified and made subject to the agreement being in the form to be approved by the landowner (see **13.4**). Also, the landowner may wish to make the obligation to sign any sale contract and to sell the promotion land or any part of it subject to a minimum price being achieved (see **13.6**) and he may wish to have some ability to deal with his land. For example, he may want to be permitted to:

- transfer the whole or any part of the promotion land to a third party who has entered into a deed of covenant with the promoter containing a covenant to be bound by and to observe and perform the obligations on the part of the landowner contained in the promotion agreement;
- grant leases or tenancies of the promotion land or any part of it, so long as such leases or tenancies do not confer security of tenure and do not prevent the

landowner from obtaining vacant possession within a specified period (three or six months) after a satisfactory planning permission has been granted;

- create easements over the promotion land with the approval of the promoter (such approval not to be unreasonably withheld); and
- charge or mortgage the promotion land or any part of it subject to the chargee/mortgagee entering into a deed of adherence containing, amongst other covenants, a covenant that on a disposal of the promotion land or any part of it the chargee/mortgagee shall procure that the buyer will be bound by the terms of the promotion agreement.

13.6 BEST PRICE AND MINIMUM PRICE

Both the promoter and the landowner will want the promotion land or (if it is to be sold in tranches) the relevant part of the promotion land to be sold for the highest price offered by a purchaser in the open market or the highest price offered having due regard to the make-up of the price and the terms associated with it. However, the landowner may not want to be obliged to sell if the market conditions are unfavourable and the gross sale proceeds or the net sale proceeds (i.e. the gross sale proceeds less all planning costs and other deductible expenditure) or the landowner's share of the net sale proceeds (i.e. the balance of the sale proceeds due to the landowner after all deductions and the payment of the promoter's fee) would be less than a specified minimum price. From the landowner's point of view, it is very important that the landowner should not be obliged to proceed with a sale if his share of the net sale proceeds will be less than a specified minimum price. This could create a problem for the promoter, however, since the promoter would be unable to recover any of the deductible expenditure incurred by it in promoting the promotion land for development if no purchaser was willing to pay a sum equal to or in excess of the minimum price or a sum which would result in the minimum purchase price requirement being satisfied and it was not possible to achieve a sale. Minimum purchase price provisions may, therefore, be resisted by the promoter, but if the landowner is adamant that he would not be prepared to proceed with a sale unless the minimum price requirement was satisfied, the promoter should consider ways of mitigating the effects of any minimum purchase price requirement. One alternative might be for the promoter to have an option to purchase the promotion land at the minimum price (or the minimum price less the promoter's fee and the deductible expenditure incurred by the promoter) within a specified period of an unacceptable offer being made. Another alternative would be for the parties to the promotion agreement to agree that:

- if the best price offered for the promotion land or any tranche within six months of the relevant land being marketed is such that the sale of the promotion land/tranche would result in the landowner receiving in his hands, after all deductions and the payment of the promoter's fee, a sum which is less than the minimum price, then the sale of the promotion land or any tranche shall be suspended for a specified period or until the date on which it is agreed that the sale of the promotion land or any tranche would achieve the minimum price requirements (whichever is the earlier);

- the sales period (see **13.3**) shall be extended by a period equal to the suspension period; and
- during the suspension period either party shall be entitled to call for a review of land values at any time in order to ascertain whether or not a sale of the promotion land or any tranche would result in the landowner receiving a sum in his hands, after all deductions and payment of the promoter's fee, equal to or in excess of the minimum price.

Another option would be for the landowner to agree to reimburse the promoter all of the deductible expenditure incurred by it following a sale of the promotion land at any time in the future. This option is likely to be resisted by a landowner.

With regard to the definition of minimum price, it could be defined as 'the sum calculated by multiplying the number of acres of land (calculated to three decimal places) comprising Net Developable Land within the land being sold by the sum of £[ ]' or 'the sum calculated by multiplying the number of gross acres of land (calculated to three decimal places) within the land being sold by the sum of £[ ]'. In other words, the minimum price could be linked to gross or net developable acreage. From the landowner's point of view, it would be sensible for the minimum price to be index linked. However, before agreeing to any minimum price requirement, the promoter should consider the likely impact of any third party land costs and/or infrastructure costs on the minimum price and whether there needs to be a mechanism for reducing the minimum price if, for example, there is a need to acquire third party land (for access or services) or to make a ransom payment. The promoter will need to consider whether any proposed minimum price requirement is realistic/likely to be achieved if there are to be substantial deductions from the sale proceeds before the balance is paid to the landowner.

13.7 PROMOTION AND PLANNING COSTS

The costs and expenses incurred by the promoter in promoting the landowner's property for development and obtaining a satisfactory planning permission will usually be paid by the promoter out of its own pocket and will be reimbursed to the promoter out of the proceeds of sale following any sale of the landowner's property.

Ideally, from the promoter's point of view, the promotion and planning costs should include:

- all costs and fees incurred in connection with the promotion of the relevant land through the planning process (including applying for and obtaining a satisfactory planning permission);
- all costs incurred by the promoter in complying with the planning obligations contained in the promotion agreement (including the cost of appealing against

a planning refusal and the cost of pursuing a planning challenge in respect of a competing site or defending a planning challenge commenced by a third party);
- any costs incurred or suffered or likely to be incurred or suffered by the promoter under all relevant planning agreements (including planning gain costs);
- any value added tax (VAT) or similar tax payable in respect of any items mentioned above to the extent that the promoter is unable to recover the same;
- CIL or any land tax which may become payable by the promoter; and
- interest on the above costs.

From the landowner's point of view, the promotion and planning costs should be reasonably and properly incurred. The landowner may also want the promotion and planning costs to be capped or to impose a requirement that the promoter must obtain the landowner's approval to expenditure above a certain level, although this is likely to be resisted by the promoter.

Where there is a possibility that the promotion land may be sold in tranches, the landowner may wish the promotion agreement to stipulate that the promoter shall only be entitled to be reimbursed a proportion (namely, the proportion that the gross acreage of the relevant tranche bears to the gross acreage of all the tranches comprised within the satisfactory planning permission) of the promotion and planning costs on a sale.

Where the promoter owns or controls adjoining land that is to be included in the proposed development area (or there is a possibility that the promoter may own or control adjoining land which will be included in the proposed development area), the landowner may wish the promotion agreement to stipulate that only a sum equal to the equalised proportion (being the proportion which the gross acreage of the promotion land having the benefit of the satisfactory planning permission bears to the gross acreage of the development area having the benefit of the satisfactory planning permission) of all promotion and planning costs shall be reimbursed to the promoter on a sale.

13.8 INFRASTRUCTURE WORKS

The parties to the promotion agreement will need to consider whether it is necessary to include any infrastructure provisions in the agreement and, if infrastructure provisions are required, they will need to be aware of the tax and other implications of imposing an obligation on the promoter to provide infrastructure.

13.8.1 Obligation to install infrastructure

Where the development site is large and it is intended that the site will be sold in phases as fully serviced parcels of land, the parties to the promotion agreement may agree that the promoter will carry out infrastructure works; and the infrastructure may need to include both on-site and off-site infrastructure. If the cost of the infrastructure is likely to be considerable, the promoter will need to think carefully before agreeing to be under an obligation to provide infrastructure: the promoter (and, indeed, the landowner) may wish to have the ability to terminate the promotion agreement if the cost of providing the infrastructure makes the project unworkable/economically unviable. For example, there may be a requirement to build a bridge or to construct a by-pass or to carry out other major road improvements at a cost which would jeopardise the financial viability of the proposed development.

Following a sale of the landowner's property, it is usual for the promoter to be reimbursed all infrastructure costs incurred by it out of the sale proceeds before they are distributed.

Ideally, from the promoter's point of view, the infrastructure costs should include:

- all costs incurred or to be incurred by the promoter in providing the infrastructure reasonably required to enable the sale of the development site as fully serviced development land capable of immediate development – infrastructure should be defined and should include all the usual infrastructure works, including on-site and off-site highway works, ground treatment works, the laying of services to the boundary of the site, landscaping works, the laying out of open spaces and play areas, etc.;
- banking and finance costs relating to the provision of the infrastructure;
- any VAT or similar tax payable in respect of infrastructure costs to the extent that the promoter is unable to recover the same; and
- interest on the costs incurred in providing infrastructure.

Where the promoter is to be obliged to install infrastructure to enable the development site to be sold in phases as fully serviced parcels, the landowner will need to be aware of a potential tax risk. It would appear that, under current legislation relating to 'transactions in land', such an obligation could give rise to a risk of the landowner being regarded as carrying out development and embarking on a trading transaction, with the sale proceeds potentially subject to income tax or corporation tax (see Income Tax Act 2007 and Finance Act 2016, s.79). There is no definition of 'development' in the tax legislation and the authors of *Land Taxation* (Gammie and de Souza, loose-leaf, Sweet & Maxwell) do not consider that dividing land into plots and laying out access roads would amount to development. They state (at para.B7.052):

> It appears from *Winterton v Edwards* that the development does not have to be substantial, and alteration of an existing building may amount to development, although it would normally imply building or preparation for building. However, it is considered that steps preparatory to the commencement of development, such as applying for planning permission, dividing the land into plots and laying out access roads are insufficient to bring a case into this situation.

However, a contrary view is taken by HM Revenue & Customs. They appear to take a much wider view of what constitutes development than the authors of *Land Taxation* and state in their Business Manual BIM60460 that development means 'any physical adaption or preparation for a new use'.

One way of avoiding the risk of HM Revenue & Customs claiming that the landowner is embarking on a trading transaction would be to provide in the promotion agreement that the land required for infrastructure must be transferred to the promoter for nil consideration before any infrastructure works are carried out and that immediately following such transfer the promoter must grant the landowner an option to call for the infrastructure land to be transferred back to him for nil consideration in the event of the promoter failing to deliver the infrastructure in accordance with the requirements of the promotion agreement or committing any other breach of the promotion agreement.

13.8.2 Infrastructure works and CIL

Both the promoter and the landowner should be made aware that the carrying out of infrastructure works may trigger a liability to pay CIL (see **5.4**). If neither party is prepared to accept liability for any CIL which may become payable upon the commencement of the infrastructure works, one possibility may be to require the purchaser of the first tranche to provide the initial infrastructure and for the carrying out of further infrastructure works and the payment of CIL to be funded out of the sales proceeds resulting from the sale of the first tranche.

If a promoter is prepared to accept any CIL liability, it will want to ensure that it is reimbursed the cost of meeting such liability out of the proceeds of sale following a sale of the promotion land. However, a promoter should think carefully before agreeing to accept responsibility for any CIL, especially where a landowner is not obliged to proceed with a sale unless a minimum purchase price is achieved, or the promotion period is subject to a longstop date.

From the landowner's point of view, where it is intended that the promotion land will be sold in phases/tranches and the promoter is to be obligated to install infrastructure, the landowner should insist, for the reasons discussed at **13.4**, on the promotion agreement containing a covenant by the promoter to pay all CIL that may become payable in relation to the promotion land and to indemnify the landowner in respect of such liability, since it is unlikely that the landowner will have the funds to discharge the liability.

As mentioned in **Chapter 5** (see **5.4**), if a planning permission permits a development to be implemented in phases then each phase of the development will be treated as a separate chargeable development under the Community Infrastructure Levy Regulations 2010 (SI 2010/948). This means, in terms of CIL liability, that the development of each phase will give rise to a separate liability to pay CIL. By obtaining a planning permission which permits phased development a landowner is, in effect, able to pay CIL in stages and the commencement of development of the first phase will not trigger a liability to pay CIL on the whole of the development site. From both the promoter's and the landowner's points of view, where a development site is large and intended to be developed in phases, a sensible planning strategy would be:

- to obtain a planning permission which permits phased development, and which contains conditions allowing separate reserved matters applications to be made in respect of each phase;
- to ensure that all financial contributions payable under a s.106 agreement are apportioned between and expressed to bind separate phases of development so that liability for the payment of such contributions is ring fenced; and
- to ensure that any obligations in a s.106 agreement relating to the delivery of works (including ground remediation works) or placing restrictions on the delivery or use of the development or restrictions on the occupation of dwellings are ring fenced and only bind the owner of the land within the specific phase of development to which the works or restrictions relate.

Whether the above strategy will be possible or not will depend upon it being acceptable to the planning authority.

One possible way of ensuring that the commencement of infrastructure works does not trigger a liability to pay CIL would be for the promoter to lodge an application for outline planning permission to develop the whole site and a separate infrastructure works planning application. It would appear that the implementation of the infrastructure works planning permission would not trigger a liability to pay CIL because CIL is payable on the floor area of a chargeable development.

13.8.3 Infrastructure works and planning obligations

The landowner will need to be made aware that the carrying out of infrastructure works is likely to trigger the payment of financial contributions and the performance of other obligations under a planning agreement. Again, the promoter should be required to covenant to comply with the obligations contained in any planning agreement and to indemnify the landowner against all costs, claims, actions, demands and liabilities arising out of any breach or non-performance of such obligations. In return, the landowner should be required to covenant with the promoter not to implement any planning permission authorising the development of the landowner's land during the subsistence of the promotion agreement.

13.9 LAND COSTS

The development of a site may require the promoter to incur various other land costs, such as the cost of acquiring land or easements reasonably necessary to facilitate access or services to the site and compensation for the termination of any tenancies. Such costs should include stamp duty land tax (SDLT), Land Registry fees and legal fees. Again, where the promoter is to receive a promotion fee which equates to a proportion of all net sale proceeds, it would be usual for the promoter to be reimbursed such costs out of the sale proceeds before they are distributed. From the landowner's point of view, the cost of acquiring any land or easements should be reasonable and subject to the approval of the landowner (not to be unreasonably withheld). Also, the acquisition of any third party land or interests should be permitted only if it is reasonably required to secure or facilitate the implementation of a planning permission and the acquisition of land upon which it is intended to construct dwellings or buildings should not be permitted.

As mentioned above in relation to promotion and planning costs (see **13.7**), where there is a possibility that the promotion land may be sold in tranches, the landowner may want the promotion agreement to stipulate that the promoter shall only be entitled to be reimbursed a proportion of any land costs incurred by the promoter on a sale. Also, where the promoter owns or controls or may own or control adjoining land, the landowner may want the promotion agreement to stipulate that the promoter shall only be entitled to be reimbursed an equalised proportion of all land costs.

13.10 MARKETING STRATEGY AND SALES

The landowner's agent or any sales agent jointly appointed by the landowner and the promoter should be required to prepare a draft marketing strategy for approval by the landowner and the promoter as soon as reasonably practicable after a satisfactory planning permission has been granted or a resolution to grant planning permission has been passed. Any dispute or disagreement between the promoter and the landowner in relation to the marketing strategy will need to be settled by an independent third party and the promotion agreement should contain a clause to this effect.

The marketing strategy should have regard to matters such as:

- the requirements of the satisfactory planning permission;
- whether the site should be sold as a whole or in tranches;
- whether the site should be sold as serviced parcels;
- the timing and manner by which infrastructure is to be provided (if at all);
- a programme for the release of the relevant land;
- the areas of land which are to be released for sale;
- the manner and method by which sales are to be achieved;
- the marketing process;
- the delivery of vacant possession;
- whether the sale documentation should include any ransom strip or any overage arrangements;
- the need for any deferred consideration proposals by a buyer to be approved and to cater adequately for the tax liabilities of the landowner;
- the need for the landowner to be protected from any liability in respect of CIL or any liability arising under a planning agreement.

Both parties should be obliged to work together to achieve a sale of the promotion land or (if it is to be sold in tranches) the first tranche as soon as reasonably practicable after the marketing strategy has been agreed.

The form of the sales documentation will need to be agreed between the promoter and the landowner and the parties will need to decide on whose solicitor should be required to deal with the sales to third parties and the distribution of the sale proceeds.

All heads of terms agreed by the landowner or the landowner's representative should be subject to the approval of the promoter (not to be unreasonably withheld) and, where the conveyancing will be dealt with by the landowner's solicitor, the promoter will want to have the ability to approve all sales documentation. The transfer of the promotion land or any part of it to a prospective buyer will need to include (amongst other provisions):

- such exceptions and reservations over the promotion land or (if it is to be sold in tranches) the relevant tranche as may be reasonably required for the existing and any future use of any retained land (i.e. such parts of the landowner's property as shall not form part of the consented land and such parts of the consented land as shall not have been acquired by a third party) and the buildings from time to time thereon (including adequate rights of way, drainage and services, rights of entry and step in rights); and
- such covenants on the part of the prospective buyer as may be reasonably required for the benefit of any retained land (including a covenant to construct roads, sewers and services to agreed capacities and to ensure that they directly connect with the boundary of the retained land, a covenant to maintain such infrastructure, a covenant to procure the adoption of estate roads and estate sewers, and a covenant to enter into any wayleave agreements, deeds of easement or other documents required to be entered into by a provider of services to any retained land) (see **7.4**).

13.11 DEFERRED PAYMENT TERMS

If an offer for the purchase of the promotion land or any part of it involves deferred payments then, from the landowner's point of view, the landowner should not be obliged to accept such an offer if the deferred payment terms would involve the landowner having to pay tax on any gain (real or notional) before he receives any of the sale proceeds to enable him to pay the tax. The promotion agreement should contain a clause to this effect. Also, the landowner may wish to include a provision in the agreement stating that if a sale involves deferred payments, the promoter's fee shall be payable in instalments, so that following the completion of a sale the landowner will only be obliged to pay the promoter an appropriate proportion of the promoter's fee with the balance to be paid as and when the deferred payments are received by the landowner.

Both the promoter and the landowner will want to ensure that any deferred payments are adequately secured by a first legal charge or other form of security acceptable to both parties.

13.12 DISTRIBUTION OF SALE PROCEEDS

The promotion agreement should set out the order of priority in which the sale proceeds will be distributed following a sale of the whole or any part of the landowner's property. The promoter will want to ensure that it is reimbursed all costs which it has incurred in respect of planning and infrastructure and land costs before any of the proceeds of sale are paid to the landowner. Where a development site is large and to be sold in tranches, the landowner may object to such costs being reimbursed to the promoter in full on the first sale and may insist that they are reimbursed to the promoter in stages (with a proportion of the deductible costs being reimbursed on each sale) (see **13.7**) This will be a matter for negotiation.

The following points, all of which relate to tax, should be noted:

1. The agreement should stipulate that all VAT due in respect of the sale proceeds must be accounted for and paid to the landowner before the proceeds of sale are distributed.
2. The promoter's fee will attract VAT and the promotion agreement should contain a provision stating that on completion of a sale the landowner will pay the promoter the promoter's fee plus VAT on such sum. The payment to the promoter will be treated as consideration for the supply of services, the services being the preparation of the relevant land for sale on behalf of the landowner, and the promoter will need to issue a VAT invoice to the landowner. In order to recover the VAT, the landowner will need to be registered for VAT and to have made an election to waive exemption from VAT. This is very important, since a failure by the landowner to opt to tax will result in the landowner having a substantial further cost to bear. (The landowner's lawyer will need to ensure that the promotion agreement does not contain a clause which prohibits the landowner from making such an election.)
3. The election by the landowner to waive exemption from VAT creates two issues for the purchaser of the promotion land. The first issue is that the purchaser will have to pay an extra 20 per cent for the land. However, if the land is sold to a property developer who is registered for VAT, it will probably be using the land to make taxable supplies and it should be able to recover the VAT paid on the purchase price for the land. Assuming that this is the case, the issue is only a cash flow issue. The second issue is that the purchaser will have to pay SDLT on the purchase price as increased by the VAT payable thereon.

   In practice, the purchaser is likely to factor the extra SDLT cost into the calculation of the price that he is prepared to pay for the land, so it will be the landowner who ends up receiving less for his land than he would have done if he had not elected to waive exemption from VAT. One possible solution to this problem may be for the parties to agree that on a sale the promoter will assign its interest in the promotion agreement to the purchaser and that the promoter and the landowner will enter into a deed of novation and assignment with the purchaser. Under this arrangement the consideration to be paid to the promoter would be a sum equal to the share of the net sale proceeds payable to the promoter under the promotion agreement.

4. On a sale of part of a development site there will be a disposal for tax purposes which may trigger a tax liability for the landowner, regardless of whether the landowner receives any of the net sale proceeds. On the first sale it is possible that the landowner may receive very little of the sale proceeds if they are to be utilised to reimburse the promoter the various costs which it has incurred and to pay the promoter its promotion fee. Nevertheless, the landowner may be liable to pay tax on any consideration paid to him by the purchaser. Clearly, this would not be a satisfactory state of affairs for the landowner and the promoter may need to offer to assist the landowner by agreeing to the deductible expenditure and the promoter's fee being paid in instalments or by making the landowner a loan to enable the landowner to meet his tax liability. For example, the promoter could agree that where any potential tax burden on the landowner can reasonably be shown to exceed any net sale proceeds due to the landowner on the date that any such tax burden arises the promoter shall on request by the landowner make a payment to the landowner of the amount of such deficit or potential deficit and such payment shall be treated as an advance on proceeds to be adjusted against payments due to the landowner on future sales.
5. If a potential sale would involve deferred payments, the landowner should not be obliged to agree to the sale if it would have adverse tax consequences for the landowner (see **13.11**).

It will be apparent from the above (and **13.8.1**) that the parties to the promotion agreement should seek advice from a tax specialist before proceeding.

13.13 SECURITY AND PROTECTING THE PROMOTION AGREEMENT

The promoter will want to ensure that the payment of its promotion fee is secured. The payment could be protected by:

- the promoter taking a legal charge over the landowner's property (however, the comments contained in **12.10** should be noted);
- the promoter having an option to purchase the landowner's property in the event of a satisfactory planning permission being granted and the landowner refusing to sell the promotion land in accordance with the provisions of the promotion agreement;
- prohibiting the landowner from dealing with his land and requiring a restriction to be entered on the landowner's title (see **12.10**).

It should be noted that:

- Prohibiting the landowner from dealing with his land without any legal charge or other form of security will not provide the promoter with complete protection. A promotion agreement is a personal agreement and, unlike a purchase contract or an option agreement, it does not create an interest in land and will not be binding on the landowner's successors in title, unless the successor in title has entered into a suitable deed of covenant with the promoter, and it is not possible to protect the promotion agreement by registering a notice of the agreement on the landowner's title. If the landowner were to sell his property prior to planning permission having been obtained by the promoter the new landowner would not be obliged to observe the obligations on the part of the landowner contained in the promotion agreement, unless the new landowner had entered into a deed of covenant with the promoter. This would be the case even if a restriction against dealing had been entered on the landowner's title, although if a restriction had been entered on the landowner's title the new landowner would have difficulty in registering the transfer to him at the Land Registry. However, best practice would be for the promoter to have, in addition to a restriction against dealing on the landowner's title, a first legal charge over the promotion land to secure the payment of the promoter's fee (even though the legal charge could be defeated by a liquidator – see **12.10.1**).
- Any application to the Land Registry to register a unilateral notice in respect of the promotion agreement is likely to be rejected by the Land Registry, but the registration of a unilateral notice would, in any event, be ineffective in protecting the interests of the promoter.
- Where the promotion land is subject to an existing charge the promoter should think carefully before entering into a promotion agreement and should require the existing charge to be discharged or (if this is not possible) the existing chargee should be required to enter into a suitable deed of adherence which contains a covenant by the chargee that if the chargee shall take possession of the promotion land then it will perform and observe all of the obligations on the part of the landowner contained in the promotion agreement, a covenant to release the promotion land from its charge upon a sale, a covenant not to sell the promotion land without procuring that the buyer enters into a deed of covenant with the promoter and a covenant to enter into a planning agreement upon request by the promoter.

13.14 DISPUTE RESOLUTION

It will be in both the promoter's and the landowner's interests for the promotion agreement to contain a suitable dispute resolution clause.

13.15 VALUE ADDED TAX

The promotion agreement should contain a provision stating that all sums due to the promoter or the landowner under the promotion agreement are exclusive of VAT and, where the promoter is entitled to receive a promoter's fee, that VAT will be payable thereon.

It will be important for the landowner to remember that he will be able to recover any VAT payable on the promoter's fee only if he is registered for VAT and has made an election to waive exemption for VAT purposes.

13.16 STAMP DUTY LAND TAX

No SDLT should be payable on any premium paid by the promoter to the landowner on entering into a pure promotion agreement, as the agreement does not create a chargeable interest in land. The promoter is simply receiving a fee for services and will not acquire any interest in land. However, where the promotion agreement is a hybrid promotion/option agreement and the promoter is granted an option to purchase the whole or part of the promotion land, SDLT may be payable on the part of the premium attributable to the grant of the option, unless the premium is below the threshold. Unless the promotion agreement is a 'pure' promotion agreement that does not involve the promoter acquiring an interest in land, it would be prudent to obtain advice from a tax specialist on whether SDLT is payable.

Also, in the event of the option being exercised, SDLT may be payable on the purchase price for the option land (with the grant and the exercise of the option being treated as linked transactions) (see **10.29**).

13.17 KEEPING A PLANNING PERMISSION ALIVE

Keeping a planning permission alive will be important and may be a challenge for a developer where there is a delay in finding a buyer for the promotion land. Where there is a delay in achieving a sale of any part of the promotion land following the grant of a satisfactory planning permission, the promoter may wish to have the ability to take such steps as may be necessary to extend or renew the satisfactory planning permission or to keep it in force before it lapses (including submitting an application for the approval of reserved matters (where the planning permission granted is an outline planning permission) or implementing the satisfactory planning permission). However, the parties to the promotion agreement will need to remember that the implementation of the satisfactory planning permission is likely to trigger the payment of financial contributions payable under any associated s.106 agreement and that it will trigger any CIL liability. The landowner should not agree to the promoter having a right to implement a planning permission.

13.18 ADVANTAGES

Promotion agreements have the following advantages:

1. On the face of it, a typical promotion agreement may be more appealing or acceptable to a landowner than an option agreement. It does not usually require the landowner to sell all of his land to the promoter. Instead, after planning permission has been obtained, the land must be marketed for sale and sold in the open market for the best price reasonably obtainable with the net proceeds of sale being distributed between the landowner and the promoter. This does not, of course, prevent a promoter from bidding for the land or acquiring an interest in the land indirectly (e.g. by entering into a collaboration agreement with another party behind the scenes whose bid for the land is accepted), but it does mean that the purchase price for the land will have been market tested (which does not happen in the case of the option agreement).
2. The promoter is less likely to agree unreasonable planning gain obligations with a local planning authority, since this will impact on its share of the proceeds of sale.
3. The interests of the promoter and the landowner are more aligned than in the case of an option agreement. For example, it will be in the interests of both parties that the open market value of the promotion land and the sale proceeds are maximised.

CHAPTER 14

Collaboration agreements between developers

14.1 WHAT IS A COLLABORATION AGREEMENT?

A collaboration agreement is another type of joint venture involving two or more parties who wish to co-operate in the purchase and/or development of land (see **Appendix E9** on the CD-ROM for an example of a collaboration agreement between two residential developers where the development site is to be acquired pursuant to an option agreement and partitioned equally between them).

Sometimes two or more developers may wish to co-operate in the purchase and/or the development of a large development site. They may wish to acquire a large development site and to partition the site between them with each developer being responsible for the development of the part of the site allocated to it and with each developer being responsible for a proportion of the costs of obtaining planning permission and constructing common infrastructure (i.e. principal roads, sewers and other services which benefit the whole of the development site). The developers may agree to acquire the site in the name of one developer (but with each developer contributing towards the purchase price) on the understanding that the developer in whose name the site is being acquired will hold the site on trust for the other developers until such time as it is partitioned; and the site may be acquired pursuant to a sale and purchase agreement or an option agreement or series of option agreements.

Alternatively, the developers may simply wish to co-operate in obtaining a planning permission to carry out a comprehensive development of land which they already own or control and in constructing infrastructure and services to serve their respective sites.

14.2 OBJECTIVES

In theory, the developers will be working towards a common goal and should not find it too difficult to reach agreement over the terms of the collaboration agreement. However, there are a number of points about which the developers will need to think.

The collaboration agreement should contain a mission statement or statement of objectives which clearly sets out the objectives of the parties. The objectives may include some or all of the following:

- acquiring the development site (which may involve the exercise of an option granted by an option agreement);
- (where the development site has been acquired by one developer) transferring the site or the net developable areas into joint names of the relevant developers;
- transferring the land required for spine and distributor roads into the joint names of the relevant developers;
- acquiring additional land for access and/or easements over adjoining land;
- promoting the site for development and applying for and using reasonable endeavours to obtain planning permission;
- co-operating in the remediation of a brownfield site;
- partitioning the development site or the net developable areas between the developers following the grant of planning permission;
- co-operating in carrying out the construction of common infrastructure (e.g. principal spine and distributor roads and sewers which benefit the allocated lands of all the developers) and common services and getting these adopted;
- sharing in agreed proportions the cost of acquiring the development site, the cost of securing planning permission, the cost of common infrastructure, and the cost of complying with the obligations contained in any statutory agreements or planning agreements relating to the development site (except in so far as they relate exclusively to land allocated to an individual developer);
- each developer constructing affordable housing on the land allocated to it in accordance with the obligations contained in the planning agreement relating to the development site; and
- co-operating in the development of the land allocated to each developer.

When deciding upon the objectives the parties to the collaboration agreement will need to consider whether the principal roads should form part of the land allocated to each party or whether they should be transferred into the joint names of the parties.

14.3 LAND PARTITION

Assuming that the development site is to be partitioned, the agreement should specify when the site is to be partitioned and it should set out the principles which are to apply in making the land allocation between the developers: the developers will not usually wish to partition the land until a satisfactory planning permission has been granted or until a resolution to grant a satisfactory planning permission has been passed.

14.3.1 Land to be partitioned with equal value between two developers

If it is intended that the net developable areas of a residential development site (i.e. the whole of the site excluding the land required for common infrastructure) should be divided equally between the developers then the agreement should state that the land to be allocated to each developer shall so far as practicable be of equal value and consist of equal areas of net developable private residential land and equal areas of affordable land or areas of net developable private residential land and affordable housing land on which equal numbers of dwellings may be constructed. The agreement should also state that the site must be divided in such a way that the land allocated to each developer will share equally in any advantages or disadvantages from the following:

- the conditions imposed by any relevant planning permission affecting the site or conditions likely to be imposed by the local planning authority on any application for approval of reserved matters;
- the physical features and ground conditions of the site;
- the layout of the principal roads (i.e. those roads which are intended to serve the whole of the site);
- the proximity to common infrastructure and common services;
- any specific issues relating to affordable housing;
- general open space requirements;
- phasing;
- density;
- marketability and value;
- any other factor affecting sales or the cost of carrying out development.

The developers will need to think about which developer should get first pick of the partitioned parcels and what should happen in the following circumstances:

- If they are unable to reach agreement as to division of the site. Usually the parties will agree to refer the matter to arbitration or to an independent expert for determination.
- If under the relevant planning permission the number of houses which may be constructed and/or occupied is restricted until a condition has been satisfied. One possibility would be to agree that each developer may build in the agreed proportions the permitted number of houses and not build beyond its share until the condition has been met.
- If during the course of the development of the site it becomes apparent that part of the site suffers from a matter which adversely affects development (such as adverse ground conditions and/or an ancient monument or other archaeological remains) and which was not taken into account when the site was partitioned between the parties. Should the developer affected by the adverse matter be entitled to compensation?
- If it is not possible to divide the areas of net developable residential land and affordable land in such a way that the land allocated to each party is of equal

value. Should the party allocated land worth more than 50 per cent of the value of the net developable residential land and the affordable land be required to make a balancing payment to the other party? If so, the parties should be required to agree a revision of the agreed proportions (50:50) for sharing costs as soon as reasonably practicable and in default of agreement the revision should be determined by an independent expert. Also, the party allocated land worth more than 50 per cent of the value of the net developable residential land and the affordable land should be required to reimburse the other party an appropriate amount in respect of the shared costs previously paid.
- If under the relevant planning permission the site must be developed in phases.

14.3.2 Land to be partitioned between more than two developers

If two or more developers wish to partition a site and share common infrastructure and common services and planning costs in unequal proportions this can be tricky. They could agree to partition the site so that they share all the net developable land or saleable square footage of dwellings in the agreed proportions. However, it should be noted that this method of partition/valuation does not take account of the fact that different types of buildings have different values (e.g. compare commercial buildings and residential dwellings; private and affordable housing; two-storey and three-storey dwellings with the same floor area, etc.).

Where a residential development site is being acquired by one developer (whether pursuant to an option or a conditional contract) with a view to it being partitioned between a number of other developers, in unequal proportions, the developers may agree that:

- Each developer is to be allocated a proportion of the total net developable private residential land within the development site and a proportion of the total affordable housing land based on the percentage of the purchase price to be paid by it (this proportion will be known as 'the agreed proportion').
- Each developer is to be responsible for its agreed proportion of all shared costs (which expression will need to be carefully defined) and all other costs and expenses payable under the collaboration agreement.

14.3.3 Land in different ownerships

Where separate parcels of land are in the ownerships of different developers and the developers agree to collaborate in obtaining a planning permission to develop all of the land within their combined ownership and the carrying out of common infrastructure works, they may agree that:

- Either each developer will be allocated a proportion of the total net developable land (which expression will need to be carefully defined) within the site representing its 'agreed proportion' of the total net developable land or, instead of the land being 'partitioned', each developer will retain its existing land holding and, if necessary, there will be a balancing land transfer or transfers between developers to ensure that each developer will own its agreed proportion of the total net developable land.

- The agreed proportions will be calculated by comparing the gross acreage of each developer's land holding with the total gross acreage of the development site.
- The cost of obtaining planning permission and carrying out common infrastructure works is to be shared in 'the agreed proportions'.

Under the above arrangement each developer will therefore be entitled to receive a proportion of the total net developable land within the site equal to the proportion which the gross acreage of its land holding bears to the total gross acreage of the whole development site.

Where each developer will retain its existing land holding and following the grant of a satisfactory planning permission it transpires that the land actually within a developer's ownership does not represent its agreed proportion of the total net developable land, there will need to be an adjustment/reconciliation which could be by way of a balancing land transfer and/or a variation of the agreed proportions. The collaboration agreement should contain an appropriate reconciliation provision to deal with this.

There may also need to be a financial adjustment if, following the grant of planning permission, the affordable housing dwellings which are to be built on the land allocated to a particular developer do not represent its agreed proportion of the affordable housing dwellings or there is a change in the anticipated tenure mix or size or location of rented and shared equity units. All of this will require careful drafting.

14.3.4 Defining 'net developable land'

As mentioned above, the expression 'net developable land' will need to be carefully defined. Net developable land will invariably include:

- all buildings and the curtilage of all buildings;
- all land required for estate infrastructure (i.e. infrastructure which benefits the land allocated to an individual developer only, such as estate roads, estate sewers and estate services); and
- land required for affordable housing.

Net developable land will usually exclude:

- facility land (i.e. land required for public open space and play areas and land required for the purpose of education, health, community use, playing fields, etc.);
- land required for primary or common infrastructure (such as principal spine and/or distributor roads (i.e. roads without direct access to dwellings) and main sewers which benefit the allocated lands of all the developers);

- land required for common services (e.g. service installations which benefit the allocated lands of all the developers);
- land required for complying with common planning obligations (apart from those relating to affordable housing).

Where there is a road which benefits the allocated lands of more than one of the developers and which also provides direct access to the dwellings on either side of the road, the developers may agree that one half of the carriageway of the road which abuts the allocated land of an individual shall comprise net developable land.

14.4 ACTION FOR JOINT PURPOSES

The agreement should set out what action is to be undertaken by the parties for their joint benefit and by whom.

This action may include:

- obtaining planning permission;
- procuring the construction and adoption of the common infrastructure and common services;
- entering into and complying with the obligations contained in a s.106 agreement;
- the laying out of public open space areas;
- the letting of contracts relating to the construction of common infrastructure and common services;
- the letting of contracts relating to other service installations;
- dealing with environmental audits and remediation on a brownfield site;
- entering into statutory infrastructure agreements relating to common infrastructure.

It would be sensible to include a provision in the agreement stating that no action is to be taken by a party until it has been approved by the other party/parties, that such approval may not be unreasonably withheld or delayed, that it will be deemed to have been given if no response to a request for approval is received within 10 working days of such request and that in the event of a dispute the matter is to be referred to and determined by an independent expert.

In relation to the construction of primary or common infrastructure, the parties to the collaboration agreement will need to consider the following:

- Should the appointment of the contractor be a joint appointment?
- The tender process – ideally, there should be a requirement for the work to be tendered to no fewer than three contractors.
- Should the contractor submitting the lowest quotation be appointed to carry out the works?
- The form of the build contract – this should be in a form and contain a building programme to be approved by all the parties (acting reasonably).

14.5 SHARED EXPENSES

The agreement should specify the types of expenses which are to be incurred by and shared between the developers and the proportions in which they are to be shared.

The shared expenses may include some or all of the following:

- the cost of complying with any obligation in a contract for purchase or option agreement;
- the cost of entering into and complying with obligations in a road or sewer adoption agreement or any other statutory agreement (except where the agreement relates exclusively to the land allocated to an individual developer);
- the costs and expenses of negotiating and completing any necessary planning agreement;
- all of the costs and expenses of complying with the obligations contained in any relevant planning agreement, including planning gain costs (except in so far as the obligations relate exclusively to the land allocated to an individual developer);
- the cost of obtaining planning permission and planning application fees;
- the costs of preparing plans and specifications for common infrastructure and common services;
- consultants' fees, including architect's fees, planning consultant's fees and highway consultant's fees;
- the cost of constructing common infrastructure and common services;
- the cost of removal or diversion of existing services;
- the cost of laying out public open space areas, including any commuted sum payable to a relevant authority;
- the cost of bonds;
- stamp duty land tax (SDLT) and Land Registry fees;
- any Community Infrastructure Levy (CIL) liability (but see **5.4**);
- the cost of demolition of buildings;
- the cost of surveys and soil investigations;
- the cost of any indemnity insurance policy.

The costs of complying with any planning agreement or infrastructure agreement should be shared between the developers in the agreed proportions, except in so far as they relate exclusively to the land allocated to a developer.

It would be sensible to include a provision in the agreement to the effect that no expenditure (or no expenditure above a specified level) is to be incurred by a party until it has been approved by the other party/parties and there should be a requirement for evidence of expenditure to be produced.

Where the collaboration agreement provides for the agreed proportions to be adjusted following the partition of the development site, the agreement should also contain a clause stating that the developers shall document any agreed revision to the agreed proportions as soon as reasonably practicable. There should also be a requirement for a financial adjustment to be made in respect of any shared costs already paid so as to ensure that all shared costs (whether already incurred or to be incurred in the future) are borne in the agreed revised proportions.

As discussed in **5.4.14**, the parties to the collaboration agreement will need to decide how any CIL liability is to be apportioned between them and whether or not it should be a shared cost or apportioned on a gross internal floor area or some other basis.

14.6 PAYMENTS

The agreement should contain provisions dealing with the mechanics for making payments which become due from one party to another and provide for interest to be paid on any late payments.

14.7 SECURITY

The covenant strength of the developers may have to be addressed and consideration given to the question of whether a guarantor or other security, such as a bond or a parent company guarantee, is required.

A developer may consider that it would be desirable to take a legal charge over the land allocated to the other developer(s), but, if this conflicts with third party financing, other security may have to be considered, such as a parent company guarantee.

Where the development site will be purchased in the name of one developer with the other developer(s) contributing towards the price, the contributing developer(s) may wish to take a charge over the site on the basis that the charge will be released once the site has been partitioned between the developers.

14.8 PLANNING OBLIGATIONS

The agreement should impose various planning obligations on each developer. For example, each developer should be obliged to covenant or undertake:

- to fully and promptly comply with the obligations contained in any relevant planning agreement and to discharge all planning conditions contained in any relevant planning permission in so far as they relate to their allocated land so as not to prejudice, delay or hinder the development of, or the occupation of dwellings on, the land allocated to the other developer(s);
- not to submit any application for planning permission or approval of reserved matters in respect of the land allocated to it which would prejudice any existing relevant planning permission or planning agreement relating to the development site;
- not to increase the number or density of dwellings to be created on the land allocated to it or the rate of construction or occupation thereof over that

approved under any existing relevant planning permission or planning agreement without the approval of the other developer(s);

- to promptly pay and contribute in the agreed proportions to all sums payable under any relevant planning agreement, except to the extent that they relate exclusively to the land allocated to an individual developer; and
- to construct affordable housing on the land allocated to it so as to fully and strictly comply with any relevant planning agreement.

14.9 INFRASTRUCTURE OBLIGATIONS

The agreement should impose infrastructure and other general obligations on each developer, such as an obligation to enter into infrastructure agreements relating to common infrastructure serving the whole of the development site, an obligation to agree on the letting of the contracts for the carrying out of the common infrastructure works and an obligation to use all reasonable endeavours to procure that the works are carried out as soon as reasonably practicable or in accordance with timescales agreed between the developers (each acting reasonably).

14.10 MUTUAL EASEMENTS

The agreement should impose an obligation on each developer to grant to the other(s) such easements as shall be reasonably necessary to enable the development occupation and use of the land allocated to each developer.

14.11 CO-OPERATION

The agreement should contain a general co-operation clause stating that each developer shall at all times act in good faith towards the other developer(s) and not do or omit to do anything which would prejudice, prevent, delay or hinder the development of the land allocated to the other developer(s).

14.12 RESOLUTION OF DISPUTES AND DEADLOCK/RETIREMENT PROVISIONS

It will be in each developer's interests for the collaboration agreement to contain a dispute resolution clause and deadlock and/or retirement provisions may also be required. In certain instances it may not be appropriate for a dispute to be settled by a third party. For example, if a deadlock is reached on a fundamental issue, such as whether a planning permission is a satisfactory planning permission or whether to appeal against a planning decision or to exercise an option, the parties may wish to have the ability to terminate the agreement or to allow a party to retire from the collaboration (see clause 5 of **Appendix E9** on the CD-ROM). Alternatively, each developer may prefer to have the right to buy out the interest of the other developer(s) in the collaboration agreement and the development site, but this may give rise to valuation issues or lead to an unsatisfactory outcome: one party may be forced to sell its interest in the site and, if that party is the owner of the site or has the benefit of an option to purchase the site, this may not be desirable. Another difficulty with deadlock provisions is that because of the possible adverse consequences of invoking the deadlock provisions no party may wish to trigger the provisions, which would mean that an impasse would arise. For all of these reasons deadlock provisions should not be automatically included in a collaboration agreement; they need to be thought about very carefully.

14.13 DURATION

The collaboration agreement should contain a clause stating that, save as otherwise mentioned in the agreement, it will continue in full force and effect until the objectives of the promotion agreement have been satisfied and the obligations of the parties under the agreement have been discharged in full.

14.14 STEP IN RIGHTS

Step in rights are important and the agreement should contain a step in rights clause which allows a party to carry out an action where another party is in default and to recover the cost of taking the action plus interest from the other party.

14.15 PRE-EMPTION RIGHTS

The developers may wish to consider including a pre-emption clause in the collaboration agreement giving each developer a right of first refusal to buy any other developer's allocated land in the event of that developer deciding to sell its land. The right of pre-emption should not apply to certain disposals, such as the disposal of individual residential dwellings or the disposal of land required for public open space or site service installations.

14.16 DECLARATION OF TRUST

If the development site is to be purchased (perhaps pursuant to an option agreement) by one developer, who will subsequently transfer part of the site to the other developer(s), with all contributing towards the purchase price and associated costs, the agreement should contain a declaration of trust provision stating that the developer acquiring the land will hold it on trust for itself and the other developer(s) as tenants in common (or that the developer who has the benefit of the option will hold its interest in the option and any land acquired under the option agreement on trust for itself and the other developer(s) as tenants in common).

14.17 DEALINGS

Where the development site will be purchased by only one developer the other developer(s) may wish to impose an obligation on the developer purchasing the site to ensure that, pending the partition of the site, a restriction against dealing is entered on the title to the site.

14.18 INSOLVENCY

The parties should consider the implications of any party becoming insolvent: they may wish to include a provision in the agreement which gives each party the right to buy any other party's interest in the agreement and any land owned or controlled by it in the event of that party becoming insolvent.

14.19 PURCHASE OF ADDITIONAL LAND

The collaboration agreement should contain a provision stating that no party will acquire any land in the vicinity of the proposed development site without consulting the other party/parties and giving them the opportunity to participate in the purchase.

14.20 ASSIGNMENT

The parties may wish to include a provision in the collaboration agreement prohibiting any party from assigning the benefit and burden of the agreement to a third party without the consent of the other party/parties.

14.21 NO PARTNERSHIP

The agreement should contain suitable a provision making it clear that no partnership is intended to be created by the parties.

14.22 VALUE ADDED TAX

The agreement should contain value added tax (VAT) provisions, including a provision that, if necessary, the developers will register themselves with HM Revenue & Customs as joint property owners of the relevant property for VAT purposes and that any input VAT credit received by the joint VAT registration will be divided between the developers in the agreed proportions.

14.23 ADVANTAGES

Collaboration agreements between developers have the following advantages:

- They are useful where a developer does not want to develop the whole of a development site and wishes to share the risk by involving another developer who will take part of the site and contribute towards planning and infrastructure costs.
- They are useful where two developers are competing for a site – by agreeing to collaborate they avoid possibly losing out or pushing up the price.
- They are useful where two or more developers own or have an interest in adjoining or neighbouring land and the local planning authority requires a comprehensive development of the area comprising the combined land holdings of all the developers.
- They do not have the tax disadvantages associated with traditional joint venture companies where landowners pool their land by transferring their respective land holdings to the joint venture company or where two developers agree to acquire and develop a site jointly in the name of a joint venture company. Where land is to be transferred into the name of a joint venture company this could trigger a capital gains tax charge. It is also likely to attract SDLT. In addition, there may be double tax hit risks: capital gains tax liability attaches to the company and may also attach to the shareholdings.

CHAPTER 15

Collaboration agreements between landowners and land pool trusts: achieving equalisation and avoiding double taxation

15.1 INTRODUCTION

A group of landowners wishing to realise the maximum development value of their land will often enter into collaboration agreements with one another, with a view to dividing the proceeds of sale between them in proportion to their holdings. This will often be accompanied by a promotion agreement, by which the landowners commission a planning promoter or developer to obtain planning permission and to market and sell the development site, although sometimes landowners will enter into a hybrid promotion/option agreement with a developer, under which the developer is granted an option to purchase part of the development site following a sale of part of the site on the open market.

The principle of dividing up the proceeds of sale so that each landowner receives a fair and reasonable proportion of the value of the whole area being developed is known as 'equalisation'. There are various mechanisms that can be used to achieve it, and the landowners will need to consider carefully which mechanism is right for them. One of the principal concerns is tax. There can be unfortunate tax implications for landowners who enter into collaboration agreements without a full understanding of the implications. In particular, care has to be taken to avoid a double charge to capital gains tax (CGT).

15.2 ACHIEVING EQUALISATION

The principle of equalisation requires that, on a sale of land within a development area owned by a number of different landowners and which benefits from planning permission, each landowner will receive a sum which represents a fair and reasonable proportion of the value of the whole of the development area. (The land being sold may include the whole of the development area or a part of it and on a sale of part the landowners may agree that each landowner will be entitled to a share of the net sale proceeds, even if he does not own land within the phase being sold, so long as he owns land which forms part of the land that benefits from the planning permission.)

Where the development area comprises bare land the relevant proportion will usually be calculated either by (a) dividing the number of gross acres comprised within an individual landowner's ownership at the time when the collaboration agreement is entered into by the total number of gross acres owned by all of the landowners at the time when the collaboration agreement is entered into, or (b) by dividing the number of gross acres comprised within an individual landowner's ownership following the grant of planning permission that benefit from the planning permission by the total number of gross acres belonging to all of the landowners that are comprised within the planning permission.

Where the development area includes bare land and buildings, the relevant proportion will usually be calculated either by (a) dividing the value of an individual landowner's landholding prior to the grant of planning permission by the total value of the land belonging to all of the landowners prior to the grant of planning permission, or (b) by dividing the value of the land within an individual landowner's ownership that benefits from planning permission on the basis that it does not benefit from any planning permission by the total value of the whole of the consented land (i.e. the land belonging to all of the landowners that is comprised within the planning permission) on the basis that it does not benefit from any planning permission.

Sometimes, where the development area includes land and buildings, the landowners will agree either (a) to carve out/exclude all buildings from the promotion agreement, or (b) to the owner of a building being paid a sum equal to the value of his building out of the net sale proceeds and to the balance of the net sale proceeds being shared between all of the landowners on a gross acreage basis (so that each landowner will receive a proportion of the balance of the net sale proceeds to be calculated by dividing the gross acreage of the land belonging to an individual owner (excluding any building) by the total gross acreage of the bare land within the whole of the development area (excluding all buildings)).

Where landowners agree to share all sale proceeds between them and to enter into a land pooling arrangement, all land on which buildings are located should be excluded from the pooling arrangement (see **15.4**).

Equalisation may be achieved in a number of different ways, including the following:

- by ensuring (through the masterplan/planning layout) that land uses are evenly distributed across the development area, so that each landowner obtains sale proceeds for his land that are proportional to the amount of land that has been contributed for development – this is not always easy to achieve where (for example) there is a requirement for substantial infrastructure (such as a by-pass, a school, a village hall or other community uses) or other land uses that do not have any development value (such as playing fields, public open spaces and balancing ponds);

- by the landowners sharing all net sale proceeds – this sounds straightforward, but can create the most difficulties in terms of tax;
- by balancing payments being made between landowners (see **15.5**); and
- by land transfers between landowners and adjustments being made to the proportion of any planning costs and infrastructure costs for which a landowner may be liable (see **15.5**).

15.3 DOUBLE TAXATION

A potential issue for landowners wishing to share all net proceeds for all sales of their different landholdings is that there may be a double tax hit (as illustrated in the case of *Burca* v. *Parkinson* [2001] STC 1298). The double tax hit arises where different landowners wish to sell their combined landholdings in tranches/phases and to apportion all net sale proceeds between them on an equalised basis with each landowner being entitled to a share of the net sale proceeds, regardless of whether or not his land is included within the sale of a tranche/phase. The owner of the tranche/phase being sold will be liable to pay CGT on the whole of the proceeds of sale, regardless of the fact that a proportion of these proceeds is shared with other landowners, and the other landowners will be liable to pay CGT on the share of the sale proceeds that they receive (so that there will be a double taxation of these sums).

The double taxation issue can be illustrated by the following example:

- Suppose that four parties each own 100 acres of land and that they enter into a collaboration agreement under which they are to share all sale proceeds equally between them.
- If Party 1 sells their land first resulting in the proceeds for a distribution of £40 million, based on the collaboration agreement, they would transfer £10 million each to Party 2, Party 3 and Party 4.
- Party 1 cannot obtain a tax deduction on the £30 million they pay to Party 2, Party 3 and Party 4, which means they pick up the CGT liability on the full £40 million. (This is because the amounts paid do not fit within any of the categories of allowable expenditure under the Taxation of Chargeable Gains Act (TCGA) 1992, s.38.)
- Party 2, Party 3 and Party 4 will also still be subject to CGT on their £10 million, which means there is a double tax assessment on £30 million. (This is because Party 2, Party 3 and Party 4 have an asset (namely, the chose in action under the collaboration agreement giving them a right to a share of the sale proceeds). When they received their share of the sale proceeds they would have derived a capital sum from the chose in action and under TCGA 1992, s.22 a disposal would have occurred.)

Double taxation will not arise:

- if the development site is sold as a whole to a single buyer/developer and each landowner receives a separate payment from the buyer/developer for his land. However, this may not be possible where the development site is very large and there is a requirement for the development site to be sold in phases to different developers, unless a sale of the whole of the development site to a large consortium of developers can be agreed. It is likely that such a sale would have to be on deferred payment terms and it is inevitable that the consortium would require a 'discount for bulk', but, on the positive side, a sale of the whole does avoid a potential double charge to CGT and the need to set up a land pool trust. (Before agreeing to deferred payment terms the landowners would want to ensure that they cater adequately for the landowners' tax liabilities and that adequate security is provided by the buyer.)
- if the development site is sold in phases and there is no sharing of sale proceeds, so that each landowner receives a payment only for land which he owns. Whether or not it will be possible to sell part of a development site that includes land belonging to only one landowner will depend on the planning layout and may be difficult. For example, it will not be possible if dwellings are located partly on one landowner's land and partly on another landowner's land. Also, equalisation may be an issue if, following the grant of planning permission, land uses have not been equally distributed across the development area and certain landowners have less net developable land/more infrastructure on their land than other landowners. However, this problem could potentially be overcome by those landowners with less developable land being compensated by the other landowners (see **15.5**).

15.4 LAND POOL TRUSTS

One possible way of avoiding the double tax hit issue is for the various landowners to create a land pool trust and to transfer/pool their respective landholdings into that trust. This would involve the landowners entering into a trust deed and then transferring their respective lands to the trustees. The trust deed would deal with, amongst other things, how any promotion premium and net sale proceeds are to be apportioned between the various beneficiaries of the trust, decision making, the trustees' powers, and the unravelling of the trust (which may involve the transfer of land back to the original owners in the event that the promotion agreement is terminated before the promotion objectives have been achieved or there is land which remains unsold after the promotion agreement has expired). The transfers to the trustees and the trust deed would usually be executed on the same day, with the transfers being executed prior to the signing of the trust deed and containing a declaration that the trustees hold the land transferred upon the trusts and with and subject to the terms, powers and provisions set out in the trust deed.

The trust will be a bare trust and the transfer/conveyance of land into the trust will not trigger a CGT liability. The decision of Knox J in *Warrington* v. *Brown* [1989] STC 577 is authority for the proposition that none of the landowners would make a disposal by contributing their land to the land pool trust. This is notwithstanding that each landowner would, in a literal sense, have disposed of a fractional share of the land which he previously owned outright. However, the values of the respective parcels contributed to the pool must equate with each other on a pro rata acreage basis. Also there should be no liability to stamp duty land tax (SDLT) on the transfer of land to the pool trust (since, assuming that the value per acre of land pooled is identical, there will be no disposal for CGT purposes) and, where the landowners wish to terminate the pooling arrangement and to transfer land back to the original landowners, no CGT or SDLT should be payable (because, again, there has been no disposal).

As pointed out by the authors of *Potter and Monroe's Tax Planning with Precedents* (11th edition, Sweet & Maxwell), it is crucial that land contributed to the land pool trust by each landowner is of equal value (within the normal tolerances of valuation) on a pro rata acreage basis. In other words, the value per acre of land contributed by each landowner must be identical. If one of the holdings is more valuable (on a pro rata acreage basis) than the others, one landowner might be treated as making a chargeable disposal on contributing his land to the trust, with a potential CGT charge. It would be advisable for valuers to be asked to provide valuations of each landowner's holding and, where a development area includes both land and buildings, the buildings should be excluded from the land pool trust.

In addition to a trust deed the landowners may wish to enter into a collaboration agreement before their landholdings are transferred to the trust that sets out how any promotion premium and net sale proceeds are to be shared between them and containing good faith and general co-operation provisions.

Sometimes landowners may wish to delay entering into a land pool trust arrangement until their land has been allocated for development and to include a provision in the collaboration agreement that they will take steps to set up a land pool trust as soon as reasonably practicable after their land has been allocated. One advantage of setting up a land pool trust after allocation is that a landowner will know whether or not his land forms part of the consented land and there will be no need for the trustees of the land pool trust to reconvey land to a landowner if his land (or any part of it) subsequently does not form part of the consented land. Another advantage of not setting up a land pool trust early is that the landowners may decide to dispense with a trust if the land allocated is not as much as originally anticipated and the development area can be sold as a whole. Prima facie it is possible to delay setting up a land pool trust until after the land is allocated or planning permission is granted. However, if the setting up of the land pool trust is delayed until after allocation or the grant of planning permission, there may be a potential problem. If under the planning permission some of the land for which consent has been granted was allocated to, say, open space and some to infrastructure, and if some of the development land had a more beneficial permission (e.g. greater density per acre or different kinds of development), the values of the respective parcels of land on an acreage basis at that stage might not be equivalent, so the creation of the pool trust at that stage could trigger a CGT liability. The same issue may arise if land uses are indicated in a draft allocation. It would seem sensible, therefore, to set up the land pool trust as soon as possible (and before the land is allocated or any land uses are indicated in a draft allocation or an indicative masterplan issued prior to the land being allocated). (Another disadvantage of delaying the setting up of a land pool trust is that if the landowners wish to claim entrepreneurs' relief and to enter into a farming partnership arrangement, a sale of the development area would need to be postponed. This is because the farming partnership will need to continue for at least a year before the development area is sold and the farming partnership is terminated in order to satisfy the conditions for obtaining entrepreneurs' relief.)

The advantages of a trust/pooling arrangement are:

- it allows landowners to share all sale proceeds regardless of whether or not their land is included in a sale and to avoid the problem of double taxation;
- it enables sale proceeds to be apportioned/shared between landowners on an equalised basis so that each landowner receives a fair proportion of the value of the whole of the development site and is not prejudiced if their land is to be used mainly for infrastructure or as public open space or a school or other use which does not have any development value;
- landowners owning land which will not come forward for development in the first phase or early phases of development will not be prejudiced, as they will receive a share of the net sale proceeds following each sale (regardless of whether or not their land is included in a sale);
- it allows landowners to share sale proceeds and (subject to certain conditions being satisfied) to claim entrepreneurs' relief. In order to claim entrepreneurs' relief, the landowners would need to enter into a farming partnership agreement (to which the trustees of the land pool trust have granted their consent) and the farming partnership would need to continue for at least a year. Where land is farmed in partnership by an individual landowner, the land will first have to cease to be a partnership asset before the new farming partnership is created (where different farming activities are carried out by the various landowners, the mechanics of the new farming partnership arrangement will need to be carefully considered); and
- only the trust will need to opt to tax/elect to waive exemption from value added tax (VAT) in order to ensure that the VAT payable on the promoter's fee can be recovered (i.e. there will be no need for each landowner to opt to tax).

The disadvantages of a trust/pooling arrangement are:

- the time and cost implications. In addition to legal fees for drafting and negotiating the promotion agreement and any collaboration agreement, it will be necessary to prepare a trust deed, to transfer the land belonging to the various landowners to the trust and to register the transfers at the Land Registry;

- there may be a need to unravel the trust in the event that the promotion agreement is terminated before the promotion objectives have been achieved or in the event that any part of the development site remains unsold after the promotion agreement has come to an end;
- (depending on what is agreed) landowners will not be able to sell their individual landholdings, although they may be able to dispose of their interest in the trust (assuming that this is permitted under the trust deed);
- where land belonging to a landowner is subject to a mortgage or legal charge, it will be necessary to obtain the consent of the mortgagee/chargee to the land being transferred to the trust and for the mortgagee/chargee to enter into a deed of adherence in which they agree to be bound by the terms of the promotion agreement. Also, a provision will need to be included in the collaboration agreement and/or trust deed stating that the cost of repaying the loan secured by the mortgage/legal charge is to be deducted from the share of the net sale proceeds due to the landowner whose land is subject to the mortgage/charge.

15.5 EQUALISATION THROUGH LAND TRANSFERS AND/OR BALANCING PAYMENTS AND/OR REDUCED LIABILITY FOR COSTS

An alternative to sharing sale proceeds may lie in balancing payments or land transfers.

Each landowner is likely to have an expectation that following the grant of planning permission his land should have a value equal to a fair and reasonable proportion of the value of the whole of the development area (e.g. a proportion to be calculated by dividing the number of gross acres comprised within an individual landowner's ownership by the total number of gross acres within the whole of the development area). It could be agreed between all the landowners that, if following the grant of planning permission an individual landowner would not on a sale of his land receive a sum which represents his agreed due proportion of the development value of the whole of the development area (because, for example, his land is to be used predominantly for infrastructure or some other use with no development value), he will be compensated by other landowners making him a balancing payment or transferring part of their developable land to him. In addition, he may want an adjustment to be made to the proportion of costs (such as infrastructure and planning costs) for which he may be liable.

Balancing payments and land transfers are not a simple solution. Determining the amount of any balancing payment may require valuations to be carried out and agreeing how different land uses (such as affordable housing) are to be valued. Alternatively, if land is to be transferred, the extent and location of that land will need to be determined. There is also the issue of how balancing payments should be protected.

15.6 PROTECTING BALANCING PAYMENTS

Where landowners decide to achieve equalisation through balancing payments, they will need to consider the question of security for such payments.

The security may comprise legal charges and/or cross-easements, cross-covenants and cross-options by one landowner in favour of others. The deed containing such arrangements will need to provide for their release upon a sale of the burdened land, once the secured obligations have been performed.

15.7 PREFERRED OPTION FOR ACHIEVING EQUALISATION AND ENSURING DELIVERABILITY

It appears to be widely accepted that a land pool trust works as a solution to the double taxation issue and, in the case of a large development site involving a number of landowners, it is probably the best way of achieving equalisation and ensuring that a scheme is capable of being delivered. As mentioned above, equalisation is achievable in other ways, such as by endeavouring to ensure that following the grant of planning permission the land owned by each landowner will consist of an agreed proportion (based on gross acreage) of the total net developable land within the development area and (if this cannot be achieved) requiring balancing payments to be made. However, land pool trusts are more straightforward and avoid the need for security arrangements, which can be complex and may be unacceptable to a promoter. They also ensure that the proposed development will be capable of being delivered and avoid the need for landowners to enter into mutual deeds of easement and/or options for easement. The promoter will want to know that the proposed development is capable of being delivered, that the landowners will not ransom each other, that on a sale of part of a development site all necessary rights of way and rights in respect of drainage and services over other parts of the development site will be granted, that the landowners will co-operate and act in good faith towards each other in connection with the sale and development of their respective lands and that they will enter into such deeds and agreements as may be required in connection with the development of the development site (including road and sewer adoption agreements, infrastructure agreements and agreements with utility companies). None of this will be a concern for the promoter if the landowners create a land pool trust and transfer their respective landholdings into the trust.

15.8 THE FORM OF THE TRUST DEED

Having decided to enter into a land pool trust the landowners will need to think about a number of matters, including the following:

15.8.1 The trust period

For how long should the trust continue to subsist? Clearly, the trust will need to continue for a period which extends beyond the date on which the promotion agreement will come to an end.

15.8.2 Restrictions on a disposal by a beneficiary of their interest in the trust

The landowners will need to consider whether a beneficiary should be prohibited from disposing of his interest in the trust or charging such interest without the consent of the other beneficiaries or whether a beneficiary should be permitted to make a disposal of his interest in the trust without obtaining such consent provided that the recipient of the disposal is bound by the terms of the trust deed.

15.8.3 Apportionment of any premium and net sale proceeds

The landowners will need to consider how any premium payable under the promotion agreement and any net sale proceeds generated by a sale of land pursuant to the promotion agreement should be apportioned between the beneficiaries of the trust. Usually any premium payable under a promotion agreement will be shared between the beneficiaries in proportion to the number of gross acres of land they each contributed to the trust. The sharing of net sale proceeds generated by a sale of land under a promotion agreement is less straightforward. Should the proportion of net sale proceeds that a beneficiary is to be entitled to receive be based on the number of gross acres of land contributed to the trust by the beneficiary or should it be based on the number of gross acres of land belonging to the beneficiary following the grant of planning permission that form part of the consented land (i.e. that are included within a satisfactory planning permission)? Put another way, should a beneficiary be entitled to a share of any net sale proceeds generated by a sale pursuant to a promotion agreement only if the land or part of the land owned by him before it was pooled forms part of the consented land or should a beneficiary be entitled to a share of any net sale proceeds even if none of the land that he contributed to the trust benefits from planning permission? The precedent for a land pool trust deed contained in *Potter and Monroe's Tax Planning with Precedents* (AR Thornhill and KJ Prosser, 11th edition, Sweet & Maxwell) assumes that upon a sale of any land transferred to the trustees, the sale proceeds will be shared between the beneficiaries in proportion to the acreages that they contributed to the trust. Under such a trust deed a beneficiary of the trust would be entitled to a share of the sale proceeds even if none of the land contributed to the trust by him formed part of the consented land. This is unlikely to be regarded as fair or reasonable by many landowners. However, notwithstanding that under the trust deed the trustees are to hold the trust property upon trust for the beneficial owners in shares which reflect the acreages contributed to the trust by each beneficial owner, there is no reason in principle why the landowners cannot agree that a beneficiary shall be entitled to receive a share of any sale proceeds which reflects the acreage of the land previously owned by him (i.e. before it was pooled) that forms part of the consented land.

15.8.4 Unsold land

The landowners will need to consider how they would like to deal with any land transferred to the trust which remains unsold after the promotion agreement has come to an end. There are a number of options available, including the following:

- transfer back to each beneficiary such part of the land originally contributed by him as has not been included within a satisfactory planning permission and transfer to the beneficiaries such part of the trust land as shall be comprised within a satisfactory planning permission and which remains unsold for them to hold as tenants in common in the same proportions as those agreed for sharing sale proceeds;
- transfer the unsold land to the beneficiaries for them to hold as tenants in common in the same proportions as those agreed for sharing sale proceeds; or
- sell the land on the open market and apportion the sale proceeds between the beneficiaries in the agreed proportions.

15.8.5 The trustees

The landowners will need to decide who the trustees of the land pool should be. There cannot be more than four trustees.

15.9 CONCLUSION

Landowners wishing to collaborate and to achieve equalisation need to consider how they intend to collaborate and to achieve equalisation and to be aware that if they intend to share all net sale proceeds between them, the transaction needs to be properly structured to avoid a potential double charge to CGT. Expert legal and tax advice should be obtained at an early stage.

CHAPTER 16

Mixed use developments

Where a development consists of a mixed use building or buildings the correct structures need to be put in place if the freeholder is going to maximise the investment value of the development and avoid infringing the pre-emption rights of residential tenants under the Landlord and Tenant Act (LTA) 1987, Part 1 when selling his freehold interest in the building. (In this chapter a reference to LTA 1987 is a reference to the Landlord and Tenant Act 1987, Part 1 and a reference to the Act is a reference to the Landlord and Tenant Act 1987.)

Suppose that a building consists of four ground floor retail units with 12 flats on the three floors above, all let on long residential leases. The freeholder will not be able to dispose of his freehold interest in the building or to grant a headlease of the common parts of the building without complying with LTA 1987, s.5 (unless the correct structures have been put in place beforehand). It would appear that the freeholder will be able to grant a lease of only the commercial space within the building without having to comply with LTA 1987, although, as discussed below, there is some doubt about this.

16.1 THE RESIDENTIAL ELEMENT – DIFFERENT STRUCTURES

The residential element of a mixed use building will usually consist of units let on long leases (generally 99 years or more) which reserve a ground rent and which have been granted for a premium. Often the ground rent will be set as high as possible and it will be subject to increase in accordance with an escalator clause. Ground rents can be a very tradeable asset, but, as discussed below, forward planning and proper structuring will be required in order to ensure that a ground rent disposal does not infringe the provisions of LTA 1987.

The freehold owner of a mixed use building will need to consider how the common parts of the building (including the structure, the exterior and common facilities) should be maintained. There are a range of alternatives available to the freeholder, including the following:

- Include service charge provisions in the long residential leases (and the leases of commercial units) which impose an obligation on the landlord to provide or to procure the provision of services for the building (including the repair and maintenance of the common parts). Where this structure is used the freeholder will need to consider whether or not it will be necessary to comply with LTA 1987, s.5 before proceeding with a sale of his freehold interest.

- Set up a management company and make the management company a party to the long residential leases and the commercial leases for the purpose of covenanting with the landlord and the tenants to provide services and upon completion of each lease issue shares in the management company to the tenant or (in the case of a management company limited by guarantee) require each tenant to become a member of the company. Where this structure is used it would be advisable for the freeholder to also become a member of the management company but with enhanced voting rights. This will enable the freeholder to retain control of the management of the building and is achieved by creating two classes of shares and issuing the freeholder with shares which provide him with enhanced voting rights. Again, where this structure is used, the freeholder will need to consider whether or not a sale of his freehold interest would be caught by LTA 1987.
- Set up a management company and let the common parts of the building (including the structure, the exterior and common facilities) or the whole building to the management company on a long lease containing service charge provisions (including a covenant by the management company to provide services) at a peppercorn rent. Where this structure is used, the long lease will need to be put in place before 50 per cent of the residential units have been let. (Note that under LTA 1987 a unit will be regarded as let if an agreement for lease in respect of that unit has been exchanged.) The grant of the long lease in favour of the management company will be subject to LTA 1987, unless the building contains commercial units with an internal floor area in excess of 50 per cent of the total internal floor area of the building, in which case LTA 1987 will not apply. Alternatively, the freeholder could enter into an agreement for lease with the management company before 50 per cent of the residential units have been let. The agreement for lease and the subsequent grant of the long lease to the management company would not be caught by LTA 1987, even if the lease was granted after the sale of the last residential unit. Once the long lease in favour of the management company has been granted the freeholder will be able to sell his freehold interest without having to comply with the requirements of LTA 1987, s.5. This is because the freeholder will not be the immediate landlord of the residential tenants (see below).

Where a long headlease of an entire building is granted to a management company before any flat lease is granted, the freeholder will want to ensure that he receives the benefit of all the premiums payable to the management company by the purchasers of the flats. This can be achieved by the freeholder retaining ownership of the management company until the last flat is sold. It will also be necessary (whether the long lease in favour of the management company is put in place before or after any of the long residential leases are granted) to include a covenant by the management company in its headlease to collect the ground rents and the insurance rents payable by the residential tenants and to pass them up to the freeholder. Also, the freeholder will want to carve out the commercial element of the building by excluding all the commercial space from the premises demised by the headlease.

It should be noted that if a management company is to be set up for the purpose of maintaining the common parts of a building then the management company should have a legal right to enter the building. If such a right of entry does not arise from a leasehold interest then the tenants of the building will need to become members of the management company, otherwise the structure will not comply with the requirements of the UK Finance Mortgage Lenders' Handbook.

16.2 GROUND RENT DISPOSALS AND PRE-EMPTION RIGHTS

Under LTA 1987, s.1(1), a landlord may not make a relevant disposal (as defined in s.4) affecting any premises to which Part 1 applies unless:

- he has in accordance with s.5 previously served a notice under that section with respect to the qualifying tenants of the flats contained in those premises (being a notice giving the qualifying tenants a right of first refusal to buy the premises); and
- the disposal is made in accordance with the requirements of ss.6–10 of the Act.

A disposal by a landlord of his reversionary interest in breach of LTA 1987 will not be void, but the qualifying tenants will be entitled to require the interest to be transferred to them for the same consideration as the consideration received by the landlord.

16.2.1 Meaning of 'premises'

Subject to certain exclusions, the pre-emption rights conferred on tenants by LTA 1987 apply to premises if:

- they consist of the whole or part of a building;
- they contain two or more flats held by qualifying tenants; and
- the number of flats held by such tenants exceeds 50 per cent of the total number of flats contained in the premises (s.1(2)).

A flat is defined in s.60(1) of the Act as a separate set of premises, whether or not on the same floor, which forms part of a building and is divided horizontally from some other part of that building and constructed or adapted for use for the purposes of a dwelling.

Note that a flat will be regarded as 'held by a qualifying tenant' if a lease of that flat has been granted to a qualifying tenant or the landlord has entered into an agreement to grant a lease of the flat to a person who will become a qualifying tenant upon the grant of the lease. Also note that a lease is defined in s.59(1) of the Act as including a sub-lease and an agreement for a lease.

Part 1 of the Act does not apply to premises if:

- any part or parts of the premises is or are occupied or intended to be occupied for non-residential use (e.g. commercial or retail use); and
- the internal floor area of that or those parts (taken together) exceeds 50 per cent of the internal floor area of the premises (taken as a whole) (s.1(3)).

Accordingly, if more than 50 per cent of the internal floor area of a mixed use building is used for commercial purposes then the provisions of LTA 1987 will not apply.

For the purpose of calculating internal floor areas, the internal floor area of any common parts is to be disregarded. 'Common parts' is defined in s.60(1) of the Act as including the structure and the exterior of a building and any common facilities within it.

16.2.2 Meaning of 'landlord'

For the purposes of LTA 1987 a person will be a landlord if he is:

- the immediate landlord of qualifying tenants of flats contained in the whole or part of the building (s.2(1)); or
- the landlord of such an immediate landlord (the superior landlord) where the immediate landlord has a tenancy for a term of less than seven years or a tenancy for a longer term but terminable within the first seven years at the option of the superior landlord (s.2(2)).

16.2.3 Meaning of 'qualifying tenants'

Subject to a few exceptions, a tenant of a flat will be a qualifying tenant unless his tenancy is:

- a protected shorthold tenancy as defined in the Housing Act 1980, s.52;
- a tenancy to which the Landlord and Tenant Act 1954, Part II applies;
- a tenancy terminable on the cessation of his employment; or
- an assured tenancy or assured agricultural occupancy within the meaning of the Housing Act 1988, Part I (LTA 1987, s.3(1)).

A tenant of a flat will not be a qualifying tenant if:

- he is the tenant not only of the flat in question but also of at least two other flats in the same building (s.3(2)); or
- his landlord is a qualifying tenant of that flat (s.3(4)).

16.2.4 Meaning of 'relevant disposal'

Subject to certain exclusions, a relevant disposal affecting premises to which LTA 1987 applies will be a disposal by the landlord of any estate or interest (whether legal or equitable) in such premises and will include:

- the disposal of any estate or interest in any common parts of such premises whether conditional or unconditional and whether or not enforceable or not enforceable by specific performance (s.4(1)); and
- entering into a contract to make such a disposal (s.4A(1)).

The use of the word 'affecting' in s.4(1) has caused some confusion with regard to the interpretation of the meaning of this section; and it is not clear whether a disposal of only retail or commercial space in a building to which LTA 1987 applies would be caught by the Act. The expression 'affecting any premises', rather than 'of premises', has led some commentators to conclude that the grant of a lease of only a shop in a mixed use building is a disposal which affects the whole building and that, logically, it is a disposal to which LTA 1987 applies. However, the authors of *Tenants' Right of First Refusal*[1] have expressed the view that, while a disposal of part of a building can be a disposal that affects the whole building and that the disposal of a shop contained within a building forming two or more flats held by qualifying tenants could be construed as a disposal to which LTA 1987 applies, this could not have been the intention of Parliament. They also point out that if the disposal of only a shop in a mixed use building was to be regarded as a disposal to which LTA 1987 applies then this would have a substantial impact on the approach previously taken to disposals of the commercial space in a building.

The following disposals will not be regarded as a relevant disposal:

- the grant of any tenancy under which the demised premises consist of a single flat;
- a disposal of any interest of a beneficiary in settled land;
- a disposal by way of security for a loan;
- a disposal to a trustee in bankruptcy or to the liquidator of a company;
- a disposal in pursuance of an order made under s.24 of the Matrimonial Causes Act 1973 or in pursuance of any of the other orders referred to in LTA 1987, s.4(2)(c);
- a disposal in pursuance of a compulsory purchase order;
- a disposal by way of gift to a member of the landlord's family or to a charity;
- a disposal by one charity to another of an estate or interest in land which prior to the disposal is functional land of the first-mentioned charity and which is intended to be functional land of the other charity once the disposal is made;

[1] For a detailed discussion about whether or not it was intended that the disposal of the commercial element only of a building was intended to be caught by LTA 1987 see A Radevsky and W Clark *Tenants' Right of First Refusal* (3rd edition, LexisNexis, 2017), para.3.12. Also, see P Dollar and S Thompson-Copsey *Mixed Use and Residential Tenants' Rights* (EG Books, 2010), para.4.04.

- a disposal consisting of the transfer of an estate or interest held on trust for any person where the disposal is made in connection with the appointment of a new trustee or in connection with the discharge of any trustee;
- a disposal consisting of a transfer by two or more persons who are members of the same family either to fewer of their number or to a different combination of members of the family (but one that includes at least one of the transferors);
- a disposal in pursuance of a contract, an option or a right of pre-emption binding on the landlord (except as provided by s.8D) (but note that under s.4A(1) an exchange of contracts to make a relevant disposal or the grant of an option or a right of pre-emption will be a relevant disposal);
- a disposal consisting of the surrender of a tenancy in pursuance of any covenant, condition or agreement contained in it;
- a disposal to the Crown;
- a disposal by a body corporate to a company which has been an associate company of that body for at least two years (see s.4(2)).

16.2.5 Offer notices

Where a landlord proposes to make a relevant disposal affecting premises to which LTA 1987 applies, he must serve an offer notice on the qualifying tenants of the flats contained in the premises in accordance with the requirements of s.5A (in the case of a disposal which consists of entering into a contract to create or transfer an interest in land), s.5B (in the case of a disposal by means of a sale at a public auction), s.5C (in the case of a disposal which consists of the grant of an option or a right of pre-emption), s.5D (in the case of a disposal which consists of a transfer or conveyance not preceded by a contract), or s.5E (in the case of a disposal for non-monetary consideration).

Disposals involving more than one building

Where a landlord proposes to make a relevant disposal involving more than one building (whether or not involving the same estate), he will be required to deal with each building separately (s.5(3)). Accordingly, where a transaction involves the disposal of two buildings, it will be necessary to sever the transaction and to treat the transaction as two separate disposals with any consideration being apportioned between the two buildings.

Requirements in the case of a contract to create or transfer an interest in land

In the case of a proposed disposal which consists of entering into a contract to create or transfer an interest in land, the offer notice must:

- contain particulars of the principal terms of the proposed disposal (including details of the property, the estate or interest to be disposed of, the deposit and the consideration required);
- state that it constitutes an offer by the landlord to enter into a contract on those terms which may be accepted by the requisite majority of the qualifying tenants of the constituent flats (i.e. qualifying tenants holding leases of more than 50 per cent of the total number of flats in the building); and
- specify a period within which the offer may be accepted – the period may not be less than two months beginning with the date of service of the notice; and
- specify a further period of not less than two months within which a person or persons may be nominated by the tenants under s.6 (see LTA 1987, s.5A).

Requirements in the case of a sale by auction

Where a landlord is proposing to make a disposal by means of a sale at a public auction, the offer notice must:

- contain particulars of the principal terms of the proposed disposal (including details of the property and the estate or interest to be disposed of);
- state that the disposal is proposed to be made by means of a sale at a public auction;
- state that the notice constitutes an offer by the landlord, which may be accepted by the requisite majority of qualifying tenants of the constituent flats, for the contract (if any) entered into by the landlord at the auction to have effect as if a person or persons nominated by them, and not the purchaser, had entered into it;
- specify a period within which the offer may be accepted – the period may not be less than two months beginning with the date of service of the notice;
- specify a further period of not less than 28 days within which a person or persons may be nominated by the tenants under s.6; and
- be served not less than four months or more than six months before the date of the auction (see LTA 1987, s.5B).

Requirements in case of grant of an option

Where a landlord proposes to make a relevant disposal consisting of the grant of an option or a right of pre-emption, the offer notice must:

- contain particulars of the principal terms of the proposed disposal (including details of the property, and the estate or interest of the landlord in the property, the consideration required by the landlord, and the principal terms on which the option or right of pre-emption would be exercisable, including the consideration payable on its exercise);

- state that the notice constitutes an offer by the landlord to grant an option or a right of pre-emption on those terms which may be accepted by the requisite majority of qualifying tenants of the constituent flats;
- specify a period within which the offer may be accepted – the period may not be less than two months beginning with the date of service of the notice; and
- specify a further period of not less than two months within which a person or persons may be nominated by the tenants under s.6 (see LTA 1987, s.5C).

Requirements in case of conveyance not preceded by contract

Where a disposal is not made in pursuance of a contract, an option or a right of pre-emption, the offer notice must:

- contain particulars of the principal terms of the proposed disposal (including details of the property, the estate, or interest to be disposed of, and the consideration required by the landlord for making the disposal);
- state that the notice constitutes an offer by the landlord to dispose of the property on those terms which may be accepted by the requisite majority of qualifying tenants of the constituent flats;
- specify a period within which the offer may be accepted – the period may not be less than two months beginning with the date of service of the notice; and
- specify a further period of not less than two months within which a person or persons may be nominated by the tenants under s.6 (see LTA 1987, s.5D).

Requirements in case of disposal for non-monetary consideration

Where the consideration required by the landlord for making the disposal does not consist, or does not wholly consist, of money, the offer notice must:

- comply with whichever is applicable of ss.5A–5D;
- state that an election may be made under s.8C (explaining its effect);
- state that the notice constitutes an offer by the landlord, which may be accepted by the requisite majority of qualifying tenants of the constituent flats, for a person or persons nominated by them to acquire the property in pursuance of ss.11–17; and
- specify a period within which the offer may be so accepted – the period may not be less than two months beginning with the date of service of the notice.

16.2.6 Ways of avoiding LTA 1987

There are a number of ways of avoiding getting caught by the provisions of LTA 1987, including the following:

- The owner of the freehold interest in a building containing two or more flats will avoid having to comply with the provisions of LTA 1987 if he enters into a contract for the sale of the freehold interest in the building before 50 per cent of the total number of flats contained in the building have been let. The contract for sale is not a disposal of 'premises' (as defined in the Act) and under LTA 1987, s.4(2) the transfer of the building pursuant to the contract will not be a 'relevant disposal'.

- Where the owner of a building containing flats is a company, that owner will be able to avoid having to comply with the provisions of LTA 1987 by transferring the freehold interest in the building to another company which has been an associated company of the owner for at least two years. If the shares in the associated company are then sold to a ground rent investor this will not be a relevant disposal under LTA 1987 – the sale of shares is not caught by LTA 1987.
- The freehold owner of a building containing flats will avoid having to comply with LTA 1987 if he interposes a reversionary lease between the freehold and the flat leases. The tenant under the reversionary lease can be required, by way of covenants in the lease, to collect the ground rents and insurance rents from the tenants of the flats and to pass them up to the freeholder. Note that the grant of the reversionary lease will be a relevant disposal under LTA 1987, unless it is granted pursuant to a contract entered into before the number of flats held by qualifying tenants is 50 per cent. However, once the reversionary lease has been granted the freeholder will be free to sell his freehold interest without having to comply with the requirements of LTA 1987, s.5.

16.3 THE COMMERCIAL ELEMENT

The freeholder will need to think about how he wants to dispose of the commercial space in a mixed use building. For example, he could grant 25-year rack rent leases of the commercial units direct to occupiers with a view to selling the commercial investment in the future. Alternatively, he could pre-sell the commercial space to an investor by granting the investor a long lease (125 years or more) of the commercial units for a premium.

Having granted long residential leases of the flats in a mixed use building, the freeholder may wish to carve out the commercial elements before selling his freehold interest by putting in place a reversionary commercial lease between the freehold and the commercial rack rent leases. In this way the freeholder will be able to retain the commercial investment.

As mentioned above, the grant of a lease of only commercial space in a mixed use building containing two or more flats held by qualifying tenants will probably not be caught by the provisions of LTA 1987. However, the risk of such a disposal being caught by the Act can be avoided by granting the commercial lease (or entering into an agreement to grant the commercial lease) before 50 per cent of the total number of flats in the building have been let.

A possible structure for a mixed use development is represented in **Figure 16.1**.

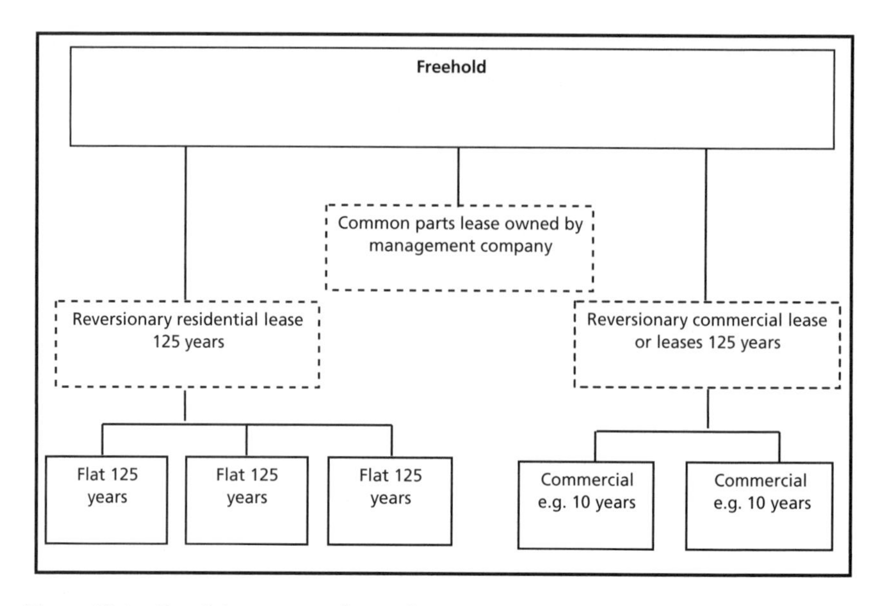

Figure 16.1 Possible structure for a mixed use development

16.4 SERVICE CHARGE

The service charge provisions that are to be included in the leases of the units in a mixed use building will need to be carefully drafted. Consistency and flexibility are key. There should be consistency between the service charge provisions contained in the long residential leases and those contained in the commercial leases. Also, the service charge provisions should be flexible and allow the landlord to recalculate the service charge if it would be fair and reasonable to do so or if there is a change in circumstances.

Commercial tenants may refuse to pay for certain heads of service charge expenditure, such as a security guard/concierge or the repair of a lift (if the lift is only to be used by the residential tenants). Equally, residential tenants may object to paying for certain heads of expenditure from which they derive little or no benefit. It may be necessary in such circumstances to have heads of expenditure that are payable by all the occupiers of the building and heads of expenditure that are payable only by a particular class of occupier.

Landlords will need to be aware that residential service charge operates under a statutory framework and that it may not be possible to load any commercial shortfall on to the residential tenants. For example, under the Landlord and Tenant Act 1985, s.19 service charge recovery is limited to reasonably incurred costs and the services or works carried out must be of a reasonable standard. Also, under ss.20 and 20ZA freeholders must comply with the consultation requirements prescribed by regulations made by the Secretary of State before carrying out any 'qualifying works' or entering into any 'qualifying long term agreement'.

APPENDICES – SECTION A

Checklists

APPENDIX A1

General property development checklist

1 Raise development land enquiries

2 Carry out pre-contract searches

- Local authority (including optional enquiries relating to common land, town and village greens and public footpaths)
- Highway authority
- Index map
- Coal mining
- Archaeological
- Environmental (environmental search agency and/or letter to Environment Agency)
- British Waterways
- Company
- Chancel repair
- Cheshire brine
- Tin mining
- Company
- Land charge
- Flood

3 Carry out technical/service enquiries

- Drainage and water
- Telephone
- Gas
- Electricity

4 Boundaries and plans

- Do the on-site boundaries accord with the title plan?
- Do the boundaries shown on any site survey plan correspond with the boundaries shown on the title plan? (The developer should always arrange for a site survey plan to be prepared prior to exchange of contracts.)
- Are boundaries clearly identifiable?
- Is a statutory declaration required?

4.1 Sale of part

- Have the boundaries been pegged out?
- Is the contract/transfer plan to a stated scale and does it show sufficient detail to be Land Registry compliant?
- Check the accuracy of the contract/transfer plan by submitting an index map search.

5 Access

- Does the development site directly abut the highway? (Check highway search.)

- Is there any evidence of a ransom strip? (Carry out site inspection and index map search.)
- Are visibility splays likely to be an issue?
  - Will they involve third party land or will the developer own all of the land required for the visibility splays? (Check planning conditions.)
- Is a right of way required?
- Is any existing right of way adequate?
  - Is it restricted or limited in any way?
  - Is it for all purposes?
  - Does it cover pedestrian and vehicular use?
  - Does it connect to an adopted highway?
  - Does it include all necessary ancillary rights?
  - Is the extent of the right of way clear/sufficient?
- Is any new right of way which is to be granted by a transfer adequate?
- Does the transfer impose all necessary obligations on the transferor in respect of maintenance, adoption, etc.?
- Will the development result in a change in the use of the site?
  - Will this result in the right of way being lost?
- Will the development result in an intensification in use of the right of way?
  - Will this result in the right of way being lost?
- Does the right of way benefit the whole of the site (or only part of the site)?
- Is a statutory declaration required? (Prescriptive right of way)
- Is defective title indemnity insurance required?
- Who is to be responsible for the maintenance, repair and adoption of the access to the site?
- Is it intended that the estate roads which are to be constructed by the developer will be adopted? If so, will they connect to an adopted highway? (Prescriptive right of way)
- Check the title to the right of way. Has a note of the right of way been entered on the title to the servient land?

6 Drainage

- Are there existing adopted sewers within the vicinity of the property? (Check drainage search.)
- Are drainage rights over third party land required? (Any deed of easement will need to be carefully drafted and should impose an obligation on the grantor to enter into an adoption agreement upon request.)
- Are existing drainage rights adequate?
  - Do they permit a full free and unrestricted right to connect to and use sewers of sufficient capacity which connect to adopted sewers?
  - Do they include all necessary ancillary rights?
- Is a right to lay new sewers required?
- Is a right to connect to and use existing sewers required?
- Are any new drainage rights which are to be granted by a transfer adequate?
- Does the right include a reference to the perpetuity period? (As from 6 April 2010 the rule against perpetuities will no longer apply to easements.)
- Will the development result in a change in the use of the site?
  - Will this result in a loss of any existing drainage easement?
- Will the development result in an intensification in the use of any existing drainage easement?
  - Will this result in a loss of the easement?
- Who is to be responsible for the maintenance, repair, adoption of the foul and surface water sewers?

- Where will surface water go?
- Are there storm water sewers within the highway?
- Will a storm water soakaway system be required?
- Will a balancing pond be required?
- Will it be necessary to obtain a deed of easement over third party land?
- Will it be necessary to requisition sewers?
- Will the drainage proposals be acceptable to the drainage authority and the Environment Agency?
- Is a statutory declaration required? (Prescriptive drainage rights)
- Is defective title indemnity insurance required?
- Is it intended that the estate sewers which are to be constructed by the developer will be adopted?
  - If so, will they connect to existing adopted sewers? (Prescriptive drainage rights)

7 Other services (water, electricity, gas and telecommunications)

- Are there existing mains services into which development will be able to link? (Check service enquiries.)
- Are service easements over third party land required?
- Are existing rights to use service installations adequate?
- Are new service media rights which are to be granted by a transfer adequate?
- Who is to be responsible for the installation, repair and maintenance of service media?

8 Adverse matters

8.1 Rights to light

- Is there a possibility that an adjoining property may have the benefit of rights to light over the site? (Check position of windows in adjoining buildings overlooking site.)
- Is there a possibility that the development may breach or infringe any rights to light?
- Should the developer enter into a rights to light agreement with the adjoining owner?
- Does the transfer contain a provision permitting the erection of buildings on the land being transferred notwithstanding that this may interfere with the access of light and air to buildings on the transferor's retained land?

8.2 Service media crossing site

- Are there any sewers, electricity cables, gas pipes or other service media crossing the development site? (Check title, technical searches and replies to development enquiries.)
- Will the proposed development be affected by any sewers or other service media crossing the site or can they be accommodated within the layout?

8.3 Wayleave agreements

- Is the site affected by any electricity wayleave agreement, telecom mast agreement/lease or any other deed or agreement in favour of a statutory undertaker or service provider? (Check title and technical searches.)
- Have copies of all wayleave and telecom mast agreements affecting the site been obtained?
- Is there a right to determine the wayleave/telecom agreement? (Remember that the statutory rights of electricity distributors and telecom operators may give the developer a problem.)

8.4 *Public footpaths*

- Are there any public footpaths crossing the site? (Check highway and local authority searches.)
- Does the route of any public footpath shown on the definitive public footpath map follow the route on the ground or has it been diverted?
- Will any public footpath crossing the site affect the development or can the footpath be accommodated within the estate layout?
- Will it be necessary to apply for a stopping up or diversion order?
  - If so, which procedure should be used?
- Are there any tracks or paths crossing the site which are not shown on the definitive public footpath map?

8.5 *Rights of way and other easements*

- Is the site subject to any express rights of way or other easements?
- Will the easements affect the development proposals?
- Is a deed of release or statutory declaration and/or title insurance required?

8.6 *Prescriptive rights and implied easements*

- Is the site subject to any prescriptive rights?
- Is the site subject to any implied rights (under the rule in *Wheeldon* v. *Burrows* or by virtue of LPA 1925, s.62)?
- Does the transfer contain a provision excluding implied easements under the rule in *Wheeldon* v. *Burrows* and s.62? (Transfer of part)

8.7 *Tree preservation orders*

- Is the site affected by a tree preservation order (TPO)? If so, has a copy of the TPO been obtained and checked?
- Will the TPO affect the development proposals?
- Does the site benefit from a detailed planning permission which overrides the TPO?
- Is the site in a Conservation Area?

8.8 *Mineral reservations*

- Is the site affected by any mineral reservation or sub-surface mineral title? (Check title and carry out index map search.)
- Is a mining rights indemnity insurance policy required?
- Does the reservation include a right to win, work and carry away minerals?
- Does the reservation include a right to enter the property and to carry out surface mining?

8.9 *Restrictive covenants*

- Is the title to the site subject to any restrictive covenants?
- Will the covenants prevent or restrict the proposed development?
- Are the covenants enforceable?
- Has there been a change in the ownership of the land burdened by the covenant?
- Is the benefit of the covenant personal to the original covenantee?
- Is the covenant personal or is it intended to be binding on the covenantor's successors in title? (i.e. Does the covenant contain words such as 'the Transferee hereby covenants with the Transferor and its successors in title that the Transferee and those deriving title under it will …'?)
- Has there been a change in the ownership of the land benefiting from the covenant?

- Is the covenant intended to benefit the successors in title of the original covenantee? (Is the land which is intended to benefit from the restrictive covenant defined or identifiable? Remember that LPA 1925, s.78 is not mandatory.)
- Does title refer to unknown restrictive covenants? (Restrictive covenant indemnity insurance)
- Is a deed of release and/or indemnity insurance required?
- Would an application to the Lands Tribunal for the covenants to be modified or discharged be successful?
- Has the covenantee sold off any part of the land benefiting from the covenant? (If so, the purchasers may also have the benefit of the covenants and indemnity insurance will be required.)

8.10 Village green registration

- Has any part of the site been registered as a town or village green?
- Has any person applied to register the site or any part of it as a village green?

8.11 Chancel repair liability

- Is the site located in an area which continues to have a potential chancel repair liability?
- Is there a need to obtain a chancel repair liability indemnity policy?

8.12 Overriding interests

- Is the site subject to any overriding interests?

9 Matters benefiting the site

- Does the site have the benefit of any rights?
  - Are these rights adequate? (Remember to check the title to any rights of way.)
- Does the site have the benefit of any covenants?
  - Are they enforceable?

10 Tenancies

- Is the site being sold with vacant possession or is the site subject to any leases?
- Do the leases exclude security of tenure and/or contain a break clause?
- How easy will it be to obtain vacant possession?

11 Surveys

- Have ground investigations been carried out?
- Is an asbestos survey required?
- Is an archaeological survey required?
- Is the vendor obliged to procure that the author of any ground or other technical report readdresses the report in favour of the developer or provides the developer with a deed of warranty or a letter of reliance signed by the author of the report?
- Is the report assignable?
- Has a copy of any deed of appointment or letter of engagement been provided?
- Have details of the relevant consultant's professional indemnity insurance cover been provided?

12 Planning permission

- Does the site benefit from a planning permission?
- Is the permission an outline or a detailed planning permission?
- When will the planning permission expire?

- Have copies of all plans which accompanied the planning application been obtained and checked?
- Does the planning permission contain any pre-commencement or Grampian conditions (i.e. conditions prohibiting development until certain actions have been taken or requirements have been satisfied)?
- Will the developer be able to comply with all of the planning conditions?
  - Will compliance with any planning condition require the approval or co-operation of a third party?
  - Does the planning permission include land outside the developer's control?
- Are there any conditions relating to off-site highway works or other off-site works?
  - Can these works be carried out without the consent of a third party?
- Does the planning permission relate to the site being acquired and other land being retained by the vendor?
  - If so, does the contract oblige the vendor to comply with all pre-commencement or Grampian conditions in so far as they relate to the retained land promptly so as not to prevent or delay the development of the site?
- Will it be possible to develop the land in stages without breaching any pre-commencement planning conditions?
  - Does the planning permission allow for the site to be developed in phases?
- Has the deadline for obtaining reserved matters approvals passed?
- Is judicial review insurance required?

13 Planning agreement

- Is the site subject to a s.106 agreement or any other planning agreement?
- Is the performance of the obligations contained in the s.106 agreement conditional upon the implementation of the planning permission/commencement of development?
- Will the owner of the site be released from all liability on parting with his interest in the site?
- Are plot purchasers and their mortgagees exempt from liability?
- Are the timescales for making financial contributions reasonable?
  - Are they linked to the commencement of development or the occupation of dwellings?
  - Is this reasonable?
- Are the affordable housing provisions acceptable to the developer?
  - Do they allow the developer to sell the affordable units for a commercial price to a social landlord of its choice?
  - Do they restrict the sale or occupations of private/open market dwellings?
  - Is the restriction reasonable?
- Will the affordable housing provisions be acceptable to a registered social landlord (RSL)?
- Will the affordable housing provisions be binding on a mortgagee or a receiver of an RSL?
- Does the s.106 agreement contain suitable mortgagee protection provisions?
- Are there any restrictions on sales or occupations of dwellings? Are they reasonable?
- Does the site plan attached to the s.106 agreement correspond with the title plan?

14 Community Infrastructure Levy (CIL)

- Is the site located in an area in which a CIL charging schedule is in force?
- Will the development of the site give rise to a liability to pay CIL?

- How is any liability to pay CIL to be dealt with?

15 Tax

15.1 Value added tax

- Is VAT payable on the purchase price?
- Is the vendor registered for VAT?
- Has the vendor elected to waive exemption from VAT?
- Has the vendor notified HMRC of the election?
- Have HMRC acknowledged receipt of the election?
- Does the contract contain a satisfactory VAT clause?
- Does the contract require the vendor to hand over a VAT invoice on completion?

15.2 Stamp duty land tax

- Is the purchaser obliged to carry out works? (Remember that stamp duty land tax may be payable on the cost of the works, as well as on the purchase price.)
- Is the transaction linked with another transaction? (Options, overage, etc.)
- Is any relief available? (Part exchanges, sub-sales)

16 Party Wall etc. Act 1996

- Will the development involve carrying out works to a party wall or excavation works near the boundary of another property?
  - If so, will it be necessary to serve a notice on an adjoining owner pursuant to the Party Wall etc. Act 1996, s.6 before commencing development?

17 Drawings, reports and copyright

- Are there any drawings or reports which have been commissioned by the vendor and on which the developer will be relying?
- Is the vendor obliged to procure that the architect who prepared the planning application drawings enters into a licence to use drawings in favour of the developer?
- Is the vendor obliged to procure that the authors of all reports commissioned by the vendor readdress the reports in favour of the developer or provide the developer with letters of reliance or duty of care agreements?

APPENDIX A2

Option agreement checklist

1 Formalities

- Is the option agreement a deed?
- Is the option supported by consideration?

2 Option fee

- Should the option fee be non-refundable but form part of the purchase price in the event of the option being exercised?

3 Option period

- Does the option agreement refer to an option period? (The rule against perpetuities no longer applies to options.)

4 Extension of option period

- Is the initial option period capable of being extended?
- Will the initial option period be automatically extended if a planning decision (including an appeal decision) or a price determination is awaited when the initial period expires?
- Will the initial option period be automatically extended if a satisfactory planning permission has been granted but less than three months have elapsed since the date of the decision notice or if a resolution to grant planning permission subject to the landowner entering into a planning agreement has been passed?
- Will the initial option period be automatically extended if the developer has purchased part of the land benefiting from a satisfactory planning permission at the expiry of the initial option period?
- Can the option period be extended on more than one occasion and to the latest of the various extension dates?
- Will the initial option period be automatically extended if an expert's determination is awaited?

5 Definition of 'planning application'

- Should the landowner have the right to approve the developer's planning application? (Most developers will be reluctant to agree to this.)

6 Definition of 'satisfactory planning permission'

- Should the developer have an absolute discretion to decide if a planning permission and any necessary planning agreement are in an acceptable form? (From the landowner's point of view a planning permission should not be regarded as satisfactory if it contains an onerous condition or it is inconsistent with planning policy guidance and/or defined option objectives.)

7 Purchase price

7.1 Market value

- Is 'market value' defined by reference to the RICS *Appraisal and Valuation Manual* or does the definition contain a detailed list of assumptions and disregards? (Most developers will prefer the latter alternative.)

7.2 Purchase price formula

- Is there a purchase price formula which requires development costs and/or planning costs to be deducted from the market value? (Any purchase price formula should be carefully checked.)
- Are the development costs to be deducted in full from the purchase price? (See 7.3.)

7.3 Development costs

- Does the agreement contain appropriate wording to ensure that there can be no double deduction of development costs?
- Does the list of development costs include any tax or levy payable to, or which may be payable to, the local planning authority (such as 'a roof tax' or the Community Infrastructure Levy) and/or to HM Government upon the implementation of any planning permission (including planning gain supplement or any equivalent form of taxation)?
- Does the agreement oblige the developer to maintain an open book policy in relation to development costs and to provide the landowner with such evidence of all costs incurred or likely to be incurred in connection with the development of the option land as the landowner shall require in order to verify the amount of the development costs?
- Does the agreement contain a provision stating that where any of the development costs relate to the development of land other than the option land then only a fair and reasonable proportion of them shall form part of the development costs to be deducted from the purchase price or taken into account in calculating the market value of the option land?
- Should there be a cap on development costs?
- Does the agreement contain a provision stating that where the option land comprises a tranche, only a fair and reasonable proportion of the development costs shall be deducted?

7.4 Minimum purchase price

- Is there a minimum purchase price? (From the landowner's point of view, it would be prudent to specify a minimum purchase price, but developers will not always agree to this.)
- Is the minimum price to be calculated by reference to gross or net developable acreage?
- What will happen if the price, as agreed or determined, is less than the minimum price? (Should the option agreement come to an end or should the agreement continue until the minimum price requirements are satisfied or until a longstop date?)

7.5 Indexation

- Is the minimum purchase price to be index linked?

7.6 Equalisation

- If the potential development site is owned by a number of different landowners then should the purchase price should be calculated on an equalised basis with each landowner receiving a proportion of the open market value of the whole development site (less a discount) as opposed to the market value of his individual land holding (less a discount)?

- Check any equalisation formula very carefully.

8 Minimum land take

- Should the developer be entitled to exercise the option only if a minimum area of the option land benefits from a satisfactory planning permission?

9 Developer's planning obligations

- Does the option agreement impose an obligation on the developer to lodge a planning application by a specified date and to appeal against a planning refusal or should the developer have an absolute discretion in this regard? (Most developers will be reluctant to agree to an obligation to appeal and will want to have the flexibility to submit a fresh planning application or appeal at their discretion, but will usually agree to appeal if planning counsel advises that there is a reasonable prospect (i.e. better than 50 per cent chance) of an appeal succeeding.)
- Does the agreement impose an obligation on the developer to use reasonable endeavours to maximise the development value of the option land and to minimise planning gain and infrastructure costs?
- Does the agreement impose an obligation on the developer to include as much of the option land within the planning application as is reasonably practicable?
- Does the agreement impose an obligation on the developer to use reasonable endeavours to minimise affordable housing requirements?

10 Landowner's planning obligations

- Does the option agreement impose an obligation on the landowner to enter into planning agreements and to procure that the landowner's mortgagee and any tenant of the option land will enter into planning agreements upon request?
- Should the developer be entitled to execute a planning agreement as attorney for the landowner?
- Is the landowner to have a right to approve a planning agreement?
- Does the option agreement impose an obligation on the developer to ensure that the planning agreement contains a clause releasing the owner from liability after he has parted with his interest in the site?
- Does the option agreement require the developer to provide the landowner with an indemnity in respect of planning obligations?

11 Planning challenges

- Does the option agreement allow for the possibility of a planning challenge/ judicial review to pass before the developer is obliged to complete the purchase of the option land following the service of an exercise notice?

12 Tranching provisions

- Does the developer need the ability to draw down the option land in phases?
- If so, is it desirable to specify a minimum size for each tranche?
- Should the minimum size relate only to land which is capable of beneficial development?
- How should each tranche be valued?

13 Price notices

- Is the developer obliged to serve a price notice within a specified period of time following the grant of a satisfactory planning permission? (This could cause a problem for the developer where there are minimum price provisions or where the development area includes land belonging to the landowner and other landowners.)

- Is the service of a price notice conditional on a satisfactory planning permission having been granted?
- Does the option agreement allow the developer to serve any number of price notices?
- Does the option agreement contain a clause stating that if a price notice is served and the option period expires before the date on which the purchase price is agreed or determined the option period will be extended?

14 Exercise notices

- Should the developer be obliged to serve an exercise notice within a specified period following agreement or determination of the purchase price of the option land for the exercise notice to be valid?
- Should the option lapse if the developer fails to comply with this requirement?
- Should this requirement apply where the purchase price, as agreed or determined, is less than the minimum price?
- Should the exercise notice be accompanied by a 10 per cent deposit?
- Does the option agreement allow the developer to serve any number of exercise notices?
- If the option agreement contains tranching provisions, should the agreement include a provision stating that it will not lapse when the initial option period expires if, prior to the expiration of that period, the developer has served an exercise notice?

15 Termination

- Should the option agreement contain a clause which allows the landowner to terminate the agreement in the event of the developer becoming insolvent or in the event of the developer committing a fundamental breach of a material term of the agreement and that breach not being remedied within a specified period? (Most developers will not wish to agree to the landowner having a right to terminate the agreement except in the case of the developer's insolvency.)

16 Easements and covenants

- If the option agreement is to contain tranching provisions then easements may need to be granted over or in favour of each tranche. Also, if the landowner owns land adjoining the option land then easements may need to be granted over the option land in favour of the landowner's retained/adjoining land.
- Do infrastructure and planning obligations need to be imposed on the developer in the transfer of the option land to the developer?
- Does the option agreement contain a clause stating that the transfer of a tranche must be in a form to be approved by the landowner and the developer and that it must contain all necessary exceptions and reservations and covenants (including covenants to provide infrastructure and to enter into infrastructure agreements and adoption agreements) for the benefit of any retained land?

17 Dealing

- Does the option agreement prohibit the landowner from dealing with the option land?
- Is there a requirement for any disponee to enter into a deed of covenant with the developer?

- Does the agreement permit a sale or the creation of a charge subject to the transferee/chargee entering into a deed of covenant with the developer?
- Should there be an absolute prohibition against any sale or disposal of the option land to another property developer or strategic land promoter?
- Should the developer have a right of pre-emption or first refusal to buy in the event of the landowner wishing to dispose of the option land?
- Should the landowner be allowed to grant leases or easements?

18 Protection

- Remember to protect the option by registering either an agreed notice or a unilateral notice of the option on the title to the option land together with a restriction against dealing or (in the case of unregistered land) a C(iv) land charge.

19 Mortgages

- Is the option land subject to any mortgage or legal charge?
- If so, has the mortgagee's consent to the option been obtained and has the mortgagee agreed to be bound by the terms of the option? (Remember that an option granted after the creation of a mortgage will not be binding on the mortgagee.)

20 Tax freezer provisions

- Are they required? (Remember that, from a developer's point of view, they should not prevent the developer from implementing a satisfactory planning permission before it lapses.)

21 Tax

- The parties will need to consider the tax implications of entering into the option agreement. The landowner should be advised to seek specialist tax advice.

22 Indemnities from the developer

- Does the option agreement require the developer to provide the landowner with an indemnity in respect of planning obligations and any CIL liability?

APPENDIX A3

Overage agreement checklist

1 Duration

- For how long should the overage agreement last? (Note: In the case of sales overage, the agreement should continue until the last dwelling/open market dwelling has been sold or until a deemed disposal date.)

2 Trigger points

Which of the following should trigger the overage payment?

- the grant of a planning permission;
- the grant of a planning permission which is immune from planning challenges and which does not contain any onerous conditions;
- the grant of a planning permission which is capable of implementation;
- the implementation of a planning permission;
- the disposal of the overage land with the benefit of a new planning permission;
- the earlier of the implementation of a planning permission and a disposal (other than a permitted disposal) with the benefit of a new planning permission;
- the disposal of the overage land for a sum which exceeds a specified base figure;
- the sale of the last open market dwelling (sales overage).

3 Overage payment

- Any formula for calculating overage should be carefully checked, particularly if there is a possibility that the overage may be paid more than once in respect of the same land or that the overage land may be developed in phases/stages.
- Consider whether any deductions need to be made (such as planning costs and the initial purchase price or a pro rata proportion of the initial purchase price). (Remember to avoid double deductions of costs and to give the developer credit for any sums previously paid.)

4 Payment date

- What should be the date for payment of the overage?
- Should the payment be linked to the grant or implementation of a planning permission?
- Should the payment be linked to the implementation of a planning permission or (if earlier) the disposal of the overage land with the benefit of planning permission? (Note: The definition of 'disposal' will need to be carefully considered. The seller's solicitor will want to ensure that it is not defined too narrowly.)
- Will the overage be payable three months after the grant of planning permission (subject to no planning challenges having been made) or within a specified period after the implementation of planning permission? (No overage should be payable until all possibility of a planning challenge/judicial review has passed.)

5 Sales overage

- Is revenue generated by sales of affordable housing dwellings to be excluded when calculating the sales overage?
- Is the cost of incentives and buyer's extras to be deducted from the overage payment?
- Does the overage agreement contain a trigger for the payment of overage in respect of unsold units?
- Does the overage agreement require (a) the sales overage to be paid on the sale of the last open market dwelling or on a longstop date (whichever is the earlier) and (b) there to be a deemed disposal of any dwellings remaining unsold on the longstop date?
- Does the overage agreement contain deemed disposal provisions which would apply in the case of a sale to a connected party or if the consideration is other than cash?
- On a sale of part of the land affected by the overage obligations, should the developer be released from the overage obligations to the extent that they relate to the land being sold?
- On the sale of part of the land affected by the overage obligations, how should the liability to pay overage be dealt with? Should the liability be apportioned between the developer and the buyer and, if so, how?

6 Multiple payments – subsequent planning permissions

- Should planning overage be payable only once (i.e. on the grant or implementation of the first planning permission) or should it be payable on each occasion that a planning permission which enhances the value of the overage land is granted? In other words, should the vendor/landowner be entitled to more than one bite of the cherry?

7 Interest

- Does the agreement provide for the payment of interest on late payments of overage?

8 Successors

- Should the provisions of the overage agreement be binding on the successors in title of the developer?
- Does the agreement make this clear?
- Is it intended that the overage obligations should not be binding on plot purchasers and/or mortgagees?
- Does the agreement make this clear?

9 Protection

- How is the overage to be protected?
- Legal charge
- Deed of covenant and restriction on title
- Restrictive covenants
- Bank bond
- Parent company guarantee

(Note:

(a) A legal charge may not be practical or acceptable to a developer's funders.
(b) If the developer becomes insolvent before the trigger date for payment of the overage then the legal charge may not be enforceable.

(c) For restrictive covenants to be enforceable certain technical requirements will need to be strictly fulfilled and the developer could apply to the Lands Tribunal to vary or release the covenant.)

10 Restrictions

- If the overage is to be protected by means of a restriction being entered on the title to the overage land then the wording of the restriction will need to be carefully considered. (The developer will want to ensure that the restriction does not prejudice plot sales or prohibit the creation of legal charges or easements in favour of statutory undertakers and utility companies.)
- Consideration will need to be given as to who should provide any certificate required in order to comply with the restriction. (Consider whether it is practical for the landowner to provide the certificate and the effect on plot sales.)
- What will happen if the landowner dies, becomes insolvent/bankrupt or cannot be found?
- Does the overage agreement impose an obligation on the landowner to provide a form RX4 on any disposal to a plot purchaser to cancel any restriction entered on the plot purchaser's title?

11 Planning obligations

- Should any planning obligations be imposed on the developer?
- Should the developer be obliged to sell the newly constructed dwellings as soon as reasonably possible?
- Do any planning obligations need to be qualified?
- Will they be acceptable to a purchaser from the developer or a mortgagee?

12 Dispute resolution clause

- Does the agreement contain a dispute resolution clause?

13 Good faith clause

- From the landowner's point of view, it may be sensible to include a good faith clause in the overage agreement.

14 Deed of release

- Does the overage agreement impose an obligation on the landowner to hand over a deed of release and a form of withdrawal of restriction upon the termination of the overage agreement?
- Does the agreement impose an obligation on the landowner to hand over a certificate required by any restriction on the title to the overage land once the requirements of the restriction have been complied with (assuming that the landowner is required to provide the certificate)?
- On a sale of part of the land affected by the overage obligations, should the developer be released from the overage obligations to the extent that they relate to the land being sold or should the developer continue to be liable for the payment of all overage?

15 No vendor's lien

- Does the overage agreement contain a clause stating that the obligation to pay overage will not give rise to a lien over the overage land?

16 Tax implications

- These will need to be considered by both the landowner and the developer. The landowner should be advised to seek specialist tax advice.

17 Excluded/permitted disposals

- Does the overage agreement contain a definition of excluded/permitted disposals? (This will usually be required by a developer, who will want to be permitted to make excluded/permitted disposals without the need for the disponee to enter into a deed of covenant with the seller. Any definition of excluded/permitted disposal will need to be carefully considered. From the landowner's point of view, it should not include a disposal to a connected person.)

APPENDIX A4

Conditional contract checklist

1 Satisfactory planning permission

- Outline or full, or outline followed by a reserved matters approval? (Remember that there is no statutory definition of full/detailed planning permission.)
- Immune from planning challenges (with developer/buyer to have a right of waiver)?
- Capable of implementation?
- Will the developer require an absolute discretion to decide if a planning permission is satisfactory or should the contract be conditional upon the grant of a planning permission containing no onerous conditions and which is immune from any planning challenges and capable of immediate implementation? (Most well-advised landowners will require the contract to be conditional upon the grant of a planning permission containing no onerous conditions.)

2 Onerous conditions

Which type of conditions should be construed as onerous?

- It makes the planning permission personal to the developer.
- It makes the planning permission limited in time.
- It limits the occupation or use of the whole or any part of the property to any designated occupier or class of occupier.
- It prevents development of any part of the property without the agreement or co-operation of an independent third party.
- It is by an objective standard unreasonable or unduly restrictive.
- When taken together with any requirement to pay Community Infrastructure Levy and all other conditions attaching to the planning permission and the obligations contained in any associated s.106 agreement it has a [materially] detrimental effect on the financial viability of the development [in the opinion of the developer (acting reasonably)].
- It requires that more than [ ] per cent of any residential development of the property be affordable housing.
- It imposes restrictions or obligations in relation to affordable housing which would be unacceptable to an affordable housing provider.

(Note: Assuming that the contract will be conditional on the planning permission containing no onerous conditions, the contract should contain a list of onerous conditions. From the developer's point of view, a planning condition should be regarded as onerous if it would have an adverse effect on the financial viability of the proposed development and the list of onerous conditions should include a 'sweeper clause' stating that a condition is to be construed as onerous if it is by an objective standard unreasonable or unduly restrictive. Both the planning permission and any planning agreement should be free from onerous conditions.)

3 Planning applications

- Will the application be for full/detailed or outline planning permission? (Remember that there is no statutory definition of full/detailed planning permission.)
- Does there need to be a reference to a minimum number of dwellings or to a minimum floor area?
- Will the application be in joint names?
- Is the seller to have a right to approve the developer's planning application?
- Does the contract allow the developer to withdraw a planning application and to submit a new or revised application?

4 The conditional period/planning period and extensions

- From the developer's point of view, the contract should refer to an initial planning period which is to be automatically extended if at the end of the initial planning period a planning decision (including an appeal decision) is awaited; or if a satisfactory planning permission has been granted but less than three months have elapsed since the date of the decision notice; or if a resolution to grant planning permission subject to the completion of a planning agreement has been passed; or if a pre-commencement planning condition remains to be satisfied; or if the decision of an expert or arbitrator is awaited in relation to a dispute, etc.
- For how long should the initial planning period last?
- Should the planning period be subject to a longstop date?

5 Developer's planning obligations

- Does the contract impose an obligation on the developer to lodge the planning application by a specified date and thereafter pursue the application expeditiously and use reasonable endeavours to obtain a satisfactory planning permission?
- Does the contract impose an obligation on the developer to keep the seller fully informed of the progress of the planning application and any appeal?
- Does the contract impose an obligation on the developer to notify the seller of all planning decisions and whether or not a planning permission is a satisfactory planning permission?

6 Appeals

- Should the developer be obliged to appeal against a planning refusal or the imposition of onerous conditions? (Most developers will prefer to have the flexibility to submit a revised planning application and/or to appeal or to terminate the contract at their sole discretion.)
- Any obligation to appeal should be qualified: the developer should not be obliged to appeal unless counsel experienced in planning matters advises that there is a reasonable prospect or better than 50 per cent chance of success.

7 Seller's obligations

- Support planning application and co-operate.
- Not make any objection.
- Not make any planning application.
- Not to do anything which would be prejudicial to the grant of planning permission or make development more difficult or expensive.
- Not to transfer, charge, lease or otherwise deal with the property.
- Promptly enter into any required planning agreement.
- Procure that any mortgagee and tenant enter into any required planning agreement.

8 Planning agreements

- Is the contract conditional upon the seller entering into any required s.106 planning agreement?
- Does the contract impose an obligation on the seller to enter into any planning agreement required as a precondition to the grant of a satisfactory planning permission?
- Does the seller have the right to approve any required planning agreement?
- Does the contract impose an obligation on the seller to procure that any mortgagee or tenant of the seller will enter into any required planning agreement?
- Does the contract impose an obligation on the developer to provide the seller with a suitable indemnity and/or to ensure that any planning agreement contains a clause releasing the seller from all liability under the agreement after he has parted with his interest in the site?

9 Planning challenges

- Notwithstanding the grant of planning permission, the planning condition should not be regarded as satisfied until the possibility of a planning challenge/judicial review has passed. Does the contract contain a clause to this effect?

10 Waiver of planning condition

- Does the contract contain a clause allowing the developer to waive the planning condition and any other condition?

11 Disputes

- Is a dispute resolution clause required? (It may not be required if the developer is to have an absolute discretion to decide whether a planning permission is satisfactory.)

12 Community Infrastructure Levy (CIL)

- Should the contract be made conditional upon any requirement to pay CIL not having, in the opinion (or reasonable opinion) of the developer, a detrimental effect on the financial viability of the proposed development?
- Do obligations in respect of any potential CIL liability need to be imposed on the seller or the developer?

13 Price adjustment provisions

- Does the contract contain or require any price adjustment clauses?

14 Protection of contract

- The developer will need to protect the contract by registering a notice of the contract on the seller's title to the property or (in the case of unregistered land) a C(iv) land charge.

APPENDIX A5

Planning promotion agreement checklist for landowners

1 Objectives for the promoter

- To maximise market value.
- To minimise the requirements for affordable housing and infrastructure.
- To minimise planning gain costs.
- To submit a planning application at the earliest possible opportunity and use reasonable endeavours to secure a satisfactory planning permission.
- To pursue a planning application with all due diligence and to appeal in the circumstances mentioned in the promotion agreement.
- Following the grant of a satisfactory planning permission, to carry out the infrastructure works required in order to sell the property as fully serviced development land. (Note: The parties will need to carefully consider whether the promotion agreement should contain any infrastructure provisions and be aware of the possible tax and other implications of carrying out infrastructure works (such as triggering planning obligations and any CIL liability).)
- To market the property for sale and to effect sales with a view to maximising the sale proceeds.

2 Promotion costs

- Is the promoter to be reimbursed all promotion costs incurred by it out of the sale proceeds?
- If so, should the promoter be reimbursed in full on the first sale or in stages (with a proportion of the promotion costs being reimbursed on each sale)?
- Should the promotion costs be subject to the approval of the landowner?
- Should the promotion costs be capped?

3 Minimum purchase price

- Should the landowner be entitled to refuse to agree to a sale if the purchase price offered is less than a specified minimum purchase price or if the landowner's share of the net sale proceeds after all deductions will be less than a specified minimum price?
- Should the landowner be entitled to refuse to agree to a sale if the purchase price offered is below a threshold sum or if it includes deferred payment terms?

4 Tax and VAT on the promoter's fee

- What is the tax status of the landowner? (If the landowner is a charity then the structure for the transaction will need to be carefully considered.)
- The promoter's fee will attract VAT. In order to recover the VAT, the landowner will need to be registered for VAT and to have made an election to waive exemption from VAT.
- The election by the landowner to waive exemption from VAT creates two issues

for the purchaser of the promotion land. The first issue is that the purchaser will have to pay an extra 20 per cent for the land. This will usually only be a cash flow issue. The second issue is that the purchaser will have to pay stamp duty land tax on the purchase price as increased by the VAT payable thereon.

5 Promotion period and extensions

- Should the promotion period be capable of extension in certain specified circumstances?
- Should the promotion period be extended if a planning permission has been granted until all the promotion land has been sold and the sale proceeds distributed between the parties?
- Should the extension provisions be subject to a longstop date?

6 Provision of infrastructure

- Should the promoter be required to provide infrastructure? (Note: This will need to be carefully considered and any infrastructure provisions will need to be carefully drafted to avoid a potential tax issue.)
- Funding of infrastructure costs – should the purchaser of the first tranche be required to provide the initial infrastructure (with the carrying out of further infrastructure works and the payment of Community Infrastructure Levy (CIL) to be funded out of the sale proceeds resulting from the sale of the first tranche)?
- The carrying out of infrastructure works may trigger a liability to pay CIL and, unless otherwise agreed, the landowners will be responsible for the payment of the CIL on the commencement of development. (From the landowner's point of view, the promoter should be responsible for payment of any CIL that may become payable and obliged to provide the landowners with suitable indemnity in respect of any CIL liability. The payment of CIL should be treated as a promotion cost to be reimbursed to the developer out of the sale proceeds.)

7 Promoter's planning obligations

- The promoter should be obliged to appoint planning and other consultants to assist it in meeting the promotion objectives.
- The landowners should have the right to approve the planning application.
- The promoter should be obliged to maximise the development value of the promotion land.
- The promoter should be obliged to use reasonable endeavours to ensure that any obligations proposed under any planning agreement are fair and reasonable and consistent with planning guidelines.
- The landowner should have the right to approve all s.106 planning agreements.
- The promoter should be obliged to submit the planning application at the earliest opportunity.
- The promoter should be obliged to appeal against a planning refusal if counsel experienced in planning matters advises that there is a reasonable prospect of success.
- The promoter should be obliged to pursue planning challenge proceedings in relation to competing sites and to defend planning challenge proceedings commenced by others.
- The landowner should have the right to approve any planning permission granted.
- The promoter should be obliged to provide the landowner with a suitable indemnity in respect of planning obligations.

8 Overage

- Should the promotion agreement require overage arrangements to be included in the documentation by which sales are to be achieved and, if so, how should any overage be apportioned between the promoter and the landowner?

9 Deferred payments

- The landowner should not be obliged to agree to a sale on deferred payment terms, unless they cater adequately for the tax liability of the landowner.
- Security?

10 Indemnity from the promoter

- Does the promotion agreement require the developer to provide the landowner with an indemnity in respect of planning obligations and any CIL liability?

APPENDIX A6

Site inspection checklist

- Are the boundaries of the site clearly defined?
- Is the site enclosed by fencing or walls along all boundaries?
- Do the on-site boundaries accord with the title plan?
- Are there any ditches and/or hedges running alongside any of the boundaries? (Note: Consider the hedge and ditch rule.)
- Does the site directly abut the highway? (Note: A highway search will not be definitive.)
- Is there a ditch between the front boundary of the site and the highway? (Note: There will be a rebuttable presumption that the ditch is not highway land and that it belongs to the owner of the site.)
- Is any apparatus belonging to a statutory undertaker or other service provider, such as an electricity substation, located on the site?
- Are there any overhead power lines crossing the site or electricity pylons or stays located on the site which may need diverting?
- Are there any buildings on adjoining land containing windows which overlook the site?
- Are there any tracks or paths crossing the site?
- Does the route of a public footpath shown on the definitive footpath map follow the route of the footpath on the ground or has there been a diversion of the definitive route?
- Is there any evidence of an adjoining owner exercising rights over the site?
- Is there any evidence of an adjoining owner encroaching on to the site?
- Are there any trees on the site which may be protected?
- Does the site have any unusual features, such as a watercourse which crosses the access to the site or which separates one part of the site from another part?
- Is there any evidence of flooding?
- Is there any Japanese knotweed or protected wildlife on the site?
- Is the frontage of the site wide enough to accommodate any visibility splays which may be required?
- Is there any evidence of the site being used for recreational purposes (e.g. dog walking or bird watching) by members of the public?
- Are there any buildings or other structures on adjoining land within 3 metres of the boundary of the site?

APPENDIX

Site Inspection Checklist

APPENDICES – SECTION B

Enquiries and report

APPENDIX B1

Development land enquiries

Land:

Seller:

Buyer:

Replies are requested to the following enquiries	The replies are as follows:
Buyer's Solicitors	Seller's Solicitors
Date:	Date:

1 Boundaries

1.1 Please mark on a plan of the Land all boundary walls, fences, hedges and ditches.

1.2 To whom do all the boundary structures belong?

1.3 Notwithstanding enquiry 1.2, which has the Seller maintained or regarded as the Seller's responsibility?

1.4 Are there any boundary structures for which no one accepts responsibility?

1.5 Has any person altered the boundaries of the Land at any time or erected any structure on or against any boundaries not in such person's full ownership and occupation?

1.6 Are the external boundaries of the Land clearly defined and marked on the ground?

1.7 When were the various boundary structures erected?

1.8 Is the Seller aware of any dispute as to the extent of such boundaries or the ownership of any ditches?

1.9 Has any adjoining owner or occupier encroached upon the boundaries of the Land?

1.10 In the case of a sale of part, please confirm that all the boundaries of the Land have been or will be pegged out prior to exchange of contracts.

1.11 Are any of the walls which separate the Land from an adjoining property party walls under the Party Wall Act etc. 1996 or by virtue of the Law of Property Act 1925, s.38 or any other statutory provision? If so, please:

(a) confirm that there have been no breaches of the Party Wall Act etc. 1996, and

(b) supply copies of any notices, counter-notices, awards and agreements relating to party structures.

1.12 Are there any discrepancies between the boundaries of the Land as shown on the title plan for the Land and the on-site boundaries?

2 Condition of the Land

2.1 Has the Land at any time been affected by subsidence, heave, raising or lowering of the water table, structural defects, flooding or defective drains? If so, please:

(a) give particulars including particulars of any work or repairs which have been done in relation to any of these matters and supply a copy of any guarantees obtained; and

(b) let us know if any claim has been made against any person in respect of any such matter and the result of such claim.

2.2 Are there any paths which cross or rights of way which are exercised or exercisable over the Land?

2.3 Are there any cables, pipelines or public or private sewers or drains (including (without limitation) fibre-optic cables or pressurised foul mains) which cross or abut the Land?

2.4 Is the Seller aware of any asbestos, high alumina cement or any other deleterious or potentially deleterious materials being or ever having been in the structure or fabric of any buildings on the Land or on the Land itself?

2.5 Are there any storage tanks pools or pits on, in or under the Land?

2.6 Are there any tunnels, underground streams, mine shafts (or anything else under the Land) which might affect the development of the Land?

2.7 Has there been any landslip on or adjacent to the Land?

2.8 Have any ponds on the Land been filled in?

2.9 Have any cattle which suffered from anthrax or foot and mouth disease been kept, slaughtered or buried on the Land?

2.10 Please confirm that the Land is not made-up ground in any respect.

2.11 Has the Seller commissioned any environmental survey or asbestos survey in respect of the Land? If so, would you please provide us with copies of all relevant ground investigation and asbestos reports. Please confirm that the reports are assignable and that the Seller will either assign the benefit of the reports to the Buyer or procure that the relevant consultants will issue fresh reports in favour of the Buyer at no cost to the Buyer.

2.12 Please confirm that there is no Japanese knotweed on the Land.

3 Environmental

3.1 Please confirm this Land has not been used as a rubbish tip, waste or industrial waste tip.

3.2 Is the Seller aware of any land within 250 metres which has been used as such a tip?

3.3 Is there any toxic or noxious material buried under the Land or has any such material been stored on the Land during or before the Seller's ownership?

3.4 Is there any asbestos or are there any PCBs on the Land?

3.5 Is the Seller aware of any of the following activities ever having been carried out on the Land or on any land within the vicinity of the Land:

(a) gas works;

(b) tanneries;

(c) dry cleaning;

(d) sewage works;

(e) landfill site;

(f) waste disposal;

(g) industrial processing;

(h) scrap yard or similar;

(i) manufacturers of printing ink;

(j) wood treatment works;

(k) any other use likely to result in land contamination by toxic or hazardous materials or otherwise?

3.6 Have any environmental audits of the Land been carried out by the Seller or the Seller's predecessors in title? If so, please provide details.

3.7 Has the Seller or (to the knowledge of the Seller) any previous owner, tenant, occupier or user of the Land or any other person:

(a) transported any toxic or hazardous materials to, from or across the Land?

(b) permitted toxic or hazardous materials to be deposited on the Land?

3.8 Have any toxic or hazardous materials migrated or threatened to migrate from any adjoining or neighbouring properties to the Land or from the Land to other property?

3.9 Have any statutory or other bodies made any environmental requirements relating to the Land? If so, please give details.

3.10 Is the Seller aware of any circumstances which could give rise to such requirements?

3.11 Have there been any civil or criminal proceedings in respect of the Land's use or occupation? If so, please give details.

3.12 Is the Seller aware of any facts which might give rise to such proceedings?

4 Adverse rights

4.1 Is the Seller aware of any rights or informal agreements specifically affecting the Land, which are exercisable by virtue of an easement, grant, wayleave, licence, consent, agreement or otherwise or which are in the nature of public or common rights? If so, please provide us with full details thereof.

4.2 Please provide us with copies of any of the following which affect the Land or any part thereof:

(a) wayleave agreements;

(b) telecommunication agreements;

(c) deeds of grant/easement;

(d) electricity substation leases.

4.3 Is the Seller aware of any unregistered interests affecting the Land which override first registration under Schedule 1 to the Land Registration Act 2002?

4.4 Is the Seller aware of any unregistered interests affecting the Land which override registered dispositions under Schedule 3 to the Land Registration Act 2002?

4.5 Please confirm that there are no tenancies, licences or any other interests of any kind affecting any part of the Land, whether formal or informal.

4.6 Is the Seller aware of:

(a) any proposals for any works on any nearby land which may affect the Land or the enjoyment thereof?

(b) any proposals for any change of use in relation to any nearby land which may affect the Land or the enjoyment thereof?

4.7 Please confirm that there are no public footpaths, bridleways or other public rights over the Land. If there are such rights please give details and indicate the routes on a plan.

4.8 Are there any openings in any fences or hedges running along the boundaries of the Land?

5 Conditions of sale

5.1 Please supply copies of any deeds and documents which you consider should be mentioned in the draft contract.

5.2 Please confirm that the Land is sold with vacant possession.

5.3 Apart from such matters as may be revealed by a local search or by the Buyer's title to the Land, please confirm that the Seller is not aware of the existence of any other encumbrances or matters affecting the Land.

6 Disputes and notices

6.1 Is the Seller aware of any past or current disputes regarding easements, covenants or other matters relating to the Land or its use?

6.2 Please give particulars of all notices relating to the Land or to matters likely to affect its use of enjoyment, given to or by any person with regard to the Land.

6.3 Apart from any matters expressly raised by these enquiries, is the Seller aware of any matters which should be brought to the attention of a buyer of the Land?

7 Title

If you have not already done so, please deduce the Seller's title to the Land.

8 Mortgagees

8.1 Is the Land subject to any mortgage or charge? If so, please provide full details of the mortgage/charge.

8.2 Is the Land subject to an unpaid vendor's lien? If so, please provide full details of the lien.

8.3 Please confirm that all charges, equitable charges and/or liens which affect the Land will be discharged on or before completion.

9 Plan

9.1 If you have not already done so, please send us a plan of the Land, showing it in relation to adjoining property and roads.

9.2 In the case of a sale of part, please confirm that the contract plan and the transfer plan will be based on a coordinated boundary survey and that they will be to a stated scale acceptable to the Land Registry with a North point and sufficient detail of surrounding areas to enable the Land to be identified.

10 Access

10.1 How is the Land accessed?

10.2 Please confirm that the Land directly abuts the public highway (and that there is no land between the Land and the public highway which is owned by a third party, i.e. a ransom strip).

10.3 Is the Seller aware of any proposed highway improvements affecting the Land or any land within 250 metres of the Land?

10.4 Is access to the Land via an unadopted roadway? If so, would you please:

(a) supply copies of any s.38 agreements relating to the unadopted roadway;

(b) confirm that the unadopted roadway connects to an adopted road.

10.5 If the Land does not directly abut a public highway, how is access to the Land obtained?

10.6 If access to the Land is via a private roadway then:

(a) Please deduce title thereto.

(b) Who is responsible for maintaining the private roadway?

(c) What other properties enjoy rights of way thereover?

(d) What sums have been paid, requested or demanded towards the upkeep and maintenance of the roadway?

(e) Is the roadway gated and, if so, who has control of the keys?

(f) Please confirm that there have been no disputes regarding the use of the roadway.

10.7 Please confirm that the Seller is not aware of any 'ransom strips' which could affect the Buyer's ability to access and service the Land.

10.8 Are there any charges payable in respect of access? If so, please give details.

10.9 Please confirm that there is no outstanding or anticipated liability for road charges or similar payments.

10.10 Please confirm that the frontage of the Land is of sufficient width to accommodate any visibility splays which may be required by the local or highway authorities in connection with the development of the Land.

10.11 Please confirm that there is sufficient room within either the Land or the highway to accommodate any road widening or other traffic management requirements which may be required by the local or highway authorities in connection with the development of the Land.

10.12 Please supply a copy of any agreement entered into under the Highways Act 1980, s.278 in respect of any road providing access to the Land.

11 Fairs and markets

Please confirm that no fairs or markets have been held or may be held upon the Land.

12 Village greens and commons

12.1 Please confirm that no part of the Land or any land over which access or drainage is taken or proposed to be taken is a town or village green or common land.

12.2 Please confirm that no part of the Land has at any time been used for sporting or recreational purposes by any of the local inhabitants and that the Seller is not aware of any pending application or threat of a pending application to register any part of the Land as a town or village green.

13 Archaeological

13.1 Please confirm that there are no ancient monuments or similar items anywhere on the Land.

13.2 Has an archaeological survey of the Land been undertaken?

14 Flooding

14.1 Please confirm that the Land is not within a flood plain.

14.2 Please confirm that the Land has not flooded during the Seller's ownership and that the Seller is not aware of any previous flooding.

15 Restrictions and easements

15.1 Please confirm that there are no covenants or restrictions which now or will on completion affect the Land or the proposed development. If there are any such, please give details.

15.2 With regard to any restrictive covenants affecting the Land:

(a) Please supply copies of the deeds imposing the covenants.

(b) If not obvious from the deeds, what evidence is there as to the identity of the land having the benefit of the covenants and what steps have been taken in order to identify such land?

(c) Have any enquiries been made of the owners of the land having the benefit with a view to negotiating a release, variation or modification? If so, please give details.

(d) Have any steps been taken in order to identify the person having the benefit of the restrictive covenants?

(e) Is the Seller aware of any assignment of the benefit of the covenants?

(f) Is the Seller aware of any person claiming to have the benefit of the covenants?

(g) Have any objections been made to the proposed development?

(h) Has the Seller, or to his knowledge, any predecessor in title tried to obtain restrictive covenant indemnity insurance cover and, if so, with what result?

(i) Has any attempt been made either by the Seller or by any other persons to vary, remove or modify such covenants and conditions, whether pursuant to the provisions of the Law of Property Act 1925, s.84 (as amended) or otherwise, or is such action contemplated?

15.3 Irrespective of whether the title is registered or not in the case of the covenants imposed post-1926, please indicate if the covenants were registered as D(ii) land charges (unless imposed in a Transfer or in an assurance inducing first registration which was registered within two months).

15.4 Does the Seller have the benefit of a restrictive covenant indemnity insurance policy? If so:

(a) Please supply a full copy of the policy together with copies of the proposal and/or copies of all relevant correspondence representing the proposal.

(b) Please confirm that the conditions of the policy have been complied with.

(c) Please confirm that the policy benefits successors in title and mortgagees.

(d) Has any claim been made under the policy?

(e) Please confirm that all material facts were disclosed to the insurers.

(f) Please confirm that the premium has been paid and that the policy is subsisting and that no indication has been received from the insurers cancelling the cover.

15.5 Have any complaints been made to the local planning authority on covenant grounds in connection with any subsisting planning permission?

15.6 Have all covenants, agreements and conditions affecting the Land or the user thereof been observed and complied with up to the date hereof? If not, please give particulars of any breach and of any complaint received.

16 Tree preservation orders

16.1 Are there any trees on the Land?

16.2 Is the Land affected by a tree preservation order (TPO)? If so, please supply full details (including a copy of the order and copies of all relevant plans) and, if a recent order, please let us know whether it has been confirmed.

16.3 If there is no existing TPO, has the local council made any visits or enquiries as a preliminary to making a TPO?

16.4 Is the Land within a Conservation Area? If so, has the Seller served any notice on the local planning authority informing the local planning authority that the Seller intends to remove or carry out works to any trees on the Land?

17 Wildlife

17.1 Is the Land affected by the Conservation of Wild Creatures and Plants Act 1975, Wildlife and Countryside Act 1981 or similar legislation?

17.2 Is the Seller aware of any bats or other protected or potentially protected species anywhere on the Land? If so, please give details.

18 Off-site costs

18.1 Please confirm that the Land is sold free from any liability to contribute towards or provide:

(a) off-site highway or drainage improvement works;

(b) open space, amenity land, playing fields, children's play areas or the like;

(c) off-site work or improvements required to bring water, gas, electricity or telecommunication services to the Land;

(d) other off-site works.

18.2 If not, please give details of all such off-site works and the estimated costs involved.

19 Drainage

19.1 Please indicate on a plan the position of the nearest public sewers.

19.2 Please explain how the connection to the public sewer system will be made. Will pumping be necessary?

19.3 If the route of any connection to the existing public foul sewers passes or will pass across an adjoining owner's land, please give details of any existing easements.

19.4 Please supply copies of any s.102 and/or s.104 agreements already in existence linking the Land with the nearest public sewer, or any such existing agreement affecting the Land itself.

19.5 Is the Seller aware of any difficulty in draining the Land to the nearest public surface and foul sewers?

20 Surface water

20.1 Where is the nearest existing public surface water sewer?

20.2 Please indicate on a plan how connection to the existing public surface water sewer is proposed.

20.3 Will pumping be necessary?

20.4 If the route of any connection to the existing surface water sewer passes or will pass across an adjoining owner's land, please give details of any existing easements.

20.5 Please supply copies of any s.102 and/or s.104 agreements already in existence linking the Land with the nearest public surface water drain, or any existing such agreement affecting the Land itself.

21 Requisition

Has any Requisition Notice, Requisition Agreement or Bond under the Water Industry Act 1991 been discussed or completed with the Water Authority? Please give full details with copies of all documents, notices, etc.

22 Water

22.1 Please indicate on a plan where the existing public water supply is, and how this will be brought to the Land.

22.2 If the water is to be brought across any adjoining or neighbouring owner's land, please give details of all existing easements.

22.3 Is there any information available as to the adequacy of the water supply for the proposed development? If any improvements are necessary to the existing system, please give details.

23 Electricity

23.1 Please indicate on a plan where the existing electricity supply is and how this will be brought to the Land.

23.2 If the electricity is to be brought across any adjoining or neighbouring owner's land, please give details of any existing easements.

23.3 Is there any information available as to the adequacy of the electricity supply for the proposed development? If any improvements are necessary to the existing system, please give details.

24 Gas

24.1 Please indicate on a plan where the existing gas supply is and how this will be brought on to the Land.

24.2 If the gas is to be brought across any adjoining or neighbouring owner's land, please give details of all existing easements.

24.3 Is there any information available as to the adequacy of the gas supply for the proposed development? If any improvements are necessary to the existing system, please give details.

25 Telephone

25.1 Please indicate on a plan where the existing telephone supply is and how this will be brought on to the Land.

25.2 If the telephone lines are to be brought across any adjoining or neighbouring owner's land, please give details of all existing easements.

25.3 Is there any information available as to the adequacy of the telephone lines for the proposed development? If any improvements are necessary to the existing system, please give details.

25.4 Are there any British Telecom or other fibre-optic or similar cables at the entrances or proposed entrances to the Land or within the Land? If so, please give details and the estimated cost of moving or dealing with them.

26 Value added tax

26.1 Has the Seller elected to waive the exemption from value added tax in respect of the Land? If so, please supply:

(a) a copy of the notice of election;

(b) details of the Seller's VAT registration number;

(c) a copy of the letter sent to HM Revenue & Customs notifying HM Revenue & Customs of the election;

(d) a copy of any letter of acknowledgement received from HM Revenue & Customs.

26.2 If no such election has been made please confirm that the Seller will not make such an election prior to completion and that a clause may be included in the contract whereby the Seller undertakes not to make such an election and in the event of breach the consideration specified in the contract shall be deemed to be inclusive of VAT.

27 Shared facilities

Please give details of any accessways, drains, wires, pipes, party walls or other facilities used in common with the owners or occupiers of any other property.

28 Use of shared facilities

Please supply copies of any agreements or documents regulating their use, liability for repair, maintenance and replacement.

29 Maintenance and cost of shared facilities

Whether or not there are any documents or agreements in respect of the shared facilities, has the Seller (or is the Seller aware that any predecessor in title has):

29.1 carried out any work on them, or been called upon to do so?

29.2 contributed towards the costs of any work, been called upon to do so or asked others to contribute?

29.3 made or received any demand for payment which is still outstanding, or is any such demand expected?

30 Employment of shared facilities

Has any person taken any action, to stop the use of any shared facility? If so, please supply full details.

31 Statutory requirements

Please supply full details of:

31.1 any notices served by any local, statutory or other competent authority in respect of the Land or its use and state whether each such notice has been complied with; and

31.2 any outstanding statutory requirement (whether communicated by formal or informal notice or without notification to the Seller) for works to the Land or its user.

32 Planning control enforcement

Is the Seller aware of any current, past or threatened enforcement action or request for compliance with planning or building regulation control made by the relevant authority? Please give details.

33 Planning and use

33.1 Has any resolution to grant planning permission to develop the Land been passed? If so, please provide a copy.

33.2 Is the Land affected or likely to be affected by any s.106 agreement? If so, please provide a copy of any existing or proposed s.106 agreement (including copies of all relevant plans).

33.3 Please also confirm that the site plan attached to any s.106 agreement corresponds with the title plan to the Land.

33.4 Please provide copies of all planning decisions affecting the Land.

33.5 In addition please supply:

(a) a copy of the applications relating thereto;

(b) a copy of all drawings submitted with those applications and referred to in the permission;

(c) copies of all material correspondence concerning the applications passing between the applicant and the planning authority;

(d) a copy of each officer's report to the planning committee;

(e) copies of all letters received by the planning authority objecting to the applications or sent direct to the applicant for consent or the Seller;

(f) a copy of any building regulation approval;

(g) evidence that all the planning conditions have been discharged.

33.6 Please state the existing actual use of every part of the Land and provide us with evidence that this is consistent with the current authorised use.

33.7 Is the Seller aware of any compulsory purchase order, or of any designation by or resolution of a local or other authority as to compulsory purchase or of any proposal to make such an order or designation, affecting the Land?

33.8 Is the Seller aware of any proposals by a local or other authority which might affect the Land?

33.9 Is any building on the Land listed?

33.10 Is the Seller aware of any proposal for making any building on the Land a listed building under the Town and Country Planning Act 1990?

33.11 Is any building on the Land of special architectural or historic interest?

34 Community Infrastructure Levy (CIL)

34.1 Is the Seller aware of any existing or future CIL liability relating to the Land? If so, please provide full details.

34.2 Has any notice relating to any existing or future CIL liability in respect of the Land been sent or received? If so, please provide full details.

34.3 If any CIL liability has been, or is to be, incurred relating to the Land, has any notice been served under the CIL regulations assuming liability for CIL?

APPENDIX B2

Highway authority enquiries

The Highways Department

[*address*]

Our ref: [*reference*]

Date: [*date*]

Dear Sirs

[*address/description of property*] (shown edged in red on the attached plan) ('the Property')

We are instructed by a prospective developer of the Property and would ask you to please reply to the following enquiries:

1. Please confirm that the Property immediately abuts onto a publicly maintainable highway and there is no intervening land between the Property and the public highway.
2. Please confirm the status of that highway (e.g. trunk, strategic, minor, public, private).
3. Please indicate on a plan the extent of the adopted highways (including verges, footpaths and cycleways) in the vicinity of the Property.
4. Please indicate on a plan any public rights of way adjacent to, abutting or going over the Property.
5. Please provide details of any proposals or schemes for road improvements or for the construction of new roads (including any by-pass) or any other road proposals or schemes which will affect the Property.
6. Please provide details of any proposal for the diversion or stopping up of any road serving the Property.
7. Please provide us with a copy of any section 38 agreement or other statutory agreement affecting any unadopted road which serves the Property.

[We enclose a cheque for £[ ] in respect of your fees for providing the above information.]

[We undertake to pay your reasonable charges for replying to the above enquiries.]

Yours faithfully

APPENDIX B3

Services enquiries

[*address of relevant utility service company*]

Our ref: [*reference*]

Your ref: [*reference*]

Date: [*date*]

Dear Sirs

Services Enquiry relating to [*address/description of property*] (shown edged in red on the attached plan) ('the Property')

We act for a prospective purchaser of the Property and would ask you to please reply to the following enquiries:

1. Are there any pipes, cables or other service apparatus belonging to your company on, over or under the Property?
2. Would you please provide us with a plan showing the location of such pipes, cables or other apparatus.
3. Are there any wayleave agreements or easements which affect the Property?
4. Would you please provide us with copies of any wayleave agreements, deeds of easement or other agreements affecting the Property.
5. Would you please provide us with a plan indicating the location of the nearest apparatus belonging to your company which would be available to serve the Property.

[We enclose a cheque for £[ ] in respect of your fees for replying to the above enquiries.]

Yours faithfully

APPENDIX B4

Environment Agency enquiries

Environment Agency

[*address*]

Our ref: [*reference*]

Your ref: [*reference*]

Date: [*date*]

Dear Sirs

[*address/description of property*] (shown edged in red on the attached plan) ('the Property')

We act for a prospective purchaser of the Property and would ask you to please reply to the following enquiries:

1. Does a landfill site form part of the Property or is there such a site within 500 metres of the Property?
2. Has the Property, or any land within 500 metres of the Property, been used for the deposit and/or recycling of refuse or waste at any time in the past?
3. Do you have any record of any part of the Property having been used for:

    3.1 Sewerage works
    3.2 Industrial processing
    3.3 Scrap yard or similar use
    3.4 Gas works
    3.5 Waste disposal?

4. Do you have any record of the Property or any land within 500 metres of it having been affected by the existence of methane gas or any other form of contamination and, if so, will any development of the Property require any special works to be carried out due to the existence of the same?
5. Are you aware of any proposals to include the Property or any part of the Property or any land within 500 metres of the Property on any Contaminated Land Register being compiled by you pursuant to the Environmental Protection Act 1990?
6. Do you have any record of the Property having been affected by:

    6.1 Flooding
    6.2 Any pollution incidents?

7. Please provide us with copies of any statutory licences or notices which you have issued in relation to the Property.

We enclose a cheque for £[ ] in respect of your fees.

Yours faithfully

APPENDIX B5

Legal report

LEGAL REPORT PREPARED FOR [ ]
RE: PURCHASE OF DEVELOPMENT LAND AT [ ]

Legal report relating to [address/description of property]

1 PRELIMINARY OBSERVATIONS

1.1 We refer to your instructions for the purchase of [address/description of property] ('the Property') from [name of vendor] ('the Vendor') for the sum of £[ ] [plus VAT]. Following receipt of your instructions we put in hand the usual preliminary searches, enquiries and pre-contract title investigations. This Report is based on the result of those searches and enquiries and on our investigation of title to the Property.

1.2 [We carried out an inspection of the Property on [ ] and this revealed [insert relevant details]]. [We have not ourselves had an opportunity to inspect the Property but we assume that an inspection has been made on your behalf.] [Unless we hear from you to the contrary, we shall assume that any inspection of the Property carried out by you has not revealed any matter which you consider should be brought to our attention. We also assume that you have made or commissioned such surveys and reports as you consider to be appropriate. Again, unless you notify us to the contrary, we shall assume that there is nothing in any such surveys/reports that you wish us to take up with the Vendor's solicitors.]

2 DESCRIPTION

2.1 The Property is shown edged in red on the plan ('the Plan') attached to this Report in Appendix [ ]. [We would ask you to please satisfy yourselves that the Plan accurately reflects the on-site boundaries of the Property and that there are no discrepancies between the Plan and the title plan for the Property.]

2.2 [The Vendor is selling part of the land within its/his ownership and the land shown edged in [blue] on the Plan is being retained by the Vendor ('the Retained Land')]. [We would recommend that the boundaries of the Property should be pegged out before you exchange contracts.]

2.3 [There is a ransom strip [between the points marked [describe] on the Plan] [along the [indicate] boundary of the Property – this is shown coloured [colour] on the Plan.] The ransom strip is excluded from the sale and does not form part of the Property.]

[Note to document user: Sale of part – The contract plan and transfer plan should be based on a coordinated boundary survey and should be to a scale acceptable to the Land Registry. The boundaries of the Property should be pegged out.]

3 TENURE AND TITLE

3.1 The whole of the Property is of [freehold/leasehold] tenure.

3.2 [The title to [part of] the Property is registered at the Land Registry with [absolute] title under title number [number] and [the Vendor] is shown as the registered proprietor. A copy of official register entries dated [date] in respect of Title Number [number] are attached to this report in Appendix [ ] together with a copy of the Land Registry title plan for the Property.]

[3.3 The title to [the remainder of] the Property is unregistered and the root of title is a conveyance [on sale] dated [date] and made between [names] ('the Conveyance'). A copy of the Conveyance is attached to this Report in Appendix [ ].]

4 BOUNDARIES

4.1 [The title deeds to the Property are silent on the question of ownership of boundary structures.] [It would appear from the title deeds that [the boundary walls separating the Property from the adjoining properties are party walls] [the boundary walls on the [left] [and] [right] hand side of the Property] [and] [at the rear] belong to the Property.]

4.2 [The Transfer of the Property to you imposes an obligation on you to construct a [fence] [boundary wall] between the points [describe] shown on the Plan.]

4.3 From looking at the Vendor's replies to pre-contract enquiries, it would appear that [the Vendor has no information regarding boundary structures].

4.4 [Our site inspection revealed that [there is a hedge and a ditch running along the boundary of the Property marked [AB] on the Plan. Please note that under the hedge and ditch rule, where two properties are separated by a hedge and a single ditch there is a presumption (in the absence of evidence to the contrary) that both the hedge and the ditch belong to the owner of the land on which the hedge is planted].]

4.5 We would recommend that: [(a) you carry out a site inspection of the Property to ensure that there are no discrepancies between the boundaries as indicated on the Land Registry title plan of the Property and the on-site boundaries and (b)] you ensure that your architects are aware of the legal boundaries of the Property and that they base all planning drawings and the estate layout drawing on the Land Registry title plan.

4.6 Please note that boundaries shown on a Land Registry Filed Plan are only general boundaries (i.e. they are not definitive).

5 ADVERSE RIGHTS COVENANTS AND OTHER ENCUMBRANCES

[Insert full details of all rights and covenants to which the Property is subject as revealed by the title documentation and pre-contract searches. Consider whether any covenants have been breached and whether the proposed development will breach any covenants or rights affecting the Property. Also consider whether a title indemnity policy should be obtained.]

[The Transfer of the Property to you ('the Transfer') will impose various obligations on you and will grant the Vendor various rights benefiting the Retained Land. A copy of the Transfer is attached to this Report in Appendix [ ].]

5.1 Restrictive covenants

5.1.1 [As you will see, the Transfer contains various restrictive covenants which will restrict your use of the Property, including the following:

[insert details of covenants contained in the Transfer]]

5.1.2 [The Property is [also] subject to the following restrictive covenants:

[insert details of covenants contained in title documents]]

5.2 Rights

5.2.1 [As you will see, the Transfer grants the following rights in favour of the Retained Land:

[insert details of rights contained in the Transfer]]

5.2.2 [The Property is subject to the following rights:

[insert details of rights contained in title documents]]

[You will need to consider whether the above mentioned rights will have any effect on your development proposals.]

[Please note that the route of the right of way granted by [insert details of relevant document containing the right] may not be varied and you will need to satisfy yourselves that it can be incorporated within your site layout and that it will not hinder your development proposals.]

[Please note that [insert details of relevant document containing the rights] does not contain any lift and shift provisions and that you will not be entitled to vary the route of the service media.]

5.3 Mineral reservations

[There are no express mineral reservations affecting the Property.]

[or]

[The Property is subject to a mineral exception and reservation [and there is a right in favour of [another] to win and work the mines and minerals beneath the Property] [with a provision for compensation in the event of damage being caused.] The party having the benefit of the mineral exception and reservation will not be entitled to carry out any mining activities without first obtaining planning permission authorising the carrying out of mining operations at the Property [and, as the Property is located in a residential area, it is perhaps unlikely that the local planning authority will be willing to grant planning permission permitting mining operations.] Nevertheless, the existence of the right to win and work minerals may deter a prospective plot purchaser from proceeding and we would recommend that you obtain a mining rights indemnity policy. We have approached [insurance company] to see whether they would be prepared to issue such a policy and we would refer you to the letter dated [date] attached to this Report in Appendix [ ]. As you will see [insurance company] are prepared to issue a mining rights indemnity policy with a limit of indemnity of £[ ] for a premium of £[ ] subject to the conditions referred to in the letter being satisfied.]

5.4 Wayleave agreements

[The Vendor's replies to our pre-contract enquiries [and the results of our technical searches] have not revealed the existence of any wayleave agreements.]

[The Property is subject to [the following wayleave agreements:] [a wayleave agreement dated [date] in favour of [name] ('the Wayleave Agreement'). A copy of [each] [the] Wayleave Agreement is attached to this Report in Appendix [ ].]]

[As you will see, the Wayleave Agreement permits the laying of underground electric cables in the position indicated on the plan attached to the Wayleave Agreement and clause [ ] of schedule [ ] states that ['this consent may be withdrawn by the Grantor upon giving to the Company 12 calendar months previous notice in writing without prejudice to the rights and powers of the Company under paragraph 6 of Schedule 4 to the Electricity Act 1989'.] Please note that under the Electricity Act 1989 a land owner requiring the removal of electrical apparatus from his land after the wayleave agreement has been terminated must serve a notice on the wayleave holder requiring it to remove its apparatus. The wayleave holder will be obliged to comply with the notice unless, within three months of the date of the notice, an application is made to the Secretary of State for the grant of a new wayleave agreement or an order authorising the compulsory purchase of the land is made. The Secretary of State will not entertain an application for a wayleave where 'land is covered by a dwelling or will be so covered on the assumption that any planning permission which is in force is acted on'. However, this does not preclude the Secretary of State from entertaining an application for a wayleave when it already exists and the wayleave holder is applying to keep its apparatus on the land, rather than to install new apparatus.]

[Remember to obtain copies of all wayleave agreements revealed by the technical searches and to consider how they will affect the development of the Property and whether they can be terminated having regard to the statutory rights of the relevant statutory undertaker/utility company.]

5.5 Public rights of way

[From looking at [the Vendor's replies to pre-contract enquiries and] the result of our local authority search it would appear that the Property is not subject to any public path or bridleway, although we would suggest that you verify this yourselves by carrying out a site inspection.]

[Please note that there is a public footpath crossing the Property – the public footpath is shown by the [blue] line on [the Plan] [the plan attached to the result of our local search]. You will need to consider whether the footpath will affect your development proposals and whether it will be necessary for you to apply for a diversion or extinguishment order. Please note that (a) there are two procedures that can be used to stop up or divert a public footpath or bridleway, namely, the procedure under section 118/section 119 of the Highways Act 1980 or the procedure under section 257 of the Town and Country Planning Act 1990; (b) under the Highways Act procedure a public path extinguishment order must not be made by the council or confirmed by the Secretary of State unless they are satisfied that it is expedient to do so having regard to the extent to which the path is used by the public and the effect of the extinguishment of the right on the land served by the path; and a public path diversion order must not be made by the council or confirmed by the Secretary of State unless they are satisfied that the diversion will not result in a substantially less convenient route; and (c) under the Town and Country Planning Act procedure the stopping up or diversion of a public footpath must be necessary to enable development to be carried out in accordance with a planning permission.]

5.6 Tree preservation

[Our searches and enquiries have not revealed the existence of any tree preservation order affecting the Property.]

[The Property is affected by a tree preservation order (TPO), a copy of which is attached to this Report in Appendix [ ]. [You will need to consider whether the TPO will have any adverse impact on your development proposals.] [Please note that it is a criminal offence to lop, top or fell a tree protected by a TPO without obtaining the consent of the local planning authority.] [As the Property is situated in a Conservation Area you will not be allowed to remove or undertake work to any trees on the Property, unless you have given the local planning authority notice of your intention to remove or undertake works to the trees and the local planning authority fails to respond to the notice within six weeks.] [Remember to check the local search and replies to pre-contract enquiries in order to ascertain whether the Property is situated in a Conservation Area. Also remember that if the Property has the benefit of a full planning permission, the implementation of which will necessitate works to TPO protected trees, the planning permission will override the TPO and a separate TPO consent will not be required.]]

5.7 Rights of light

[The title deeds to the Property have not disclosed the existence of any rights to light in favour of any adjoining properties. However, this does not mean that such rights do not exist. In many cases rights to light will have arisen not as a result of having been expressly created, but due to the actual enjoyment of light from neighbouring land over a long period (at least 20 years). You should therefore check whether there are any buildings on adjoining land containing windows which overlook the Property and consider whether your proposed development will obstruct the access of light to such windows.]

[The Property is subject to [the following] rights to light declarations in favour of adjoining land:

[insert rights]]

6 RIGHTS AND COVENANTS BENEFITING THE PROPERTY

[Insert full details of all rights and covenants which benefit the Property as revealed by the title documentation and consider whether the rights are adequate.]

[The Property does not have the benefit of any express rights or covenants.]

[The Property has the benefit of the following rights:]

[The Property has the benefit of the following covenants:]

[As you will see, the Transfer grants the following rights in favour of the Property:]

7 TENANCIES

[The Property is not subject to any leases.]

[or]

7.1 [The Property is being sold subject to various [business/agricultural] tenancies, brief details of which are attached to this report in Appendix [ ].]

7.2 [In order to bring the business tenancies to an end, it will be necessary to serve a section 25 notice to quit on each tenant stating that the landlord will oppose the grant of a new lease on redevelopment grounds. The notice to quit will need to specify the date on which the landlord requires possession and such date may not be more than 12 months nor less than six months before the lease term will expire (or, if the lease term has already expired, not more than 12 months or less than six months from the date of the notice to quit). Please note that:

7.2.1 In order to successfully oppose the grant of a new lease on redevelopment grounds, a landlord will have to show that he has a firm intention to demolish or reconstruct the demised premises. Ideally, the landlord should obtain the necessary permission by the hearing, but failure to do so will not be fatal, since the test is whether there is a reasonable prospect of getting consent. Provided the landlord can establish his intention as a matter of fact, his motive for carrying out the work is irrelevant. A landlord who is seeking to oppose the grant of a new lease on redevelopment grounds should therefore ensure that, if a corporation, there is a present and appropriately worded resolution, that any requisite consents and approvals (for example, planning permission or listed building consents) have been obtained, that plans and specifications have been prepared, that either a building contract has been entered into for the proposed works or at least that evidence is available that a contract will be entered into in good time, that the necessary finance for the project is or can be made available, and that the project will not be held up by some impediment, such as a tenant of another part of the building who cannot be removed.

7.2.2 The intention of the landlord to demolish or reconstruct the property has to be established as at the date upon which the application is heard by the court.

7.2.3 Any tenant whose statutory right of renewal is successfully opposed by a landlord on the ground that the landlord has a firm intention to redevelop the demised premises will be entitled to compensation. The amount of compensation will be [the rateable value of the demised premises] [twice the rateable value of the demised premises]. The rateable value is ascertained at the date of service of the landlord's section 25 notice to quit or the landlord's notice of opposition to a section 26 request by the tenant for a new tenancy.

7.2.4 Under the Landlord and Tenant Act 1927 a tenant of business premises may also be entitled to compensation at the end of the lease for authorised improvements which benefit the landlord.]

8 CONTAMINATED LAND LIABILITY

It is possible that under the legislation relating to contaminated land an owner or occupier of contaminated land may be responsible for cleaning up the contamination even where the owner did not cause or knowingly permit the contamination. Although the legislation follows the principle that, where feasible, the 'polluter pays', there are exceptions to this principle and it is possible for liability for contamination to be transferred from a seller to a buyer. For example, a seller may avoid liability by providing the buyer with sufficient information to make the buyer aware of the contamination or by permitting the buyer to carry out his own environmental survey; and in transactions between large commercial organisations permission from the seller for the buyer to carry out his own survey will normally be taken as sufficient indication that the buyer has the necessary information. We would therefore recommend that, if you have not already done so, you thoroughly investigate the ground conditions of the Property before proceeding to exchange contracts to purchase the Property.

[We would draw your attention to the provisions of clause [ ] of the Purchase Contract, which effectively transfer all liability for contamination from the Vendor to you.]

[Attached to this Report in Appendix [ ] is a copy of the [Sitecheck search] prepared by [ ]. As you will see, this concludes that [ ].]

[We understand that you have made or will be making arrangements for ground investigations to be carried out at the Property. Unless we hear from you to the contrary, we shall assume that the ground investigations do not reveal anything unexpected.]

[We understand that you have been provided with a ground investigation report carried out by [ ]. [It is a term of the Purchase Contract that the Vendor will procure that the report is re-addressed in your favour or that the author of the report provides you with a letter of reliance in the form of the draft letter of reliance attached to this Report in Appendix [ ].] [Also attached to this Report in Appendix [ ] is a copy of the deed of appointment/letter of engagement signed by the author of the report.]]

We have raised environmental enquiries of the Vendor and these have revealed the following:

[insert findings]

[Our usual enquiries of the local authority [did not reveal any particular problems] but these enquiries are far from conclusive as to the risks of existence of any contaminated land.]

[We have raised environmental enquiries of the Environment Agency and these have revealed the following:

[insert findings]]

9 PLANNING

[Insert full details of all relevant planning permissions and planning agreements and list all planning obligations and pre-commencement/Grampian conditions. Does any planning permission include land other than the Property? If so, will this have any impact on the development of the Property? When will the planning permissions lapse?]

[9.1 As you know, the Property is currently [agricultural land/an industrial property] and does not benefit from any [residential] planning consent. [However, your purchase of the Property will be conditional on your obtaining [an implementable] planning permission for [residential] development – see paragraph [ ] of this Report.] [We understand that you have spoken to the planners and that you are aware of their likely planning gain requirements.]]

[9.1 The Property has the benefit of the following planning permissions ('the Planning Permissions'):

[Copies of the Planning Permissions are attached to this Report in Appendix [ ].]]

9.2 [The Planning Permissions are all conditional planning permissions and we would draw your attention in particular to the following conditions:]

9.3 [The Property is affected by a planning agreement dated [date] ('the section 106 Agreement'). A copy of the section 106 Agreement is attached to this Report in Appendix [ ] and we would draw your attention in particular to the following:]

10 SEARCHES AND ENQUIRIES

10.1 Attached to this Report in Appendix [ ] are copies of the following:

(a) Pre-contract development enquiries and replies
(b) Local authority search
(c) Chancel repair liability search
(d) Index map search
[(e) Environmental search agency [and] [Letter from the Environment Agency dated [ ]]]
[(f) Title enquiries and replies]
[(g) Coal mining report]
[(h) Land charge search certificates]
[(i) Company search against the Vendor]
[(j) British Waterways search]
[(k) Archaeological search]
[(l) Flood search]

10.2 We would ask you to carefully read through the above enclosures and to contact us if you have any queries.

11 REPLIES TO ENQUIRIES

With regard to the Vendor's replies to our pre-contract development enquiries, we would draw your attention in particular to the following:

[insert replies to enquiries]

12 COAL MINING SEARCH

[As you will observe, the coal mining report, reveals that:

[insert findings]]

13 INDEX MAP SEARCH

[Our index map search of the Property has not revealed the existence of any sub-surface mineral title and our index map search of the land adjoining the front boundary of the Property has revealed that the title to that land is unregistered.]

14 LOCAL SEARCH

With regard to the local authority search, you will note that this reveals, amongst other matters, the following:

[(a) The Property is situated in a Smoke Control Area.]
[(b) [ ] Road is a public highway maintainable at the public's expense.]
[(c) The foul drainage from the Property drains to a public sewer.]
[(d) The statutory sewer map indicates that there is a public sewer or disposal main within the boundaries of the Property in respect of which a vesting declaration has been made or which is the subject of a section 104 agreement.]
[(e) There is a public footpath crossing the Property.]

[(f) The Property is [not] situated in a Conservation Area.]

[(g) No part of the Property has been registered as common land or a town or village green. However, please note that if there is a pending application to register any part of the property as a town or village green then this would not be revealed by a local authority search.]

[(h) The Property is situated in a Mineral Consultation Area. This means that the planning authority has undertaken to consult with the local mineral extraction industries before granting any planning permission to develop the Property and planning permission might be refused if it would impede the extraction of minerals.]

15 CHANCEL SEARCH

As you will observe, the chancel search reveals that the Property is located within a parish which [has no] [continues to have a] potential chancel repair liability. [Please note that a clear chancel search does not establish beyond all doubt that a property has no chancel repair liability. The search is based on certain records and will not be conclusive. The expression 'no record of risk' means:

(a) No record of risk is held by the National Archive within the relevant Inland Revenue Indices for the subject parish.

(b) The Property is within a parish with evidence of risk but the Property is situated within a tithe district that has no risk per the records described.

(c) The records held by the National Archive details that the total liability is held by the Church Commissioners, Cathedrals and/or education establishments.]

16 FLOODING

As you will observe, the [environmental search] [sitecheck search] [flood search] reveals that [the Property is [not] affected by flooding].

17 ACCESS AND HIGHWAYS

17.1 We understand that access to the Property [is/will be] via [describe access] which [(as stated above)] is an [adopted/unadopted] road.

17.2 Attached to this Report in Appendix [ ] is a letter dated [date] from [specify] Council regarding the extent of the public highway abutting the Property. As you will see, according to the Council's records, the extent of the adopted highway is as shown coloured in [colour] on the plan attached to the Council's letter. We would suggest that you ask your highway consultants to overlay the title plan and the highway plan provided by the Council to ensure that there is no intervening strip of land between the highway and the boundary of the Property across which access to the Property is to be gained. [It would appear from the plan attached to the Council's letter that the Property directly abuts the public highway, but we cannot be certain that this is the case. You should be aware that a highway search is not definitive: it is based on the Council's records and these may not be entirely accurate. For this reason, we have also carried out an index map search in respect of the land immediately abutting the front boundary of the Property and this has revealed [that the title to such land is unregistered].]

17.3 [Please note the conditions contained in the planning permission dated [date] (see Appendix [ ]) relating to [access/off-site highway works/visibility splays]. [You will need to ensure that [the creation of the new access to the Property/the off-site highway works/the visibility splay requirements] do not involve third party land over which you have no control.]]

[or]

[The development of the Property will involve the creation of a new access road and improvements to the highway and you should ensure that your architects take into account all visibility splay requirements and that the splays do not encroach on to adjoining land.]

18 DRAINAGE

18.1 We understand that you have made or will be making your own enquiries of [name of water company] regarding:

(a) the existence of any public sewers under the Property; and
(b) the proximity of foul and surface water sewers into which the Property will be able to link.

Unless you notify us to the contrary, we shall assume that your technical team have satisfied themselves that (a) there are no sewers within the boundaries of the Property which will affect your development proposals; (b) there are existing adopted foul and surface water sewers into which you will be able to link without the need to cross third party land; and (c) the existing sewers are of sufficient capacity to serve the Property once fully developed.

18.2 [Please note the conditions contained in the planning permission dated [ ] relating to drainage.]

18.3 Attached to this Report in Appendix [ ] is a copy of our drainage search. You will note that:

[(a) The public sewer map does not show any public sewers within the boundary of the Property.]

[insert findings]

19 OTHER SERVICES

19.1 We understand that you have made or will be making your own enquiries of the various utility companies regarding:

(a) the supply of services to the Property (including the supply of water, gas and electricity); and
(b) the existence of any pipes, cables or other apparatus on, under or above the Property.

Unless you notify us to the contrary, we shall assume that you have satisfied yourselves on these matters.

19.2 [Attached to this Report in Appendix [ ] are copies of the following searches:

(a) Electricity search
(b) Gas search
(c) BT search

Please note the positioning of the apparatus belonging to the various utility service providers. Again, unless you notify us to the contrary, we shall assume that your technical team are satisfied that you will be able to connect to the mains water, electricity, gas and telecommunications systems without the need to cross any third party land.]

20 VALUE ADDED TAX

The Vendor has [not] elected to waive exemption from value added tax ('VAT') in respect of the Property. Accordingly, [no] VAT will be payable on the Purchase Price. [Attached to this Report in Appendix [ ] are copies of the following:

(a) the Vendor's VAT election to waive exemption from VAT;
(b) the Vendor's letter notifying HM Revenue & Customs of the election; and
(c) the letter of acknowledgement from HM Revenue & Customs.]

21 PURCHASE CONTRACT

21.1 [A copy of the agreed form of sale and purchase agreement ('the Purchase Contract') is attached to this Report in Appendix [ ]. We do not propose to comment in detail on the terms of the Purchase Contract and would ask you to read through this document carefully.]

21.2 We would draw your attention to the following:

21.2.1 Price

The Purchase Price for the Property is £[ ] [plus VAT]. [The Purchase Contract requires the Vendor to hand over a valid VAT invoice on completion.]

21.2.2 Deposit

A deposit of £[ ] [plus VAT] will be payable on exchange of contracts. The deposit will be held by the Vendor's solicitors as [stakeholders] [agents].

21.2.3 Vacant possession/tenancies

The Property is being sold [with vacant possession] [subject to the tenancies referred to in paragraph [ ] above.]

21.2.4 Conditions

The Purchase Contract is [not conditional upon planning or any other matter] [conditional upon your obtaining [detailed] planning permission for the [residential] development of the Property [in a form acceptable to you] [containing no Onerous Conditions (as defined)] before the Planning Period (as defined) expires. [Please note:

(a) The definition of 'Acceptable Planning Permission' contained in clause [ ] of the Purchase Contract. [As you will see, for the Planning Permission to be regarded as acceptable it must [be in a form and contain conditions acceptable to you in your absolute discretion] [not contain any Onerous Conditions].]
(b) The definition of 'Planning Application' contained in clause [ ] of the Purchase Contract. [As you will see, it includes further planning applications and the revision of a planning application.]
(c) The definition of 'Development' contained in clause [ ] of the Purchase Contract.
(d) The definition of 'Onerous Condition' contained in clause [ ] of the Purchase Contract. As you will see, a condition is to be regarded as onerous if:

[(i)
(ii)
(iii)
(iv)]

(e) The definition of 'Planning Condition' contained in clause [ ] of the Purchase Contract. [As you will see, for the Planning Condition to be satisfied the Acceptable Planning Permission must be immune from challenge [and capable of implementation].]

(f) The definition of 'Planning Period' contained in clause [ ] of the Purchase Contract. [As you will see, it includes the Initial Planning Period of [ ] months [as extended in accordance with the provisions of clause [ ] of the Purchase Contract.]]

[(g) The Purchase Contract obliges you to lodge a planning application within [ ] months of the date of the Purchase Contract and to use reasonable endeavours to obtain an Acceptable Planning Permission as soon as reasonably possible [and to appeal against a Planning Refusal]. [You will not be obliged to appeal against a Planning Refusal as defined.]]

[(h) If the Planning Condition has not been satisfied by [ ] [the expiration of the Planning Period] then the Purchase Contract may be terminated by either party serving notice on the other party in accordance with the provisions of clause [ ] of the Purchase Contract and the provisions of clauses [ ] will then apply.]

[(i) The Planning Condition may be waived by you at any time.]

[(j) The Purchase Contract imposes an obligation on the Vendor to enter into any section 106 agreement required as a precondition of an Acceptable Planning Permission being granted.]

[(k) The Purchase Contract obliges you to provide the Vendor with a copy of any planning decision not later than [10] Working Days after notice of the planning decision has been received by you and to notify the Vendor within [20] Working Days after the planning decision has been received by you whether or not you consider the planning permission to be an Acceptable Planning Permission.]

[(l) Notwithstanding the grant of planning permission, the Planning Condition shall not be treated as satisfied until (i) the Challenge Period (as defined) has expired without any Challenge Proceedings (as defined) having been commenced or (ii) if any Challenge Proceedings are commenced with the Challenge Period then they have been exhausted leaving in place an Acceptable Planning Permission.]]]

21.2.5 Completion

The date fixed for completion is [date].

21.2.6 Insurance

[The risk of insuring the Property will pass to you on exchange of contracts. You will therefore need to arrange for the Property to be insured as from the date of exchange.]

21.2.7 Title Guarantee

The Vendor is selling the Property with [full/limited] title guarantee.

21.2.8 [Obligations

The Purchase Contract imposes the following obligations on the Purchaser:]

21.2.9 Guarantor

[Insert information where appropriate]

21.2.10 Licence to use drawings

[Insert information where appropriate]

21.2.11 Reports

[Insert information where appropriate]

21.2.12 Environmental

[Insert information where appropriate]

22 SUMMARY OF MAIN RISKS

We would briefly summarise the main risks involved in proceeding with this transaction as follows:

[describe as appropriate]

23 CERTIFICATE OF TITLE

23.1 On the basis of our enquiries and investigations to date, we are of the opinion that, subject to such observations, qualifications or outstanding matters made or referred to in this Report, the Property has a good and marketable title.

23.2 We will report to you on our Land Registry searches and Requisitions on Title in due course, after which time we hope to give you our final confirmation that the Property has a good and marketable title.

23.3 This Report has been prepared for [ ] in connection with the purchase of the Property and should not be relied upon by any other party or used for any other purpose.

[Signature]

[Date]

APPENDICES – SECTION C

Transfers and deeds

APPENDIX C1

Sample form: Transfer of part granting and reserving rights (where transferee is obliged to provide infrastructure under the contract)

HM Land Registry
Transfer of part of registered title(s)

Any parts of the form that are not typed should be completed in black ink and in block capitals.

If you need more room than is provided for in a panel, and your software allows, you can expand any panel in the form. Alternatively use continuation sheet CS and attach it to this form.

For information on how HM Land Registry processes your personal information, see our Personal Information Charter.

Guidance	Panel
Leave blank if not yet registered.	1 Title number(s) out of which the property is transferred:
When application for registration is made these title number(s) should be entered in panel 2 of Form AP1.	2 Other title number(s) against which matters contained in this transfer are to be registered or noted, if any:
Insert address, including postcode (if any), or other description of the property transferred. Any physical exclusions, such as mines and minerals, should be defined.	3 Property:
Place 'X' in the appropriate box and complete the statement.	The property is identified
For example 'edged red'.	☐ on the attached plan and shown:
For example 'edged and numbered 1 in blue'.	☐ on the title plan(s) of the above titles and shown:
Any plan lodged must be signed by the transferor.	
Remember to date this deed with the day of completion, but not before it has been signed and witnessed.	4 Date:
Give full name(s) of **all** of the persons transferring the property.	5 Transferor:
Complete as appropriate where the transferor is a company.	For UK incorporated companies/LLPs Registered number of company or limited liability partnership including any prefix: For overseas companies (a) Territory of incorporation: (b) Registered number in the United Kingdom including any prefix:
Give full name(s) of **all** the persons to be shown as registered proprietors.	6 Transferee for entry in the register:
Complete as appropriate where the transferee is a company. Also, for an overseas company, unless an arrangement with HM Land Registry exists, lodge either a certificate in Form 7 in Schedule 3 to the Land Registration Rules 2003 or a certified copy of the constitution in English or Welsh, or other evidence permitted by rule 183 of the Land Registration Rules 2003.	For UK incorporated companies/LLPs Registered number of company or limited liability partnership including any prefix: For overseas companies (a) Territory of incorporation: (b) Registered number in the United Kingdom including any prefix:

Guidance	Panel
Each transferee may give up to three addresses for service, one of which must be a postal address whether or not in the UK (including the postcode, if any). The others can be any combination of a postal address, a UK DX box number or an electronic address.	7 Transferee's intended address(es) for service for entry in the register:
	8 The transferor transfers the property to the transferee
Place 'X' in the appropriate box. State the currency unit if other than sterling. If none of the boxes apply, insert an appropriate memorandum in panel 12.	9 Consideration ☐ The transferor has received from the transferee for the property the following sum (in words and figures): ☐ The transfer is not for money or anything that has a monetary value ☐ Insert other receipt as appropriate:
Place 'X' in any box that applies. Add any modifications.	10 The transferor transfers with ☐ full title guarantee ☐ limited title guarantee
Where the transferee is more than one person, place 'X' in the appropriate box. Complete as necessary. The registrar will enter a Form A restriction in the register *unless*: – an 'X' is placed: – in the first box, or – in the third box and the details of the trust or of the trust instrument show that the transferees are to hold the property on trust for themselves alone as joint tenants, *or* – it is clear from completion of a form JO lodged with this application that the transferees are to hold the property on trust for themselves alone as joint tenants. Please refer to *Joint property ownership* and *practice guide 24: private trusts of land* for further guidance. These are both available on the GOV.UK website.	11 Declaration of trust. The transferee is more than one person and ☐ they are to hold the property on trust for themselves as joint tenants ☐ they are to hold the property on trust for themselves as tenants in common in equal shares ☐ they are to hold the property on trust:
Use this panel for: – definitions of terms not defined above – rights granted or reserved – restrictive covenants – other covenants – agreements and declarations – any required or permitted statements – other agreed provisions. The prescribed subheadings may be added to, amended, repositioned or omitted. Any other land affected by rights granted	12 Additional provisions **12.1 DEFINITIONS** **'Affecting Matters'** means the covenants, exceptions, reservations, rights and other matters (other than charges of a financial nature) contained or referred to in the Property and Charges Registers of title number(s) [ ] as at the date of this Transfer;

or reserved or by restrictive covenants should be defined by reference to a plan.

'the Estate Roads' means the roads and footpaths now constructed or to be constructed in the future on the Property;

'the Estate Sewers' means the foul and surface water sewers now constructed or to be constructed in the future within the Property;

'Parties' means the parties to this Transfer;

'Plan' means the plan or plans attached to this Transfer;

'Relevant Authority' means all or any of the following as appropriate:

(a) such authority or body as shall have responsibility under statute for highway matters;

(b) such authority or body as shall have responsibility under statute for drainage matters;

(c) such authority or body as shall have responsibility under statute for planning matters;

(d) such authority or body as shall have responsibility under statute for environmental matters;

(e) any utility company concerned with the installation of Service Media and the provision of Services;

(f) any other authority, company, body, corporation or organisation concerned with the control of development or the adoption of roads or sewers or the protection of wildlife and/or the environment or having jurisdiction in relation to the development of the Property and the Retained Land and/or the infrastructure serving the same;

'Retained Land' means [the land shown edged in blue on the Plan] [the land now or formerly comprised within title numbers [ ] excluding the Property];

'Service Media' means conduits, sewers, drains, pipes, cables, pumping systems, channels, balancing ponds and other service media for the supply of Services;

'Services' means water, gas, electricity, telephone, telecommunications, cable television, surface water drainage, foul drainage and similar services.

12.2 In this Transfer references to 'the Transferor' and 'the Transferee' shall be deemed to include their respective successors in title and references to the Retained Land and the Property shall be references to the whole and each and every part of such land respectively.

12.3 The Property is transferred **TOGETHER WITH** the rights set out in the First Schedule hereto and **EXCEPTING AND RESERVING** to the Transferor and its successors in title and their respective tenants, servants and invitees and all others authorised by the Transferor the rights referred to and set out in the Second Schedule hereto for the benefit of the Retained Land and any building or buildings now or hereafter erected thereon.

12.4 TRANSFEREE'S COVENANTS

The Transferee **HEREBY COVENANTS** by way of indemnity only and not further or otherwise with the Transferor to observe and perform the Affecting Matters in so far as the same respectively affect the Property and are still effective and to indemnify and keep indemnified the Transferor and its successors in title from all costs, claims and actions arising out of any future breach and non-observance thereof so far as aforesaid.

[NOTE: This transfer does not contain any infrastructure obligations or impose any restrictive covenants on the Transferor or the Transferee.]

12.5 AGREEMENTS AND DECLARATIONS

It is hereby agreed and declared as follows:

12.5.1 Rights of light and air

12.5.1.1 Neither the Transferee nor the persons deriving title under it shall become entitled whether by implication, prescription or otherwise to any right of light or air or other right or easement (except as herein contained) which would restrict or interfere with the free use by the Transferor of the Retained Land or any part or parts thereof for building or other purposes.

12.5.1.2 Neither the Transferor nor the persons deriving title under it shall become entitled whether by implication, prescription or otherwise to any right of light or air or other right or easement (except as herein contained) which would restrict or interfere with the free use by the Transferee of the Property or any part or parts thereof for building or other purposes.

12.5.2 Rights of third parties

Unless the right of enforcement is expressly provided it is not intended that a third party should have the right to enforce any terms of this Transfer pursuant to the Contracts (Rights of Third Parties) Act 1999 but this does not affect any rights which are available apart from that Act.

12.5.3 Implied rights

Section 62 of the Law of Property Act 1925 and the rule in *Wheeldon* v. *Burrows* do not apply to this Transfer and no legal or other rights are granted over the Retained Land for the benefit of the Property except for those expressly granted by this Transfer.

12.5.4 Rights reserved and granted

12.5.4.1 Unless otherwise stated, the rights hereby granted are granted for use by the Transferee in common with the Transferor and all persons lawfully entitled to exercise them and the rights hereby reserved are reserved for use by the Transferor in common with the Transferee and all persons lawfully entitled to exercise them.

12.5.4.2 The rights hereby reserved and granted shall not be exercised over land which has been or is being or is intended to be developed by the construction of buildings or their curtilages [or over shared access areas not intended to be made available for general use] [or (except for acceptable rights of way) over land to be dedicated as public open space].

12.5.4.3 Any rights of entry on land shall be exercised only upon reasonable notice and at reasonable times (except in cases of emergency).

12.5.4.4 All requisite consents from any Relevant Authority for connections to and construction of any roads and/or Service Media pursuant to the rights hereby reserved and granted shall be obtained by the person exercising the rights prior to effecting the same.

12.5.4.5 The person exercising the rights shall cause as little damage and disturbance as reasonably possible and shall make good all damage caused as soon as reasonably practicable.

12.5.4.6 [Connections to Service Media and Estate Sewers shall only be made to the extent that there is capacity therefor and the Transferee shall not be obliged to upsize or oversize the Service Media or Estate Sewers.]

12.5.4.7 [The person exercising the rights hereby reserved shall (if so requested) consent to the Estate Roads and/or the Service Media and/or Estate Sewers over or through which the rights are exercised becoming adopted and/or maintainable at the public expense [and pending adoption shall contribute a fair and reasonable proportion (according to user) of the costs of inspecting, cleansing, repairing maintaining renewing or replacing the Estate Roads and/or the Service Media and/or the Estate Sewers over or through (or into) which the rights are exercised.]]

12.5.4.8 [Rights of way over the Estate Roads shall not be exercised until the same shall have been constructed to base course level.]

12.5.5 Co-operation

[The parties to this Transfer agree the one with the other and undertake with each other that they will co-operate with each other and act in the utmost good faith with each other in connection with this Transfer [and will without delay join in any necessary agreements reasonably required by the other (subject to any reasonable indemnities being given and reasonable provision for costs being made) required for the development of either party's land and/or the adoption of any roads and Service Media and any connections thereto].]

12.5.6 Application

The Transferor and the Transferee hereby apply to the Chief Land Registrar to enter into the Registers of the Titles to the Property and the Retained Land such of the rights, reservations, exceptions, covenants and conditions contained or referred to herein as are capable of registration.

IN WITNESS whereof this Transfer has been executed by the Transferor and the Transferee as a Deed on the date and year first before written

THE FIRST SCHEDULE before referred to
Rights Granted

The following rights for the Transferee, its successors in title of all or any parts of the Property and their respective tenants and servants and invitees in common with the Transferor and all others so entitled:

1. [To use roads

The full and free right to go, pass and repass with or without vehicles at all times and for all purposes over and along any roads and on foot only over any footpaths now constructed or to be constructed at any time in the future on the Retained Land.]

2. [To connect to and use sewers

The full and free right to connect to and to use any sewers now laid or to be laid at any time in the future within the Retained Land together with the right (upon reasonable prior written notice) to enter upon the Retained Land but only so far as strictly necessary with workmen and equipment for the purpose of (a) making connections with such sewers and/or (b) testing, cleaning, maintaining, renewing and repairing such sewers and the connections thereto.]

3. [To connect to and use Service Media

The full and free right to connect to and use any Service Media now laid or to be laid in the future within the Retained Land together with the right (upon reasonable prior written notice) to enter upon the Retained Land but only so far as strictly necessary with workmen and equipment for the purpose of (a) making connections with such service media and/or (b) testing, cleaning, maintaining, renewing and repairing such service media and the connections thereto.]

4. [To lay new Service Media

[The full and free right to lay new Service Media under the Retained Land at any time in the future together with the right (upon reasonable prior written notice) to enter upon the Retained Land but only so far as is strictly necessary for the purpose of laying and thereafter repairing, maintaining, inspecting and replacing such service media].]

5. Right of entry

5.1 [The right to enter upon such parts of the Retained Land as shall be reasonably necessary at any time for any of the following purposes: (a) connecting to, inspecting, maintaining, repairing or cleansing any roads and sewers now laid or to be laid within the Retained Land and (b) laying, connecting to, inspecting, maintaining, repairing, renewing and cleansing any Service Media.]

5.2 The right at all times to enter after reasonable notice (except in the case of emergency) upon such part of the Retained Land as shall be reasonably necessary for the purpose of constructing, repairing, maintaining and replacing any part of any dwellinghouse or boundary fence to be erected on the Property or for any other reasonable purpose connected with the proposed development of the Property.]

THE SECOND SCHEDULE before referred to
Rights Reserved

The following rights for the Transferor, its successors in title of all or any parts of the Retained Land and their respective tenants, servants and invitees in common with the Transferee and all others lawfully entitled to exercise the rights:

1. To use the Estate Roads

The full and free right to connect to the Estate Roads and the full and free right to go, pass and repass with or without vehicles at all times and for all purposes over and along the Estate Roads [(and the routes thereof pending construction)] and on foot only over any associated footpaths [until the same are adopted by the Relevant Authority as highways maintainable at the public expense.]

2. To connect to and use the Estate Sewers

The full and free right to connect to and to use the Estate Sewers together with the right (upon reasonable prior written notice) to enter upon the Property but only so far as strictly necessary with workmen and equipment for the purpose of (a) making connections with the Estate Sewers and/or (b) testing, cleaning, maintaining, renewing, repairing and upgrading the Estate Sewers and the connections thereto [until the same are adopted or taken over by the Relevant Authority].

3. To connect to and use Service Media

The full and free right to connect to and use the Service Media now laid or to be laid at any time in the future within the Property together with the right (upon reasonable prior written notice) to enter upon the Property but only so far as strictly necessary with workmen and equipment for the purpose of (a) making connections with such service media and/or (b) testing, cleaning, maintaining, renewing and repairing such service media and the connections thereto.

4. To lay new Service Media

[The full and free right to lay new Service Media under the Property at any time in the future together with the right (upon reasonable prior written notice) to enter upon the

Property but only so far as is strictly necessary for the purpose of laying and thereafter repairing, maintaining, inspecting and replacing such service media.]

5. Rights of entry

5.1 The right to enter upon such parts of the Property as shall be reasonably necessary at any time for the purposes of (a) connecting to, inspecting, maintaining, repairing or cleansing the Estate Roads and the Estate Sewers and (b) laying, connecting to, inspecting, maintaining, repairing, renewing and cleansing any Service Media.

5.2 [The right at all times to enter after reasonable notice (except in the case of emergency) upon the Property for the purpose of constructing, repairing, maintaining, and replacing any part of any dwellinghouse or boundary fence to be erected within the Perpetuity Period on the Retained Land or for any other reasonable purpose connected with the development of the Retained Land.]

The transferor must execute this transfer as a deed using the space opposite. If there is more than one transferor, all must execute. Forms of execution are given in Schedule 9 to the Land Registration Rules 2003. If the transfer contains transferee's covenants or declarations or contains an application by the transferee (such as for a restriction), it must also be executed by the transferee.

If there is more than one transferee and panel 11 has been completed, each transferee must also execute this transfer to comply with the requirements in section 53(1)(b) of the Law of Property Act 1925 relating to the declaration of a trust of land. Please refer to *Joint property ownership* and *practice guide 24: private trusts of land* for further guidance.

Remember to date this deed in panel 4.

13 Execution

EXECUTED as a DEED
By the TRANSFEROR
acting by:

Director/Authorised signatory

Secretary/Authorised signatory

EXECUTED as a DEED
By the TRANSFEREE
acting by:

Director/Authorised signatory

Secretary/Authorised signatory

WARNING
If you dishonestly enter information or make a statement that you know is, or might be, untrue or misleading, and intend by doing so to make a gain for yourself or another person, or to cause loss or the risk of loss to another person, you may commit the offence of fraud under section 1 of the Fraud Act 2006, the maximum penalty for which is 10 years' imprisonment or an unlimited fine, or both.

Failure to complete this form with proper care may result in a loss of protection under the Land Registration Act 2002 if, as a result, a mistake is made in the register.

Under section 66 of the Land Registration Act 2002 most documents (including this form) kept by the registrar relating to an application to the registrar or referred to in the register are open to public inspection and copying. If you believe a document contains prejudicial information, you may apply for that part of the document to be made exempt using Form EX1, under rule 136 of the Land Registration Rules 2003.

APPENDIX C2

Sample form: Transfer of part reserving rights for benefit of retained land (including a right of way over estate roads and a road corridor) with transferee infrastructure obligations

HM Land Registry
Transfer of part of registered title(s)

Any parts of the form that are not typed should be completed in black ink and in block capitals.

If you need more room than is provided for in a panel, and your software allows, you can expand any panel in the form. Alternatively use continuation sheet CS and attach it to this form.

For information on how HM Land Registry processes your personal information, see our Personal Information Charter.

Guidance	Panel
Leave blank if not yet registered.	1 Title number(s) out of which the property is transferred:
When application for registration is made these title number(s) should be entered in panel 2 of Form AP1.	2 Other title number(s) against which matters contained in this transfer are to be registered or noted, if any:
Insert address, including postcode (if any), or other description of the property transferred. Any physical exclusions, such as mines and minerals, should be defined. Place 'X' in the appropriate box and complete the statement. For example 'edged red'. For example 'edged and numbered 1 in blue'. Any plan lodged must be signed by the transferor.	3 Property: [ ] The property is identified ☒ on the attached plan and shown: Edged in red [excluding the Ransom Strip] ☐ on the title plan(s) of the above titles and shown:
Remember to date this deed with the day of completion, but not before it has been signed and witnessed.	4 Date:
Give full name(s) of **all** of the persons transferring the property. Complete as appropriate where the transferor is a company.	5 Transferor: [ ] For UK incorporated companies/LLPs Registered number of company or limited liability partnership including any prefix: For overseas companies (a) Territory of incorporation: (b) Registered number in the United Kingdom including any prefix:
Give full name(s) of **all** the persons to be shown as registered proprietors. Complete as appropriate where the transferee is a company. Also, for an overseas company, unless an arrangement with HM Land Registry exists, lodge either a certificate in Form 7 in Schedule 3 to the Land Registration Rules 2003 or a certified copy of the constitution in English or Welsh, or other evidence permitted by rule 183 of the Land Registration Rules 2003.	6 Transferee for entry in the register: [ ] For UK incorporated companies/LLPs Registered number of company or limited liability partnership including any prefix: For overseas companies (a) Territory of incorporation: (b) Registered number in the United Kingdom including any prefix:

Each transferee may give up to three addresses for service, one of which must be a postal address whether or not in the UK (including the postcode, if any). The others can be any combination of a postal address, a UK DX box number or an electronic address.	7 Transferee's intended address(es) for service for entry in the register:
	8 The transferor transfers the property to the transferee
Place 'X' in the appropriate box. State the currency unit if other than sterling. If none of the boxes apply, insert an appropriate memorandum in panel 12.	9 Consideration ☒ The transferor has received from the transferee for the property the following sum (in words and figures): [ ] together with value added tax thereon in the sum of [ ]] ☐ The transfer is not for money or anything that has a monetary value ☐ Insert other receipt as appropriate: The consideration for this transfer is as set out in panel 12.
Place 'X' in any box that applies. Add any modifications.	10 The transferor transfers with ☒ full title guarantee ☐ limited title guarantee
Where the transferee is more than one person, place 'X' in the appropriate box. Complete as necessary. The registrar will enter a Form A restriction in the register *unless*: – an 'X' is placed: – in the first box, or – in the third box and the details of the trust or of the trust instrument show that the transferees are to hold the property on trust for themselves alone as joint tenants, *or* – it is clear from completion of a form JO lodged with this application that the transferees are to hold the property on trust for themselves alone as joint tenants. Please refer to *Joint property ownership* and practice guide *24: private trusts of land* for further guidance. These are both available on the GOV.UK website.	11 Declaration of trust. The transferee is more than one person and ☐ they are to hold the property on trust for themselves as joint tenants ☐ they are to hold the property on trust for themselves as tenants in common in equal shares ☐ they are to hold the property on trust:

Use this panel for:
- definitions of terms not defined above
- rights granted or reserved
- restrictive covenants
- other covenants
- agreements and declarations
- any required or permitted statements
- other agreed provisions.

The prescribed subheadings may be added to, amended, repositioned or omitted.

Any other land affected by rights granted or reserved or by restrictive covenants should be defined by reference to a plan.

12 Additional provisions

12.1 DEFINITIONS

'Adoption Agreement' means an agreement pursuant to section 38 of the Highways Act 1980 or section 104 of the Water Industry Act 1991 and **'relevant Adoption Agreement'** shall be construed accordingly;

'Affecting Matters' means the covenants, exceptions, reservations, rights and other matters (other than charges of a financial nature) contained or referred to in the Property and Charges Registers of title number [ ];

'**Affordable Housing**' means affordable housing as the phrase is defined in the National Planning Policy Framework dated July 2018 published by the Ministry of Housing, Communities and Local Government and any guidance amending or replacing it;

'Approval' means approval in writing which shall not be unreasonably withheld or delayed and the terms **'Approve'**, **'Approving'** and **'Approved'** shall be construed accordingly;

'Connected Person' has the meaning given to it in section 839 of the Income and Taxes Act 1988;

'Deed of Covenant' means a deed of covenant in substantially the same form as the draft deed of covenant annexed to this Transfer with such amendments thereto as the circumstances may require and/or as the Transferor may reasonably require [and the Transferee shall Approve];

'Development' means the development of the Property in accordance with the Planning Permission [and all required Reserved Matters Approvals (if any)] [or any other planning permission relating to the development of the Property [that has been Approved by the Transferor]];

'Disposition' means one or more of the following in respect of the Property or any part of it;

(a) the transfer or assent of the whole or any part of the Property, whether or not for valuable consideration; or

(b) the grant of a lease over the whole or any part of the Property, whether or not for valuable consideration; or

(c) [the grant of any Security over the whole or any part of the Property; or]

(d) [the grant of a deed of easement; or]

(e) [entering into restrictive covenants or positive covenants; or]

(f) [the grant of a building lease or a building licence;]

'Drainage Agreement' means an agreement pursuant to section 104 of the Water Industry Act 1991 for the making up and adoption of the Estate Sewers;

'Estate Roads' means the roads and associated footpaths, street lighting and other street furniture and any cycleways to be constructed on the Property in connection with the proposed

Development [pursuant to the Services Specification and] in accordance with the obligations set out in Part II of the Third Schedule and which are [intended to serve both the Property and the Retained Land and all buildings from time to time erected on the Retained Land] [and] to abut and lead from the adopted highway known as [ ] up to and to directly connect with the boundary of the Retained Land between the points marked [AB] on the Plan (or as close thereto as the Relevant Authority shall permit) and to have a carriageway with a minimum width of [ ] metres with footpaths measuring at least [ ] metres wide on either side [and a [ ] metre wide cycleway] [and which are to be in the appropriate position shown coloured [brown] on the Plan or any substituted route thereof Approved by the Transferor **PROVIDED ALWAYS THAT** such road shall lead from the adopted highway known as [ ] up to and directly connect with the boundary of the Retained Land between the points marked [AB] on the Plan (or as close thereto as the Relevant Authority shall permit) and have a carriageway with a minimum width of [ ] metres with footpaths measuring at least [ ] metres in width on either side [and a [ ] metre wide cycleway]];

[NOTE: The Transferor should seek advice from a highway consultant regarding the width of the Estate Roads. How wide will the Estate Roads need to be in order to satisfy the highway authority's requirements for a road serving any future development on the Retained Land?]

'Estate Sewers' means the foul and surface water sewers to be constructed within the Property in connection with the proposed Development [pursuant to the Services Specification] [and which are intended to serve both the Property and the Retained Land [once fully developed]] and which are to connect to adopted foul and surface water sewers [in the public highway];

'Excluded Disposal' means one or more of the following in respect of the Property (excluding the Road Corridor) or any part thereof (unless made to a Connected Person):

(a) a transfer at arm's length to a bona fide purchaser for valuable consideration of one or more individual dwellings erected upon the Property (including the curtilage thereof and any separate garage(s) and shared driveway) together with the grant of all easements required for their proper use and enjoyment;

(b) the grant at arm's length to a bona fide purchaser for a premium of a lease of a flat or apartment (including any parking space and any garden) together with the grant of all easements required for its proper use and enjoyment;

(c) a transfer of the freehold reversion of any dwellings let on long leases;

(d) a transfer of any land and/or the grant of a lease required for an electricity substation, gas governor, sewerage or water pumping station, balancing lagoon or other site service installations;

(e) a disposal of any part of the Property required for general open space or a play area or internal roads that may be imposed by or agreed with the local authority in connection with the Planning Permission or the Planning Agreement or any other planning agreement relating to the Property;

(f) a transfer of any land or dwellings required by any planning permission or planning agreement for Affordable Housing;

(g) the transfer of any land to a local authority or other statutory body pursuant to a planning obligation under the Planning Agreement or any other planning agreement in relation to the Property;

(h) the grant of a wayleave agreement or deed of easement to a service supply company or statutory body;

(i) [the grant of Security to secure the repayment of money entered into at arm's length with a genuine financing institution on the condition that the Transferee procures that the financing institution enters into a deed with the Transferor (in a form to be Approved by the Transferor) containing (without limitation) the following:

(i) a covenant by the financing institution that on a disposal by the financing institution of the Property or any part of the Property subject to the Security the financing institution shall procure that the buyer will be bound by the obligations on the part of the Transferee contained in this Transfer;
(ii) a covenant by the financing institution to release the Property or the relevant part of it from the Security on completion of the sale of the Property or any relevant part of it; and
(iii) a covenant by the financing institution to enter into any planning agreement or infrastructure agreement required in connection with the development of the Property in order solely to consent to the same;]

'Expert' means a person having appropriate professional qualifications and experience and who shall be appointed (in default of agreement) on the application of either Party by the president or other most senior available officer of the Relevant Body;

'the Land' means the Property and the Retained Land;

'Parties' means the Transferor and the Transferee and 'Party' means either the Transferor or the Transferee as the context admits;

[**'Permitted Development'** means the development of the Property pursuant to the Planning Permission [and all required Reserved Matters Approval (if any)];

'Plan' means the plan or plans annexed to this Transfer;

'Planning Agreement' means the agreement dated [ ] and made between (1) [ ] (2) [ ] (3) [ ] (4) [ ] and (5) [ ] pursuant to section 106 of the Town and Country Planning Act 1990;

'Planning Permission' means the [outline] planning permission granted [on Appeal] on [ ] (Reference: [ ]) authorising [the residential development of the Property] [or any other planning permission relating to the development of the Property [that has been Approved by the Transferor]];

[**'Ransom Strip'** means the [1 metre] [500mm] [300mm] wide strip of land between the points marked [ ] on the Plan which is being retained by the Transferor and which forms part of the land registered under title number [ ];]

'Relevant Authority' means all or any of the following in relation to the Property as appropriate:

(a) such authority or body as shall have responsibility under statute for highway matters;

(b) such authority or body as shall have responsibility under statute for drainage matters;

(c) such authority or body as shall have responsibility under statute for planning matters;

(d) such authority or body as shall have responsibility under statute for environmental matters;

(e) any utility company concerned with the installation of Service Media and the provision of Services;

(f) any other local or competent authority or body having jurisdiction in relation to the development of the Property and/or the infrastructure serving the same

and the expression 'Relevant Authorities' shall be construed accordingly;

'**Relevant Body**' means one of the following:

(a) in respect of a dispute of a planning nature, the Royal Town Planning Institute;

(b) in respect of a dispute of a valuation or surveying nature, the Royal Institution of Chartered Surveyors;

(c) in respect of a dispute of an engineering nature, the Institution of Civil Engineers;

(d) in respect of a dispute in relation to the respective rights, duties and obligations of the Parties under this Transfer or the terms of any document to be entered into under this Transfer, the Law Society of England and Wales;

[**'Reserved Matters Application'** means an application for the approval of reserved matters pursuant to the Planning Permission or any other planning permission relating to the development of the Property];

[**'Reserved Matters Approval'** means the issue of a reserved matters approval following a Reserved Matters Application];

'Retained Land' means the land retained by the Transferor being the land now comprised within title number [ ] excluding the Property;

'Road Agreement' means an agreement pursuant to section 38 of the Highways Act 1980 for the making up and adoption of the Estate Roads;

'Road Corridor' means (where the Estate Roads do not connect with the boundary of the Retained Land between the point marked [AB] on the Plan) the corridor of land lying between the Estate Roads and the boundary of the Retained Land between the points [AB] shown on the Plan being [not less than [ ] metres wide and of sufficient width to build a road and associated footpaths thereon [to adoptable standard] to serve the Retained Land and any dwellings erected thereon in the future together with any cycleway that may be required] [the same width as the Estate Roads] and leading from and fully abutting the section of the Estate Roads lying closest to the boundary of the Retained Land between the points marked [AB] on the Plan up to and connecting with and fully abutting upon the boundary of the Retained Land between the points marked [AB] on the Plan and in such ultimate position as shall be determined in accordance with clause 1.1 of Part II of the [Second] Schedule hereto [together with such sight lines as may be required for visibility splays];

[NOTE: Width of Road Corridor to be agreed. The Transferor should seek advice from a highway consultant as to what the width of the Estate Roads should be in order to satisfy the requirements of the highway authority in relation to roads serving any future development on the Retained Land.]

'Security' means a legal charge, debenture or any other form of security;

'Service Media' means sewers, drains, pipes, cables, pumping systems, channels, balancing ponds and other service media for the supply of Services;

'Services' means water, gas, electricity, telephone, telecommunications, surface water drainage, foul drainage and similar services;

['**Services Specification'** means the specification attached to this Transfer at Appendix [ ] relating to the design and size of the Estate Roads and the Estate Sewers that are to be constructed by the Transferee in the course of carrying out the Development;]

'Sight Line Areas' means such areas within the Property as shall be required to be retained as sight line areas in connection with the Relevant Authority's visibility splay requirements for the construction of the Estate Roads and any other roads and footpaths leading to the Retained Land (including any road and footpaths to be constructed in the future within the Road Corridor) in such ultimate position as shall be determined in accordance with clause 1.1 of Part II of the [Second] Schedule hereto.

12.2 In this Transfer references to 'the Transferor' and 'the Transferee' shall be deemed to include their respective successors in title and references to the Property and to the Retained Land shall be references to the whole and each and every part of such land respectively.

12.3 The Property is transferred [**TOGETHER WITH** the rights set out in the First Schedule hereto and] **EXCEPTING AND RESERVING** to the Transferor and its successors in title and their respective tenants, servants and invitees and all others authorised by the Transferor or its successors in title (including in particular the Relevant Authorities) for the benefit of the Retained Land and any building or buildings now or hereafter erected thereon the rights referred to and set out in the [Second] Schedule hereto and together with the benefit of but **SUBJECT TO** the terms and provisions of the Planning Agreement so far as they relate to and affect the Property.

12.4 TRANSFEREE'S COVENANTS

12.4.1 The Transferee **HEREBY COVENANTS** by way of indemnity only and not further or otherwise with the Transferor to observe and perform the Affecting Matters in so far as the same affect the Property and are still effective and to indemnify and keep indemnified the Transferor and its successors in title from all costs, claims and actions arising out of any future breach and non-observance thereof so far as aforesaid.

12.4.2 The Transferee **HEREBY COVENANTS** with the Transferor to observe and perform the obligations set out in clauses [ ] of the Planning Agreement and to indemnify and keep indemnified the Transferor and its successors in title from all costs claims and actions arising out of any future breach or non-performance thereof.

12.4.3 For the benefit and protection of the Retained Land or any part or parts thereof and so as to bind the Property or any part or parts thereof into whosesoever hands the same may come the Transferee **HEREBY COVENANTS** with the Transferor and its successors in title that the Transferee and those deriving title under it will at all times hereafter comply with the restrictive covenants set out in Part I of the [Third] Schedule hereto.

12.4.4 The Transferee **HEREBY COVENANTS** with the Transferor to comply with the positive covenants set out in Part II of the [Third] Schedule hereto.

12.5 AGREEMENTS AND DECLARATIONS

It is hereby agreed and declared as follows:

12.5.1 Rights of light and air

The Parties shall not by implication, prescription or otherwise become entitled to any right of light or air which would restrict or interfere with the free use of the Parties' respective parts of the Land or any other land adjoining the Property and/or the Retained Land.

12.5.2 Rights of third parties

Unless the right of enforcement is expressly provided, it is not intended that a third party should have the right to enforce any terms of this Transfer pursuant to the Contracts (Rights of Third Parties) Act 1999 but this does not affect any rights which are available apart from that Act.

12.5.3 Implied rights

Section 62 of the Law of Property Act 1925 and the Rule in *Wheeldon* v. *Burrows* do not apply to this Transfer and no legal or other rights are granted over the Retained Land for the benefit of the Property or granted over the Property for the benefit of the Retained Land except for those expressly granted or reserved by this Transfer.

12.5.4 Reserved rights

12.5.4.1 Any rights of entry on land shall be exercised only upon reasonable notice and at reasonable times (except in cases of emergency when no notice shall be required).

12.5.4.2 Unless otherwise stated, the rights hereby reserved are not exclusive and are to be used in common with others and all persons lawfully entitled to use them.

12.5.4.3 All requisite consents from any Relevant Authority for connections to and construction and/or laying of roads and/or Service Media pursuant to the rights hereby reserved shall be obtained by the person exercising the rights prior to effecting the same.

12.5.4.4 The person exercising the rights hereby reserved shall cause as little damage and disturbance as reasonably possible and shall make good all damage caused as soon as reasonably practicable.

12.5.4.5 [Connections to Service Media and Estate Sewers shall only be made to the extent that there is capacity therefor and the Transferee shall not be obliged to oversize the Service Media or the Estate Sewers.]

12.5.4.6 [The person exercising the rights hereby reserved shall (if so requested) consent to the Estate Roads and/or the Service Media and/or Estate Sewers over or through which the rights are exercised becoming adopted and/or maintainable at the public expense [and pending adoption shall contribute a fair and reasonable proportion (according to user) of the costs of inspecting, cleansing, repairing, maintaining, renewing or replacing the Estate Roads and/or the Service Media and/or the Estate Sewers over or through (or into) which the rights are exercised].]

12.5.4.7 [Rights of way over the Estate Roads shall not be exercised until the same shall have been constructed to base course level.]

12.5.4.8 [The Transferee shall be entitled to alter the position of the Estate Roads and/or the Estate Sewers and/or the Service Media within the Property with the Approval of the Transferor subject to:

(a) the Transferor Approving the proposed new route of the Estate Roads and/or the Estate Sewers and/or the Service Media; and

(b) the Transferee obtaining all the necessary consents and approvals to the proposed works; and

(c) the Transferee complying with the requirements of the Relevant Authority in relation to the works; and

(d) the Transferee entering into a suitable deed of easement with the Transferor in a form to be Approved by the Transferee and the Transferor prior to commencing any alterations.

Any dispute regarding this clause 12.5.4.8 or the form of the said deed of easement shall be referred to and determined by an Expert in accordance with clause 12.6.]

12.5.5 <u>Good faith</u>

The Transferee acknowledges that it is the intention of the Transferee to act in good faith towards the Transferor in connection with this Transfer and agrees not to do or omit to do anything which would ransom the Transferor or hinder or prevent the Transferor from gaining access to the Retained Land [(via the Estate Roads and the Road Corridor)] or developing the Retained Land (it being acknowledged that the Retained Land may be developed in the future).

12.5.6 Restriction and Excluded Disposal

The Transferor acknowledges that in the event of the Transferee making an Excluded Disposal after the date of this Transfer it is not intended that any restriction entered on the title to the Property in accordance with clause 12.8 of this Transfer shall be entered on the title to the land which is the subject of the Excluded Disposal and in the event of such a restriction being entered on the title to land which is the subject of an Excluded Disposal the Transferor shall promptly take such steps as shall be necessary to remove the restriction (including completing and signing such Land Registry form as may be appropriate) [and in default hereby authorises the Transferee to remove such restriction].

12.6 DISPUTE RESOLUTION

Unless otherwise provided in this Transfer any dispute or difference between the Parties regarding any of the provisions of this Transfer shall be referred to the Expert. The Expert shall act as expert and not as arbitrator and his decision shall be final and binding on the Parties and the following provisions shall apply:

(a) The Expert shall give the Parties the opportunity to make representations to him before making his decision.

(b) The Expert shall be entitled to obtain opinions from others if he so wishes.

(c) The Expert shall give reasons for his decision.

(d) The Expert shall comply with any time limits or other directions agreed by the Parties.

(e) The charges and expenses of the Expert shall be borne equally between the Parties or in such other proportions as the Expert may direct.

12.7 APPLICATION

The Transferor and the Transferee hereby apply to the Chief Land Registrar to enter into the Registers of the Titles to the Property and the Retained Land such of the rights, reservations, exceptions, covenants and conditions contained or referred to herein as are capable of registration.

12.8 RESTRICTION

12.8.1 The Transferor and the Transferee hereby apply to the Chief Land Registrar for the entry of the following restriction upon the proprietorship register of the title to the Property in the following terms (or as near thereto as the Land Registry will permit):

'Restriction – no disposition of the registered estate by the proprietor of the registered estate or the proprietor of any registered charge, not being a charge registered before the entry of this restriction, is to be completed by way of registration without a certificate signed by [ ] or his conveyancer that the provisions of paragraph [3] of Part I of the [Third] Schedule of the Transfer dated [*date*] made between [ ] and [ ] have been complied with or do not apply.'

IN WITNESS whereof this Transfer has been executed by the Transferor and the Transferee as a Deed the date and year first before written

THE FIRST SCHEDULE before referred to

Rights Granted

1. [To lay a sewer

The full and free right to lay and thereafter maintain, repair, renew and use a [surface water]/[foul] sewer in the position shown by [a broken blue line on the Plan] and the full and free right at reasonable times and upon giving a reasonable period of notice to enter on and dig up and excavate so much of the Retained Land as may be strictly necessary from time to time with or without workmen, plant and equipment for the purposes aforesaid.]

[NOTE: Consider whether any rights are required over the Retained Land.]

THE [SECOND] SCHEDULE before referred to

Rights Reserved

1. [Temporary right of way

The right to pass and repass with or without vehicles at all times and for all purposes over the Property along a route to be Approved by the Transferee for the purpose of gaining access to and from the Retained Land pending the construction of the Estate Roads **PROVIDED THAT** this right shall cease once the Estate Roads have been constructed to base course level.]

2. To connect to and use the Estate Roads

The full and free right, following the construction of the Estate Roads to base course level, to connect to the Estate Roads and the full and free right to go, pass and repass with or without vehicles at all times and for all purposes over and along the Estate Roads (once they have been constructed to base course level) and any Road Corridor and any roads constructed within any Road Corridor in the future.

3. To connect to and use the Estate Sewers

The full and free right, following the construction of the Estate Sewers, to connect to and to use the Estate Sewers together with the right (upon reasonable prior written notice) to enter upon the Property (excluding any part of the Property comprising or intended to comprise a dwelling and its curtilage) but only so far as strictly necessary with workmen, plant machinery and equipment for the purpose of (a) laying new Service Media in order to connect to the Estate Sewers, (b) making connections with the Estate Sewers or (c) testing, cleaning, maintaining, renewing, repairing and upgrading the Estate Sewers and the connections thereto.

4. To connect to and use existing and new Service Media

The full and free right to use the existing Service Media within the Property serving the Retained Land and the full and free right to connect to and use any new Service Media to be laid in the future within the Property together with the right (upon reasonable prior written notice) to enter upon the Property (excluding any part of the Property comprising or intended to comprise a dwelling and its curtilage) but only so far as strictly necessary with workmen, plant, machinery and equipment for the purpose of making connections with and for the purpose of testing, cleaning, maintaining, renewing, repairing and upgrading such service media and the connections thereto.

5. To lay new Service Media

The full and free [and exclusive] right to lay and thereafter use new Service Media in, on, under or over the Property (excluding any part of the Property comprising or intended to comprise a dwelling and its curtilage) together with the right (upon reasonable prior written notice) to enter upon the Property but only so far as is strictly necessary for the purpose of laying and thereafter repairing maintaining inspecting and replacing such Service Media.

6. Rights of entry

6.1 The right to enter and remain upon any Road Corridor and such other parts of the Property as shall be reasonably necessary at any time (and with or without workmen, plant, equipment and machinery) for the purpose of constructing the Sight Line Areas and/or for the purpose of constructing within any Road Corridor a road and footpaths with all ancillary works and laying Service Media in, under, over or on the Road Corridor to serve the Retained Land.

6.2 The right to enter and remain upon such parts of the Property (excluding any part of the Property comprising or intended to comprise a dwelling and its curtilage) as shall be reasonably necessary at any time (and with or without workmen, plant, equipment and machinery) for the purposes of (a) connecting to, inspecting, maintaining, repairing, renewing or cleansing the Estate Roads and the Estate Sewers, (b) maintaining and repairing the Sight Line Areas and the Road Corridor and (c) laying, connecting to, inspecting, maintaining, repairing, renewing, cleansing, upgrading and augmenting any Service Media.

6.3 The right at all times to enter after reasonable notice (except in the case of emergency) upon the Property with or without workmen, plant, equipment and machinery for the purpose of constructing, repairing, maintaining and replacing any part of any dwellinghouse or boundary fence to be erected on the Retained Land or for any other reasonable purpose connected with the development of the Retained Land.

7. [Step in rights

The right in the event of default by the Transferee to perform the positive obligations set out in Part II of the [Third] Schedule hereto in accordance with the provisions of Part II of the [Third] Schedule hereto to enter upon the Property and (at the cost of the Transferee) to carry out such works and/or take such action as may be necessary and to act as attorney and agent of the Transferee for the purpose of executing a relevant document to remedy any breach **PROVIDED ALWAYS THAT** (a) before exercising such right the Transferor shall serve seven days' prior written notice on the Transferee and (b) the Transferor shall be entitled to exercise such right only if the Transferee shall fail within such seven-day period to promptly and diligently take steps to complete any works which are outstanding and such other action as may be necessary **PROVIDED THAT** if, due to exceptionally adverse weather conditions or other circumstances reasonably outside the Transferee's control and which could not have been foreseen, there is delay by the Transferee in promptly and diligently taking steps to complete any works which are outstanding then the said seven-day period shall be extended by such period as is reasonable in all the circumstances.]

THE [THIRD] SCHEDULE before referred to

Transferee's covenants

PART I

Transferee's Restrictive Covenants

1. Use

1.1 Not to use the Property or any part of it for any purpose other than for [the construction of residential accommodation and use of the same as residential accommodation with associated curtilages, garages, parking areas, private driveways and ancillary structures and service apparatus and roads and footpaths serving the same].

1.2 [Not to carry out any development on the Property except for the Permitted Development.]

2. Planning

2.1 [Not to make or cause to be made any objections, claims or comments of any description on any application for planning permission made by the Transferor in respect of any part of the Retained Land and/or any adjoining land or any appeal or public enquiry arising from such application.]

2.2 [Not to vary the Planning Permission or the Planning Agreement or submit a new or revised planning application to develop the Property without the Approval of the Transferor.]

3. Dispositions

Not to make any Disposition of the Property or any part of it without procuring that the disponee prior to each such disposal delivers to the Transferor a deed of covenant with the Transferor in the form of the Deed of Covenant **PROVIDED THAT**

(a) In no event shall a Deed of Covenant be required in respect of an Excluded Disposal.

(b) The Transferee and any person who has previously executed the Deed of Covenant shall be released from all obligations upon a successor giving a further Deed of Covenant to the extent that the successor covenants to observe such obligations in the further Deed of Covenant.

[NOTE: Consider whether the Transferor should be prohibited from making any Dispositions other than a Permitted Disposition (i.e. an Excluded Disposal).]

4. Not to hinder development

Not to do or agree to do or omit to do anything which would prejudice delay or hinder or prevent the development of the Retained Land by the Transferor.

5. No nuisance

5.1 Not to cause or permit to be done in or upon the Property or any part thereof any act or thing which may be or become a nuisance[, annoyance or disturbance] to the owners or occupiers for the time being of the Retained Land or any part thereof **PROVIDED THAT** the development and use of the Property for [residential] purposes shall not be a breach of this covenant.

5.2 Not to obstruct or permit to be obstructed any rights or easements hereby reserved in favour of the Retained Land.

5.3 Not to use the Property or permit the same to be used to provide access or services to any land other than the Retained Land and the Property unless so required by the Transferor.

5.4 Not at any time to obstruct or impede in any way access to or egress from the Retained Land over the Estate Roads and any Road Corridor.

5.5 Not to erect or place or permit to be erected or placed any building, tree, shrub or other structure on any Road Corridor or the Sight Line Areas.

5.6 Not to use or permit any Road Corridor to be used or designated as public open space.

5.7 Not to erect any walls, fences or other structures along any boundary between the Property and the Retained Land that would prevent the Transferor from gaining access to and from the Retained Land.

6. Road Corridor

6.1 Not to make any Disposition of any Road Corridor other than to the Transferor or as directed by the Transferor.

6.2 Not to grant any rights or easements or create any incumbrances over any Road Corridor [without the consent of the Transferor who shall have an absolute discretion to give or refuse such consent] [without the Approval of the Transferor].

7. [Commencement of development

Not to commence any development of the Property without obtaining the Approval of the Transferor to the route and specification of the proposed Estate Roads and any proposed Road Corridor and having obtained such approval not to construct the Estate Roads other than in the position shown and in accordance with the detailed plans that have been approved by the Transferor]

PART II

Transferee's Positive Covenants

1. Estate Roads and Road Corridor

1.1 As soon as reasonably practicable after the date of this Transfer and prior to commencing any development of the Property, to consult with the Transferor and to submit detailed plans of the route of the proposed Estate Roads and any proposed Road Corridor and the location of the Sight Line Areas to the Transferor for Approval and it is agreed between the Transferor and the Transferee:

1.1.1 that the Transferor shall be reasonable in refusing approval if the proposed Road Corridor does not connect to and fully abut the boundary of the Retained Land between the points marked [AB] on the Plan or if the alignment of the purposed Road Corridor or the location of the Sight Line Areas is such that it would prevent adoption by the Relevant Authority of the road footpath or Service Media to be laid within the Road Corridor in the future;

1.1.2 the Estate Roads shall lead to and connect with the boundary of the Retained Land between the points marked [AB] on the Plan (or as close thereto as the Relevant Authority shall agree);

1.1.3 [the Estate Roads shall be of sufficient width and capacity to serve the Development and any development in the future on the Retained Land; and]

1.1.4 if the Relevant Authority will not agree to the Estate Roads leading to and connecting with the boundary of the Retained Land then the estate layout of the Property shall include the Road Corridor.

1.2 As soon as reasonably possible after the date of this Transfer (but not before obtaining the Approval of the Transferor to the route of the proposed Estate Roads and Road Corridor) to apply for and thereafter use reasonable endeavours to obtain the approval of the Relevant Authority to the design and layout of the Estate Roads.

1.3 To commence the construction of the Estate Roads within [ ] months after receipt of the relevant technical approval of the Relevant Authority [and by no later than [ ]].

1.4 At the expense of the Transferee to construct the Estate Roads in a good and workmanlike manner using good quality materials [and to a standard required for adoption] and in accordance with the requirements of the Relevant Authority such construction to base course to be completed by no later than [[ ] months after the date on which the relevant technical approvals have been obtained from the Relevant Authority] [and in any event by no later than [ ] months after the date of this Transfer].

1.5 At the expense of the Transferee to apply the final wearing course to the Estate Roads and to complete the construction of the footpaths and street lighting along the Estate Roads as quickly as reasonably practicable after the construction of the Estate Roads to base course level [and in any event by no later than [ ]].

1.6 To maintain the Estate Roads at all times to the satisfaction of the Relevant Authority and to comply with the agreements for construction, maintenance and adoption thereof at all times.

1.7 Following the obtaining of technical approval to the design and construction of the Estate Roads and the Transferor having Approved the route of the Estate Roads, to provide the Transferor with a plan or plans detailing the exact positions of the Estate Roads and any Road Corridor and Sight Line Areas and to enter into any supplemental deed that is necessary formally to document the agreement reached as to the exact positions of the Estate Roads and any Road Corridor.

2. Estate Sewers

2.1 As soon as reasonably possible after the date of this Transfer (but not before obtaining the Approval of the Transferor to the route of the Estate Roads and the proposed Road Corridor) to apply for and thereafter use reasonable endeavours to obtain the approval of the Relevant Authority to the design and layout of the Estate Sewers.

2.2 At the expense of the Transferee to construct the Estate Sewers in a good and workmanlike manner using good quality materials and to a standard required for adoption with connection points to or as close to the boundaries of the Retained Land as the Relevant Authority shall permit such sewers [to be of such capacity as shall be sufficient to drain the whole of the Property when fully developed and the Retained Land and] to be completed ready for connection and use [within [ ] months from the date of the relevant technical approvals by the Relevant Authority] [and in any event by no later than [ ] months after the date of this Transfer].

2.3 To maintain the Estate Sewers at all times to the satisfaction of the Relevant Authority and to comply with the agreements for construction, maintenance and adoption thereof at all times.

3. Service Media

3.1 At the expense of the Transferee to provide or secure the installation of [gas, water, electricity, and telecommunications] with connection points to or close to the boundaries of the Retained Land such service media:

(a) to be installed in a good and workmanlike manner to a standard required by the appropriate relevant supplier;
(b) to be of sufficient capacity to serve the Property when fully developed for residential purposes and the Retained Land;
(c) to be installed within [ ] months from the date of this Transfer.

4. Planning

To comply with the conditions referred to in the Planning Permission and the obligations contained in the Planning Agreement.

5. Grant wayleaves

To enter into any wayleave agreement, deed of easement or other documents reasonably required by the Transferor in connection with the installation and maintenance of any Service Media installed within the Property by the Transferor after the date of this Transfer for the benefit of Retained Land or as required by the provider of any of the Services as a condition of the provider of those Services installing and/or adopting new Service Media within the Property for the benefit of the Retained Land or allowing connections to be made to any existing or any new Service Media for the benefit of the Retained Land subject to the Transferor agreeing to pay the reasonable legal costs of signing such deed or agreement and subject to the Transferor providing the Transferee with an indemnity in respect of the obligations contained in such deed or agreement.

6. Adoption Agreements

6.1 To [use reasonable endeavours to] enter as soon as reasonably practicable after the date of this Transfer [(and in any event by no later than [ ] months after the date of this Transfer)] into a Road Agreement with the Relevant Authority in relation to the Estate Roads and to give to the Relevant Authority such security as is normally required.

6.2 To [use reasonable endeavours to] enter as soon as reasonably practicable after the date of this Transfer [(and in any event by no later than [ ] months after the date of this Transfer)] into a Drainage Agreement with the Relevant Authority in relation to the Estate Sewers and to give to the Relevant Authority such security as is normally required.

6.3 To provide the Transferor with full certified copies of the Road Agreement and the Drainage Agreement (including colour copies of all relevant plans) within 10 working days after the same have been concluded.

6.4 Upon receipt of written notice from the Transferor to enter into any relevant Adoption Agreement (as landowner but not for any other purpose) in respect of (a) the road, footpaths and foul and surface water sewers laid within any Road Corridor and (b) in respect of any connections made to the Estate Sewers and/or any sewers laid within the Property by the Transferor as soon as reasonably practicable provided that the Transferee shall have no responsibility for the construction or maintenance of such road, footpath, sewers and connections and subject to the Transferor providing the Transferee with a suitable indemnity in respect of the obligations contained in such agreement and to meeting the Transferee's reasonable and proper legal costs.

7. Fencing

[To erect [close boarded] fencing of a type and specification to be Approved by the Transferor along the boundary marked [ ] on the Plan within [ ] months after the date of this Transfer [and thereafter to keep the same in good and substantial repair and condition at all times].]

8. Costs arising as a result of Transferee's default

[To pay to the Transferor on demand all costs and expenses incurred by the Transferor in the event of the Transferee failing to comply with the positive obligations contained in the immediately preceding paragraphs 1 to 7.]

9. [Transfer Road Corridor

Within [10] days of receipt of a request in writing from the Transferor to transfer any Road Corridor to the Transferor for nil consideration and with full title guarantee and free from all incumbrances. The transfer of any Road Corridor to the Transferor shall be in such form as the Transferor shall reasonably require and the Transferee shall Approve and shall include all necessary rights, including rights to use the Estate Roads, the Estate Sewers and the Service Media within the Property and to lay new Service Media and associated covenants.]

10. Surface Road Corridor

To surface the Road Corridor with [stone having a width of [ ] metres and a depth of [ ]mm] before the occupation of the first dwelling.

11. Good faith

11.1 To act in good faith towards the Transferor in connection with this Transfer.

11.2 [(Without prejudice to the generality of paragraph 11.1) not to do or omit to do anything that would ransom the Transferor or hinder or prevent the Transferor from gaining access to or developing the Retained Land and to promptly join in any agreement reasonably required by the Transferor for the development of the Retained Land subject to the Transferor agreeing to pay the Transferee's proper and reasonable legal costs and providing the Transferee with a suitable indemnity and the agreement being in the form that has been Approved by the Transferee.]

The transferor must execute this transfer as a deed using the space opposite. If there is more than one transferor, all must execute. Forms of execution are given in Schedule 9 to the Land Registration Rules 2003. If the transfer contains transferee's covenants or declarations or contains an application by the transferee (such as for a restriction), it must also be executed by the transferee.

If there is more than one transferee and panel 11 has been completed, each transferee must also execute this transfer to comply with the requirements in section 53(1)(b) of the Law of Property Act 1925 relating to the declaration of a trust of land. Please refer to *Joint property ownership* and practice guide 24: *private trusts of land* for further guidance.

Remember to date this deed in panel 4.

13 Execution

SIGNED as a DEED
by [ ]
in the presence of:

SIGNED as a DEED
by [ ]
in the presence of:

EXECUTED as a DEED
by [ ]
acting by:

Director

Director/Secretary

EXECUTED as a DEED
by [ ]
acting by:

Director

Director/Secretary

WARNING
If you dishonestly enter information or make a statement that you know is, or might be, untrue or misleading, and intend by doing so to make a gain for yourself or another person, or to cause loss or the risk of loss to another person, you may commit the offence of fraud under section 1 of the Fraud Act 2006, the maximum penalty for which is 10 years' imprisonment or an unlimited fine, or both.

Failure to complete this form with proper care may result in a loss of protection under the Land Registration Act 2002 if, as a result, a mistake is made in the register.

Under section 66 of the Land Registration Act 2002 most documents (including this form) kept by the registrar relating to an application to the registrar or referred to in the register are open to public inspection and copying. If you believe a document contains prejudicial information, you may apply for that part of the document to be made exempt using Form EX1, under rule 136 of the Land Registration Rules 2003.

APPENDIX C3

Sample form: Transfer of part reserving and granting rights with transferee and transferor covenants (including transferor infrastructure covenants)

Form TP1 on the following page is Crown copyright material and is reproduced with the permission of the Controller of Her Majesty's Stationery Office.

HM Land Registry
Transfer of part of registered title(s)

Any parts of the form that are not typed should be completed in black ink and in block capitals.

If you need more room than is provided for in a panel, and your software allows, you can expand any panel in the form. Alternatively use continuation sheet CS and attach it to this form.

For information on how HM Land Registry processes your personal information, see our Personal Information Charter.

Guidance	Panel
Leave blank if not yet registered.	1 Title number(s) out of which the property is transferred:
When application for registration is made these title number(s) should be entered in panel 2 of Form AP1.	2 Other title number(s) against which matters contained in this transfer are to be registered or noted, if any:
Insert address, including postcode (if any), or other description of the property transferred. Any physical exclusions, such as mines and minerals, should be defined. Place 'X' in the appropriate box and complete the statement. For example 'edged red'. For example 'edged and numbered 1 in blue'. Any plan lodged must be signed by the transferor.	3 Property: Land at [*location*] The property is identified ☐ on the attached plan and shown: ☐ on the title plan(s) of the above titles and shown:
Remember to date this deed with the day of completion, but not before it has been signed and witnessed.	4 Date:
Give full name(s) of **all** of the persons transferring the property. Complete as appropriate where the transferor is a company.	5 Transferor: [*company name*] (Company Number: [ ]) For UK incorporated companies/LLPs Registered number of company or limited liability partnership including any prefix: For overseas companies (a) Territory of incorporation: (b) Registered number in the United Kingdom including any prefix:
Give full name(s) of **all** the persons to be shown as registered proprietors. Complete as appropriate where the transferee is a company. Also, for an overseas company, unless an arrangement with HM Land Registry exists, lodge either a certificate in Form 7 in Schedule 3 to the Land Registration Rules 2003 or a certified copy of the constitution in English or Welsh, or other evidence permitted by rule 183 of the Land Registration Rules 2003.	6 Transferee for entry in the register: [*company name*] (Company Number: [ ]) For UK incorporated companies/LLPs Registered number of company or limited liability partnership including any prefix: For overseas companies (a) Territory of incorporation: (b) Registered number in the United Kingdom including any prefix:

Guidance	Panel
Each transferee may give up to three addresses for service, one of which must be a postal address whether or not in the UK (including the postcode, if any). The others can be any combination of a postal address, a UK DX box number or an electronic address.	7 Transferee's intended address(es) for service for entry in the register: [*address(es)*]
	8 The transferor transfers the property to the transferee
Place 'X' in the appropriate box. State the currency unit if other than sterling. If none of the boxes apply, insert an appropriate memorandum in panel 12.	9 Consideration ☐ The transferor has received from the transferee for the property the following sum (in words and figures): [ ] [together with value added tax thereon in the sum of [ ]] ☐ The transfer is not for money or anything that has a monetary value ☐ Insert other receipt as appropriate:
Place 'X' in any box that applies. Add any modifications.	10 The transferor transfers with ☐ full title guarantee ☐ limited title guarantee
Where the transferee is more than one person, place 'X' in the appropriate box. Complete as necessary. The registrar will enter a Form A restriction in the register *unless*: – an 'X' is placed: – in the first box, or – in the third box and the details of the trust or of the trust instrument show that the transferees are to hold the property on trust for themselves alone as joint tenants, *or* – it is clear from completion of a form JO lodged with this application that the transferees are to hold the property on trust for themselves alone as joint tenants. Please refer to *Joint property ownership* and *practice guide 24: private trusts of land* for further guidance. These are both available on the GOV.UK website.	11 Declaration of trust. The transferee is more than one person and ☐ they are to hold the property on trust for themselves as joint tenants ☐ they are to hold the property on trust for themselves as tenants in common in equal shares ☐ they are to hold the property [*complete as necessary*]:

Use this panel for:
- definitions of terms not defined above
- rights granted or reserved
- restrictive covenants
- other covenants
- agreements and declarations
- any required or permitted statements
- other agreed provisions.

The prescribed subheadings may be added to, amended, repositioned or omitted.

Any other land affected by rights granted or reserved or by restrictive covenants should be defined by reference to a plan.

12 Additional provisions

12.1 DEFINITIONS

'Access Road' means the road and associated footpaths, street lighting and other street furniture which are to be constructed by the Transferor on the Retained Land in accordance with the Specification and the obligations set out in Part II of the Fourth Schedule hereto and which are intended to serve both the Property and the Retained Land when fully developed and which are shown [coloured brown] on the Plan [or any substituted route thereof agreed (with the Approval of the Transferee) between the Transferor and the Relevant Authority **PROVIDED ALWAYS THAT** such road shall lead from the adopted highway known as [ ] up to and directly connect with the boundary of the Property [and have a carriageway with a minimum width of [ ] metres with footpaths measuring at least [ ] metres wide on either side]];

[NOTE: This Transfer assumes that the Access Road will connect with the boundary of the Property (and that there is no need for road corridor provisions – see Appendix C2). It is suitable for use where the Property and Retained Land are to be developed pursuant to an existing planning permission authorising the development of the Property and Retained Land. The Transfer imposes infrastructure obligations on the Transferor (including an obligation to construct the Access Road) and contains mutual planning obligations with the Transferor being obligated to comply with the conditions of the planning permission in so far as they relate to the Retained Land and the obligations in the associated planning agreement (except in so far as they have been made the responsibility of the Transferee) and the Transferee being obligated to comply with such planning conditions in so far as they relate to the Property and such planning obligations in so far as they relate solely to the Property and have not been made the responsibility of the Transferor.]

'Affecting Matters' means the covenants, exceptions, reservations, rights and other matters (other than charges of a financial nature) contained or referred to in the Property and Charges Registers of title numbers [ ] as at the date of this Transfer;

'**Affordable Housing**' means affordable housing as the phrase is defined in the National Planning Policy Framework dated July 2018 published by the Ministry of Housing Communities and Local Government and any guidance amending or replacing it;

'Approved' means approved by the relevant Party in writing acting reasonably and with reasonable promptness [and which shall be deemed to have been given if no response is received or if no reasons are given for any refusal of approval in each case within [10] Working Days of a request for approval] and any dispute between the Parties about whether the relevant Party is acting reasonably shall be determined by the Expert in accordance with clause [12.7] and the expressions **'Approve'** and **'Approval'** shall be construed accordingly;

'Connected Person' has the meaning given to it in section 839 of the Income and Corporation Taxes Act 1988;

'Disponee' means a person to whom a Disposition is made;

'Disposition' means one or more of the following in respect of the

Property or any part of it [or, as the case may be, the Retained Land or any part of it]:

(a) the transfer or assent of the whole or any part of [the Property] [the relevant property], whether or not for valuable consideration;

(b) the grant of a lease over the whole or any part of [the Property] [the relevant property], whether or not for valuable consideration;

(c) [the grant of any Security over the whole of any part of [the Property] [relevant property];]

(d) [the grant of a deed of easement;]

(e) [entering into restrictive covenants or positive covenants;]

(f) [the grant of a building lease or a building licence;]

(g) [any other disposition of the whole or any part of [the Property] [the relevant property] whether or not for valuable consideration;]

'Drainage Agreement' means an agreement pursuant to section 104 of the Water Industry Act 1991 for the making up and adoption of the Estate Sewers;

'Excluded Disposal' means one or more of the following in respect of the whole or any part of the Property [or, as the case may be, the whole or any part of the Retained Land] unless made to a Connected Person:

(a) a transfer at arm's length to a bona fide purchaser for valuable consideration of one or more individual dwellings erected upon [the Property] [the relevant property] (including the curtilage thereof and any separate garage(s) and shared driveway) together with the grant of all easements required for their proper use and enjoyment;

(b) the grant at arm's length to a bona fide purchaser for a premium of a lease of a flat or apartment (including any parking space and any garden) together with the grant of all easements required for its proper use and enjoyment;

(c) a transfer of the freehold reversion of any dwellings let on long leases;

(d) a transfer of any land and/or the grant of a lease required for an electricity substation, gas governor, sewerage or water pumping station, balancing lagoon, or other site service installations;

(e) a disposal of any part of [the Property] [relevant property] required for general open space or a play area or internal roads that may be imposed by or agreed with the local authority in connection with the Planning Permission or the Planning Agreement or any other planning agreement relating to the Property;

(f) a transfer of any land or dwellings required by any planning permission or planning agreement for

Affordable Housing;

(g) the transfer of any land to a local authority or other statutory body pursuant to a planning obligation under the Planning Agreement or any other planning agreement relation to [the Property] [the relevant property]; or

(h) the grant of a wayleave agreement or deed of easement to a service supply company or statutory body;

(i) [the grant of Security to secure the repayment of money entered into at arm's length with a genuine financing institution on the condition that the Transferee [or the Transferor (as the case may be)] procures that the financing institution enters into a deed with the Transferor] [the other Party] (in a form to be Approved by [the Transferor] [the other Party]) containing (without limitation) the following:

(i) a covenant by the financing institution that on a disposal by the financing institution of [the Property] [the relevant property] or any part of [the Property] [relevant property], subject to the Security the financing institution shall procure that the buyer will be bound by the obligations on the part of [the Transferee] [or the Transferor (as appropriate)] contained in this Transfer;

(ii) a covenant by the financing institution to release [the Property] [the relevant property] or the relevant part of it from the Security on completion of the sale of the [Property] [the relevant property] or any relevant part of it; and

(iii) a covenant by the financing institution to enter into any planning agreement or infrastructure agreement required in connection with the development of [the Property] [the relevant property] in order solely to consent to the same;]

'the Estate Sewers' means the foul and surface water sewers which are to be constructed by the Transferor in accordance with the Specification and the obligations set out in Part II of the Fourth Schedule hereto in connection with the proposed [residential] development of the Property and the proposed [commercial/retail] development of the Retained Land and which are intended to serve both the Property and the Retained Land when fully developed and which are to connect to adopted foul and surface water sewers **PROVIDED THAT** such expression shall not include any such sewers serving solely the Property;

'Expert' means be a person having appropriate professional qualifications and experience and who shall be appointed (in default of agreement between the Parties) on the application of either Party by the president or other most senior available officer of the Relevant Body;

'Parties' means the Transferor and the Transferee and **'Party'** means either the Transferor or the Transferee as the context admits;

'Plan' means the plan or plans annexed to this Transfer;

'Planning Agreement' means the agreement dated [*date*] made between (1) [ ] Council (2) [ ] (3) [ ] and (4) [ ];

'Planning Permission' means the [outline] planning permission dated [*date*] and numbered [ ] authorising the development of the Property and the Retained Land;

'Property' means the property transferred by the Transferor to the Transferee by this Transfer;

'Relevant Authority' means all or any of the following in relation to the Property as appropriate:

(a) such authority or body as shall have responsibility under statute for highway matters;

(b) such authority or body as shall have responsibility under statute for drainage matters;

(c) such authority or body as shall have responsibility under statute for planning matters;

(d) such authority or body as shall have responsibility under statute for environmental matters;

(e) any utility company concerned with the installation of Service Media and the provision of Services;

(f) any other local or competent authority or body having jurisdiction in relation to the development of the Property and the Retained Land and/or the infrastructure serving the same;

'Relevant Body' means one of the following:

(a) in respect of a dispute of a planning nature, the Royal Town Planning Institute;

(b) in respect of a dispute of a valuation or surveying nature, the Royal Institution of Chartered Surveyors;

(c) in respect of a dispute of an engineering nature, the Institution of Civil Engineers;

(d) in respect of a dispute in relation to the respective rights, duties and obligations of the Parties under this Transfer or the terms of any document to be entered into under this Transfer, the Law Society of England and Wales;

'Retained Land' means the land shown edged in blue on the Plan [(being the land now comprised within title number [ ] excluding the Property)];

'Road Agreement' means an agreement pursuant to section 38 of the Highways Act 1980 for the making up and adoption of the Access Road;

'Section 278 Agreement' means an agreement pursuant to section 278 of the Highways Act 1980 relating to the Section 278 Works;

[**'Section 278 Works'** means any off-site highway works which are to be carried out by the Transferor in connection with the construction of the Access Road pursuant to section 278 of the

Highways Act 1980;]
'Security' means a legal charge, debenture or any other form of security;

'Service Media' means conduits, sewers, drains, pipes, cables, pumping systems, channels, balancing ponds and other service media for the supply of Services;

'Services' means water, gas, electricity, telephone, telecommunications, cable television, foul water drainage, surface water drainage and similar services;

'Specification' means the specification and drawings annexed to this Transfer and initialled on behalf of the Parties;

'Transferee's Deed of Covenant' means a deed of covenant [in substantially the same form as the draft deed of covenant annexed to this Transfer at Appendix [ ] with such amendments (if any) as the Transferor may require and the Transferee shall Approve)] [containing a covenant in favour of the Transferor (for the benefit of the Transferor and the Transferor's successors in title), the owners for the time being of the Retained Land and each and every part of the Retained Land to perform the positive covenants (mutatis mutandis) set out in Part II of the [Third] Schedule hereto [such deed to be in a form to be Approved by the Transferor]];

'Transferor's Deed of Covenant' means a deed of covenant [in substantially the same form as the draft deed of covenant annexed to this Transfer at Appendix [ ] with such amendments (if any) as the Transferee may require and the Transferor shall Approve)] [containing a covenant in favour of the Transferee (for the benefit of the Transferee and the Transferee's successors in title), the owners for the time being of the Property and each and every part of the Property to perform the positive covenants (mutatis mutandis) set out in Part II of the [Fourth] Schedule thereto [such deed to be in a form to be Approved by the Transferee];

12.2 In this Transfer references to 'the Transferor' and 'the Transferee' shall be deemed to include their respective successors in title and references to the Retained Land and the Property shall be references to the whole and each and every part of such land respectively.

12.3 The Property is transferred **TOGETHER WITH** the rights set out in the First Schedule hereto and **EXCEPTING AND RESERVING** to the Transferor and all others authorised by the Transferor the rights referred to and set out in the Second Schedule hereto [and together with the benefit of but **SUBJECT TO** the terms and provisions of the Planning Agreement so far as they relate to and affect the Property].

12.4 TRANSFEREE'S COVENANTS

12.4.1 The Transferee **HEREBY COVENANTS** by way of indemnity only and not further or otherwise with the Transferor to observe and perform the Affecting Matters in so far as the same respectively affect the Property and are still effective and to indemnify and keep indemnified the Transferor and its successors in title from all costs, claims, and actions arising out of any future breach and non-observance thereof so far as aforesaid.

12.4.2 For the benefit and protection of the Retained Land or any part or parts thereof and so as to bind the Property or any part or parts thereof into whosesoever hands the same may come the Transferee **HEREBY COVENANTS** with the Transferor and its successors in title that the Transferee and those deriving title under it will at all times hereafter comply with the restrictive covenants set out in Part I of the [Third] Schedule hereto.

12.4.3 The Transferee **HEREBY COVENANTS** with the Transferor to comply with the positive covenants set out in Part II of the [Third] Schedule hereto.

12.4.4 [The Transferee **HEREBY COVENANTS** with the Transferor to indemnify the Transferor from and against all costs, expenses, claims, demands, actions and liabilities arising out of any breach or non-performance of the provisions of the [Third] Schedule hereto.]

12.5 TRANSFEROR'S COVENANTS

12.5.1 For the benefit and protection of the Property or any part or parts thereof and so as to bind the Retained Land into whosesoever hands the same may come the Transferor **HEREBY COVENANTS** with the Transferee and its successors in title that the Transferor and those deriving title under it will at all times hereafter comply with the restrictive covenants set out in Part I of the [Fourth] Schedule hereto.

12.5.2 The Transferor **HEREBY COVENANTS** with the Transferee to comply with the positive covenants set out in Part II of the [Fourth] Schedule hereto.

12.5.3 [The Transferor **HEREBY COVENANTS** with the Transferee to indemnify the Transferee from and against all costs, expenses, claims, demands, actions and liabilities (and losses in respect of paragraph 7 of Part II of the Fourth Schedule) arising out of any breach or non-performance of the provisions of the Fourth Schedule hereto.]

12.6 AGREEMENTS AND DECLARATIONS

It is hereby agreed and declared as follows:

12.6.1 <u>Rights of light and air</u>

12.6.1.1 Neither the Transferee nor the persons deriving title under it shall become entitled whether by implication prescription or otherwise to any right of light or air or other right or easement (except as herein contained) which would restrict or interfere with the free use by the Transferor of the Retained Land or any part or parts thereof for building or other purposes.

12.6.1.2 Neither the Transferor nor the persons deriving title under it shall become entitled whether by implication prescription or otherwise to any right of light or air or other right or easement (except as herein contained) which would restrict or interfere with the free use by the Transferee of the Property or any part or parts thereof for building or other purposes.

12.6.2 Rights of third parties

Unless the right of enforcement is expressly provided it is not intended that a third party should have the right to enforce any terms of this Transfer pursuant to the Contracts (Rights of Third Parties) Act 1999 but this does not affect any rights which are available apart from that Act.

12.6.3 Implied rights

Section 62 of the Law of Property Act 1925 and the rule in *Wheeldon* v. *Burrows* do not apply to this Transfer and no legal or other rights are granted over the Retained Land for the benefit of the Property except for those expressly granted by this Transfer.

12.6.4 Rights reserved and granted

12.6.4.1 Unless otherwise stated, the rights hereby granted are granted for use by the Transferee in common with the Transferor and all other persons lawfully entitled to exercise them and the rights hereby reserved are reserved for use by the Transferor in common with the Transferee and all persons lawfully entitled to exercise them.

12.6.4.2 The rights hereby reserved and granted shall not be exercised over land which has been or is being or is intended to be developed by the construction of buildings or their curtilages or over shared access areas not intended to be made available for general use or (except for acceptable rights of way) over land to be dedicated as public open space.

12.6.4.3 Any rights of entry on land shall be exercised only upon reasonable notice and at reasonable times (except in cases of emergency).

12.6.4.4 All requisite consents from any Relevant Authority for connections to and construction of any roads and/or Service Media pursuant to the rights hereby reserved and granted shall be obtained by the person exercising the rights prior to effecting the same.

12.6.4.5 The person exercising the rights shall cause as little damage and disturbance as reasonably possible and shall make good all damage caused as soon as reasonably practicable.

12.6.4.6 [The person exercising the rights hereby granted shall (if so requested) consent to the Access Roads and/or the Service Media and/or Estate Sewers over or through which the rights are exercised becoming adopted and/or maintainable at the public expense [and pending adoption shall contribute a fair and reasonable proportion (according to user) of the costs of inspecting, cleansing, repairing, maintaining, renewing or replacing the Access Roads and/or the Service Media and/or the Estate Sewers over or through (or into) which the rights are exercised].]

12.6.4.7 [Rights of way over the Access Road shall not be exercised until the same shall have been constructed to base course level].

12.6.4.8 [The Transferor shall be entitled to alter the position of the Access Road and/or the Estate Sewers and/or the Service Media within the Retained Land with the Approval of the Transferee subject to:

(a) the Transferee Approving the proposed new route of the Access Road and/or the Estate Sewers and/or the Service Media; and

(b) the Transferor obtaining all the necessary consents and approvals to the proposed works; and

(c) the Transferor complying with the requirements of the Relevant Authority in relation to the works; and

(d) the Transferor entering into a suitable deed of easement with the Transferee in a form to be Approved by the Transferee and the Transferor prior to commencing any alterations.

Any dispute regarding this clause 12.6.4.8 or the form of the said deed of easement shall be referred to and determined by an Expert in accordance with clause 12.7.]

12.6.5 Co-operation and good faith

The Parties agree the one with the other and undertake with each other that they will co-operate with each other and act in [the utmost] good faith with each other and will without delay join in any necessary agreements reasonably required by the other (subject to any reasonable indemnities being given and reasonable provision for costs being made) required for the development of either Party's land and/or the adoption of the Access Road, the Estate Sewers and any Service Media and any connections thereto.

12.6.6 [Attorney

12.6.6.1 The Transferor as security for the observance of the obligations contained in paragraph 7 of Part II of the Fourth Schedule hereto hereby irrevocably appoints the Transferee and any person nominated by the Transferee as its attorney and agent for the purpose of signing, executing, sealing and delivering on behalf of the Transferor any of the documents referred to in paragraphs [5] and [6] of Part II of the [Fourth] Schedule hereto.

12.6.6.2 The Transferee as security for the observance of the obligations contained in paragraph 4 of Part II of the Third Schedule hereto hereby irrevocably appoints the Transferor and any person nominated by the Transferor as its attorney and agent for the purpose of signing, executing, sealing and delivering on behalf of the Transferee any of the documents referred to in paragraphs [3] and [4] of Part II of the [Third] Schedule hereto.]

12.6.7 Restriction and Excluded Disposal

The Transferor acknowledges that in the event of the Transferee making an Excluded Disposal after the date of this Transfer it is not intended that any restriction entered on the title to the Property in accordance with clause [12.9.2] of this Transfer shall be entered on the title to the land which is the subject of the Excluded Disposal and in the event of such a restriction being entered on the title to land which is the subject of an Excluded Disposal the Transferor shall promptly take such steps as shall be necessary to remove the restriction (including completing and signing such Land Registry form as may be appropriate) and in default hereby authorises the Transferee to remove such restriction.

12.7 DISPUTE RESOLUTION

12.7.1 Unless otherwise provided in this Transfer any dispute or difference between the Parties regarding any of the provisions of this Transfer shall be referred to the Expert. The Expert shall act as expert and not as arbitrator and his decision shall be final and binding on the Parties and the following provisions shall apply:

12.7.1.1 The Expert shall give the Parties the opportunity to make representations to him before making his decision.

12.7.1.2 The Expert shall be entitled to obtain opinions from others if he so wishes.

12.7.1.3 The Expert shall give reasons for his decision.

12.7.1.4 The Expert shall comply with any time limits or other directions agreed by the Parties.

12.7.1.5 The charges and expenses of the Expert shall be borne equally between the Parties or in such other proportions as the Expert may direct.

12.8 APPLICATION

The Transferor and the Transferee hereby apply to the Chief Land Registrar to enter into the Registers of the Titles to the Property and the Retained Land such of the rights, reservations, exceptions, covenants and conditions contained or referred to herein as are capable of registration.

12.9 RESTRICTIONS

12.9.1 The Transferor and the Transferee hereby apply to the Chief Land Registrar for the entry of the following restriction upon the proprietorship register of the title to the Retained Land in the following terms (or as near thereto as the Land Registry will permit):

'Restriction – no disposition of the registered estate [(other than a charge)] by the proprietor of the registered estate or the proprietor of any registered charge, not being a charge registered before the entry of this restriction, is to be registered without a certificate signed by the conveyancer acting for the registered proprietor that the provisions of paragraph [1] of Part I of the [Fourth] Schedule of the Transfer dated [ ] made between [ ] and [ ] have been complied with or do not apply.'

12.9.2 The Transferor and the Transferee hereby apply to Chief Land Registrar for the entry of the following restriction upon the proprietorship register of the title to the Property in the following terms (or as near thereto as HM Land Registry will permit):

'Restriction – no disposition of the registered estate [(other than a charge)] by the proprietor of the registered estate or the proprietor of any registered charge, not being a charge registered before the entry of this restriction, is to be registered without a certificate signed by the conveyancer acting for the registered proprietor that the provisions of paragraph [4] of Part I of the [Third] Schedule of the Transfer dated [ ] made between [ ] and [ ] have been complied with or do not apply.'

12.9.3 [Upon satisfaction of the Transferor's obligations contained in [paragraphs [ ] of] of Part II of the Fourth Schedule the Transferee shall at the request of the Transferor release the Transferor from such obligations and procure the cancellation of the restriction in respect thereof entered on the proprietorship register of the title to the Retained Land and in each case upon such terms as the Transferor shall reasonably require.]

12.9.4 [Upon satisfaction of the Transferee's obligations contained in [paragraphs [ ] of] Part II of the Third Schedule hereto the Transferor shall at the request of the Transferee release the Transferee from such covenants and procure the cancellation of the restriction entered upon the proprietorship register of the title to the Property and in each case upon such terms as the Transferee shall reasonably require.]

IN WITNESS whereof this Transfer has been executed by the Transferor and the Transferee as a Deed the date and year first before written.

THE FIRST SCHEDULE before referred to

Rights Granted

The following rights for the Transferee, its successors in title of all or any parts of the Property and their respective tenants and servants and invitees in common with the Transferor and all others so entitled:

1. To connect to and use the Access Road

1.1 The full and free right to connect to the Access Road after it has been constructed to base course level.

1.2 The full and free right to go, pass and repass with or without vehicles at all times and for all purposes over and along the Access Road after it has been constructed to base course level and any connection thereto.

2. To connect to and use the Estate Sewers

The full and free right, following the construction of the Estate Sewers, to connect to and to use the Estate Sewers together with the right (upon reasonable prior written notice) to enter upon the Retained Land (but not any part of the Retained Land comprising a building) but only so far as strictly necessary with workmen and equipment for the purpose of (a) laying new Service Media in order to connect to the Estate

Sewers and/or (b) making connections with the Estate Sewers and/or (c) testing, cleaning, maintaining, renewing and repairing the Estate Sewers and the connections thereto.

3. To connect to and use the Service Media

The full and free right to connect to and use the Service Media now laid or to be laid at any time in the future within the Retained Land (but not any part of the Retained Land comprising a building) together with the right (upon reasonable prior written notice) to enter upon the Retained Land but only so far as strictly necessary with or without workmen, plant, machinery and equipment for the purpose of (a) making connections with such service media and/or (b) testing, cleaning, maintaining, renewing and repairing such service media and the connections thereto.

4. To lay and use new Service Media

The full and free right to lay and use new Service Media in, on, under or over the Retained Land (excluding any part of the Retained Land comprising or intended to comprise a dwelling and its curtilage) together with the right (upon reasonable prior written notice) to enter upon the Retained Land but only so far as is strictly necessary for the purpose of laying and thereafter repairing, maintaining, inspecting and replacing such Service Media.

5. Right of entry

5.1 The right to enter and remain upon such parts of the Retained Land (excluding any part of the Retained Land comprising or intended to comprise a dwelling and its curtilage) as shall be reasonably necessary at any time (and with or without workmen, plant, equipment and machinery) for any of the following purposes: (a) connecting to, inspecting, maintaining, repairing, renewing or cleansing the Access Road or the Estate Sewers and (b) laying, connecting to, inspecting, maintaining, repairing, renewing, cleansing, upgrading and augmenting any Service Media.

5.2 The right at all times to enter after reasonable notice (except in the case of emergency) upon such part of the Retained Land as shall be reasonably necessary (but not any part of the Retained Land comprising a building) for the purpose of constructing, repairing, maintaining and replacing any part of any dwellinghouse or boundary fence to be erected on the Property or for any other reasonable purpose connected with the proposed [residential] development of the Property.

6. [Step in rights

The right in the event of default by the Transferor to perform the positive obligations set out in Part II of the Fourth Schedule hereto in accordance with the provisions of Part II of the Fourth Schedule hereto to enter and remain upon the Retained Land (but not any part of the Retained Land comprising a building) and (at the cost of the Transferor) to carry out such works and/or take such action as may be necessary **PROVIDED ALWAYS THAT** (a) before exercising such right the Transferee shall serve [seven] days' prior written notice on the Transferor and (b) the Transferee shall be entitled to exercise such right only if the Transferor shall fail within such [seven]-day period to promptly and diligently take steps to complete any works which are outstanding and such other action as may be necessary **PROVIDED THAT** if due to exceptionally adverse weather conditions or other circumstances reasonably outside the Transferor's control and which could not have been foreseen there is delay by the Transferor in promptly and diligently taking steps to complete any works which are outstanding then the said [seven]-day period shall be extended by such period as is reasonable in all the circumstances.]

THE SECOND SCHEDULE before referred to

Rights Reserved

The following rights for the Transferor, its successors in title of all or any parts of the of the Retained Land and their respective tenants and servants and invitees in common with the Transferee and all others so entitled:

1. To connect to and use Service Media

   The full and free right to connect to and use the Service Media now laid or to be laid at any time in the future within the Property **TOGETHER WITH** the right (upon reasonable prior written notice) to enter upon the Property (but not any part of the Property comprising a dwelling or its curtilage) but only so far as strictly necessary with workmen and equipment for the purpose of making connections with such Service Media and testing, cleaning, maintaining, renewing and repairing such Service Media and the connections thereto.

2. Right of entry

   The right at all times for the Transferor and its successors in title and all persons authorised by the Transferor or its successors in title with servants workmen and others to enter after reasonable prior written notice (except in the case of emergency) upon such part of the Property as shall be reasonably necessary (but not any part of the Property comprising a building or its curtilage) for the purpose of constructing, repairing, maintaining and replacing the Access Road and the Estate Sewers and any other services or for any other reasonable purpose connected with the proposed [residential] development of the Retained Land.

THE THIRD SCHEDULE before referred to

Transferee's covenants

Part I

Transferee's Restrictive Covenants

1. No nuisance

1.1 [Not to cause or permit to be done in or upon the Property or any part thereof any act or thing which may be or become a nuisance [annoyance or disturbance] to the owners or occupiers for the time being of the Retained Land or any part thereof **PROVIDED ALWAYS THAT** the development of the

Property and its subsequent use for [residential] purposes shall not be a breach of this obligation.]

1.2 Not to obstruct or permit to be obstructed any rights or easements hereby granted in favour of the Retained Land.

2. Hinder development

Not to do or agree to anything which will delay, hinder or prevent the development of the Retained Land **PROVIDED ALWAYS THAT** the [residential] development of the Property shall not be a breach of this obligation.

3. No mud on roads

To use all reasonable endeavours not to deposit or permit or suffer to be deposited by any person involved in any proposed development of the Property or the supply of goods or services thereto mud or debris or other materials on the Access Road or any other road constructed or to be constructed on the Retained Land and without undue delay remove any such mud or debris or other materials deposited in breach hereof by the Transferee or its contractor and any other person involved in the development of the Property.

4. Deed of Covenant

4.1 Not to make any Disposition of the whole or any part of the Property without procuring that the Disponee prior to each such Disposition delivers to the Transferor a deed of covenant with the Transferor in the form of the Transferee's Deed of Covenant **PROVIDED THAT**:

4.1.1 in no event shall a Transferee's Deed of Covenant be required in respect of an Excluded Disposal;

4.1.2 the Transferee and any person who has previously executed the Transferee's Deed of Covenant shall be released from all obligations upon a successor giving a further Transferee's deed of covenant to the extent that the successor covenants to observe such obligations in the further Transferee's Deed of Covenant.

Part II

Transferee's Positive Covenants

1. Compliance with Planning Permission

To comply with [the conditions of the Planning Permission] [conditions [ ] of the Planning Permission and the remaining conditions] in so far as they relate to the Property [other than conditions [ ] which shall be the Transferor's responsibility].

[NOTE: Consider carefully and amend as required. It would be sensible to refer to the specific planning conditions that the Transferee will be obliged to comply with.]

2. [Compliance with Planning Agreement

To comply or procure compliance with the obligations set out in [the [ ] Schedule of] the Planning Agreement in so far as the same are still subsisting and relate solely to the Property.]

[NOTE: Consider carefully and amend as required. It would be sensible to refer to the specific planning obligations that the Transferee will be obliged to comply with.]

3. [Grant wayleaves

To enter into any wayleave agreement, deed of easement, adoption agreement or other document reasonably required by the provider of any of the Services as a condition of the provider of those Services installing and/or adopting Service Media or allowing connections to be made to Service Media for the benefit of the Retained Land subject to the Transferor providing the Transferee with a suitable indemnity in respect of the obligations contained in such document and agreeing to pay the Transferee's reasonable professional and legal fees.]

4. [Adoption agreements

Upon receipt of written notice from the Transferor to [use reasonable endeavours to] enter into an adoption agreement in respect of the Service Media referred to in paragraph 1 of the Second Schedule hereto subject to the Transferor providing the Transferee with a suitable indemnity in respect of the obligations contained in such adoption agreement and agreeing to pay the Transferee's reasonable professional and legal fees.]

5. Costs arising as a result of the Transferee's default

[To pay to the Transferor on demand all costs and expenses properly incurred by the Transferor in the event of the Transferee failing to comply with the positive obligations contained in the immediately preceding paragraphs 1 to 4.]

THE FOURTH SCHEDULE before referred to

Transferor's covenants

PART I

Transferor's Restrictive Covenants

1. Deed of covenant

1.1 Not to make any Disposition of the whole or any part of the Retained Land without procuring that the Disponee prior to each such Disposition delivers to the Transferee a deed of covenant with the Transferee in the form of the Transferor's Deed of Covenant **PROVIDED THAT**:

1.1.1 In no event shall a Transferor's Deed of Covenant be required in respect of an Excluded Disposal.

1.1.2 The Transferor and any person who has previously executed the Transferor's Deed of Covenant shall be released from all obligations upon a successor giving a further Transferor's Deed of Covenant to the extent that the successor covenants to observe such obligations in the further Transferor's Deed of Covenant.

2. Not to hinder development

Not to do or agree to do or omit to do anything which would prejudice, delay or hinder or prevent the development of the Property by the Transferee **PROVIDED ALWAYS** that the development of the Retained Land and its subsequent use for [commercial and/or retail] purposes shall not be a breach of this obligation.

3. No nuisance

3.1 [Not to cause or permit to be done in or upon the Retained Land or any part thereof any act or thing which may be or become a nuisance [annoyance or disturbance] to the owners or occupiers for the time being of the Property or any part thereof **PROVIDED ALWAYS** that the development of the Retained Land and its subsequent use for [commercial and/or retail] purposes shall not be a breach of this obligation.]

3.2 Not to obstruct or permit to be obstructed any rights or easements hereby granted in favour of the Property.

4. No mud on roads

To use all reasonable endeavours not to deposit or permit or suffer to be deposited by any person involved in any proposed development of the Retained Land or the supply of goods or services thereto mud or debris or other materials on the Access Road or any other road constructed or to be constructed on the Retained Land and without undue delay remove any such mud or debris or other materials deposited in breach hereof by the Transferor or its contractor and any other person involved in the development of the Retained Land.

5. [No development
Not to develop or use the Retained Land or any part thereof for residential purposes until completion of the sale of the last unit to be built on the Property.] **[NOTE: Amend or delete as required.]**

PART II

Transferor's Positive Covenants

1. Access Road

1.1 [The Transferor shall forthwith apply for and use [all] reasonable endeavours to obtain the approval of the Relevant Authority to the design and layout of the Access Road [and the Section 278 Works].]

1.2 The Transferor shall commence the construction of the Access Road [and the Section 278 Works] [within [28 days] after receipt of the technical approval of the Relevant Authority [and] [by no later than [ ]] [(time to be of the essence)].

1.3 The Transferor shall at the expense of the Transferor construct the Access Road in a good and workmanlike manner and to a standard required for adoption and in accordance [with the Specification and] the requirements of the Relevant Authority such construction to base course to be completed [within [four] months after the date on which the relevant technical approval is obtained from the Relevant Authority] [and by no later than] [[24] months after the date of this Transfer] [(time to be of the essence)] [**PROVIDED THAT** if due to exceptionally adverse weather conditions or other circumstances reasonably outside the Transferor's control and which could not have been foreseen there is delay by the Transferor in completing any works then the said period shall be extended by such period as is reasonable in all the circumstances].

1.4 The Transferor shall at the expense of the Transferor apply the final wearing course to the Access Road as quickly as reasonably practicable after the construction of the Access Road to base course level [and in any event no later than [one month] after completion of the sale of the last unit on the Property].

1.5 The Transferor shall at the expense of the Transferor complete the construction of the footpaths and street lighting along the Access Road as quickly as reasonably practicable after the construction of the Access Road to base course level [and in any event by no later than [ ]].

1.6 The Transferor shall [use [all] reasonable endeavours to] procure the adoption of the Access Road as soon as reasonably possible after completion of the construction of the Access Road.

1.7 [The Transferor shall as soon as reasonably practicable enter into the Section 278 Agreement.]

1.8 [The Transferor shall at the expense of the Transferor construct the Section 278 Works in a good and workmanlike manner using good quality materials and in accordance with the requirements of the Relevant Authority such construction to be completed by no later than [ ] [**PROVIDED THAT** if due to exceptionally adverse weather conditions or other circumstances reasonably outside the Transferor's control and which could not have been foreseen there is delay by the Transferor in completing any works then the said period shall be extended by such period as is reasonable in all the circumstances].

1.9 The Transferor shall maintain the Access Road at all times to the satisfaction of the Relevant Authority and shall comply with the agreements for construction, maintenance and adoption thereof at all times.

2. Estate Sewers

2.1 [The Transferor shall forthwith apply for and use [all] reasonable endeavours to obtain the approval of the Relevant Authority to the design and layout of the Estate Sewers.]

2.2 The Transferor shall commence the construction of the Estate Sewers [within [four] months after the date on which the relevant technical approval is obtained from the Relevant Authority] [and] [by no later than [ ]] [time to be of the essence].

2.3 The Transferor shall at the expense of the Transferor construct the Estate Sewers in a good and workmanlike manner using good quality materials and to a standard required for adoption [in accordance with the Specification and in accordance with the requirements of the Relevant Authority] [with connection points to or as close to the boundaries of the Property as the Relevant Authority shall permit] such sewers and drains to be of sufficient capacity to serve both the Property and the Retained Land when fully developed and to be completed ready for connection and use [within [ ] months of the date on which the relevant technical approval is obtained] [and] [by no later than [ ] [(time to be of the essence)] [**PROVIDED THAT** if due to exceptionally adverse weather conditions or other circumstances reasonably outside the Transferor's control and which could not have been foreseen there is delay by the Transferor in completing any works then the said period shall be extended by such period as is reasonable in all the circumstances].

2.4 The Transferor shall [use [all] reasonable endeavours to] procure the adoption of the Estate Sewers as soon as reasonably possible after completion of the construction of the Estate Sewers.

2.5 The Transferor shall maintain the Estate Sewers at all times to the satisfaction of the Relevant Authority and shall comply with the agreements for construction, maintenance and adoption thereof at all times.

3. Service Media

The Transferor shall at the expense of the Transferor provide or secure the installation of gas, water, electricity and telecommunications in a good and workmanlike manner and using good quality materials and to a standard required by the appropriate relevant supplier [and in accordance with the Specification] [with connection points to or close to the boundaries of the Property] and such service media shall be of sufficient capacity to serve the Property when fully developed and] installed and available for connection and use by no later than [ ] [**PROVIDED THAT** if due to exceptionally adverse weather conditions or other circumstances reasonably outside the Transferor's control and which could not have been foreseen there is delay by the Transferor in completing any works then the said period shall be extended by such period as is reasonable in all the circumstances].

4. Planning compliance

4.1 The Transferor will at its own cost comply with [the conditions of the Planning Permission] [conditions [ ] of the Planning Permission and the remaining conditions] in so far as they relate to the Retained Land [other than conditions [ ] of the Planning Permission which shall be the Transferee's responsibility].

[NOTE: Consider carefully and amend as required. It would be sensible to refer to the specific planning conditions that the Transferor will be obliged to comply with.]

4.2 [The Transferor will at its own cost comply or procure compliance with the obligations contained in the Planning Agreement in so far as the same are still subsisting and have not been made the responsibility of the Transferee under this Transfer so that the development and occupation of the Property is not prejudiced or delayed].

[NOTE: Consider carefully and amend as required. It would be sensible to refer to the specific planning obligations that the Transferor will be obliged to comply with.]

5. Grant wayleaves

The Transferor shall grant such further rights and easements to and/or enter into such covenants as shall be required by a Relevant Authority providing Services to the Property as a condition of installing Service Media or allowing connections to be made to Service Media for the benefit of the Property and/or as may be required by a Relevant Authority in connection with the development of the Property and shall enter into any deed or agreement that may be [reasonably] required by the Relevant Authority subject to the Transferee providing the Transferor with a suitable indemnity in respect of the obligations contained in such documents and agreeing to pay the Transferor's reasonable professional and legal costs.

6. Adoption agreements

6.1 The Transferor shall [use [all] reasonable endeavours to] enter as soon as reasonably practicable [(but in any event by no later than [12] months after the date of this Transfer)] into a Road Agreement with the Relevant Authority in relation to the Access Road and give to the Relevant Authority such security as is normally required.

6.2 The Transferor shall [use [all] reasonable endeavours to] enter as soon as reasonably practicable [(and in any event within [12] months of the date of this Transfer)] into a Drainage Agreement with the Relevant Authority in relation to the Estate Sewers and give to the Relevant Authority such security as is normally required.

6.3 The Transferor shall provide the Transferee with full certified copies of the Road Agreement and the Drainage Agreement (including colour copies of all relevant plans) within 10 working days after the same have been concluded.

6.4 The Transferor shall upon receipt of written notice from the Transferee promptly enter into any relevant adoption agreement in respect of any new Service Media laid by the Transferee within the Retained Land and/or any connections made to the Estate Sewers within the Retained Land by the Transferee [provided that the Transferor shall have no responsibility for the construction of such Service Media and connections and subject to the Transferee providing the Transferor with a full and complete indemnity in respect of the obligations contained in such agreement and to meeting the Transferor's reasonable and proper legal costs.]

7. [Costs arising as a result of Transferor's default

To pay to the Transferee on demand all costs and expenses properly incurred by the Transferee in the event of the Transferor failing to comply with the positive obligations contained in the immediately preceding paragraphs 1 to 6].

The transferor must execute this transfer as a deed using the space opposite. If there is more than one transferor, all must execute. Forms of execution are given in Schedule 9 to the Land Registration Rules 2003. If the transfer contains transferee's covenants or declarations or contains an application by the transferee (such as for a restriction), it must also be executed by the transferee.

If there is more than one transferee and panel 11 has been completed, each transferee must also execute this transfer to comply with the requirements in section 53(1)(b) of the Law of Property Act 1925 relating to the declaration of a trust of land. Please refer to *Joint property ownership* and *practice guide 24: private trusts of land* for further guidance.

Remember to date this deed in panel 4.

13 Execution

EXECUTED as a DEED by the **TRANSFEROR** acting by:

Director

Director/Secretary

EXECUTED as a DEED by the **TRANSFEREE** acting by:

Director

Director/Secretary

WARNING
If you dishonestly enter information or make a statement that you know is, or might be, untrue or misleading, and intend by doing so to make a gain for yourself or another person, or to cause loss or the risk of loss to another person, you may commit the offence of fraud under section 1 of the Fraud Act 2006, the maximum penalty for which is 10 years' imprisonment or an unlimited fine, or both.

Failure to complete this form with proper care may result in a loss of protection under the Land Registration Act 2002 if, as a result, a mistake is made in the register.

Under section 66 of the Land Registration Act 2002 most documents (including this form) kept by the registrar relating to an application to the registrar or referred to in the register are open to public inspection and copying. If you believe a document contains prejudicial information, you may apply for that part of the document to be made exempt using Form EX1, under rule 136 of the Land Registration Rules 2003.

APPENDIX C4

Sample form: Standard plot sale transfer

HM Land Registry

Transfer of part of registered title(s)

Any parts of the form that are not typed should be completed in black ink and in block capitals.

If you need more room than is provided for in a panel, and your software allows, you can expand any panel in the form. Alternatively use continuation sheet CS and attach it to this form.

For information on how HM Land Registry processes your personal information, see our Personal Information Charter.

Notes	Panel
Leave blank if not yet registered.	1 Title number(s) out of which the property is transferred:
When application for registration is made these title number(s) should be entered in panel 2 of Form AP1.	2 Other title number(s) against which matters contained in this transfer are to be registered or noted, if any:
Insert address, including postcode (if any), or other description of the property transferred. Any physical exclusions, such as mines and minerals, should be defined.	3 Property:
Place 'X' in the appropriate box and complete the statement.	The property is identified
For example 'edged red'.	☐ on the attached plan and shown:
For example 'edged and numbered 1 in blue'.	☐ on the title plan(s) of the above titles and shown:
Any plan lodged must be signed by the transferor.	
Remember to date this deed with the day of completion, but not before it has been signed and witnessed.	4 Date:
Give full name(s) of **all** of the persons transferring the property.	5 Transferor:
Complete as appropriate where the transferor is a company.	For UK incorporated companies/LLPs Registered number of company or limited liability partnership including any prefix: For overseas companies (a) Territory of incorporation: (b) Registered number in the United Kingdom including any prefix:
Give full name(s) of **all** the persons to be shown as registered proprietors.	6 Transferee for entry in the register:
Complete as appropriate where the transferee is a company. Also, for an overseas company, unless an arrangement with HM Land Registry exists, lodge either a certificate in Form 7 in Schedule 3 to the Land Registration Rules 2003 or a certified copy of the constitution in English or Welsh, or other evidence permitted by rule 183 of the Land Registration Rules 2003.	For UK incorporated companies/LLPs Registered number of company or limited liability partnership including any prefix: For overseas companies (a) Territory of incorporation: (b) Registered number in the United Kingdom including any prefix:

Guidance	Panel
Each transferee may give up to three addresses for service, one of which must be a postal address whether or not in the UK (including the postcode, if any). The others can be any combination of a postal address, a UK DX box number or an electronic address.	7 Transferee's intended address(es) for service for entry in the register:
	8 The transferor transfers the property to the transferee
Place 'X' in the appropriate box. State the currency unit if other than sterling. If none of the boxes apply, insert an appropriate memorandum in panel 12.	9 Consideration ☐ The transferor has received from the transferee for the property the following sum (in words and figures): ☐ The transfer is not for money or anything that has a monetary value ☐ Insert other receipt as appropriate:
Place 'X' in any box that applies. Add any modifications.	10 The transferor transfers with ☐ full title guarantee ☐ limited title guarantee
Where the transferee is more than one person, place 'X' in the appropriate box. Complete as necessary. The registrar will enter a Form A restriction in the register *unless*: – an 'X' is placed: – in the first box, or – in the third box and the details of the trust or of the trust instrument show that the transferees are to hold the property on trust for themselves alone as joint tenants, *or* – it is clear from completion of a form JO lodged with this application that the transferees are to hold the property on trust for themselves alone as joint tenants. Please refer to *Joint property ownership* and practice guide *24: private trusts of land* for further guidance. These are both available on the GOV.UK website.	11 Declaration of trust. The transferee is more than one person and ☐ they are to hold the property on trust for themselves as joint tenants ☐ they are to hold the property on trust for themselves as tenants in common in equal shares ☐ they are to hold the property on trust:

Use this panel for:
- definitions of terms not defined above
- rights granted or reserved
- restrictive covenants
- other covenants
- agreements and declarations
- any required or permitted statements
- other agreed provisions.

The prescribed subheadings may be added to, amended, repositioned or omitted.

Any other land affected by rights granted or reserved or by restrictive covenants should be defined by reference to a plan.

12 Additional provisions

12.1 DEFINITIONS

'Boundary Structure' means any wall, fence, hedge, tree, retaining wall or other structure on any boundary of the Property;

'Building' means a house, bungalow, other structure with living quarters, garage, car port constructed or to be constructed on the Estate by the Transferor;

'Estate' means all the land (except the Property) now or formerly comprised in the title number(s) in Panel 1 and Panel 2 (if any) [and which is known as [ ];

'Estate Roads' means all roads, verges, footpaths now or within the Perpetuity Period constructed within the Estate which are intended to become maintainable at public expense;

'Estate Sewers' means the surface water and foul sewers now or within the Perpetuity Period constructed within the Estate which are intended to become public sewers;

'Perpetuity Period' means 80 years from 1 January 2009;

'Plan' means the plan or plans annexed to this Transfer;

[**'Planning Agreement'** means the agreement dated [*date*] and made between (1) [ ] Council (2) [ ] and (3) [ ] under or by virtue of section 106 of the Town and Country Planning Act 1990;]

'Plot' means each plot on the Estate intended for residential occupation and **'Plots'** means all or any number of those plots;

'Projections' means all foundations, chimneys, eaves, guttering, drainpipes, fence posts, wall piers and similar projections (and, temporarily during the course of construction and for essential maintenance, scaffolding);

'Relevant Authority' means all statutory corporations, local or other authorities and all bodies exercising statutory rights powers or obligations which will include but is not limited to highway, planning, drainage, water, electricity, gas and telecommunications suppliers and any other authority or body or company to which the powers of such authority body or company are delegated;

'Restriction Period' means the period expiring on the earlier of expiry of five years from the date of this Transfer or the date the Transferor has developed and physically left the Estate;

'Service Media' means all conducting media and apparatus (excluding the Estate Sewers) for foul and surface water drainage, gas, light, water, oil, electricity, telephone, electronic transmissions and similar services now or within the Perpetuity Period constructed within the Estate or the Property;

'Shared Access' means the area (if any) which forms or is intended to form the site of an access drive and/or footpath jointly serving the Property and adjoining or neighbouring dwellings but not intended to become public highway and will include (for the avoidance of doubt) those areas which also run beneath a structure (with or without living quarters) constructed by the Transferor above ground level;

12.2 DECLARATIONS

It is agreed and declared by the Transferor and the Transferee as follows:

12.2.1 Section 62 of the Law of Property Act 1925 and the rule in *Wheeldon* v. *Burrows* do not apply to this Transfer and no legal or other rights are granted over the Estate for the benefit of the Property or granted over the Property for the benefit of the Estate except for those expressly granted or reserved by this Transfer.

12.2.2 The expressions the 'Transferor' and the 'Transferee' include their respective successors in title unless specifically excluded.

12.2.3 The singular includes the plural and the masculine includes the feminine and vice versa and where there are two or more persons included in the Transferee any obligation or agreement in this deed will bind them both individually and jointly.

12.2.4 All future rights granted in this transfer must be exercised within the Perpetuity Period which is to be the perpetuity period applicable to this transfer.

12.2.5 The covenants in clause 12.5 are enforceable between the Transferor and the Transferee and also between the purchasers of Plots on the Estate but no building scheme will be created by this transfer and the Transferor may modify waive or release any covenants set out in clause 12.5.

12.2.6 The covenants in clause 12.5 will cease to be binding between the Transferor and the Transferee (but not as between the Transferee and any other owner of any part of the Estate) after expiry of the Restriction Period.

12.2.7 The Transferor is not liable to the Transferee or his successors in title for any breaches of covenants or conditions committed by the purchasers or lessees on any other Plot and the Transferor is not obliged to take proceedings to enforce those covenants, restrictions, stipulations and conditions.

12.2.8 The Transferor is not bound by any scheme of development of the Estate as shown on any plans or documents and is entitled to sell the Estate in such plots or parcels and subject to such rights, declarations and covenants as it considers appropriate and is entitled to vary the same and vary the layout of the Estate as it considers fit.

12.2.9 Any person exercising the rights in clauses 12.3 and 12.4 will not do so unreasonably and will cause as little damage and inconvenience as reasonably possible and will repair any damage caused as quickly as possible.

12.2.10 The Transferee will if requested by the Transferor enter into any necessary deed of grant or variation in respect of easements relating to the Service Media, Estate Sewers or Estate Roads.

12.2.11 All Boundary Structures separating the Property and the Estate (except those adjoining the Estate Road or public highways or marked with an inward or outward 'T' on the Plan) and any walls separating Buildings on the Property from any other Buildings on the Estate are party Boundary Structures and are to be maintained accordingly.

12.2.12 The use of any Shared Access Service Media or Boundary Structure and any other things now or to be constructed by the Transferor intended for shared use by the Transferee and the owners of any other parts of the Estate is conditional on the Transferee paying a fair proportion of the costs incurred in their inspection, maintenance and renewal by the Transferor or any person sharing their use and/or enjoyment and any dispute about the amount to be paid will be settled by the written certificate of an independent surveyor acting as an expert appointed by agreement between the parties to the dispute or failing agreement by the President of the Royal Institution of Chartered Surveyors on the application of any party to the dispute.

12.3 RIGHTS GRANTED

The following rights are granted to the Transferee and all others authorised by the Transferor (in common with all other persons having a similar right).

12.3.1 A right of way over:

12.3.1.1 the Estate Roads until they become maintainable at public expense;

12.3.1.2 any Shared Access (but on foot only over footpaths) which serves the Property but is not within the red edging on the Plan.

12.3.2 A right to use the Estate Sewers until they become maintainable at public expense.

12.3.3 The right to use, inspect, maintain and renew any Service Media on the Estate which serve the Property.

12.3.4 The right of support and protection to the Property and any Building on the Property from the Estate.

12.3.5 The right to keep and use on adjoining parts of the Estate any Projections from the Property as constructed by the Transferor.

12.3.6 The right to enter upon adjoining parts of the Estate (except the site of any electricity, gas, water, telephone or other services substation, governor, pumping station, tank or similar apparatus which is vested in or under the control of any Relevant Authority) to inspect maintain or renew any part of the Property or any of any part of the Estate which attach to the Property.

12.4 RIGHTS RESERVED

Except as mentioned below these rights are reserved to the Transferor for the benefit of any part or parts of the Estate and any other land acquired by the Transferor within the Perpetuity Period which is capable of benefiting from them and also for the benefit of any Relevant Authority and of any other persons authorised by them or by the Transferor.

12.4.1 Rights of way with or without vehicles at all times over any Shared Access which is part of the Property but the use of which is shared and serves any other parts of the Estate or any land adjoining the Estate.

12.4.2 Rights to use the Estate Sewers (if any) crossing the Property until they become maintainable at public expense.

12.4.3 Rights to use, inspect, maintain and renew any Service Media which cross the Property.

12.4.4 Rights of support and protection from the Property for any land or Buildings adjoining the Property.

12.4.5 Rights to keep and use on the Property any Projections from any Buildings adjoining the Property now or to be constructed by the Transferor.

12.4.6 Rights to enter on the Property to inspect, maintain or renew any part of any building or structure adjoining the Property constructed by the Transferor or any Shared Access or Service Media serving the Property and other Buildings.

12.4.7 The right for the Transferor (for these purposes excluding its successors in title to the Plots) and for the Relevant Authority and of any other persons authorised by them or authorised by the Transferor to enter the Property:

12.4.7.1 to connect to and alter any existing Service Media and to lay new Service Media;

12.4.7.2 to tie in adjoining Buildings and other structures and to construct any Projections and any walls or fences relating to adjoining land or Buildings;

12.4.7.3 for the purpose of complying with the proper requirements of any Relevant Authority;

12.4.7.4 to plant trees or shrubs or to carry out landscaping operations or to fulfill the requirements of any relevant planning permission;

12.4.7.5 to re-locate any Boundary Structure or other boundary marker (in respect of which the Transferee will not be entitled to object or to claim compensation) if as a result of a subsequent as built survey it is shown that such Boundary Structure or marker has not been erected in the position shown on the Plan;

12.4.7.6 at any time during the Restriction Period to erect, maintain and keep any advertisement board or hoarding or directional sign on the Property such boards or signs to be of such size, dimensions and design as the Transferor in its absolute discretion determines subject to the Transferor making good any damage caused to the Property by the exercise of such right.

Include words of covenant.

Restrictive covenants by the transferee

12.5 TRANSFEREE'S COVENANTS

The Transferee so as to bind the Property and each and every part and to benefit the Estate and each and every part covenants with the Transferor (and as a separate covenant with every other person who is now the owner of any part of the Estate) to observe and perform the following covenants, restrictions and stipulations and conditions but not so as to render the Transferee personally liable for any breach after he has disposed of his legal interest in the Property.

12.5.1 Not to use the Property for any purpose other than as or incidental to one private residential dwelling and not to use the Property for any trade or business.

12.5.2 Not to do or permit or suffer to be done on the Property anything which may be or become a nuisance or annoyance or cause damage to the Transferor or to the owners, tenants or occupiers of any adjoining or neighbouring property.

12.5.3 Not to erect or construct within the Restriction Period any building or other structure whatsoever whether temporary or permanent on the Property without the prior consent in writing of the Transferor and if required any Relevant Authority and to pay such reasonable administration fee as the Transferor reasonably requires.

12.5.4 Not within the Restriction Period to alter the external appearance of the Building on the Property without the prior written consent of the Transferor and to pay such reasonable administration fee as the Transferor reasonably requires.

12.5.5 Not to erect any walls, fences or other structures nor allow any hedge to grow on the Property between any Building on the Property and the Estate Roads except as provided as at the date of this transfer.

12.5.6 Not to erect or exhibit on the Property any hoarding, structure, notice board or sign of any kind for advertising or other purpose except that after the Restriction Period has expired the Transferee may erect one notice or sign not exceeding one half square metre advertising the Property for sale.

12.5.7 Not to park or cause or suffer or permit to be parked any commercial vehicle, caravan, trailer, boat or unroadworthy vehicle on the Property between any building on the Property and the Estate Road.

12.5.8 Not to park on or obstruct the Estate Roads or the Shared Access (if any).

12.5.9 Not to park any commercial vehicle exceeding 1000 Kg GVW on the Property or on any part of the Estate (including any unadopted Estate Roads).

12.5.10 Not to keep or feed or breed or permit to be kept or fed or bred on the Property animals or birds other than the keeping (but not breeding) of a maximum of two normal household domestic pets.

12.5.11 Not to cut down, damage, neglect or remove any existing tree or hedge on the Property or any other plant planted pursuant to the requirements of the local planning authority.

12.5.12 To keep any garden (front and back) forming part of the Property well cultivated, tidy and free from weeds and not to permit the same to become unsightly, untidy or a nuisance to the Transferor or other adjoining owners or occupiers.

12.5.13 To keep grassed or planted any unenclosed parts of the garden of the Property excluding areas of hard surface constructed by the Transferor and to maintain in the position as previously existing or erected by the Transferor any Boundary Structure (together with any garden hedges, fences and walls not forming the boundary with an adjoining Plot on the Estate) in good condition, repairing or renewing to their original specification as necessary provided that hedges will be maintained so as not to exceed 3 metres in height.

12.5.14 To maintain repair and renew at the Transferee's sole cost any Boundary Structure on any boundary of the Property marked with an inward 'T' on the Plan (if any) or adjoining any Estate Road or public highway.

12.5.15 To keep in good condition and repair such parts of the Shared Access and Service Media (if any) as are within the Property.

12.5.16 To contribute on demand a fair proportion of the cost of inspecting, repairing and renewing the Service Media and the Shared Access (if any) which serve the Property jointly with other parts of the Estate or adjoining land and any Boundary Structure separating the Property and the Estate (except those adjoining the Estate Road or public highways or marked with an inward or outward 'T' on the Plan).

12.5.17 Immediately on request to execute any easement, deed or document required by a Relevant Authority in respect of the provision, maintenance or adoption of the Estate Roads or Estate Sewers or Service Media.

12.5.18 Not to do or permit or suffer to be done upon the Property or the Estate any act or thing which:

12.5.18.1 may impede the adoption or the vesting in the Relevant Authority of the Estate Roads or Estate Sewers or the Service Media which is or are intended to be so adopted or vested; or

12.5.18.2 may result in loss or damage to or interference with any Estate Road, Estate Sewer or Service Media within the Property which may be or become maintainable at the public expense or which is used jointly with the Transferor or with the owners or occupiers of the Estate or any adjoining or neighbouring land.

12.5.19 Not without the written consent of the appropriate Relevant Authority to plant or permit trees, shrubs or other plants to grow to a height exceeding 0.3 metres on any highway, verge or visibility splay or on that part of the Property between any sight line denoted on the Plan and any existing or intended public highway.

12.5.20 Not without the prior written consent of the Relevant Authority to cultivate, erect or place or suffer to be erected or placed any structure or other thing on or over the service strip (if any) between the boundary of the Property and the footpath or carriageway of the Estate Road and to maintain it as a grassed area.

12.5.21 Not to construct, erect, place, plant or permit upon, under or over the easement strip shown on the Plan (if any) or on or over any Shared Access or on or within 3 metres of the Estate Sewers (if any) or any part thereof, any building wall or other structure, erection or works of any kind whatsoever whether permanent or temporary or any trees or large shrubs without the prior written consent of the appropriate Relevant Authority.

12.5.22 Not to erect or place on the Property any satellite dish other than on the side or rear elevation of any dwelling on the Property and of a colour in keeping with the external appearance of the dwelling provided always that no satellite dish may be erected without permission from the Relevant Authority if required or on any elevation directly overlooking any public open space.

12.6 INDEMNITY COVENANTS BY THE TRANSFEREE

The Transferee covenants with the Transferor to observe and perform the covenants contained in the Charges Register of the title referred to above so far as they affect the Property and to indemnify the Transferor in respect of any costs, claims, demands and expenses arising from any future breach thereof.

12.7 TRANSFEROR'S COVENANTS

12.7.1 The Transferor covenants with the Transferee to construct and maintain the Estate Roads and the Estate Sewers intended to serve the Property and intended for adoption to the requirements of the appropriate Relevant Authority and to indemnify the Transferee against all costs, claims and demands arising from any failure to do so until the Estate Roads and Estate Sewers are adopted.

12.7.2 [The Transferor covenants with the Transferee to indemnify the Transferee against all liabilities resulting from non-performance or non-observance by the Transferor of the terms of the Planning Agreement].

The transferor must execute this transfer as a deed using the space opposite. If there is more than one transferor, all must execute. Forms of execution are given in Schedule 9 to the Land Registration Rules 2003. If the transfer contains transferee's covenants or declarations or contains an application by the transferee (such as for a restriction), it must also be executed by the transferee.

If there is more than one transferee and panel 11 has been completed, each transferee must also execute this transfer to comply with the requirements in section 53(1)(b) of the Law of Property Act 1925 relating to the declaration of a trust of land. Please refer to *Joint property ownership* and practice guide *24: private trusts of land* for further guidance.

Remember to date this deed in panel 4.

13 Execution

SIGNED as a DEED by
[*company name*] acting by:

Director

Director/Secretary

SIGNED as a DEED by
[*company name*] acting by:

Director

Director/Secretary

WARNING
If you dishonestly enter information or make a statement that you know is, or might be, untrue or misleading, and intend by doing so to make a gain for yourself or another person, or to cause loss or the risk of loss to another person, you may commit the offence of fraud under section 1 of the Fraud Act 2006, the maximum penalty for which is 10 years' imprisonment or an unlimited fine, or both.

Failure to complete this form with proper care may result in a loss of protection under the Land Registration Act 2002 if, as a result, a mistake is made in the register.

Under section 66 of the Land Registration Act 2002 most documents (including this form) kept by the registrar relating to an application to the registrar or referred to in the register are open to public inspection and copying. If you believe a document contains prejudicial information, you may apply for that part of the document to be made exempt using Form EX1, under rule 136 of the Land Registration Rules 2003.

APPENDIX C5

Sample form: Plot sale transfer with management company provisions

HM Land Registry
Transfer of part of registered title(s)

Any parts of the form that are not typed should be completed in black ink and in block capitals.

If you need more room than is provided for in a panel, and your software allows, you can expand any panel in the form. Alternatively use continuation sheet CS and attach it to this form.

For information on how HM Land Registry processes your personal information, see our Personal Information Charter.

Leave blank if not yet registered.	1 Title number(s) out of which the property is transferred:
When application for registration is made these title number(s) should be entered in panel 2 of Form AP1.	2 Other title number(s) against which matters contained in this transfer are to be registered or noted, if any:
Insert address, including postcode (if any), or other description of the property transferred. Any physical exclusions, such as mines and minerals, should be defined.	3 Property:
Place 'X' in the appropriate box and complete the statement.	The property is identified
For example 'edged red'.	☐ on the attached plan and shown:
For example 'edged and numbered 1 in blue'.	☐ on the title plan(s) of the above titles and shown:
Any plan lodged must be signed by the transferor.	
Remember to date this deed with the day of completion, but not before it has been signed and witnessed.	4 Date:
Give full name(s) of **all** of the persons transferring the property.	5 Transferor:
Complete as appropriate where the transferor is a company.	For UK incorporated companies/LLPs Registered number of company or limited liability partnership including any prefix: For overseas companies (a) Territory of incorporation: (b) Registered number in the United Kingdom including any prefix:
Give full name(s) of **all** the persons to be shown as registered proprietors.	6 Transferee for entry in the register:
Complete as appropriate where the transferee is a company. Also, for an overseas company, unless an arrangement with HM Land Registry exists, lodge either a certificate in Form 7 in Schedule 3 to the Land Registration Rules 2003 or a certified copy of the constitution in English or Welsh, or other evidence permitted by rule 183 of the Land Registration Rules 2003.	For UK incorporated companies/LLPs Registered number of company or limited liability partnership including any prefix: For overseas companies (a) Territory of incorporation: (b) Registered number in the United Kingdom including any prefix:

Each transferee may give up to three addresses for service, one of which must be a postal address whether or not in the UK (including the postcode, if any). The others can be any combination of a postal address, a UK DX box number or an electronic address.

7 Transferee's intended address(es) for service for entry in the register:

8 The transferor transfers the property to the transferee

Place 'X' in the appropriate box. State the currency unit if other than sterling. If none of the boxes apply, insert an appropriate memorandum in panel 12.

9 Consideration

☐ The transferor has received from the transferee for the property the following sum (in words and figures):

☐ The transfer is not for money or anything that has a monetary value

☐ Insert other receipt as appropriate:

Place 'X' in any box that applies.

Add any modifications.

10 The transferor transfers with

☐ full title guarantee

☐ limited title guarantee

Where the transferee is more than one person, place 'X' in the appropriate box.

11 Declaration of trust. The transferee is more than one person and

☐ they are to hold the property on trust for themselves as joint tenants

☐ they are to hold the property on trust for themselves as tenants in common in equal shares

Complete as necessary.

☐ they are to hold the property on trust:

The registrar will enter a Form A restriction in the register *unless*:

- an 'X' is placed:
  - in the first box, or
  - in the third box and the details of the trust or of the trust instrument show that the transferees are to hold the property on trust for themselves alone as joint tenants, *or*
- it is clear from completion of a form JO lodged with this application that the transferees are to hold the property on trust for themselves alone as joint tenants.

Please refer to *Joint property ownership* and *practice guide 24: private trusts of land* for further guidance. These are both available on the GOV.UK website.

Use this panel for:
- definitions of terms not defined above
- rights granted or reserved
- restrictive covenants
- other covenants
- agreements and declarations
- any required or permitted statements
- other agreed provisions.

The prescribed subheadings may be added to, amended, repositioned or omitted.

Any other land affected by rights granted or reserved or by restrictive covenants should be defined by reference to a plan.

12 Additional provisions

12.1 DEFINITIONS

'Accountant' means an independent accountant to be appointed by the Management Company who is a member of a body of accountants established in the United Kingdom and for the time being recognised by the Secretary of State for the purpose of the Companies Act 2006;

'Accountants Certificate' means a written statement containing a breakdown of the Expenses and specifying the Service Charge payable by the Transferee which will be conclusive and binding on the Management Company, the Transferee and the Transferor as regards all matters contained, specified or certified therein (other than any question of law) to the extent permitted by statute;

'Boundary Structure' means any wall, fence, hedge, tree, retaining wall or other structure on any boundary of the Property;

'Building' means a house, bungalow, other structure with living quarters, garage, car port, constructed or to be constructed on the Estate by the Transferor;

'Common Parts' means all landscaped areas (if any) within the Estate, [any pumping station, the Services (which do not fall within the boundaries of other Plots but which are intended to serve the Property and the other Plots on the Estate),] and any other areas and facilities intended to be used in common by the Property and the other Plots (but excluding any areas and facilities which become or which are intended to become adopted or which fall within the boundaries of other Plots) including (without prejudice to the generality thereof) the area shown on the Plan as land owned and maintained by the Management Company; **[NOTE: Amend as necessary]**

'Estate' means all the land (except the Property and the site of any electricity substation, gas governor or water pumping station) now or formerly comprised in the title number in Panel 2 and on which the Transferor is carrying out development and which is known as [ ] together with any other land acquired or which may be acquired by the Transferor within the Perpetuity Period adjacent to or adjoining such land to form part of or ancillary to the proposed development of such land;

'Estate Roads' means all roads, verges, footpaths now or within the Perpetuity Period constructed within the Estate which are intended to become public highway;

'Estate Sewers' means the surface water and foul sewers now or within the Perpetuity Period constructed within the Estate which are intended to become public sewers;

'Expenses' means in respect of each Financial Year the costs incurred by the Management Company in carrying out its obligations as specified in clause 12.10 under the heading 'Obligations of the Management Company' and the expenses incurred by the Management Company as specified in clause 12.11 under the heading 'The expenses incurred by the Management Company in carrying out its obligations';

'Financial Year' means the period from 1 January in each year to 31 December in each year or such other annual period as the Management Company may in its absolute discretion determine;

'Interim Payment' means such amount as in the opinion of the Surveyor fairly represents 50 per cent of the Service Charge for the current Financial Year;

'Management Company', **'Managing Agents'** means The [ ] Management Company Limited (CRN [ ]) registered office [ ] the managing agents for the time being of the Management Company or if none the Management Company;

'Perpetuity Period' [80] years from [*date*];

'Plan' means the attached plan;

[**'Planning Agreement'** means the agreement dated [ ] and made between [ ] Council (1) [ ] (2) and [ ] (3) under or by virtue of section 106 of the Town and Country Planning Act 1990];

'Plots' means each plot on the Estate intended for residential occupation;

'Projections' means all foundations, chimneys, eaves, guttering, drainpipes, fence posts, wall piers and similar projections (and, temporarily during the course of construction and for essential maintenance, scaffolding);

'Relevant Authority' means all statutory corporations, local or other authorities and all bodies exercising statutory rights powers or obligations which will include but is not limited to highway, planning, drainage, water, electricity, gas and telecommunications suppliers and any other authority or body or company to which the powers of such authority body or company are delegated;

'Restriction Period' means the period expiring on the earlier of expiry of five years from the date of this Transfer or the date the Transferor has developed and physically left the Estate;

'Service Charge' means such proportion as may be reasonably determined by the Management Company of the Expenses [(a) the cost to the Management Company of carrying out its obligations hereunder during the financial year in question and (b) the expenses incurred by the Management Company in carrying out such obligations during the financial year in question;]

'Service Media' means all conducting media and apparatus (excluding the Estate Sewers) for foul and surface water, drainage, gas, light, water, oil, electricity, telephone, electronic transmissions and similar services now or within the Perpetuity Period constructed within the Estate or the Property;

'Shared Access' means the area (if any) which forms or is intended to form the site of an access drive and/or footpath jointly serving the Property and adjoining or neighbouring dwellings but not intended to become public highway and will include (for the avoidance of doubt) those areas which also run beneath a structure (with or without living quarters) constructed by the Transferor above ground level;

'Surveyor' means any surveyor employed by the Management Company.

12.2 DECLARATIONS

It is agreed and declared by the Transferor and the Transferee as follows:

12.2.1 Section 62 of the Law of Property Act 1925 and the rule in *Wheeldon* v. *Burrows* do not apply to this Transfer and no legal or other rights are granted over the Estate for the benefit of the Property or granted over the Property for the benefit of the Estate except for those expressly granted or reserved by this Transfer.

12.2.2 The expressions the 'Transferor', the 'Management Company' and the 'Transferee' include their respective successors in title unless specifically excluded.

12.2.3 The singular includes the plural and the masculine includes the feminine and vice versa and where there are two or more persons included in the Transferee any obligation or agreement in this deed will bind them both individually and jointly.

12.2.4 All future rights granted in this transfer must be exercised within the Perpetuity Period which is to be the perpetuity period applicable to this transfer.

12.2.5 No building scheme will be created by this transfer and the Transferor may modify, waive or release any covenants set out in clause 12.5.

12.2.6 The covenants in clause 12.5 are enforceable between the Transferor and the Transferee and also between the purchasers of Plots on the Estate.

12.2.7 The covenants in clause 12.5 will cease to be binding between the Transferor and the Transferee (but not as between the Transferee and any other owner of any part of the Estate) after expiry of the Restriction Period.

12.2.8 The Transferor is not liable to the Transferee or his successors in title for any breaches of covenants or conditions committed by the purchasers or lessees on any other plot on the Estate and the Transferor is not obliged to take proceedings to enforce those covenants, restrictions, stipulations and conditions.

12.2.9 The Transferor is not bound by any scheme of development of the Estate as shown on any plans or documents and is entitled to sell the Estate in such plots or parcels and subject to such rights, declarations and covenants as it considers appropriate and is entitled to vary the same and vary the layout of the Estate as it considers fit.

12.2.10 Any person exercising the rights in clauses 12.3 and 12.4 will not do so unreasonably and will cause as little damage and inconvenience as reasonably possible and will repair any damage caused as quickly as possible.

12.2.11 The Transferee will if requested by the Transferor enter into any necessary deed of grant or variation in respect of easements relating to the Service Media, Estate Sewers or Estate Roads.

12.2.12 All Boundary Structures separating the Property and the Estate (except those adjoining the Estate Road or public highways or marked with an inward or outward 'T' on the Plan) and any walls separating Buildings on the Property from any other Buildings on the Estate are party Boundary Structures and are to be maintained accordingly.

12.2.13 The use of all Shared Accesses, Service Media and Boundary Structures and any other things now or to be constructed by the Transferor intended for shared use by the Transferee and the owners of any other parts of the Estate is conditional on the Transferee paying a fair proportion of the costs incurred in their inspection, maintenance and renewal by the Transferor or any person sharing their use and/or enjoyment and any dispute about the amount to be paid will be settled by the written certificate of an independent surveyor acting as an expert appointed by agreement between the parties to the dispute or failing agreement by the President of the Royal Institution of Chartered Surveyors on the application of any party to the dispute.

12.3 RIGHTS GRANTED

The following rights are granted to the Transferee and all others authorised by the Transferor (in common with all other persons having a similar right).

12.3.1 A right of way over:

12.3.1.1 the Estate Roads until they become maintainable at public expense;

12.3.1.2 any Shared Access (but on foot only over footpaths) which serves the Property but is not within the red edging on the Plan.

12.3.2 A right to use the Estate Sewers until they become maintainable at public expense.

12.3.3 The right to connect to and use, inspect, maintain and renew any Service Media on the Estate which serve the Property.

12.3.4 The right of support and protection to the Property and any Building on the Property.

12.3.5 The right to keep and use on adjoining parts of the Estate any Projections from the Property as constructed by the Transferor.

12.3.6 The right to enter upon adjoining parts of the Estate to inspect, maintain or renew any part of any Shared Access which serves the Property and any part of the Property or the Service Media serving the Property.

12.3.7 The right to the benefit of all covenants by other owners of any part of the Estate which attach to the Property.

12.3.8 A right to use the Common Parts for all reasonable purposes connected with the use of the Property.

12.4 RIGHTS RESERVED

Except as mentioned below these rights are reserved for the benefit of any part or parts of the Estate and any other land acquired by the Transferor within the Perpetuity Period which is capable of benefiting from them and also for the benefit of the Management Company and any Relevant Authority and of any other persons authorised by them or by the Transferor.

12.4.1 Rights of way with or without vehicles at all times over any Shared Access which is part of the Property but the use of which is shared and serves any other parts of the Estate or any land adjoining the Estate.

12.4.2 Rights to connect to and use, inspect, maintain and renew any Service Media which cross the Property.

12.4.3 Rights to keep and use on the Property any Projections from any Buildings adjoining the Property now or to be constructed by the Transferor.

12.4.4 Rights to tie in adjoining Buildings and of support and protection from the Property for any land or Buildings adjoining the Property.

12.4.5 Rights to enter on the Property to inspect, maintain or renew any Shared Access forming part of the Property and any part of any building adjoining the Property constructed by the Transferor.

12.4.6 Rights to enter the Property to alter any existing Service Media and to lay new Service Media and to use, inspect, maintain and renew any Service Media.

12.4.7 Rights to enter the Property in order to construct any Projections and any walls or fences relating to adjoining land or Buildings.

12.4.8 Rights to enter the Property for the purpose of complying with the proper requirements of the Management Company and/or any Relevant Authority.

12.4.9 Rights to enter the Property to plant trees or shrubs or to carry out landscaping operations or to fulfil the requirements of any relevant planning permission.

12.4.10 Rights to enter the Property for the purpose of re-locating any Boundary Structures or other boundary markers (in respect of which the Transferee will not be entitled to object or to claim compensation) if as a result of a subsequent as built survey it is shown that such Boundary Structures or markers have not been erected in the position shown on the Plan.

12.4.11 Rights of support and protection for the Estate by the Property.

12.4.12 The right for the Transferee only at any time during the Restriction Period to erect, maintain and keep any advertisement board or hoarding or directional sign on the Property such boards or signs to be of such size dimensions and design as the Transferor in its absolute discretion determines subject to the Transferor making good any damage caused to the Property by the exercise of such right.

12.5 TRANSFEREE'S COVENANTS

The Transferee so as to bind the Property and each and every part and to benefit the Estate and each and every part covenants with the Transferor (and as a separate covenant with every other person who is now the owner of any part of the Estate) to observe and perform the following covenants, restrictions and stipulations and conditions but not so as to render the Transferee personally liable for any breach after he has disposed of his legal interest in the Property.

12.5.1 Not to use the Property for any purpose other than as or incidental to one private residential dwelling and not to use the Property for any trade or business.

12.5.2 Not to do or permit or suffer to be done on the Property anything which may be or become a nuisance or annoyance or cause damage to the Transferor or to the owners, tenants or occupiers of any adjoining or neighbouring property.

12.5.3 Not to erect or construct within the Restriction Period any building or other structure whatsoever whether temporary or permanent on the Property without the prior consent in writing of the Transferor and if required any Relevant Authority and to pay such reasonable administration fee as the Transferor reasonably requires.

12.5.4 Not within the Restriction Period to alter the external appearance of the dwellinghouse on the Property without the prior written consent of the Transferor.

12.5.5 Not to erect any walls, fences or other structures nor allow any hedge to grow on the Property between any Building on the Property and the Estate Roads except as provided as at the date of this transfer.

12.5.6 Not to erect or exhibit on the Property any hoarding, structure, notice board or sign of any kind for advertising or other purpose except that after the Restriction Period has expired the Transferee may erect one notice or sign not exceeding one half square metre advertising the Property for sale.

12.5.7 Not to erect or place on the Property any satellite dish other than on the side or rear elevation of any dwelling on the Property and of a colour in keeping with the external appearance of the dwelling provided always that no satellite dish may be erected without permission from the Relevant Authority if required or on any elevation directly overlooking any public open space.

12.5.8 Not to cut down, damage, neglect or remove any existing tree or hedge on the Property or any other plant planted pursuant to the requirements of the local planning authority.

12.5.9 To keep any garden front and back forming part of the Property well cultivated, tidy and free from weeds and not to permit the same to become unsightly, untidy or a nuisance to the Transferor or other adjoining owners or occupiers.

12.5.10 To keep grassed any unenclosed parts of the garden of the

Property excluding planted areas and areas of hard surface and to keep all parts of the garden neat and tidy and to maintain in the position as previously existing or erected by the Transferor any Boundary Structures (together with any garden hedges, fences and walls not forming the boundary with an adjoining Plot on the Estate) in good condition, repairing or renewing to their original specification as necessary **PROVIDED THAT** hedges will be maintained so as not to exceed 3 metres in height.

12.5.11 Not to keep or feed or breed or permit to be kept or fed or bred on the Property animals or birds other than the keeping (but not breeding) of a maximum of two normal household domestic pets.

12.5.12 Not to park or cause or suffer or permit to be parked any commercial vehicle, caravan, trailer, boat or unroadworthy vehicle on the Property between any building on the Property and the Estate Road.

12.5.13 Not to park on or obstruct the Estate Roads or the Shared Access (if any).

12.5.14 Not to park any commercial vehicle exceeding 1000 Kg GVW on the Property or on any part of the Estate (including any unadopted Estate Roads).

12.5.15 To maintain, repair and renew any Boundary Structure on any boundary of the Property marked with an inward 'T' on the Plan (if any).

12.5.16 To keep in good condition and repair such parts of the Shared Access and Service Media (if any) as are within the Property.

12.5.17 To contribute on demand a fair proportion of the cost of inspecting, repairing and renewing the Service Media and the Shared Access (if any) which serve the Property jointly with other parts of the Estate or adjoining land.

12.5.18 Not without the prior written consent of the Relevant Authority to cultivate, erect or place or suffer to be erected or placed any structure or other thing on or over the service strip (if any) between the boundary of the Property and the footpath or carriageway of the Estate Road and to maintain it as a grassed area.

12.5.19 Not to construct, erect, place, plant or permit upon, under or over the easement strip shown on the Plan (if any) or on or over any Shared Access or on or within 3 metres of the Estate Sewers (if any) or any part thereof, any building, wall or other structure, erection or works of any kind whatsoever whether permanent or temporary or any trees or large shrubs without the prior written consent of the appropriate Relevant Authority.

12.5.20 Immediately on request to execute any easement deed or document required by a Relevant Authority in respect of the provision, maintenance or adoption of the Estate Roads or Estate Sewers or Service Media.

12.5.21 Not to do or permit or suffer to be done upon the property or the Estate any act or thing which:

12.5.21.1 may impede the adoption or the vesting in the Relevant Authority of the Estate Roads or Estate Sewers or the Service Media which is or are intended to be so adopted or vested or;

12.5.21.2 may result in loss or damage to or interference with any Estate Road, Estate Sewer or Service Media within the Property which may be or become maintainable at the public expense or which is used jointly with the Transferor or with the owners or occupiers of the Estate or any adjoining or neighbouring land.

12.5.22 Not without the written consent of the appropriate Relevant Authority to plant or permit trees, shrubs or other plants to grow to a height exceeding 0.3 metres on any highway verge or visibility splay or on that part of the Property between any sight line denoted on the Plan and any existing or intended public highway.

12.6 INDEMNITY COVENANTS BY THE TRANSFEREE

The Transferee covenants with the Transferor to observe and perform the covenants contained in the Charges Register of the title referred to above so far as they affect the Property and to indemnify the Transferor in respect of any costs, claims, demands and expenses arising from any future breach thereof.

12.7 TRANSFEROR'S COVENANTS

12.7.1 The Transferor covenants with the Transferee to construct and maintain the Estate Roads and the Estate Sewers intended to serve the Property and intended for adoption to the requirements of the appropriate Relevant Authority and to indemnify the Transferee against all costs, claims and demands arising from any failure to do so until the Estate Roads and Estate Sewers are adopted.

12.7.2 [The Transferor covenants with the Transferee to indemnify the Transferee against all liabilities resulting from non-performance or non-observance by the Transferor of the terms of the Planning Agreement.]

12.8 MANAGEMENT COMPANY PROVISIONS

12.8.1 **Declarations**

It is agreed and declared by the Transferor and the Transferee and the Management Company as follows:

12.8.1.1 that the Management Company will not be liable for any breach of the covenants contained in this transfer unless and until a notice in writing has been received by the Management Company specifying the breach and the Management Company has had a reasonable opportunity to remedy the same;

12.8.1.2 that the Transferee will not be entitled to enforce any of the covenants while any sums payable by the Transferee under the terms of this transfer are in arrears or the Transferee is otherwise in substantial breach of the covenants on his part contained in this transfer;

12.8.1.3 the Management Company will not be liable or

responsible for any loss or damage suffered by the Transferee or any visitor or employee of the Transferee or any other person including any other person occupying the Property to themselves, their personal effects or to the Property by reason of any neglect or default of the Management Company or of any agent, contractor, employee or licensee of the Management Company by reason of theft or otherwise from any part of the Common Parts or by reason of any defect or want of repair in the Common Parts or on any part thereof or in equipment provided thereon or the absence of lighting in or upon the Common Parts or any part thereof or from any other cause except in so far as any such liability may be covered by the Management Company under insurance effected by the Management Company.

12.9 POSITIVE COVENANTS BY THE TRANSFEREE WITH THE MANAGEMENT COMPANY

The Transferee covenants with the Management Company:

12.9.1 On the 1st January and the 1st July in each year to pay on account of the Service Charge the Interim Payment in advance.

12.9.2 Upon receipt of the Accountant's Certificate forthwith to pay to the Management Company the balance (if any) of the Service Charge mentioned therein after allowing for payments on account.

12.9.3 To pay to the Management Company on a full indemnity basis all costs incurred by the Management Company or its solicitors in enforcing payment of monies due from the Transferee under the terms of this Transfer.

12.9.4 Not to transfer the Property or any part thereof without (i) first notifying the Management Company in writing of the intention to do so; and (ii) simultaneously requiring the relevant transferee to become a member of the Management Company and upon completion of such transfer to enter into a deed of covenant with the Management Company (in a form to be approved (such approval not to be unreasonably withheld or delayed) by the Management Company) to observe and perform the covenants set out herein.

12.9.5 Upon the transfer of the Property or upon the devolution of the legal estate therein howsoever arising the Transferee will immediately give to the Management Company or its Solicitors notice in writing thereof with full registration of such particulars and will pay a reasonable fee but not less than £40.00 plus VAT for the notice and the Management Company covenants with the Transferee that upon receipt of such notice and upon payment of any unpaid Service Charge it will give to the person lodging the same a certificate in accordance with clause 12.13.

12.9.6 To comply with the rules from time to time made by the Management Company in connection with the running and management of the Common Parts and to ensure that any occupiers and/or lessees of the Property comply with such rules.

12.10 OBLIGATIONS OF THE MANAGEMENT COMPANY

Subject to the due performance by the Transferee of his obligations to pay the Interim Payment and the Service Charge the Management Company covenants with the Transferee:

12.10.1 To keep the Common Parts in good repair and condition and to clean, renew, maintain, replace, repair and cultivate as appropriate in accordance with the principles of good estate management the Common Parts.

12.10.2 To keep the Common Parts properly lit as the Management Company in the interests of good estate management deems appropriate.

12.10.3 To pay all rates and other outgoings assessed or charged upon the Common Parts.

12.10.4 To effect insurance against the liability of the Management Company to third parties against such risks and in such amount and through such insurers, underwriters and through such agency as the Management Company in its absolute discretion thinks fit and to make all payments necessary for effecting and maintaining such policy or policies of insurance within seven days after they become payable and to produce to the Transferee on demand (but not more than once in each year) the said policy or policies and the receipt for or other evidence of every such payment.

12.10.5 To carry out such additional works and provide such additional services as it may consider necessary or beneficial to the residents of the Property and the other Plots from time to time.

12.10.6 In advance of (or as early as may be in) each Financial Year to determine and notify in writing to the Transferee (or to procure that the Surveyor so determines and notifies) the amount of the Interim Payment PROVIDED that if in the opinion of the Surveyor the Interim Payment should continue the same as in the previous Financial Year no further notification need be given.

12.10.7 That it will as soon as practicable on or after the end of each Financial Year cause the amount of the Expenses for such year to be determined by the Accountant and the Accountants Certificate to be issued.

12.10.8 To hold any monies received by the Transferee from time to time by way of Service Charge and not actually expended by it or otherwise dealt with so as to be an allowable expense calculating the Management Company's Income Tax liability upon trust to expend them upon the matters in this clause hereinbefore mentioned and subject thereto upon trust for the Transferee absolutely.

12.11 THE EXPENSES INCURRED BY THE MANAGEMENT COMPANY IN CARRYING OUT ITS OBLIGATIONS

12.11.1 The costs of employing contractors to carry out any of the Management Company's obligations under this transfer or if any repairs, redecorations, renewals, maintenance, cultivation or cleaning are carried out by the Management Company itself their normal charges (including profit) in respect thereof.

12.11.2 The fees and disbursements paid to any surveyor or the Managing Agents employed by the Management Company in respect of the management of the Common Parts.

12.11.3 The fees and disbursements paid to any accountant, solicitor or other professional person in relation to the preparation, auditing or certification of any account of the costs, expenses, outgoings and matters referred to in this schedule.

12.11.4 A reasonable sum for administrative expenses and where no Managing Agent is appointed management expenses to be retained by the Management Company **PROVIDED THAT** such sum may be determined from time to time by the Accountant whose determination will be final and binding.

12.11.5 Any Value Added Tax or tax of a similar nature payable in respect of any costs, expenses, outgoings or matters falling within any clause under this heading.

12.11.6 Paying any taxes which may be assessed or charged on the Service Charge.

12.11.7 Such sum as is estimated by the Managing Agents or if none the Management Company (whose decision will be final) to provide a reserve to meet part or all of any sums or any of the costs, expenses, outgoings and matters mentioned in the foregoing paragraphs which the Managing Agents (or if none the Managing Company) anticipate will or may arise such calculation to have regard to the monies at any time standing to the credit of such reserve fund.

12.11.8 All other expenses (if any) incurred by the Management Company in or about the maintenance and proper and convenient management and running of the Common Parts and any interest paid on any money borrowed by the Management Company to defray any expenses incurred by it and specified under this heading.

12.11.9 Paying or making such provisions as the Management Company thinks fit for pensions annuity or retirement or disability benefits for staff on the termination of their employment.

12.11.10 Carrying out such repairs to any part of the Common Parts for which the Management Company may be responsible and supplying such other services for the benefit of the Transferee and the owners of other properties on the Development and carrying out such improvements, works or additions as the Management Company considers necessary in the general interest of the Transferee and other such persons.

12.12 ADJUSTMENT OF SERVICE CHARGE

If in the reasonable opinion of the Management Company the Transferee's liability hereunder to contribute towards the costs and expenses incurred by the Management Company in complying with its obligations hereunder is inequitable (having regard to the expenditure incurred or the premises in the Development or any other cause) the Management Company is at liberty in its discretion to adjust such liability to a fair and reasonable amount or proportion (to be certified by the Surveyor) and this procedure will be repeated as often as circumstances require.

12.13 RESTRICTION

The parties apply to the Chief Land Registrar to enter a restriction on the Proprietorship Register of the title to the Property in the following terms (or as close thereto as the Land Registry will permit):

'No disposition of the registered estate other than a charge by the proprietor of the registered estate is to be registered without a certificate signed on behalf of [ ] Management Company Limited of [ ] by its Secretary or Conveyancer that the provisions of Clauses 12.9.4 AND 12.9.5 of the Transfer dated [date] referred to in the Charges Register have been complied with.'

The transferor must execute this transfer as a deed using the space opposite. If there is more than one transferor, all must execute. Forms of execution are given in Schedule 9 to the Land Registration Rules 2003. If the transfer contains transferee's covenants or declarations or contains an application by the transferee (such as for a restriction), it must also be executed by the transferee.

If there is more than one transferee and panel 11 has been completed, each transferee must also execute this transfer to comply with the requirements in section 53(1)(b) of the Law of Property Act 1925 relating to the declaration of a trust of land. Please refer to *Joint property ownership* and practice guide *24: private trusts of land* for further guidance.

Remember to date this deed in panel 4.

13 Execution

Signed as a DEED by

In the presence of:

Witness signature:

Witness name:

Witness occupation:

Witness address:

WARNING
If you dishonestly enter information or make a statement that you know is, or might be, untrue or misleading, and intend by doing so to make a gain for yourself or another person, or to cause loss or the risk of loss to another person, you may commit the offence of fraud under section 1 of the Fraud Act 2006, the maximum penalty for which is 10 years' imprisonment or an unlimited fine, or both.

Failure to complete this form with proper care may result in a loss of protection under the Land Registration Act 2002 if, as a result, a mistake is made in the register.

Under section 66 of the Land Registration Act 2002 most documents (including this form) kept by the registrar relating to an application to the registrar or referred to in the register are open to public inspection and copying. If you believe a document contains prejudicial information, you may apply for that part of the document to be made exempt using Form EX1, under rule 136 of the Land Registration Rules 2003.

APPENDIX C6

Deed of covenant (to be entered into by the transferor's successor in title)

DATED: 20[ ]

(1) [ ]

and

(2) [ ]

DEED OF COVENANT

(to be entered into by a successor in title of the Transferor)

relating to

[ ]

PARTICULARS

Date:	[ ]
New Owner:	[Company name] (Company registration number [ ]) [of] [whose registered office is at] [ ]
Adjoining Owner:	[insert details of the original transferee or the successor in title of the original transferee]
Original Transfer:	A transfer of the Property [and other land] dated [ ] made between [ ] (1) and [ ] (2)
Original Transferor:	[ ]
the Covenants:	The covenants and obligations of the Original Transferor contained in clause [ ] of the Original Transfer
Property:	The property known as [ ] [being part of the land] registered at the Land Registry under title number(s) [ ] [and shown edged red on the attached plan]
Retained Land:	The property shown edged in [blue] on the attached plan
[**Relevant Part**]:	That part of the Retained Land to be purchased by the New Owner and shown [ ] on the attached plan

THE DEED OF COVENANT is made on the date set out in the Particulars

BETWEEN

(1) the New Owner; and
(2) the Adjoining Owner.

BACKGROUND

(A) The New Owner has agreed to purchase [the Retained Land] [the Relevant Part].
(B) The Adjoining Owner is the owner of the Property.
(C) The New Owner has agreed to enter into this Deed of Covenant pursuant to the terms of the Original Transfer.

OPERATIVE PROVISIONS

1 CONSTRUCTION

1.1 References to the New Owner are to the New Owner and its successors in title to [the Retained Land] [the Relevant Part] and references to the Adjoining Owner are to the Adjoining Owner and its successors in title and express assigns.
1.2 References to [the Retained Land] [the Relevant Part] include the whole and every part of [the Retained Land] [the Relevant Part].
1.3 The parties to this Deed do not intend that any of its terms will be enforceable by virtue of the Contracts (Rights of Third Parties) Act 1999 by any person not a party to it.
1.4 The Particulars form part of this Deed.

2 COVENANT

The New Owner covenants [jointly and individually] with the Adjoining Owner that the New Owner:

2.1 will comply with the Covenants in so far as the same are still subsisting and to the extent that the obligations comprised in the Covenants remain to be discharged [so far as they relate to the Relevant Part] and will indemnify the Adjoining Owner against all costs, damages, expenses, liabilities and losses arising from their breach occasioned after the date hereof; and
2.2 will not effect any transfer of [the Retained Land] [the Relevant Part] or any part of it without procuring that the transferee enters into a direct covenant with the Adjoining Owner on the terms of this Deed of Covenant [provided that:

2.2.1 [in no event shall a Deed of Covenant be required in respect of any transfer of one or more individual dwellings on [the Retained Land] [the Relevant Part] or the freehold reversion of such dwellings sold on long leasehold or the transfer of any land for a substation, pumping station or similar service facilities or of open space, land or the transfer of any land which is to be adopted or the transfer of any land required for affordable housing under a planning agreement];
2.2.2 the New Owner and any person who has previously executed a Deed of Covenant shall be released from all obligations upon a successor giving a further Deed of Covenant to the extent that the successor covenants to observe such obligations in the further Deed of Covenant].

3 RESTRICTION

The New Owner covenants with the Adjoining Owner to apply to the Land Registry as soon as reasonably practicable after the date of this Deed for a restriction to be entered against the Title Number [to be allocated] to [the Retained Land] [the Relevant Part] in the following form:

> 'No disposition [(other than a charge)] by the proprietor of the registered estate or by the proprietor of any registered charge, not being a charge registered before the entry of this restriction, is to be registered without a certificate signed by [a conveyancer] [the applicant for registration or their conveyancer] that the provisions of clause 2.2 of the Deed of Covenant dated [date] made between [ ] [ ] (1) and [ ](2) have been complied with [or do not apply].'

4 EXECUTION

The New Owner has executed this Deed of Covenant as a deed and it is delivered on the date set out in the Particulars.

THE COMMON SEAL of [ ] was affixed to this Deed in the presence of [ ]

Director

Director/Secretary

EXECUTED as a DEED by [ ] acting by [ ]

Director

Director/Secretary

APPENDIX C7

Deed of covenant (to be entered into by the transferee's successor in title)

DATED: 20[ ]

(1) [ ]

and

(2) [ ]

DEED OF COVENANT

(to be entered into by a successor in title of the Transferee) relating to

[ ]

PARTICULARS

Date:	[ ]
New Owner:	[company name] (Company registration number [ ]) [of] [whose registered office is at] [ ]
Adjoining Owner:	[insert details of transferor or successor in title of the transferor]
Original Transfer:	A transfer of the Property [and other land] dated [ ] made between [ ] (1) and [ ] (2)
Original Transferee:	[ ]
The Covenants:	The covenants and obligations of the Original Transferee contained in clause [ ] of the Original Transfer
Property:	The property known as [ ] [being part of the land] registered at the Land Registry under title number(s) [ ] [and shown edged red on the attached plan]
Retained Land:	The property shown edged in [blue] on the attached plan
[**Relevant Part**]:	That part of the Property to be purchased by the New Owner and shown [ ] on the attached plan

THIS DEED OF COVENANT is made on the date set out in the Particulars

BETWEEN:

(1) the New Owner; and
(2) the Adjoining Owner.

BACKGROUND

(A) The New Owner has agreed to purchase [the Property] [the Relevant Part].
(B) The Adjoining Owner is the owner of the Retained Land.
(C) The New Owner has agreed to enter into this Deed of Covenant pursuant to the terms of the Original Transfer.

OPERATIVE PROVISIONS

1 CONSTRUCTION

1.1 References to the New Owner are to the New Owner and its successors in title to [the Property] [the Relevant Part] and references to the Adjoining Owner are to the Adjoining Owner and its successors in title and express assigns.
1.2 References to [the Property] [the Relevant Part] include the whole and every part of [the Property] [the Relevant Part].
1.3 The parties to this Deed do not intend that any of its terms will be enforceable by virtue of the Contracts (Rights of Third Parties) Act 1999 by any person not a party to it.
1.4 The Particulars form part of this Deed.

2 COVENANT

The New Owner covenants [jointly and individually] with the Adjoining Owner that the New Owner:

2.1 will comply with the Covenants in so far as the same are still subsisting and to the extent that the obligations comprised in the Covenants remain to be discharged [so far as they relate to the Relevant Part] and will indemnify the Adjoining Owner against all costs, damages, expenses, liabilities and losses arising from their breach occasioned after the date hereof; and
2.2 will not effect any transfer of [the Property] [the Relevant Part] or any part of it without procuring that the transferee enters into a direct covenant with the Adjoining Owner on the terms of this Deed of Covenant [provided that:

2.2.1 [in no event shall a Deed of Covenant be required in respect of any transfer of one or more individual dwellings on [the Property] [the Relevant Part] or the freehold reversion of such dwellings sold on long leasehold or the transfer of any land for a substation pumping station or similar service facilities or of open space, land or the transfer of any land which is to be adopted or the transfer of any land required for affordable housing under a planning agreement];
2.2.2 [the New Owner and any person who has previously executed a Deed of Covenant shall be released from all obligations upon a successor giving a further Deed of Covenant to the extent that the successor covenants to observe such obligations in the further Deed of Covenant]].

3 RESTRICTION

The New Owner covenants with the Adjoining Owner to apply to the Land Registry as soon as reasonably practicable after the date of this Deed for a restriction to be entered against the Title Number [to be allocated] to [the Property] [the Relevant Part] in the following form:

> 'No disposition [(other than a charge)] by the proprietor of the registered estate or by the proprietor of any registered charge, not being a charge registered before the entry of this restriction, is to be registered without a certificate signed by [a conveyancer] [the applicant for registration or their conveyancer] the provisions of clause 2.2 of the Deed of Covenant dated [date] made between [ ] [ ] (1) and [ ] (2) have been complied with [or do not apply].'

4 EXECUTION

The New Owner has executed this Deed of Covenant as a deed and it is delivered on the date set out in the Particulars.

THE COMMON SEAL of [ ] was affixed to this Deed in the presence of [ ]

Director

Director/Secretary

EXECUTED as a DEED by [ ] acting by [ ]

Director

Director/Secretary

APPENDIX C8

Deed of covenant (to be entered into by the grantor's successor in title)

DATED: 20[ ]

(1) [ ]

and

(2) [ ]

DEED OF COVENANT

(to be entered into by a successor in title of the Grantor) relating to

[ ]

PARTICULARS

Date:	[ ]
New Owner:	[company name] (Company registration number [ ]) [of] [whose registered office is at] [ ]
Adjoining Owner:	[insert details of original grantee or the party who currently owns the land which benefits from the deed of easement]
Original Deed:	A deed of easement dated [ ] made between [ ] (1) and [ ] (2) relating to the Property
the Covenants:	The covenants and obligations of [ ] contained in clause [ ] of the Original Deed
Property:	The property known as [ ] [being part of the land] registered at the Land Registry under title number(s) [ ] [and shown edged red on the attached plan]
[**Relevant Part**]:	That part of the Property to be purchased by the New Owner and shown [ ] on the attached plan

THIS DEED OF COVENANT is made on the date set out in the Particulars

BETWEEN

(1) the New Owner; and
(2) the Adjoining Owner.

BACKGROUND

(A) The New Owner has agreed to purchase [the Property] [the Relevant Part].

(B) The Adjoining Owner is the owner of the land which has the benefit of the rights granted by the Original Deed.

(C) The New Owner has agreed to enter into this Deed of Covenant pursuant to the terms of the Original Deed.

OPERATIVE PROVISIONS

1 CONSTRUCTION

1.1 References to the New Owner are to the New Owner and its successors in title to [the Property] [the Relevant Part] and references to the Adjoining Owner are to the Adjoining Owner and its successors in title and express assigns.

1.2 References to [the Property] [the Relevant Part] include the whole and every part of [the Property] [the Relevant Part].

1.3 The parties to this Deed do not intend that any of its terms will be enforceable by virtue of the Contracts (Rights of Third Parties) Act 1999 by any person not a party to it.

1.4 The Particulars form part of this Deed.

2 COVENANT

The New Owner covenants [jointly and individually] with the Adjoining Owner that the New Owner:

2.1 will comply with the Covenants in so far as the same are still subsisting and to the extent that the obligations comprised in the Covenants remain to be discharged [so far as they relate to the Relevant Part] and will indemnify the Adjoining Owner against all costs, damages, expenses, liabilities and losses arising from their breach occasioned after the date hereof; and

2.2 will not effect any transfer of [the Property] [the Relevant Part] or any part of it without procuring that the transferee enters into a direct covenant with the Adjoining Owner on the terms of this Deed of Covenant [provided that:

2.2.1 [in no event shall a Deed of Covenant be required in respect of any transfer of one or more individual dwellings on [the Property] [the Relevant Part] or the freehold reversion of such dwellings sold on long leasehold or the transfer of any land for a substation, pumping station or similar service facilities or of open space, land or the transfer of any land which is to be adopted or the transfer of any land required for affordable housing under a planning agreement];

2.2.2 [the New Owner and any person who has previously executed a Deed of Covenant shall be released from all obligations upon a successor giving a further Deed of Covenant to the extent that the successor covenants to observe such obligations in the further Deed of Covenant]].

3 RESTRICTION

The New Owner covenants with the Adjoining Owner to apply to the Land Registry as soon as reasonably practicable after the date of this Deed for a restriction to be entered against the Title Number [to be allocated] to [the Property] [the Relevant Part] in the following form:

'No disposition [(other than a charge)] by the proprietor of the registered estate or by the proprietor of any registered charge, not being a charge registered before the entry of this restriction is to be registered without a certificate signed by [a conveyancer] [the applicant for registration or their conveyancer] that the provisions of clause 2.2 of the Deed of Covenant dated [ ] made between [ ] (1) and [ ] (2) have been complied with [or do not apply].'

4 EXECUTION

The New Owner has executed this Deed of Covenant as a deed and it is delivered on the date set out in the Particulars.

THE COMMON SEAL of [ ] was affixed to this Deed in the presence of [ ]

Director

Director/Secretary

EXECUTED as a DEED by [ ] acting by [ ]

Director

Director/Secretary

APPENDIX C9

Deed of covenant (to be entered into by a party to whom a transferee is making a subsequent disposal (e.g. a buyer, a tenant or a chargee))

DATED: 20[ ]

(1) [ ]

and

(2) [ ]

DEED OF COVENANT

(to be entered into by a party to whom a transferee is making a disposal) relating to [ ]

PARTICULARS

Date:	[ ]
Covenantor:	[insert details of the party to whom the original transferee is making a disposal]
Adjoining Owner:	[insert details of transferor or successor in title of the transferor]
Original Transfer:	A transfer of the Property [and other land] dated [ ] made between [ ] (1) and [ ] (2)
Original Transferee:	[ ]
Covenants:	The covenants and obligations of the Original Transferee contained in clause [ ] of the Original Transfer
Property:	The property known as [ ] [being part of the land] registered at the Land Registry under title number(s) [ ] [and shown edged red on the attached plan]
Retained Land:	The property shown edged in [blue] on the attached plan
[Relevant Part]:	That part of the Property [to be purchased by the Covenantor] [which is to be subject to [the Charge] [the Lease]] and which is shown [ ] on the attached plan

[Charge:	A legal charge over [the Property] [the Relevant Part] dated the same date as this Deed of Covenant granted by the Original Transferee in favour of the Covenantor]
[Lease:	A lease of [the Property] [the Relevant Part] dated the same date as this Deed of Covenant made between (1) the Original Transferee and (2) the Covenantor]

THIS DEED OF COVENANT is made on the date set out in the Particulars

BETWEEN

(1) the Covenantor; and
(2) the Adjoining Owner.

BACKGROUND

(A) [The Covenantor has agreed to purchase [the Property] [the Relevant Part] from the Original Transferee.] [The Original Transferee has agreed to grant the Covenantor a lease of [the Property] [the Relevant Part].]

[The Original Transferee has agreed to create a legal charge over [the Property] [the Relevant Part] in favour of the Covenantor.]

(B) The Adjoining Owner is the owner of the Retained Land.
(C) The Covenantor has agreed to comply with the Covenants [in so far as they relate to the Relevant Part] and to enter into this Deed of Covenant pursuant to the terms of the Original Transfer.

OPERATIVE PROVISIONS

1 CONSTRUCTION

1.1 References to the Covenantor are to the Covenantor and its successors in title and permitted assigns and references to the Adjoining Owner are to the Adjoining Owner and its successors in title and express assigns.
1.2 References to [the Property] [the Relevant Part] include the whole and every part of [the Property] [the Relevant Part].
1.3 The parties to this Deed do not intend that any of its terms will be enforceable by virtue of the Contracts (Rights of Third Parties) Act 1999 by any person not a party to it.
1.4 The Particulars form part of this Deed.

2 COVENANTOR'S OBLIGATIONS

2.1 Subject to the provisions of clause 2.2 of this Deed of Covenant, the Covenantor covenants [jointly and individually] with the Adjoining Owner to comply with the Covenants [so far as they relate to the Relevant Part] and to indemnify the Adjoining Owner against all costs, damages, expenses, liabilities and losses arising from any breach of any the Covenants occurring after the date of this Deed of Covenant.
2.2 [The covenants contained in clause 2.1 will end on the expiry of the term of years granted by the Lease.]

[The covenants contained in clause 2.1 will not apply unless the Covenantor enters [the Property] [the Relevant Part] as a mortgagee in possession or otherwise exercises its rights or remedies as a mortgagee and will end on the date that the Covenantor releases [the Property] [the Relevant Part] from the Charge.]

3 EXECUTION

The Covenantor has executed this Deed of Covenant as a deed and it is delivered on the date set out in the Particulars.

THE COMMON SEAL of [ ] was affixed to this Deed in the presence of [ ]

....
Director

....
Director/Secretary

EXECUTED as a DEED by [ ] acting by [ ]

....
Director

....
Director/Secretary

APPENDIX C10

Deed of adherence (to be entered into by a mortgagee/chargee in favour of a promoter)

DATED: 20[ ]

(1) [ ]

and

(2) [ ]

DEED OF ADHERENCE

relating to a promotion agreement relating to land at [ ]

THIS DEED OF ADHERENCE is made on [ ]

BETWEEN

1. [ ] (company number [ ]), of [ ] (the '**Chargee**'); and
2. [ ] (company number [ ]), whose registered office is at [ ] (the '**Promoter**').

BACKGROUND

(A) The Property is subject to the Legal Charge.
(B) The Promoter and the Owner have on [ ] OR [or about the date of this Deed] entered into the Promotion Agreement.
(C) The Chargee has agreed to be a party to this Deed and to be bound by and to comply with the terms of the Promotion Agreement on the terms hereinafter appearing.

OPERATIVE PROVISIONS

1 DEFINITIONS

1.1 In this Deed the following expressions have the following meanings:

'**Approved**' means approved by the relevant Party in writing acting reasonably and with reasonable promptness;

'**Infrastructure Agreement**' means any agreement, obligation or undertaking to be made pursuant to the following or similar legislation: section 38 or 278 of the Highways Act 1980, section 104 of the Water Industry Act 1991, Electricity Act 1989, Gas Act 1986, Flood and Water Management Act 2010 or any provision of similar intent with any appropriate authority as to the water supply to or drainage of surface water and effluent from the Property or any part of it or any agreement with any competent authority or body relating to any other services or access;

'**Legal Charge**' means the legal charge dated [ ] in favour of the Chargee and referred to in entry numbers [ ] of the charges register of title number [ ];

'**Owner**' means [ ], of [ ];

'**Parties**' means the Promoter and the Chargee, and 'Party' shall be construed accordingly;

'**Planning Act**' means the Town and Country Planning Act 1990 (as amended by the Planning and Compulsory Purchase Act 2004 and the Planning Act 2008) together with any amendment modification or re-enactment of it and any legislation subordinate to it;

'**Planning Agreement**' means any of the following:

(a) any agreement or unilateral planning obligation in respect of the Property or any part or parts of it to be made pursuant to section 106 of the Planning Act;

(b) any agreement in respect of the Property or any part or parts of it to be made pursuant to section 111 of the Local Government Act 1972;

'**Promotion Agreement**' means a promotion agreement in the form of the draft promotion agreement attached to this Deed at Appendix I;

'**Property**' means the land at [ ] as more particularly described in the Promotion Agreement.

2 INTERPRETATION

2.1 This Deed shall be governed by and construed in accordance with English law and each party agrees to submit to the exclusive jurisdiction of the English courts over any claim or matter arising under or in connection with this Deed.

2.2 Reference to 'taking possession' of the Property (or words of like intent or effect) shall include (inter alia) any analogous action taken by or on behalf of the Chargee directly or by a receiver, administrative receiver, agent or other person or persons appointed by or on behalf of the Chargee whether under the terms of the Charge, pursuant to statute, or on some other basis.

2.3 Reference to the Property shall include each and every part of it and, as the case may be, any part of it.

3 CHARGEE CONSENT AND COVENANTS

3.1 The Chargee consents to the Owner entering into the Promotion Agreement and registering a restriction on the titles to the Property on the terms set out in the Promotion Agreement (or as near thereto as the Land Registry will permit).

3.2 The Chargee hereby covenants with the Promoter:

3.2.1 that if the Chargee shall take possession of the Property then the Chargee will observe and perform and be bound by all of the obligations on the part of the Owner contained in the Promotion Agreement (and which have not been performed at the date of this Deed) as though the Chargee were a party to the Promotion Agreement in place of the Owner;

3.2.2 that on a disposal of the Property or any part thereof the Chargee shall procure that the disponee will be bound by the terms of the Promotion Agreement;

3.2.3 (without prejudice to the generality of the foregoing clause) that on a disposal of the Property or any part thereof the Chargee shall procure that the disponee shall enter into a deed of covenant with the Promoter agreeing to be bound by and to observe and perform and be bound by the obligations of the Owner contained in the Promotion Agreement as if the Promotion Agreement had originally been entered into by the Buyer (such deed to be in a form to be Approved by the Promoter);

3.2.4 that upon request in writing by the Promoter the Chargee shall enter into such Planning Agreement or Infrastructure Agreement for the purposes of the Promotion Agreement as the Promoter shall require, for the purpose of consenting to its terms.

This Deed has been duly executed and delivered as a Deed by the parties on the date hereof.

EXECUTED as a **DEED**

by [ ]

EXECUTED as a DEED by [ ] acting
by a director in the presence of:

....
Director

Signature of witness ....
Name (in BLOCK CAPITALS) ....
Address ....
....
....
....

APPENDIX I

[Copy of the Promotion Agreement]

APPENDIX C11

Deed of release of restrictive covenants

DATED: 20[ ]

(1) [ ]

and

(2) [ ]

DEED OF RELEASE OF COVENANTS

relating to land at [ ]

PARTICULARS

Date:	[ ]
Owner:	[company name] (company number [ ]) [of] [whose registered office is at] [ ]
Covenantor:	[ ] (company number [ ]) [of] [whose registered office is at] [ ]
[Mortgagee:	[company name] (company number [ ]) [of] [whose registered office is at] [ ]]
Owner's Land:	The freehold property at [ ] shown edged in red on the Plan and being the land comprised in [title number [ ]] [a conveyance dated [ ] and made between [ ] (1) and [ ] (2)]
Covenantor's Land:	The freehold property at [ ] shown edged in blue on the Plan and being the land comprised in [title number [ ]] [a conveyance dated [ ] and made between [ ] (1) and [ ] (2)]

THIS DEED OF RELEASE is made on the date set out in the Particulars

BETWEEN

(1) the Owner, and
(2) the Covenantor

BACKGROUND

(A) By the Original Deed the Covenantor's Land became subject to the Covenants;
(B) The Covenants were made for the benefit of the Owner's Land;

(C) The Covenantor's Land [is now] [remains] vested in the Covenantor;
(D) The Owner's Land [is now] [remains] vested in the Owner.

1 DEFINITIONS

In this Deed where the context so admits the following expressions have the following meanings:

'**Covenants**' means [the covenants contained in clause [ ] of the Original Deed] [those of the covenants contained in clause [ ] of the Original Deed which are set out in the Schedule];

'**Original Deed**' means a [transfer] [conveyance] dated [ ] made between [ ] and [ ] relating to the Covenantor's Land;

'**Plan**' means the plan attached to this Deed [which is for the purposes of identification only].

2 INTERPRETATION

2.1 Unless the context otherwise requires references in this Deed to clauses, schedules and paragraphs are to clauses, schedules and paragraphs in this Deed and references to a clause or paragraph include a sub-clause or sub-paragraph respectively.
2.2 The headings to a clause in this Deed are for reference only and do not affect its interpretation.
2.3 Words importing one gender include all other genders and words importing the singular include the plural and vice versa.
2.4 A reference to a person includes an individual or corporation, company, firm or partnership or government body or agency, whether or not legally capable of holding land.
2.5 References in this Deed to the Owner's Land and the Covenantor's Land include any part of them.
2.6 Where two or more people form a party to this Deed the obligations they undertake may be enforced against them jointly or against each individually.
2.7 If any provision of this Deed is held to be illegal, invalid or unenforceable, the legality and enforceability of the remainder of this Deed are to be unaffected.
2.8 The Particulars form part of this Deed and words and expressions set out in the Particulars are to be treated as defined terms in this Deed.

3 RELEASE

In consideration of the sum of [ ] pounds (£[ ]) paid by the Covenantor to the Owner (receipt of which the Owner acknowledges) the Owner hereby releases with [full] [limited] title guarantee the Covenantor and its successors in title and the Covenantor's Land from the Covenants to the intent that the Covenants are extinguished from the date of this Deed.

4 CANCELLATION OF REGISTRATIONS

4.1 [The Owner covenants that it will within seven days of the date of this Deed apply to HM Land Registry for cancellation of:

4.1.1 entry [ ] of the [ ] Register of title number [ ]; and
4.1.2 entry [ ] of the [ ] Register of title number [ ].]

[The Owner covenants that it will within seven days of the date of this Deed apply to HM Land Charges Department for the cancellation of any land charges entry relating to the Covenants.]

5 RIGHT TO EFFECT RELEASE

The Owner covenants that it has full power and authority to effect the release and the extinguishment of the Covenants.

6 CONTINUING EFFECT

The parties to this Deed agree and declare that except for the release contained in clause 3 the Original Deed shall remain in full force and effect.

7 [MORTGAGEE CONSENT

The Mortgagee consents to the release of the Covenants and the cancellation of the entries referred to in clause 4 above.]

This Deed has today been duly executed and delivered by the parties.

APPENDIX C12

Deed of release of easements

DATED: 20[ ]

(1) [ ]

and

(2) [ ]

and

(3) [ ]

DEED OF RELEASE OF EASEMENTS

relating to land at [ ]

PARTICULARS

Date:	[ ]
Grantor:	[company name] (company number [ ]) [of] [whose registered office is at] [ ]
Grantee:	[company name] (company number [ ]) [of] [whose registered office is at] [ ]
[**Mortgagee:**	[company name] (company number [ ]) [of] [whose registered office is at] [ ]]
Grantor's Land:	The freehold property at [ ] shown edged in red on the Plan and being the land comprised in title number [ ] [a conveyance dated [ ] and made between [ ] (1) and [ ] (2)]
Grantee's Land:	The freehold property at [ ] shown edged in blue on the Plan and being the land comprised in title number [ ] [a conveyance dated [ ] and made between [ ] (1) and [ ] (2)]

THIS DEED OF RELEASE is made on the date set out in the Particulars

BETWEEN

(1) the Grantor; and
(2) the Grantee.

BACKGROUND

(A) By the Original Deed the Grantor's Land became subject to the Rights;
(B) The Rights were made for the benefit of the Grantee's Land;
(C) The Grantor's Land [is now] [remains] vested in the Grantor;
(D) The Grantee's Land [is now] [remains] vested in the Grantee.

1 DEFINITIONS

In this Deed where the context so admits the following expressions have the following meanings:

'**Original Deed**' means a [transfer] [conveyance] dated [ ] made between [ ] and [ ] relating to the Grantor's Land;

'**Plan**' means the plan attached to this Deed [which is for the purposes of identification only];

'**Rights**' means [the rights contained in clause [ ] of the Original Deed] [those of the rights contained in clause [ ] of the Original Deed which are set out in the Schedule].

2 INTERPRETATION

2.1 Unless the context otherwise requires references in this Deed to clauses, schedules and paragraphs are to clauses, schedules and paragraphs in this Deed and references to a clause or paragraph include a sub-clause or sub-paragraph respectively.
2.2 The headings to a clause in this Deed are for reference only and do not affect its interpretation.
2.3 Words importing one gender include all other genders and words importing the singular include the plural and vice versa.
2.4 A reference to a person includes an individual or corporation, company, firm or partnership or government body or agency, whether or not legally capable of holding land.
2.5 References in this Deed to the Grantor's Land and the Grantee's Land include any part of them.
2.6 Where two or more people form a party to this Deed the obligations they undertake may be enforced against them jointly or against each individually.
2.7 If any provision of this Deed is held to be illegal, invalid or unenforceable, the legality and enforceability of the remainder of this Deed are to be unaffected.
2.8 The Particulars form part of this Deed and words and expressions set out in the Particulars are to be treated as defined terms in this Deed.

3 RELEASE

In consideration of the sum of [ ] pounds (£[ ]) paid by the Grantor to the Grantee (receipt of which the Grantor acknowledges) the Grantee hereby releases with [full] [limited] title guarantee the Grantor and its successors in title and the Grantor's Land from the Rights to the intent that the Rights are extinguished from the date of this Deed.

4 CANCELLATION OF REGISTRATIONS

[The Grantee covenants that it will within seven days of the date of this Deed apply to HM Land Registry for cancellation of:

4.1 entry [ ] of the [ ] Register of title number [ ]; and
4.2 entry [ ] of the [ ] Register of title number [ ].]

[The Grantee covenants that it will within seven days of the date of this Deed apply to HM Land Charges Department for the cancellation of any land charges entry relating to the Rights.]

5 [RIGHTS TO EFFECT RELEASE

The Grantee covenants that it has full power and authority to effect the release and the extinguishment of the Rights.]

6 CONTINUING EFFECT

The parties to this Deed agree and declare that except for the release contained in clause 3 the Original Deed shall remain in full force and effect.

7 [MORTGAGEE CONSENT

The Mortgagee consents to the release of the Rights and the cancellation of the entries referred to in clause 4 above.]

This Deed has today been duly executed and delivered by the parties.

SCHEDULE

Rights

SIGNED as a DEED and delivered by [ ]
in the presence of:

Witness signature:

Witness name:

Witness address:

Witness occupation:

SIGNED as a DEED and delivered by
[ ]
in the presence of:

Witness signature:

Witness name:

Witness address:

Witness occupation:

EXECUTED as a DEED by [ ] acting by two directors or one director and the company secretary

....
Director

....
Director/Secretary

NOTE

If the Grantee's Land is subject to a mortgage or charge it will be necessary for the mortgagee/chargee to be made a party to the deed of release for the purpose of consenting to its terms.

APPENDIX C13

Deed of easement and covenant

DATED: 20[ ]

(1) [ ]

and

(2) [ ]

DEED OF EASEMENT AND COVENANT

relating to land at [ ]

[**NOTE**: This deed is intended to be for guidance purposes only and will need to be adapted/tailored to the needs of the parties and the particular transaction and reflect any agreed heads of terms. Wording and clauses in square brackets should be carefully considered. The deed contains infrastructure obligations imposing an obligation on the grantor to construct an access road and new service media to serve the grantee's land. If not required they will need to be deleted and other consequential amendments will need to be made to the deed.]

PARTICULARS

Date:	[ ]
Grantor:	[company name] (company number [ ]) [of] [whose registered office is at] [ ]
Grantee:	[company name] (company number [ ]) [of] [whose registered office is at] [ ]
Grantor's Land:	The freehold property at [ ] shown edged in [red] on Plan [ ] and being the land registered at the Land Registry under title number [ ]
Grantee's Land:	The freehold property at [ ] shown edged in [blue] on Plan [ ] and being the land registered at the Land Registry under title number [ ]
[**Mortgagee:**	[ ] [of] [whose registered office is at] [ ]]

THIS DEED OF EASEMENT AND COVENANT is made on the date set out in the Particulars

BETWEEN

1. the Grantor; [and]
2. the Grantee; [and]
[3. the Mortgagee.]

BACKGROUND

(A) The Grantor is the owner of the Grantor's Land and the Grantee is the owner of the Grantee's Land.

(B) The Grantor has agreed to grant the Rights to the Grantee and to enter into the Covenants for the benefit of the Grantee's Land and any building or buildings now or hereafter erected thereon.

[(C) The Mortgagee has agreed to be made a party to this Deed for the purpose of consenting to the grant of the Rights and the Grantee entering into the Covenants.]

OPERATIVE PROVISIONS

1 DEFINITIONS AND INTERPRETATION

1.1 In this Deed the following words and expressions have the following meanings:

['**Access Road**' means the access road [(having a minimum width of [ ] metres)], footpaths [(having a minimum width of [ ] metres)] and any cycle paths and all associated street lighting, drainage and street furniture to be constructed by the Grantor over the [Grantor's Land] [those parts of the Grantor's Land shown coloured [brown] on Plan [ ]] in accordance with [the Access Road Specification and] the terms set out in Schedule [6] and which access road and footpaths are to abut and lead from the adopted highway known as [ ] up to and to directly connect with the boundary of the Grantee's Land at the point(s) marked [ ] on Plan [ ] (or as close thereto as the Relevant Authority shall permit;]

['**Access Road Specification**' means the proposed technical specification showing the proposed route (including its start and end points), width and capacity of the Access Road [(taking into account the current and proposed uses of the Grantee's Land)], the location of any Sight Line Areas, the standard of construction of the Access Road [to achieve an adoptable standard] and the programme of works for its construction [in the form attached to this Deed at Appendix [ ]] [to be agreed in accordance with paragraph [1.1] of Schedule [6]];]

'**Approved**' means approved by the relevant Party in writing acting reasonably and with reasonable promptness [and approval shall be deemed to have been given if no response is received or if no reasons are given for any refusal of approval in each case within [10] Working Days of a request for approval] [and any dispute between the Parties about whether the relevant Party is acting reasonably shall be determined by an Expert in accordance with the provisions of clause [5] of this Deed] and the terms '**Approval**' and '**Approve**' shall be construed accordingly;

['**Connected Person**' has the meaning given to it in section 839 of the Income and Corporation Taxes Act 1988;]

'**Covenants**' means the restrictive covenants set out in Schedule 2 and the positive covenants set out in Schedule 3;

'**Deed of Covenant**' means a deed of covenant [in such form as the Grantee shall reasonably require to be entered into by any party to whom the Grantor makes a Disposal containing a covenant in favour of the Grantee and its successors in title for the benefit of the Grantee's Land to observe and perform the Covenants] [in substantially the same form as the draft deed of covenant attached to this Deed at Appendix [ ] with such amendments thereto as the circumstances may require and/or such amendments as the Grantee may require and the Grantor shall Approve]. Any dispute between the Parties regarding the form of the Deed of Covenant shall be settled by an Expert in accordance with the provisions of clause [5] of this Deed;

'**Disposal**' means a transfer, assent, lease, mortgage, charge, grant of legal or equitable easements, the entering into of restrictive or positive covenants or any other disposition of the whole or any part of the Grantor's Land [or, as the case may be, the Grantee's Land], whether or not for valuable consideration;

'**Expert**' means a person having appropriate professional qualifications and experience and who shall be appointed (in default of agreement between the Parties) on the application of either Party:

(a) in regard to any matter or thing of a planning nature arising out of or connected with the subject matter of this Deed, by the President for the time being of the Royal Town Planning Institute;
(b) in regard to any matter or thing of a valuation or surveying nature arising out of or connected with the subject matter of this Deed, by the President for the time being of the Royal Institution of Chartered Surveyors;
(c) in regard to any matter of an engineering nature arising out of or connected with the subject matter of this Deed, by the President for the time being of the Institution of Civil Engineers;
(d) in regard to the respective rights, duties or obligations of the Parties under this Deed or the terms of any form of document to be entered into under this Deed, by the President for the time being of the Law Society;

['**New Service Media**' means Service Media for the supply of [ ] to be installed or constructed by the Grantor in, on, under or over [the Grantor's Land] [those parts of the Grantor's Land shown coloured [ ] on the Plan] in accordance with the terms set out in Schedule [6];]

'**Parties**' means the Grantor and the Grantee and '**Party**' shall be construed accordingly;

['**Permitted Disposal**' means any of the following in relation to the Grantor's Land [or, as the case may be, the Grantee's Land] unless [in, either case,] made to a Connected Person:

(a) the disposal of [part of the Grantor's Land] [part of the relevant property] by way of transfer of the freehold or the grant of a lease [for a term exceeding 21 years] in each case to a service authority or utility company in order to provide Services to or from the [Grantor's Land] [relevant property];
(b) the grant of any easement or wayleave to a service authority or utility company in order to provide Services to or from the [Grantor's Land] [the relevant property];
(c) the disposal of part of the [Grantor's Land] [relevant property] by way of transfer of the freehold or the grant of a lease for the dedication of highway or of public open space pursuant to section 106 of the Town and Country Planning Act 1990 or sections 38 or 278 of the Highways Act 1980;
(d) [the grant of a lease over the whole or any part of the [Grantor's Land] [relevant

property] at an open market rent without taking a premium for a term not exceeding [five] years without the right for the tenant to renew the lease, contracted out of the security of tenure provisions in sections 24 to 28 of the Landlord and Tenant Act 1954 and which permits the use of the [Grantor's Land] [relevant property] only for [ ] without any right for the tenant to apply to the landlord for a change of the use authorised by the lease;]

(e) [the disposal at arm's length to a bona fide purchaser and for valuable consideration of one or more fully constructed houses and their gardens for occupation as a private dwelling or dwellings whether with or without a separate garage together with the grant of all easements required for their proper use and enjoyment;]
(f) [the grant at arm's length to a bona fide purchaser for a premium of a lease of a flat or apartment including any garden and garage or parking space together with the grant of all easements required for its proper use and enjoyment;]
(g) [the transfer of the freehold reversion of any dwellings let on long leases;]
(h) [a disposal of any land required for an electricity substation, gas governor, sewerage or water pumping station or any other site service installations;]
(i) [the disposal of land to a local authority or other statutory body pursuant to an obligation in a Planning Agreement;]
(j) [the grant of an easement over or the giving of a covenant affecting any part of the [Grantor's Land] [relevant property] [that, in either case, does not materially affect the value of the [Grantor's Land] [relevant property] and does not materially increase the value of the property benefiting from the easement or covenant] [that does not adversely affect the Rights];]]

'**Plan 1**' means the plan numbered [ ] annexed to this Deed at Appendix [ ];

'**Plan 2**' means the plan numbered [ ] annexed to this Deed at Appendix [ ];

'**Planning Agreement**' means an agreement or undertaking with any Relevant Authority made under, or varying an existing agreement made under:

(a) section 106 of the Town and Country Planning Act 1990 (as amended by the Planning and Compulsory Purchase Act 2004 and the Planning Act 2008);
(b) section 111 of the Local Government Act 1972;
(c) section 38, 184 or 278 of the Highways Act 1980;
(d) section 33 of the Local Government (Miscellaneous Provisions) Act 1982;
(e) section 98, 104 or 106 of the Water Industry Act 1991; or
(f) section 2 of the Local Government Act 2000;

'**Relevant Authority**' means all or any of the following as appropriate:

(a) such authority or body as shall have responsibility under statute for drainage matters;
(b) such authority or body as shall have responsibility under statute for highway matters;
(c) such authority or body as shall have responsibility under statute for planning matters;
(d) such authority or body as shall have responsibility under statute for environmental matters;
(e) any utility company or body concerned with the installation of Service Media and the supply of Services;
(f) any other local or competent authority or body having jurisdiction in relation to the development of the Grantor's Land and the Grantee's Land or the infrastructure serving the same;

'**Rights**' means the rights set out in Schedule 1;

['**Road Corridor**' means where the Access Road does not connect with the boundary of the Grantee's Land at the point marked [ ] on Plan [ ] (the **Terminus**), the corridor of land:

(a) lying between the section of the Access Road that is closest to the Terminus and the Terminus;
(b) having the same width as the Access Road at the point that is closest to the Terminus; and
(c) in such ultimate position as shall be determined in accordance with paragraph [1.10] of Schedule [6];]

'**Service Media**' means conduits, sewers, drains, pipes, cables and other service media for the supply of Services;

'**Services**' means water, gas, electricity, telephone, telecommunications and electronic data transmission, surface water drainage, foul drainage and similar services;

['**Services Specification**' means the specification showing the proposed route, capacity, standard of construction and the programme of works for the New Service Media [(taking into account the current and future uses of the Grantee's Land)] [in the form attached to this Deed at Appendix [ ]] [to be agreed in accordance with paragraph [2.3] of Schedule [6]];]

['**Sight Line Areas**' means such areas within the Grantor's Land as shall be required to be maintained as sight line areas in connection with the Relevant Authority's visibility splay requirements for the construction of the Access Road and any other roads and footpaths leading to the Grantee's Land (including any to be constructed in the future within the Road Corridor) in such ultimate position as shall be determined in accordance with paragraph [1.10] of Schedule [6];]

'**Successor**' means any person to whom a Disposal is made;

'**Working Day**' means any day other than Saturday, Sunday and any bank or public holiday and 'Working Days' shall be construed accordingly.

1.2 In this Deed:

1.2.1 the clause headings do not affect its interpretation;
1.2.2 unless otherwise indicated, references to clauses and Schedules are to clauses of and Schedules to this Deed and references in a Schedule to a Part or paragraph are to a Part or paragraph of that Schedule;
1.2.3 references to any statute or statutory provision include references to:

a) all Acts of Parliament and all other legislation having legal effect in the United Kingdom; and
b) any subsequent statutes directly or indirectly amending, consolidating, extending, replacing or re-enacting that statute and also include any orders, regulations, instruments or other subordinate legislation made under that statute;

1.2.4 references to Grantor's Land and Grantee's Land include any part of them;
1.2.5 references to the Grantor and the Grantee include their respective successors in title;
1.2.6 words importing one gender include all other genders and words importing the singular include the plural and vice versa;
1.2.7 a reference to a person includes an individual or corporation, company, firm or partnership or government body or agency;

1.2.8 'including' means 'including, without limitation';
1.2.9 where two or more people form a party to this Deed, the obligations they undertake may be enforced against them all jointly or against each individually; and
1.2.10 if any provision is held to be illegal, invalid or unenforceable, the legality, validity and enforceability of the remainder of this Deed are to be unaffected.

1.3 The Particulars form part of this Deed and words and expressions set out in the Particulars are to be treated as defined terms in this Deed.

1.4 [The Parties to this Deed do not intend that any of its terms will be enforceable by virtue of the Contracts (Rights of Third Parties) Act 1999 by any person not a party to it.]

2 GRANT

2.1 [In consideration of £[ ] [plus value added tax] (receipt of which is acknowledged] the Grantor **GRANTS** the Rights to the Grantee [in fee simple] [for a term of [ ] years] with [full] [limited] title guarantee for the benefit of the Grantee's Land.

2.2 No legal or other rights over the Grantor's Land for the benefit of the Grantee's Land are granted by this Deed except for the Rights.

2.3 Unless otherwise stated, the Rights are not exclusive and are granted for use in common with the Grantor and all other persons lawfully entitled to exercise them.

3 THE GRANTOR'S OBLIGATIONS

3.1 For the benefit and protection of the Grantee's Land and each and every part thereof and so as to bind the Grantor's Land and each and every part thereof into whosesoever hands the same may come the Grantor **HEREBY COVENANTS** with the Grantee and its successors in title that the Grantor and those deriving title under it will at all times hereafter comply with the restrictive covenants set out in Schedule 2.

3.2 The Grantor **HEREBY FURTHER COVENANTS** with the Grantee to comply with the positive covenants set out in Schedule 3.

4 THE GRANTEE'S OBLIGATIONS

4.1 For the benefit and protection of the Grantor's Land and each and every part thereof and so as to bind the Grantee's Land and each and every part thereof into whosesoever hands the same may come the Grantee **HEREBY COVENANTS** with the Grantor and its successors in title that the Grantee and those deriving title under it will at all times hereafter comply with the restrictive covenants set out in Schedule 4.

4.2 [The Grantee **HEREBY FURTHER COVENANTS** with the Grantor to comply with the positive covenants set out in Schedule 5.]

5 DISPUTE RESOLUTION

5.1 Unless otherwise provided in this Deed, any dispute or difference between the Parties regarding any of the provisions of this Deed shall be referred to the Expert for determination. The Expert shall act as expert and not as arbitrator and his decision shall be final and binding on the Parties, save in the case of manifest error or fraud, and the following provisions shall apply:

5.1.1 The Expert shall give the Parties the opportunity to make representations to him before making his decision.
5.1.2 The Expert shall be entitled to obtain opinions from others if he so wishes.

5.1.3 The Expert shall give reasons for his decision.
5.1.4 The Expert shall comply with any time limits or other directions agreed by the Parties.
5.1.5 The charges and expenses of the Expert shall be borne equally between the Parties or in such other proportions as the Expert may direct.

6 LAND REGISTRY APPLICATIONS

6.1 The Grantor consents to the entry of a notice of the Rights and a notice of the Covenants in the appropriate registers of the title to the Grantor's Land.

6.2 The Grantee agrees to apply forthwith to the Land Registry for the Rights and the Covenants to be noted on the title to the Grantor's Land.

7 REGISTRATION OF RESTRICTION (GRANTOR'S LAND)

The Grantor and the Grantee hereby apply to the Chief Land Registrar for the entry of the following restriction upon the proprietorship register of the title to the Grantor's Land in the following terms (or as near thereto as the Land Registry will permit):

> 'No disposition of the registered estate by the proprietor of the registered estate or the proprietor of any registered charge, not being a charge registered before the entry of this restriction, is to be registered without a certificate signed by [ ] or their conveyancer that the provisions of paragraph [7] of Schedule 2 to the deed of easement and covenant dated [ ] and made between (1) [ ] and (2) [ ] have been complied with or that they do not apply.'

[8 REGISTRATION OF RESTRICTION (GRANTEE'S LAND)

The Grantor and the Grantee hereby apply to the Chief Land Registrar for the entry of the following restriction upon the proprietorship register of the title to the Grantee's Land in the following terms (or as near thereto as the Land Registry will permit):

> 'No disposition of the registered estate by the proprietor of the registered estate or the proprietor of any registered charge, not being a charge registered before the entry of this restriction, is to be registered without a certificate signed by [ ] or their conveyancer that the provisions of paragraph [3] of Schedule [4] to the deed of easement and covenant dated [ ] and made between (1) [ ] and (2) [ ] have been complied with or do not apply.']

[9 MORTGAGEE'S CONSENT

9.1 The Mortgagee consents to the grant of the Rights and to the Covenants and also to the registration of notice of them in the charges register of the title to the Grantor's Land.

9.2 If the Mortgagee exercises its power of sale to sell the whole or any part of the Grantor's Land it shall comply with the obligations on the Grantor contained in paragraph [7] of Schedule 2.]

IN WITNESS whereof the Parties have executed this Deed as a deed the day and year first before written.

SCHEDULE 1 – THE RIGHTS

The following rights for the Grantee, its successors in title of all or any parts of the Grantee's Land and their respective tenants, servants and invitees and all others authorised by the Grantee or its successors in title:

1 RIGHT OF WAY

1.1 [A right of way at all times and for all purposes with or without vehicles over and along the roads and the footpaths shown coloured [ ] on Plan [ ] together with a right to connect to such roads and footpaths.]

1.2 [The right, following the construction of the Access Road, to use the Access Road at all times and for all purposes for access to and from the Grantee's Land together with the right to connect to the Access Road.]

1.3 [A right of way at all times and for all purposes with or without vehicles over any Road Corridor that may be required to provide access to the Grantee's Land in accordance with the terms of this Deed.]

1.4 [A right of way at all times and for all purposes with or without vehicles over any road constructed on any Road Corridor in the future.]

2 SERVICES

2.1 The full and free right to connect to and use any existing Service Media in, on, under or over the Grantor's Land for the passage of Services to and from the Grantee's Land.

2.2 [The full and free right to connect to and use any New Service Media installed or constructed by the Grantor in, on, under or over the Grantor's Land for the passage of Services to and from the Grantee's Land.]

2.3 [The [exclusive] right to install at any time after the date of this Deed and thereafter use Service Media in, on, under or over the Grantor's Land.]

2.4 [The full and free right to connect to and thereafter use, repair, maintain, renew and inspect any Service Media installed after the date of this Deed within any Road Corridor.]

3 ENTRY

3.1 [The right to enter and remain upon [those parts of the Grantor's Land that are not built upon] [so much as is necessary of the Grantor's Land] on giving the Grantor reasonable prior notice in writing (except in case of emergency when no notice shall be required) with or without workmen, plant, equipment and machinery to:

3.1.1 connect to any existing Service Media in, on, under or over the Grantor's Land;

3.1.2 [connect to any New Service Media installed by the Grantor after the date of this Deed in, on, under or over the Grantor's Land];

3.1.3 [install, connect to, repair, re-lay, alter, clean, maintain, replace, enlarge and renew any Service Media permitted under the rights granted by paragraph 2.3 of this Schedule;]

3.1.4 [repair, maintain, decorate, replace, renew and clean any buildings or fences on the Grantee's Land or boundary fences or party walls between the Grantor's Land and the Grantee's Land and to erect scaffolding on the Grantor's Land in the exercise of this right;]

3.1.5 [connect to, repair, maintain, replace, renew[, enlarge] and clean [the Access Road] [any roads and footpaths over which rights are granted by this Deed];] and

3.1.6 [construct, connect to, repair, maintain, replace, renew and clean a new road and/or Service Media within the Road Corridor].]

4 SUPPORT

[The right of support for the Grantee's Land and any buildings on it from the Grantor's Land and any buildings on it.]

5 LIGHT AND AIR

[The right of uninterrupted and unimpeded access of light and air over the Grantor's Land to any buildings from time to time on the Grantee's Land.]

6 BUILDING

[The right to build new buildings upon and to rebuild, extend, alter or carry out any other works to any buildings from time to time on the Grantee's Land in such manner as the Grantee may wish notwithstanding that it may interfere with or diminish the passage of light and air to any buildings from time to time on the Grantor's Land.]

7 [STEP IN RIGHTS

The right in the event of default by the Grantor to perform the positive obligations set out in Schedule 3 [and/or Schedule [6]] in accordance with the provisions of Schedule 3 [and/or Schedule [6]] to enter upon the Grantor's Land and (at the cost of the Grantor) to carry out such works and/or take such action as may be reasonably necessary to remedy any breach [**PROVIDED ALWAYS THAT** (a) before exercising such right the Grantee shall serve 14 days' prior written notice on the Grantor and (b) the Grantee shall be entitled to exercise such right only if the Grantor shall fail within such 14-day period to promptly and diligently take steps to complete any works which are outstanding and such other action as may be necessary **PROVIDED THAT** if due to circumstances reasonably outside the Grantor's control and which could not have been foreseen there is delay by the Grantor in promptly and diligently taking steps to complete any works which are outstanding then the said 14-day period shall be extended by such period as is reasonable in all the circumstances.]]

8 [The rights granted in the above paragraphs of this schedule are subject to the following provisions:

8.1 Any rights of entry shall be exercised only upon reasonable notice and at reasonable times (except in cases of emergency when no notice shall be required).

8.2 All requisite consents from any Relevant Authority for connections to and construction and/or laying of roads and/or Service Media pursuant to the rights hereby granted must be obtained by the person exercising the rights prior to effecting the same.

8.3 The person exercising the rights hereby granted shall cause as little damage and disturbance as reasonably possible and shall make good all damage caused as soon as reasonably practicable.

8.4 The person exercising the rights hereby granted shall (if so requested) consent to the roads and/or Services over or through which the rights are exercised becoming adopted and/or maintainable at the public expense [and pending adoption shall contribute a fair and reasonable proportion (according to user) of the costs of inspecting, cleansing, repairing, maintaining, renewing or replacing the roads and/or the Services over or through (or into) which the rights are exercised].

8.5 [Rights of way over any roads shall not be exercised until the same shall have been constructed to base course level.]

8.6 [Connections to Service Media within the Grantor's Land shall only be made to the extent that there is a capacity therefor.]]

SCHEDULE 2 – GRANTOR'S RESTRICTIVE COVENANTS

1 [NUISANCE

Not to do anything in or upon the Grantor's Land that may be or may grow to be a [legal] nuisance, [annoyance or disturbance to the Grantee] [provided that the development and use of the Grantor's Land for [residential] purposes shall not be a breach of this covenant].]

2 USER

2.1 [Not to use that part of the Grantor's Land shown hatched [ ] on Plan [ ] for any purpose whatsoever other than as a well-maintained [landscaped area/visibility splay] [and so that no tree or shrub planted on it exceeds [ ] metres in height].]

2.2 Not to do or omit to do anything that would ransom the Grantee or prevent the Grantee from exercising any of the Rights.

2.3 Not to do or omit to do anything that would prevent the Grantee from developing the Grantee's Land or that would hinder such development.

3 [LIGHT AND AIR

Not to do anything on the Grantor's Land that would or might interfere with or diminish the access of light and air to the existing windows and openings of the buildings now or in the future upon the Grantee's Land.]

4 SERVICE MEDIA

4.1 Not to overload any Service Media within the Grantor's Land beyond their designated capacity.

4.2 Not to discharge into any Service Media within the Grantor's Land anything that is or could be corrosive, harmful or that could cause any obstruction of them.

4.3 [Not to connect to any Service Media constructed by the Grantee pursuant to its rights in paragraph 2.3 of Schedule 1 without the Approval of the Grantee to the programme of works for the connection to such Service Media. The Grantee may withhold Approval if, in its reasonable opinion, the proposed use of such Service Media by the Grantor would overload the capacity of such Service Media having regard to the Grantee's use and proposed uses of the Grantee's Land and the Grantor's use and proposed use of the Grantor's Land.]

5 [SIGHT LINES AND ROAD CORRIDOR

5.1 Not to build any temporary or permanent building, wall or structure on the Sight Line Areas [or any Road Corridor].

5.2 Not to alter the ground levels within the Sight Line Areas [or any Road Corridor].

5.3 Not to plant any trees, shrubs or other plants within the Sight Line Areas [or any Road Corridor].

5.4 Not to use or permit the Sight Line Areas [or any Road Corridor] to be used or designated as public open space.

5.5 Not to use the Sight Line Areas [or any Road Corridor] for any purposes that may endanger or prevent the use of the Access Road or that may make the use of the Access Road more difficult or expensive.

5.6 Not to grant any rights or easements over the Sight Line Areas [or any Road Corridor] [without the Approval of the Grantee] [without the consent of the Grantee who shall have an absolute discretion to give or withhold that consent].]

6 NOT TO OBSTRUCT RIGHT OF WAY

6.1 Not to park on or otherwise obstruct any part of the [Access Road] [any road constructed on the Grantor's Land].

6.2 Not to erect any fencing or other structures along the boundaries of the Grantor's Land that would prevent the Grantee using the rights of way granted by paragraph [1] of Schedule 1.

7 [DISPOSALS OF THE GRANTOR'S LAND

7.1 [[Unless a Disposal is a Permitted Disposal], the Grantor shall not make a Disposal of the Grantor's Land unless its Successor:

7.1.1 executes a Deed of Covenant on or before the date of the deed or document effecting the Disposal and delivers it to the Grantee's solicitors;

7.1.2 pays the proper and reasonable legal costs and expenses of the Grantee's solicitors in respect of the preparation and approval of the Deed of Covenant together with any value added tax on those costs and expenses; and

7.1.3 makes an application to the Land Registry on form RX1 (at the same time as the transfer in favour of the Successor is sent to the Land Registry for registration) for a restriction in the form of the restriction referred to in clause 7 of this Deed to be entered onto the proprietorship register of the title number(s) under which the Grantor's Land is registered with that restriction being entered in priority to any other restrictions, charges or other entries on the register to be made following the registration of the Successor as the registered proprietor of the Grantor's Land.]

7.2 [In the case of a disposal that is not a Permitted Disposal of the Grantor's Land, if the Grantee receives a duly executed Deed of Covenant, the Grantee shall consent to the registration of a Disposal at the Land Registry for the purposes of the restriction referred to in clause 7 of this Deed.]

7.3 [In the case of a Permitted Disposal of the Grantor's Land, the Grantor shall:

7.3.1 consent to the registration of the Permitted Disposal at the Land Registry for the purposes of the restriction referred to in clause 7 of this Deed; and

7.3.2 release the restriction registered over those parts of the Grantor's Land that were the subject of the Permitted Disposal within two weeks of being requested to do so if it is necessary for registration of the Permitted Disposal.]]

SCHEDULE 3 – GRANTOR'S POSITIVE COVENANTS

1 [ACCESS ROAD [AND NEW SERVICE MEDIA]]

[To comply with the obligations set out in Schedule [6].]

2 SERVICE MEDIA

2.1 To repair, maintain, clean, replace and renew any Service Media over which rights are granted by this Deed, including any New Service Media installed by the Grantor after the date of this Deed [but not any Service Media constructed by the Grantee pursuant to the rights granted in paragraph [2.3] of Schedule 1].

2.2 To [use reasonable endeavours to] enter into an adoption agreement with the Relevant Authority in relation to any new foul or surface water sewer forming part of the New Service Media as soon as reasonably practicable after the date of this Deed (and by no later than [ ]) and to give the Relevant Authority such security as is normally required.

2.3 To promptly enter into any wayleave agreement, deed of easement or other documents [reasonably] required by the Grantee in connection with the installation and maintenance of any Service Media installed by the Grantee after the date of this Deed within the Grantor's Land for the benefit of the Grantee's Land.

[The Grantee shall:

2.3.1 pay the proper and reasonable costs of the Grantor; and
2.3.2 agree to indemnify the Grantor in respect of any liability incurred by the Grantor under those documents.]

2.4 To promptly enter into any wayleave agreement, deed of easement, adoption agreement or other documents if [reasonably] required by the provider of any of the Services as a condition of the provider of those Services installing and/or adopting Service Media in, on, under or over the Grantor's Land for the benefit of the Grantee's Land or allowing connections to be made to existing Service Media for the benefit of the Grantee's Land.

[The Grantee shall:

2.4.1 pay the reasonable costs of the Grantor; and
2.4.2 agree to indemnify the Grantor in respect of any liability incurred under those documents.]

3 ROAD AND PATHS

3.1 To repair, maintain, replace, renew, clean, light, remove obstructions from and, where necessary, grit any roads and paths over which rights are granted by this Deed.

3.2 To [use reasonable endeavours to] enter into an adoption agreement with the Relevant Authority in relation to the Access Road as soon as reasonably practicable after the date of this Deed [and by no later than [ ]] and to give the Relevant Authority such security as is normally required.

3.3 [To promptly enter into any agreements properly and reasonably required by the Relevant Authority to ensure that any roads and footpaths constructed pursuant to the rights granted by paragraph [1.2] and [1.3] of Schedule 1 are adopted as part of the public highway. [The Grantee shall:

3.3.1 pay the proper and reasonable costs of the Grantor; and
3.3.2 agree to indemnify the Grantor in respect of any liability incurred by the Grantor under those agreements.]]

4 PLANNING AGREEMENTS

4.1 To enter into any Planning Agreements properly and reasonably required by the Grantee and Approved by the Grantor to facilitate the development of the Grantee's Land. [The Grantee shall:

4.1.1 pay the proper and reasonable costs of the Grantor; and
4.1.2 agree to indemnify the Grantor against any liability incurred by the Grantor under those Planning Agreements.]

5 [ACCESS ROAD CORRIDOR

5.1 Within [20] days of receipt of a request in writing from the Grantee at any time during the period commencing on the date of completion of construction of the Access Road to base course level or [12] months after the date on which the relevant technical approvals to the design and construction of the Access Road have been obtained from the Relevant Authority (whichever is the earlier) and expiring 20 years after the date of this Deed, to transfer the Road Corridor to the Grantee.

5.2 The transfer of the Road Corridor to the Grantee pursuant to paragraph 5.1 shall:

5.2.1 be for nil consideration;
5.2.2 be with full title guarantee;
5.2.3 be free from all incumbrances;
5.2.4 be in a form to be Approved by the Grantor and the Grantee;
5.2.5 include all necessary rights, including rights to use the Access Road and Service Media within the Grantor's Land and to lay new Service Media and associated covenants.]

6 GOOD FAITH

6.1 To act in good faith towards the Grantee in connection with this Deed.

6.2 (Without prejudice to the generality of paragraph 6.1) to promptly join in any agreement reasonably required by the Grantee for the development of the Grantee's Land (it being acknowledged by the Grantor that the Grantee's Land may be developed in the future).

Any agreement must:

6.2.1 be subject to a suitable indemnity being given by the Grantee and reasonable provisions for costs being made;
6.2.2 not adversely affect [in any material way] the proposed development of the Grantor's Land; and
6.2.3 be in a form that has been Approved by the Grantor and the Grantee.

SCHEDULE 4 – GRANTEE'S RESTRICTIVE COVENANTS

1 SERVICE MEDIA

1.1 Not to overload any Service Media laid or to be laid within the Grantor's Land beyond their designated capacity.

1.2 Not to discharge into any Service Media laid or to be laid within the Grantor's Land anything that is or could be corrosive or harmful or that could cause any obstruction of them.

1.3 [Not to connect to any Service Media laid or to be laid within the Grantor's Land unless the programme of works for the connection to the Service Media has been Approved by the Grantor.] [This restriction does not apply in respect of any Service Media installed by the Grantee pursuant to the rights in paragraph [2.3] of Schedule 1.]

2 NOT TO OBSTRUCT RIGHT OF WAY

Not to park on or otherwise obstruct any part of the road [shown coloured [brown] on Plan [ ]] [or the Access Road].

3 [DISPOSALS OF THE GRANTEE'S LAND

3.1 [[Unless a Disposal is a Permitted Disposal,] the Grantee shall not make a Disposal of the Grantee's Land unless its Successor:

3.1.1 executes a Deed of Covenant on or before the date of the deed or document effecting the Disposal and delivers it to the Grantor's solicitors;

3.1.2 pays the proper and reasonable legal costs and expenses of the Grantor's solicitors in respect of the preparation and approval of the Deed of Covenant together with any value added tax on those costs and expenses; and

3.1.3 makes an application to the Land Registry on form RX1 (at the same time as the transfer in favour of the Successor is sent to the Land Registry for registration) for a restriction in the form of the restriction referred to in clause [8] of this Deed to be entered onto the proprietorship register of the title number(s) under which the Grantee's Land is registered with that restriction being entered in priority to any other restrictions, charges or other entries on the register to be made following the registration of the Successor as the registered proprietor of the Grantee's Land.]

3.2 [In the case of a disposal that is not a Permitted Disposal of the Grantee's Land, if the Grantor receives a duly executed Deed of Covenant, the Grantor shall consent to the registration of a Disposal at the Land Registry for the purposes of the restriction referred to in clause [8] of this Deed.]

3.3 [In the case of a Permitted Disposal of the Grantee's Land, the Grantee shall:

3.3.1 consent to the registration of the Permitted Disposal at the Land Registry for the purposes of the restriction referred to in clause [8] of this Deed; and

3.3.2 release the restriction registered over those parts of the Grantee's Land that were the subject of the Permitted Disposal within two weeks of being requested to do so if it is necessary for registration of the Permitted Disposal.]]

SCHEDULE 5 – GRANTEE'S POSITIVE COVENANTS

[1 MAINTENANCE COSTS

1.1 To pay to the Grantor within 14 days of written demand [ ] per cent [a fair and reasonable proportion according to use] of the proper and reasonable costs incurred by the Grantor in complying with the obligations in paragraph [2.1] and paragraph [3.1] of Schedule 3 together with any value added tax payable on the costs.

1.2 If the costs referred to in paragraph 1.1 are not paid in accordance with that paragraph to pay interest at [4] per cent above the base rate from time to time of [ ] on any sums not paid for the period from and including the date of demand to and including the date of payment of the outstanding sums.]

[2. GOOD FAITH

2.1 To act in good faith towards the Grantor in connection with this Deed.]

SCHEDULE 6 – DEVELOPMENT WORKS

1 [ACCESS ROAD

1.1 Before constructing the Access Road the Grantor shall consult with the Grantee as soon as reasonably practicable after the date of this Deed [and by no later than [ ]]

and shall obtain the Approval of the Grantee to the route of the Access Road and (if required) the location of the Road Corridor and the Sight Line Areas, the standard of construction of the Access Road [to achieve an adoptable standard] and the programme of works for its construction prior to commencing the construction of the Access Road.

1.2 The Grantor shall:

1.2.1 use reasonable endeavours to persuade the Relevant Authority to agree to the Access Road leading to and directly connecting with the boundary of the Grantee's Land at the point marked [ ] on Plan [ ];

1.2.2 upon request in writing from the Grantee, provide the Grantee with evidence that this obligation has been complied with.

1.3 If the Relevant Authority will not agree to the Access Road leading to and connecting with the boundary of the Grantee's Land at the point marked [ ] on Plan [ ], the estate layout of the Grantor's Land shall include the Road Corridor or such of the Road Corridor as shall be necessary to provide access to the Grantee's Land at the point marked [ ] on Plan [ ] in accordance with the provisions of this Deed.

1.4 Subject to obtaining the Approval of the Grantee to the route of the Access Road and any Road Corridor, the Grantor shall apply for and use reasonable endeavours to obtain the necessary technical approval of the Relevant Authority to the design and layout of the Access Road as soon as reasonably practicable after the date of this Deed and by no later than [ ]. [The owners of the Grantor's Land shall:

1.4.1 keep the Grantee fully informed of all progress in this regard;

1.4.2 upon request in writing from the Grantee, provide the Grantee with any information that the Grantee requests in relation to the obtaining of that technical approval.]

1.5 The Grantor shall at their own expense construct the Access Road to base course level by no later than [ ] months after the date on which the relevant technical approvals to the design and construction of the Access Road have been obtained from the Relevant Authority. The construction of the Access Road shall be carried out:

1.5.1 in a good and workmanlike manner; and

1.5.2 using good quality materials; [and]

1.5.3 in accordance with the Access Road Specification; [and]

1.5.4 [to a standard required for adoption; and]

1.5.5 in accordance with the requirements of the Relevant Authority.

1.6 The Grantor shall at their own expense apply the final wearing course to the Access Road and shall complete the construction of the footpaths and street lighting along the Access Road as quickly as reasonably practicable and by no later than [ ].

1.7 [The Grantor shall use reasonable endeavours following completion of the construction of the Access Road to procure that the Access Road is adopted by the Relevant Authority.]

1.8 [The Grantor and the Grantee acknowledge that the location of the Access Road, any Road Corridor and any Sight Line Areas as shown on Plan [ ] are approximate positions as at the date of this Deed.]

1.9 Following the obtaining of technical approval to the design and construction of the Access Road and the Grantee having Approved the route of the Access Road and any Road Corridor under this Schedule, the Grantor shall provide the Grantee with a plan or plans detailing the exact positions of the Access Road and any Road Corridor and Sight Line Areas.

1.10 The Grantee and the Grantor agree to enter into any supplemental deed that is necessary formally to document the agreement reached as to the exact positions of the Access Road and any Road Corridor.]

2 [NEW SERVICE MEDIA

2.1 [Before constructing the New Service Media, the Grantor shall consult with the Grantee as soon as reasonably practicable after the date of this Deed and by no later than [ ] to:

2.1.1 ensure that the capacity of the New Service Media will, if constructed, be reasonably satisfactory for connection to, and use by the owners of, the Grantee's Land taking into account the current and proposed uses of the Grantee's Land; and

2.1.2 obtain their Approval to the routes of the New Service Media, the standard of their construction and the programme of works for their construction.]

2.2 [Subject to obtaining the Approval of the Grantee to the route and capacity of the New Service Media,] the Grantor shall apply for and use reasonable endeavours to obtain the necessary technical approval of the Relevant Authority to the design and layout of the New Service Media as soon as reasonably practicable after the date of this Deed and by no later than [ ]. [The owners of Grantor's Land shall:

2.2.1 keep the Grantee fully informed of all progress in this regard;

2.2.2 upon request in writing from the Grantee, provide the Grantee with any information that the Grantee requests in relation to the obtaining of that technical approval.]

2.3 The Grantor shall at their own expense construct the New Service Media by no later than [ ] months after the date on which the relevant technical approvals to the design and construction of the New Service Media have been obtained from the Relevant Authority. The construction of the New Service Media shall be carried out:

2.3.1 in a good and workmanlike manner; and

2.3.2 using good quality materials; [and]

2.3.3 [in accordance with the Services Specification; and]

2.3.4 [in the case of sewers, to a standard required for adoption; and]

2.3.5 in accordance with the requirements of the Relevant Authority.

2.4 [The Grantor shall use reasonable endeavours following the construction of any new sewer forming part of the New Service Media to ensure its adoption as a public sewer.]]

[**NOTE**: Include this Schedule if the Grantor is to be obliged to construct an access road and service media to serve the Grantee's Land.]

EXECUTED as a DEED by [ ] acting by two directors or one director and the company secretary

....

Director

....

Director/Secretary

EXECUTED as a DEED by [ ] acting by two directors or one director and the company secretary

....
Director

....
Director/Secretary

APPENDIX C14

Deed of easement (foul and surface water sewers)

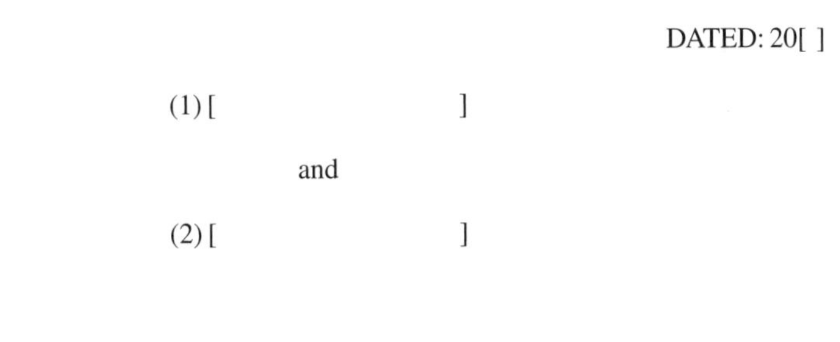

DATED: 20[ ]

(1) [ ]

and

(2) [ ]

DEED OF EASEMENT (FOUL AND SURFACE WATER SEWERS)

relating to land at [ ]

PARTICULARS

Date:	[ ]
Grantor:	[company name] (company number [ ]) [of] [whose registered office is at] [ ]
Grantee:	[company name] (company number [ ]) [of] [whose registered office is at] [ ]
Grantor's Land:	The freehold property at [ ] shown edged in [red] on Plan [ ] and being the land registered at the Land Registry under title number [ ]
Grantee's Land:	The freehold property at [ ] shown edged in [blue] on Plan [ ] and being the land registered at the Land Registry under title number [ ]
[**Mortgagee:**	[ ] [of] [whose registered office is at] [ ]]

THIS DEED OF EASEMENT is made on the date set out in the Particulars

BETWEEN

(1) the Grantor; [and]
(2) the Grantee; [and]
[(3) the Mortgagee.]

BACKGROUND

(A) The Grantor is the owner of the Grantor's Land and the Grantee is the owner of the Grantee's Land.

(B) The Grantor has agreed to grant the Rights to the Grantee for the benefit of the Grantee's Land.

[(C) The Mortgagee has agreed to be made a party to this Deed for the purpose of consenting to the grant of the Rights.]

OPERATIVE PROVISIONS

1 DEFINITIONS AND INTERPRETATION

1.1 In this Deed the following words and expressions have the following meanings:

'**Approval**' means approval in writing which shall not be unreasonably withheld or delayed [and which shall be deemed to have been given if no response is received or if no reasons are given for any refusal of approval in each case within 10 Working Days of a request for approval] and the terms 'Approving', 'Approved' and 'Approve' shall be construed accordingly;

'**Covenants**' means the restrictive and positive covenants contained in clause 3 of this Deed;

'**Deed of Covenant**' means a deed of covenant [in such form as the Grantee shall reasonably require to be entered into by any party to whom the Grantor makes a Disposal containing a covenant in favour of the Grantee and its successors in title for the benefit of the Grantee's Land to comply with all of the Covenants] [in substantially the same form as the attached draft deed of covenant with such amendments as the circumstances may require and/or such amendments as the Grantee may require and the Grantor shall Approve]. Any dispute between the Parties regarding the form of the Deed of Covenant shall be referred to and determined by an arbitrator appointed in accordance with clause [5];

'**Disposal**' means a transfer, assent, lease, mortgage, charge, grant of a legal or equitable easement, the entering into of positive or restrictive covenants or any other disposition of the whole or any part of the Grantor's Land, whether or not for valuable consideration;

'**Disponee**' means any person to whom a Disposal is made;

'**Drainage Authority**' means such authority or body as shall have responsibility under statute for drainage matters;

'**Easement Strip**' means the strip of land [shown coloured [yellow] on the Plan] having a width of [ ] metres on either side of the Sewer;

'**Necessary Consents**' means all planning permissions, approvals, consents, licences and certificates required by any Relevant Authority for the construction of the Sewer;

'**Parties**' means the Grantor and Grantee and 'Party' shall be construed accordingly;

'**Plan 1**' means the plan numbered [ ] annexed to this Deed at Appendix [ ];

'**Relevant Authority**' means all or any of the following as appropriate:

(a) such authority or body as shall have responsibility under statute for drainage matters;

(b) such authority or body as shall have responsibility under statute for planning matters;
(c) such authority or body as shall have responsibility under statute for environmental matters;
(d) any utility company or body concerned with the installation of Service Media and the supply of Services;

'**Rights**' means the rights set out in the Schedule to this Deed;

'**Service Media**' means conduits, sewers, drains, pipes, cables and other service media for the supply of Services;

'**Services**' means water, gas, electricity, telephone, telecommunications, surface water drainage, foul drainage and similar services;

'**Sewer**' means the [foul water] [surface water] [foul and surface water] sewer constructed pursuant to the Rights and includes not only the sewer pipe but also any pumps, control chambers and other accessories or apparatus;

['**Specification**' means [the specification (if any) attached to this Deed at Appendix [ ]] [a specification to be Approved by the Grantor];]

'**Working Day**' means any day other than Saturday, Sunday and any bank or public holiday and 'Working Days' shall be construed accordingly.

1.2 In this Deed:

1.2.1 the clause headings do not affect its interpretation;
1.2.2 unless otherwise indicated, references to clauses and Schedules are to clauses of and Schedules to this Deed and references in a Schedule to a Part or paragraph are to a Part or paragraph of that Schedule;
1.2.3 references to any statute or statutory provision include references to:

(a) all Acts of Parliament and all other legislation having legal effect in the United Kingdom; and
(b) any subsequent statutes directly or indirectly amending, consolidating, extending, replacing or re-enacting that statute and also include any orders, regulations, instruments or other subordinate legislation made under that statute;

1.2.4 references to Grantor's Land and Grantee's Land include any part of them;
1.2.5 references to the Grantor and the Grantee include their respective successors in title;
1.2.6 words importing one gender include all other genders and words importing the singular include the plural and vice versa;
1.2.7 a reference to a person includes an individual or corporation, company, firm or partnership or government body or agency;
1.2.8 'including' means 'including, without limitation';
1.2.9 where two or more people form a party to this Deed, the obligations they undertake may be enforced against them all jointly or against each individually; and
1.2.10 if any provision is held to be illegal, invalid or unenforceable, the legality, validity and enforceability of the remainder of this Deed are to be unaffected.

1.3 The Particulars form part of this Deed and words and expressions set out in the Particulars are to be treated as defined terms in this Deed.

1.4 The Parties to this Deed do not intend that any of its terms will be enforceable by virtue of the Contracts (Rights of Third Parties) Act 1999 by any person not a party to it.

1.5 Where the Approval of a Party is required under this Deed and the Parties are unable to reach agreement the matter shall be referred to and determined by an arbitrator in accordance with the provisions of clause [5].

2 GRANT

2.1 [In consideration of £[ ] (receipt of which is acknowledged)] the Grantor **GRANTS** the Rights to the Grantee in fee simple with [full/limited] title guarantee for the benefit of the Grantee's Land.

2.2 No legal or other rights over the Grantor's Land for the benefit of the Grantee's Land are granted except for the Rights.

3 THE GRANTOR'S OBLIGATIONS

3.1 The Grantor so as to bind the Grantor's Land into whosesoever hands it may come and for the benefit and protection of the Grantee's Land and each and every part thereof **COVENANTS** for itself and its successors in title to observe and perform at all times after the date of this Deed the following stipulations and restrictions:

3.1.1 that nothing shall be done or suffered to be done upon the route of the Sewer which may in any way interfere with or damage the Sewer or interfere with or obstruct the Grantee's access thereto and without prejudice to the generality of the foregoing that no building or other erection shall be constructed and no trees planted over the route of the Sewer without the consent of the Grantee;

3.1.2 that the ground cover or depth of soil over the Sewer will not in any way be altered without the Approval of the Grantee;

3.1.3 that no excavations in or over the route of the Sewer will be carried out without prior notification and affording a representative of the Grantee the opportunity of being in attendance;

3.1.4 that the Grantee shall be permitted access to [the Grantor's Land] [the Easement Strip] with or without workmen, machinery and equipment at all reasonable times and on reasonable notice for the purposes of laying, connecting to, inspecting, repairing, maintaining, renewing[, enlarging] and replacing the Sewer;

3.1.5 that the Grantor will not make any Disposal of [the Grantor's Land] [the Easement Strip] or any part of it without procuring that the Disponee enters into a Deed of Covenant.

3.2 The Grantor **FURTHER COVENANTS** with the Grantee:

3.2.1 to promptly enter into any wayleave agreement, deed of easement or other documents [reasonably] required by the Grantee in connection with the installation and maintenance of the Sewer. [The Grantee shall:

3.2.1.1 pay the proper and reasonable costs of the Grantor; and

3.2.1.2 agree to indemnify the Grantor in respect of any liability incurred by the Grantor under those documents;]

3.2.2 to promptly enter into any wayleave agreement, deed of easement, adoption agreement or other documents if [reasonably] required by the Drainage Authority as a condition of the Sewer being installed and/or adopted or allowing connections being made to the Sewer. [The Grantee shall:

3.2.2.1 pay the reasonable costs of the Grantor; and
3.2.2.2 agree to indemnify the Grantor in respect of any liability incurred under those documents;]

3.2.3 to act in good faith towards the Grantee in connection with this Deed [and (without prejudice to the generality thereof) not do anything to hinder or prevent the exercise of the Rights or the development of the Grantee's Land].

4 THE GRANTEE'S OBLIGATIONS

The Grantee so as to bind the Grantee's Land into whosesoever hands it may come for the benefit of the Grantor's Land **COVENANTS** for itself and its successors in title with the Grantor to observe and perform at all times after the date of this Deed in relation to the Grantee's Land the following stipulations and restrictions:

4.1 that the Grantee will keep the Grantor indemnified against all losses, claims, costs, expenses and damages which the Grantor may suffer or incur by reason of anything done or omitted to be done by the Grantee or its workmen, agents and others authorised by the Grantee in connection with exercise of the Rights;

4.2 that the Grantee will cause as little damage as reasonably possible to the Grantor's Land in the exercise of the Rights and that it will make good as soon as reasonably possible any damage actually occasioned to the reasonable satisfaction of the Grantor and will pay reasonable compensation for any damage not capable of being made good;

4.3 that before commencing the construction of the Sewer the Grantee shall:

4.3.1 carry out a full investigation of the Grantor's Land to ensure that no damage or disturbance is caused to existing pipes, wires or other service media in or under the Grantor's Land;
4.3.2 obtain all Necessary Consents to the construction of the Sewer from the Relevant Authority; and
4.3.3 give the Grantor reasonable notice of the Grantee's intention to commence the construction of the Sewer;

4.4 that the Grantee shall construct the Sewer in a good and workmanlike manner and in accordance with all Necessary Consents, all relevant statutes and current codes of building practice [and the Specification].

5 ARBITRATION

In the event of any dispute or difference arising between the Parties as to the construction of this Deed or any part thereof or as to the rights, duties or obligations of the Parties hereunder or as to any other matter in any way arising out of or connected with the subject matter of this Deed (unless provision for some other method of determining any matter is made in this Deed) the same shall be referred to an arbitrator (acting as an arbitrator) to be agreed by the Parties or in default of agreement to be appointed by the President for the time being of the Law Society of England and Wales on the application of either Party and such arbitration shall be conducted in accordance with and subject to the Arbitration Act 1996.

6 REGISTRATION OF RESTRICTION

The Grantor and the Grantee hereby apply to the Land Registry for the entry of the following restriction upon the proprietorship register of the title to the Grantor's Land in the following terms (or as close thereto as the Land Registry shall permit):

'No disposition of [the registered estate] [the part of the registered estate shown shaded [yellow] on the title plan] by the proprietor of the registered estate or the proprietor of any registered charge, not being a charge registered before the entry of this restriction, is to be registered without a certificate signed by [ ] [a conveyancer] [the applicant for registration or their conveyancer] that the provisions of clause 3.1.5 of the deed of grant dated [ ] and made between [ ] and [ ] have been complied with.'

[**NOTE**: The part of the registered estate to be shown shaded yellow on the title plan would be any Easement Strip shown on any plan attached to this Deed.]

7 LAND REGISTRY APPLICATIONS

7.1 The Grantor consents to the entry of a notice of the Rights and a notice of the Covenants in the appropriate registers of the title to the Grantor's Land.

7.2 The Grantee agrees to forthwith apply to the Land Registry for the Rights and the Covenants to be noted on the title to the Grantor's Land.

8 [MORTGAGEE'S CONSENT

8.1 The Mortgagee consents to the grant of the Rights and to the Covenants and also to the registration of them in the charges register of the title to the Grantor's Land.

8.2 If the Mortgagee exercises its power of sale to sell the whole or any part of the Grantor's Land, it shall comply with the obligations of the Grantor contained in clause 3.1.5 of this Deed.]

IN WITNESS whereof the parties have executed this document as a deed the day and year first before written.

SCHEDULE – THE RIGHTS

The following rights for the Grantee, its successors in title of all or any parts of the Grantee's Land and their respective tenants, servants and invitees and all others authorised by the Grantee or its successors in title.

1. The right to lay and thereafter to connect to, use, maintain, repair, renew, alter, relay, inspect[, enlarge] or remove a [foul water] [surface water] [foul and surface water] sewer under the Grantor's Land in the approximate position shown by [a broken [blue] line on Plan [ ]] [or such alternative route as shall be Approved by the Grantor].
2. The right at reasonable times and upon giving a reasonable period of notice (save in case of an emergency where no notice will be necessary) to enter on and dig up and excavate [so much of the Grantor's Land as may be reasonably necessary] [the Easement Strip] with or without workmen, plant, machinery and equipment for any of the purposes mentioned in paragraph 1 above.

   [**PROVIDED THAT** the Grantor shall be entitled to alter the position of the Sewer with the Approval of the Grantee subject to:

   (a) the Grantee Approving the proposed new route of the Sewer; and
   (b) the Grantor obtaining all the necessary consents and approvals to the proposed alterations; and
   (c) the Grantor complying with the requirements of the Relevant Authority in relation to the relevant construction works; and
   (d) the proposed alterations not adversely affecting or being prejudicial in any way to the exercise of the Rights; and
   (e) the Grantor entering into a new deed of easement with the Grantee in substantially the same form as this Deed but with the Rights to apply to the

altered position of the Sewer. Any dispute or disagreement between the Parties regarding this clause or the new deed of easement shall be referred to and determined by an arbitrator in accordance with clause 5.]

EXECUTED as a DEED by [ ] acting by two directors or one director and the company secretary

....

Director

....

Director/Secretary

APPENDIX C15

Deed of assignment and novation (affordable housing)

DATED: 20[ ]

(1) [ ]

and

(2) [ ]

and

(3) [ ]

and

(4) [ ]

and

(5) [ ]

ASSIGNMENT AND NOVATION

Affordable Housing (plots [ ]) at

[ ]

DEED OF EASEMENT (FOUL AND SURFACE WATER SEWERS)

relating to land at [ ]

[**NOTE**: This Agreement assumes that the Seller has entered into two separate agreements, namely, a land agreement and a building agreement, with the affordable housing provider and that the Seller is proposing to transfer a proportion of the plots on which the affordable housing dwellings are to be constructed to the Buyer]

THIS DEED is made on [ ]

BETWEEN

1. [ ], a company incorporated in England and Wales (company number [ ]) whose registered office is at [ ] ('the Seller'); and
2. [ ], a company incorporated in England and Wales (company number [ ]) whose registered office is at [ ] ('the Buyer'); and
3. [ ], a company incorporated in England and Wales (company number [ ]) whose registered office is at [ ] ('the Association'); and
4. [ ], a company incorporated in England and Wales (company number [ ]) whose registered office is at [ ] ('the Seller's Surety'); and
5. [ ], a company incorporated in England and Wales (company number [ ]) whose registered office is at [ ] ('the Buyer's Surety').

1 DEFINITIONS

1.1 In this Deed the following words and expressions shall have the following meanings:

'Association's Obligations'	all obligations of the Association under the Main Agreements relating to the Dwellings and each plot on which the Dwellings are intended to be constructed;
'Building Agreement'	the Agreement dated [ ] and made between the Seller (1) the Seller's Surety (2) and the Association for the construction of affordable housing units on the Property;
[**'Deposit'**	[has the same meaning as in the Land Agreement];]
'Dwellings'	the affordable housing units (comprising plots [ ]) to be constructed upon the Sale Property in accordance with the Main Agreements details of which are set out in the schedule hereto;
[**'Golden Brick Payments'**	[has the same meaning as in the Land Agreement];]
'Land Agreement'	the Agreement dated [ ] made between the Seller (1) the Seller's Surety (2) and the Association (3) for the sale of the Property;
'Main Agreements'	the Land Agreement and the Building Agreement;
'Parties'	the Seller, the Buyer and the Association;
'Plan'	the plan annexed hereto;
'Property'	has the same meaning as in the [Building Agreement] [Land Agreement];
'Retained Land'	[the Property excluding the Sale Property;]
'Sale Property'	the part of the Property shown edged in [red] on the Plan;
'Seller's Obligations'	all obligations of the Seller under the Main Agreements relating to the Dwellings;
'Surety Obligations'	all obligations of the Seller's Surety under the Main Agreements relating to the Dwellings.

1.2 The clause headings are included for convenience only and shall not affect the interpretation of this Deed.

2 RECITALS

2.1 The Seller has entered into the Main Agreements for the provision and sale of affordable housing at the Property.

2.2 The Seller has requested and the Association has agreed that the Seller shall be entitled to assign and novate the benefit and burden of the Main Agreements to the Buyer in so far as they relate to the Dwellings and each plot upon which the Dwellings are intended to be constructed.

2.3 The Association has agreed to release and discharge the Seller from the Seller's Obligations upon the Buyer accepting the Seller's Obligations in substitution for the Seller as if the Buyer had originally been a party to the Main Agreements in place of the Seller but only in so far as the Main Agreements relate to the Dwellings.

2.4 The Association has further agreed to release and discharge the Seller's Surety from the Surety Obligations upon the Buyer's Surety accepting the Surety Obligations in substitution for the Seller's Surety as if the Buyer's Surety had originally been a party to the Main Agreements but only in so far as the Main Agreements relate to the Dwellings.

2.5 The Buyer has agreed with the Association to transfer the Sale Property to the Association and to construct the Dwellings on the Sale Property in accordance with the Seller's Obligations and the Main Agreements.

3 OPERATIVE PROVISIONS

3.1 In consideration of the assumption by the Buyer of the Seller's Obligations in accordance with clause 5 of this Deed:

3.1.1 the Association agrees to the Seller assigning to the Buyer the benefit and burden of the Seller's Obligations;

3.1.2 the Association agrees with the Buyer to observe and perform the Association's Obligations;

3.1.3 the Association releases and discharges the Seller from the Seller's Obligations from the date of this Deed (but not from any liability in respect of any antecedent breaches);

3.1.4 for the avoidance of doubt the Association agrees with the Seller that in the event of a default by the Buyer in the performance of the Seller's Obligations the Association will not seek any redress against the Seller for the default of the Buyer.

3.2 In consideration of the assumption by the Buyer's Surety of the Surety Obligations in accordance with clause 6 of this Deed the Association releases and discharges the Seller's Surety from the Surety Obligations from the date of this Deed.

4 ASSIGNMENT AND NOVATION

In consideration of the assumption by the Buyer of the Seller's Obligations the Seller assigns to the Buyer the benefit and burden of the Seller's Obligations and the benefit of the Association's Obligations.

5 COVENANTS BY THE BUYER

In consideration of the agreement and release by the Association contained in clause 3 and of the assignment in clause 4 of this Deed the Buyer undertakes and covenants with the Association and the Seller that with effect from and on the date of this Deed the Buyer will accept, perform and be bound by the Seller's Obligations and will assume all of the Seller's Obligations (including without limitation all of the Seller's Obligations from the date of the Main Agreements (save in respect of any antecedent breach of the Seller)) in substitution for the Seller as if the Buyer had been named as an original party to the Main Agreements but only in so far as the Main Agreements relate to the Dwellings.

6 COVENANT BY THE BUYER'S SURETY

In consideration of the agreement contained in clause 3 and the release contained in clause 3.2 the Buyer's Surety undertakes and covenants with the Association that with effect from the date of this Deed the Buyer's Surety will accept, perform and be bound by the Surety Obligations and will assume all of the Surety Obligations (including without limitation all of the Surety Obligations from the date of the Main Agreements (save in respect of any antecedent breach by the Seller)) in substitution for the Seller's Surety as if the Buyer's Surety had been named as an original party to the Main Agreements.

7 COVENANT BY THE SELLER

In consideration of the assumption by the Buyer of the Seller's Obligations in accordance with clause 5 of this Deed the Seller undertakes and covenants with the Buyer to observe and perform all of the obligations on the part of the Seller contained in the Main Agreements in so far as they relate to the Retained Land and the infrastructure and dwellings to be constructed thereon.

8 CONTINUING FORCE AND EFFECT

This Deed shall be deemed to incorporate in full all of the terms and provisions of the Main Agreements as if they had been set out in this Deed in full and save to the extent the Main Agreements have been varied by this Deed the Seller and the Buyer hereby acknowledge and declare that the Main Agreements shall continue in full force and effect.

9 RIGHTS OF THIRD PARTIES ACT

A person who is not a party to this Deed has no right under the Contracts (Rights of Third Parties) Act 1999 to enforce any term of this Deed but this does not affect any right or remedy of a third party which exists or is available apart from that Act.

10 [DEPOSIT AND GOLDEN BRICK PAYMENT

The Seller shall on the date of this Deed pay to the Buyer the sum of £[ ] being a proportion of the Deposit [and all the Golden Brick Payments paid by the Association to the Seller prior to the date of this Deed] and such sum shall be held by the Buyer on terms identical to those contained in clause [ ] of the Land Agreement.]

IN WITNESS this Deed was executed by the parties to this Deed and delivered upon dating it.

SCHEDULE – DETAILS OF DWELLINGS

Plot number	Unit type	Tenure	Price

EXECUTED as a DEED by the affixing of the Common Seal of [ ] in the presence of two authorised signatories

....

Authorised signatory

....

Authorised signatory

EXECUTED as a DEED
[ ] acting by two Directors or a Director and the Company Secretary

....

Director

....

Director/Secretary

EXECUTED as a DEED by the Affixing of the Common Seal [ ] in the presence of two Directors or a Director and the Company Secretary

....

Director

....

Director/Secretary

EXECUTED as a DEED
[ ] acting by two Directors or a Director and the Company Secretary

....

Director

....

Director/Secretary

EXECUTED as a DEED
[ ] acting by two Directors or a Director and the Company Secretary

....
Director

....
Director/Secretary

APPENDIX C16

Reliance letter

[TO BE TYPED ON THE HEADED NOTEPAPER OF [CONSULTANT]]

To: [buyer]

[address]

Date: [ ] [20]

Dear Sirs

LAND AT [ ] (shown edged in red on the attached plan) ('Property')

We refer to our report in respect of the Property dated [ ] (Ref: [ ]) ('**Report**') prepared for [ ] ('**Client**'). In consideration of the sum of £1.00 (receipt of which we hereby acknowledge):

1. We confirm that in carrying out the agreed services relating to the [audit/survey] of the Property and the preparation of the Report, we exercised all the reasonable skill, care and attention to be expected of a competent and appropriately qualified [insert as applicable] consultant, experienced in carrying out investigations and preparing reports of a similar nature, value and complexity to the Report.
2. We acknowledge that you will be acquiring an interest in the Property and that you wish to rely upon the contents of the Report and we agree that you and your successors in title and third parties granted an interest in the Property may use and rely upon the Report as if the Report was originally commissioned by you.
3. We confirm that the Report may be regarded as having been issued by us in your favour and that we shall owe you the same duty of care (but no greater) that we owe to the Client subject to all of the matters contained or referred to in the Report.
4. We confirm that we maintain professional indemnity insurance with a limit of not less than [ ] pounds (£[ ]) [the amount of cover is to be reasonable and proper having regard to the nature and value of the consultant work carried out] [on each and every claim basis] [in the annual aggregate] in respect of our services and that we will maintain such insurance [for a period of 12 years after the date of this letter] [provided that such insurance is available in the market at commercially reasonable rates].

5. We confirm that the benefit and the rights granted under this letter may be assigned or licensed without our consent to any party taking all or any part of your interest in the Property and any party providing finance in connection with the Property.
6. We hereby grant to you a non-exclusive irrevocable royalty free licence to copy, use, adapt and reproduce the Report and any plans and drawings prepared by us in any format including electronic format for any purpose related to the Property including (without limitation) construction, completion, reconstruction, modification, extension, repair, use, letting, sale and advertisement.

Yours sincerely

For and on behalf of [ ]

APPENDICES – SECTION D

Model clauses

APPENDIX D1

Model clauses

1 BOUNDARY ADJUSTMENT

If prior to commencing the proposed [residential] development of the Property the Seller [reasonably] considers that it is necessary for an adjustment to be made to the boundaries of the Property then the Buyer and the Seller shall consult and shall endeavour to agree such adjustments to the boundaries of the Property [as may be necessary to enable the Reserved Matters Approval and/or any other necessary consents to be obtained] [as may be [reasonably] required by the Seller] and they will act reasonably and in good faith towards each other in agreeing such adjustments [and the Buyer shall not be entitled to object to any change if the change will not involve any material reduction in the total area of the Property [or if the Seller shall transfer additional land to the Buyer adjacent to the Property so as to keep the total area of the Property the same]]. Following agreement of any amendments to the boundaries of the Property occurring after the Completion Date the Buyer and the Seller will promptly enter into any deed or deeds of rectification of the Transfer necessary to give effect to such amendment provided that the Buyer's reasonable and proper costs, fees and expenses (including Land Registry fees) are paid by the Seller.

2 BOUNDARY ADJUSTMENT

1. It is intended that the Property shall be developed as residential dwellings but acknowledged by the Parties that:
   (a) the layout for the development of the Site (including the location of the estate roads and the positioning of the dwellings) has not yet been approved by the Local Planning Authority; and
   (b) changes to the extent and/or location of the Property and/or the boundaries of the Property may need to be made in order to comply with the requirements of the Local Planning Authority.
2. If in order to satisfy the requirements of the Local Planning Authority in relation to the development of the Site it shall be necessary to change the location of the dwellings and/or to change the extent of the Property and/or the location of the Property and/or to adjust or move or reposition the boundaries of the Property then the Parties shall act in good faith towards each other and co-operate with each other and use all reasonable endeavours to agree the necessary changes provided always that the total area of the Property shall not be less than the existing area of the Property as shown on the Plan and shall not exceed [ ] acres of Net Developable Land.
3. Any dispute between the Parties regarding clauses 1 and 2 above shall be settled by an expert in accordance with the provisions of clause [ ] of this Agreement.

3 EXCLUDING IMPLIED RIGHTS

Section 62 of the Law of Property Act 1925 and the rule in *Wheeldon* v. *Burrows* do not apply to this Transfer and no legal or other rights are granted over the Retained Land for the benefit of the Property or granted over the Property for the benefit of the Retained Land except for those expressly granted or reserved by this Transfer.

4 EXCLUDING LIABILITY

A mortgagee of the Site will not incur any liability for any breach of the obligations contained in this Agreement unless and until it becomes a mortgagee in possession of the Site or appoints a receiver or administrative receiver under a security.

5 EXCLUDING LIABILITY UNTIL SITE IS ACQUIRED BY DEVELOPER

The Developer acknowledges and declares that this Deed has been entered into by the Owner with its consent and that the Site shall be bound by the obligations contained in this Deed and that the [Option Agreement] [Purchase Agreement] shall be subject to this Deed provided that the Developer shall have no liability under this Deed unless it becomes the owner of the Site in which case it too will be bound by the obligations contained in this Deed as the person deriving title from the Owner.

6 RELEASE FROM LIABILITY

No party shall be liable for any breach of the covenants, restrictions or obligations contained in this Agreement if the party has no interest in the Site or any part in respect of which any breach occurs and no party shall be liable for any breach of the covenants, restrictions or obligations contained in this Agreement occurring after he has parted with his interest in the Site or any part in respect of which such breach occurs but without prejudice to liability for any subsisting breach of covenant, restriction or obligation prior to parting with such interest.

7 EXCLUDING LIABILITY

The obligations under this Agreement shall not be enforceable against the individual owners or occupiers or mortgagees of any individual residential unit constructed on the [Site] [Land] pursuant to the [Planning] Permission.

8 DISPOSAL OF AFFORDABLE HOUSING; OWNER UNABLE TO SECURE A SALE TO A REGISTERED PROVIDER

1. In the event that having taken reasonable steps to do so the Owner is unable to secure contracts for the sale or other disposal of the Affordable Housing Units to a Registered Provider by [occupation of 50 per cent of the Market Units] or in the event that the Registered Provider terminates a contract and the Owner having taken reasonable steps to do so is unable to secure a further contract [on the same commercial terms] then the Owner shall be free to dispose of the Affordable Housing Units as such other Affordable Housing tenure in accordance with the NPPF as agreed with the Council (acting reasonably).
2. In the event that having taken reasonable steps to do so the Owner is unable to secure the sale of the Affordable Housing Units in accordance with paragraph 1 above within a period of three months then the Owner may elect to pay the Affordable Housing Commuted Sum to the Council in lieu of the provision of Affordable Housing and on

payment of the Affordable Housing Commuted Sum the Owner's obligations shall no longer be binding on the Owner.

9 MORTGAGEE PROTECTION PROVISIONS

The covenants and restrictions contained in [Affordable Housing Schedule] shall not bind:

(a) mortgagees or chargees (or receivers appointed by such mortgagees or chargees) of the Registered Provider [provided that the mortgagee, chargee or receiver appointed by such mortgagee or chargee shall first have complied with the Chargee's Duty];
(b) any Affordable Housing Unit acquired from the parties referred to in sub-paragraph (a) above; or
(c) any Protected Tenant or any mortgagee or chargee of a Protected Tenant or any person deriving title from the Protected Tenant or any successor in title thereto and their respective mortgagees and chargees.

'**Chargee's Duty**' means prior to seeking to dispose of any Affordable Housing Unit pursuant to a power of sale or other remedies under the terms of a mortgage or charge a mortgagee or chargee (or receiver appointed by a mortgagee or chargee) must have first used reasonable endeavours to seek to dispose of the said Affordable Housing Unit to an alternative Registered Provider for a period of three months from such mortgagee or chargee notifying the Council in writing of its intention to exercise its power of sale **PROVIDED THAT** in exercising such reasonable endeavours the mortgagee, chargee or receiver shall not be required to (a) act contrary to its duties under the charge or mortgage; or (b) dispose of the Affordable Housing Unit for a price lower than [the open market value of the dwellings] [required to recover all monies due under the charge or mortgage].

'**Protected Tenant**' means any tenant of Affordable Housing who:

(a) has exercised the right to acquire pursuant to the Housing Act 1996 or statutory provision for the time being in force (or any equivalent contractual right)
(b) has exercised any statutory right to buy (or any equivalent contractual right);
(c) has been granted a shared ownership lease (or similar arrangement where a share is owned by the tenant) and the tenant has subsequently purchased from the Registered Provider all the remaining share so that the tenant owns the entire unit of Affordable Housing.

10 WARRANTY: SDLT RELIEF

The [plot purchaser] acknowledges that [the developer] will apply for stamp duty land tax relief pursuant to section 58A of and Schedule 6A to the Finance Act 2003 on the transfer of the Property to [the developer].

The [plot purchaser] warrants that [the plot purchaser] occupied the Property as [the plot purchaser's] only or main residence immediately prior to completion of this contract and intends to occupy the Plot as [the plot purchaser's] only or main residence.

The [plot purchaser] will indemnify [the developer] in respect of any claims, costs, penalties or interest payable by [the developer] to HM Revenue & Customs arising from or incurred as a result of [the plot purchaser] breaching the warranty contained in this clause [ ].

11 STEP IN RIGHTS

1. If either Party ('the Defaulting Party') shall fail to make any payments or to carry out any works or to comply with any other obligations on its part contained in this Agreement then the other Party ('the Innocent Party') may serve written notice ('the

Default Notice') on the Defaulting Party requiring the Defaulting Party to take immediate action to remedy the breach within such reasonable period [(which shall not exceed 20 Working Days)] as shall be specified therein.

2. If [no action is taken to remedy the breach or] the breach is not remedied within the period stipulated in the Default Notice then the Innocent Party shall be entitled to:

   2.1 enter upon such part of the Property and/or the Retained Land as may be necessary and take such action as it shall [(in its absolute discretion)] think fit to ensure that the breach is remedied, including (but not by way of limitation) making such payments and/or carrying out such works and/or entering into such agreements or deeds as it shall consider to be necessary;

   2.2 act as attorney and agent of the Defaulting Party for the purpose of executing relevant documents to remedy any breach;

   2.3 recover from the Defaulting Party the [reasonable and proper] costs and expenses incurred by the Innocent Party in remedying the breach; and

   2.4 charge the Defaulting Party interest at the Interest Rate on the costs incurred by the Innocent Party in remedying the breach and a supervision fee representing 5 per cent of such costs.

12 LICENCE AND COPYRIGHT TO USE PLANS

The Vendor confirms that the Purchaser shall have a royalty free irrevocable licence and copyright to use all plans drawings elevations and other documents relating to the proposed [residential] development of the Property including (without prejudice to the generality thereof) all plans drawings and elevations submitted with the planning application for the proposed [residential] development. Without prejudice to the generality of this clause [ ] the Vendor will procure at the Vendor's expense that a licence (in the form of the attached draft licence) is granted to the Purchaser on or before the Completion Date for use on the Property only in respect of all drawings, plans and other documents submitted as part of or in connection with the planning permission relating to the development of the Property including without limitation the following plans and drawings prepared by [ ].

13 CHALLENGE PROCEEDINGS

Notwithstanding the grant of Planning Permission, the Planning Condition shall not (unless the Purchaser serves a notice pursuant to clause [ ] waiving the Planning Condition) be treated as satisfied until (i) [three months] [eight weeks (or such longer period as may from time to time be prescribed by statute or the Civil Procedure Rules for commencing Challenge Proceedings)] from the grant of an Acceptable Planning Permission have expired without any Challenge Proceedings having been commenced or (ii) if any Challenge Proceedings are commenced within such [three-month period] [eight-week or longer period] then they have been exhausted leaving in place an Acceptable Planning Permission.

14 CHALLENGE PROCEEDINGS

(a) Completion of the sale and purchase of the Property shall take place at the offices of the Vendors' Solicitors or such other place as they shall reasonably direct on or before 1.00pm on the date occurring three months and 10 Working Days after the Planning Condition has been satisfied or waived by the Purchaser (as the case may be) when the balance of the Purchase Price shall be paid.

(b) The time period of three months and 10 Working Days referred to in the immediately preceding clause will be suspended if Challenge Proceedings are commenced prior to completion and shall only continue running once the Challenge Proceedings have been finally determined and the Acceptable Planning Permission upheld.

(c) If the Challenge Proceedings result in the Acceptable Planning Permission being quashed, modified or invalidated then this Agreement may be rescinded on five Working Days' notice in writing by either the Vendor or the Purchaser to the other or its solicitors and upon such rescission this Agreement shall forthwith cease and determine (but without prejudice to any rights already accrued at that date in favour of either party hereto against the other in respect of any antecedent breach or non-observance or any obligation herein contained) and the Vendor will forthwith pay the Deposit to the Purchaser **PROVIDED THAT** the Vendor's notice to rescind shall be void if prior to the expiration of the said five Working Days the Purchaser serves notice of waiver.

15 DEFINITION OF 'PLANNING CONDITION'

'**Planning Condition**' means the grant of an Acceptable Planning Permission during the Conditional Period and for the purposes of this Agreement the date of grant shall be deemed to be the first Working Day after the latest of the following dates have occurred with reference to that permission:

(a) (in the case of a permission issued by the local planning authority) the date which is [three months] [eight weeks (or such longer period as may from time to time be prescribed by statute or the Civil Procedure Rules for commencing Challenge Proceedings)] from the date of issue of the permission (provided that no Challenge Proceedings were commenced in respect of it by such date);

(b) (in the event of a permission issued by the Secretary of State) the date which is [three months] [eight weeks (or such longer period as may from time to time be prescribed by statute or the Civil Rules Procedure for commencing Challenge Proceedings)] from the date printed on the letter or other instrument given by or on behalf of the Secretary of State notifying such grant (provided that no Challenge Proceedings were commenced in respect of it by such date);

(c) (in the event that any Challenge Proceedings have been commenced in respect of a permission) the date on which such Challenge Proceedings are finally determined and the permission is finally granted or upheld whether after a reference back to the Secretary of State or the local planning authority or any other relevant authority (as the case may be) and so that such permission is no longer open to challenge in any way by the issue of further proceedings.

16 NO DOUBLE DEDUCTION OF COSTS

Notwithstanding any other provision of this Agreement, there shall be no deduction of a Development Cost [or a Planning Cost] from the Price if it has already been deducted in calculating the Market Value [or if it was deducted on the purchase of a previous Tranche] so there cannot be a double recovery of any Development Cost [or Planning Cost].

17 EQUALISATION

If the local planning authority shall indicate that it is not prepared to agree to the Property being developed in isolation and that it will require a comprehensive development of the Property and other land ('Additional Land') or if the Planning Application and the Satisfactory Planning Permission shall include the Property or part of the Property and Additional Land then the Developer will use [all] reasonable endeavours to enter into suitable collaboration agreements or option agreements with the owners of the Additional Land containing equalisation provisions which provide for the purchase price to be calculated on an equalised basis and any liabilities in relation to any Planning Agreement, the Satisfactory Planning Permission, Development Costs and Infrastructure to be apportioned fairly between the Landowner and the owners of the Additional Land and (subject to such agreements being entered into) the Developer [and the Landowner shall use reasonable endeavours to enter into any necessary variation to the terms of this Agreement].

18 EQUALISATION

If during the Option Period it becomes apparent that additional land is required to be comprised in an Application to maximise the chances of a Satisfactory Planning Permission being granted the Developer shall at its own expense use [all] reasonable endeavours to procure that agreements with the proprietors of such land are entered into on reasonable commercial terms [which are previously approved by the Owners (such approval not to be unreasonably withheld or delayed)] which equalise the Infrastructure Costs and value of the Property and such additional land and which allow an Application to be submitted in relation to the Property and such additional land together. Any dispute regarding this clause is to be determined by an independent expert in accordance with clause [ ] of this agreement.

19 APPROVAL OF PLANNING AGREEMENT

The Owner will be entitled to [withhold approval to any Planning Agreement] [refuse to enter into any Planning Agreement] if and only if the Planning Agreement:

1. imposes obligations which are not in accordance with local or national planning policies at the time the Planning Agreement is to entered into; or
2. contains obligations which infringe the tests referred to in paragraph 56 of the National Planning Framework dated July 2018; or
3. contains a provision which will or is likely to reduce materially the value of the Owner's adjoining land; or
4. requires the Owner to grant any rights or enter into covenants which will [materially] affect the Owner's adjoining land; or
5. requires the Owner to transfer or dispose of land not forming part of the Property[; or
6. imposes obligations which are inconsistent with the Option Objectives].

20 RESTRICTION AND EXCLUDED DISPOSALS

The Transferor acknowledges that in the event of the Transferee making an Excluded Disposal after the date of this Transfer it is not intended that any restriction entered on the title to the Property in accordance with clause [ ] of this Transfer shall be entered on the title to the land which is the subject of the Excluded Disposal and in the event of such a restriction being entered on the title to the land which is the subject of an Excluded Disposal the Transferor shall promptly take such steps as shall be necessary to remove the restriction (including completing such Land Registry Form as may be appropriate) and in default hereby authorises the Transferee to remove such restriction.

21 NO VENDOR'S LIEN

The Developer and the Seller hereby both acknowledge and agree that the provisions of this Overage Agreement and the obligation to pay overage hereunder shall not give rise to a vendor's lien over the Property or any part thereof in favour of the Seller or any other party.

Index